Fourth Edition

ASSESSMENT OF EXCEPTIONAL STUDENTS

Educational and Psychological Procedures

Ronald L. Taylor

Florida Atlantic University

Allyn and Bacon
Boston • London • Toronto • Sydney • Tokyo • Singapore

Series Editor: Ray Short
Editorial Assistant: Christine Svitila
Marketing Manager: Kris Farnsworth
Senior Editorial Production Administrator: Susan McIntyre
Editorial Production Service: Ruttle, Shaw & Wetherill, Inc.
Composition Buyer: Linda Cox
Manufacturing Buyer: Megan Cochran
Cover Administrator: Linda Knowles

Library of Congress Cataloging-in-Publication Data

Taylor, Ronald L., [date]
    Assessment of exceptional students : educational and psychological
procedures / Ronald L. Taylor.--4th ed.
        p.   cm.
    Includes bibliographical references (p.   ) and indexes.
    ISBN 0-205-18859-1
    1. Handicapped children--Education--United States.   2. Handicapped
children--United States--Psychological testing.   3. Educational
tests and measurements--United States.   4. Special education--United
States.   I. Title.
LC4031.T36   1997
371.9'0973--dc20   96-10691
                                                                   CIP

Printed in the United States of America

10   9   8   7   6   5   4   3   2   01   00   99   98   97

CONTENTS

PREFACE

Assessment is an area that is constantly changing. New laws, philosophies, and assessment instruments and techniques quickly make information in this field obsolete. A tremendous amount of change has occurred in the four years since publication of the third edition of this book. This fourth edition includes information that reflects those changes. Specifically, this edition includes:

1. A separate chapter on portfolio assessment and other alternative assessment procedures.
2. A separate chapter on the assessment of written expression.
3. Information related to assessing students with Attention Deficit Disorder and Attention Deficit/Hyperactivity Disorder.
4. Information related to assessing children with autism.
5. An update of legislation affecting assessment.
6. Expanded coverage of curriculum-based assessment and other teacher-oriented assessment procedures.
7. An update of philosophical movements that affect assessment practices (e.g., inclusion).
8. Descriptions and discussions of more than thirty new or revised tests.
9. An updated review of the literature that includes approximately 150 new references.

Obviously, other changes have also been made, and many of the procedures or instruments that are outdated have been eliminated (or greatly reduced if they are outdated but still used). The fourth edition has, however, kept most of the general features of previous editions.

The text is divided into six major parts. Part I, Introduction to Assessment: Issues and Concerns, begins with a chapter that traces the historical, philosophical, and legal foundations of assessment. The second chapter serves as a general introduction to educational and psychological assessment. It poses several questions that must be answered prior to assessing any student, and it also proposes an assessment model. Chapter 3 addresses practical considerations that should be taken into account during the assessment process, whereas Chapter 4 focuses on the controversial area of labeling and classification. Part II, Informal Procedures: Basic Tools for Teachers, includes chapters related to observation (Chapter 5), criterion-referenced testing and error analysis (Chapter 6), curriculum-based assessment and measurement (Chapter 7), and portfolio and other alternative assessment procedures (Chapter 8).

Part III, consisting of Chapters 9 through 12, provides a discussion and overview of the instruments and procedures most widely used to assess an individual's underlying *abilities*. This includes chapters on the assessment of intelligence (Chapter 9), adaptive behavior (Chapter 10), behavioral/emotional status (Chapter 11), and language (Chapter 12). Part IV focuses on the assessment of *achievement*, including general academic areas (Chapter 13), reading (Chapter 14), mathematics (Chapter 15), and written expression (Chapter 16). The following format is used to describe the instruments in these two parts: A general description is followed by a more specific description of subtests or other components of each test; a discussion about how the scores are interpreted; a subsection focusing on technical characteristics, including standardization, reliability, and validity, and a review of the relevant research (discussed later). Finally, for each test described, an overview box summarizes the information and suggests uses for the test.

The Review of Relevant Research section for each test is a feature unique to this textbook, and it describes the literature that practitioners will find useful for test selection, administration, and interpretation. Specifically, these reviews highlight studies dealing with the reliability and validity of the instruments, as well as their use with special education students. The research studies were located by a computer search. The information yielded by the search was cross-checked against the following periodicals: *Diagnostique, Learning Disability Quarterly, Remedial and Special Education, Journal of Learning Disabilities, Journal of Special Education, Exceptional Children, Psychology in the Schools, Journal of School Psychology, Education and Training in Mental Retardation, Mental Retardation, American Journal of Mental Retardation, Gifted Child Quarterly*, and *Educational and Psychological Measurement*. For the fourth edition, literature from 1991 through 1995 was updated.

Part V, Special Assessment Considerations, includes a description of assessment procedures and instruments relevant for early childhood (Chapter 17), and older students with vocational/transitional needs (Chapter 18). The book concludes with two case studies in which the assessment process is followed from initial identification through the development of an Individualized Education Program (IEP).

A number of unique features have been retained in the fourth edition:

1. A pragmatic approach to assessment is emphasized. .
2. A summary matrix is provided for most chapters. This matrix presents information about specific instruments and techniques in a format that allows easy comparison of the instruments for suggested use and target population. The matrix also includes a statement of any special considerations of which a user should be aware. Finally, for each instrument or technique, the matrix gives the educational relevance for exceptional students. The matrices are directly related to the assessment model proposed in Chapter 2.
3. Both informal and formal assessment procedures are included, with emphasis on how each kind of procedure fits into the assessment process.
4. A thorough review of relevant research is provided for each norm-referenced instrument. The review emphasizes the use of the test with exceptional students.
5. An overview box is provided for each test. The overview summarizes the age range, technical adequacy, and suggested use for the test. This feature adds to the value of this book as a reference text.
6. The book examines instruments and techniques both for students with mild disabilities and for students with severe disabilities. The two case studies in Chapter 19 reflect this emphasis.
7. An instructor's manual that includes test questions and activities is available.

Needless to say, many individuals deserve my sincere appreciation and thanks. Although many provided feedback and suggestions, several deserve specific acknowledgment. Thanks to reviewers Lamoine J. Miller, Northeast Louisiana University; Tim Heron, The Ohio State University; and Nancy Halhuber, Eastern Michigan University. My thanks go to Steve Richards and Rod Van Dyke for their contributions to Chapter 18; to graduate students Geny Lima and Andrea Presberg for their assistance in compiling information; to Barbara Truzzolino and Cindy Carson for their secretarial and technical assistance; and to my wife and sons for their perseverance, patience, and support.

Part I

INTRODUCTION TO ASSESSMENT: ISSUES AND CONCERNS

Assessment is a critical component of the educational process. It allows educators and other professionals to make relevant educational decisions. Some individuals downplay the importance of assessment, believing that time spent assessing would better be spent teaching. If, however, appropriate assessment procedures are conducted, the information obtained can be used to enhance the teaching process.

In this section, several issues important to the establishment of appropriate assessment procedures will be discussed. The potential uses as well as the limitations of assessment will be considered. Assessment does not occur in a vacuum; neither is it left totally to the discretion of the assessor. Many important historical events and philosophical movements have shaped the assessment procedures found in today's schools. Similarly, there have been significant court cases and legislation that mandate certain assessment practices. These areas, discussed in Chapter 1, will provide the reader with the *historical framework* for developing assessment procedures.

Assessment should also be practical and efficient. One important issue is knowing when to apply what assessment procedure. This requires, among other things, understanding the types and purposes of various assessment sources. Such information will be provided and an assessment model will be presented in Chapter 2. This will give the reader a *conceptual framework* for developing assessment procedures.

Assessment certainly is more than the simple administration of a test. Nonetheless, testing is an integral part of the assessment process. Because tests supply only a *sample* of a student's behavior, it is important to understand all the variables that can affect test performance. More importantly, these variables must be considered when making decisions based on that test performance. These practical considerations related to the testing process and tests themselves are discussed in Chapter 3. One of the most controversial uses of assessment information is to make labeling and classification decisions. Chapter 4 is devoted to a critical discussion of this important area.

AFTER READING PART I YOU SHOULD BE ABLE TO:

- Identify historical events, philosophical movements, litigation, and legislation that have had an effect on assessment procedures in today's schools.
- Identify important questions that should be asked before initiating any assessment, resulting in a more efficient and practical process.
- Identify factors that can affect assessment results, including those related to the examiner, the examinee, and the test itself.
- Identify the important issues and problems related to the use of assessment information for labeling and classification purposes.

1

ASSESSMENT: HISTORICAL, PHILOSOPHICAL, AND LEGAL CONSIDERATIONS

Areas Included

Historical Events

Philosophical Movements

Relevant Assessment Litigation

Bias in Testing

Appropriateness of Assessment Procedures

Relevant Legislation

P.L. 94-142

P.L. 99-457

P.L. 101-476

P.L. 101-336

Assessment refers to the gathering of relevant information to help an individual make decisions. The educational and psychological assessment of exceptional students, specifically, involves the collection of information that is relevant in making decisions regarding appropriate goals and objectives, teaching strategies, and program placement. The assessment process should include the general education teacher, special education teacher, school psychologist, specialists, therapists, and any other individuals involved in a student's educational program. Assessment should be an active, ongoing process that has a clearly specified purpose. Further, it can and should be an individualized process, as individualized as instructional strategies are. Not only is it inappropriate, but it is also practically impossible to use the same group of tests with all exceptional students; by definition, this population has unique characteristics and concerns that require an individualized approach.

Although educational and psychological assessment has been considered synonymous with testing, it involves much more than the simple acts of administering and scoring tests and reporting test scores. It includes the careful analysis of the information provided by various instruments and techniques (including tests), which should result in functional, relevant, appropriate decisions. The choice of which instrument or technique to use and the decision about which method of analysis or interpretation is best largely depends on the goal or purpose for the assessment. This textbook focuses on this pragmatic issue that emphasizes the appropriate use of various instruments and techniques, depending on the specific purpose for the assessment.

Before addressing these pragmatic issues that will shape the assessment process, it is important to discuss other factors that have had, and will continue to have, an effect on assessment policies and procedures used in the schools. These include historical events and philosophical movements, court cases (litigation), and legislation that directly or indirectly affect assessment practices. In this chapter, a chronology of the historical, philosophical, and legal events that have influenced assessment practices is presented, followed by a summary of the legislation that has led to, or has been a result of, those events.

HISTORICAL EVENTS AND PHILOSOPHICAL MOVEMENTS

Early Twentieth Century

Before special education became a formal field, most assessment issues were related to the measurement of the areas of intelligence and personality. This reflected the beginnings of the special education field with its roots in medicine and psychology. Alfred Binet had perhaps the first major influence on the use of assessment instruments with exceptional individuals. He and Theodore Simon were asked by the Ministry of Education in France to develop an intelligence test that could be used to differentiate individuals with and without mental retardation. Their test was translated into English in 1908 and was revised by Terman in 1916 and called the Stanford-Binet. This marked the first formal attempt to provide an objective measure of intelligence.

1920s–1950s

Attempts at measuring personality characteristics and emotional status were popular over the next three decades, using a variety of instruments tied primarily to the fields of psychology and psychiatry. These included the development of projective tests such as the Rorschach Ink Blot Test (Rorschach, 1932), thematic picture tests such as the Thematic Apperception Test (Murray, 1943), and personality inventories such as the Minnesota Multiphasic Personality Inventory (Hathaway & Meehl, 1951). These tests are still used today, although their relevance in education has been questioned (see Chapter 11 for a discussion). Also during this period, there was increased interest in the measurement of achievement. Many group achievement tests such as the Metropolitan Achievement Tests were developed more than fifty years ago and continue to be revised as educational demands and curricula in the schools change.

1960s

In the 1960s, the role of assessment, particularly through standardized testing, became increasingly popular. This also mirrored the coming of age of the field of special education itself. When the term *learning disabilities* was coined in 1963, the door opened for the development of tests that went beyond the measurement of intelligence, personality, and achievement. During this period, primarily as a result of the application of the medical/neurological model, "process testing" became very popular. This included perceptual-motor tests and other instruments designed to measure how a student processed information. Examples of such tests are the Illinois Test of Psycholinguistic Ability (Kirk, McCarthy, & Kirk, 1968) and the Developmental Test of Visual Perception (Frostig, Lefever, & Whittlesey, 1966). The Developmental Test of Visual Perception was recently revised (Hammill, Pearson, & Voress, 1993). Appendix A provides a brief description of several instruments that have been used as process tests. The overemphasis on perceptual-motor testing, in particular, had quite an influence on the field of assessment.

Misuses of Perceptual-Motor Tests

Perceptual-motor theorists such as Kephart, Cratty, and Frostig were partially responsible for the movement toward perceptual-motor testing during the 1960s. These theorists emphasized the importance—in fact, the necessity—of perceptual-motor skills in the acquisition of academic skills. The problem was that many professionals stressed perceptual-motor development to the exclusion of academic-skill development. In other words, people assumed that development of perceptual-motor skills would "generalize" to academic areas, because such skills were considered a crucial component of the academic skills. Historically, this movement led to (1) the use of perceptual-motor tests to predict achievement; (2) the use of perceptual-motor tests to help determine "modality strength and weaknesses" for teaching purposes; and (3) the development of remedial programs specifically designed for perceptual-motor skills. Each of these purported uses is discussed separately.

Use of Tests to Predict Achievement.   In general, research on the use of perceptual-motor tests to predict achievement was disappointing. At best, most tests showed moderate correlations with achievement. Hammill and Larsen (1974) reviewed more than thirty research studies that investigated the relationship of auditory-visual integration with reading disability. They concluded that "apparently a large percentage of children who perform adequately on tests of auditory perception experience difficulty in learning to read; and an equally sizeable percentage who do poorly on these same tests have no problems in reading." Similarly, Larsen and Hammill (1975) reviewed more than sixty studies of visual perception and school learning and found no support for the relationship between tested visual-perceptual problems and academic achievement.

Use of Tests to Determine Modality Preference.   One of the least-understood issues in the area of special education is that of "modality teaching." According to proponents of this model (for example, Johnson & Myklebust, 1967; Wepman, 1967), children should be classified as primarily auditory or primarily visual learners, according to their scores on certain tests. The children should then be taught through their strong modality (for example, phonics for auditory learners; sight-word for visual learners). Although this approach might have intuitive appeal, little empirical evidence has suggested that the model is a valid one. In a careful analysis of the existing literature on the subject, Arter and Jenkins (1977) found that only one of fourteen studies supported the modality-teaching model. That study (Bursuk, 1971) differed from the others in that secondary-level students were used and reading comprehension was the dependent measure (all other studies used elementary students and tested beginning-reading skills). Arter and Jenkins (1977) gave several possible explanations for the general lack of support for the modality-preference model:

1. Modality strength may be an irrelevant factor in teaching.
2. Other uncontrolled factors may conceal the effects of modality teaching.
3. The instruments used to determine modality preference are ineffective and technically inadequate.
4. The criterion measures used to determine learning might be insensitive.

Whatever the reason, little empirical evidence has supported this widely used model. It does stand to reason, however, that using an indirect measure, such as a perceptual-motor test, to determine modality preference for *academic learning* is not the best way to find out the desired information. Why not determine modality preference directly, by measuring the effects of various instructional procedures on learning rate?

Use of Perceptual-Motor Training Programs.   Research in this area has been fairly straightforward. There is little or no evidence that perceptual-motor training improves academic ability (Hallahan & Cruickshank, 1973; Hallahan & Kauffman, 1976; Larsen & Hammill, 1975). In fact, Kavale and Mattson (1983), using a metaanalysis procedure, found that perceptual-motor training was not an effective intervention technique for improving academic, cognitive, or even perceptual-motor skills. They titled their article "One Jumped Off the Balance Beam: Metaanalysis of Perceptual-Motor Training" as an analogy to *One Flew Over the Cuckoo's Nest*, the Ken Kesey novel in which mental patients endured the harsh, and usually illogical, authority of the head nurse until one patient finally rebelled and escaped. Kavale and Mattson comment: "Perceptual-motor interventions are not effective treatments for exceptional children. Perceptual-motor training results in little or no improvement for trained subjects but will probably continue until its apparent futility becomes recognized and one falls off the balance beam." Interestingly, there has been some official movement to deemphasize the use of perceptual-motor training. In 1986, the Council for Learning Disabilities published a position statement that opposed the measurement and training of perceptual and perceptual-motor functions as a part of learning disabilities services.

Early 1970s

Partially as a result of the backlash against perceptual-motor testing, the 1970s brought a somewhat negative view of standardized testing in special education. This negativism was fueled by court cases accusing the schools of discriminatory use of assessment information and charging that many of the tests themselves were discriminatory (discussed later in this chapter). Also at this time, the behavioral model became prominent; included in this model was an emphasis on observation and a de-emphasis on the use of test data on which inferences had to be made. Indeed, there was almost a moratorium against the use of many standardized tests in special education; certainly there was a widespread acknowledgment of their limitations.

Late 1970s and Early 1980s

To further cloud the issue, the passage of P.L. 94-142 (discussed later in this chapter) mandated certain assessment procedures (e.g., nondiscriminatory evaluation) and implied the need for various types of assessment procedures. For example, P.L. 94-142 required that students receive a specific label in order to receive funding; this implied the need for standardized norm-referenced tests. (Chapter 4 addresses the important issue of labeling and classification.) Further, the requirement of an Individualized Education Program suggested the need for more precise informal measures. Suffice it to say that in the late 1970s and early 1980s there was a shift in emphasis to more informal assessment tempered by the realization that more formal assessment procedures would need to be used as well. The philosophy stated in Chapter 2 and applied throughout this book is that *both* types of assessment procedures can and should be helpful. The appropriate use of both types occurs when the purpose for the evaluation is matched to the type of assessment procedure and when the strengths and limitations of both approaches are recognized.

Mid-1980s–Early 1990s

In the mid-1980s, a major philosophical movement affected the field of education and its assessment practices. In an article entitled "Educating Children with Learning Problems: A Shared Responsibility," Madeleine Will (1986) summarized several reasons why and how the concept of special education might be changed. Will, who was assistant secretary of the Office of Special Education and Rehabilitative Services in the U.S. Office of Education, was in a unique position both to evaluate the state of special education and to suggest any necessary changes. She noted, for example, that the current system separated regular[1] and special education, stigmatized certain students as being handicapped, and addressed failure of students rather than prevention of problems. She also noted that whereas approximately 10 percent of the school population might be eligible to receive special education, another 10–20 percent had significant problems in school yet did not qualify for special education. Will's recommendation was to have regular educators and special educators "collectively contribute skills and resources to carry out individual educational plans based on individualized educational needs." Specifically, she suggested that assessment and intervention strategies be employed before the referral for special education to try to prevent the identification of a child as handicapped. Figure 1.1 shows a model for *prereferral intervention* that emphasizes the amount of assessment and intervention that should take place before a referral is made. Will also suggested that we need to emphasize the *curriculum-based assessment* procedures discussed in Chapter 7.

This Regular Education Initiative (REI) was implemented on a trial basis in a number of states and local school districts. Although the pros and cons of the initiative are still being debated, many changes have been made in assessment practices as a result.

Early 1990s–Present

Partially as an extension of the REI, educational reform efforts are continuing in the 1990s. The most notable, as well as controversial, is *full inclusion*. Proponents of full inclusion believe that *all* students, regardless of the type or severity of their disability, should be taught in the general education classroom at their home school. Their reasoning is that these students are a minority group and denying them access to the general education classroom violates their civil rights (e.g., Stainback & Stainback, 1992). Critics point out that full inclusion violates the concept of *least restrictive environment* that is mandated by federal law (discussed later in this chapter). Some confusion also exists over *how* full inclusion should be implemented. Should it involve the general education teacher working with the students without disabilities and the special education teacher working with those with disabilities in the same classroom? Team teaching all students? Using the special education teacher as a consultant? Mutually planning the curriculum

---

[1]Although the term *regular education* was preferred during this time period, the more accepted term *general education* is used throughout the remainder of this book.

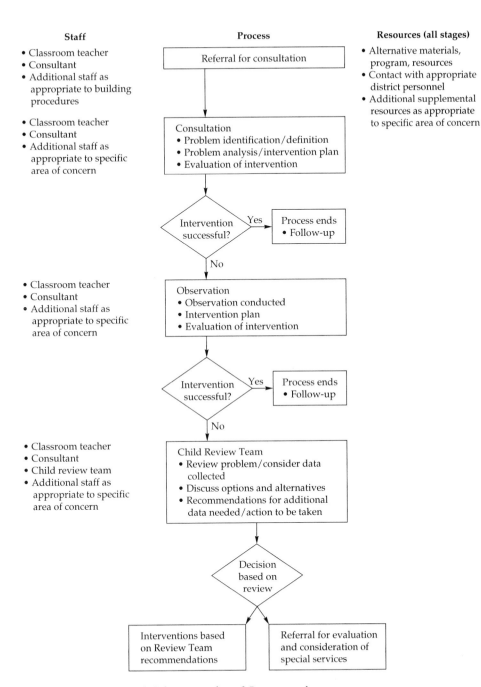

Staff

- Classroom teacher
- Consultant
- Additional staff as appropriate to building procedures

- Classroom teacher
- Consultant
- Additional staff as appropriate to specific area of concern

- Classroom teacher
- Consultant
- Additional staff as appropriate to specific area of concern

- Classroom teacher
- Consultant
- Child review team
- Additional staff as appropriate to specific area of concern

Process

Referral for consultation

Consultation
- Problem identification/definition
- Problem analysis/intervention plan
- Evaluation of intervention

Intervention successful? — Yes → Process ends
- Follow-up

No

Observation
- Observation conducted
- Intervention plan
- Evaluation of intervention

Intervention successful? — Yes → Process ends
- Follow-up

No

Child Review Team
- Review problem/consider data collected
- Discuss options and alternatives
- Recommendations for additional data needed/action to be taken

Decision based on review

Interventions based on Review Team recommendations

Referral for evaluation and consideration of special services

Resources (all stages)

- Alternative materials, program, resources
- Contact with appropriate district personnel
- Additional supplemental resources as appropriate to specific area of concern

FIGURE 1.1   A Model for Prereferral Intervention

From J. Graden, A. Casey, and S. Christenson. Implementing a Prereferral Intervention System: Part I. The Model. *Exceptional Children*, 1985, *51*, 380. Copyright © 1985 by the Council for Exceptional Children.

and teaching all the students? Indeed, the term holds different meanings for different people. The effect of full inclusion on assessment is straightforward, however. It means that the general education teacher will become much more involved in the overall process.

Another visible movement is the shift toward *alternative assessment* procedures. This category includes authentic, performance-based, and portfolio techniques. Their common link is that they provide direct measurement of student learning and progress and focus on the process rather than the product of learning (Rivera, 1993). Wolf, LeMahieu, and Eresh (1992) noted that these approaches tap higher-level thinking and problem-solving skills that emphasize the critique of the student work as part of a dynamic, ongoing process. For example, instead of a teacher determining how many words a student can read compared with others (traditional assessment), he or she might determine the student's attitude toward reading, develop a list of the books the student has read, create a tape of the student reading, and obtain the student's self-evaluation (portfolio assessment). Portfolio assessment is discussed in depth in Chapter 8.

RELEVANT ASSESSMENT LITIGATION[2]

The majority of the court cases related to assessment practices, particularly the earlier ones, focused on the discriminatory use of tests with ethnic minority children. Many of these cases also helped lead to the nondiscriminatory evaluation clause of P.L. 94-142, discussed later in this chapter. Those cases included *Hobson v. Hanson, Diana v. California, Guadalupe v. Tempe, Larry P. v. Riles, PASE v. Hannon,* and *Marshall v. Georgia.* Later cases focused more on assessment practices such as the timely delivery of assessment procedures. These included *Jose P. v. Ambach* and *Luke S. & Hans S. v. Nix et al.* Each of these cases is summarized next.

Hobson v. Hanson *(1968)*

This was the first major case focusing on the misuse or discriminatory use of test scores. The plaintiff charged that test scores were being used to "track" minority students, particularly black students, into the lower track of the educational programs. The court found the grouping of students for tracking purposes to be unconstitutional due to its discriminatory nature.

Diana v. State Board of Education *(1970)*

This case was filed in California on behalf of nine Spanish-speaking children who were placed into classes for students with mental retardation based on their scores

---

[2]In the sections on litigation and legislation, terminology specific to each case or law is used to maintain historical integrity. Throughout the remainder of the book, current terminology is used (e.g., "student with a disability" instead of "handicapped student").

from intelligence tests administered in English. Among the consent decrees from this case, several had particular relevance: (1) language competence should be assessed, (2) tests in the student's primary language should be subsequently administered, (3) more emphasis should be placed on nonverbal measures for students whose primary language is not English, and (4) students who are placed incorrectly should be appropriately reevaluated.

Guadalupe v. Tempe *(1972)*

This case was similar to the *Diana* case with similar conclusions. In addition, however, this case noted the importance of evaluating adaptive behavior before labeling a student as having mental retardation. (Adaptive behavior is discussed in Chapter 10.)

Larry P. v. Riles *(1971)*

The *Larry P.* case focused on the alleged cultural bias of intelligence tests. This is perhaps the best-known and certainly the most complex court case that has dealt with assessment issues. In fact, the case has surfaced and resurfaced for more than fifteen years in appeals and was the basis for another court case, *Crawford v. Honig* (1988). There are purportedly more than ten thousand pages of transcripts related to the case (Reschly, Kicklighter, & McKee, 1988). The *Larry P.* case was first filed in 1971. Several injunctions were imposed until 1977, followed by an eight-month trial. Finally, in 1979, Judge Peckham reached the following conclusions: (1) intelligence tests are biased, (2) the use of intelligence tests to classify black children as having mental retardation was prohibited, and (3) the overrepresentation of black children as having educable mental retardation must be eliminated. The state of California appealed the decision, but it was upheld by a two-to-one vote in 1984. In 1986, the *Larry P.* plaintiffs again went to court charging that overrepresentation of black students had not changed markedly since the early 1970s, although the label had changed to "learning handicapped" (Reschly, 1991). The result was the complete prohibition of intelligence tests for the purpose of identifying or placing black students into special education. Further, an intelligence test could not be used with a black student *even with parental consent.* This last point is the basis for the previously mentioned *Crawford v. Honig*, in which black parents argued discrimination because their children *could not* be evaluated using an intelligence test. One can clearly see the impact that the *Larry P.* case has had on assessment procedures overall and in California in particular.

PASE v. Hannon *(1980)*

Ironically, another court case almost identical to the *Larry P.* case was heard in the state of Illinois with the opposite conclusions. Provided with similar evidence, Judge Grady ruled that intelligence test bias had an insignificant influence on psychoeducational assessment and that the overrepresentation was not regarded as discriminatory (Reschly, 1991). Clearly, this confused the overall issue of test bias. It did, however, help formulate the professional question of whether or not the right issue is being debated. Is it the tests that are biased or are tests being used in a biased fashion (Taylor, 1990)?

Marshall v. Georgia *(1984)*

In a related case, the plaintiffs alleged that overrepresentation of black students in special education was caused by violations of procedural regulations and improper interpretation of state and federal guidelines regarding classification and placement. Although the issues of intelligence tests and IQs were discussed, they clearly took a subordinate role (Reschly, Kicklighter, & McKee, 1988). Again in this case the defense of the school district was supported, although procedural violations were acknowledged and prereferral intervention guidelines were established (Reschly, 1991). It would appear that, for the most part, the specific allegations against test bias will probably be debated outside the courtroom in the future.

Jose P. v. Ambach *(1983)*

This suit filed against New York City was concerned with the appropriate delivery of services. Specifically, the plaintiffs noted the delays in providing services to students referred for special education. The judge sided with the plaintiffs and, among other things, charged that the district must provide a *timely evaluation* after a student is referred. This was defined as a maximum of thirty days from referral to evaluation.

Luke S. & Hans S. v. Nix et al. *(1982)*

This case was similar to that of *Jose P.* There were estimates that as many as ten thousand students were not being evaluated within the sixty day period after referral noted in Louisiana's guidelines. The court agreed with the plaintiffs and noted that the state should provide greater assessment *before* the referral is made (prereferral assessment). The case also resulted in more training of both general and special educators in the area of assessment.

SIGNIFICANT LEGISLATION

Along with philosophical movements and litigation comes legislation. Interestingly, although in some cases the philosophical movements and litigation have led to legislation, in others the legislation has led to philosophical movements and litigation. Among the relevant legislation that affects assessment practices is P.L. 94-142 as well as various amendments to that law, including P.L. 99-457 and P.L.

101-476. Each of these laws, as well as the Americans with Disabilities Act (ADA) of 1990, are discussed next.

Public Law 94-142: Education for All Handicapped Children Act

The law that has had perhaps the most impact on the field of special education is the Education for All Handicapped Children Act (P.L. 94-142). Regardless of any future changes in legislation, and even though federal legislation cannot override state laws, P.L. 94-142 has had a profound effect on assessment practices in special education. The law emphasized the following six principles (*Federal Register*, 1977):

1. *Zero reject:* All handicapped children should be provided with a free, appropriate public education.

2. *Nondiscriminatory evaluation:* This principle is defined as avoiding discrimination in the

   . . . procedures used . . . to determine whether a child is handicapped and the nature and extent of the special education and related services that the child needs. The term means procedures used selectively with a child and does not include basic tests administered to or procedures used with all children in a school, grade or class (Federal Register, p. 42494).

   This definition implies that the principle of nondiscriminatory evaluation covers classification as well as the determination of the most appropriate educational program.

3. *Individualized Education Programs (IEPs):* All students with disabilities must have an IEP; among other components, IEPs should include (1) documentation of the current level of performance; (2) annual goals; (3) short-term objectives; and (4) evaluation procedures and schedules for determining the mastery of short-term objectives. Other requirements include documentation of the type and duration of the planned services, and information related to the extent of general education programming.

4. *Least restrictive environment:* This is perhaps the most publicized and least understood principle of P.L. 94-142. Although it implies that children with disabilities should be educated with children without disabilities to the maximum extent possible, it is not synonymous with mainstreaming. The idea of the law is that, ultimately, a child with a disability should be mainstreamed; however, the law does not require that a child be mainstreamed if the type or severity of the disability precludes the child's successful performance in a mainstream environment. As is mentioned earlier, the current emphasis on full inclusion is also related to the least restrictive environment concept.

5. *Due process:* This principle refers to a system of checks and balances that seeks to ensure the fairness of educational decisions and the accountability of both the professionals and the parents who make those decisions (Strickland & Turnbull, 1990).

6. *Parental participation:* This principle ensures that parents are informed of decisions made about their children and encourages their participation in the decision-making process.

In reality, all of these principles addressed by P.L. 94-142 indirectly affect or are affected by assessment. The two principles that have direct relevance are *nondiscriminatory evaluation* and *parental participation*.

Nondiscriminatory Evaluation

Although it included no suggested procedures or specific definition of nondiscriminatory evaluation, P.L. 94-142 did outline acceptable assessment guidelines in considerable detail. Six points were included in those guidelines.

1. *Tests and other evaluation material*

   a. *should be provided and administered in the child's native language or other mode of communication, unless it is clearly not feasible to do so.* Considerable research points to the unfairness of using inappropriate tests with certain populations. Examples include using intelligence tests requiring motor responses for individuals with cerebral palsy or tests using visual input for partially sighted children and auditory input for persons with hearing impairment. Similarly, using tests in English for children whose primary language is not English is no longer considered appropriate. Although these examples are obvious, they demonstrate the need to ensure the measurement of skills through the dominant mode of communication.

   b. *should have been validated for the specific purpose for which they are used.* The validity of tests and other assessment materials is an absolute prerequisite for a meaningful evaluation (see Chapter 3).

   c. *should be administered by trained personnel in conformity with the instructions provided by the producer.* The American Psychological Association's *Standards for Educational and Psychological Tests* (1985) includes several guidelines for test administrators. At the very least, persons involved in evaluation should be thoroughly familiar with the instrument used and should be knowledgeable about the general area of assessment. The degree of expertise necessary, at least in terms of test administration, depends somewhat on the test used. To administer some tests (such as the WISC-III and the Stanford-Binet-4), certification and licenses are necessary. Some test publishers also indicate the examiner qualifications of specific tests in their catalog. American Guidance Service, for example, will not sell a test to a person who does not have the qualifications to administer it. The amount of preparation required to administer most tests, however, is left to the examiner's discretion. Such factors as test length, type of test, and degree of subjectivity in the scoring criteria should be considered in determining when an examiner is considered to be trained. Because of differences in length of administration and sophistication of scoring, for example, it will take more preparation to administer a test such as the Differential Abilities Scale than to administer the Wide Range Achievement Test-3.

2. *Tests and other evaluation materials should include instruments tailored to assess specific areas of educational need, and not merely instruments designed to provide a single general IQ.* This simply means that the bottom line is the individual's actual educational ability or disability. Procedures aimed at determining those needs, therefore, become the core of the evaluation. Intelligence testing alone is not considered sufficient to determine a student's educational status.

3. *Tests should be selected and administered so as to best ensure that for a child with impaired sensory, manual, or speaking skills, the test accurately reflects the child's aptitude or achievement level or whatever other factors the test purports to measure, rather then reflecting the child's impaired sensory, manual, or speaking skills (except where those skills are the factors that the test purports to measure).* This point essentially means that the test results should not be affected by the child's disability. For instance, a child with a reading problem should not be given a written math test stressing word problems to determine arithmetic achievement.

4. *No single procedure should be used as the sole criterion for determining an appropriate educational program for a child.* Again, the obvious implication is that a child can no longer be placed according to the results of a single instrument. Several of the previously discussed court cases that focus on the use of a single IQ to determine placement helped lead to this mandate.

5. *The evaluation should be made by a multidisciplinary team or group of persons including at least one teacher or other specialist with knowledge in the area of the suspected disability.* One important component is the inclusion of the teacher or other professional who has the most knowledge of the disability. This requires the teacher to become an active part of the assessment process. The multidisciplinary approach also requires communication among the evaluators to avoid replication of test procedures and to enhance interpretation of the results.

6. *The child should be assessed in all areas related to the suspected disability, including, where appropriate, health, vision, hearing, social and emotional status, general intelligence, academic performance, communicative status, and motor abilities.* This point again emphasizes the multidisciplinary approach to assessment.

The search for nondiscriminatory evaluation procedures has been frustrating. Duffey, Salvia, Tucker, and Ysseldyke (1981) identified eleven proposed solutions that had been tried. Among these were development of culture-fair, culture-free, or culture-specific tests; translation of existing tests; alteration of administrative procedures; and a moratorium on testing. Unfortunately, none of these approaches has been a panacea. As an example, Padilla and Garza (1975) noted that difficulties are encountered when tests are translated from one language to another. One example is an intelligence test item in which the examiner shows his or her thumb and asks, "What do you call this finger?" They point out that the formal word for thumb in Spanish is *pulgar*, but that this word is rarely used; most Spanish-speaking children would probably respond "dedo gordo," a common colloquial phrase meaning "fat finger." This answer would be scored as incorrect, according to the scoring criteria in the manual.

Parental Participation

P.L. 94-142 specified that parents must be kept informed about, and give their consent to, any evaluation of their child. The parents should receive written notification that includes the following types of information:

1. The reason for the evaluation and the person(s) who requested it.
2. The evaluation procedures and instruments that will be used. The parents have a right to evaluate those instruments.
3. A statement that they have the right to refuse the evaluation, but that an impartial hearing might be necessary to determine the outcome.
4. A statement that they have the right to an independent evaluation (usually paid for by the parents).

In addition, schools must allow parents to inspect their child's educational records (including assessment information) and provide them the opportunity to question the appropriateness of any of the included material. In general, this part of the law establishes that parents have the right, if not the obligation, to be aware of all steps in the special education process.

Public Law 99-457: Education of the Handicapped Act Amendments of 1986

Although there have been several amendments to P.L. 94-142, the one that perhaps has had the greatest impact on the area of assessment has been P.L. 99-457. Among the recommendations in this amendment was the need to identify and establish programs for infants and toddlers (children from birth to age 2) with disabilities. Specifically, P.L. 99-457 stated that there is an urgent and substantial need

1. *to enhance the development of handicapped infants and toddlers and to minimize their potential for developmental delay,*
2. *to reduce the educational costs to our society, including our Nation's schools, by minimizing the need for special education and related services after handicapped infants and toddlers reach school age,*

3. *to minimize the likelihood of institutionalization of handicapped individuals and maximize the potential for their independent living in society, and*

4. *to enhance the capacity of families to meet the special needs of their infants and toddlers with handicaps* (P.L. 99-457, Sec. 671; 1986).

The amendment defined handicapped infants and toddlers as children from birth to age 2 who are experiencing developmental delays, as measured by appropriate diagnostic instruments and procedures, in areas such as cognitive development, physical development, language and speech development, psychosocial development, or self-help skills. The law goes on to state that others who might qualify are those children who have a diagnosed physical or mental condition that has a high probability of resulting in developmental delay or children who are at risk of having substantial developmental delays should early intervention not be provided. The inclusion of "at-risk" children is up to the individual state's discretion, however. P.L. 99-457 also mandates that all states applying for P.L. 94-142 funds must serve all children ages 3 to 5 who have disabilities. In fact, considerable fiscal support available for the preschool population will be eliminated if the state does not meet the mandate.

This increased emphasis on early intervention created a need for more and improved diagnostic procedures for young children from birth through age 5. This resulted in the creation of new developmental tests and the revision of several older ones. Chapter 17 addresses infant and early childhood assessment.

Public Law 101-476: Education of the Handicapped Act Amendments of 1990

In 1990, President Bush signed the Amendments to the Education of the Handicapped Act that changed its name to the Individuals with Disabilities Education Act (IDEA). All of the references to *handicaps* noted in P.L. 94-142 and subsequent amendments were replaced by the term "disabilities." For example, the phrase "handicapped infants and toddlers" was replaced with "infants and toddlers with disabilities."

Although the most sweeping changes in P.L. 101-476 dealt with the authorization of grants for special programs and services, a few of the changes did have some influence on assessment practices. Among them were an emphasis on transition services that includes vocational evaluation (discussed in Chapter 18) and a requirement that a statement of needed transition services be placed in a student's IEP by at least the age of 16. Another change was the inclusion of traumatic brain injury and autism as separate categories of disability.

Public Law 101-336: Americans with Disabilities Act

Another major piece of legislation passed in 1990 was the Americans with Disabilities Act (ADA), which is essentially a civil rights act for individuals with disabilities. The law requires that accommodations must be made by schools, employers, and government agencies to allow persons with disabilities to participate to the fullest extent possible in daily living activities (Hallahan & Kauffman, 1994). This includes elimination of physical barriers (e.g., requiring ramps for wheelchair access) and modification of equipment (e.g., providing a relay service with an interpreter for an employee with a hearing impairment).

Unlike IDEA, which is relevant only until a person is age 21, ADA covers individuals of all ages. Thus, it is relevant to postsecondary settings and assessment of adults with disabilities. Implicit in this law is accommodation for individuals with disabilities when they are being assessed. For example, a college student with a learning disability might need extended time to complete an exam. Similarly, a student with a visual impairment might need to be evaluated using an enlarged print version of the test.

SUMMARY

A number of historical, philosophical, and legal events have played an important role in shaping the assessment policies and procedures that are used in the schools today. Historically, interest in the development and use of standardized tests, particularly in the areas of intelligence, personality, and achievement, grew in the first half of the twentieth century. In the 1960s, with the development of special education as a formal field, the interest in standardized testing increased, particularly in tests designed for use with students with learning disabilities. The 1970s, however, brought a somewhat negative attitude toward testing, partially as a result of discriminatory test practices and the overreliance on certain types of standardized tests (e.g., process tests). In the mid-1980s, proponents of the Regular Education Initiative reemphasized the limitations of standardized testing and stressed the importance of informal measures, particularly curriculum-based assessment. There is a general agreement that both types of assessment have their place if used appropriately. With the current emphasis on inclusion, the role of the general educator in the assessment process becomes an extremely important one. It will be necessary for the general educator and the special educator to work collaboratively to design and refine the assessment process.

Legally, the area of assessment has been affected by both litigation and legislation. Most court cases have dealt with the discriminatory use of tests (e.g., *Diana* and *Larry P.*) or with timely delivery of assessment services (e.g., *Jose P.*). The most relevant legislation has been P.L. 94-142 with its specific requirements for (among other things) the development of an Individualized Education Program, the use of nondiscriminatory procedures, and the delineation of parents' rights in the assessment process. Other legislation that has affected assessment are P.L. 99-457, which increased emphasis on infants and preschool children, and P.L. 101-476, which emphasized the importance of the assessment of a student's need for transitional services and added the categories of traumatic brain injury and autism. Finally, the ADA ensures that there can be no discrimination against individuals with disabilities. This implies that the necessary accommodations must be made during any assessment.

2

THE ASSESSMENT PROCESS:
A PROPOSED MODEL

Areas Included

Why Assess?

How Is the Process Initiated?

What Procedures Should Be Used?

Who Should Assess?

When Should Assessment Be Conducted?

What Should Be Done with the Results?

An Assessment Model

Before any assessment procedure is initiated, the prerequisite questions listed above must be addressed. The answers to these prerequisite questions serve as a basis for an assessment model discussed later in this chapter. A discussion of each of these questions and possible answers follows.

WHY ASSESS?

Any person who is involved in the assessment process should know why the assessment is being conducted. There are many purposes for assessment, and with careful planning more than one purpose can usually be addressed. Among the many purposes for assessment are (1) initial identification or screening; (2) determination and evaluation of teaching programs and strategies; (3) determination of current performance level and educational need; (4) decisions about classification and program placement; and (5) development of Individualized Education Programs (including goals, objectives, and evaluation procedures).

Initial Identification (Screening)

Typically, individuals who might require special services or special education are initially identified through assessment procedures. These can be either informal procedures (such as observation or analysis of work products) or more formal procedures (such as achievement or intelligence tests). In other words, assessment can be used to identify individuals who warrant further evaluation.

Assessment can also be used to screen individuals who are considered to be at high risk for developing various problems. These individuals do not yet demonstrate deficiencies requiring special attention, but they do demonstrate behaviors that suggest possible problems in the future. Identification of such individuals allows the careful monitoring of those potential trouble areas and occasionally implies the use of a program designed to "prevent the problem." For instance, children who lag behind in language skills before entering kindergarten might be monitored closely after they enter school to make sure that they do not fall behind in language-oriented areas. It might also be possible to initiate a language-stimulation program before kindergarten as a preventive measure.

Assessment for initial identification purposes, therefore, is used to identify individuals who might need additional evaluation or who might develop problems in the future. It is also possible to use assessment to identify those students for whom some type of immediate remedial program is warranted. In other words, assessment can be used to determine those students for whom prereferral intervention is necessary.

Determination and Evaluation of Teaching Programs and Strategies

One of the more important roles of assessment is to help determine appropriate teaching programs and strategies. For this purpose, assessment information can be used in four ways. First, prior to a student's receiving special education, it can be used to assist the general education teacher in determining what to teach and the best method for teaching it. Second, assessment procedures can also serve as a method to evaluate the effectiveness of the particular teaching program or strategy. Many times a formal referral for special education can be avoided if assessment information is used in this way. In other words, assessment data can be used to develop and evaluate prereferral intervention programs. Suppose, for example, that a teacher, Ms. Jones, had a student, Jim, who was performing inconsistently in the area of spelling. The teacher, before referring Jim for formal assessment to determine if he was eligible for special education services, decided to assess him informally. On the basis of the assessment, she determined that Jim was sounding out and spelling words purely on their phonetic representation. For instance, "decision" was spelled "dasishun," and "enough" was spelled "enuff." Ms. Jones then initiated an appropriate remedial program that, among other things, emphasized spelling rules. She reevaluated Jim periodically and determined that her teaching program had been effective, thus avoiding an unnecessary referral for a special education program.

Third, in determining appropriate programs and strategies, assessment can provide prereferral information to document the need for a formal referral. Suppose, for instance, that the remedial program in the preceding example did *not* work. The documentation from that experience could be used to help justify a referral for possible special education services. Fourth, this information can be incorporated into the individualized education program for students who are eligible for and who ultimately receive special education. Particularly relevant would be information that documents which teaching strategies or approaches have been used, both successfully and unsuccessfully.

In a survey of state departments of education, Carter and Sugai (1989) found that the majority strongly advocated the use of prereferral intervention and noted the crucial role played by the general educator. It is important to note that in most cases prereferral assessment and intervention are the responsibility of the general education teacher. In fact, Bahr (1994) reported data indicating that 92 percent of the general education teachers were responsible for implementing prereferral intervention programs, as compared with only 22 percent of the special education teachers. The importance of prereferral assessment and intervention has become so apparent that commercial products are available to help teachers in this process. One example is the *Prereferral Intervention Manual and Prereferral Checklist* (McCarney, 1993). This instrument aids identification of the most common learning and behavioral problems and provides suggested intervention strategies and activities for each. A computerized version is also available.

Determination of Current Performance Level and Educational Need

Since the mandate of P.L. 94-142, students who receive special education must have a clearly identified need that is not being currently met by their programs. This is accomplished by evaluating each student's current level of performance and could involve, among other things, measurement of preacademic, academic, or social skills. By using information for this purpose, the teacher or examiner can document the subject(s) and skill(s) for which each student needs special assistance. This information would also include the student's strengths and weaknesses and possible teaching strategies. In other words, assessment data for this purpose are used (1) to identify general areas in which the student needs additional help; (2) to identify both strengths and weaknesses of the student; and (3) to determine possible teaching strategies and remedial approaches for the student.

Decisions about Classification and Program Placement

The use of assessment data for classification purposes is controversial. Theoretically, individuals are classified to indicate similarities and relationships among their educational problems and to provide nomenclature that facilitates communication within the field (Hardman, Drew, Egan, & Wolf, 1993). With minor exceptions, it is currently also necessary to classify students to receive federal funds for special education services. On the negative side, attention has focused on the stigmatizing effect of such labels and the disproportionately high number of minority students labeled. (Classification and labeling are discussed in depth in Chapter 4.)

A placement decision is usually made at the time of classification, and assessment data are used to help make that decision. As noted previously, P.L. 94-142 required that individuals be placed in the least restrictive environment. Although this is often interpreted as mainstreaming, it suggests that students be placed into as "normal" an educational setting as is deemed appropriate, that is, one that provides optimum chance for success. This has traditionally resulted in a decision (using assessment information) to determine which "least restrictive" placement would be best for a child on a continuum from, for example, separate school, self-contained classroom, resource room, to the general education classroom. The emphasis has been placed on the student and on determining the setting in which the student will best learn and perform.

In the mid-1980s, emphasis shifted to investigating more creative settings that might be appropriate for students with different ability levels. One example was the *Adaptive Learning Environments Model* (ALEM). This model, developed and field tested at the University of Pittsburgh, contained twelve design components that allowed (1) early identification of learning problems through diagnostic-prescriptive monitoring, (2) description of students' needs in instructional rather than labeling terms, (3) the development of individually designed educational plans, and (4) the teaching of self-management skills (Wang & Birch, 1984). To meet these objectives, the ALEM included such things as involving the family, encouraging multi-age grouping of students based on instructional needs, and changing staffing patterns to provide an interface between general and special education. Unfortunately, the research on the effectiveness of the ALEM has been criticized. Bryan and Bryan (1988) noted, for example, a general lack of control subjects. Similarly, Anderegg and Vergason (1988) pointed out that ALEM was subject to problems in personnel, funding, and practical application. Wang and Zollers (1990) argued that ALEM was effective but acknowledged that it required systematic staff development and organizational support.

As noted in Chapter 1, the most recent emphasis among many special education professionals is on full inclusion, in which all students, regardless of type or severity of disability, are placed in the general education classroom. If this trend continues, assessment information will be used more to determine how instructional environment, materials, and strategies must be modified to accommodate students' needs rather than to determine which educational placement is most appropriate.

Development of the Individualized Education Program

If a student receives formal special education services and receives federal funding, he or she must have an *Individualized Education Program* (IEP), another requirement mandated by P.L. 94-142. Even if the law changes regarding requirement for delivery of special education services, the IEP should still be considered as best practice and should not be eliminated. The IEP functions as a "contract" to identify goals, objectives, and timelines for delivery of services. P.L. 101-476 and P.L. 99-457 have also mandated the development of *Individualized Transition Programs (ITPs)* and *Individualized Family Service Programs (IFSPs)*. ITPs are designed to assist students in the transition from school to the working world, whereas IFSPs have been used to assist families who have a child with a disability.

For an IEP, the following information must be included:

1. Documentation of the student's current level of performance
2. Indication of the specific services and type of program to be provided, including timelines for delivery of services
3. Annual goals
4. Short-term objectives
5. Procedures and schedules for evaluating goals and objectives

The first two requirements were discussed earlier; the other three requirements are extremely important and will be discussed as separate purposes. Also note that if assessment data is used for these five purposes, the legal requirement for the development of IEPs will be met.

Determination of Goals

Assessment data can help determine realistic goals for students. Typically, the goals identified for students are annual; that is, they project approximately one year in advance what a student should be doing. Goals are, as a rule, fairly general; they more or less delineate those major areas for which more specific and short-term objectives will be identified. An example of a goal might be, "Student will correctly add two-digit numbers with carrying."

Determination of Objectives

Assessment data are also important in determining appropriate objectives for students. The objectives that are identified for exceptional students are a sequential breakdown of those skills that provide a link between the student's current performance level and the projected annual goals. Assume, for instance, that a student can only add one-digit numbers with a sum of less than ten (current performance level). Using the goal cited in the preceding section, it might be possible to identify two objectives that are the necessary steps to reach the goal. These objectives might be: (1) student will correctly add one-digit numbers with a sum greater than ten and (2) student will correctly add two-digit numbers without carrying.

Objectives are usually thought of either as *general* (projecting at what level a student will be performing in approximately three to six months) or *short-term* (stating the immediate objective on which the student should be working). Figure

Current Level of Performance	What the student can currently do
Short-Term Objective	What the student should be working on in the immediate future
General Objective	What the student should be able to do in three to six months
Goal	What the student should be able to do in a year

FIGURE 2.1   Steps in the IEP Process

2.1 shows the progression that is followed in the IEP process and how the objectives fit into that progression.

To ensure that goals and objectives are appropriately determined, Tymitz-Wolf (1982) developed a checklist to serve as guidelines (Figure 2.2). Many assessment instruments and techniques are developed by following a sequential framework and are particularly relevant for identifying specific objectives. In reality, goals and objectives are usually determined simultaneously, using the same or similar assessment data. It is possible, however, that the information for goals and for objectives could come from different sources.

Evaluation of Goals and Objectives

An often-overlooked area in which assessment plays a major role is that of *program evaluation;* this refers to the constant monitoring of the appropriateness and effectiveness of the goals and objectives designed for each student. The evaluation of goals and objectives has three major aspects: (1) the determination of objective criteria; (2) the determination of appropriate evaluation procedures; and (3) the determination of evaluation schedules (Strickland & Turnbull, 1990).

The *determination of objective criteria* suggests that the goals and objectives be stated in terms of standards of time and accuracy. The following example, for instance, clearly states the criteria: "Given a worksheet with ten problems of two-digit addition (without carrying), the student will correctly solve the problems in twenty minutes or less with at least 90 percent accuracy." This aspect (determining objective criteria) can be addressed, therefore, by carefully writing the objective to include time and accuracy standards.

The *appropriate evaluation procedure* will depend on a number of factors. In practice, more formal procedures are used to evaluate goals and general objectives, whereas informal procedures are used to measure short-term objectives. In general, the schedule for evaluating goals and objectives should be determined when the IEP is developed. Also, it is helpful to determine who is responsible for the evaluation. Table 2.1 on page 26 gives a schedule that could be followed in evaluating an IEP.

1. Does the goal statement refer to target areas of deficit?	OR	Have I written a goal which is unrelated to remediation needs described in present level of performance and assessment information?
2. Given the assessment data, is it probable that this goal could be achieved in a year (i.e., annual period for the IEP)?	OR	Is the goal so broad that it may take two or more years to accomplish?
3. Does the goal contain observable terms with an identified target-area for remediation?	OR	Have I used words which fail to accurately describe the problem area or direction I am taking?
4. Have goals been written for each area of deficit?	OR	Do I have dangling data (data which indicate a need for remediation but have been overlooked)?
5. Is the scope of the objective appropriate?	OR	Have I written any objectives that encompass the entire year, thus making them annual goals?
6. Do the objectives describe a subskill of the goal?	OR	Have I failed to determine the hierarchy needed to teach the skill? • Did I simply rephrase the goal statement? • Did I describe a terminal skill, but only less of it?
7. Are the objectives presented in a sequential order?	OR	Have I listed the objectives in random order, unrelated to the way the skill would logically be taught?
8. Do the objectives show a progression through the skill to meet the goal?	OR	Do the objectives emphasize only one phase of a particular skill?
9. Does the objective contain an appropriately stated condition?	OR	Have I failed to describe the exact circumstances under which the behavior is to occur? • Have I described irrelevant or extraneous materials? • Does the condition refer to an isolated classroom activity?
10. Does the objective contain an appropriately stated performance using observable terms?	OR	Is the mode of performance (e.g., oral, different from the desired goal (e.g., written)?
11. Does the objective contain an appropriately stated standard?	OR	Is the standard unrelated to the assessment information and level of performance? • Am I using the performance statement as a standard? • Am I using percentages when the behavior requires alternative ways to measure? • Have I chosen arbitrary percentages?

FIGURE 2.2   Checklist for IEP Goals and Objectives

From Barbara Tymitz-Wolf. Guidelines for Assessing IEP Goals and Objectives. *Teaching Exceptional Children*, 1982, 14, 200. Copyright © 1982 by the Council for Exceptional Children. Reprinted by permission.

TABLE 2.1   Schedule for Evaluating an IEP

Component	Schedule for Evaluation	Person Primarily Responsible
1. Short-term instructional objective	Daily or weekly	Teacher(s)
2. General objective	2–6 months	Teacher(s), parents, and other staff
3. Annual goals	Once a year	Representative of public agency, teacher, and other staff
4. Delivery of services	2–6 months and at least twice a year	Representative of public agency, teacher, and other staff

From: S. Larsen and M. Poplin. *Methods for Educating the Handicapped: An Individualized Education Program Approach* (Boston: Allyn & Bacon, 1980). Copyright © 1980 by Allyn & Bacon. Reprinted by permission.

HOW IS THE PROCESS INITIATED?

After a student has been initially identified as having some type of problem or potential problem, decisions must be made about what to do next. As previously discussed, one option is to gather prereferral information and initiate a prereferral intervention program. In other words, the student is further assessed by the teacher who made the initial identification. In other situations, a formal referral is initiated to obtain the necessary assessment service. Each school or school district has different procedures for referring individuals for assessment. All those involved in assessment should be thoroughly familiar with the referral procedures used in their school or facility and with the services that are available.

Two points regarding referrals deserve further comment. The first is that, as a rule, an individual should not be referred until preliminary assessment data have been collected. For instance, instead of simply referring a child who is "acting up" in class, the documentation should include information about the type of behavior, the frequency or duration of the behavior, and the conditions under which the behavior occurs (time of day, behavioral antecedents, and consequences). In other instances, however, more extensive assessment can be done, including academic testing. As previously mentioned, many times a formal referral might be avoided by collecting this prereferral information and implementing a prereferral intervention program. Usually the severity of the problem dictates when, and if, a formal referral is necessary. In reality, students who receive special education provided by federal funds go through the formal referral process.

The second point is that the referral should include the prereferral assessment data and other specific information such as the type and effectiveness of any prereferral intervention strategies. Nothing is more frustrating than to refer a student for assessment, wait months for a report of the results, and find that you only learned what you already knew or that a program that you had already tried was recommended. This unnecessary situation can be avoided by carefully communicating what is already known about the individual and specifying clearly why you want the assessment. Figure 2.3 shows a referral form that might be more meaningful than many currently in use. A referral form such as this can be modi-

---

Please complete the following checklist if you need an educational assessment of a student in your class. This information will assist us in responding to your request. Please return the completed form to _____ (school psychologist).

Teacher: Referral Problem:
Student:
Date of Birth:
Date of Referral:

A. Priority for assessment
     _____1. *Urgent*—cannot program without further information
     _____2. *Important*—need information to develop most appropriate program
     _____3. *Useful*—need information to refine teaching program

B. Reason for referral
     _____1. To determine current level of academic functioning
     _____2. To compare with previous testing
     _____3. To establish educational objectives
     _____4. To determine student's learning style
     _____5. To consider student for possible special education program
     _____6. To receive information regarding possible behavior-intervention program
     _____7. Other (Please explain)

C. Type of assistance needed
     _____1. Formalized objective tests (i.e., battery of achievement and diagnostic testing)
     _____2. Classroom observation with formal and information testing
     _____3. Classroom observation, information assessment, and diagnostic prescriptive teaching assistance (involvement with child and teacher both in and out of the classroom)

D. Work products
If the referral problem is in the academic area, please attach any examples of student's performance.
If the referral is in a nonacademic area, please include any relevant observational data.

E. Please attach any information regarding intervention or remediation strategies that have already been tried to deal with the referral problem.

FIGURE 2.3   Example of a Referral Form

fied to the needs of each school. Moreover, the time spent completing such a form will be well spent.

WHAT PROCEDURES SHOULD BE USED?

Typically, people think of "giving tests" when they think of assessment. Although tests are typically included in the assessment process, the two terms are certainly not synonymous. Tests are merely a means of obtaining behavioral samples that give examiners a *quantitative* measure in a specific area. Thus, we might find out that John has an IQ of 102, Bill scored at the 3.6 grade level in reading, or Jane correctly completed 89 percent of her two-digit addition problems. In short, *tests are simply devices to which individuals are exposed that give a quantitative characterization of one or more traits of those individuals.* Nevertheless, tests are used extensively in the assessment of exceptional students. They can be classified in various ways. For educational purposes, however, three comparisons are most relevant. These are norm-referenced versus criterion-referenced tests, speed versus power tests, and group versus individual tests.

Norm-Referenced Tests

A *norm-referenced test* is one in which a person's score is compared to a specific reference group. The reference group is also called the *normative* or *standardization sample* and provides the norms on which to base the comparison. Norm-referenced tests are typically used when a person is interested in how a student performs in a certain area relative to other individuals. Because norm-referenced tests compare an individual's performance to those individuals in the normative sample, it is important to know the makeup and characteristics of the sample. These tests address the question of *how much* rather than *what* a person knows or can do and are normed on either an age scale or a point scale. In an *age scale,* a person's performance on a test is compared to a typical performance by a person of the same age. This is determined by the percentage of individuals at various age levels who respond correctly to a test item. For instance, a particular test might be norm-referenced for 3- through 8-year-old children. Certain items on the test will be scaled for each age level. Thus, for those items scaled for 6-year-old children, some 4- to 5-year-old children should answer them correctly, most 6-year-old children should, and almost all 7- to 8-year-olds should.

Point scales include test items that are of different levels of difficulty but that are not specifically tied to age-related percentages. In such a scale, items passed are added (this figure becomes the *raw score*). The raw score can then be converted to one of a variety of *derived scores* that compare the raw score to the performance of a group of subjects of known demographic characteristics, such as age, sex, and geographic area (Salvia & Ysseldyke, 1995). Thus, the derived scores give relative meaning to the raw scores. A number of derived scores are used in educational and psychological testing. The most common are age equivalents, grade equivalents, quartiles, deciles, percentiles, and standard scores. These scores are briefly defined in the next section. Other types of scores are defined in later chapters that provide descriptions of the specific norm-referenced tests.

Age and Grade Equivalents

Age and grade equivalents are both considered *developmental* scores. Both types of scores attempt to transform a raw score into the "average" performance of a particular age group or grade level. Age equivalents are expressed in years and months. For instance, suppose that during the standardization of a particular intelligence test, the mean (or median in some tests) number of correct responses was eighty for all individuals 6 years, 6 months old. Any person taking that test who obtained a raw score of 80 would have an age equivalent of 6 years, 6 months (6-6).

Grade equivalents are expressed in years and tenths of years. The calendar year is actually divided into ten parts, nine of which represent the nine months of the academic year, and the last of which represents the summer months. Thus, a 7.2 would be interpreted seventh grade, second month. Like age equivalents, grade equivalents are based on the average performance of the standardization sample. Grade equivalents are often used inappropriately to measure gains in achievement and to identify exceptional students. For instance, a student with an average IQ in grade 6.7 who scores at the 3.2 grade level in achievement might be considered as having a learning disability. The use of grade equivalents has certain intuitive appeal, because educators often think in such terms regarding academic ability. For teaching purposes, however, a grade equivalent (e.g., 4.1) indicates a student's performance relative to the standardization sample of the test, not to placement within a curriculum. In other words, one should not assume that the student who receives the 4.1 grade equivalent should be placed in a beginning fourth grade curriculum.

This emphasis on grade equivalents (as well as age equivalents) has been seriously questioned. Burns (1982), for instance, noted that grade equivalents lack sensitivity, are based on extrapolated scores for upper and lower ends of most tests, and have different standard deviations for different age groups. Berk (1981) stated "there is no technically sound reason to justify their use in the identification, diagnosis, and remediation of learning disabilities" (p. 137). This statement is true for all special education students as well. Green (1987) cautioned the use of these scores with secondary-level students in particular. The criticism of grade equivalents has led to major recommendations against their use. The International Reading Association, for example, encouraged a moratorium on the use of grade equivalents. Similarly, Bryk, Deabster, Easton, Luppescu, and Thom (1994), in an examination of the Chicago public school system noted the problems of using grade equivalents to document educational improvement. Interestingly, however, Huebner (1989) noted that the widespread use and criticism of grade equivalents has increased evaluators' awareness and has led to their more accurate interpretation.

Quartiles, Deciles, and Percentiles

Quartiles, deciles, and percentiles are all indications of the percentage of scores (determined from the standardization sample) that fall below a person's raw score. Quartiles divide the distribution of scores from the standardization into four equal parts, deciles into ten equal parts, and percentiles into one hundred equal parts. Thus, for example, the first quartile (Q_1) is the point at which 25 percent of the scores fall below; the eighth decile (D_8) is the point at which 80 percent of the scores fall below; and the twenty-third percentile (P_{23}) is the point at which 23 percent of the scores fall below. In other words, if a person's raw score on a test was at the Q_1, D_8, or P_{23}, it would be equal to or higher than, respectively, 25 percent, 80 percent, or 23 percent of the scores on which the test was normed. Of these three types of scores the most widely used is the percentile. The score itself is often referred to as a *percentile rank*.

Standard Scores

Standard scores are transformed raw scores with the same mean and standard deviation. The *mean* represents the average score, and the *standard deviation* reflects the variability of a set of scores. In the standardization of a test, approximately 34 percent of the subjects score within one standard deviation of the mean; approximately 14 percent score between one and two standard deviations; only about 2 percent score between two and three standard deviations. Thus, approximately 68 percent of the subjects score between ± 1 standard deviations, and approximately 96 percent score between ± 2 standard deviations. For instance, assume that a test has a mean of 100 and a standard deviation of 15. This means that the average score of those subjects in the standardization sample was 100 and that 68 percent scored between 85 and 115. Similarly, 96 percent scored between 70 and 130. Because of its statistical base, standard deviation plays an important role in the determination of extent of strength or weakness in a student's abilities. Figure 2.4 gives a visual representation of the relationship of percentile ranks and a variety of standard scores with different means and standard deviations.

There are many types of standard scores, including z scores, *T* scores, stanines, and scaled scores. In general, standard scores allow for the direct comparison of raw scores of individuals of different ages (or other characteristics). Suppose, for example, that a scaled score for a particular test had a mean of 10 and a standard deviation of 3. Child A, age 6-2, had a *raw score* of 15. Child B, age 12-4, had a raw score of 32. It is possible (depending on the standardization) that both children would have *scaled scores* of 10 (representing the average performance).

Normal Curve Equivalents

Normal curve equivalents (NCEs) are, in a sense, a combination of standard scores and percentile ranks. NCE is expressed as a standard score with a mean of 50 and a standard deviation of 21.06. The atypical standard deviation results from dividing the normal curve into one hundred equal intervals.

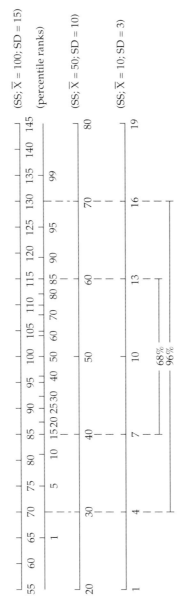

FIGURE 2.4   Relationship of Various Types of Derived Scores

SS = Standard score.

Scoring and Interpretation of Norm-Referenced Tests

The scoring of many norm-referenced tests can be tedious and frequently results in errors including computational errors and the misuse of statistical tables. For this reason, it is important that test examiners are properly trained and careful when doing mathematical calculations and using tables to convert raw scores to derived scores. For this reason also computer scoring programs are available for many tests. For example, one test publisher—Pro-Ed—has a computer program called PRO-SCORE for many of its tests. This program provides a printout that includes background information on the child, raw scores, percentiles, standard scores, and descriptions of all the subtests, profiles of subtests and subtest combinations (composites), and significance testing of the comparisons of all the composites. Other publishers (e.g., Western Psychological Services) provide a Test Report FAX Service. The examiner simply faxes the answer sheets to the publisher who then returns a fax of an interpretive report within minutes.

Simply reporting derived scores, whether they are determined through hand-scoring or computer scoring, is not sufficient. For example, suppose that a person obtained a percentile rank of 52 on a spelling test. This would indicate that he or she performed slightly above average in spelling compared to the normative sample. To really understand what that means, however, it is necessary to *consider the task demands of the test itself.* In other words, what did the student have to do to score well on the test? Did he have to orally spell words? Write words from dictation? Identify the correct spelling of a word from four choices? Each of these skills might be called "spelling"; it is possible, however, that one might make a mistake in assuming that the student with a 52nd percentile rank is about average in the area of written spelling if the score is based on oral spelling. Often the name of a test or subtest does not imply the specific task demands. Frequently, in fact, the name of the test or subtest has little to do with what the examinee actually has to do. It is therefore imperative that those task requirements be determined and considered when interpreting the results. This can be one of the drawbacks of computer-generated test reports.

Criterion-Referenced Tests and Curriculum-Based Assessment

A criterion-referenced test, as opposed to a norm-referenced test, does not specifically compare an individual's score to other people's scores. Rather, it measures an individual's mastery of content. For instance, instead of discovering that Joan scored at the 63rd percentile in math (norm-referenced test), you might find that she can add and subtract one-digit numbers correctly 100 percent of the time, but can add and subtract two-digit numbers correctly only 25 percent of the time (criterion-referenced test). In a criterion-referenced test you learn specifically *what a person knows,* instead of *how much a person knows compared to others.* Criterion-referenced tests are often "teacher made" and thus pinpoint the exact areas included in an individual's curriculum. In fact, many criterion-referenced tests are developed based on specific educational objectives. This is accomplished by sequencing the objectives (task analysis) and developing test items that measure each objective (discussed in Chapter 6). There are also, however, a number of commercially prepared criterion-referenced tests that measure both academic skills and developmental skills.

For teaching purposes, the advantage of using criterion-referenced tests is that they usually provide more specific information about a person's ability level than do norm-referenced tests. In fact, IEPs can usually be developed much more easily from criterion-referenced test data. The disadvantages of criterion-referenced tests are that you do not get comparative information and, unless you use a commercially prepared test, you must take the time to develop the instrument.

An area that has received considerable attention in the past decade is *curriculum-based assessment* (CBA). CBAs use the expected curricular outcomes of the school as their content. In reality, they are very similar in nature to criterion-referenced tests. If, for example, a school were using the Macmillan reading series, then CBAs would use the content of that series for the test items. A type of CBA, referred to as *curriculum-based measurement* (CBM), has also become popular. CBM includes a more standardized methodology and typically focuses on items representing an entire annual curricular area (Fuchs, Fuchs, Hamlett, & Allinder, 1989). Chapter 7 discusses CBA and CBM in greater depth and provides examples.

Power versus Speed Tests

Norm-referenced and criterion-referenced tests can measure power or speed. A *power test* is one designed to measure a full range of skills or abilities without a time limit. In a power test you are more interested in how much a person knows than in how fast he or she can perform. Usually, test items are of increasing difficulty, so that a person taking the test will answer some but not all correctly. A *speed test* is one in which the time element becomes important. With speed tests, the examiners are more concerned with how many test items a person can complete within a specific time limit. Usually the level of difficulty for each item is such that given unlimited time, all the items could be completed. In reality, many tests in special education are a combination of speed and power.

Individual versus Group Tests

Norm-referenced and criterion-referenced tests can also be individually or group administered. Certain advantages and disadvantages are inherent in each type of test. Group tests yield information in a shorter amount of time. For instance, it might be possible to obtain achievement scores for an entire class in two or three hours. However, you lose the opportunity to observe an individual's approach to a certain task. In short, group tests are usually administered for screening, and individual tests are administered for diagnostic, classification, and program-placement purposes. Certainly, both types of tests have their place in the assessment process.

Other Assessment Procedures

As previously mentioned, assessment involves more than simply the administration, scoring, and interpretation of tests. Any and all *relevant* information about an individual should be gathered. This information can be meaningful in its own right, and it can also help put the test data into proper perspective. Although the sources of such information are virtually limitless, several specific sources are frequently used in assessing exceptional individuals. These include the use of *inventories, checklists,* and *observation.* Both formal and informal checklists and inventories can be used to help locate behavior that can be observed later or assessed in depth. Observation is an invaluable tool that is always used, but not always systematically. (Observational assessment and its very important role in the overall process are discussed in Chapter 5.)

Other sources of assessment information involve the study of school records, discussion with parents and previous or current teachers, analysis of the home and academic environments, medical and developmental histories, and error analysis of specific work samples.

School records can and should be more than a collection of meaningless data accumulated in a file folder. They should contain relevant information about previous assessments, specific documentation of behavioral observations, and information relating to teaching strategies or intervention programs that have been implemented. This type of knowledge can eliminate a tremendous amount of duplication of services in two ways. First, it will help avoid a situation in which a child is overtested. For instance, in some schools the psychologist, general classroom teacher, learning disability specialist, and speech therapist might all give the same test within a short period of time. That problem can be eliminated if the school records are used as a central data bank. Second, use of the information in the school records can help avoid a waste of time in recommending or implementing a program that has already been tried and found ineffective.

Discussions with parents and teachers can also be helpful, although you should be aware of the possibility of biased information. In addition to obtaining valuable information about the specific nature of an individual's problem, you can also obtain an historical perspective. For example, you might discover whether any factors in the person's home life have suddenly changed. You might also find out whether the primary language spoken in the home is the same as that used in school. In addition, you can determine whether the child behaves differently at home than at school. If, for instance, a child has problems at school but not at home, certain conditions can often be identified in the home environment that can be replicated in the school environment.

Discussions with parents and analyses of the home environment are sensitive areas. Care must be taken not to imply blame or in any manner make the parents feel threatened or uncomfortable. To avoid this, some structured approach is usually helpful. Also avoid asking questions that are irrelevant to the student's problem or situation. Any information gathered should serve a useful purpose.

Another source of information is the medical and developmental history of an individual. Again, this is a sensitive area, in which only information that is potentially relevant to the assessment process should be obtained. Most medical and developmental histories are used in the early identification or prediction of some type of special problem or in the search for a cause or prognosis for a particular type of problem (particularly for more severe problems). If one of these is the goal for the assessment, an in-depth evaluation of developmental milestones and pre-, peri-, or postnatal infections, intoxications, or other events might be relevant. You must keep in mind, however, that knowing the cause of a problem does not necessarily imply an appropriate treatment program. Also, asking this information of a parent of a 7-year-old child with spelling problems probably would be unnecessary and might cause undue anxiety in that parent. ("Why are they asking me these questions? Do they suspect brain damage or retardation?") In other words, collect the information if there is a reason, but do not collect it if you are not going to use it or do not know what to do with it.

One often-overlooked source of information is the work that is collected daily during routine class time. Work products, like test results, are samples of a student's behavior and can be analyzed and interpreted in much the same way. Careful analysis of the kinds of errors made on work products can provide a lot of invaluable information (error analysis is discussed in depth in Chapter 6). Figure 2.5 provides examples of types of errors that could be made on a simple arithmetic worksheet.

The first problem in Figure 2.5 is an example of the use of a wrong operation; the person added instead of subtracting. The second example contains an obvious computational error. The third problem is an example of a defective algorithm; this means that there were procedural errors in an attempt to apply the correct process (in this example, subtracting the smaller number from the larger, regardless of placement). The answer to the last problem appears to be a random error. Clearly, each type of error would require a different remedial strategy.

$$
\begin{array}{cc}
\begin{array}{r} 38 \\ -21 \\ \hline 59 \end{array} &
\begin{array}{r} 53 \\ \times\,2 \\ \hline 116 \end{array}
\end{array}
$$

Wrong operation   Computation error

$$
\begin{array}{cc}
\begin{array}{r} 685 \\ -497 \\ \hline 212 \end{array} &
\begin{array}{r} 463 \\ \times\,25 \\ \hline 185 \end{array}
\end{array}
$$

Defective algorithm   Random error

FIGURE 2.5   Examples of Error Analysis in Arithmetic

More recently, a number of *alternative assessment procedures* have been gaining popularity. One procedure that is particularly helpful is portfolio assessment. Using this approach, the student and teacher compile representative examples of the student's work. For example, a portfolio in the area of reading might include classroom tests, audiotapes, the teacher's observational notes, the student's self-evaluation, progress notes, and a list of books the student has read. The intent is to focus on both the process and the product of learning. Valencia (1990) compared portfolio assessment of academic areas to artists' portfolios, in which samples of work are used to exemplify the breadth and depth of their expertise. Portfolio assessment as well as other alternative assessment procedures are discussed in Chapter 8.

In summary, a number of techniques and types of instruments are available to assess exceptional students. In general, these approaches are thought of as being *informal procedures* or *formal procedures.* Informal assessment procedures include observation, teacher-made tests, error analyses, and the use of portfolio assessment. Formal assessment procedures include norm-referenced tests, as well as commercially prepared inventories and criterion-referenced tests. The choice of procedure depends largely on the purposes for the assessment. Table 2.2 matches the purposes with recommended formal and informal procedures.

TABLE 2.2   Matching the Purposes and Types of Assessment Procedures

Purpose	Type	
	Formal	Informal
1. Initial identification (screening)	Screening and readiness tests; achievement tests	Criterion-referenced tests; observation; curriculum-based assessment
2. Determination and evaluation of teaching programs and strategies	Depends on area of need	Criterion-referenced tests; error analysis; curriculum-based assessment; portfolios
3. Determination of current performance level and educational need	Achievement or diagnostic academic tests; other tests (depending on area of need)	Criterion-referenced tests; observation; curriculum-based assessment
4. Decisions about classification and program placement	Intelligence, achievement, adaptive-behavior and classroom-behavior measures	Observation and criterion-referenced tests, used to supplement formal testing
5. Development of IEPs (goals, objectives, teaching strategies)	Commercially prepared inventories and criterion-referenced tests	Criterion-referenced tests; observation; error analysis; portfolios
6. Evaluation of IEPs	Some norm-referenced tests	Criterion-referenced tests; observation; portfolios

Three points should be made about Table 2.2. First, these are merely *suggestions* for types of assessment procedures that can be used for various purposes. There are times when other tests or measures are more beneficial for the purpose stated. Conversely, not all the procedures mentioned need to be used in all situations. Second, you should determine whether to use informal procedures, formal procedures, or a combination of the two. For many purposes, either type will give the desired information. Third, there is a great deal of overlap in the types of procedures used; in other words, results from specific assessment procedures can often be used for more than one purpose (e.g., an error analysis of norm-referenced test results). Acknowledging this point and planning the procedures in advance will result in a more efficient, more practical assessment.

WHO SHOULD ASSESS?

Answering this question is very important for several reasons. First, it can help avoid having more than one person administer the same test or battery of tests. In addition, it raises the questions of why the assessment is needed and how the results will be used. As noted previously, assessment can and perhaps should be performed by everyone involved with the education or training of an individual. This might include general education teachers, special education teachers, specialists, therapists, school psychologists, and parents. Each has a unique perspective that might prove invaluable. This does not mean that everyone should always be involved. Sometimes a teacher's assessment in the classroom is all that is needed. Other instances call for in-depth assessment by a number of professionals. Again, to a large extent, the purpose for assessment will determine who assesses.

With the current emphasis on full inclusion, it has become almost mandatory to include both the special education teacher and the general education teacher in the assessment process at all times. Teachers are perhaps in the best position to assess their students effectively. First, there is a strong rapport between the teacher and student that might bring out the student's best effort. Second, the student can usually be assessed in the classroom, which typically reduces the common fear of testing. Third, the teacher can assess at the most appropriate times and not have to wait for an outside evaluator who often is working under a tight schedule.

WHEN SHOULD ASSESSMENT BE CONDUCTED?

Time of assessment depends largely on the answer to the question, Who will assess? If the evaluator is someone other than the teacher or other individual who routinely works with the student, the issue of when to assess becomes one of scheduling. In other words, the student is usually pulled out of class and evaluated at a time that fits into both the examiner's and the student's schedule. Clearly, this is not always the most appropriate or beneficial time but is dependent on a number of factors, such as case loads or priorities for assessment. For this reason, it is even more important that teachers use discretion in referring students for further assessment and that they help in establishing priorities regarding who needs assessing the most. If every child in a class is referred for assessment, chances are that many students who do not really need this service will be evaluated, whereas others who need it will not be evaluated until later.

If a student is evaluated by the teacher (who, as previously stated, should do at least some of the assessment), the issue of scheduling takes on new meaning. The student will not usually be taken out of the classroom, and so assessment time is either incorporated into or separated from teaching time. For example, it might be possible to administer an informal test to a student before and after group instruction in a certain academic area. It might also be possible to assess individually during the day when the rest of the class is busy doing some other type of assignment (such as individual seat work, workbooks, or small-group projects). As noted previously, it is also possible to evaluate all or some of the students in the class based on the content of the curriculum (CBA or CBM). Finally, materials for a portfolio can be routinely gathered and assembled for later analysis.

One way of looking at assessment in the classroom (and anywhere else, for that matter) is to think of a filtering process in which you begin with information for a number of individuals and gradually collect more on those who need more assessment. For instance, a group-achievement test or curriculum-based assessment might be given as a first step to an entire class of thirty (Figure 2.6). The assessment at this stage could be incorporated into the teaching time. From these results, the teacher might identify 10 percent, or three students, who need further testing. As a second step, a more individualized achievement test could be given to those 10 percent to determine specific areas of academic strengths and weaknesses. This testing could be given while the rest of the class is working on other assignments. Suppose one person performed poorly in math and another in spelling, while another had some minor problems in reading. As a third step, the teacher or other evaluator could then test the first two students' academic areas through diagnostic testing and find out what the students know within the area and possibly determine reasons why the students are having problems. This assessment could be done either within or outside the classroom setting, depending on who assesses. For the third student, a prereferral intervention program could be initiated. Steps one and two could easily be administered by the teacher and, *if necessary*, by other professionals. It is at this point that the teacher typically makes the referral decision.

It is important to note that this is only an example of a sequence in which assessment might occur. Many times these specific steps will not be followed. If a teacher has a student who is clearly having serious problems—academic, emotional, or physical—then a referral is usually made with observational and supporting data but not necessarily with formalized test results.

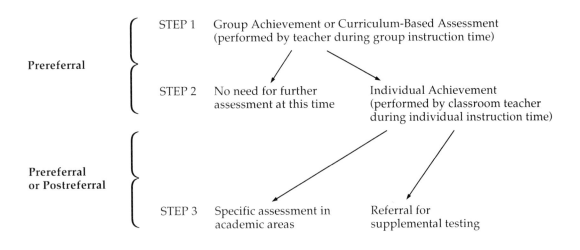

Prereferral

STEP 1   Group Achievement or Curriculum-Based Assessment
(performed by teacher during group instruction time)

STEP 2   No need for further
assessment at this time

Individual Achievement
(performed by classroom teacher
during individual instruction time)

Prereferral
or Postreferral

STEP 3   Specific assessment in
academic areas

Referral for
supplemental testing

FIGURE 2.6   Example of a Teacher-Initiated Assessment

WHAT SHOULD BE DONE WITH THE RESULTS?

In a certain sense, this should be the first question asked. If you cannot answer it, you probably should not initiate the assessment. Too much time and energy are wasted on testing students and writing reports that are filed in folders and never used. If assessment data are collected, there should be a clearly specified means of using the results. What happens with the results depends largely on the purpose for assessment. For example, if you are assessing for initial identification purposes, the results might be used to determine the need for and type of further assessment or to monitor certain kinds of behavior that are considered high risk. Conversely, data for classification and program-placement decisions might be used more formally, usually evaluated by a multidisciplinary team of professionals. Information for program planning might be used informally by a teacher to initiate or modify a teaching strategy, or it might be formally used to develop an IEP, ITP, or IFSP. Whoever is involved in assessment should take the time to learn the policies governing dissemination of assessment data in his or her school or other educational setting. Knowing this information can expedite the effective use of assessment data and can increase communication among the various professionals involved in assessment.

AN ASSESSMENT MODEL

Assessment should be a dynamic, continuous process undertaken with a clearly specified goal in mind. The process should be monitored and should be flexible enough to be modified if necessary. One way to view assessment is to break it

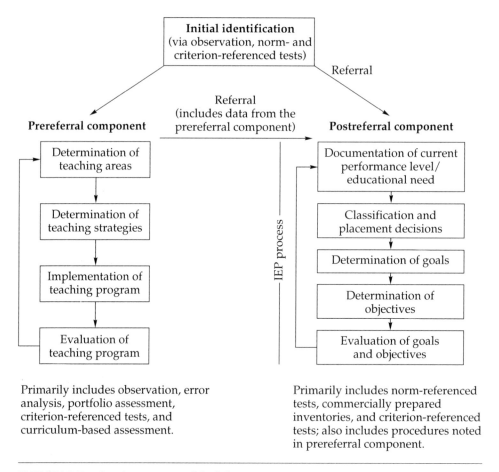

FIGURE 2.7   An Assessment Model

down into two components: prereferral and postreferral (Figure 2.7). The goal of the *prereferral component* is to develop and implement a teaching or remedial program and to monitor the effectiveness of the program by observing the student's progress. Assessment in this component is conducted before making a referral for special education services and will, it is hoped, result in no referral at all. This component is heavily weighted toward informal assessment procedures, such as observation, error analysis of work products, portfolio assessment, curriculum-based assessment, and teacher-made tests. Note that the *purposes* for assessment are closely tied to the assessment model. If the purpose is identified, the appropriate steps in the model can be followed. Norm-referenced tests are also used occasionally. The prereferral component is usually implemented by the teacher within the student's current educational setting.

The *postreferral component* includes the documentation of an educational need and usually results in decisions about classification and program placement. It also might result in the development of a formalized IEP that includes the goals, objectives, instructional strategies, and timeline for implementing and evaluating goals and objectives. This component includes both formal assessment (norm-referenced tests, also commercially prepared inventories and criterion-referenced tests) as well as informal assessment procedures. A multidisciplinary approach (including the teacher) is used during this component.

It is entirely possible that *both* components might be included in the assessment of a particular student. Where possible, it is better to go through the prereferral assessment first. In fact, this is a requirement in many states. This will often yield enough information to deal with the situation that required the assessment. If further assessment is necessary, important prereferral information can be incorporated into the assessment at the time of the referral. On the other hand, with certain students, a referral may be justified as the first step, as soon as a problem has been identified. This is particularly true for children whose problems are severe and who definitely need supplementary or alternative programming. *Note that the procedures used and the information gathered in the prereferral component are of great value in the postreferral component.* In a sense, the entire prereferral component could also be considered as part of the postreferral component (particularly the documentation of educational need and IEP development steps).

SUMMARY

It is essential that the legal and philosophical factors that relate to special education be considered when planning assessment strategies. It is also important to answer several questions before any assessment begins. These questions are (1) Why assess? (2) How is the process initiated? (3) What procedures should be used? (4) Who should assess? (5) When should assessment be conducted? and, (6) What should be done with the results? Answering these questions will save time and avoid unnecessary or irrelevant assessment. It is possible, and in fact probable, that the answers to these questions will change once the process begins. It is up to you to keep thinking about them *throughout* the process. One way to do that is to think of assessment as a continuous, dynamic process, requiring constant monitoring and modification. When assessment is looked at in this way, who should be involved and how the results should be used will be clear. An assessment model was proposed that ties directly into this pragmatic philosophy. Once the specific purpose for the assessment was identified in the model, the procedures and steps to follow were delineated.

3

PRACTICAL CONSIDERATIONS

Areas Included

Factors Affecting Test Results

Factors Related to the Examinee

Factors Related to the Examiner and the
Examiner-Examinee Interaction

Factors Related to the Test

Several considerations must be addressed before conducting any type of assessment procedure. Although these considerations are relevant for all formal as well as informal assessment procedures, they are primarily related to norm-referenced testing. This relevance lies in the format and types of questions as well as in the kind of emphasis placed on the scores of norm-referenced tests.

FACTORS AFFECTING TEST RESULTS

Three principal classes of factors can affect an individual's performance on a test and can minimize the meaning of, and in some cases invalidate, the test results. They are factors related to (1) the person being tested, (2) the examiner and the examiner–examinee interaction, and (3) the test itself. Each will be discussed separately.

Factors Related to the Examinee

Anxiety and Motivation

The first major potential source of error consists of factors related to the examinee. Among these are such obvious factors as anxiety and motivation. All of us have probably experienced test phobia or test anxiety and know how it can affect performance. Fleege, Charlesworth, Burts, and Hart (1992) found that stress behaviors during testing were noted as early as kindergarten. Turner, Beidel, Hughes, and Turner (1993) investigated test anxiety among African American children and found the prevalence to be 41 percent. Unfortunately, some attempts at reducing test anxiety have resulted in reduced anxiety but no improvement in test performance (Kass & Fish, 1991). There is, however, some evidence that eliminating time pressure reduces anxiety and improves test performance (Plass & Hill, 1986) and that a pretest review can minimize anxiety (Mealy & Host, 1992).

Similarly, lack of motivation may suggest that an "I don't know" response to a test question means "I don't care." Anxiety and motivational factors might be minimized by ensuring that a test environment is positive, supportive, and nonthreatening. Extra time spent establishing rapport might also help eliminate this source of error.

Test Wiseness

Another factor that may influence the student's performance on tests is the effect of practice, that is, repeated administrations of the same test or same type of test. Practice can occur through routine test-taking or through coaching. Test wiseness has been suggested as an important consideration in the testing of both minority children (Dreisbach & Keogh, 1982) and students with learning disabilities (Scruggs & Lifson, 1986), who have been shown to have deficits in their test-taking ability. Johns and VanLeirsburg (1992) concurred that students from different cultural groups as well as special education students could benefit from test-taking strategies.

There is evidence suggesting that test performance can be improved through practice of test-taking skills (Dreisbach & Keogh, 1982; Putnam, 1992; Scruggs & Marsing, 1988). One example of a strategy for improving math problem-solving performance was offered by Beattie and Enright (1993). They suggested that the student use the following five-step blueprint:

Study the problem
Organize the facts
Line up a plan
Verify the plan
Examine your answer

In fact, books and manuals including strategies and exercises for improving test-taking skills have been developed (e.g., Ciardi, 1990; Gall, 1990).

There are also some data to support the idea that certain types of test performances are more amenable to coaching than others. In a series of studies (Scruggs & Mastropieri, 1986; Scruggs, Mastropieri, & Tolfa-Veit, 1986), it was found that students with learning disabilities and behavior disorders improved more on tasks such as word-study skills and mathematical concepts than on reading comprehension after coaching (consisting of teaching them to attend to the appropriate stimulus, mark answers correctly, use time wisely, and avoid careless errors). They hypothesized that two factors led to this result. First, the word-study and mathematical concepts have complicated formats that would ordinarily confuse students. Second, continued poor performance in reading comprehension was the result of problems in deductive reasoning and other deficits not related to the coaching per se. Enright, Beattie, and Algozzine (1992) also found that mathematics test performance could be improved by including a systematic review of the content as well as the format of the test during math instruction.

A "test to test test wiseness" was developed to identify students who lack test-taking skills (Parrish, 1982). The interesting question that must be asked is, "Should students be trained if they are identified as having these deficiencies?" On the one hand, if the goal is to get an accurate'picture of how much a person knows, any disadvantage a person might have that is unrelated to the test content should be eliminated. On the other hand, training students might result in test scores that are not reflective of their true classroom performance. Scruggs, Mastropieri, and Tolfa-Veit (1986) discussed this issue and suggested the need for research to determine the best practice to follow. It would seem that, once again, the *purpose* of the testing is important in that decision. Regardless of the purpose, the specific test items should not be taught; only instruction in test-taking skills should be considered.

Health and Emotional State

Other factors that can affect the test taker's performance are health and emotional state. Time should be spent to determine whether a student is performing "typically" at the time of evaluation. A teacher is perhaps in the best position to make this judgment, and this is one of the many advantages of teacher assessment. If examiners other than the teacher (or other person familiar with the child) administer the tests, they should consult with the teacher to get this important information.

Type of Disability

Depending on the type of disability that a student has, a number of factors might bias test results. These include (1) test content, (2) motivation or cognitive arousal, (3) physical access to the testing materials, and (4) response techniques (Cole, D'Alonzo, Gallegos, Giordano, & Stile, 1992). For example, a student with a reading problem would be at a disadvantage on a timed math test that included story problems. Similarly, a young student with cerebral palsy would have difficulty on an intelligence test that included block building and other fine-motor tasks. Most states, in fact, that have large-scale assessment programs for accountability purposes allow for certain modifications for students with disabilities. These include changes in presentation format, response format, and setting and timing of the test (Hanley, 1995). Unfortunately, many teachers know little about what modifications are allowed (Siskind, 1993).

Factors Related to the Examiner and the Examiner–Examinee Relationship

Differences in Administration and Interpretation

The next major factor affecting test results relates to the examiner and the examiner–examinee relationship. One of the most common sources of error is differences in test administration and test interpretation. Assessment instruments, particularly norm-referenced tests, are designed to be administered in a standard, similar manner. However, many factors during the assessment process make this difficult to do. As noted previously, modifications under certain conditions (particularly during group testing) are acceptable. However, examiners who evaluate students individually often differ in the amount of variation to the standard instructions and conditions. One reason for such variation is that examiners' personalities and methods of interacting with examinees result in differences in rapport and amount of feedback given, both of which can greatly affect the testing situation. For example, differences in the amount of reinforcement and verbal approval might affect test scores, particularly for younger students (Bradley-Johnson, Graham, & Johnson, 1986). In one study, Breuning and Zella (1978) found that for an experimental group, individualized incentives increased IQ scores an average of thirteen points over a control group. Marlaire and Maynard (1990) stressed that the entire process of testing is an "interactional phenomenon."

Other factors should also be considered regarding the effects of reinforcement on test-taking behavior, including the age of the student being tested. Bradley-Johnson, Graham, and Johnson (1986) reported that almost all studies using rewards with early elementary-age children have found increases, whereas those using students in the sixth grade or above have not. Other differences occur when test examiners are confronted with a unique, atypical, or ambiguous answer. Sattler, Andres, Squire, Wisely, and Maloy (1978) found that when examiners (regardless of their level of training) were asked to score "ambiguous" responses on the Wechsler Intelligence Scale for Children-Revised[1] (WISC-R), there was considerable disagreement. Consider the following example of an interaction between the examiner and examinee on the comprehension subtest of the WISC-R:

EXAMINER: What are you supposed to do if you find someone's wallet or pocketbook in a store?

EXAMINEE: I'd give it to the person behind the counter.

EXAMINER: What should you do if you see thick smoke coming from the window of your neighbor's house?

EXAMINEE: Call the police and call an ambulance.

---

[1]The WISC-R is an earlier version of the Wechsler Intelligence Scale for Children-III (WISC-III) discussed in Chapter 9.

EXAMINER: What are some reasons why we need policemen?

EXAMINEE: Because people are always fighting and there are drugs around here.

If these answers are scored according to the criteria stated in the WISC-R manual, the student would receive a 2 (indicating best response) for the first two questions and a 0 (indicating an incorrect response or no credit) for the last question. What if, however, the student comes from a tough neighborhood where fighting and drugs are associated with the police? Would you score the response as incorrect in accordance with the WISC-R scoring criteria? Would you give some credit because the response was correct, given the student's environment? No doubt, many examiners would respond differently to this example, depending on their philosophy of assessment and the reason for the evaluation. Because standardized tests imply a standard format for administration and scoring, violations result in invalid findings. One rule of thumb is to adhere strictly to the standard administration and scoring guidelines when possible and to state precisely why and where you differ if it is necessary to do so.

Differences of interpretation are especially obvious when more subjective scoring systems are used. In many situations, a question has no right or wrong answer, but the answers have varying degrees of correctness. The area in which interpretation of results varies the most is probably projective testing, which is discussed in Chapter 11.

Examiner Bias

Another examiner-related source of error is examiner bias. This is not necessarily conscious bias. Depending on the information you have heard about a particular student, you might have a tendency to give the benefit of the doubt or to be somewhat more conservative with the scoring. McDermott (1981), in reviewing the possible sources of "biasing cues," indicated that empirical evidence suggests that the evaluator's knowledge of special education placement, race, sex, social class, and cultural background significantly affects diagnostic decisions. For example, Payette and Clarizio (1994) found that girls were more likely to be incorrectly classified as having a learning disability than boys, even when obtaining the same discrepancy between their IQ and achievement scores. In addition, O'Reilly (1989) found that information related to reason for referral (giftedness or learning disability) resulted in significant bias regarding assessment and classification. One general guideline is to make use of the information that you have about an individual but make a conscious effort to avoid being biased. Also, it helps to be aware that some bias will probably still exist.

The reason for testing can also affect the scoring. If you know that good students are being routinely evaluated, there might be a tendency to give them positive scores for ambiguous answers. If, however, you know that the "class troublemaker" is being evaluated for possible special education placement, you might not be as liberal in your scoring. Again, these are not necessarily conscious biases but, rather, biases that are tied into expectations. For example, Ysseldyke,

Algozzine, Regan, and McGue (1981) found that many students are classified for and receive special education simply because they are referred. In a more recent study, Fugate, Clarizio, and Phillips (1993) reported that approximately one out of every two students who are referred are placed into special education. In addition, the decision regarding the *type* of test to administer can be affected by certain factors. Huebner (1989a) found that school psychologists' decisions about further psychoeducational testing were affected by students' achievement test scores but not by their race or socioeconomic status. Previous test performance within a testing session might also bias the examiner. For example, if students were doing well up to a point, there might be a tendency to give them credit for answers of questionable quality later in the test.

Race of Examiner

The racial differences between examiner and examinee have received widespread attention. For years, it was assumed, for instance, that African American children would score higher on tests if the examiner was also African American. An analysis of the research, however, suggested that the race of the examiner does not have a significant effect on test performance. Sattler and Gwynne (1982) reviewed twenty-seven published articles in which the race of examiner was explored empirically; in twenty-three of the twenty-seven studies, no significant effect was found. They concluded that "some writers have simply declared by fiat that white examiners impair the intelligence test scores of black children. Unfortunately, this declaration is not justified by the available research, as the present review and as past reviews have shown. In everyday clinical and school encounters, there are probably individual cases in which a white examiner adversely affects a black person's performance on intelligence tests, but the research suggests that these situations are infrequent" (p. 207). Similarly, Graziano (1982) reviewed fifteen years of research and found no biasing effect of examiner race. Fuchs and Fuchs (1989), however, found that *familiarity* with the examiner did have an effect on Hispanic and African American children's test performance.

Culture and Language of the Examiner

Similarly, the cultural, language, and dialect differences of the examiner and the examinee have been explored to determine if they affect test performance. Padilla and Garza (1975) noted that "when a Spanish-surnamed examinee and a non-Spanish–surnamed examiner sit across from each other in a testing situation, there is often a wider gulf separating them than just the table. Typically, there is a linguistic, cultural, and socioeconomic gap between them, associated with their different sets of life experiences. An examiner who is not sensitive to these differences will surely have a negative influence on the outcome of the child's performance" (pp. 55–56). Hilton (1991) suggested that school personnel involved in assessment should be trained in cultural awareness. Hing-McGowan (1994) even developed a test data collection form that can be used to analyze tests for cultural fairness. The available research suggests that the effect of the language differences of both the examiner and test diminishes as the Spanish-speaking child spends more time in English-speaking schools (Clarizio, 1982). Wolfram (1990) also reported on the important role of dialect differences and its biasing effect on testing. Hilton (1991) went so far as to say that incorrect answers that reflect dialect differences should be accepted as correct responses.

Scoring Errors

The last source of examiner error is scoring errors. Although this is an area in which extra care can and should be taken, scoring errors do exist. They can cause problems leading to incorrect educational programming and, in some cases, incorrect classification. For example, Sherrets, Gard, and Langner (1979), in a study of thirty-nine examiners' scorings of two hundred intelligence test protocols, noted that 90 percent of the examiners made some kind of scoring error. The largest error would have raised the student's IQ by nine points or lowered it by seven points. Interestingly, 32 percent of the protocols included some type of simple addition error. Similarly, Hunnicutt, Slate, Gamble, and Wheeler (1990) and Slate, Jones, Murray, and Coulter (1993) found examiner errors on 83 percent and 100 percent of the intelligence test protocols they checked, respectively. They also found that the IQ should have been different in about 50 percent of the tests. The tendency to make scoring errors apparently begins early in a professional's career. Slate and Jones (1990) reported that students in a graduate course in assessment made an average of almost nine errors per test protocol; Giacobbe and Traynelis-Yurck (1989) found that when undergraduate students were asked to administer and score a vocabulary test, more than 70 percent made some type of error. In addition, it appears that even tests that are relatively simple to administer and score are subject to scoring errors. For example, Peterson et al. (1991) noted mistakes on 95 percent of the protocols for the Wide Range Achievement Test-Revised, a widely administered test.

Factors Related to the Test

The last factor that can affect test results relates to the test itself. This involves the test's technical adequacy (for example, validity and reliability) or its possible bias against certain types of students.

Validity

Validity refers to the extent to which a test measures what it purports to measure. Three major types of validity are included in a discussion of assessment instruments: criterion-related validity, content validity, and construct validity.

Criterion-related validity refers to the extent to which a person's score on a certain test correlates with a criterion measure (usually that person's score on another test). The correlation coefficient that this comparison yields is called a *validity coefficient*. Correlation coefficients indicate the degree of relationship between two variables. They range from a –1.00 (perfect negative correlation) to +1.00 (perfect positive correlation). A +1.00 correlation means that as the values of the first variable change, the values of the second variable change in the same direction. Alternately, a –1.00 correlation means that as the values of the first variable change, the values of the second variable change in the opposite direction. Very rarely, however, do correlations reach –1.00 or +1.00. Usually, correlations are expressed as a positive or negative two-digit decimal, such as .63 or –.86 or .75. In assessment, positive correlations are used almost exclusively. In measuring criterion-related validity, the closer the decimal is to +1.00, the more valid the instrument is with respect to the criterion measure. No cut-off point exists that makes a test either valid or not valid; in general, however, a validity coefficient of less than .70 for individual tests and less than .60 for group-administered tests probably should be interpreted with caution.

An example of establishing criterion-related validity is shown in Table 3.1, giving the data from two intelligence tests.

By using the formula for determining correlation coefficients, you can determine that Intelligence Test 1 (test to be validated) correlates .86 with Intelligence Test 2 (criterion measure). This type of criterion-related validity is called *concurrent validity*, and it quantifies the degree to which a test correlates with a criterion measure administered at roughly the same time.

The other type of criterion-related validity is *predictive validity*, which refers to the extent to which test results correlate with a criterion measure that is given at some future time. To establish the predictive validity of the Scholastic Aptitude Test (SAT), for instance, the SAT scores (test to be validated) of individuals in high

TABLE 3.1   Example of Criterion-Related Validity

Subject	Intelligence Test 1 (Test to Be Validated)	Intelligence Test 2 (Criterion Measure)
Ron	97	94
Roni	89	96
Muriel	109	113
Mark	78	85
Juanita	98	95
Ruth	116	110
Helen	93	89
Stuart	100	109
Jay	100	97
Sherri	84	89
Scott	97	99
Randi	98	104
Sonny	102	99
Michael	108	112
JoAnn	89	90
Daniel	93	98
Evan	87	85
Erin	97	107
Lauren	108	110
Eric	111	106

school might be correlated with these individuals' grade-point averages (criterion measure) after their freshman year in college. The closer the correlation is to +1.00, the greater the predictive validity of the SAT.

Regarding criterion-related validity, it is important to be aware that a test is only as valid as the criterion measure. If authors report high correlations between their test and a criterion test that is not considered valid, this correlation does not make the authors' test valid. You must learn to look not only at the magnitude of the correlation coefficient, but also at the criterion measure itself. Suppose, for instance, that you were interested in establishing the validity of a new intelligence test. You chose as your criterion measure the Terrible Test of Intelligence, a technically inadequate test in its own right. A high correlation would indicate that the new test measures areas similar to those measured in the historically inadequate Terrible Test.

Content validity refers to the extent to which a test accurately measures the sample of behaviors under consideration. Salvia and Ysseldyke (1995) noted three factors that should be considered in establishing content validity:

1. Appropriateness of the test items (that is, are the items appropriate in age level and content?)
2. Completeness of the item sample (that is, does the test include a broad sample of tasks in the measured domain?)
3. Appropriateness of the way in which the test items measure the content (that is, the type of task required, such as multiple choice, fill in the blank, or true-false)

Suppose, for example, that a test was developed to measure spelling for students in first through sixth grades. If the test had a number of extremely difficult items (for example, *pulchritude, unctuous*), it would not be *appropriate*. If the test only included simple two-letter words (for example, *do, an, of*), it would not be *complete*. If it required an examinee to indicate whether a word was spelled correctly using a true-false format, it might not be measuring spelling in an *appropriate way*.

Establishing content validity is extremely important, yet doing so is not as straightforward as determining criterion-related validity. One way to maximize content validity is to consider what needs to be measured and how it will best be measured during test construction. The determination of content validity usually involves some type of expert judgment. In the above example, a group of teachers familiar with spelling curricula might be asked to judge the content validity of the spelling test.

Construct validity has to do with the extent to which a test measures some type of theoretical characteristic or concept. Self-concept and reasoning ability are two examples of these relatively abstract constructs that are difficult to define and subsequently difficult to measure. In general, the establishment of construct validity includes the careful identification and definition of the construct and then the derivation and verification of hypotheses concerning test performance related to the construct (Gronlund, 1988).

Construct validity is usually established through careful empirical studies using certain statistical procedures. Two procedures are frequently used for this purpose. The first involves the intercorrelation among test items to determine if the test primarily measures a single construct. The second involves procedures to establish a positive correlation of the test scores with other measures that supposedly measure the same construct and a negative correlation with other measures that supposedly do not (American Psychological Association, 1985).

Reliability

Another important quality of a test is reliability. Reliability refers to the consistency of a test. If a test is not reliable, it is not dependable, stable, predictable, or accurate (Kerlinger, 1986). Lack of these traits is obviously undesirable in an assessment instrument designed to identify educational needs. If a test is not reliable, by definition it cannot be valid (Salvia & Ysseldyke, 1995). However, just because a test is reliable, it is not necessarily valid; in other words, results on a test could be consistent, but they could consistently measure the wrong thing. Four kinds of reliability are most commonly reported: test-retest, equivalent form, internal, and interscorer.

Test-retest is probably the most common form of reliability, and it quantifies the extent to which results from a test remain consistent over time. Test-retest reliability is established by correlating the test results of a group of individuals with the same individuals' test results after a relatively short period of time (usually about two weeks, but time varies with the type of test). Table 3.2 gives hypothetical data demonstrating the test-retest reliability of an intelligence test. The resulting correlation coefficient is .92, a figure that indicates a generally high test-retest reliability. Usually, a reliability coefficient of at least .90 is desirable for individual diagnostic tests, .80 for group-administered tests, and .60 for screening tests (Salvia & Ysseldyke, 1995).

Equivalent-form reliability is established by using alternate forms of an instrument that measure the same skills. The correlation of scores quantifies the similarity of the two forms and gives some indication of the degree to which they are interchangeable. For example, two forms of a mathematics test might include different test items to measure knowledge of the same concepts. Equivalent-form reliability would be established by administering the two forms to the same population and correlating the resulting scores. In establishing equivalent-form reliability, it is important that the time between administration of the two forms be as short as possible. This eliminates the possibility that other factors might affect the test performances. Equivalent-form reliability is also referred to as alternate-form reliability.

Another method of establishing reliability that is, in a sense, a combination of the two previously discussed approaches is *test-retest with alternate forms.* This involves administering one form of a test to a group of individuals at a given time and then administering the alternate form of the test to the same group after a short period of time has passed. Many argue that this is the best method of estimating test error (e.g., Anastasi, 1988). One should note, however, that the result-

TABLE 3.2   Example of Test-Retest Reliability

Subject	Score on Intelligence Test (First Administration)	Score on Intelligence Test (Second Administration)
Ron	97	89
Roni	89	87
Muriel	109	109
Mark	78	80
Juanita	98	96
Ruth	116	119
Helen	93	99
Stuart	100	103
Jay	100	100
Sherri	84	82
Scott	97	93
Randi	98	99
Sonny	102	105
Michael	108	104
JoAnn	89	90
Daniel	93	97
Evan	87	84
Erin	97	104
Lauren	108	110
Eric	111	107

ing correlation coefficient is lower than those yielded by the test-retest or alternate form techniques.

Internal reliability is determined using a variety of procedures. This type of reliability refers to the internal consistency of a test and is computed using statistical procedures such as coefficient alpha and Kuder-Richardson formulae. Another procedure, called *split-half*, involves the correlation of one half of a test with the other half (for example, odd-numbered items versus even-numbered items, first half versus second half). In a sense, this provides an estimate of the alternate-form reliability of the total test.

Interscorer reliability, sometimes referred to as interrater reliability, is concerned with how consistently a test is scored or a behavior is rated by two examiners. In the first type, a test might be administered to a group of students and given to two individuals to score. The results of the two individuals' scoring of the tests for the student could be correlated to provide a reliability coefficient. In the second type, usually involved in behavioral observation, the percentage of agreement between two individuals observing the same behavior is computed.

Other Technical Characteristics

Another reliability-related characteristic that is often reported is the *standard error of measurement* (SEM). The SEM represents an attempt to account for the possible variability or error involved in the scoring and interpretation of a test. Because no tests are absolutely reliable, a person's *true score*—score on a test if the test were totally reliable—is never known. Individual scores on tests, therefore, can be thought of as estimates of true scores. The greater the reliability of a test the smaller the SEM (and vice versa).

The SEM provides a range that more accurately reflects how closely people's scores on a test approach their true scores. For instance, if Bob scored 110 on a given test whose SEM was 2.4, then approximately two-thirds of the time his true score would fall somewhere between 107.6 and 112.4. In general, the lower the SEM, the more confident you can be that a person's score on a test is an accurate estimate of the true score. Conversely, the larger the SEM for a test, the less confident you can be. The SEM is extremely important when labeling and classification are considered. Many tests include *confidence bands* that are determined from the SEM. This allows the user to see the range of scores that represent the student's true score. The 90 percent range is frequently used. In other words, a test user can plot both the student's obtained score and the range that indicates where the student would score 90 percent of the time.

Another type of technical information that should be considered is the nature of the *norm*, or population used to standardize a norm-referenced test. Because an individual's score on a norm-referenced test is derived through comparison with the standardization population, it is extremely important that the nature of that population is known. Are you comparing a student's performance to a random sample of children across the United States? Males from lower socioeconomic, rural areas? Students with severe retardation living in institutions? Obviously, the score that the student receives needs to be interpreted relative to those who comprise the normative sample. An "average" score would be interpreted differently when compared to the three populations just mentioned, for example. It is best to have a representative sample that considers characteristics such as gender, race, geographic region, and parents' education. It is important to remember that the norm does not necessarily refer to normal but to the types of individuals included in the standardization sample.

Many tests also have basals and ceilings. Although not considered technical characteristics in a traditional sense, basals and ceilings are important to understand for both correct administration and interpretation. Basals and ceilings are used in power tests in which the difficulty level of the items progresses from easy to hard. The *basal* of a test is the point at which the examiner assumes that the student could answer easier items. The *ceiling* of a test is the point at which the examiner assumes that the student would miss more difficult items. The use of a basal and ceiling allows the examiner to save time by not administering items that are probably too easy or too difficult for the student. For example, suppose the basal rule of a test was three in a row correct while the ceiling rule was three in a row incorrect. You start administering the test at item 30 (as noted in the manual according to the age of the student). Items 32–34 were correct and items 41–43 were incorrect. You would assume that all items before 32 (1–31) are correct and all items past 43 are incorrect. Therefore, certain assumptions are being made about the student's performance.

Possible Test Bias

A test is often considered biased when individuals with certain characteristics (for example, different ethnic groups, geographic regions, economic levels, or gender) consistently score differently when it is administered under similar conditions. For example, a test might be considered biased if, when administered in a consistent fashion, Hispanic students score lower than white children, males lower than females, or rural children lower than urban children.

There are actually several possible reasons why individuals with certain characteristics might score lower on a particular test. One explanation is that the differences in test scores are a result of bias in the test itself. Another explanation is that the differences in test performance reflect true differences and therefore are not the result of test bias. These differing interpretations of the same phenomenon have resulted in heated debate regarding test bias, particularly in the area of intelligence testing. Considerable attention was addressed in the 1970s to the bias of intelligence tests against ethnic minority students (see Hobbs, 1975; Mercer, 1972, 1973; Samuda, 1975). A number of court cases investigating the discriminatory nature of intelligence testing resulted from this attention. Unfortunately, the results from litigation have provided little additional insight into the issue of bias in testing. As noted in Chapter 1, in some cases, such as *Larry P. v. Riles*, (1979), the decision implied bias in the tests, whereas in others (*PASE v. Hannon*, 1980), the decision did not support test bias.

What is evident from the history of contradiction regarding test bias is the need for a clear definition of bias or at least a delineation of the types of bias that can be empirically explored. Reschly (1980) identified nine common definitions, four of which are particularly relevant to this discussion. These are mean-difference bias, item bias, psychometric bias, and factor-analytic bias.

Mean-difference bias is perhaps the most common definition of bias and is the one described in the previous discussion. It asks the question, Do individuals with different characteristics score differently on the same test? Because certain groups do score lower on certain types of tests, those tests have been considered biased against those groups. As discussed previously, the causes of those differences in scores are subject to considerable controversy.

Item bias refers to the situation in which specific items on a test are considered to be outside the life experiences of certain individuals. For example, a potentially biased item for a lower socioeconomic, rural child might be "How far is it from New York to Los Angeles?" (from WISC-R, one of the tests involved in litigation). Other items might be considered biased if a certain type of typical, stereotyped response is considered the correct answer. For example, one item that appeared in the WISC-R is, "What is the thing to do if a boy (or girl) much smaller than yourself starts to fight with you?" The answer that receives the most credit is to "walk

```
1. Alley apple
   a. Brick              c. Dog
   b. Piece of fruit     d. Horse

2. Deuce and a quarter
   a. Money              c. A house
   b. A car              d. To like

3. The eagle flies
   a. The blahs          c. Pay day
   b. Movie              d. Deficit

Correct answers:
1. (a)
2. (b)
3. (c)
```

**FIGURE 3.1   Examples from the Black
Intelligence Test of Cultural Homogeneity**

away," although many individuals have argued that this would not be an appropriate response (or behavior) of an inner-city child.

Williams (1972) developed a test to illustrate the point that administering a test that includes items to which a person has not been exposed results in biased decisions. His test, called the Black Intelligence Test of Cultural Homogeneity (BITCH), included one hundred vocabulary words that he thought would be a better predictor of learning ability for African American children than traditional intelligence test items. Figure 3.1 shows examples from this test.

The difficulty with deciding which items on a test are biased is that it requires subjective judgment, a problem that has resulted in experimental investigation and criticism. For example, when studying the performance of children of different ethnic groups, researchers have not found significant differences on items assumed to be biased (Sandoval, 1979). In addition, there is actually little agreement among raters on which items should be considered biased (Sandoval & Miille, 1980).

Other types of bias include *psychometric bias* and *factor-analytic* bias. Psychometric bias is determined by asking the question, Are the technical characteristics (for example, validity and reliability) similar for individuals with different characteristics? Factor-analytic bias involves the use of a statistical procedure in which items (or subtests) are grouped together because they correlate highly with one another and have low correlations with other factors identified by the same process. To determine this type of bias, one would see if similar or different factors on a test were identified for the groups of individuals under investigation. This type of bias is related to psychometric bias, because it essentially focuses on the issue of construct validity.

The controversy regarding the issue of bias in testing, particularly intelligence testing, raises important questions and, once again, should make us look carefully at the uses and limitations of test scores. Perhaps educators should be less concerned about whether or not specific tests are biased and more concerned about the appropriate uses of the tests and the possible use of test scores for discriminatory purposes. Many intelligence tests, for example, have proved relatively good predictors of school performance (measured by achievement test scores), regardless of the ethnic background of the student (see Oakland, 1977; Reschly & Reschly, 1979). On the other hand, the results of these tests should not be overemphasized, and their use in major educational decisions should be avoided (Clarizio, 1982). Certainly, equating these scores with "intellectual potential" is inappropriate (discussed in Chapter 9). The Alliance of Black School Educators (1984) cogently reported their position on the use of "biased" tests:

> *Testing in order to rank children by intellect, to rank them by cognitive or behavioral style, or to rank them with "nonbiased" assessment procedures is malpractice, in our opinion, unless such practices can be demonstrated by valid research to result in significant and meaningful changes in achievement for our children.* (p. 28)

SUMMARY

Several considerations must be addressed during assessment. These considerations or factors pertain specifically to formal assessment procedures, although they can also provide guidelines for informal procedures.

The first factor that could affect test results is related to the person being tested (the examinee). Included in this category are such factors as anxiety, motivation, previous test experience, health and emotional status, and attitudes of the person being tested. The second major factor relates to the examiner. In this category, test administration and interpretation differences, styles of interacting with the examinee, bias, racial or cultural differences between the examiner and examinee, and scoring errors were discussed. The last major factor is in the test itself, including its validity, reliability, standard error of measurement, and possible bias. All three of these factors should be considered throughout the assessment. Acknowledging these factors will help reduce some of the error and put assessment data into proper perspective. Specifically, these factors should be considered during test selection, administration, and interpretation. Such consideration should give a test user some idea of the limitations of assessment information and, when relevant, some idea of appropriate generalization of assessment data.

4

ASSESSING TO LABEL: ISSUES AND CAVEATS

Areas Included

Preliminary Considerations
Procedures
    Learning Disabilities
    Mental Retardation
    Emotional Disturbance/Behavior Disorders
    Gifted and Talented
    Educational Disadvantage
Caveats
    Factors That Affect Test Results
    Problems with Definitions
    Variability within Categories
    Differences in Eligibility Criteria
    Stability of Categories

The use of assessment data for labeling and classification is a controversial yet important issue in special education, and it is a crucial component in the post-referral assessment process. The pros and cons of labeling have been argued, debated, and analyzed for years. The major goals and purposes of labeling and classifying in special education are to identify children with significant educational problems, to indicate similarities and relationships among the educational problems, and to provide information that allows professional communication within the field (Hardman, Drew, Egan, & Wolf, 1993).

In the 1970s and 1980s, however, the way was paved for noncategorical or generic approaches to classification. This development was primarily the result of pressure by critics who were highly vocal in their dislike of labeling. Among their criticisms were that the various disabilities lacked acceptable definitions, that the number of minority students labeled was disproportionately high, that not enough appropriate, identifiable educational programs were available to prescribe after classification, and that labels had a possible stigmatizing effect. This last criticism was the most controversial and was the focus of considerable research in the 1970s and early 1980s. For example, several researchers (including Algozzine & Sutherland, 1977; Jacobs, 1978; and Taylor, Smiley, & Ziegler, 1983) found that when labels such as mental retardation, emotional disturbance, and learning disability were used, teachers' expectations were lower and negative attitudes developed. On the other hand, in what has become a classic review of the subject, MacMillan, Jones, and Aloia (1974) found no conclusive evidence that the label "mentally retarded" had any biasing effect. That review, however, was conducted over two decades ago.

Apparently, labeling is a complex issue that involves both the label and the behavior of the labeled student (Dusek & O'Connell, 1973; Good & Brophy, 1972). Reschly and Lamprecht (1979), for example, found that teachers' expectancies of labeled students' behavior changed when they observed behavior inconsistent with the label. Undoubtedly, the debate over the effects of labeling will continue as long as labels are used.

Despite these controversies and the long history of research, labeling and classification have continued, primarily as a means of establishing priorities and obtaining funds for educational programming. Public Law 94-142, for instance, carefully defined those children for whom special education is warranted:

> *Handicapped children means those children evaluated as being mentally retarded, hard of hearing, deaf, speech impaired, visually handicapped, seriously emotionally disturbed, orthopedically impaired, other health impaired, deaf-blind, multi-handicapped, or as having specific learning disabilities, who because of those impairments need special education and related services.* (p. 121a.5)

P.L. 101-476, although changing the term *handicapped children* to *children with disabilities,* kept the categorical designations.[1] P.L. 101-476 noted that the term *children with disabilities* means children with mental retardation, hearing impairments including deafness, speech or language impairments, visual impairments including blindness, serious emotional disturbance, orthopedic impairments, autism, traumatic brain injury, other health impairments, or specific learning disabilities. (Note that autism and traumatic brain injury were added.).

---

[1]At the time of publication, Congress was debating the reauthorization of P.L. 101-476 (10EA). One point under consideration was the elimination of categories with funding based on a flat percentage of the school population.

It should be pointed out that the Regular Education Initiative (discussed in Chapter 1) and other similar movements have suggested that labels should not be used to identify students who need additional services. However, if the labels noted in federal legislation are no longer used, other labels—either formal or informal—will undoubtedly take their place.

PRELIMINARY CONSIDERATIONS

The term *norm-referenced testing* is often considered synonymous with labeling. But although labeling and classification usually require the administration of norm-referenced tests, these are certainly not the only purposes of such tests. Furthermore, because of several factors, the use of assessment data for labeling is anything but an exact science. Among these factors are those mentioned in Chapter 3, as well as the inexact and changing definitions of the various labels.

Other considerations regarding labeling and classification include:

1. In many situations, labeling and classification are unnecessary. It is important to work with a student to see if a referral and possible label can be avoided (prereferral intervention).

2. The types of tests (and the tests themselves) used to label students differ from examiner to examiner.

3. The criteria used to determine various labels differ considerably from state to state. It is entirely possible that a student might receive one label in a particular state and a different or no label in another state. These different criteria also result in significant variation in the percentages of students who are labeled. Hallahan, Keller, and Ball (1986), for example, noted that the percentage of students labeled as having a learning disability ranged from 3.06 (Indiana) to 8.73 (Rhode Island). Similarly, the percentages for students with mental retardation and emotional disturbance ranged from .67 (three states) to 4.77 (Alabama) and .09 (Mississippi) to 3.45 (Delaware), respectively.

4. Although students are often labeled and classified on the basis of educational and psychological assessment, this is not always prudent. The advantages of using such an approach (for example, added services) must be weighed against the disadvantages (for example, possible stigmatizing effects).

PROCEDURES

Not all exceptional children are initially identified through educational and psychological assessment. Many children with disabilities, such as those with orthopedic impairments, hearing impairments, or traumatic brain injury, are identified through medical and other procedures. Even in these situations, however, assessment data are usually used to document the need for special education and to establish specific goals and objectives.

Classification on the basis of educational and psychological assessment becomes particularly important in situations in which the label or diagnosis depends primarily on the student's intellectual and academic skills or emotional and behavioral status. For example, gifted students and those with learning disabilities, mental retardation, or behavior disorders are often identified through educational and psychological assessment data. It might be more appropriate to state that these types of students are determined to be eligible for special education using educational and psychological tests.

How can test data be used for labeling purposes? Usually, a battery of tests is administered to a student, and the results are examined for certain patterns. The same test battery, however, is not appropriate for all students. As mentioned in Chapter 2, individualizing the assessment procedure is extremely important. Although tests vary greatly, at least some measure of individual intelligence, achievement, adaptive behavior, and emotional and behavioral characteristics is usually obtained as a basis for classification. In general, although some informal and criterion-referenced tests may be used, norm-referenced tests are usually administered. After the selected instruments are administered and scored, the results can be used in deciding the possible classification, if any, of the student.

The following section reviews the definitions of the various labels used in special education and examines their implications for assessment. An *assessment profile* is mentioned for each type of exceptional student. This profile (which includes measures of intelligence, achievement, adaptive behavior, and emotional and behavioral characteristics) is meant as an example to demonstrate how data might be used. More important, the profiles are presented to show how difficult it really is to use assessment as a basis for labeling. As will be discussed, differences in definitions and eligibility criteria for various labels as well as the differences in characteristics of students with the same label make the formulation of a "typical" assessment profile difficult indeed.

Learning Disabilities

Since the term *learning disabilities* was introduced in 1963, professionals have disagreed about its definition. Of the many definitions available, the one proposed by the National Advisory Committee on Handicapped Children (1968) is accepted by many special educators and was only slightly modified by P.L. 94-142. That definition states:

> *Children with specific learning disabilities exhibit a disorder in one or more of the basic psychological processes involved in understanding or in using spoken or written language. They may be manifested in disorders of listening, thinking, talking, reading, writing, spelling, or arithmetic. They include conditions which have been referred to as perceptual handicaps, brain injury, minimal brain dysfunction, dyslexia, developmental aphasia, etc. They do not include learning problems which are primarily due to visual, hearing, or motor handicaps, to mental retardation, emotional disturbance, or to environmental disadvantage.* (p. 34)

In 1988, a proposed definition was developed by the Interagency Committee on Learning Disabilities (ICLD), a group consisting of thirteen federal agencies. The major modification proposed added social skills deficits as a possible characteristic of learning disabilities and acknowledged that learning disabilities might coexist with attention deficit disorder. The ICLD definition follows:

Learning disabilities is a generic term that refers to a heterogeneous group of disorders manifested by significant difficulties in the acquisition and use of listening, speaking, reading, writing, reasoning, or mathematical abilities, or of social skills. These disorders are intrinsic to the individual and presumed to be due to central nervous system dysfunction. Even though a learning disability may occur concomitantly with other handicapping conditions (e.g., sensory impairment, mental retardation, social and emotional disturbance) with socioenvironmental influences (e.g., cultural differences, insufficient or inappropriate instruction, psychogenic factors), and especially attention deficit disorder, all of which may cause learning problems, a learning disability is not the direct result of those conditions or influences.

Also in 1988, the National Joint Committee for Learning Disabilities (NJCLD) modified their earlier 1981 definition that included a reaction to the ICLD definition. That definition reads

Learning disabilities is a general term that refers to a heterogeneous group of disorders manifested by significant difficulties in the acquisition and use of listening, speaking, reading, writing, reasoning, or mathematical abilities. These disorders are intrinsic to the individual and presumed to be due to central nervous system dysfunction and may appear across the life span. Problems in self-regulatory behaviors, social perception, and social interaction may exist with a learning disability but do not by themselves constitute a learning disability. Although a learning disability may occur concomitantly with other handicapping conditions (for example, sensory impairment, mental retardation, serious emotional disturbance) or with extrinsic factors (such as cultural differences, insufficient or inappropriate instruction) they are not the direct result of those conditions or influences.

There is certainly no consensus regarding the definition of learning disabilities.

Hammill (1990) reviewed eleven definitions of learning disabilities and found that although there was considerable agreement among them, the NJCLD definition appeared to include the best descriptive statements. Regardless of which definition is used, one common diagnostic criterion is the documentation of a discrepancy between expected and actual performance. In a survey of the definitions used by all fifty states, three factors emerged in 75 percent or more of their criteria for identifying learning disabilities. Those were exclusion (such as problems not caused by another disability) and language and academic problems usually expressed by some type of discrepancy formula (Mercer, King-Sears, & Mercer, 1990).

Historically, students with learning disabilities (LD) have been assumed to have normal or low normal intelligence but have problems in at least one area of achievement. Heward and Orlansky (1992) noted that the most common characteristic of children with learning disabilities is a significant achievement deficiency in the presence of adequate overall intelligence (i.e., a discrepancy between aptitude and achievement). Aptitude-achievement formulae used to identify students with LD differ significantly, and their use can greatly influence the types of students being identified. For example, Reynolds (1985a) noted that grade-level discrepancy criteria typically will deny learning disability services to students with IQs that are above average, whereas most standard score models will deny services to students with below-average IQs. In general, the entire area of aptitude-achievement discrepancies has been criticized because of their lack of empirical support and the statistical flaws inherent in many of the formulae. Evans (1990) reported that the regression model formula was the best although the issue of classification is still dependent on the tests used. In other words, it is possible that the same student could be given different batteries of tests resulting in different classification decisions using the same formula. In addition, Siegel (1989) argued that IQ should not be used in such formulae because they do not measure potential and are not independent of achievement. In fact, the Council for Learning Disabilities has recommended that the use of discrepancy formulae be abandoned. Wood (1991) also urged that *educational significance*, not just statistical significance, be considered when using the formulae. It should be noted, however, that discrepancy formulae are still being used widely; Hickman and Bevins (1990), for example, recently published a computer program to perform discrepancy analyses. Evans (1992), in fact, reported that 89 percent of the school psychologists he surveyed had used a computer-based discrepancy model and that 62 percent used it regularly.

Because of the differences in definition and criteria used in the field of learning disabilities, it is difficult to identify a specific assessment profile for this population. A review of the characteristics of the LD population confuses the matter even more. As an example, Rivers and Smith (1988) reviewed the assessment profiles of two hundred students with LD and found that many had below-average IQs and did not have aptitude-achievement discrepancies. The following profile represents a pattern of assessment results that *might* be found for a student with LD. Note the variability in each of the areas included.

SAMPLE ASSESSMENT PROFILE: LEARNING DISABILITY (LD)

INTELLIGENCE: Average or low average performance
ACHIEVEMENT: Variable or low average performance
ADAPTIVE BEHAVIOR: Average or variable performance
EMOTIONAL AND BEHAVIORAL CHARACTERISTICS: Variable
    performance

Thus, if a student were administered a battery of tests and the scores resulted in this profile, this student might be considered as having a learning disability. Some regulations also require the assessment of deficits in information processing; such deficits are usually measured by specific perceptual-motor, aptitude, or language tests (see Appendix A).

Mental Retardation

Although various classification systems are still used for students with mental retardation, the most accepted system is one proposed by the American Association on Mental Retardation (AAMR) (Luckasson, 1992). According to that system,

> Mental retardation *refers to substantial limitations in present functioning. It is characterized by significantly subaverage intellectual functioning, existing concurrently with related limitations in two or more of the following applicable adaptive skill areas: communication, self-care, home living, social skills, community use, self-direction, health and safety, functional academics, leisure, and work. Mental retardation manifests before age eighteen.*

The AAMR further states that "significantly subaverage intellectual functioning" is defined by a score on a standardized intelligence test that is 70–75 or below. Although the criterion is specifically stated, the interpretation is not as straightforward. Wodrich and Barry (1991), in a survey of actual practices, found that more than 25 percent of the school psychologists were flexible and would identify a student as having retardation who had an IQ above the cut-off point. The 1992 AAMR definition also made several notable changes to previous definitions. First, they eliminated the various levels of retardation and the accompanying IQ criteria (see Table 4.1 on page 66 for the old levels). The levels of mental retardation were replaced with the levels of support services needed by the individual with mental retardation. Those levels are intermittent, limited, extensive, and pervasive (see Table 4.2 on page 66). Second, they stressed even more the adaptive behavior component by identifying and defining ten adaptive skill areas (an individual must have deficits in at least two of the areas). Those are:

1. Communication
2. Self-care
3. Home living
4. Social skills
5. Community use
6. Self-direction
7. Health and safety
8. Functional academics
9. Leisure
10. Work

TABLE 4.1   AAMD Levels of Mental Retardation

Level of Retardation	IQ Range
Mild	50–55 to approx. 70
Moderate	35–40 to 50–55
Severe	20–25 to 35–40
Profound	Below 20 or 25

From H. Grossman, *Classification in Mental Retardation*, 1983.
Copyright © American Association on Mental Deficiency.

The translation of the adaptive behavior criteria to practice is also somewhat problematic. For one thing, the adaptive-behavior test score sufficient to indicate a deficit is not clear. Wodrich and Barry (1991) reported that only 50 percent of the school psychologists surveyed used 70 as a cutoff (usually two standard deviations below the mean).

In achievement, students with mental retardation (MR) also perform significantly below their peers (e.g., Taylor, Sternberg, & Richards, 1995). In general, achievement by students with MR is consistent with their intellectual level, although some evidence suggests that they are lower than expected in reading skills relative to their IQ (MacMillan, 1982).

TABLE 4.2   Definition and Examples of Intensities of Supports

Intensity of Support	Definition
Intermittent	Supports on an "as needed basis." Characterized by episodic nature, person not always needing the support(s), or short-term supports needed during life-span transitions (e.g., job loss or an acute medical crisis). Intermittent supports may be high or low intensity when provided.
Limited	An intensity of supports characterized by consistency over time, time-limited but not of an intermittent nature, may require fewer staff members and less cost than more intense levels of support (e.g., time-limited employment training or transitional supports during the school to adult provided period).
Extensive	Supports characterized by regular involvement (e.g., daily) in at least some environments (such as work or home) and not time-limited (e.g., long-term support and long-term home living support).
Pervasive	Supports characterized by their constancy, high intensity, provided across environments; potential life-sustaining nature. Pervasive supports typically involve more staff members and intrusiveness than do extensive or time-limited supports.

From R. Luckasson, *Mental Retardation: Definition, Classification, and Systems of Support*, 1992. Copyright © American Association on Mental Retardation.

Other than the individual differences noted in everyone, few patterns of classroom behavior are typical of students with MR. Three that tend to surface are a lack of motivation, poor self-concept, and difficulty making friends (Hallahan & Kauffman, 1994). A sample profile for a student with MR, therefore, might look like the following:

SAMPLE ASSESSMENT PROFILE: MENTAL RETARDATION (MR)

INTELLIGENCE: Low performance
ACHIEVEMENT: Low performance
ADAPTIVE BEHAVIOR: Low performance
EMOTIONAL AND BEHAVIORAL CHARACTERISTICS: Variable
   performance

Emotional Disturbance/Behavior Disorders

Emotional disturbance is extremely difficult to define. In fact, there is little agreement about what term to use to refer to individuals with emotional or behavioral problems. Emotional disturbance, emotional handicap, and behavior disorder, among other terms, have all been used. There is also a considerable amount of subjectivity about what constitutes an emotional or behavioral problem. Indeed, there is no consensus and no universally accepted definition, although Bower's definition (1969) is the one most widely used by educators and is the basis for the definition used in P.L. 101-476. That definition reads:

I. . . . A condition exhibiting one or more of the following characteristics over a long period of time and to a marked degree, which adversely affects educational performance.

   A. An inability to learn which cannot be explained by intellectual, sensory, or health factors.

   B. An inability to build or maintain satisfactory interpersonal relationships with peers and teachers.

   C. Inappropriate types of behavior or feelings under normal circumstances.

   D. A general pervasive mood of unhappiness or depression.

   E. A tendency to develop physical symptoms, pains, or fear associated with personal or school problems.

II. The term includes children who are schizophrenic. The term does not include children who are socially maladjusted unless it is determined that they are seriously emotionally disturbed.

As a basis for assessment, this definition is frustrating because it is subjective. Individual interpretations of "inappropriate behavior or feelings," "unhappiness," and "depression" can differ, leading to application of the emotionally disturbed classification to a wide range of children. Social, cultural, and situational expectations confuse the assessment even more.

More recently, in fact, a new definition has been proposed that was developed by the Task Force of the Mental Health and Special Education Coalition. That definition reads:

I. Emotional and behavioral disorders mean a disability that is characterized by behavioral or emotional responses in school so different from appropriate age, culture, or ethnic norms that they adversely affect educational performance, including academic, social, vocational, or personal skills. Such a disability

   A. is more than a temporary, expected response to stressful events in the environment;
   B. is consistently exhibited in two different settings, at least one of which is school-related;
   C. is unresponsive to direct intervention applied in general education, or the child's condition is such that general education interventions would be insufficient.

II. Emotional and behavioral disorders can coexist with other disabilities.

III. This category may include children and youth with schizophrenic disorders, affective disorders, anxiety disorders, or other sustained disorders of conduct or adjustment when they adversely affect educational performance in accordance with section I. (Forness & Knitzer, 1992; p. 13)

This proposed definition uses different terminology, although it still requires subjective interpretation.

The assessment profile of the individual with emotional or behavioral problems is also somewhat confusing. For example, documentation of a typical cognitive, academic, and behavioral performance is difficult. By definition, intellectual deficits should not be the cause of that individual's inability to learn. This implies that to be correctly classified as having an emotional disturbance, a person should score within the normal range of intelligence. Kauffman (1993) noted that as a group, children with emotional disturbance score in the low normal range but that their scores have a wide range.

Kauffman further noted that low achievement goes hand in hand with behavior disorders, although it is not clear if the behavior problem causes the low achievement, or vice versa. In general, however, the achievement of these students is as variable as their scores on intelligence tests. Tamkin (1960) found that in achievement, 41 percent of the disturbed children he studied were above grade level, and only 32 percent were below. Other researchers (including Bower, 1969; Motto & Wilkins, 1968) found that children with emotional disturbance were significantly below their peers in academic achievement. These apparently contradictory findings may derive at least in part from the variations in the type and severity of the problems that led to the classification.

Children with emotional disturbance frequently demonstrate behavior problems in the classroom. To a certain extent, they also tend to have problems in adaptive behavior. Kauffman (1993) mentioned the following four kinds of behavior that are typically associated with children with emotional or behavior problems: (1) hyperactivity, distractibility, and impulsivity; (2) aggression; (3) withdrawal, immaturity, and inadequacy; and (4) juvenile delinquency and deficiencies in moral development.

Although it is very difficult to determine an assessment profile for students who have emotional disturbance or behavior disorders, such a profile might look like the following:

SAMPLE ASSESSMENT PROFILE: EMOTIONAL OR BEHAVIOR PROBLEMS

INTELLIGENCE: Average or low average performance
ACHIEVEMENT: Variable or low average performance
ADAPTIVE BEHAVIOR: Variable performance
EMOTIONAL AND BEHAVIORAL CHARACTERISTICS: Low
  performance

Gifted and Talented

In recent years, gifted children have been receiving more and more attention. In a certain sense, however, definitions of *gifted* are just as ambiguous as definitions of other exceptional categories—if not more so. The generally accepted definition was set forth in Section 902 of the Gifted and Talented Children's Act (P.L. 95-561) and reported in the *Congressional Record* (1978).

> *The term* gifted and talented children *means children and, whenever applicable, youth who are identified at the preschool, elementary, or secondary level as possessing demonstrated or potential abilities that give evidence of high performance capabilities in areas such as intellectual, creative, specific academic or leadership ability, or in the performing and visual arts, and who by reason thereof, require services or activities not ordinarily provided by the school.* (H-12179)

In general, a subtle distinction is made between the terms *gifted* and *talented*. Gifted often refers to cognitive and creative superiority in combination with strong motivation, whereas talented refers to a special ability, aptitude, or accomplishment (Hallahan & Kauffman, 1994). Kirk and Gallagher (1993), however, pointed out a substantial positive correlation between intellectual ability and talented performance.

Although superior academic achievement is common in children who are gifted, some professionals estimate that as many as 15 to 20 percent of gifted children do not achieve at their expected level (Kirk & Gallagher, 1993). Lack of interest, of motivation, or of self-confidence could all be contributing factors.

In terms of behavioral characteristics, Terman's longitudinal study (Terman, 1925; Terman & Oden, 1959) is perhaps the most exhaustive. Terman found that scores for children who are gifted were average or above average in virtually every character trait measured. An exception might occur in unmotivated or underachieving gifted students, who might demonstrate some inappropriate classroom behavior. In terms of adaptive behavior, the definition and description of children who are gifted implies that the majority are average or above. Exceptional leadership skills, for instance, are not uncommon in gifted students (Kirk & Gallagher, 1993).

The following profile is offered for gifted children:

SAMPLE ASSESSMENT PROFILE: GIFTED

INTELLIGENCE: High performance
ACHIEVEMENT: High or variable performance
ADAPTIVE BEHAVIOR: Average or high performance
EMOTIONAL AND BEHAVIORAL CHARACTERISTICS: Average or
    variable performance

Educational Disadvantage

Even though *educationally disadvantaged* is not an officially accepted classification for exceptional children, it is included here because many children who are classified as having mental retardation, emotional or behavioral problems, or learning disabilities probably should fall within this classification. Educationally disadvantaged refers to those students who are not doing well in school yet are not disabled in the traditional sense. These children often come from low socioeconomic groups or non-Anglo cultures in which English may be a second language. The concept *educationally disadvantaged* does not imply that the students it refers to cannot be exceptional in some other way; rather, it means that they are often labeled as such when they should not be.

It has long been recognized that educationally disadvantaged students typically perform poorly on intelligence tests (Kaufman & Doppelt, 1976; Mercer, 1973). Because intelligence tests predict achievement fairly well (see Chapter 9), such children also usually do poorly on achievement tests. One striking difference between these students and students with MR (who also score low on intelligence and achievement tests) is their behavior *outside the classroom.* Mercer (1973) distinguished between clinically retarded children (who have difficulties with day-to-day living skills) and quasi-retarded children (who get along well in the community, hold jobs, and develop social relationships with co-workers and friends). She referred to the "six-hour retarded child" as the one who has retarded performance only during school hours. Analogously, the assessment profiles for educationally disadvantaged children resemble those for children with MR, with the exception that educationally disadvantaged children have average scores in the area of adaptive behavior.

The profile for an educationally disadvantaged student might look something like this:

SAMPLE ASSESSMENT PROFILE: EDUCATIONAL DISADVANTAGE

INTELLIGENCE: Low performance
ACHIEVEMENT: Low performance
ADAPTIVE BEHAVIOR: Average performance
EMOTIONAL AND BEHAVIORAL CHARACTERISTICS: Variable
   performance

CAVEATS

Many problematic issues must be considered when assessment data are used for labeling and classification. Table 4.3 on page 72 presents an overall matrix for the test profiles of the exceptional categories discussed. It would be wonderful if the process were as simple and clear cut as Table 4.3 may seem to imply. Unfortunately, this is not the case. As mentioned previously, some of the causes for the difficulty in using assessment data as a basis for classification are (1) the factors that affect test results; (2) the changing and variable definitions of the categories of exceptional children; (3) the variation among children within these categories; and (4) the different eligibility criteria used by different states.

Factors That Affect Test Results

Virtually all the factors that can affect tests results that were mentioned in Chapter 3 should be considered during labeling and classification. As much care as possible should be taken in eliminating, or at least minimizing, those variables. Proper test selection, adherence to administration and scoring criteria (or documentation of any modification), sensitivity before and during the testing session, and a full understanding of the limitations of tests—that is, their use solely as samples of behavior—are all necessary. Attending to all these factors might seem to be a formidable task, but careful planning and thought beforehand will make the procedure easier.

Problems with Definitions

The differing opinions on definition and prevalence of the various categories of exceptional students make labeling and classification even harder. Most definitions are subjective enough to allow a multitude of interpretations. Hence, a student might be considered as having a learning disability in one evaluator's

TABLE 4.3 Test-Profile Matrix

	Learning Disability	Mental Retardation	Emotional Disturbance	Educational Disadvantage	No Disability	Gifted
Intelligence	A–LA	L	A–LA	L	A	H
Achievement	V–LA	L	LA–V	L	A	H–V
Adaptive Behavior	A–V	L	V	A	A	A–H
Emotional and Behavioral Characteristics	V	V	L	V	A	A–V

A = Average   L = Low   LA = Low-average
H = High   V = Variable

opinion, but not in another's. Two other considerations also apply: (1) the periodic changes in definitions and terminology within the field of special education; and (2) the resulting confusion about which classification system to use. There are many examples of changing definitions and their subsequent effect on the use of assessment data for assigning labels. The previously discussed proposed definitions for learning disabilities (by the NJCLD) and emotional/behavioral disorder (by the Task Force of the Mental Health and Special Education Coalition) are two. The AAMR definition of mental retardation provides more specific requirements for adaptive behavior deficits and other changes that might affect assessment.

The result of changing definitions was explored by Taylor (1980), who looked at the systems used in classifying mental retardation. He found that the American Association on Mental Deficiency (AAMD) classification system was used in only 28 percent of the articles in the journals published by the AAMD between 1973 and 1979. In approximately 27 percent of the articles, the educational classifications *educable* and *trainable* were used, and in 40 percent, the subjects were simply classified as mentally retarded, with no mention of the classification system used. In a follow-up study, Taylor and Kaufmann (1991) reported that the use of the AAMD/AAMR system almost doubled during the 1980s, although no classification system was used for almost 25 percent of the studies.

Variability within Categories

The variability of test scores of individuals within each category also causes problems. Although the matrix shown in Table 4.3 may show the typical pattern of the test scores, in reality, scores vary greatly within each category. For instance, regarding intelligence, students with learning disabilities are often thought of as being average; their reported IQs, however, are often below 90. Similarly, students with emotional disturbance should have average IQs, yet as a group, they tend to score in the low average range, implying that at least some of these students score below average.

Careful analysis of the research into the use of norm-referenced instruments with exceptional students, unfortunately, indicates that many of these instruments have definite limitations. Also, the severity of the children's disabilities obviously will affect their test performance. In general, this chapter, particularly concerning mental retardation and emotional disturbance, relates to the assessment of students with mild or moderate disabilities. In most cases, children who have severe or profound mental retardation or emotional disturbance (for example, autism) are extremely difficult to test in the traditional manner and are usually identified through other means, such as medical diagnosis.

Differences in Eligibility Criteria

As noted previously, there is tremendous variability regarding the specific criteria used to identify special education students. The possibility of a student with a specific label losing (or changing) that label when moving to an area that uses different criteria is one to consider. The different aptitude–achievement discrepancy formulae used to identify students with learning disabilities is a good example of this point. An individual might be considered as having a learning disability using one formula and as not by using another, even though the same test scores are used. Another issue to consider is changes in criteria within a specific area. For example, Frankenberger and Fronzaglio (1991) reported that 40 percent of the states revised their guidelines for identifying students with learning disabilities between 1988 and 1990.

Stability of Categories

Because of all the reasons previously discussed, it is likely that a person's label might change even without differences in eligibility criteria. In a study designed to determine the stability of the categorical designations that an individual might receive, Wolman, Thurlow, and Bruininks (1989) followed more than five hundred special education students throughout their school years. They found that approximately 25 percent had at least one change in their labels. They also found that the change was more likely to occur during the secondary years and was more likely to result in a change to a label that most considered a more serious disability.

SUMMARY

Labeling and classification have advocates and critics. It is clear that in many situations the procedures are necessary to obtain proper educational services. They might also be viewed as techniques for assigning priority to those who are in need of additional help, although Will (1986) estimated that probably another 20 percent of the student population are not labeled who do need additional help. On the other hand, potential dangers also lurk in labeling and classifying children. The issues of overrepresentation of minorities and the possible stigmatizing effects of labels should be considered. Perhaps it is most important to remember that assessment for labeling and classifying is not an exact science—not only because of the limitations in the tests themselves, but also because of the ambiguity in the definitions of types of exceptional children.

Too often, people have taken an all-or-none approach to labeling and classification, either believing that any child needing additional help should be labeled, or that no child should be subjected to the process, regardless of the circumstances. Perhaps a more pragmatic approach is in order. If a student is initially identified as needing help, every effort could be made to provide this help by informally adapting the environment, curriculum, or materials (that is, by using prereferral intervention procedures). Doing so might even include consultation with the most appropriate specialists.

If this approach does not work, the teacher should be aware of the implications of labeling and weigh them against the potential value of the services available. In other words, the question should be asked: "Is it worth it to put a child through the referral and subsequent assessment process?" At times the answer to the question will be yes, and at other times it will be no. The information included in this chapter should help you in making those decisions. Figure 4.1 is a flow chart that summarizes the decision-making process involved in labeling and classification.

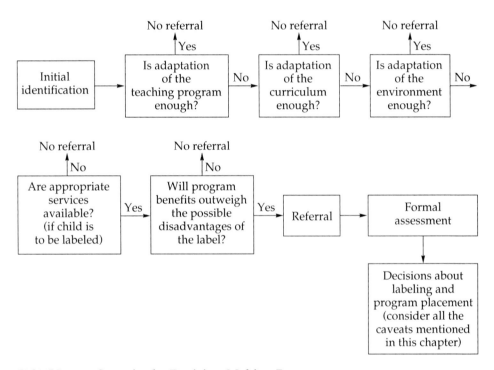

FIGURE 4.1   Steps in the Decision-Making Process

Part **II**

INFORMAL PROCEDURES: BASIC TOOLS FOR TEACHERS

Most assessment can and should be incorporated into the students' "routine" daily schedule. In other words, teachers should be aware of the importance of gathering information that is provided during the instructional process. In many cases, such data can be routinely collected through *observation* (discussed in Chapter 5) and *analysis of work products* (discussed in Chapter 6). In other cases, the teacher can use the curriculum or a student's Individualized Education Program (IEP) to develop a *criterion-referenced instrument* (discussed in Chapter 6) or a *curriculum-based assessment instrument* (discussed in Chapter 7). These types of tests provide the teacher with relevant information on which to base instructional decisions. The teacher might also use *alternative assessment procedures,* such as portfolio assessment, to gather meaningful educational information (discussed in Chapter 8).

As noted in Chapter 2, all of these informal procedures are important *throughout* the assessment process. They are crucial to the prereferral component and can provide much-needed information for developing prereferral intervention programs and documenting referrals of students for special education. Conversely, these approaches are invaluable in developing and evaluating educational programs *after* a student has been identified as needing special education services (postreferral component).

For each technique that is described in this section, the following information is provided:

1. A summary matrix that presents information about specific instruments and techniques in a format allowing easy comparison of the instruments for suggested use and target population. The matrix also includes a statement of any special considerations of which a user should be aware. In addition, for each technique, the matrix gives the educational relevance for exceptional students. The matrices are directly related to the assessment model proposed in Chapter 2.

2. An introduction box for each technique identifying the suggested use and the suggested user.

AFTER READING PART II YOU SHOULD BE ABLE TO:

- Identify the components involved in observational assessment, including the appropriate recording procedures.
- Identify the steps involved in developing a criterion-referenced test.
- Identify the steps involved in conducting an error analysis in the areas of reading, mathematics, and spelling.
- Identify the steps involved in developing a curriculum-based assessment instrument.
- Identify the similarities and differences between curriculum-based assessment and curriculum-based measurement.
- Identify several types of alternative assessment procedures.
- Identify the uses and limitations of portfolio assessment.

5

OBSERVATIONAL ASSESSMENT

Instruments and Procedures Included

Student Observation—Informal Systems
    Goals of Observation
    An Observational Model
    Other Uses of Data
Student Observation—Formal Systems
Observation of the Environment

Observation is undoubtedly the most pervasive and widely used method of assessment. Virtually every second spent during a day in the classroom yields a tremendous amount of observational data. The key, however, is to use the observational data in a systematic and meaningful way. As mentioned in Chapter 2, the collection of prereferral information is important in determining the course and method of evaluation. Observational data certainly fit into this category of prereferral assessment. Such data can be used to determine and evaluate a teaching or behavioral program that in turn can be used to identify those students who will need more in-depth formal evaluation. Observation can also be helpful in developing and monitoring Individualized Education Programs (IEPs) for both academic and nonacademic behavior. On the other hand, observation of the educational *environment* can also provide important information for making educational decisions.

Observation is perhaps the most objective method of assessment. In fact, it is generally thought of as the most direct method of obtaining assessment data with the least amount of inference by the evaluator. Keller (1980) noted that "observation involves description of behaviors which requires little, if any, inference by observers. Further, the use of observation involves direct measurement of behaviors in settings of concern to the child being referred and of concern to the referral agent. The result of its use is a more direct and close relationship between assessment and intervention, with a minimum, or at least reduction, of inferential leaps relative to a reliance upon standardized tests solely" (p. 21).

When most people think of observation as an assessment tool, they think about observing student behavior to obtain information that will aid in educational decision making. However, as noted previously, observation of the educational *or* instructional environment can also provide valuable information.

Observational techniques can be classified as either formal or informal. Formal approaches include observational packages that usually include specific coding and scoring systems. Informal approaches—by far more commonly used—include observation with the observer already present in the setting; observation with an outside observer in the setting; and observation with the observer not present in the setting. These types of informal approaches are particularly relevant when student behavior is being observed.

STUDENT OBSERVATION—INFORMAL SYSTEMS

WHY USE INFORMAL STUDENT OBSERVATION?

Screening and identification; informal determination and evaluation of teaching programs and strategies; documentation of need for further evaluation or referral; development and evaluation of IEPs

WHO SHOULD USE IT?

Primarily teachers; also school psychologists and parents

In the most widely used of the three informal procedures, the observer is already present in the natural environment. In this approach, many times the teacher is the primary evaluator or observer. It is also possible that peers—or even the target child—could perform these observations. Theoretically, the primary advantage of observation by someone already present is that in the absence of an external observer, the observed child should "act naturally." Observation of the child's behavior in the natural setting, with no changes in the schedule or routine or environment, should give a truer measure of the problem behavior. This procedure also has disadvantages. First, it is often difficult to manage (or find) the time to collect observational data. This is particularly true for the teacher. It is possible to have teachers' aides collect this information, but again, the time element is extremely crucial.

The second type of informal procedure uses an external or outside observer in the natural setting. The observer can be a psychologist, parent, volunteer, principal, or any school staff member who does not routinely work with the child in that setting (usually the classroom). The advantage of this procedure is that it allows the teacher to continue in the routine daily schedule. The observers can work at times that are appropriate both for the child and for themselves. The disadvantage of this approach is that it may cause reactivity (the effect of an observer on the behavior of the observed individual) that might bias the results.

Many researchers (including Boehm & Weinberg, 1987; Repp, Nieminen, Olinger, & Brusca, 1988) have discussed the issue of reactivity and its effects on observational assessment. Haynes (1978), in fact, indicated a number of ways in which reactivity could be reduced. These included decreasing the conspicuousness of the observer and minimizing the interaction between the observed person and the observer.

The third informal procedure involves an observer who is not present in the natural setting. This approach usually includes an artificial apparatus such as a one-way mirror or a videotape or audiotape that can later be transcribed. The advantage of this approach is that the child sees no observer, so that reactivity becomes less of an issue. The apparatus itself, however, can have some reactive effect on the child (Boehm & Weinberg, 1987). Obviously, the less obtrusive the apparatus, the more "naturally" a child will behave. This approach can be time-consuming (particularly using tapes) or restrictive (not every classroom has one-way mirrors).

With each of these informal observation procedures, it is extremely important to obtain reliable, valid information. For maximum reliability in obtaining information, observers should use specific operational definitions and collect interrater reliability data—that is, more than one person should observe the behavior until all observers reach agreement. For maximum validity, information should be collected by observing the behavior in the environment in which it is a problem. Also, the observation must measure a representative sample of the person's behavior. In general, ensuring the reliability and validity of informal observation is often overlooked, an unfortunate oversight that could have a negative effect on the decisions made about the observed student.

Goals of Observing Student Behavior

Keller (1980) delineated four general uses of observation. Those were directly assessing problems in the setting of concern, monitoring an intervention program, measuring the effectiveness and generalization of an intervention, and enhancing collaborative consultation among school personnel. Cartwright and Cartwright (1984) outlined more specific uses of observation for educational decision making. Those included (1) early detection of problems; (2) making decisions about entry behaviors; and (3) making instructional decisions. Another important goal of observation that incorporates many of the previously mentioned uses is to provide a model to allow teachers to increase, decrease, or maintain certain academic or social behaviors of their students.

Early Detection of Problems

Observation to detect problems is an informal way of screening. It simply means that the observer notes that a student is starting to experience difficulty in some area. This observation is usually based on the observer's knowledge of "typical" or "expected" development or on a comparison to other individuals who have similar characteristics (for example, same age and gender). This can lead to more formal assessment to determine the extent and possible cause of the problem.

Making Decisions about Entry Behaviors

In a sense, making decisions about entry behaviors is similar to determining a student's current level of performance. In other words, it allows an observer to determine what behaviors in a given area a student already possesses. This requires that the observer critically analyze the student's needs to determine which behaviors should be observed. This usually involves some type of ecological assessment, or analyzing the environments within which the student exists or will exist to determine those behaviors necessary to function as independently as possible. These might be academic skills for younger students with mild disabilities, more functional "survival" skills, such as recognizing danger signs or completing job applications, for older students with disabilities, or independent living skills for students who have more severe disabilities. By determining a student's entry level in specified areas, the observer will have a good idea where to begin a more in-depth evaluation.

Making Instructional Decisions

Another use of observation is to help make instructional decisions. As Cartwright and Cartwright (1984) noted, "If you have been able to collect information about a child's history of successes with different instructional materials, then you are better able to select appropriate teaching methods and materials that can be used with some assurance of effectiveness with the child." Using observation for this purpose is important in planning prereferral intervention strategies.

Student Observation: A Model

One important goal of observational assessment is to provide information that will enable a teacher to increase, decrease, or maintain specific academic and non-academic behaviors. This can be easily accomplished if a four-step model is followed. Those four steps are:

1. Careful identification of the target behavior
2. Precise and appropriate measurement of the target behavior
3. Systematic introduction of intervention or remedial programs
4. Evaluation of program effectiveness

Identification of the Target Behavior

The success of any program designed to change behavior will depend largely on how well the target behavior is defined. It is extremely important that behaviors be identified in terms that are precise, observable, and measurable. Terms such as *aggression, hyperactivity, poor-self-concept,* and *academically slow* are too vague and general to have any practical value. These terms also mean different things to different people, making it difficult to obtain reliable measurement. As Taylor and Marholin (1980) noted, "Behaviors presented in terms of traits, personality characteristics, and labels are too general and open to idiosyncratic interpretation to be of much value. If behaviors are defined objectively, few or no inferences are necessary to detect behaviors when they occur." For example, aggression might be defined as "strikes out at others with fists or objects" or "verbally abuses others by using curse words or a loud tone of voice." Similarly, poor self-concept might be defined as "makes negative statements about self," and hyperactivity might be considered as "gets out of seat at inappropriate times."

In the above examples, the behaviors are precise, observable, and measurable; yet even these could be still further defined to include the setting and a clarification of terms. For example, it might be acceptable for a child to raise his or her voice on the playground. Or it might be necessary to indicate at which times or in which situations getting out of a seat is considered inappropriate. In every instance when the behavior is defined, the student, the situation, and the anticipated goal or outcome should be kept in mind. For every child labeled distractible, the term distractibility might be defined differently. You should strive to be specific enough so that if other people were to observe and measure the behavior they would be able to obtain the same or similar results. It is also important to be aware of the possibility of "observer drift," a situation in which the observer gradually shifts from the initial definition of the target behavior (Alberto & Troutman, 1995; Repp et al., 1988).

Measurement of the Target Behavior

The accurate, careful recording of behavioral data is extremely important. Informal observational assessment requires the evaluator to develop and implement a unique measurement system. Typically, lack of time or misunderstanding of the importance of objective data leads to the use of some type of subjective system. Subjective systems include evaluations such as, "John seems to be doing much better in the area of self-help skills," or "Sally appears to be getting out of her seat less often than she used to."

Observational data are usually recorded as frequently as possible, ideally daily, thus giving the observer a much better idea of the changes in behavior as a function of environmental interventions and of the teaching program. The observational data are usually recorded on a graph or chart, thereby presenting a visual display of the change in behavior over time.

Initially, data are collected when no specific intervention program is in effect (or when the current, unsuccessful program is in effect). These preintervention data are called *baseline data* and correspond roughly to a *pretest* in traditional assessment measures. Usually baseline data are collected until they stabilize or show a consistent pattern. If a consistent pattern does not emerge, further definition of the target behavior might be necessary.

Before initiating an observational assessment, it is necessary to choose both the recording devices and the recording procedures that will be used. The choice of recording procedure is particularly important and is largely dependent on the type of behavior that is being observed. The general issue of recording devices and several specific recording procedures are discussed next.

Recording Devices.   Three basic tools are necessary to observe and record behavior: a timer, a counter, and a graph or chart. For all the observational approaches, the issue of time is important. Certain recording procedures, however, require more exact timekeeping devices. The most common are the stopwatch, the clock or watch with a second hand, and the calculator with a stopwatch or timer. Devices for counting behaviors include wrist counters, abacus beads, and the basic pencil-and-paper technique. The wrist counter is worn like a watch. By pushing a button on the counter, the observer keeps a cumulative tally. Abacus beads can also be worn on the wrist. They consist of rows of beads that represent place values (ones, tens, hundreds). Pencil-and-paper tallies are widely used. There are a limitless number of pencil-and-paper techniques, although Tukey (1977) developed a standard system. Alessi (1980) described Tukey's system:

> In this system, dots and lines are used to tally counts. The first count is represented by a single dot (.), the second by two dots (. .), the third by three dots (. :) and the fourth by four dots(: :). The dots are placed so as to outline a box. The numbers five, six, seven, and eight are then represented by completing the box sides with lines, in any order: Five = ɪ :, six = ⌐:, seven = ⌐ɪ, eight = ⊏, nine = ⊠, and ten = ⊠. Fewer errors in both tabulation and summation are likely using this system as compared with others (such as |, ||, |||, ||||). The dot and box system also takes much less space on the protocol. (pp. 36–37)

More expensive and sophisticated devices are also available. For example, Datamyte (Electro General Corporation) and MORE (Observational Systems, Inc.) are hand-held data collectors that include a measure of time and a counter. These systems also have solid-state memory and optional features that allow interface with a computer for data storage and analysis. These instruments are relatively expensive and overly sophisticated for everyday classroom use.

The last basic tool is the graph or chart, which offers a visual representation of observed behaviors. In the most common graph, the data are plotted along a vertical line (ordinate) and a horizontal line (abscissa). The ordinate usually represents the unit of behavioral measure (such as frequency or percentage), and the abscissa represents the unit of time (Alberto & Troutman, 1995). Figure 5.1 demonstrates this approach. Graphs such as this are usually drawn on plain or graph paper. More sophisticated charts are also available. One example is the *Standard*

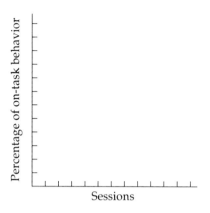

FIGURE 5.1   Example of a Graph

Behavior Chart (SBC) that is used in precision teaching. The SBC is a semilogarithmic chart that is based on a ratio rather than an ordinal scale (Figure 5.2 on page 86). Essentially, this means that the vertical axis is scaled proportionally so that, for instance, the distance between 1 and 5 is the same as the difference between 100 and 500. This allows the plotting of behavior that occurs as frequently as one thousand times per minute or as infrequently as one time in one thousand minutes on the same 9 1/2-by-11-inch chart. The SBC uses *frequency* (defined as number of behaviors divided by number of minutes observed) as its primary measure. The advantage of a system such as this is that it is interpretable by all who are familiar with the chart (an advantage that is rare when individuals develop their own systems). The SBC also allows a standard measure of learning rate (called *celeration*) and variability (called *bounce*).

Recording Procedures.   One important issue is the choice of recording procedures. Clearly, certain recording procedures are more appropriate for certain types of behavior. A description of each type of recording procedure follows, with examples of appropriate use.

Event Recording. Event recording, sometimes referred to as frequency recording, involves counting the number of behaviors that occur within a certain time limit —for instance, the number of times Bill gets out of his seat during a fifty-minute science period, or the number of correct problems Alex completes during a fifteen-minute mathematics session. By including both the number of behaviors and the time interval, it is possible to convert the data to a standard period. This is accomplished by using the following formula:

$$\text{frequency} = \frac{\text{number of behaviors observed}}{\text{number of minutes or hours spent observing}}$$

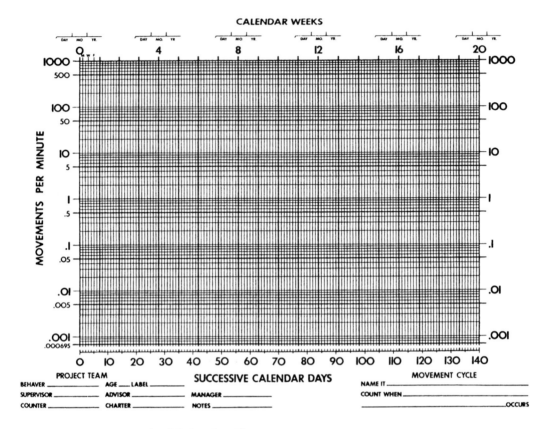

FIGURE 5.2   The Standard Behavior Chart

From Behavior Research Company, Kansas City, Kansas. Reprinted by permission.

This allows the observer to record for different time periods without misrepresenting the data. For instance, suppose a teacher noted that Karl was getting more aggressive because he kicked his playmate seven times during recess on Monday and ten times on Tuesday and Wednesday. If, in fact, recess was twenty minutes on Monday and thirty minutes on Tuesday and Wednesday, then Karl decreased, not increased, his frequency of kicking.

Event recording is best used when the behavior has a discrete beginning and ending and when occurrences can be easily counted, particularly if a permanent product is left (such as the number of windows broken or the number of words spelled correctly). It is not a good method to use if the behavior occurs at an extremely high rate (for example, pencil tapping) or for an extended period of time (for example, staring out the windows). The example of Sandy demonstrates the use of event recording.

EXAMPLE: SANDY

Mr. Harper, a third-grade teacher, is concerned about his student Sandy, who is constantly getting into trouble on the way to the lunchroom. Sandy will speak to anyone and everyone she sees, even though she has been told to remain quiet while in the hallway. Mr. Harper decided to implement a behavior-change program aimed at decreasing her talking episodes. The following preintervention or baseline data were collected:

	M	Tu	W	Th	F
Time observed (in minutes)	4	8	6	5	7
Number of behaviors	3	9	7	8	7
Frequency	0.75	1.13	1.17	1.60	1.00

Next, he implemented his behavior-change program, and the following data were collected:

	M	Tu	W	Th	F
Time observed (in minutes)	7	8	6	7	5
Number of behaviors	7	4	3	2	1
Frequency	1.0	0.50	0.50	0.29	0.20

Figure 5.3 is a graph of these data.

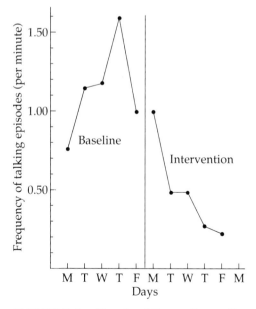

FIGURE 5.3   Graph of Event-Recording Data

Duration Recording. Suppose you had a student who would get out of his or her seat at the beginning of an instructional period and stay out until the end. In this case, the frequency of the behavior would be irrelevant, and event recording would not be the most appropriate method for measuring the behavior. For a problem in which the important factor is the amount of time a person spends engaging in the target behavior, duration recording should be used. Because duration measures require constant attention and monitoring of the time, a stopwatch or clock with a second hand is almost a must. This need for a constant monitoring of the time is a major disadvantage of duration recording, and it usually dictates that only one child at a time be observed. The example of Jimmy represents the use of duration recording.

EXAMPLE: JIMMY

Ms. Lambert was concerned that her student Jimmy would frequently be off task during individual seat work. Typically, he would start his work but lose interest rather quickly. At that point, he would tap his pencil, look out the window, or in some other way avoid completing the task. Ms. Lambert decided to implement a program designed to increase Jimmy's on-task behavior. First, she would measure the amount of time Jimmy actually spent on task. She defined on-task behavior as keeping his eyes on his paper. She decided to observe him for a ten-minute period each day. The following baseline data were recorded:

	M	Tu	W	Th	F
Minutes spent on-task	3	2	6	4	5

She then implemented her behavioral program with Jimmy, and it resulted in the following data:

	M	Tu	W	Th	F
Minutes spent on-task	6	7	9	10	10

Figure 5.4 is the visual representation of these data.

Latency Recording. Suppose you had a student who typically wandered around the room and visited with his friends even after the bell rang, signaling him to sit in his chair. In this situation, both event recording and duration recording would be inappropriate. Latency recording would be the recording procedure of choice. Latency recording measures the amount of time that elapses between the signaling of a stimulus (such as the sound of the bell) and the initiation of a behavior (sitting in a chair). Latency recording, like duration recording, has the basic disadvantage of requiring constant attention to the time. The example of Les demonstrates the use of latency recording.

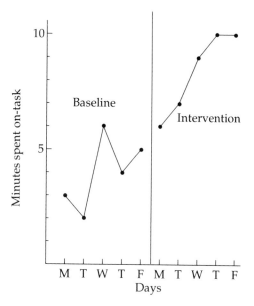

FIGURE 5.4   Graph of Duration-Recording Data

EXAMPLE: LES

Ms. Jones was concerned about one of her students, Les. When she instructed the class to begin solving written math problems, Les would drop his pencil, stare out the window, or demonstrate other avoidance behaviors. She wanted to develop a program to minimize the amount of time he took before he started writing his answers. She therefore chose a latency-recording procedure to measure the amount of time it took him to start writing after she gave the instructions. The following baseline data were collected:

	M	Tu	W	Th	F	M
Number of seconds elapsed	42	18	36	41	39	44

She then developed a program for Les and put it into effect. The following data were then recorded:

Tu	W	Th	F	M	Tu	W	Th
25	15	20	14	12	10	10	5

Figure 5.5 shows these data.

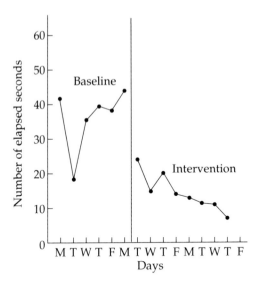

FIGURE 5.5   Graph of Latency-Recording Data

Interval Recording. Another useful procedure for recording observations is interval recording. Interval recording measures the occurrences or nonoccurrences of the target behavior during specified time intervals marked off within an overall observation period. This procedure is appropriate for behaviors that occur at a high frequency or for extended periods of time, and it indicates the pattern of behavior. Suppose, for instance, that Susan is off task a considerable amount of time during her five-minute workbook session. Interval recording would make it possible to determine if a pattern exists (such as primarily at the beginning or end of the session) as well as to specify the percentage of off-task behavior. (Of course, the term *off task* would need to be carefully defined.) To set up an interval-recording system, the overall observation period can be divided into smaller time intervals. A five-minute period divided into fifteen-second intervals, for example, would yield twenty time intervals. The observer simply indicates whether or not the behavior occurs during any portion of each time interval. It should be noted that the length of the interval is important. For example, Repp et al. (1988) noted that smaller intervals are more accurate than large intervals. Typically, a plus (+) is given for the presence of the behavior and a minus (–) for the absence. In this example, the target behavior (off-task behavior) was observed during the first, second, third, fifth, sixth, seventh, eighteenth, nineteenth, and twentieth intervals:

+	+	+	–	+	+	+	–	–	–
–	–	–	–	–	–	–	+	+	+

These data indicate that the student was off task during a
of the intervals, primarily during the beginning and end

Momentary Time Sampling. Momentary time sampling is a
ing. During momentary time sampling, the individual is
(for example, every fifteen seconds). The observer must indicate whether or not
the target behavior is exhibited *at those particular times.* One advantage of both
interval recording and momentary time sampling is that more than one child can
be observed at one time. One potential disadvantage of both interval recording
and momentary time sampling is that some type of cue must signal the time to
record. A number of cuing systems are available, such as a kitchen timer or an
audiotape with a signal prerecorded at certain intervals. Another disadvantage is
that only limited conclusions can be drawn on the behavior recorded. For example, it might be possible that the behavior occurs frequently but not at the specific time that it was observed (Alberto & Troutman, 1995).

Introduction of Intervention Programs

As noted in the previous examples of Sandy, Jimmy, and Les, after a specific behavior or skill has been carefully identified, defined, and recorded, it is time to
systematically introduce some type of intervention or remedial program in an attempt to change the behavior in the desired direction. Using whatever information is available, including observational data, the teacher (or other change agent)
will make the decision on the nature of the intervention procedure. The key is to
attempt to demonstrate that changes in the target behavior are related to the introduction of the intervention program. If an effective procedure can be found for a
specific behavior for a given individual, that same procedure might also be effective for other behaviors in the same individual or for the same behavior with different individuals. For this reason it is important to be specific and not attempt to
change too many behaviors or introduce a "shotgun approach" to intervention. It
is possible that behavioral changes might occur, but the value of the data for assessment purposes will be minimized.

Evaluation of the Intervention Program

This is an important step in the observational model and, coincidentally, one that
is often overlooked. It essentially involves recording (using the same procedures
as were used in the collection of baseline data) to determine if the initiation of the
intervention program had an effect on the target behavior. If change occurs in the
desired direction, the information can be used to plan future instructional programs. If the behavior does not change, or changes in the opposite direction, it
signals the need for trying a different approach, or perhaps the need to identify a
different target behavior that might be within the student's behavioral repertoire.
For example, it might be possible that a target behavior identified for a student
might be too difficult, and an easier or prerequisite behavior would be more appropriate as a target.

The previously described SBC is used in a system called *precision teaching* (Lindsley, 1964), which incorporates the four-step observation model to make instructional decisions. Precision teaching usually involves six steps. They are:

1. Pinpoint the exact behavior (academic or social) that you wish to change.
2. Record the number of behaviors observed and the number of minutes spent observing.
3. Calculate the frequency by dividing the number of behaviors by the number of minutes.
4. Plot these frequencies on the SBC.
5. Make a systematic change in the environment or instructional program.
6. Use the SBC regularly to observe the effects of the instructional or environmental changes on the pinpointed behavior.

Steps 1, 2, 5, and 6 are the same as those described in the four-step model of identifying the target behavior, measuring the target behavior, introducing the intervention program, and evaluating the intervention program.

Other Uses of Student Observational Data

Observational data can be used for a variety of purposes. In addition to those previously described, another purpose is to document that a problem exists. One procedure for this purpose is called the *referred-student/comparison-student* approach (as in Walker & Hops, 1976). In such an approach, data are collected simultaneously on the target subject as well as on a control subject who is the same age and gender and who is not experiencing difficulties. Such data collection can lead to the development of "local micronorms" that reflect the degree to which certain behaviors are considered acceptable by the teacher or other observer (Alessi, 1980). For instance, suppose a teacher was concerned about a student's (Karen) out-of-seat behavior. Using a momentary time sampling, the observer would observe Karen as well as another student to determine their percentages of out-of-seat behavior. It would also be possible to collect this data for the entire class (that is, percentage of children out of seat at any given time). The following data might be collected:

	Out of Seat
Karen	85%
Control subject	5%
Class	3%

These data can be used to help decide the relative inappropriateness of Karen's behavior.

Similarly, Deno (1980) described a system using *peer sampling.* This system involved, first, the recording of four key behaviors (noisemaking, out-of-seat activity, physical contact or destruction of objects, and off-task activity) of a target subject and a peer and, second, a comparison of the data. In any approach such as this, however, the significance assigned to the magnitude of the discrepancy between the data for the target subject and the data for peers must be subjective.

STUDENT OBSERVATION—FORMAL SYSTEMS

WHY USE FORMAL STUDENT OBSERVATION?

Screening and identification; informal determination and evaluation of teaching programs and strategies; documentation of need for further evaluation or referral; development and evaluation of IEPs

WHO SHOULD USE IT?

Primarily teachers; also school psychologists and parents

In addition to the informal observation procedures used to assess student needs and instructional programs, more formal observational systems are also available. These systems usually include some type of coding or notational procedure so that behaviors can be categorized in some meaningful way. For example, Bramlett and Barnett (1993) described a system, called the Preschool Observation Code, that was specifically developed for use with young children. Similarly, Rotholz, Kamps, and Greenwood (1989) developed a system called the Code for Instructional Structure and Student Academic Response-Special Education (CISSAR-SPED) that is used with students with autism or developmental disabilities. Prasad (1994) also described an observational system that stresses social interactions; these include initiating the interaction, turn taking, and responding to the interaction.

In fact, many formal systems allow for the coding of behavioral interactions rather than the behavior of the student in isolation. For example, the Behavioral Coding System (Patterson, Reid, Jones, & Conger, 1975) includes fourteen behavior categories. In this system, numbers are assigned to the target child and those who interact with him. For example, 2YE*-1IG* might represent an interaction in which the mother yelled and the target child ignored the outburst. The advantage of formal systems is that they allow for greater communication among individuals observing a student. For example, if a student were being observed at home by his parents and at school by his teacher, the coded results would allow each of the observers to understand what was happening in the other environment.

Observer							Sheet No.			Subject								
Date							Academic Activity											
Structured			Unstructured				Group			Individual			Transitional					

Subject	AP	CO	TT+	IP+	VO	AT	PN	DS	DI	NY	NC	PL	TT–	(IP–)	IL	SS	LO	NA	IT
Peer 1	AP	CO	TT+	IP+	VO	(AT)	PN	DS	DI	NY	NC	PL	TT–	IP–	IL	SS	LO	NA	IT
Subject	AP	CO	TT+	IP+	VO	(AT)	PN	DS	DI	NY	NC	PL	TT–	IP–	IL	SS	LO	NA	IT
Peer 2	AP	CO	TT+	IP+	VO	AT	PN	DS	DI	NY	NC	PL	TT–	IP–	IL	SS	(LO)	NA	IT
Subject	AP	CO	(TT+)	IP+	VO	AT	PN	DS	DI	NY	NC	PL	TT–	IP–	IL	SS	LO	NA	IT
Peer 3	AP	CO	TT+	IP+	VO	(AT)	PN	DS	DI	NY	NC	PL	TT–	IP–	IL	SS	LO	NA	IT
Subject	AP	CO	TT+	IP+	VO	AT	PN	DS	DI	(NY)	NC	PL	TT–	IP–	IL	SS	LO	NA	IT
Peer 4	AP	CO	TT+	IP+	VO	(AT)	PN	DS	DI	NY	NC	PL	TT–	IP–	IL	SS	LO	NA	IT
Subject	AP	CO	TT+	IP+	VO	AT	PN	DS	DI	NY	NC	PL	TT–	IP–	(IL)	SS	LO	NA	IT
Peer 5	AP	CO	TT+	IP+	VO	AT	(PN)	DS	DI	NY	NC	PL	TT–	IP–	IL	SS	LO	NA	IT

FIGURE 5.6 **Example of Coded Behavior Interactions**

Other systems have been developed exclusively for the school environment but retain the coding systems for behavior interactions. One example is the *Manual for Coding Discrete Behaviors in the School Setting* (Cobb & Ray, 1975). This system uses nineteen behavior categories; both the behaviors of the target child and his/her peers are alternately observed in six-second intervals. Figure 5.6 shows an example of the interaction for the following sequence. (Note: IP– = inappropriate interaction with peers, AT = attending, TT+ = appropriate talking with teacher, LO = looking around, NY = noisy, IL = inappropriate locale, and PN = physical negative.)

Albert is a fourth-grade student in a self-contained learning-disability classroom with five other students. He is involved in a structured individual task of using the dictionary to define certain vocabulary words. The following sequence is observed during the six-second intervals:

1. Albert is talking with a student about a television show. The student responds.
2. Peer 1 is looking at the dictionary.
3. Albert is looking at the dictionary.
4. Peer 2 is staring out the window.
5. Albert is asking the teacher about alphabetizing.
6. Peer 3 is writing a definition.
7. Albert is banging his dictionary on the desk. The teacher tells him to stop.
8. Peer 4 is reading the dictionary.
9. Albert leaves his seat to visit a friend. His friend gets mad and tears a page out of the dictionary.
10. Peer 5 is pulling the hair of his friend.

OBSERVATION OF THE INSTRUCTIONAL ENVIRONMENT

WHY USE OBSERVATION OF THE INSTRUCTIONAL ENVIRONMENT?

Analysis of instructional environment

WHO SHOULD USE IT?

Teachers

Although assessment of student behavior is the primary use of observational data, the assessment of the student's instructional environment is another role of observation. Both types of observation have a common goal of improving instructional practices that will positively affect the student.

According to Cartwright and Cartwright (1984), four components of the instructional environment should be considered. These components (which actually interact constantly) are teacher behaviors, space and objects in the environment, time variables, and the management and teaching procedures that are used within the instructional environment. For example, it might be possible to observe teachers and provide feedback on their behavior. It might be observed that a teacher is inadvertently reinforcing an annoying student behavior by attending to it whenever it occurs. It might also be possible that a student is much more distractible when placed in an open classroom setting, thus implying that moving him to a more structured setting would be advisable. Time variables are important in setting up schedules that optimize the chance for student success.

Although most observation of instructional environments is done informally, and sometimes inconsistently, a few formalized approaches and instruments have been designed to achieve this goal. For example, the *Stanford Research Institute Classroom Observation Instrument* (Stallings, 1977) was developed to measure the relationship between the instructional environment and student behavior. Both the physical environment and the interaction between student and teacher are examined. More recently, Ysseldyke and Christenson (1992) developed *The Instructional Environment Scale-II* (TIES-II), which is described as a comprehensive methodology for assessing an individual student's instruction.

TIES-II is a set of observation and interview forms used with teachers and parents. Specifically, information is gathered through observation of the student in a classroom setting and through interviews with the student and the student's teacher and parents. The following is a list of the twelve *Instructional Environment* components used to analyze the classroom environment.

Instructional Match: Instruction is clear and effective; directions are presented in sufficient detail.
Teacher Expectations: Expectations of student performance are realistic yet high.

Classroom Environment: Classroom is positive and supportive; time is used effectively.

Instructional Presentation: Instruction is presented in a clear and effective manner.

Cognitive Emphasis: Thinking skills necessary to complete tasks are communicated to the student.

Motivational Techniques: Teacher uses good strategies to increase student interest and effort.

Relevant Practice: Student is given adequate opportunities for practice.

Academic Engaged Time: Student is actively engaged in tasks and is redirected by teacher if not.

Informed Feedback: Student receives appropriate feedback for correct and incorrect performance.

Adaptive Instruction: Curriculum is modified to meet student needs.

Progress Evaluation: Teacher uses direct and frequent measures of student progress.

Student Understanding: Student knows what to do in the classroom.

In addition, five *Home Support for Learning* components in TIES-II involve a parent interview. Those components are Expectations and Attributions, Discipline Orientation, Effective Home Environment, Parent Participation, and Structure for Learning.

SUMMARY MATRIX

The summary for all chapters that describe instruments or techniques will be in the form of a *summary matrix.* This matrix will allow the reader to compare and contrast the instruments or techniques in terms of their suggested use, target population, and relevance for exceptional students. The matrix includes the following specific components (and their definitions):

A. Suggested use

1. *Screening and initial identification (prereferral):* Use of assessment data to identify individuals who need further evaluation, remedial help, or both.
2. *Informal determination and evaluation of teaching programs and strategies (prereferral):* Use of assessment data

    a. to assist the general-education teacher in identifying and evaluating appropriate objectives and teaching strategies,

    b. to help document the need for a formal referral, and

    c. to assist in the development of IEPs for students who receive special education.

3. *Determination of current performance level and educational need (postreferral):* Use of assessment data to determine

   a. general areas in which a student needs remediation or assistance,
   b. strengths and weaknesses, and
   c. possible teaching strategies and approaches.

4. *Decisions about classification and program placement (postreferral):* use of assessment data to determine special education eligibility and to identify the most appropriate program setting for the student.

5. *Development of IEP (postreferral):* use of assessment data to identify annual goals.

6. *Objectives of IEP (postreferral):* use of assessment data to identify appropriate objectives.

7. *Evaluation of IEP (postreferral):* use of assessment data to monitor student progress toward meeting the identified goals and objectives.

B. Target population

1. *Mild/moderate:* refers to individuals whose special needs are usually met within a mainstreamed or inclusive classroom, resource room, or self-contained classroom. This category may include students with mild or moderate mental retardation, learning disabilities, behavior disorders, or other types of disabilities whose problems are not considered severe.

2. *Severe/profound:* refers to individuals whose special needs might be met within an inclusive classroom, self-contained classroom, special school, or residential setting. This category may include students with severe or profound mental retardation, multiple disabilities, sensory disabilities (blind or deaf), or other individuals who have significant impairments.

3. *Preschool:* includes individuals from birth through approximately age 5.

4. *Elementary age:* includes individuals from ages 6 through approximately 12 (kindergarten through grade 6).

5. *Secondary age:* includes individuals from approximately ages 13 through 18 or 20 (grade 7 through grade 12).

6. *Adult:* includes individuals who because of their age no longer receive public-school services (usually older than 18 or 21).

C. *Special considerations:* Includes a brief statement of any particular advantage or disadvantage, technical characteristic, or other consideration that is relevant to each instrument or technique.

D. *Educational relevance for exceptional students:* Provides a rating of the relative applicability of each instrument or technique for exceptional students. The ratings are "very limited," "limited," "adequate," "useful," and "very useful." This rating is based on information such as the type of data yielded, the technical adequacy of an instrument, and research related to the instrument or technique.

Instrument or Technique	Suggested Use							Target Population						Special Considerations	Educational Relevance for Exceptional Students
	Prereferral			Postreferral											
	Screening and Initial Identification	Informal Determination and Evaluation of Teaching Programs and Strategies	Determination of Current Performance Level and Educational Need	Decisions about Classification and Program Placement	IEP Goals	IEP Objectives	IEP Evaluation	Mild/Moderate	Severe/Profound	Preschool	Elementary Age	Secondary Age	Adult		
Event Recording	X	X	X		X	X	X	X	X	X	X	X	X	Use when the frequency of a behavior is important; behavior should have a discrete beginning and ending	useful
Duration Recording	X	X	X		X	X	X	X	X	X	X	X	X	Use when the amount of time during which behavior occurs is important; requires constant monitoring	useful
Latency Recording	X	X	X		X	X	X	X	X	X	X	X	X	Requires constant monitoring	useful
Interval Recording	X	X	X		X	X	X	X	X	X	X	X	X	Use for behaviors that occur at a high frequency or for an extended time	useful
Momentary Time Sampling	X	X	X		X	X	X	X	X	X	X	X	X	More than one person can be observed at a time; requires a cue to signal when to record	useful
Behavioral Coding System	X	X					X	X		X	X	X	X	Use in home and school; codes behavioral interactions; has a complex scoring system	adequate
Manual for Coding Discrete Behaviors in the School Setting	X	X					X	X		X	X	X	X	Use in the school setting; requires observation of the target subject and control subjects	adequate
The Instructional Environment Scale–II		X						X			X	X		Provides qualitative evaluation of learning environment; also looks at teacher behaviors	useful

6

CRITERION-REFERENCED TESTING AND ERROR ANALYSIS

Areas Covered

Criterion-Referenced Tests
An Overview of Principles

Procedures

An Example

What to Teach versus How to Teach
Error Analysis

CRITERION-REFERENCED TESTS

WHY USE CRITERION-REFERENCED TESTS?

Determination and evaluation of objectives and teaching strategies; gathering of prereferral information; development and evaluation of IEPs

WHO SHOULD USE THEM?

Teachers

When people refer to tests used in schools, they usually think of traditional norm-referenced instruments such as achievement tests or intelligence tests.

These instruments can be helpful in making certain types of decisions including screening, eligibility, and the determination of strengths and weaknesses. These types of traditional assessment instruments have some shortcomings, however (Gable & Hendrickson, 1990). As noted in Chapter 2, norm-referenced tests (NRTs) show how an individual performs compared to others but provide little information that can be used for the development of specific instructional programs. The instruments typically used for those decisions are criterion-referenced tests (CRTs). Gronlund (1988) noted that whereas there are many similarities in the development of NRTs and CRTs, there are also some basic points of difference. For example, in a NRT the intended learning outcome may be described in either general or specific terms; in a CRT the intended outcome tends to be described in more specific terms. Second, a NRT usually covers a broad range of areas with few items per area; a CRT usually measures a more limited domain with numerous items per area. Finally, a NRT is designed so that the items can *discriminate* among students, whereas a CRT is designed so that the items will *describe* student performance on specific learning tasks.

An Overview of Principles

CRTs are particularly helpful in determining *what* to teach. For this reason, they are frequently used to determine appropriate goals and objectives for a student. Many CRTs have been developed and published commercially and will be discussed elsewhere in this textbook. This chapter, however, will focus on the principles and procedures that teachers and diagnosticians can use to develop their own CRTs. As mentioned in Chapter 2, CRTs focus more on an individual's mastery of content (for example, John can complete 90 percent of his two-digit addition problems correctly) than on a comparison of that individual with others (for example, John scored at the 63rd percentile in arithmetic).

By developing your own test, you can ensure that relevant objectives and items are included in the instrument. However, it is necessary to design and construct the CRT in a systematic, meaningful fashion. Gronlund (1973) suggested the following six principles to follow in developing a CRT. Criterion-referenced testing requires:

1. A clearly defined and delimited domain of learning tasks
2. Instructional objectives clearly defined in behavioral (performance) terms
3. Standards of performance clearly specified
4. Student performance adequately sampled within each area of performance
5. Test items selected on the basis of how well they reflect the behavior specified in the instructional objectives
6. A scoring and reporting system that adequately describes student performance on clearly defined learning tasks[1] (pp. 3–5)

---

[1]Reprinted with permission of Macmillan Publishing from *Preparing Criterion-Referenced Tests* by Norman E. Gronlund. Copyright © 1973 by Norman E. Gronlund.

Each of these six principles will be discussed in greater detail.

Principle 1: Clearly Define and Delimit Domain of Learning Tasks

Criterion-referenced testing is most effective when it focuses on a specific set of instructional objectives. Identifying the skill or skills for which a CRT will be developed is simplest if certain procedures are kept in mind. First, certain skills are more amenable to this type of testing. Gronlund (1973) noted that the basic skill areas (for example, arithmetic) are easier to measure than loosely structured areas (for example, social studies). In either case, however, the skills should be broken down into manageable units. This is usually accomplished through a task analysis of the instructional objective to be measured.

Task analysis refers to the identification and sequencing of behaviors that are necessary components of the skill required for an individual to complete a task. Figure 6.1 gives an example of a task analysis. Note that each step is a prerequisite for later steps in the task analysis.

Task Analysis of Objective: The child is able to alphabetize the following list of words, each of which has been placed on a separate card: stop, ask, dinner, name, boy.

1. Child can write the alphabet in the correct order.
2. Given a stack of 26 flash cards, each containing a different letter of the alphabet, the child can place the cards in alphabetical order.
3. Given a stack of 26 flash cards, each containing a word beginning with a different letter of the alphabet, the child can place the cards in alphabetical order *with* the help of an alphabet chart.
4. Given a stack of 26 flash cards, each containing a word beginning with a different letter of the alphabet, the child can place the cards in alphabetical order *without* the help of an alphabet chart.
5. Given a stack of 15 flash cards, each containing a different letter of the alphabet, the child can place the cards in alphabetical order *with* the help of an alphabet chart (therefore, some letters of the alphabet are missing).
6. Given a stack of 15 flash cards, each containing a different letter of the alphabet, the child can place the cards in alphabetical order *without* the help of an alphabet chart.
7. Given a stack of 15 flash cards, each containing a word beginning with a different letter of the alphabet, the child can place the cards in alphabetical order *with* the help of an alphabet chart.
8. Given a stack of 15 flash cards, each containing a word beginning with a different letter of the alphabet, the child can place cards in alphabetical order *without* the help of an alphabet chart.
9. The child is able to alphabetize the following list of words, each of which has been placed on a separate card: *stop, ask, dinner, name, boy.*

FIGURE 6.1   Example of a Task Analysis

From A. R. Frank, "Breaking Down Learning Tasks: A Sequence Approach," *Teaching Exceptional Children, 6.* Copyright © 1973 by the Council for Exceptional Children. Reprinted with permission.

Two issues concerning task analysis should be mentioned. The first concerns the determination of how small or incremental the steps should be. For instance, it might be possible to have two equally valid task analyses, one with one hundred steps and another with ten steps. The choice of which task analysis you would use as the basis for a CRT would depend largely on the type of student for whom the test was designed. A student with profound mental retardation, for example, might need a much more sensitive sequential breakdown than a student with a learning disability.

The second issue concerns the kind of skill for which a task analysis is planned. It is much easier to task-analyze nonacademic skills (such as tying a shoe or dialing the telephone) than academic skills (such as identifying words by sight or multiplying two-digit numbers). Lidz (1979) noted that in general there is little consensus on how to identify and sequence the objectives in a task analysis. Again, the choice of objectives or subcomponents might depend on the type of student.

Principle 2: Define the Objectives in Behavioral Terms

This principle requires that an objective be defined in such a way that its mastery must be observed in student behavior. In other words, students must demonstrate that they have met an objective. "The student must complete correctly arithmetic problems involving the multiplication of three-digit numbers by two-digit numbers with carrying" is an objective that requires a specific behavioral performance. "Understands multiplication" does not. Swezey (1981) further noted that a good objective should specify the conditions and standards. The condition refers to the situations under which a student's performance is evaluated. The standard refers to the level of performance required (discussed next).

Principle 3: Specify Standards of Performance

One extremely important issue in the development of criterion-referenced tests is to determine what the criteria should be—that is, what criterion level a student must meet if an observer is to assume that the student has mastered that skill. Criteria in general tend to be determined arbitrarily. One teacher might feel that a student must answer 90 percent of mathematical problems correctly, and another teacher might feel 95 percent must be completed satisfactorily. One guide to use is to identify which students appear to have mastered a particular skill, and then to determine their performance level. This level could then be taken as a standard for mastery.

Another important issue is *maintenance* of the behavioral performance. Can it be assumed that a student has mastered a skill if he or she meets a 90 percent criterion for only one day? In defining mastery, it is also important to indicate how many times a student must meet the criterion level.

Principle 4: Adequately Sample Student Performance

As a rule, the more items a test has in a specific area, the better picture the test provides of the student's true ability in that area. It is necessary to be practical, however, in deciding how many items to use. Several factors affect this decision.

First, the number of test items will depend on the skill being measured. More items measuring the execution of simple addition could feasibly be included, for example, than items demonstrating the ability to handle money and make change. Second, for some skills, the complete sample of the skill can be described in the test items (Gronlund, 1973). These include skills such as identifying letters of the alphabet or writing numbers from one to twenty. In general, it is advisable that at least twice as many test items are created as will actually be used in the test. If necessary, the extra items could be used to develop alternate forms of the test (Swezey, 1981).

Principle 5: Develop Test Items That Reflect the Behavior Specified in the Instructional Objectives

Criterion-referenced testing uses a direct approach in obtaining information. In other words, a specific instructional area is determined, behaviors are identified that are associated with that area, and test items are developed to measure those behaviors. In evaluating the test results, therefore, little inference needs to be made. The test yields specific, relevant information, such as, "Trisha is having difficulty adding two-digit numbers requiring carrying, because she missed ten out of ten problems of this type," as opposed to general, relatively meaningless information, such as, "Trisha is having difficulty adding two-digit numbers because she is functioning at the 1.6 grade level in mathematics." Gronlund (1988) proposed eight questions that should be asked to determine if the test items have been properly constructed. These include, "Does each item present a clearly formulated task?" "Is the item free of extraneous clues?" "Is each test item independent?" and "Are the items as a group free from overlapping?"

Principle 6: Include a Scoring System That Describes Student Performance on Specific Learning Tasks

This principle incorporates many of the previously mentioned points. It means that a CRT should indicate, first, the area and objective to be measured, and second, the specific behavior to be measured, including the standard of performance required of the student. Conversely, the results of a CRT include the exact performance level of the student in a specific area.

Development of Criterion-Referenced Tests: Procedures

The following steps can act as guidelines for developing a CRT.

Step 1: Identify Skill to Be Measured

Problem.   Determine the skills to be measured.

Comments.   The skills that should be measured can be determined in a number of ways. Hopefully, a student's IEP will reflect his or her educational needs and will indicate those areas that need to be assessed. Therefore, if the student is not receiving special education services and no IEP is available, a careful analysis of the areas covered in your curriculum will identify a number of goals. In some situations, school or district policy will determine the skills to be covered.

Step 2: Identify Objectives

Problem.   Identify the specific subskills or objectives to be measured.

Comments.   Again, objectives can be identified in a number of ways. If a student has an IEP, it will state the objectives. Unfortunately, many IEPs do not include good sequential objectives. As a result it may be necessary to perform a task analysis of the skill.

Step 3: Develop Test Items

Problem.   Develop materials and test items for each objective.

Comments.   If the objective is associated with a finite, easily manageable number of behaviors (such as counting from one to ten), *each* behavior can be included in the test. If this is not possible, the test should cover as many items as feasible. More test items can be developed for simple skills (such as multiplying three-digit numbers by two-digit numbers) than for more complex skills (such as reciting Middle English poems). In general the evaluator should ask several questions such as, "Are the intended learning outcomes stated in measurable terms?" "Is each test item relevant to an important learning outcome?" and "Is there an adequate number of items for each interpretation to be made?" (Gronlund, 1988). If the answer is not yes to all the questions, the items should be modified. Figure 6.2 also provides a series of questions based on the *type* of item that is developed. After the items have been developed, they must be put together in a meaningful way. Watanabe and Algozzine (1989) suggested that items should be grouped that measure the same skill or content area and should be placed in progressive order of difficulty.

Step 4: Determine Standard of Performance

Problem.   Determine criteria for evaluating performance.

Comments.   In developing a CRT, it is important to establish criteria to indicate when a student has mastered a particular skill. Although the criteria could relate to *speed* (for example, can read twenty sight words in two minutes), they usually involve accuracy, specifically the percentage of items passed. Although determining the criteria or the standard of performance is usually left up to the teacher's (or other testmaker's) discretion, certain standards are typically used more than others. Frequently, 90 or 95 percent of the items must be passed before mastery is assumed. As noted previously, however, there is a great deal of flexibility in deter-

A. Multiple-Choice Items

1. Does the stem of the item present a single, clearly formulated problem?
2. Is the stem stated in simple, readable language?
3. Is the stem worded so that there is no repetition of material in the alternatives?
4. Is the stem stated in positive form, wherever possible?
5. If negative wording is used in the stem, is it emphasized (by underlining or caps)?
6. Is the intended answer correct or clearly best?
7. Are all alternatives grammatically consistent with the stem and parallel in form?
8. Are the alternatives free from verbal clues to the correct answer?
9. Are the distracters plausible and attractive to the uninformed?
10. Is the relative length of the correct answer varied, to eliminate length as a clue?
11. Has the alternative "all of the above" been avoided and "none of the above" used only when appropriate?
12. Is the position of the correct answer varied so that there is no detectable pattern?

B. True–False Items

1. Does each statement contain one central, significant idea?
2. Is the statement so precisely worded that it can be unequivocally judged true or false?
3. Are the statements brief and stated in simple language?
4. Are negative statements used sparingly and double negatives avoided?
5. Are statements of opinion attributed to some source?
6. Have specific determiners (such as, always, sometimes, may) and other clues (such as, length) been avoided?

C. Matching Items

1. Does each matching item contain only homogeneous material?
2. Is the list of items short with the brief responses on the right?
3. Is the list of responses longer or shorter than the list of premises, to provide an uneven match?
4. Do the directions clearly state the basis for matching and that the responses can be used once, more than once, or not at all?

D. Interpretive Exercises

1. Is the introductory material relevant to the learning outcomes to be measured?
2. Is the introductory material new to the examinees?
3. Is the introductory material as brief as possible?
4. Do the test items call forth the performance specified in the learning outcomes?
5. Do the test items meet the criteria of effective item writing that apply to the type of objective item being used?

E. Short-Answer Items

1. Is the item stated so that a single, brief answer is possible?
2. Has the item been stated as a direct question wherever possible?
3. Do the words to be supplied relate to the main point of the item?
4. Are the blanks placed at the end of the statement?
5. Have extraneous clues (such as "a" or "an," and length of the blank) been avoided?
6. Where numerical answers are to be given, have the expected degree of precision and the units in which they are to be expressed been indicated?

F. Essay Test

1. Is each question restricted to the measurement of complex learning outcomes?
2. Is each question relevant to the learning outcome being measured?
3. Does each question present a clearly defined task?
4. Are all examinees directed to answer the same questions (unless the outcome requires a choice)?
5. Has ample time been allowed for answering, and has a time limit been suggested for each question?
6. Have adequate provisions been made for scoring the essay answers?

G. Performance Test

1. Have the performance outcomes to be measured been clearly specified?
2. Does the test situation reflect an appropriate degree of realism for the outcomes being measured?
3. Do the instructions clearly describe the test situation?
4. Are the observational forms well designed and appropriate for the performance being evaluated?

FIGURE 6.2   Questions to Ask before Developing CRT Items

From Norman E. Gronlund, *How to Construct Achievement Tests*, 4th ed. Copyright © 1988 Allyn & Bacon. Reprinted with permission.

mining those criteria. One should keep in mind that identifying a cutoff for mastery will impose "a false dichotomy on a continuum of proficiency" (Berk, 1984). In other words, if 90 percent correct is determined to be the criterion level for mastery, a person who correctly answered 89 percent of the items on a one hundred item test would not have "mastered" the skill involved, whereas a person who answered one more correctly would have.

Gronlund (1988, pp. 119–120) noted that when a testmaker is setting the performance standards, several considerations should be taken into account. Those are:

1. Set mastery level on a multiple-choice test at 85 percent correct.
2. Increase the level if essential for next stage of instruction.
3. Increase the level if essential for safety (for example, mixing chemicals).
4. Increase the level if test or subtest is short.
5. Decrease the level if repetition is provided at next stage.
6. Decrease the level if tasks have low relevance.
7. Decrease the level if items are extremely difficult.
8. Adjust the level up or down as teaching experience dictates.

Standards can also be calculated empirically by determining the performance levels of students who, in the testmaker's eyes, have already mastered a particular objective. It is also a good idea to indicate how many times a student must reach criterion level before mastery is assumed.

Step 5: Administer the Test

Problem.   Administer the CRT.

Comment.   After the test has been developed carefully, it can be administered to the student(s) for whom it was intended. One frequently overlooked area has to do with ensuring that the student is given proper instructions on how to take the criterion-referenced test. Swezey (1981) indicated that general test instructions should include the following type of information:

1. The purpose of the test
2. The time limits for the test
3. A description of the test conditions (e.g., "You may use scratch paper if you wish.")
4. A description of the test standards (e.g., "In order to receive credit you must get the exact answer.")
5. A description of the test items (e.g., "Reduce fractions in your answers to the lowest common denominator.")
6. The general test regulations (e.g., "Continue to the next page when you see a finger pointing at the bottom of a page; stop when you see a stop sign at the bottom of the page.")

Step 6: Score the Test

Problem.   Score the CRT.

Comment.   After the test has been developed and appropriately administered, it is necessary to score the test. This usually will involve determining the number of correct and incorrect items for each skill area and determining the percentage of mastery. Obviously, scoring the instrument will depend on the type of items used and the purpose for the testing. For example, if rate were more important than accuracy it might only be necessary to count the correct responses (e.g., the number of words read in a one-minute period).

Johnson and Harlow (1989) noted that the CRT model calls for a large number of items that go into depth and detail. Subsequently, a great deal of clerical work is necessary. They argued that teachers should consider using computers to score, analyze, and profile the data obtained from CRTs.

Step 7: Interpret the Test

Problem.   Interpret the CRT.

Comments.   Suppose that in the measurement of a specific skill, ten subcomponents or objectives were determined. For each of these ten objectives, ten test items were developed, resulting in a CRT of one hundred items. Is it necessary to administer all one hundred items? Probably not. The goal of a CRT is to provide specific information for instructional purposes. Two approaches might be appropriate. First, on the basis of the information available about a student (for example, work products, results of tests to document educational need), the test user might know that the student has mastered some of the earlier objectives and can therefore skip them. Another approach might be to administer the items for objective 10 (goal) first, and work backwards to the items for objectives 9, 8, 7, and so on. If a student reaches mastery for the items for objective 5, for instance, it could be assumed that the student also has mastery over items in objectives 1 through 4. Thus, a teacher might gain from the test an indication of the immediate short-term objective (objective 5) as well as a list of sequential objectives (6 through 9) leading to the goal (objective 10).

Development of Criterion-Referenced Tests: An Example

The following is an example of the development of a CRT.

Step 1: Identify Skill to Be Measured

Subtraction of whole numbers (with renaming).

Step 2: Identify Objectives

1. Given problems requiring the subtraction of numbers 1–18 from numbers 1–18, the student will provide the correct answers.
2. Given problems requiring the subtraction of 0 from numbers 1–10, the student will provide the correct answers.
3. Given problems requiring the subtraction of a one-digit number from a two-digit number without renaming, the student will provide the correct answers.
4. Given problems requiring the subtraction of a two-digit number from a two-digit number without renaming, the student will provide the correct answers.
5. Given problems requiring the subtraction of three-digit numbers from three-digit numbers without renaming, the student will provide the correct answers.
6. Given problems requiring the subtraction of a one-digit number from a two-digit number with renaming, the student will provide the correct answers.
7. Given problems requiring the subtraction of a two-digit number from a two-digit number with renaming, the student will provide the correct answers.
8. Given problems requiring the subtraction of a three-digit number from a three-digit number with renaming, the student will provide the correct answers.

Step 3: Develop Test Items

1.	18	8	13	7	11	14	4	17	9	15
	−9	−4	−11	−1	−10	−6	−2	−7	−3	−12
2.	9	5	3	8	1	4	7	2	6	10
	−0	−0	−0	−0	−0	−0	−0	−0	−0	−0
3.	17	14	26	48	79	23	65	89	55	96
	−5	−2	−4	−6	−3	−2	−1	−7	−3	−5
4.	28	39	45	13	86	64	78	57	92	40
	−16	−17	−22	−11	−45	−32	−23	−34	−81	−10
5.	865	752	279	370	143	666	478	607	191	754
	−652	−241	−124	−230	−121	−351	−352	−506	−180	−322
6.	18	55	62	27	76	91	36	44	82	17
	−9	−7	−8	−9	−8	−3	−9	−5	−4	−8
7.	84	28	31	82	65	97	56	33	41	92
	−35	−19	−22	−64	−17	−38	−29	−16	−25	−83
8.	985	257	381	973	444	543	674	278	626	552
	−796	−179	−193	−588	−255	−358	−596	−179	−337	−274

Step 4: Determine Standard of Performance

The student must correctly answer at least nine out of ten problems (90 percent) before mastery is assumed. Further, the student must reach criterion level for three consecutive days before mastery is assumed.

Step 5: Administer, Score, and Interpret Test

On the information gathered prior to the administration of the CRT (for example, test data to document educational need, work samples), the teacher was able to determine that the student knew his basic number facts and had no problems with one-digit numbers. Therefore, the criterion-referenced testing began with objective 3—subtraction of a one-digit number from a two-digit number without renaming.

First Administration	Second Administration	Third Administration
1. Not administered (NA)	1. NA	1. NA
2. NA	2. NA	2. NA
3. 90%	3. 100%	3. 90%
4. 20%	4. 40%	4. 30%
5. 10%	5. 20%	5. 20%
6. 0%	6. 0%	6. 0%
7. NA	7. NA	7. NA
8. NA	8. NA	8. NA

These results suggest that the student has mastered objectives 1–3, is having difficulty and is somewhat inconsistent with objectives 4 and 5, and does not know how to do objectives 6–8. The immediate objective for this student would be to subtract multidigit numbers without renaming. The goal would be to teach the concept of renaming. The teacher would progress from objectives 4–8 and re-evaluate using the CRT as skills are taught.

WHAT TO TEACH VERSUS HOW TO TEACH

Although CRTs are helpful in determining students' performance in specific curriculum areas, they do have their limitations. For example, a CRT will tell a teacher *what to teach* but gives little information about *how to teach* that skill effectively (Cohen & Spence, 1990). Put another way, most CRTs are more interested in measuring *product* rather than *process*. Swezey (1981), however, argued that CRTs could be designed to measure process as well as product. His distinction was that a product refers to something tangible that can be easily measured, whereas a process usually refers to the degree to which a student follows procedures correctly regardless of the outcome (e.g., did the student use the right strategy in solving a computation problem but made a mistake that resulted in the wrong answer?). This example illustrates this point:

```
  1
 48
+97
———
155
```

The student knew to carry the one to the tens place but made an error in adding $1 + 4 + 9$. This information would indicate that additional instruction in renaming might not be necessary but that addition of three one-digit numbers might be warranted.

One method that can be used to help determine the process or strategies a student is using when engaging in academic tasks is *error analysis.*

Error Analysis

WHY USE ERROR ANALYSIS?

Determination and evaluation of teaching strategies; gathering of prereferral information; development and evaluation of IEPs.

WHO SHOULD USE IT?

Teachers

A great deal of information can be determined from the type of error a student makes in routine school work products that are easily obtained. Similarly, when test results (CRT or NRT) are examined, the type as well as the number of errors can provide meaningful information. Suppose, for example, that in the previous computation problem the following solution was given:

```
  48
+ 97
————
1315
```

This would indicate that the student *does* need instruction in renaming because he added the ones and tens column separately.

Gable and Hendrickson (1990) provided several suggestions for maximizing the usefulness of error analysis. For example, they suggested that at least five items are necessary for a given skill before error analysis is used. They also noted that as a first step, a teacher should choose one subject area and one student rather than attempting to analyze errors for an entire class. The following are specific guidelines for conducting error analyses in the areas of reading, mathematics, and spelling.

Reading

Error analysis in reading can focus on oral reading, reading comprehension, or both. A procedure called *miscue analysis,* for example, addresses oral reading, comprehension, and word analysis skills.

Oral Reading.   Analyzing errors made during oral reading and word recognition can provide important information that can be useful in developing instructional plans for students. For example, a student who substitutes a different word (e.g., *suit* for *shout*) might require different teaching procedures from a student who incorrectly sounds out phonetically a given word (e.g., *tut* for *toot*). Usually, error types such as omissions, substitutions, mispronunciations, repetitions, insertions, reversals, or hesitations are noted when conducting an error analysis of word recognition (Evans, Evans, & Mercer, 1986).

Morsink and Gable (1990) reported a four-step procedure for the analysis of word recognition errors. The first step involves the *actual sampling of the oral reading.* They suggest that the student should read from graded material from a basal series or other instructional material at a level at which the student can comprehend approximately 60 percent of the information. In other words, one should choose a reading passage that is neither too difficult nor too easy for the student. The second step is to *identify possible error patterns and confirm those patterns through retesting.* To identify error patterns, Morsink and Gable (1990) suggested that both qualitative information and quantitative information be gathered. A chart similar to that found in Figure 6.3 on page 112 can help in determining the type of error pattern that exists. Retesting is important to determine if the problem is consistent or is due perhaps to other factors such as lack of motivation or inattention. It is also possible that retesting might help to determine other relevant diagnostic information. For example, Salvia and Hughes (1990) noted that it is important to distinguish between words that a student can read without time constraints and words that a student cannot read at all. This distinction is important because different teaching procedures are required for increasing word fluency and for teaching unknown words.

It is important that a consistent coding or notation system and perhaps a scoring system be used that allows for greater communication among those who see the error analysis (for example, the general and special education teachers). Figure 6.4 on page 113 is an example of a notation system that might be used for coding reading errors. Miller (1986) has suggested a scoring system whereby one point is deducted for an error that affects comprehension and one-half point is deducted for minor errors that do not affect comprehension. The points are totaled and divided by the number of words in the paragraph to obtain a percentage of correct words.

The third step is to *interview the student.* This involves asking the student what type of approach to reading he or she is using. For example, an incorrect word could be shown to the student, who is then asked, "Were you trying to sound out this word or were you trying to figure it out by looking at the other words in the sentence?" Information from these types of questions can provide important in-

Student _____   Dates _____

Material/Level _____

_____

	Error Type/Number	Prioritized Instruction	
Ignore Punctuation			Proficiency
Hesitation			
Repetition			
Insertion			Transition
Self-Correct			
Substitution			Acquisition
Teacher Aid			
Mispro-nounce			

Number of Readings_____

Average Number of Words _____

Average Time of Readings _____

Correct Rate _____   Error Rate _____

FIGURE 6.3   Error Analysis Chart for Oral Reading

Error Type	Notation	Example
Omissions	Circle the word, words, or part of a word that is omitted.	He did not want to go in(to) his friend's house.
Substitutions	Write the substituted word above the correct word.	She put the coins in the bag.
Mispronunciations	Write the mispronounced word above the correct word.	*thife* The man is a thief.
Repetitions	Draw a wavy line under the repeated word or words.	He wants a truck for his birth-day.
Insertions	Write in the insertion. Indicate with a caret.	*dark* The doll has brown hair.
Reversals	For a letter reversal within a word, write the substituted word above the corrected word.	*top* They were cooking soup in the pot.
	For reversals of words draw a line indicating the transposition of words.	He|looked|quickly for his homework.
Hesitations	Indicate with a slash mark.	The park was close/to the school.
Unknown or aided	Underline the word(s) after waiting a sufficient time for a response.	The boys were <u>exhausted</u> from their hike.
Omission of punc-tuation marks	Cross out the punctuation mark that was omitted.	The little girl put on her coat_x She went outside.
Self-corrected errors	Write the incorrect word and place a check beside it.	*bike* ✓ He wants a new bike for his birthday.

FIGURE 6.4   Notation System for Indicating Oral Reading Errors

From S. Evans, W. Evans, and C. Mercer, *Assessment for Instruction.* Copyright © 1986 by Allyn and Bacon, Inc.

sight into the method of reading that the student is using. The last step involves *recording the results of the error analysis.* This could be a simple chart in which the type and number of errors as well as instructional priorities are identified.

Reading Comprehension.   Morsink and Gable (1990) suggested the use of the same four-step procedure in evaluating the errors in reading comprehension. For the first step, *obtaining the sample,* they suggest a procedure in which the teacher asks the student to read from a passage and to then tell what the story was all about. The teacher then notes the key thought units recalled and separates these into areas such as main ideas, actual details, sequential events, or inferences.

For the second step, *identifying the errors and retesting,* the teacher should probe further if it is noted that the student is having difficulty with a particular aspect of comprehension. This can be accomplished by asking specific detailed questions. Morsink and Gable (1990) also noted that this is a good time to focus on the student's understanding of vocabulary words. They suggest that for each error made during word recognition, the teacher can indicate that word in text and ask, "What does _____ mean?" This might also provide important information. For example, Salvia and Hughes (1990) noted that in literal comprehension, the most important areas are related to vocabulary and grammar. In other words, many errors in literal comprehension may be due to the student's lack of knowledge of the meaning of the words or the grammatical structure used in the passage. They also note that when the student does understand the words and grammar, lack of comprehension could result from such things as slow reading in which the train of thought is lost.

In the third step, *interviewing the student,* the student is asked directly about the type of strategies or procedures being used to complete the comprehension exercise. To illustrate, "The student with difficulty in simple literal comprehension may say, 'I just try to remember what it says but when there are so many things, I can't remember them all.' This type of response indicates the absence of a workable strategy for recall" (Morsink & Gable, 1990). For the final step, *recording the findings,* they suggest that a chart be developed that includes the type and number of the errors that are made. In the areas of critical reading, for example, the findings may address making inferences, sequence of events, main idea or summary, and/or recall of factual detail. Again, based on this information, prioritized instruction can be identified.

Miscue Analysis.   *Miscue analysis* is an informal process for assessing oral-reading deficits. Specifically, miscue analysis yields information on skills in oral reading, comprehension, and word analysis by providing a systematic method for studying the patterns of reading errors. Although any method of analyzing the errors can be used, the *Reading Miscue Inventory* (Goodman & Burke, 1972) is perhaps the most popular. Goodman, Watson, and Burke (1987) described the steps in conducting a miscue analysis. First, an appropriate reading selection is made, the student reads the selection, and the oral reading is audiotaped. Next, the student retells the story. Finally, the pattern of errors are studied both qualitatively and quantitatively. The areas that are addressed are syntactic acceptability, semantic acceptability, meaning change, graphic similarity, sound similarity (does the reading error sound similar to the correct word?), and correction (did the reader attempt to self-correct?).

Mathematics

Error analyses in mathematics are relatively simple, because, as a rule, a written product is available; thus, the teacher has a tremendous amount of potential information from the students' routine math work in school. Several in-depth studies have been conducted to determine the typical extent and types of mathematics errors. Lankford (1972) studied the computational errors of 176 seventh-grade students from various regions in the United States. He found, for example, five major types of errors in addition and seven in subtraction, multiplication, and division. Miller and Milam (1987) specifically looked at the error patterns of students with learning disabilities in the areas of multiplication and division. They found that poor memory for basic multiplication and addition facts was the most common multiplication error, whereas omitting the remainder was the most common division error. The area of subtraction has been studied relatively extensively. Frank, Logan, and Martin (1982) found that students with learning disabilities had a definite pattern to their subtraction errors rather than making random errors. Cebulski and Bucher (1986) reported that borrowing and inversion (subtracting smaller number from larger regardless of their position) errors were most common.

Ashlock (1990) has written a widely used book that addresses error patterns in arithmetic computation. The problems in Figure 6.5 on page 116 are examples of the error types discussed by Ashlock. As can be seen from the examples shown in the box, it is important to do more than just note whether a problem is worked out correctly. The pattern of error can yield meaningful information, particularly in determining the teaching strategy that is most appropriate.

Enright, Gable, and Hendrickson (1988), described a nine-step model for diagnosing and remediating errors in mathematics computation. Each of these steps will be presented with a brief discussion.

Step 1: Obtain Samples

This involves gathering multiple samples of the student's mathematics computation work. Enright et al. recommend that samples should include at least three to five items for each subskill measured.

Step 2: Interview the Student

The diagnostic interview is a helpful technique in math error analysis. Using this procedure, the examiner asks the students to "talk their way through" the arithmetic problems as they are solving them. In many cases, the examiner will clearly be able to see where and why the student is making an error. Take the following as an example:

$$3\overline{\smash{)}63}^{\,12} \qquad 4\overline{\smash{)}124}^{\,13} \qquad 2\overline{\smash{)}148}^{\,47} \qquad 5\overline{\smash{)}155}^{\,13}$$

The student commented, "three into six is two, I put the 2 in the ones column. three into three is one, so I put that here." In this situation, the student understands division facts but probably is confused because addition, subtraction, and multiplication problems are all solved from right to left. He inappropriately generalized that procedure to division. The student responded in a similar fashion to the other three problems. Underhill, Uprichard, and Heddens (1982) provided

Addition examples:

(1)   82
    + 41
    123

(2)   68
    + 39
    917

(3)   45
    + 35
    710

Error Pattern: The student is adding the 1s column and the 10s column independently without carrying or noting the place value in the sum.

Subtraction examples:

(1)   63
    − 37
    34

(2)   49
    − 27
    22

(3)   81
    − 19
    78

Error pattern: The student is subtracting the smaller number from the larger number in each column regardless of their positions as subtrahend or minuend.

Multiplication examples:

(1)   83
    × 4
    362

(2)   63
    × 5
    355

(3)   48
    × 2
    106

Error Pattern: The student is adding the carried digit before instead of after multiplying. In the first example, for instance, the student multiplied 3×4, wrote the 2, carried the 1, and added this to 8. The student then calculated 4×9 rather than $(4 \times 8) + 1$.

Division examples:

(1) $\dfrac{13}{3\overline{)93}}$
  9
  3
  3

(2) $\dfrac{81}{4\overline{)72}}$
  4
  32
  32

(3) $\dfrac{32}{6\overline{)138}}$
  12
  18
  18

Error Pattern: The student is dividing correctly but is writing down the answer from right to left.

FIGURE 6.5   Examples of Math Errors

more detailed guidelines for conducting diagnostic interviews in the area of mathematics.

Step 3: Analyze Errors and Identify Error Patterns

A variety of major error types have been used in classification. Salvia and Hughes (1990) summarized five distinct types of computational errors. These were a lack of prerequisite skills; wrong operation (e.g., adding instead of subtracting); an obvious computational error; a defective algorithm (when a student tries to apply the correct operation but makes errors in making the necessary steps); and random responses. Gable and Coben (1990) also included grouping errors (mistakes in placing digits in the proper column when regrouping) in addition to those just listed.

To assist in the analysis, Enright et al. suggested the use of a computational error chart (see Figure 6.6 on page 118) that indicates the type and number of errors made. As an exercise, try to identify the type of error for each of the following examples using the error chart in Figure 6.6.

1.	2.	3.	4.	5.
48	91	35	43	45
+8	× 4	−25	× 6	+23
416	157	60	308	67

ANSWERS

1. Grouping (student correctly added but did not carry)
2. Random (no apparent pattern)
3. Wrong operation (student added instead of subtracted)
4. Defective algorithm (student correctly multiplied but added 1 to 4 before multiplying)
5. Computational error (student added 5 + 3 incorrectly)

Step 4: Select Primary Error Pattern and Show the Precise Error to the Student

The information presented in Figure 6.6 might be shared with the student as a means of providing corrective feedback.

Step 5: Demonstrate a Correct Computational Procedure as Part of the Corrective Feedback Mechanism

The teacher should demonstrate the correct computational procedure and leave the completed problem as a permanent model.

Step 6: Select a Corrective Strategy

At this point, the error pattern has been determined and feedback has been provided to the student about why the answer was incorrect and how to determine the correct answer. Now it is necessary to determine instructional strategies that might be helpful in teaching the correct procedure. As an example of this, Enright et al. suggested that color coding the signs, such as green for plus, red for minus, when a student is using the wrong operation might help draw attention to the appropriate operation to complete.

Step 7: Introduce Appropriate Practice

This involves a structured series of practice exercises that reinforces the correct computational procedure that has been taught.

Student _____   Dates _____

Material _____ No. of Problems/Digits _____

Problem Class _____

	Error Type/Number	Corrective Strategy
Wrong Operation		
Computa-tional		
Defective Algorithm		
Grouping		
Random		
Other		

Beginning Time _____   Ending Time _____
Corrects per Minute _____   Errors per Minute _____

Peer Standards
High Performer—Corrects per Min. _____   Errors per Min. _____
Med Performer—Corrects per Min. _____   Errors per Min. _____
Low Performer—Corrects per Min. _____   Errors per Min. _____

FIGURE 6.6   Computation Error Chart

Step 8: Identify and Apply Normative Standards

Essentially, this refers to the establishment of criteria that the teacher feels is necessary to indicate that the child has mastered a particular computational procedure. In a sense, this is similar to establishing criteria for mastery noted in criterion referenced testing.

Step 9: Evaluate Performance

This refers to the ongoing assessment that is necessary in the diagnostic remedial process.

Spelling

A tremendous amount of information can be gleaned from looking at types of spelling errors. As in the analysis of arithmetic errors, spelling-error analysis is also relatively easy because a written product is usually available. Perhaps the most common types of spelling errors are phonological substitutions (such as "desishun" for "decision") and omissions (such as "namly" for "namely"). Thomas (1979) reported the results of a study that determined types of spelling errors made by 450 students. He found that substitutions and omissions accounted for approximately 38 percent of all errors. Other errors included confused pronunciation (such as *denist* for *dentist*), doubling (such as *citty* for *city*), insertions (such as *biteing* for *biting*), transpositions (such as *freind* for *friend*) and homonyms (such as *see* for *sea*), plus some unclassified errors.

The information obtained from a careful look at error types suggests certain remedial strategies. For example, a student with transpositional errors might have difficulty learning or remembering spelling rules. A student with homonym errors might have problems attending to or understanding the meaning of words. Thomas (1979) identified potential causes and remedial procedures for each of these eight types of errors.

The following misspelled words provide an exercise for conducting an error analysis:

Actual Word	Student's Spelling	Type of Error
1. Enough	Enuff	_____
2. Believe	Belive	_____
3. Motel	Mottel	_____
4. Nerve	Nerv	_____
5. Has	Haz	_____
6. Good	Goode	_____
7. Carrying	Carring	_____
8. Eight	Ate	_____
9. Towel	Towle	_____
10. Girls	Grils	_____

Answers: (1) PS (2) O (3) D (4) O (5) PS (6) I/A (7) O (8) H (9) T (10) T
Key: PS—phonological substitution   O—omission
      D—doubling   I—insertion
      A—addition   H—homonym
      T—transposition

Silva and Yarborough (1990) also provided a model for understanding and analyzing spelling errors. In their model, they encourage the analysis of actual writing samples rather than isolated spelling words. They use three major areas of errors: language/dialect, orthographic rules/convention, and learned lexicon/ visual memory. Each major area has subcategories. For example, a language/dialect error could involve a wrong or missing ending or affix (e.g., irresponsible for unresponsible). An orthographic rule/convention error might include those related to doubling (e.g., skiped for skipped) or the silent *e* rule (e.g., ninty for ninety). The learned lexicon/visual memory error might involve homonym confusion, compound word errors, reversals, and added or missing syllables as examples.

To conduct a spelling error analysis, Hendrickson and Gable (1990) suggested a five-step process:

Step 1: Obtain a Sample

It is recommended that word lists, paragraphs, or stories be dictated to the student.

Step 2: Interview the Student

This procedure can be used to identify spelling strategies that the student uses. Questions such as, "How do you remember how to spell new words that you learn?" can help better determine how the student approaches the reading process.

Step 3: Analyze and Classify the Errors

The analysis might involve some method of objectively scoring the errors. This is particularly helpful if the number of words sampled remains constant and the student is frequently reevaluated. Hendrickson and Gable summarized five approaches that can be used in scoring spelling errors. These are whole word, syllables, sound cluster, letters in place, and letter sequences. These approaches differ in the extent to which the spelling error is analyzed and scored. For example, using the syllable approach the word "city" would be scored 1/2 if it was spelled "cite" (ci/<u>te</u> note: underlined portion is scored as an error). If the word were spelled "site" the score would be 0/2 (<u>si</u>/<u>te</u>). Using the letter-in-place approach, "cite" would be scored 3/4 (c/i/t/<u>e</u>) and "site" would be scored 2/4 (<u>s</u>/i/ t/<u>e</u>). Hendrickson and Gable note that the whole-word approach (the word is scored right or wrong) is the most logical for typical classroom use but that the others are more precise and might be helpful for more serious spelling problems.

Regardless of the scoring system used, it is important to look at the *pattern* of the errors. Hendrickson and Gable suggest using a spelling error chart that indicates the *type* of errors (vowels, consonants, or rules and patterns) and whether the error *tendency* is to omit, delete, or substitute letters, or to change their order.

Step 4: Select a Corrective Strategy

By classifying the words misspelled as regular, irregular, or predictable, instructional strategies can be identified. For example, if a student consistently missed predictable words (those that conform to traditional spelling words), the instructional strategy would be different than for irregular words that might require the use of certain memory strategies. Hendrickson and Gable (1990) also provide guidelines for selecting and implementing instructional strategies that are beyond the scope of this discussion.

Step 5: Implement Strategy and Evaluate Its Effect

This would involve continuous monitoring to determine the effectiveness of the instructional program.

Instrument or Technique	Suggested Use							Target Population						Special Considerations	Educational Relevance for Exceptional Students
	Prereferral			Postreferral											
	Screening and Initial Identification	Informal Determination and Evaluation of Teaching Programs and Strategies	Determination of Current Performance Level and Educational Need	Decisions about Classification and Program Placement	IEP Goals	IEP Objectives	IEP Evaluation	Mild/Moderate	Severe/Profound	Preschool	Elementary Age	Secondary Age	Adult		
Criterion-Referenced Test	X	X	X		X	X	X	X	X	X	X	X	X	Can be developed by the teacher on the basis of a student's curriculum; determination of criteria is arbitrary	very useful
Error Analysis—Reading	X	X	X					X			X	X		Provides information on oral reading and comprehension	very useful
Error Analysis—Mathematics	X	X	X					X			X	X		Relatively easy to do, written products (math problems) are readily available	very useful
Error Analysis—Spelling	X	X	X					X			X	X		Relatively easy to do, written products (spelling words) are readily available	very useful

7

CURRICULUM-BASED ASSESSMENT

Areas Covered

Criterion-Referenced CBA
  Development of a CBA Instrument
  Uses and Limitations
Curriculum-Based Measurement
  Computer-Based CBM
  Uses and Limitations
CBA and CBM: An Integrated Model

WHY USE CURRICULUM-BASED ASSESSMENT?

Determination and evaluation of objectives and teaching strategies; gathering of prereferral information; development and evaluation of IEPs

WHO SHOULD USE IT?

Teachers

During the past decade, curriculum-based assessment (CBA) has received widespread attention in the area of special education. The concept of CBA is certainly not new and has been employed in schools for a number of years. The emphasis on CBA in special education is more a result of philosophical changes than technological changes regarding test construction. The Regular Education Initiative discussed in Chapter 1, for instance, placed heavy emphasis on the use of CBA.

Idol, Nevin, and Paolucci-Whitcomb (1986) noted that interest in CBA seemed to develop as a means of coping with low-achieving and special-needs learners who were mainstreamed into general education. They further noted that the CBA model fits nicely into a noncategorical model in which the emphasis is on testing curricular-based skills instead of testing for labeling purposes. Clearly, the current emphasis on full inclusion of students with disabilities in the general education classroom has led to increased use of CBA procedures.

CBA involves the measurement of the level of a student in terms of the *expected curricula outcomes of the school* (Tucker, 1985). In other words, the assessment instrument is based on the content of the student's curriculum (Taylor, Willits, & Richards, 1988). CBA actually refers to a variety of different procedures. Some types of CBA are relatively informal, others are more formal and standardized (Fuchs & Fuchs, 1989). In fact, there has been some confusion as to what professionals are talking about when they refer to the term CBA. Shinn, Rosenfeld, and Knutson (1989) investigated the professional literature regarding CBA procedures and categorized them into four models. The first was *CBA for instructional design* in which the determination of instructional needs is based on students' continuous performance in the existing curriculum. The second, *curriculum-based evaluation,* is characterized by the measurement of specific subcomponents of a curricular task. The other two—*criterion-referenced CBA* and particularly *curriculum-based measurement* (CBM)—are the most widely researched and used and will be discussed in detail.

CRITERION-REFERENCED CBA

Most criterion-referenced or informal CBA procedures are based on a task-analytic model that can be applied to developmental (hierarchical) curricula, spiraling curricula (organized by levels with concepts repeated at later levels), and unestablished (individualized to student need) curricula (Spruill, 1990). A number of guidelines have been suggested for developing an informal CBA instrument. Blankenship (1985) suggested that the first step should be to list the skills presented in the curriculum, write an objective for each skill, develop items for each listed objective, and then administer the test before and after a structured program has been initiated. Cohen and Spence (1990) identified a five-step process that involved identifying the purpose of the CBA, developing the test specifications for curriculum objectives, constructing and revising the test items, administering the CBA instrument, and finally, graphing the student's performance. Similarly, Salvia and Hughes (1990) expanded somewhat on these previously mentioned steps and suggested the following:

1. Specify reasons for decisions.
2. Analyze the curriculum.
3. Formulate the behavioral objectives.
4. Develop appropriate assessment procedures.
5. Collect data.

6. Summarize data.
7. Display the data.
8. Interpret data and make decisions.

It should be noted that the steps outlined by these various authors are similar to the steps noted in Chapter 6 in terms of developing a criterion-referenced test (CRT). In fact, this type of CBA is essentially a CRT with the content of the curriculum dictating the content of the instrument.

CBA instruments can be developed for any type of curriculum. Usually, the content of the test reflects several levels of the curriculum. For example, if the curriculum area were reading, it would be desirable to develop tests that would include passages selected from each level of the reading series. If the test was focused on spelling, items could be randomly chosen from each lesson at each level in a spelling series. A teacher can then choose to give the entire CBA or only portions related to a given skill area.

It is generally recommended that a student be evaluated on three separate days using three separate forms of the test (Idol, Nevin, & Paolucci-Whitcomb, 1986). In other words, three forms should be developed that cover the same content but that have different items. By administering these three forms, one can get a better picture of the student's true ability and help to control for sporadic performance (White & Liberty, 1976). CBA instruments are also frequently group-administered. By reproducing the tests, it is possible to administer them to an entire class to find out where they are in relation to the curriculum.

Development of a Criterion-Referenced CBA Instrument: An Example

Using the procedures outlined for developing a CRT that was noted in Chapter 6, it is possible to give an example of how to develop an informal CBA instrument.

Step 1: Identify Skill to Be Measured

The curriculum area chosen for the CBA was mathematics. The first step was to look at the mathematics curriculum for the student and determine the skill areas included in that curriculum. Suppose that the student uses the Scott, Foresman, and Co. mathematics curriculum. The teacher would analyze that curriculum and determine what specific skill areas it covered. (NOTE: For this example, only a portion of the mathematics curriculum was analyzed for ease of discussion.) Analysis showed that the following skills were included in the part of the mathematics curriculum selected:

digit writing
place value
greater than/lesser than concept
addition
subtraction
missing addends

If the entire curriculum had been analyzed, a chart could have been developed that included all of the skill areas covered, the sequence of the skills, and even the page numbers in the curriculum where the skills are taught.

Step 2: Identify Objectives

When breaking down skill areas into objectives, a *summary sheet* is sometimes used that allows the teacher to determine the specific concepts to be tested as well as the number of items that measure each objective and the standards of performance. Table 7.1 shows the summary sheet for this CBA instrument.

TABLE 7.1   Summary Sheet for a Mathematics CBA

Concepts	Problem Numbers	Day 1	Day 2	Day 3	Total Score 5/6	Mastery 5/6
Writing digits	1,2	/2	/2	/2	/6	/6
Place value	3,4	/2	/2	/2	/6	/6
Comparing numbers	5,6	/2	/2	/2	/6	/6
Add basic facts 0–10	7,21	/2	/2	/2	/6	/6
Add basic facts 11–20	8,22	/2	/2	/2	/6	/6
Add 2 digits (no renaming)	9,24	/2	/2	/2	/6	/6
Add 1 (renaming)	10,26	/2	/2	/2	/6	/6
Add 3 digits (no renaming)	11,28	/2	/2	/2	/6	/6
Add 2 (renaming)	12,30	/2	/2	/2	/6	/6
Add 3 or more numbers	13,32	/2	/2	/2	/6	/6
Add 4 digits (renaming)	14,30	/2	/2	/2	/6	/6
Subt. basic facts 0–10	15,23	/2	/2	/2	/6	/6
Subt. basic facts 11–20	16,25	/2	/2	/2	/6	/6
Subt. 2 digits (no renaming)	17,27	/2	/2	/2	/6	/6
Subt. 2 digits (1 renaming)	18,29	/2	/2	/2	/6	/6
Subt. 3 digits (no renaming)	19,31	/2	/2	/2	/6	/6
Subt. 3 digits (1 renaming)	20,33	/2	/2	/2	/6	/6
Missing addends (1)	35,36	/2	/2	/2	/6	/6

Adapted from L. Idol, A. Nevin, and P. Paolucci-Whitcomb, *Models of Curriculum-Based Assessment.* Copyright © 1986 by Aspen Publishers, Inc. Reprinted with permission of Aspen Publishers, Inc.

Step 3: Develop Test Items

Figure 7.1 displays the test developed from the portion of the mathematics curriculum analyzed. Note that the "problem numbers" heading in Table 7.1 relates to the items in the test itself. The test in Figure 7.1 would be one of three tests developed that measure the same areas.

Step 4: Determine Standards of Performance

Table 7.1 indicates that the student is required to correctly answer five out of six items for each objective to reach mastery. The criteria are based on the student's performance on the three tests together.

Give the number:
1. 9 tens, 6 ones   2. 3 thousand, 7 hundred forty-one

_____   _____

Tell what place 7 holds:
3. 271 _____   4. 8,726 _____

Compare the numbers. Use > or < :
5. 32 _____ 49   6. 2 × 3 _____ 10

Add:

7. 2	8. 7	9. 42	10. 76	11. 231
+6	+5	+21	+17	+243

12. 373	13. 7+2+5 = _____	14. 3692
+147		+2345

Subtract:

15. 8	16. 11	17. 87	18. 76	19. 588	20. 349
−7	−4	−43	−59	−164	−187

Add or subtract:

21. 4	22. 6	23. 9	24. 55	25. 15
+3	+3	−4	+31	−8

26. 24	27. 79	28. 401	29. 82	30. 242
+36	−25	+296	−37	+369

31. 865	32. 4+4+6 = _____	33. 824	34. 4654
−321		−717	+1975

Fill in the missing number:
35. 3 + _____ = 9   36. 57 − _____ = 39

FIGURE 7.1   Sample Math CBA

Step 5: Administer and Interpret the CBA Instrument

Each of the three tests were administered on consecutive days to the entire class. Table 7.2 shows the test results for one student in the class. These results would indicate that this particular student was having no problems with writing digits, understanding place value and comparing numbers, and addition and subtraction of single- and multiple-digit numbers without renaming. The student, however, apparently had no idea how to "carry" or "borrow" when adding and subtracting and had not mastered how to supply missing addends. It would be pos-

TABLE 7.2   Results from the CBA

Concepts	Problem Numbers	Day 1	Day 2	Day 3	Total Score 5/6	Mastery 5/6
Writing digits	1,2	2/2	2/2	2/2	6/6	6/6
Place value	3,4	2/2	2/2	2/2	6/6	6/6
Comparing numbers	5,6	2/2	2/2	2/2	6/6	6/6
Add basic facts 0–10	7,21	2/2	2/2	2/2	6/6	6/6
Add basic facts 11–20	8,22	2/2	2/2	2/2	6/6	6/6
Add 2 digits (no renaming)	9,24	2/2	1/2	2/2	5/6	5/6
Add 1 (renaming)	10,26	0/2	0/2	0/2	0/6	0/6
Add 3 digits (no renaming)	11,28	2/2	2/2	1/2	5/6	5/6
Add 2 (renaming)	12,30	0/2	0/2	0/2	0/6	0/6
Add 3 or more numbers	13,32	2/2	1/2	2/2	5/6	5/6
Add 4 digits (renaming)	14,30	0/2	0/2	0/2	0/6	0/6
Subt. basic facts 0–10	15,23	2/2	2/2	2/2	6/6	6/6
Subt. basic facts 11–20	16,25	2/2	2/2	2/2	6/6	6/6
Subt. 2 digits (no renaming)	17,27	1/2	2/2	2/2	5/6	5/6
Subt. 2 digits (1 renaming)	18,29	0/2	0/2	0/2	0/6	0/6
Subt. 3 digits (no renaming)	19,31	2/2	2/2	2/2	6/6	6/6
Subt. 3 digits (1 renaming)	20,33	0/2	0/2	0/2	0/6	0/6
Missing addends (1)	35,36	1/2	1/2	1/2	3/6	3/6

Adapted from L. Idol, A. Nevin, and P. Paolucci-Whitcomb, *Models of Curriculum-Based Assessment*. Copyright © 1986 by Aspen Publishers, Inc. Reprinted with permission of Aspen Publishers, Inc.

sible, therefore, to have a good idea which skill—renaming—to teach this student. Further, the teacher could group the students in the class according to performance, so that students with similar deficits could be taught together.

Uses and Limitations of Criterion-Referenced CBA Instruments

Overall, the research support for CBA procedures has been positive. Among the strengths of CBA noted are its ability to lead to student improvement (Galagan, 1985) and its use as an effective communication tool with parents (Marston & Magnusson, 1985). Clearly, its primary advantage is in allowing increased instructional decision making (Howell & Morehead, 1987).

Although the majority of information about CBA is positive, proponents and critics alike agree that CBA procedures have certain limitations. For example, Heshusius (1991) argued that the CBA model was simplistic and did not consider the learning process itself. He further argued that CBA use creates a situation in which the teacher is virtually teaching the test. He instead argued for holistic evaluation that emphasizes process and ecological testing. Taylor, Willits, and Richards (1988) also noted some limitations to CBA and mentioned several issues that CBA users should consider. Among those considerations were that the validity of the curriculum on which the CBA instrument is based will affect the validity of the instrument and that the term *CBA* is so broad that many people have interpreted it differently. Shinn (1988) also noted that no uniform approach to the development of CBA procedures incorporated a consistent, identifiable set of objectives.

CURRICULUM-BASED MEASUREMENT (CBM)

One of the more widely researched models of CBA is CBM, developed by Deno and his associates at the University of Minnesota (Deno, 1985; Deno & Fuchs, 1987). Whereas CBA is a more generic term that usually refers to informal and nonstandardized assessment (including the previously discussed criterion-referenced CBA), CBM is a standardized, empirically derived version. CBM differs from informal CBA in at least two ways: First, it focuses measurement on the annual curriculum so that the items represent an entire school year's content. For example, spelling might include a twenty-word test drawn randomly from the entire pool of words for the year. Secondly, it uses a standardized methodology with documented reliability and validity (Fuchs, Fuchs, Hamlett, & Allinder, 1989). Shinn et al. (1989) also noted that informal CBA instruments are used primarily as pretests and mastery tests before instruction begins, whereas CBM is an ongoing evaluation process for use after an instructional program is initiated. Fuchs and Fuchs (1990) noted the following characteristics of the CBM model:

1. Selection of one long-term goal instead of a series of short-term curricular steps

2. Measurement of standard behaviors that have documented reliability, validity, and sensitivity
3. Use of prescribed measurement methods
4. Incorporation of rules that provides systematic procedures for summarizing and evaluating the information
5. Accommodation of any instructional paradigm

One of the hallmarks of the CBM model is the importance of instructional decision making based on the student's progress within the curriculum. Therefore, when CBM procedures are used, it is important to determine the *trend line* or *progress line* of the student's performance (based on graphed data points) and compare that with the goal established for the student. If the trend line indicates that progress is slower than expected (in relation to the goal), an instructional change is suggested. If the trend line indicates that progress is faster than expected, the goal is modified accordingly. The progress line can be determined informally by visually drawing a line through the data that appears to best fit the trend. The accuracy of this approach has been questioned, however (Tawney & Gast, 1984). Some relatively simple approaches can be used to increase the reliability of the trend line. Examples of these approaches are the *quarter-intersect method* and a modification of this procedure called the *split-middle method* (White & Haring, 1980). The following steps describe the two procedures. In addition, the steps are visually depicted in Figure 7.2.

Step 1.　Divide the data into two equal parts. With an odd number of data points, the line will be through the middle (median) data point going from left to right. With an even number the line will be between two data points.

Step 2.　For each half, draw a vertical line at the mid-date. This will be the middle data point from left to right for an odd number of data points or between the middle data points for an even number.

Step 3.　For each half, draw a horizontal line through the mid-rate line (the middle data point or between the two middle data points counting from bottom to top). Note that this line may pass though more than one data point (as depicted in Figure 7.2).

Step 4.　Draw a line that passes through the intersection created in steps 1 and 2. This is the *quarter-intersect method*.

Step 5.　Move the line (always in a parallel fashion) up or down until there are equal numbers of data points on or above the line and on or below the line. This is the *split middle method*.

Fuchs and Fuchs (1990) provided an excellent description of the use of CBM in the area of reading. The following example summarizes their description.

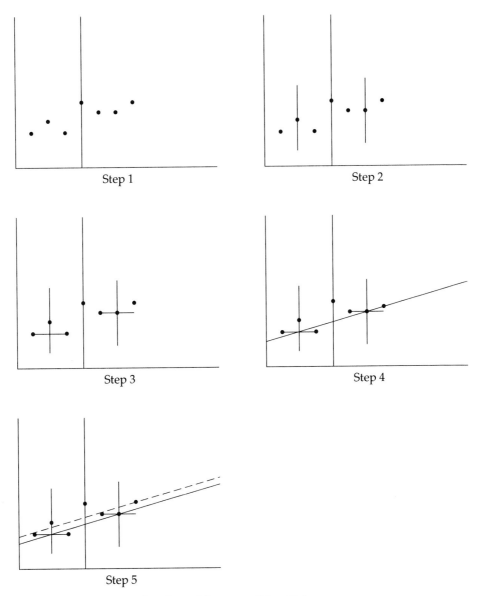

Step 1

Step 2

Step 3

Step 4

Step 5

**FIGURE 7.2   Determination of Progress Line Using
Quarter-Intersect and Split-Middle Methods**

1. The teacher determines that by the end of the year the student should be proficient on third-grade level material (proficiency defined as reading at least ninety words per minute correctly with no more than five errors). This constitutes the long-term goal.

2. The teacher assesses the student at least twice weekly, each time on a different passage, randomly sampled in the third-grade curricular text. The teacher states a standard set of directions, has the student read orally for one minute from the text, and scores the number of correctly and incorrectly read words.

3. The teacher charts the student's performance on graph paper, with the performance criterion of ninety words per minute placed on the graph at the intersection of the goal date and criterion level. A goal line connecting the baseline level and date and the goal criterion and date is drawn onto the graph. Figure 7.3 shows an example of such a graph in which the student correctly read twenty-nine words in the first week of September with the goal set at ninety words correct by the end of May.

4. The teacher provides an instructional program and continues to assess and graph the student's performance.

5. Whenever at least eight scores have been collected, the teacher analyzes the adequacy of the student's progress and then draws a line of best fit through the student's data.

6. At this point the teacher determines the effectiveness of the teaching program. If the student's actual progress is steeper than the goal line, the teacher increases the goal (Figure 7.4). This would indicate that the date of the goal could be moved to mid-January. If the student's progress is less steep than the goal line, the teacher changes the instructional program to address the student's instructional needs (Figure 7.5). This figure shows that the student's improvement was not consistent with the projected goal.

Note that the CBM procedure relies heavily on decision making based on visual inspection of the data. In other words, the assessment information is used continually to monitor progress and to aid the teacher in instructional decision making.

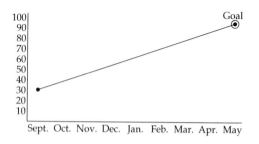

• Words read correctly per minute

FIGURE 7.3   Graph Reporting Baseline Performance and Goal/Date for Student in the Area of Oral Reading

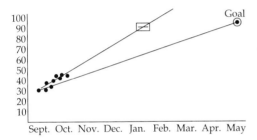

• Words read correctly per minute
▱ Projected goal date based on trend line

FIGURE 7.4   Graph Indicating That Goal Date Should Be Changed

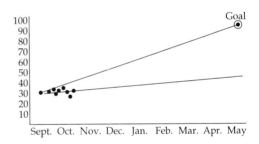

• Words read correctly per minute

FIGURE 7.5   Graph Indicating That Instructional Change Is Necessary

Computer-Based CBM

More recently, the use of computers to monitor and assist in CBM decision making has become increasingly widespread. Computers are helpful in the mechanical aspects of scoring and in helping teachers with analysis. They lead to more accurate information that enhances teacher decision making (Fuchs, Fuchs, & Hamlett, 1993). Specific programs have been designed to help teachers score, graph, and analyze student performance data (Hasselbring & Moore, 1990). An example of a computer-based measurement technique is *Monitoring Basic Skills Progress* (Fuchs, Hamlett, & Fuchs, 1990), a computer program package that is available for reading, spelling, and mathematics.

Monitoring Basic Skills Progress

Monitoring Basic Skills Progress (MBSP) comprises three software programs that were designed using the CBM model. As such, they allow the student to take a series of short tests at a given grade level that are automatically scored by the computer. It also provides feedback to the student and saves the student's scores and responses. Finally, it summarizes the performance for the teacher by providing a graph of the student's scores across the school year and a profile.

The three programs are *Basic Reading, Basic Spelling,* and *Basic Math.* The materials for each program include a sample student disk, a master student disk, and a teacher disk. In addition, information related to the reliability and validity of each program is included in the manuals. The sample student disk contains assessment information for several students to give the teacher an idea of the types of graphs and skill profiles that will be presented. The master student disk contains the software that allows the students to take the tests. The master is used to make an individual student disk for each student. The teacher disk allows the teacher to examine student assessment information. The MBSP manuals include guidelines to help teachers make instructional decisions by interpreting the graphs and skill

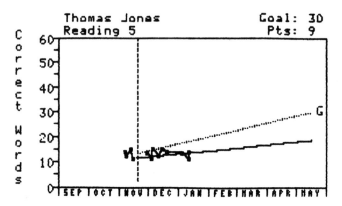

FIGURE 7.6   Sample Performance Pattern for Recommended Teaching Change

profiles that are generated by the computer. The guidelines include suggestions for monitoring goals, adjusting instructional programs, and comparing the relative effectiveness of different instructional components. The skill profile provides such information as the objectives that the student has mastered, partially mastered, not mastered, or were not attempted. The graphs provide a visual representation of the student's progress over time. Figure 7.6 shows an example of a student's graph where performance indicated that an instructional change was necessary. All disks require an Apple II computer with at least one disk drive and 64K of memory.

Basic Reading Tests.   The tests used for *Basic Reading* are on separate Story Disks (one for each grade level from one to six). The tests use a "maze" procedure (see Chapter 14 for a detailed discussion of this procedure). In the MBSP, the maze procedure is set up so that every seventh word in a four hundred-word reading passage is deleted and replaced with a blank. The students read the story and when they get to a blank they press the spacebar to get three choices to replace the blank. The student indicates the correct choice and then goes to the next blank. It is recommended that the student take a test every week (twice a week for special education students). The test is automatically scored and saved, and a graph similar to that in Figure 7.7 is created.

Basic Spelling Tests.   *Basic Spelling* includes thirty lists of twenty spelling words at each of six grade levels. The words are dictated by the teacher and the student types the responses into the computer. As in *Basic Reading*, the computer then scores the responses, provides feedback to the student, and generates graphs and profiles for the teacher to analyze.

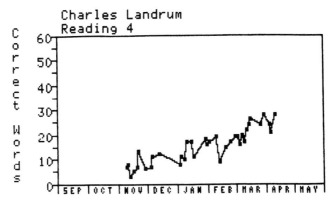

**FIGURE 7.7   Sample Printed Graph Format to
Distribute to Students**

Basic Math Tests.   There are thirty twenty-five-item mathematics tests available
for each of six grade levels. The computer automatically administers the tests at
the grade level designated by the teacher. The same scoring and feedback features
noted in the other programs are available. A separate booklet with 180 mathematics tests also comes with the package.

Uses and Limitations of CBM

Similar to the research on CBA, the professional literature has generally supported the use of CBM procedures, particularly for enhancing instructional decision making. Shapiro and Eckert (1994), in fact, reported that school psychologists significantly and consistently rated CBM as more acceptable than standardized achievement measures. In addition to the use of CBM to make instructional decisions, other purposes have also been identified. For example, Shinn and Habedank (1992) argued that CBM could be used to determine eligibility for special education. CBM could also be used to identify potential candidates for reintegration into general education. Shinn, Habedank, Rodden-Nord, and Knutson (1993) developed local norms of low-level reading students in general education. When applied to special education students, they found that 40 percent could be reintegrated into the general education classroom. Yet another purpose might be grouping for instruction. For example, Wesson, Vierthaler, and Haubrich (1989) reported that the use of CBM required less than five minutes per student to establish reading groups that were similar to those established over a seven-month period based on teacher recommendation. More formal uses of CBM have been the development of classwide decision-making strategies (Fuchs, Fuchs, Bishop, & Hamlett, 1992), and the development of oral reading fluency norms (Hasbrouck & Tindal, 1992).

The majority of research on CBM has been conducted to determine ways to improve instructional decision making. It has been reported that the appropriate selection of the long-term goal used in CBM procedures has been a problem for teachers (Fuchs, Fuchs, & Hamlett, 1989) and that they need specific recommendations on how to incorporate CBM feedback into instructional planning (Fuchs, Fuchs, Hamlett, Phillips, & Bentz, 1994). It has also been shown that if they know the actual student responses and not just the graphed responses teachers can more effectively make instructional decisions (Fuchs, Fuchs, Hamlett, & Allinder, 1991). As a result, skill analysis programs such as that noted in the MBSP have been developed to provide more specific information for the teacher. Fuchs, Fuchs, Hamlett, and Allinder (1991), in fact, found that teachers' effective use of CBM data improved when the teachers were provided with skills analyses as well as the graphed performance of the students' skills. Another related finding is that *greater student achievement* is noted when consultation (computerized, systematic, and instructional) is provided for teachers within a CBM model than when no CBM is used or CBM is used without consultation (Fuchs, Fuchs, Hamlett, & Ferguson, 1992). Interestingly, McCurdy and Shapiro (1992) found that self-monitoring or peer monitoring that used CBM was as effective as teacher monitoring. This might lead to student self-evaluation using CBM procedures. In addition, other refinements and suggestions for maximum decision making are being made.

Some limitations of CBM procedures are also noted in the professional literature. One criticism is that CBM emphasizes the isolation of skills rather than the examination of the learning process itself. Also, it tends to view learning in a linear fashion and the use of the graphs may oversimplify the learning process (Coleman, 1990). Gable (1990) also noted that CBM procedures are not always useful for designing interventions. In other words, although they can effectively indicate when a program change is needed, they do not provide the type of information that would help in determining the nature of an effective program. As an example of this, Frank and Gerken (1990) found that CBM probes were insufficient in making program decisions for students with mild retardation. Finally, some general drawbacks of CBM are the time and logistics required to implement CBM in a practical, meaningful way (Yell, Deno, & Marston, 1992).

CBA AND CBM: AN INTEGRATED MODEL

There are clear similarities and differences in the CBA and CBM procedures discussed in this chapter. Both procedures have many advantages over traditional assessment methods. Cohen and Spence (1990) summarized several of these advantages. First, they provide increased communication for parents, teachers, and students about instructional decisions and student progress. Second, they have increased sensitivity and a direct impact on the student's curriculum. Third, they allow for peer referencing. In other words, they allow the teacher to determine the student's growth in comparison to a set of predetermined criteria (CBA) or in comparison to other students' progress (CBM). Finally, they noted that the use of these procedures reduces bias in teacher referrals.

Should the CBA and CBM procedures discussed in this chapter be viewed and used in isolation? No. Each provides important information in the evaluation process. Shapiro (1990), in fact, proposed an integrated model for CBA. He suggested that the first step should be to assess the academic environment through interviews and observation. The second step should be to assess the grade level of the student across the curriculum material. The third step should be to assess the instructional level within the correctly placed grade level. The fourth step should be to determine when instructional modification is necessary as new skills are acquired. The last step should be to assess the student's progress. Given the information presented in this chapter, CBA would be appropriate for step 3 (as a pre-test) and step 5 (as mastery tests or probes). CBM would be appropriate for steps 2, 4, and 5.

Another model proposed to help individuals develop effective and meaningful curriculum-based assessment instruments was offered by King-Sears (1994), who suggested naming the model with the mnemonic APPLY. The APPLY model is essentially a combination of the criterion-referenced CBA and the CBM methods already discussed and uses the following steps:

1. **Analyze** the curriculum. The first step in developing a CBA is curriculum analysis. Care should be taken to look at the curriculum in collaboration with appropriate professionals. For example, if the student is placed in general education for all or part of the day, the general education teacher should become involved. Similarly, if vocational training is important then collaboration with potential employers might be relevant. The curriculum must be analyzed to determine short-term objectives (as in criterion-referenced CBA) and long-term objectives (as in CBM), and these should be identified considering the individual characteristics of the student who will be administered the instrument.

2. **Prepare** items to match curriculum objectives. Among the issues involved in preparing items is the consideration of the type of measurement to be used for evaluating a specific objective. The discussion in Chapter 6 regarding item development of criterion-referenced tests would be particularly relevant here. Another consideration is the use both of items that measure basic facts and items that measure higher-level thinking skills. It is important to avoid a simplistic skill-by-skill analysis and to include probes that will ensure that the student can apply or perform this skill in realistic situations. This is a strong basis for the use of alternative assessment procedures discussed in Chapter 8. King-Sears (1994) noted "All items must (a) match the behavior and conditions stated in the objective, (b) be directly measurable, (c) link student performance to curriculum objectives, and (d) be considered as overall indicators of critical performance necessary for students within a given curriculum."

3. Probe frequently. It is important to probe or to sample frequently students' behavior related to the objectives found in the CBA. Although there is no specific time suggestion regarding how often the student should be tested, the goal of CBA (identification of appropriate objectives and monitoring of progress) dictates that the more frequent the assessment the more valuable the information received.

4. Load data using a graph format. It is important that results from a CBA be visually displayed so that data trends are obvious. Although the specific results of the CBA, when reported in numerical scores can also be meaningful, they often are not interpreted appropriately until a visual analysis is provided.

5. Yield to results—revisions and decisions. Without using the results of the CBA, the whole process is somewhat meaningless. In reality, the data derived from the CBA should dictate the decisions to be made in the classroom; this might include revising the instructional program, changing the method of instruction, using more probes, or changing the behavioral objectives themselves.

Instrument or Technique	Suggested Use							Target Population						Special Considerations	Educational Relevance for Exceptional Students
	Prereferral			Postreferral											
	Screening and Initial Identification	Informal Determination and Evaluation of Teaching Programs and Strategies	Determination of Current Performance Level and Educational Need	Decisions about Classification and Program Placement	IEP Goals	IEP Objectives	IEP Evaluation	Mild/Moderate	Severe/Profound	Preschool	Elementary Age	Secondary Age	Adult		
Criterion-Referenced CBA	X	X	X		X	X	X	X		X		X		Uses the actual curriculum as the content of the testing	very useful
Curriculum-Based Measurement	X	X	X		X	X	X	X			X	X		A more standardized version of CBA	very useful
Monitoring Basic Skills Progress	X	X	X		X	X	X	X			X			A computerized version of CBM; available in reading, math, and spelling	useful

8

PORTFOLIO ASSESSMENT AND OTHER ALTERNATIVE PROCEDURES

Areas Covered

Performance Assessment
Authentic Assessment
Portfolio Assessment
Large-Scale Portfolio Projects
Purposes for Portfolio Assessment
Portfolio Development
Development of a Portfolio: An Example

The field of educational assessment is changing. Several alternative assessment procedures have received widespread attention as a result of a dissatisfaction with more traditional norm-referenced tests. The area that has received the most criticism has been standardized achievement testing (particularly group achievement testing). Hart (1994) noted that, in part, dissatisfaction with standardized tests has grown as emphasis has shifted from the use of achievement test data for "low-stakes assessment" to "high-stakes assessment." Low-stakes assessment refers to the use of assessment data for individual diagnostic purposes or for evaluating the effects of instruction. The use of high-stakes assessment, on the other hand, might result in student promotion, the teacher's evaluation, or perhaps a school district's certification. Among the reasons why standardized testing has been criticized are:

- It puts too much value on recall and rote learning at the expense of understanding and reflection;
- It promotes the misleading impression that a single right answer exists for almost every problem or question;
- It turns students into passive learners who need only recognize, not construct, answers and solutions;
- It forces teachers to focus more on what can be easily tested than on what is important for students to learn; and
- It trivializes content and skill development by reducing whatever is taught to a fill-in-the-bubble format. (p. 7)

As a result of this dissatisfaction with standardized testing, several changes in the assessment field have occurred. Meltzer and Reid (1994) noted that educational assessment

A. Is becoming holistic and dynamic
B. Is becoming multidimensional
C. Is beginning to address metacognitive processes and strategic learning
D. Is beginning to account for the ongoing interactions among developmental and curriculum effects
E. Is becoming continuous with instruction

In fact, the changes in assessment have largely been a result of changes in curricular and instructional practices (see Figure 8.1).

This movement has resulted in a number of alternative approaches such as *performance assessment, authentic assessment,* and *portfolio assessment.* Although these approaches have been used for years in general education, they have recently been gaining attention in the area of special education. With the current emphasis of inclusion of exceptional students in the general education classroom, this interest will undoubtedly continue. All of these alternative approaches have several points in common. First, they directly examine the student's achievement as an ongoing process and measure the student's abilities in various academic areas. There are, in fact, several similarities to all the various terms used in alternative assessment. For example, Worthern (1993) noted that they are all viewed as alternatives to traditional multiple-choice standardized achievement tests and that they refer to direct examination of student performance on relevant tasks. Poteet, Choate, and Stewart (1993) pointed out that the one major difference between traditional and alternative assessment is the type of response required by the student. Whereas traditional norm-referenced tests require students to select and mark correct responses, alternative assessment approaches require the students to produce, construct, demonstrate, or perform a task. Finally, Wiggins (1989) likened traditional tests that are arbitrarily timed, superficial exercises to drills on the practice field rather than performance in an actual game. He further

From	To
• Acquisition of pieces of knowledge as an end in itself	• Embedding knowledge in a conceptual framework and using knowledge as a tool for solving problems
• Emphasis on separate areas of content	• Content integration
• Emphasis on one right answer	• Emphasis on students' reasoning and problem-solving processes
• Students as passive participants in learning	• Students as active participants in constructing learning
• Teachers as transmitters of knowledge	• Teachers as facilitators of learning
• Evaluation as measuring student mastery	• Evaluation as a means of improving instruction, learning, and programs
• Students working alone, quietly	• Cooperative learning
• Learning to write	• Writing to learn
• Computer-Assisted Instruction in computer labs	• Classroom-based technology to enhance instructional opportunities

FIGURE 8.1   Shifts in Instructional Practices

stated that we typically learn too much about a student's short-term recall and too little about what is the most important—a student's habits of mind. Figure 8.2 provides the definitions of many terms currently used in the alternative assessment movement.

Alternative Assessment: Assessments that are not standardized, multiple-choice, norm-referenced.

Performance Assessment: An alternative assessment that requires the student to *do* (produce, demonstrate, perform, create, construct, apply, build, solve, plan, show, illustrate, convince, persuade, or explain) some task.

Authentic Assessment: A performance assessment that requires the *application* of knowledge to real-life, real-world settings, or a simulation of such a setting using real-life, real-world activities.

Portfolio Assessment: A performance assessment of observable evidence or products completed by the student over time. Portfolio assessment may or may not be "authentic."

FIGURE 8.2   Definitions of Common Terms

PERFORMANCE ASSESSMENT

WHY USE PERFORMANCE ASSESSMENT?

Determination and evaluation of objectives and teaching strategies; gathering of prereferral information; monitoring progress; parent conferencing

WHO SHOULD USE IT?

Teachers

Performance assessment requires the student to perform some activity that demonstrates mastery of the competencies necessary to perform the task. Performance assessment is actually not new. For example, the work-sample method of assessment noted in Chapter 18 (vocational assessment) has been around for years. This requires an individual to perform specific job requirements to determine whether the individual has mastered the skills. The key is to shift from a simple multiple-choice format for assessing students' knowledge and skills to a more practical application of that information.

Fuchs (1994) describes a performance assessment task in the area of mathematics: A group of five families on your block is going to have a garage sale in which clothes, toys, and books will be sold. Your family has twelve items to sell and will need eighteen square feet to display these items; the Hamletts have thirteen items and need twenty square feet; the Phillips, seven items and ten square feet; the Garcias, fifteen items and fifteen square feet; the Nguyens, ten items and thirty square feet. Rental tables measure 6 feet by 2.5 feet and cost six dollars per day. The garage where the sale will be held is twenty feet by thirty feet. Newspaper advertising costs $11 for the first ten words and $1.50 for each additional word.

1. How many tables will you need? Explain how you got this number.
2. Draw a diagram showing how the tables can be arranged in the garage to allow the customers to move about with at least four feet between tables.
3. Write an ad for your sale that includes enough information.
4. How much money do you have to earn from your sale for the families to break even?

The students are aware of the scoring system and the criteria used to determine the scores. Their responses will be classified as exemplary, competent, minimal, inadequate, or no attempt, based on a rubric that specifies the characteristics of responses in each of these categories.

This example demonstrates that performance assessment requires the student to do more than simple arithmetic computations. In fact, it taps a number of different areas as the student applies the information in a variety of ways. Elliott (1994) provided several guidelines for teachers to follow in order to make performance assessment meaningful. These included selecting assessment tasks that clearly relate to what is being taught; providing students with statements, standards, and models of acceptable performance; and encouraging students to complete self-assessments of their performance.

Unfortunately, performance assessment is not without its critics. As noted previously, one use of these procedures has been to evaluate students in large-scale, statewide testing programs (high-stakes assessment). Mehrens (1992) pointed out that it is difficult, if not impossible, to keep the exact content of these types of exams secure. Thus, new performance assessments have to be developed each year, adding to the costs and making cross-year comparisons of growth difficult. Coutinho and Malouf (1993) also agreed that the expenses of performance assessment are greater than those of pencil-and-paper tasks and that the amount of time involved in the administration, scoring, and interpretation is considerable. There have been attempts to address this issue, however. For example, American Guidance Service publishes a series of assessment books for students in grades three through eight. These include performance-based tasks of reading, language arts, mathematics, and integrated subjects. Similarly, Karlsen (1993) has developed a commercially published program called the *Language Arts Assessment Portfolio*. This provides performance-based tasks as well as a portfolio folder to display the results.

One must also be aware of the *purpose* for the performance assessment and its subsequent limitations. Baker (1993) argued that although performance assessment has been viewed as equally useful for both accountability (high stakes) and for improving classroom learning (low stakes), the technical aspects of performance assessment must be more stringent when it is used for high-stakes assessment. Coutinho and Malouf (1993), however, point out that performance assessment requires subjectivity of scoring and that examiner objectivity and reliability may be a problem. Baker also noted that we do not know enough about the effectiveness of performance assessment as a stand alone procedure for its use in low-stakes assessment to determine individual student accomplishments. Finally, Burger and Burger (1994) suggested that whereas performance-based assessment does provide additional information to that yielded from norm-referenced tests, it is unclear if this information is any better. Thus, it appears that the expense and time concerns as well as technical limitations of performance assessment might create some problems for high-stakes assessment. Further, the exact value of the information obtained from these procedures for low-stakes assessment is not clear.

Finally, the exact role of performance assessment when used with individuals with disabilities also is unclear. Coutinho and Malouf (1993) noted three critical issues that must be addressed in this area. Those are: (1) What are the significant policy, procedural, and technical considerations regarding students with disabilities and large-scale performance assessment programs? (2) What are appropriate uses of performance assessment with children and youth with disabilities? and (3) How should special education contribute to the productive use of performance assessment in the schools? In other words, at this point relatively little is known about the uses of performance assessment with students with disabilities. One example was provided by Vitali (1993), who noted that whereas teachers do tend to focus instruction on the content of standardized multiple-choice tests, the same was not true when performance-based assessment was used. Ironically, this implies that the content of the performance-based assessment does not carry over into instructional practices, a goal of alternative assessment. Vitali concluded that teachers simply did not know how to teach the performance-based assessments, nor did they feel they could do so within the current educational constraints.

AUTHENTIC ASSESSMENT

WHY USE AUTHENTIC ASSESSMENT?

Determination and evaluation of objectives and teaching strategies; gathering of prereferral information; monitoring progress; parent conferencing

WHO SHOULD USE IT?

Teachers

Poteet et al. (1993) noted that *performance assessment* becomes *authentic assessment* when it requires realistic demands and is set in a real-life context. However, because the school setting is a major real life context for many students, particularly younger students, the distinction between performance and authentic assessment is not always clear. The terms, in fact, are sometimes used interchangeably. Again, authentic assessment is also not new. For example, when an individual is being assessed in the area of vocal music, typically he or she must sing and is evaluated according to various criteria; it is not simply the person's knowledge of the music, the notes, and the tempo. Howell, Bigelow, Moore, and Evoy (1993) noted that whereas a more traditional achievement test might ask a student to spell words or punctuate sentences to measure written language skills, an authentic measure might ask the student to write a story about the pursuit of a dream. The student would first generate details regarding character and plot, then write a rough draft, then read the rough draft to class members to get ideas to improve their work and finally edit, rewrite, and proofread their work. Examples of authentic assessment in a variety of areas follow (Poteet et al., 1993):

> *Reading:* Actual or audio- or videotape of reading to a peer
> *Science:* Original investigation and report of findings
> *Oral Expression:* Phone call to request information
> *Social Studies:* Design of museum exhibit on topic of interest
> *Written Expression:* Article for school paper

The Arts: Design and decoration of bulletin board
Mathematics: Monitoring a savings account

The determination of what constitutes authentic assessment requires some degree of value judgment. For example, Coutinho and Malouf (1993) indicated that the task must be considered examples of "valued performances" in order to be considered authentic. Others, such as Archbald and Newmann (1988), pointed out that authentic assessment tasks should be worthwhile, significant, and meaningful. Similar to performance assessment, authentic assessment also has limitations when it is used for high-stakes assessment purposes. Miller and Seraphine (1993) felt that authentic assessment was good for classroom assessment uses but not for accountability purposes.

PORTFOLIO ASSESSMENT

WHY USE PORTFOLIO ASSESSMENT?

Determination and evaluation of objectives and teaching strategies; gathering of prereferral information; monitoring progress; parent conferencing

WHO SHOULD USE IT?

Teachers

The alternative assessment approach that has the most direct relevance for the classroom teacher is *portfolio assessment*. Paulson, Paulson, and Meyer (1991, p. 60) defined a portfolio as "a purposeful collection of student works that exhibits the students' efforts, progress, and achievement in one or more areas. The collection must include student participation in selecting contents, the criteria for selection, the criteria for judging merit and evidence of student self-reflection." In other words, portfolio assessment contains the observable evidence of the products of performance assessment and other sources of information. The portfolio, therefore, can serve as an excellent means of allowing a teacher to discuss progress with a student, parents, or other teachers. This approach moves away from a skill-by-skill approach to assessment, toward a more holistic evaluation that focuses on the *process* of learning, as well as the *product* of learning (Mathews, 1990). Valencia (1990) in describing a portfolio in the area of reading, compared it to an artist's portfolio in which samples of work are used to exemplify the artist's depth and breadth of expertise. Included in a typical reading portfolio might be samples of student work such as classroom tests, audiotapes, teacher's observational notes, the student's self-evaluation, and progress notes. Figure 8.3 on page 148 provides examples of different types of assessment portfolios.

If designed and used correctly, portfolio assessment can be integrated with classroom instruction and can represent significant authentic work that requires

Reading Portfolio
- Audiotape of oral reading of selected passages
- Original story grammar map
- Transcript of story retelling
- Log of books read with personal reactions, summaries, vocabulary
- Representative assignments; responses to pre-postreading questions
- Favorite performance
- Journal entries including self-evaluation

Science Portfolio
- Representative work samples
- Student-selected best performance
- Report from hands-on investigation
- Notes on science fair project
- Journal entries including self-evaluation

Writing Portfolio
- Scrapbook of representative writing samples
- Selected prewriting activities
- Illustrations/diagrams for one piece
- Log/journal of writing ideas, vocabulary, semantic maps, compositions, evaluations
- Conference notes, observation narratives
- Student-selected best performance
- Self-evaluation checklists and teacher checklists

Social Studies Portfolio
- Representative work samples
- Student-selected best performance
- Design of travel brochure, packet or itinerary of trip
- Notes on history fair project
- Journal entries including self-evaluation

Mathematics Portfolio
- Reports of mathematical investigations
- Representative assignments
- Teacher conference notes
- Descriptions and diagrams of problem-solving processes
- Video, audio, or computer-generated examples of work
- Best performance
- Journal entries including self-evaluation

Arts Portfolio
- Best performance
- Favorite performance
- First, middle, and final renderings of projects
- Tape of performance
- Journal entries including self-evaluation

Generic Portfolio
- Learning progress record
- Report cards
- Personal journal
- Tests
- Significant daily assignments
- Anecdotal observations
- Photographs
- Awards
- Personal goals

FIGURE 8.3   Examples of Assessment Portfolios

Reprinted by permission of Love Publishing Company, Denver, Colorado. From J. Poteet, J. Choate, and S. Stewart (1993). Performance assessment and special education: Practices and prospects. *Focus on Exceptional Students, 26*(1).

complex thinking skills and provides a more sensitive portrait of the student's strengths and weaknesses. It also encourages teachers and students to reflect on the progress and to adjust instruction accordingly (Herman, Gearhart, & Baker,

1993). Nolet (1993) in reviewing the research on portfolios noted five characteristics that were consistently reported.

1. Portfolios involve samples of student behavior collected over time, rather than during a single testing situation.
2. Portfolio assessment employs data generated from multiple procedures and under a variety of stimulus and response conditions.
3. Assessment portfolios are intended to sample tasks regularly performed in a natural or authentic context.
4. Portfolio assessment typically involves at least two types of data: raw data consisting of student's actual work and summarization data compiled by the teacher.
5. The process of selecting materials for inclusion generally involves at least some degree of student participation.

Large-Scale Portfolio Projects

Portfolio assessment, like other alternative assessment procedures, has been used for high-stakes assessment. Mathews (1990) described a school district–wide portfolio assessment procedure. Included in the portfolio was the following:

1. A reading development checklist (measuring attitudes toward reading, concepts about print, strategies for word identification and comprehension)
2. Writing samples
3. Lists of books read by the student
4. A reading comprehension test
5. Other information such as anecdotal records and student self-evaluation

In fact, several states have developed portfolio projects that are widespread in the schools. One example is the Vermont Portfolio Project that initially began in 137 schools. Fourth- and eighth-grade students develop portfolios in the areas of written expression and mathematics. In general, the results indicated that the students' writing skills were good, although their math abilities needed improvement. More importantly, the results indicated that the students did not present their results clearly; fewer than half of the students assembled their portfolios in a clear manner. This indicated the need for training both teachers and students in the portfolio process. In 1991, Kentucky enacted the Kentucky Education Reform Act. One significant component of this piece of legislation was an assessment system that included portfolios of students' work in writing and mathematics, as well as student achievements on "performance events" in the areas of math, science, social studies, arts and humanities, and vocational education (Guskey, 1994). Rhode Island has also developed a statewide assessment project that incorporates the use of portfolios. Snider, Lima, and DeVito (1994) made several recommendations regarding portfolio assessment based on their experience with the Rhode Island project. Those included:

- Those involved must share a fundamental belief that all students can learn and achieve at high levels.
- Participants must embrace the concept that good assessment looks like good instruction.
- Students must be ready to take more responsibility for their own learning and be willing to accept the teacher as a facilitator or coach rather than solely as a lecturer.
- School and district administration support must be evident for portfolio assessment procedures to succeed.
- Teachers must be given the time to learn about portfolio assessment, to try out numerous activities, and to experience successes as well as failures.
- Teachers must be provided with adequate technical assistance in portfolio assessment, for the great majority of classroom teachers are neither trained nor experienced in these procedures. (p. 87)

Some, however, believe that large-scale portfolio assessment is not appropriate. Purves (1993) argued that portfolios should be used for individual, not group assessment. Again, the lack of technical characteristics, such as reliability data, also support the use of the procedure more for individualized instruction rather than for accountability purposes.

Purposes for Portfolio Assessment

Whereas the use of portfolio assessment on a large scale is becoming more popular, its primary use is for low-stakes purposes. Although there are a variety of consistent descriptions of portfolio assessment for these purposes, there is little consensus regarding the goals or procedures for using portfolio assessment. Nolet (1992) suggested that portfolio assessment is a process of collecting multiple forms of data to support inferences about student performance in a skill or content area that cannot be measured directly by a single measure. He also noted that portfolios have been used for a variety of reasons, including formative and summative evaluation of student's performance in elementary and high schools. Farr and Tone (1994) made the distinction between a *working portfolio* and a *show portfolio*. The working portfolio includes examples of daily work, whereas the show portfolio would have selected samples of the student's work and would be used for conferences and other more formal evaluation purposes. These have also been referred to as the *instructional portfolio* and *assessment portfolio* (Nolet, 1992), and the *master portfolio* and *assessment portfolio* (Hewitt, 1995). Swicegood (1994) stated five possible purposes for a portfolio. The first is to provide a concrete display of the learner's best work and the learner's development. The second is to obtain multidimensional assessment information over time. The third reason is to produce a concrete display of the range of learning abilities, and the fourth is to share a tool for student and teacher reflection on learning goals. The last purpose is to encourage dialogue and collaboration among educators and between the teacher and the student. Wesson and King (1992) suggested that portfolio information could be used in conjunction with curriculum-based measurement (CBM) (discussed in Chapter 7). They believed that portfolios could be used for instructional planning and that CBM could be used to evaluate the instructional plans. Portfolio assessment has even been used to identify minority children who are gifted and who are not identified through more traditional measures, such as intelligence tests (Coleman, 1994; Hadaway & Marek-Schroer, 1994).

Portfolio Development

Although any number of entries can be included in a portfolio, it is important to be systematic in choosing those that will ultimately be included. As noted previously, the purpose for the assessment to a certain extent will dictate the type of information included. Nolet (1992), again using the analogy of an artist portfolio, indicated that the *context* is important. For example, an artist providing a portfolio of work to a committee who would award the contract to build a library, would show different examples than when the same artist would make a presentation to a real estate developer. Likewise, the context for which the educational portfolio will be used must be considered.

Vavrus (1990) identified five decisions that must be made before a teacher puts together a portfolio assessment. The first decision is *what it should look like.* A good portfolio should have both a physical structure and a conceptual structure. The physical structure is the actual arrangement of the entries in the portfolio, such as the subject area and the chronological order, whereas the conceptual structure refers to the learning goals that are set for the student and the corresponding portfolio entries that best reflect those goals. Nolet (1992) also noted that *portfolio format* is important and could include some type of expandable file folder, laser disks, or computers. As an example of the use of technology in portfolio assessment, Edyburn (1994) described the *Grady Profile,* an integrated series of Hypercard stacks that serve as a electronic portfolio for students' work. The actual work samples can be stored in three formats: sound (by microphone), graphics (by a scanner), and video. Each student has a complete set of stacks that serve as his or her portfolio and is protected by a password. Figure 8.4 on page 152 shows one of several screens that can be accessed through the Grady Profile. This screen would allow an individual to both review the students' reading skills and hear a recording of the student actually reading.

The second decision is *what goes in* the portfolio. This determination is sometimes totally left up to the student, whereas other times it is teacher driven. Usually there is some joint decision making (Nolet, 1992). Six questions must be answered before you can decide what goes into a portfolio.

1. Who is the intended audience for the portfolio?
2. What will this audience want to know about student learning?
3. Will the selected documents show aspects of student growth or will they corroborate evidence that test scores have already documented?
4. What kinds of evidence will best show student progress toward learning goals?

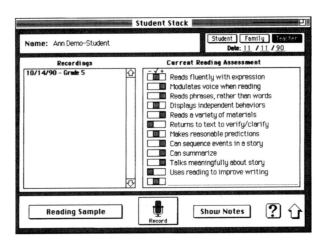

FIGURE 8.4   Reading Sample Card from the Grady Profile

From D. Edyburn (1994). An equation to consider: The portfolio assessment knowledge base + technology = The Grady Profile. *LD Forum, 19*(4). Reprinted by permission, Council for Learning Disabilities.

5. Will the portfolio contain best work, or a progressive record of student growth, or both?
6. Will the portfolio include more than finished pieces, such as ideas, sketches and revisions?

Swicegood (1994) investigated the contents of several portfolios and identified four major areas or categories of information that emerged. The first area was measures of behavior and adaptive functioning. This included entries such as observations, interviews about interests, videotapes of student behavior, and social skills and peer ratings. The second was measures of academic and literacy growth. Entry examples included writing samples collected over time, photographs of student projects, classroom tests, informal assessment (such as criterion-referenced tests or curriculum-based assessment), and running anecdotal records. The third area was measures of strategic learning and self-regulation. Examples of entries included student self-evaluations of task performance, interviews with the student about how they approach classroom tasks, student descriptions of strategies and operations used in observation, and ratings of study skills. The last area was measures of language and cultural aspects. These included entries such as a primary language sample, simulation in role plays, and cultural interviews with the student and parents.

The actual content of the portfolio will depend on the specific goals that are set for the student. Examples for entries for documenting progress in literacy might be samples from writing folders, excerpts from writing journals and literature logs, audiotapes of oral reading, and portions of projects that require reading and writing. Conversely, in the area of math the student might include samples of computations, explanations of why mathematical processes work for solutions to open-ended questions. Also included in any portfolio should be documentation of the students' self-evaluations and self-reflections. As John Dewey once said, "We learn by doing if we reflect on what we've done."

Knight (1992) provided the following excerpt from one of her eigth-grade students' portfolio that indicates the degree of reflection that goes into the selection of portfolio materials.

I chose these papers from my portfolio because they show my best work and my worst work. They portray both sides of my academic performance in math this last semester. The 45% math test is in my portfolio because it shows that I have some problems in math. It shows my bad work. It shows that sometimes I have a bad day. It shows also that I forgot to study (ha, ha, ha). I can sum up three papers in this paragraph. Those are the Personal Budget, the James project, and the $2,000 lottery project. On all of these papers I did really well. That shows that I tend to do much better on those projects, especially the creative ones. I have a bit more fun doing them rather than doing just normal take-home math assignments, these papers definitely show me at my best. (p. 72)

The third decision that a teacher must make is *how and when to select the entries*. This relates to the *conditions* under which the material is produced. Are typical performances included, or should exemplary work only be included? Again, this ties into the goal for why the portfolio is being assembled. For example, the end of a unit, semester, or school year are good times to select work samples that best demonstrate student growth. Vavrus also suggests creating a time line and identifying regular times during the year for selecting student work. This also provides a time line for the student who can prepare portfolio entries.

The fourth decision is related to *evaluating the portfolio*. The key to scoring or evaluating the portfolio is to set standards that relate to the student goals. These standards should be determined ahead of time, and the portfolio can be evaluated in terms of meeting those standards or on growth demonstrated toward meeting those standards. This setting of standards is a difficult and somewhat subjective process and might be facilitated by consulting with other teachers and getting their interpretations of mastery or high performance. Another method might be to identify at what level the student would be working at in an inadequate, satisfactory, or exemplary level. This is usually accomplished through the development of a rubric. A *rubric* is a set of criteria that provide a description of various levels of student performance as well as a value to each of the levels. Rubrics also serve as a means of communicating the purpose and requirements of the work that the student is completing. Fischer and King (1995, p. 29–30) provided the following steps for developing a rubric.

Step 1.   Start by making a list of the most important components or expectations of a learning activity. These might include the process, content, mechanics, presentation, variety and number of source materials, neatness, and other factors.

Step 2. Determine the criteria you will use for a scale. It might start with *Excellent* or 5 and scale down. Write a description or number for as many additional categories as you desire. Rubrics using more than six criteria descriptions are more difficult to use.

Step 3. Write a description of the performance expected for each criterion. Include the components you previously identified as important to this activity in your description of performance at each level. Some criteria on the scale may have more components assigned to them than others.

The development of a rubric can be somewhat time-consuming, and there is still the issue of reliability to address. One method used to increase reliability is *benchmarking*. A benchmark is an example of a piece of work chosen to illustrate the various levels of accomplishment for each of the criteria (Hewitt, 1995). This provides a guideline by which the students' work can be scored. This determination of benchmarks is, in itself, somewhat subjective and time-consuming. In fact, Rivera (1993) indicated both a lack of evidence supporting reliability and validity of portfolio assessment, and a need for further research in this area.

The last decision has to do with *how to pass the portfolios on.* A portfolio should not end when the school year ends, but could and should be passed on with the student to the next grade or the next teacher. Valencia (1990), in discussing the contents of a portfolio, noted that care must be taken not to simply have a holding file for various unrelated samples of isolated skill tests, but that it should be related to the district's curricular goals and objectives.

One final suggestion, provided by Swicegood (1994), is that a portfolio should contain a table of contents that groups the pieces included into sections, for example, (1) samples of daily work, (2) interviews and attitudes, (3) behavioral observations, (4) student reflections, and (5) teacher reaction. The table of contents should be based on the nature of the student's portfolio. Figure 8.5 provides a checklist of what constitutes a complete portfolio.

DEVELOPMENT OF A PORTFOLIO: AN EXAMPLE

This section illustrates the previously described steps in developing a portfolio. This is only an example. There is a great deal of flexibility in determining the contents and evaluation procedures of portfolios. The actual development of any given portfolio depends on a number of factors, including the subject area, the intended audience, and the purpose for the assessment.

This portfolio was being developed for Mike, a seventh-grade student with learning disabilities. At Mike's middle school the teachers worked in teams and had a specified number of students assigned to them. Included on the team were all the content area teachers for the group of students as well as a special education teacher who worked with those exceptional students assigned to the team.

A Complete Portfolio Will Include:

- *A completed table of contents:* may represent the student's current mode of communication; written, pictorial, audiotape.

- *A letter to the reviewer* written or dictated by the student (or a collaborative effort of a student and a nondisabled peer) that describes the portfolio and its contents.

- *Seven to ten entries* that represent the breadth of entries (types, contexts, and domain areas). Each entry must include the original question, task, or problem posed, a name, a title, and a date. Entries must be arranged in the order presented in the table of contents.

- *A student's weekly schedule* and description of its use indicating types of activities, opportunities for choice, and interactions with nondisabled peers.

- *A sample of the student's current mode(s) of communication* and description of use. May use as evidence the table of contents, letter to the reviewer, or student schedule.

- *A letter from a family member or caregiver* validating the contents of the portfolio.

An Incomplete Portfolio Fails to Include:

- A table of contents.
- A student letter to the reviewer.
- At least seven entries (not including the letters).
- A student activities schedule and description of its use.
- Validation letter from family member or caregiver.

FIGURE 8.5   Checklist for a Complete Portfolio

Mike's team included his English teacher, Ms. Brewer; history teacher, Ms. Yuran; geography teacher, Mr. Lee; science teacher, Ms. Novello; mathematics teacher, Ms. Massey; and special education teacher, Mr. Wald. This team approach allowed for collaborative planning and conferencing with parents when appropriate. Mr. Wald wanted to develop a portfolio for Mike in the area of written expression. This had been a difficult area for Mike in the past although improvement was noted in the previous year by his sixth-grade team.

STEP ONE: Determine Structure of the Portfolio

Determine physical structure. Mr. Wald decided to coordinate the portfolio; he requested entries from each of the content area teachers. He chose a simple expandable file folder as the best way to hold and display Mike's work. He separated the portfolio according to content areas and also included a section on self-reflections and a section on teacher comments.

Determine conceptual structure. Because Mr. Wald was interested in determining progress in Mike's written expression areas, he requested that each teacher provide representative samples of Mike's writing. The determination of the representative samples would be made jointly by Mike and each teacher.

STEP TWO: Determine Contents of the Portfolio

Determine purpose of the portfolio. As just noted, the purpose of Mike's portfolio was to document progress over time in the area of written expression.

Determine intended audience. Mike's portfolio was developed with many people in mind; included were Mike's parents, all of Mike's teachers, and Mike himself.

Determine audience needs. Based on the intended audience, the portfolio was developed in such a way that both qualitative and quantitative growth could be demonstrated over time. This would allow Mike's parents to see the differences in his written expression throughout the school year, provide the teachers with examples of how Mike was writing in the other content areas, and would also serve as a basis for self-reflection on Mike's part.

Determine type of entries. As noted, the entries were chosen jointly by Mike and each of his teachers. Mike was instructed to vary the types of writing samples that he chose from each classroom. In other words, he was told to take examples of creative work, of responses to essay questions, poems, reports, and so on. This would provide a good variety of writing samples on which to base his progress.

STEP THREE: Determine Selection Process

Every two weeks, on Thursday, Mike's teachers would put all of his written material in a folder and send it home so that he could decide which of the pieces were the most representative of his work. He was told not to pick his best work, or examples where he felt he had not done a good job. In other words, he was told to pick those that represented the most consistent type of writing sample.

Initially, the teachers met with Mike to show him examples of what they thought were representative. It was his responsibility after that point to make the determination. The next day he would meet with his teachers, show them the samples he had chosen, and would confer to determine if, in fact, they were representative. The teachers questioned Mike about his choices. Figure 8.6 shows a sample from science chosen by Mike and Ms. Novello during the beginning of the year. Mike had to write a poem using the science vocabulary words that he was learning that week. Figure 8.7 shows the example of writing chosen from Mike's English class for an entry during the middle of the year. His assignment was to write a brief description of three books that he had recently read and liked best.

a perfect world to me is
a world without wars
a world without pollution
a world with no endangered animals
and a world with every animal
flying, swimming and walking free.
That is what a perfect world is to
me.

FIGURE 8.6 Portfolio Entry from Science Class

Rating scale 1 forget it, 2 poor, 3 fair, 4 good,
5 got to read it

Book ratings from 1 to 5
The three best books I read were
Congo, Jurassic Park, and Goosebumps.
Congo is about an expedition sent
into the Congo to find out what happened
to the first expedition. The first was
killed by an unknown predator. With
the second expedition is, Amy, the gorilla with
a 620 sign vocabulary, and a man looking
for the lost city of Z inja and millions of
diamonds. I rate this book a 4. P.S. Congo
is a real place in Africa.
Jurassic Park is about a group of people
invited to a theme park only to notice they
are surrounded by prehistoric dinosaurs. Once
they finish their tour in the cars, Nedry shuts
the dinosaur gates down. The movie is different
than the book. I rate this book a 5. P.S. This will
probably happen in 48 years.
Goosebumps is one of many book series
It is about 3 kids who go to a carnival
but this one is very different with real
freaks, a lagoon monster, and a roller coaster
that puts you in another dimension this isn't
your everyday carnival. I rate this book
a 3. P.S. you choose the story.

FIGURE 8.7 Portfolio Entry from English Class

He also was asked to develop a rating system and to rate each book. Finally, Figure 8.8 shows an example from his history class in which he wrote about his favorite historical person. This sample was chosen toward the end of the school year.

STEP FOUR: Determine Evaluation Criteria

In order to provide a more quantitative measure of Mike's growth, it was necessary to develop a scoring rubric.

Determine most important components. Mr. Wald, who was responsible for developing the scoring rubric, investigated the literature in the area of written expression and conferred with Ms. Brewer, Mike's English teacher. He found that five components of written language were frequently mentioned: ideation, handwriting, spelling, usage, and mechanics. (See Chapter 16 for a discussion of these areas).

Determine scaling of the rubric. Mr. Wald decided to keep the scoring system relatively simple. He used a four-point scale: four = outstanding, three = good, two = fair, one = poor.

Write a description of the expected performance. Mr. Wald next provided a description of what was considered outstanding, good, fair, and poor in each of the five areas of written expression. Table 8.1 shows the completed scoring rubric incorporating the criteria and the description of each performance level.

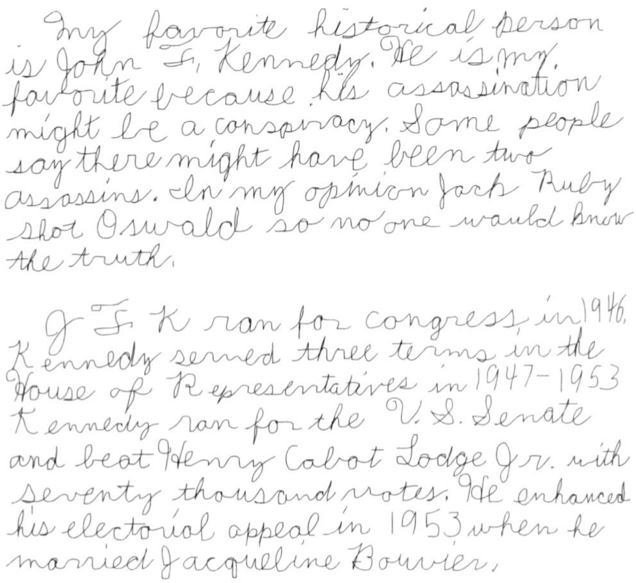
My favorite historical person is John F. Kennedy. He is my favorite because his assassination might be a conspiracy. Some people say there might have been two assassins. In my opinion Jack Ruby shot Oswald so no one wauld know the truth.

J F K ran for congress, in 1946. Kennedy served three terms in the House of Representatives in 1947–1953 Kennedy ran for the U. S. Senate and beat Henry Cabot Lodge Jr. with seventy thousand votes. He enhanced his electorial appeal in 1953 when he married Jacqueline Bouvier.

FIGURE 8.8 Portfolio Entry from History Class

TABLE 8.1   Scoring Rubric for Written Expression

	Ideation	Handwriting	Spelling	Usage	Mechanics (e.g., capitalization and punctuation)
4 Out-standing	Writing style and quality are very appropriate for intended purpose	Writing is very neat and legible	Few, if any, errors made	Use of vocabulary and syntax very appropriate for intended purpose	Few if any grammatical errors made
3 Good	Writing style and quality relatively appropriate for intended purpose	Writing is relatively neat and legible	Some errors are made	Use of vocabulary and syntax is relatively appropriate for intended purpose	Some grammatical errors made; starting to affect the meaning of the passage
2 Fair	Writing style and quality are somewhat inappropriate for intended purpose	Writing is becoming illegible	Several errors are made; begins to affect the meaning of the passage	Use of vocabulary and syntax somewhat inappropriate for intended purpose	Several grammatical errors made; starting to affect the meaning of the passage
1 Poor	Writing style and quality are not appropriate for intended purpose	Writing is illegible	Frequent errors are made; affects meaning of passage	Use of vocabulary and syntax is not appropriate for intended purpose	Frequent grammatical errors made; affects meaning of passage

STEP FIVE: *Determine Evaluation Procedures*

Because the goal of the portfolio was to document progress over time, a summary sheet was developed that showed Mike's scores throughout the school year (Figure 8.9). This provided a quantitative representation of his progress. The scores presented are an average of the ratings from Mr. Wald and the content area teacher for each subject.

STEP SIX: *Determine Procedures to Utilize Portfolio Data*

Self-reflection. In addition to making his biweekly choices, Mike was asked to answer a series of questions about his selections. Figure 8.10 on page 161 shows Mike's responses to several questions about his writing sample shown in Figure 8.7 (page 157).

Portfolio conferencing. Twice during the year, at the middle and at the end, Mr. Wald scheduled an appointment with Mike's parents to go over his general progress. As part of that conference, the portfolio was used to indicate his progress in the area of written language. Both the writing samples themselves, as well as the quantitative scoring were presented and discussed.

Passing it on. When Mike goes to the eighth grade he will be assigned to a different team; he will also have a different learning disabilities teacher.

Ideation

English	1.5	2	2	2.5	3	3	3	3	3	3.5	3.5	4	4	4	3.5
Science	2	2	1.5	2	2	2	2.5	3	3	3	4	3.5	3	3	3
History	2	2	2.5	2	3	3	3	3	3	3	3	4	4	3.5	3.5
Geography	2	2	2.5	2	2.5	3	3	3	4	3	3.5	3.5	4	4	4
Mathematics	1.5	1.5	1	1.5	2	2	2	2	2.5	3	3	2.5	3	3	3

Handwriting

English	2	2	2	2	2	2	3	3	3	3.5	3	3	3	3	3
Science	2	2	2	2	2.5	2.5	2	2	3	3	3	3	3	3	3
History	2	2	2	2	2	2	2	2	2	3	3	3	3	3	3
Geography	2	2	2	2	2	2.5	2	3	3	3	3	3	3	3	3.5
Mathematics	1	1	1	1.5	2	2	2	2	2	2.5	3	3	3	3	3

Spelling

English	2	2	2.5	3	3	3	3	3.5	4	4	4	4	4	4	4
Science	3	3	3	3	3	3	3.5	3	3	3.5	4	4	4	4	4
History	3	3	3	3	3	3	3	3.5	4	4	4	4	4	4	4
Geography	2	3	3	3	3	3.5	3	4	4	4	3.5	4	4	4	4
Mathematics	2	2	2	3	3	3	3	3	3	3	4	4	3.5	4	4

Usage

English	2	2	3	3	3	3	3	3.5	3.5	4	4	4	4	4	4
Science	2.5	3	3	3	3	3	3	3	3	3	3	3	3.5	4	3.5
History	3	3	3	3	4	3	3	3	3	4	4	4	3.5	4	4
Geography	3	3	3	3	3	4	3	4	3	4	4	4	4	4	4
Mathematics	2	2	2	2.5	3	2.5	3	3	3	3	3	3	3	3	3

Mechanics

English	2	2	2	2	2	3	2.5	3	3	3	3	3	3	4	3.5
Science	2	2	2	2	2	2	2.5	2.5	3	3	3	4	4	4	3.5
History	2	2	2	3	2	3	3	3	3	3	4	4	4	4	4
Geography	2	2	2	3	3	3	3	3	3	3.5	3	4	3	4	4
Mathematics	1.5	2	2	2	2	2	2	2	2.5	3	3	3	3	3	3

FIGURE 8.9   Summary Sheet for Rubric

Mr. Wald plans on meeting with Mike's new teacher in the fall to go over the portfolio and the scoring rubric, and to encourage Mike's new team to continue the portfolio process through the eighth grade. Mike responded favorably to the responsibility of determining his portfolio entries and was pleased to be involved in this self-reflection process.

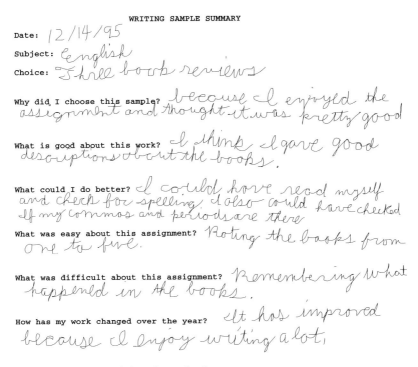

WRITING SAMPLE SUMMARY

Date: 12/14/95

Subject: English

Choice: Three book reviews

Why did I choose this sample? because I enjoyed the assignment and thought it was pretty good

What is good about this work? I think I gave good descriptions about the books.

What could I do better? I could have read myself and check for spelling. I also could have checked if my commas and periods are there

What was easy about this assignment? Rating the books from one to five.

What was difficult about this assignment? Remembering what happened in the books.

How has my work changed over the year? It has improved because I enjoy writing a lot.

FIGURE 8.10   Writing Sample Summary

Instrument or Technique	Suggested Use							Target Population						Special Considerations	Educational Relevance for Exceptional Students
	Prereferral			Postreferral											
	Screening and Initial Identification	Informal Determination and Evaluation of Teaching Programs and Strategies	Determination of Current Performance Level and Educational Need	Decisions about Classification and Program Placement	IEP Goals	IEP Objectives	IEP Evaluation	Mild/Moderate	Severe/Profound	Preschool	Elementary Age	Secondary Age	Adult		
Performance Assessment	X	X	X		X	X	X	X		X	X	X		Requires the student to apply information instead of selecting the correct response	useful
Authentic Assessment	X	X	X		X	X	X	X		X	X	X		Application of performance assessment in real-life, meaningful situations	useful
Portfolio Assessment	X	X	X		X	X	X	X		X	X	X		Collection of student work used for a variety of purposes; usually includes self-reflection	very useful

Part **III**

ASSESSMENT OF ABILITIES

One of the hallmarks of educational and psychological assessment is the measurement of an individual's abilities. Ability assessment involves the measurement of hypothetical constructs (i.e., underlying abilities) and is distinguished from the assessment of achievement (discussed in Part IV). As will be discussed, however, there is some question whether this ability/achievement distinction represents a true dichotomy. The abilities, and their subsequent assessment, that are discussed in this part are *intelligence, adaptive behavior, emotional/behavioral status,* and *language.*

As noted in Chapter 4, evaluation of the areas discussed in this section are important to help determine eligibility decisions. For example, the areas of intelligence and adaptive behavior are measured to help determine the label of mental retardation. In addition, IQ is used as a measure of aptitude in many states to help determine the aptitude/achievement discrepancy that is necessary for a label of learning disability. Language testing is used to help determine those who are eligible for programs for students with speech and language impairments, whereas emotional/behavioral testing is used with students suspected of having problems in those particular areas.

Perhaps more importantly, these types of tests can also be used to provide information about a student's strengths and weaknesses in each of the areas. They might also be used to identify general educational goals for the student and to identify areas that require further assessment. Finally, they are frequently used to make assumptions about an individual's underlying abilities. Often, ability tests are administered by ancillary personnel such as school psychologists, social workers, or speech-language clinicians (depending on the area tested). Teachers, however, do administer some of the tests discussed in this section. Further, it is important that teachers be familiar with these areas because they will see assessment information related to them.

Both formal and informal tests and procedures are included in these chapters. For each test described in this section the following information is included:

1. A summary matrix is provided that presents information about specific instruments and techniques in a format that allows easy comparison of the instruments for suggested use and target population. The matrix also includes a statement of any special considerations of which a user should be aware. In addition, for each instrument, the matrix gives the educational relevance for exceptional students. The matrices are directly related to the assessment model proposed in Chapter 2.
2. A thorough review of relevant research is provided for each norm-referenced instrument. The review emphasizes the use of the test with exceptional students.
3. An overview box is provided for each test. The overview summarizes the age range, technical adequacy (for norm-referenced tests), and suggested use for each instrument.

In addition, information is presented related to how each type of test best fits into the overall assessment process.

AFTER READING PART III YOU SHOULD BE ABLE TO:

- Identify critical issues related to the assessment of intelligence.
- Identify alternative methods of measuring intelligence.
- Identify the various uses of adaptive behavior testing.
- Identify the advantages of using language samples.
- Identify the various philosophical approaches of measuring emotional/behavioral status.
- Identify the strengths and weaknesses of the major instruments used to measure intelligence, adaptive behavior, language, and emotional/behavioral status.

9

ASSESSMENT OF INTELLIGENCE

Instruments and Procedures Included

Alternatives to Traditional Tests
Intelligence Tests
Group Tests
Detroit Tests of Learning Aptitude–3
Differential Ability Scales
Kaufman Assessment Battery for Children
Stanford-Binet–Fourth Edition
Wechsler Intelligence Scale for Children–III
Woodcock-Johnson–Revised
Additional Instruments
Cognitive Levels Test
Goodenough-Harris Drawing Test
Kaufman Brief Intelligence Test
McCarthy Scales of Children's Abilities
Slosson Full-Range Intelligence Test
Slosson Intelligence Test–Revised

For routine screening, Mrs. McMillan gave her fourth-grade class a group intel-ligence test. One of her students, Phillip, scored significantly below the rest of the class. Mrs. McMillan had been concerned about Phillip ever since he transferred into her class from another state. She had been collecting prereferral intervention data that justified a referral for possible placement in a special education pro-gram. After she referred Phillip, the school psychologist administered an in-dividual intelligence test to help make a decision about Phillip's eligibility for special education.

Intelligence testing is one of the most debated issues in special education. Intelligence tests have both their staunch supporters and their vehement critics. Legal battles have been fought over whether these instruments have their place in the field of education. Suffice it to say that the debate is far from over and that ignoring the issue will not make it go away.

Historically, intelligence has been an enigmatic concept. It is a much-valued construct or quality that is extremely difficult to define. Is intelligence the same as verbal ability? Analytical thinking? Academic aptitude? Strategic thinking? The ability to cope? Different theorists might argue for each, or a combination, of these abilities. Similarly, they might ask whether intelligence is, or should be, defined in the same way for individuals of different cultural, ethnic, or social backgrounds.

As noted in Chapters 1 and 3, intelligence tests have been the focus of considerable debate because of their alleged bias against ethnic minority students. Research on the presence of bias in intelligence testing is fairly straightforward. Individuals from different cultural, ethnic, and socioeconomic groups do score differently on most measures of intelligence, particularly those that are verbal. Empirical investigation of the tests themselves (much of which was conducted as a result of the court cases regarding discriminatory evaluation) suggests that they are not statistically biased. Perhaps educators should be less concerned about whether or not a test is biased and more concerned about the uses of test data for discriminatory purposes. For instance, it has long been known that verbally-oriented intelligence tests are valid predictors of school performance (measured by achievement tests), regardless of the racial or ethnic background of the student (Oakland, 1977; Reschly & Reschly, 1979). The use of these tests to predict teachers' ratings of students is somewhat more speculative, however (Partenio & Taylor, 1985; Reschly & Reschly, 1979). Their use in making major educational decisions is inappropriate (Clarizio, 1982). Certainly, test-based statements regarding "intellectual potential" should be avoided. In other words, intelligence tests have been criticized (probably erroneously) because incorrect or inappropriate decisions have been made from intelligence test data. The problem is not necessarily inherent in the test itself; it is more a function of what we, as professionals, are doing with the tests.

One reason for this misunderstanding is that a distinction between "potential" and "performance" has not always been made. Many professionals have used intelligence tests as if they measured "intellectual potential." The tests, however, are much more accurate in reflecting what individuals have been taught and the material to which they have been exposed. Even performance on nonverbal analytical tasks is affected by a person's experience with similar tasks.

Several alternatives to traditional intelligence testing, however, have been receiving more and more attention. These alternative approaches will be discussed briefly, and an analysis of several intelligence measures widely used in special education will then follow.

ALTERNATIVES TO TRADITIONAL TESTS

Traditional intelligence testing has been referred to as static assessment; as such, it does not measure the extent to which a student will profit from instruction (Campione, 1989). This static approach has been criticized when used to identify students with mental retardation and to assess culturally different minority-group children. Another criticism of traditional intelligence tests is that they are based on a too narrowly defined concept of intelligence (Naglieri, Das, & Jarman, 1990). Bransford, Delclos, Vye, Burns, and Hasselbring (1987) also noted three arguments for moving away from traditional intelligence testing:

1. Traditional assessment is more concerned with products rather than processes of learning.
2. Traditional assessment does not address the responsiveness of the individual to instruction.
3. Traditional assessment does not provide prescriptive information that would be helpful for effective instruction.

These criticisms have led to a number of attempts to devise alternative techniques for measuring learning potential. These techniques are usually referred to as *dynamic assessment.* According to Haywood, Brown, and Wingenfeld (1990), dynamic assessment is characterized by (1) use of a test-teach-test paradigm; (2) emphasis on assessment of process, not product; (3) attempts to specify obstacles to more effective learning; (4) attempts to specify conditions that will allow more effective performance; and (5) attempts to distinguish between performance and potential.

There are, however, limitations to dynamic assessment. For example, Jitendra and Kameenui (1993) noted that dynamic assessment varies in its definition, theoretical foundation, and procedural requirement. They also pointed out that another primary concern is the large amount of time it takes to conduct dynamic assessment because of the individualized nature of the testing. It is possible, however, that the use of computers will help to minimize this concern. Additionally, dynamic assessment procedures also have limited reliability, although they do have validity (Laughon, 1990). Several of these procedures are discussed in the following sections.

Learning Potential Assessment Strategy (Budoff, 1973)

Budoff was one of the first to use a test-train-retest paradigm to measure an individual's ability to learn from teaching. The procedure was developed initially for adolescents who had been classified as educably mentally retarded (EMR). Using nonverbal measures (for example, Raven's Progressive Matrices, Koh's Block Designs), Budoff pretested the subjects, trained or coached the subjects on problem-solving strategies, and posttested the subjects twice over a one-month period. He then classified the subjects as *high scorers* (pretest scores are high—gain little from training); *gainers* (pretest scores are low—gain from training); and *nongainers* (pretest scores are low—gain little from training). Budoff supported such a model to identify those students who are *educationally* as opposed to *mentally* retarded.

Learning Potential Assessment Device (Feuerstein, Haywood, Rand, Hoffman, & Jensen, 1984)

Feuerstein and colleagues' approach, like Budoff's, uses a test-train-retest paradigm. The Learning Potential Assessment Device (LPAD) consists of four nonverbal tasks (including the Raven's Progressive Matrices). The training in the LPAD, however, is somewhat different from Budoff's training. Feuerstein encourages the examiner to interact constantly with the examinee to maximize the probability of solving the problem. Feuerstein suggests that results from his measure can be used to identify appropriate teaching strategies as well as to supply information helpful in classifying a student. Frisby and Braden (1992), however, argued that the LPAD lacked the technical adequacy to replace more traditional assessment.

Paired-Associate Learning

Paired-associate learning is certainly not a new technique. In experimental psychology, it has been a commonly used technique to measure memory and other skills. Paired-associate learning requires a subject to learn a novel set of associated items. For instance, a student might be told "ball–chair; brick–curtain; plant–tape; book–tree; plate–roof." The first word of each pair is then told to the subject who, in turn, must provide the associated word. Typically, the number of trials necessary for the subject to complete the associations is used as the measure of learning. Both meaningful and nonmeaningful associations have been used within this paradigm. The use of paired-associate learning is based on the assumption that learning new material is a good indication of learning ability. Kratochwill (1977) pointed out, however, that this technique measures only rote memory, which is merely one of many skills necessary for achievement in school.

Chronometric Techniques

More recently, chronometric techniques such as reaction time and speed of information processing (e.g., speed of memory retrieval) have been suggested as measures of intelligence (e.g., Jensen, 1993). Vernon (1990) noted that such approaches place no emphasis on previous learning or acquired knowledge yet are strongly correlated with standardized IQ measures.

INTELLIGENCE TESTS: GENERAL PURPOSE AND DESCRIPTION

WHY USE INTELLIGENCE TESTS?

Screening and identification (group tests); decisions about classification and program placement (individual tests)

WHO SHOULD USE THEM?

School psychologists, guidance personnel; information also used by teachers

As previously noted, intelligence tests are relatively good predictors of school performance (particularly, of achievement test scores). They are much less accurate in measuring the "learning potential" of an individual. Reschly (1979) reported a type of "surgeon general's warning" that can be used to help avoid misinterpretation of results from intelligence tests:

> *IQ tests measure only a portion of the competencies involved with human intelligence. The IQ results are best seen as predicting performance in school, and reflecting the degree to which children have mastered middle class cultural symbols and values. This is useful information, but it is also limited. Further cautions— IQ tests do not measure innate-genetic capacity and the scores are not fixed. Some persons do exhibit significant increases or decreases in their measured IQ.* (p. 24)

Intelligence tests fall into two major categories: group administered and individually administered. Group-administered intelligence tests are similar in structure and format to group-administered achievement tests. They measure, in fact, similar areas. Group intelligence tests usually have different levels that are used with individuals in certain grades. Typically, they include some combination of measures of language ability, memory skills, comprehension, analogical reasoning, and reading and mathematics aptitude.

Fields and Kumar (1982) surveyed ninety teachers and found that 30 percent found little or no use for the scores from group intelligence tests. Even though such a relatively large number of the teachers thought the information was limited, approximately 85 percent still used it. These tests, however, should be used for *rough screening only.* The determination and use of IQs on the basis of these group tests is not advised. Table 9.1 on page 170 summarizes the areas measured by some of the more popular group intelligence tests.

TABLE 9.1   Frequently Used Group-Administered Intelligence Tests

Name	Areas Measured (Scores Available)[1]
Analysis of Learning Potential (Durost, Gardner, Madden, & Prescott, 1971)	Overall learning potential, mathematics, reading
California Test of Mental Maturity (Sullivan, Clark, & Tiegs, 1970)	Logical reasoning, spatial relationships, numerical reasoning, verbal concepts, memory, language, nonlanguage
Cognitive Abilities Test (Thorndike & Hagen, 1994)	Verbal, quantitative, nonverbal
Kuhlmann-Anderson Test (Kuhlmann & Anderson, 1982)	Verbal, quantitative
Lorge-Thorndike Intelligence Tests (Lorge, Thorndike, & Hagen, 1966)	Verbal, nonverbal, composite
Otis-Lennon School Ability Test (Otis & Lennon, 1989)	Analogies, classifying, reasoning, sequencing
Short Form Test of Academic Aptitude (Sullivan, Clark, & Tiegs, 1970)	Sequences, analogies, memory, verbal reasoning, cognitive skills

[1]All the above instruments have several levels designed to be used with individuals from kindergarten (in some cases prekindergarten) through grade twelve.

Individual intelligence tests vary tremendously in their format and content. Some intelligence tests (or tests that purportedly measure intelligence) measure only one skill such as vocabulary or visual analogy. Other more popular instruments are multiskilled—that is, they measure many components of the intelligence construct. There are also a number of tests that have been developed for or are used primarily with special populations. For example, the Perkins-Binet Intelligence Scale, the Leiter International Performance Scale, and more recently, the Comprehensive Test of Nonverbal Intelligence are designed in such a way to circumvent the person's specific visual, auditory, or physical disability (see Appendix B).

Individual intelligence testing, until recently, has been a crucial, even mandatory component in the formal assessment process. It is still required to determine eligibility for special education in the vast majority of states.

This section focuses on six tests that are commonly used in special education. The Detroit Tests of Learning Aptitude–3 (DTLA-3) is the second revision of an old and popular test. The Differential Ability Scales is relatively new and increasingly popular. The Kaufman Assessment Battery for Children (K-ABC) is a widely researched instrument. The Stanford-Binet Intelligence Scale–Fourth Edition is the most recent version of the "grandfather" of intelligence tests. The Wechsler Intelligence Scale for Children–Third Edition (WISC-III) is the latest revision of the most popular instrument. The Woodcock-Johnson–Revised measures cognitive ability and achievement. (The achievement section is discussed in Chapter 13.)

Detroit Tests of Learning Aptitude–3

The Detroit Tests of Learning Aptitude–3 (DTLA-3) (Hammill, 1991) is the second major revision of a test that was originally published in 1935. The original and earlier revised versions were criticized for a number of reasons, including a limited standardization sample and questionable validity. The DTLA-2 (Hammill, 1985) included a more representative normative group, added four new subtests, and dropped many subtests from the earlier versions. The DTLA-2, however, retained (with some format and name changes) seven of the subtests from the earlier versions. The DTLA-3 made further changes, revising six subtests, dropping three subtests, and adding three new subtests. The DTLA-3 takes approximately one to two hours to administer, depending on the age and ability level of the examinee. Basal and ceiling rules are used to minimize administration time.

Description of Subtests

Word Opposites (50 items)—The examinee is asked to give the opposite of vocabulary words such as *hot, crooked,* and *remember.*

Design Sequences (12 items)—The student is shown a card with a series of pictures on it. Next, the student is shown another card with the same pictures in a different order and is asked to put them in the same order as before.

Sentence Imitation (30 items)—Sentences such as "In summer, we go north where it is cool" are read to the examinee, who must repeat them exactly.

Letter Sequences (12 items)—The student is briefly shown a card with a series of letters printed on it and is asked to write them down in the exact order.

Story Construction (3 stories)—The student is asked to look at a picture and make up a story about it. The story is scored according to certain criteria related to conceptual and creative attributes, among others.

Design Reproduction (23 items)—The examinee is shown a geometric figure for 5 seconds and then asked to draw it from memory.

Basic Information (40 items)—The student is asked a basic question such as "What planet is closest to the sun?" and must give an oral answer.

Symbolic Relations (30 items)—This subtest requires the student to use visual reasoning to solve a series of problems in which a series of pictures or designs forms a pattern that would lead to a correct answer to complete the pattern.

Word Sequences (30 items)—The student is asked to repeat a series of words ranging from *man-horse-song* to *ear-pig-skate-rope-wool.*

Story Sequences (8 items)—The student is shown a series of four to eight pictures and must put them in the correct sequence to tell a story.

Picture Fragments (27 items)—The student is shown an incomplete picture and must identify what it is.

Interpretation of Results

Raw scores from each individual subtest can be converted to standard scores (mean = 10; standard deviation = 3), percentile ranks, and age equivalents. In addition, several composite scores are available in three major domains. These are determined by combining various subtest scores. There is also a General Mental Ability Quotient (GMAQ) that consists of all eleven subtests in combination and an Optimal Mental Ability Score that is determined by using the four highest subtest scores. Each of these latter scores have a mean of 100 and a standard deviation of 15. A list of the various composite scores and their respective domains follows:

Linguistic Domain

Verbal Aptitude
Nonverbal Aptitude

Attentional Domain

Attention-Enhanced Aptitude
Attention-Reduced Aptitude

Motoric Domain

Motor-Enhanced Aptitude
Motor-Reduced Aptitude

Finally, Theoretical Composite scores can be determined that include the subtests most highly associated with various theoretical models of intelligence (e.g., fluid versus crystallized). Results from the DTLA-3 can be plotted on a profile sheet for visual interpretation. Also, additional interpretive guidelines can be found in the manual.

Technical Characteristics

Normative Sample. A stratified sample of more than twenty-five hundred students from thirty-six states were included in the standardization. Race, ethnicity, gender, residence, and geographic area were matched to the U.S. population.

Reliability. Test-retest reliability coefficients ranged from .77 to .96 for the subtests and .81 to .96 for the composites based on a limited sample. Internal consistency ranged from .81 to .94 and .89 to .96 for the subtests and composite scores, respectively.

Validity. Arguments for content and construct validity are presented in the manual. Concurrent-validity coefficients using the DTLA-2, K-ABC, and Woodcock-Johnson–Revised are reported. DTLA-3 subtest coefficients were low to moderate, whereas the composite coefficients were moderate with those measures. The correlation between the GMAQ and the global IQs from the other tests were in the .80s–.90s range.

Review of Relevant Research

No research on the DTLA-3 was located. In a review of the DTLA-3, Schmidt (1994) noted that it had an impressive standardization and adequate overall validity and reliability. She also noted that some subtests could be used with students with visual or hearing impairments. Information related to the DTLA-2 might be relevant for the DTLA-3, although research on the earlier editions must be interpreted cautiously due to format and standardization differences. Stehouwer (1985) reviewed the DTLA-2 and noted that it appeared potentially useful for identifying students' strengths and weaknesses, although it was still necessary to determine the test's validity and reliability. In one empirical study, Silverstein (1986b) factor-analyzed the test and noted that none of the factors corresponded to any of the composite scores that were yielded. This finding questions the construct validity of the instrument. Further research is obviously needed on the DTLA-3.

OVERVIEW: DETROIT TESTS OF LEARNING APTITUDE–3

- *Age level*—6–18 years old
- *Type of administration*—Individual
- *Technical adequacy*—Good standardization, adequate reliability, questionable validity
- *Scores yielded*—Standard scores, percentile ranks, age equivalents
- *Suggested use*—The DTLA-2 and DTLA-3 are certainly an improvement over the original DTLA. However, validity data that give meaning to the various composite scores are lacking. As noted in the manual, one should not compare composite scores from different domains. It is probably best to acknowledge that the DTLA-3 is an *aptitude* test, not an instrument to determine how an individual processes information. Therefore, the Global Composite score is probably the best to interpret as an overall measure of learning aptitude. At present, the test should be interpreted cautiously until more information is available attesting to its uses and limitations. It should be noted that there is also a DTLA–Primary for children ages three to nine and a DTLA–Adult.

Differential Ability Scales

The Differential Ability Scales (DAS) (Elliot, 1990) is an individually administered battery of cognitive and achievement tests for individuals ages 2 1/2 through 17. The DAS is an updated revision of the British Ability Scales. The DAS is organized into a cognitive battery that includes two levels, preschool and school age, and the school achievement tests. Each of these will be discussed separately.

Description

Cognitive Battery—Preschool Level.   The preschool level of the cognitive battery is further broken down into two sublevels, one suitable for children ages 2 1/2 to 3 1/2, the other for children ages 3 1/2 to 6. For each level, both core subtests and diagnostic subtests provide supplemental information. The preschool level 2 1/2 to 3 1/2 includes the following four core subtests:

> *Block Building (12 items)*—Requires the child to copy two- and three-dimensional designs with wooden blocks.
> *Verbal Comprehension (36 items)*—Requires the child to point to pictures or manipulate objects in response to oral instructions.
> *Picture Similarities (32 items)*—Requires the child to identify pictures that share a common element or concept.
> *Naming Vocabulary (26 items)*—Requires the child to identify objects or pictures by name.

For 3 1/2 to 6 year olds, the subtests include three of the four previously described subtests (Verbal Comprehension, Naming Vocabulary, and Picture Similarities), plus the following three subtests:

> *Pattern Construction (26 items)*—Requires the child to construct a design using flat squares or solid cubes with black and yellow patterns.
> *Early Number Concepts (28 items)*—Requires the child to answer questions about number, size, or numerical concepts.
> *Copying (20 items)*—Requires the child to reproduce a line drawing provided by the examiner.

As mentioned, diagnostic subtests are also available for testing the preschool child. They are administered for additional probing to gather more comprehensive information. For 2 1/2 to 3 1/2 year olds, the diagnostic subtests are Recall of Digits and Recognition of Pictures. For 3 1/2 to 6 year olds, the same two subtests plus Block Building, Matching Letter-Like Forms, and Recall of Objects are used.

Cognitive Battery—School Age.   For the school-age level, ages 6 through 17, there are six core subtests:

> *Recall of Designs (21 items)*—Requires the individual to reproduce a line drawing that is presented for five seconds and then removed.
> *Word Definitions (42 items)*—The individual must tell the meaning of words ranging from *gift* to *hirsute*.
> *Pattern Construction (26 items)*—Discussed in preschool battery.
> *Matrices (33 items)*—Requires the individual to select from four or six choices the figure that correctly completes an incomplete matrix of abstract figures.

Similarities (34 items)—The individual must identify how three objects or pictures are similar or go together.

Sequential and Quantitative Reasoning (39 items)—The individual must either complete a series of abstract figures by providing one that is missing or find a relationship within two pairs of numbers and apply that relationship to find a missing number.

There are three diagnostic subtests for the school-age level. Those are Recall of Digits, Recall of Objects, and Speed of Information Processing.

School Achievement Tests.

Basic Number Skills (48 items)—Requires the individual to solve computational problems presented on a worksheet.

Spelling (70 items)—Requires the individual to write the correct spelling of words ranging from *in* to *ichthyosaurus*.

Word Reading (90 items)—Requires the individual to read orally words ranging from *the* to *tertiary*.

Interpretation of Results

Various scoring options are available on the DAS. The following is a description of those scores as they are presented in the test manual:

Cognitive subtests—Percentile ranks and T-scores (mean = 50, standard deviation = 10) are provided for each of the individual cognitive subtests. These tables used are on the basis of *ability scores* that are obtained by converting the raw scores using information found in the record form.

General Conceptual Ability and Cluster scores—For each level, a General Conceptual Ability (GCA) score (similar to an IQ) can be determined using a combination of the core subtests. The GCA is presented as a standard score with a mean of 100 and a standard deviation of 15. In addition, at the 3 1/2- to 6-year-old level, a Verbal Ability and Nonverbal Ability Cluster score can be obtained. Similarly, for the school-age level, Verbal Ability, Nonverbal Reasoning Ability, and Spatial Ability Cluster scores can be determined. These scores also are based on a mean of 100 and a standard deviation of 15.

The School Achievement Tests—These individual tests can be interpreted by use of standard scores (mean of 100, standard deviation of 15) and percentiles by both age and grade.

Age Equivalents—These scores are available for all cognitive and achievement subtests.

Score Comparisons—This provides information helpful in profile analysis, including such things as determination of aptitude-achievement discrepancies. Information regarding statistical significance of score differences is also presented.

Technical Characteristics

Normative Sample.   Approximately thirty-five hundred children were included in the sample. The sample was stratified by gender, race or ethnicity, current education, and geographic region. In addition, for the preschool population, stratification was based on educational preschool enrollment. The technical handbook for the DAS provides extensive descriptions of the tryout and standardization samples. Care was taken to ensure that percentages in the sample were similar to those in the U.S. population.

Reliability.   Internal reliabilities for the preschool level of the cognitive battery were in the .70s and .80s for subtests and in the high .80s and .90s for the GCA and Cluster scores. A similar pattern, but with somewhat higher coefficients, was recorded for the school-age level and for the achievement tests.

Test/retest reliabilities for the preschool subtests were low to moderate. Test/retest coefficients for the Cluster scores and GCA were higher, ranging from .79 to .94. For the school-age subtests, correlation coefficients were somewhat higher, whereas the Cluster and GCA coefficients were similar to that in the preschool population. Interrater reliability was also determined for four subtests for which that type of reliability would be relevant. Those coefficients ranged from .90 for Copying subtests to .96 for Similarities subtest.

Validity.   The author provides a considerable amount of evidence for construct validity, including intercorrelations of subtests and composites and results of a factor analysis that supports the cluster scores. Concurrent validity for the DAS for the preschool level with the Wechsler Preschool and Primary Scale of Intelligence–Revised (WPPSI-R) as the criterion was reported. The overall correlation between the GCA and the Full Scale IQ was .89. Correlations between the subtests of the DAS and the WPPSI-R were considerably lower. Coefficients with the Stanford-Binet–4 were also provided with an overall correlation of .77 with the full-scale scores. Correlations with other intelligence measures were in the .60s to .70s range. At the school-age level, correlations with the WISC–R at different age levels ranged from .84 to .91. Coefficients with the Stanford-Binet–4 ranged from .85 to .88; the correlation with the K-ABC was .75. The manual also includes correlations between various subtests and other instruments such as language and measures of nonverbal intellectual functioning.

Correlations between the three achievement tests and the same intellectual measures range from approximately .50 to .70. Correlations between the achievement tests and other achievement measures were higher, generally ranging in the .70 to .80 range. One advantageous feature is the reporting of DAS score profiles of special populations including gifted, and those with mental retardation, learning disabilities, and reading disabilities. This information provides the breakdown of the representation of those types of students in the standardization sample and their subsequent performance on the DAS.

Review of Relevant Research[1]
- The construct validity of the DAS was supported through the use of confirmatory factor analysis (Stone, 1992a & 1992b).
- Independent interpretation of the verbal and nonverbal scales is supported (McIntosh, Mulkins, Pardue-Vaughn, Barnes, & Gridley, 1992).
- Six subgroups of students with learning disabilities were identified using the DAS (McIntosh & Gridley, 1993).
- Platt, Kamphaus, Keltgen, and Gilliland (1991) reviewed the DAS and the available research on the instrument. They noted that it has many strong qualities, including good psychometric characteristics and the use of extended norms that allow the calculation of GCAs as low as 25. They had questions, however, about the nonverbal reasoning and spatial factors and whether the individual subtests should be interpreted.
- Kercher and Sandoval (1991) found that children with reading disabilities displayed a characteristic pattern, performing poorly in achievement and Recall of Digits and Recall of Objects.
- Stone (1994) suggested that the Speed of Information Processing subtest on the DAS would be a good measure to use to identify students who are gifted.

Summary of Research Findings
At the time of the completion of this book, limited research had been reported. In general, however, reports have been favorable; particularly related to the validity of the DAS.

OVERVIEW: DIFFERENTIAL ABILITY SCALES

- *Age level*—Ages 2 1/2 through 17
- *Type of administration*—Individual
- *Technical adequacy*—Good standardization, good reliability and validity (particularly construct validity)
- *Scores yielded*—Percentile ranks, standard scores, age equivalents, grade equivalents
- *Suggested use*—The DAS appears to be one of the better constructed individual intelligence tests. The manuals are thorough, and the technical handbook provides comprehensive descriptions of individual studies regarding its development and subsequent validation. The attention paid to the preschool level is worthy of note. Unlike many other instruments, the DAS reports technical characteristics of the preschool level in some detail, and the information is easy to find in the manual. In addition, the preschool subtests can be administered in significantly less time than many

---

[1]Note: Terminology used in this section throughout the book is consistent with that reported by the author(s) of the original research.

other instruments designed for the same age such as the WPPSI–R or the McCarthy Scales. In fact, the school-age level can also be administered relatively quickly (forty-five to sixty-five minutes). Another notable characteristic is the use of both core and diagnostic subtests as well as guidelines for "extended" and "out-of-level" testing when individuals who are performing considerably lower or higher than others of the same chronological age are evaluated. Although more research is needed to investigate its usefulness, it appears to be a well-developed instrument that will provide an option to other traditional intelligence measures usually employed.

The Kaufman Assessment Battery for Children

The Kaufman Assessment Battery for Children (K-ABC) (Kaufman & Kaufman, 1983) is a widely researched addition to the available intelligence measures. According to the authors, the K-ABC is a measure of both intelligence and achievement (acquired knowledge) for children of ages 2 1/2 through 12 1/2. The theoretical basis for the instrument is drawn heavily from cognitive psychology and neuropsychology. The authors define and measure intellectual ability as the child's ability to perform problems requiring sequential and simultaneous processing. *Sequential processing* refers to the ability to arrange stimuli in sequential or serial order. *Simultaneous processing* requires an individual to integrate and synthesize spatial or analogic information.

Description
The K-ABC has sixteen subtests. Three subtests comprise the sequential-processing scale; seven subtests comprise the simultaneous-processing scale; and six subtests comprise the achievement scale. Certain subtests are appropriate for certain age levels.

Sequential Processing

Hand Movements (ages 2 1/2 through 12 1/2)—This subtest requires the child to reproduce a series of hand movements demonstrated by the examiner.
Number Recall (ages 2 1/2 through 12 1/2)—In this subtest, the child must repeat a series of verbally presented digits.
Word Order (ages 4 through 12 1/2)—The child must touch a series of pictures in the same sequence that is verbally presented by the examiner.

Simultaneous Processing

Magic Window (ages 2 1/2 through 4)—The child must identify a picture that is exposed only partially at any one time.
Face Recognition (ages 2 1/2 through 4)—The child is exposed briefly to a photograph that shows one or two faces and must pick out the faces from a photograph of a group of faces.

Gestalt Closure (ages 2 1/2 through 12 1/2)—The child must name an object that is only partially drawn.

Triangles (ages 4 through 12 1/2)—The child is required to reproduce various models using identical triangle puzzle pieces.

Matrix Analogies (ages 5 through 12 1/2)—The child must choose a picture that best completes a visual analogy.

Spatial Memory (ages 5 through 12 1/2)—The child is shown a page with several pictures placed in certain areas and must remember the placement of the pictures.

Photo Series (ages 6 through 12 1/2)—The child must place several photographs of an event (for example, a candle melting) in chronological order.

Achievement

Expressive Vocabulary (ages 2 1/2 through 4)—The child must name objects in a photograph.

Faces and Places (ages 2 1/2 through 12 1/2)—The child must name a fictional character, place, or well-known person shown in a photograph.

Arithmetic (ages 3 through 12 1/2)—The child must demonstrate school-related mathematics abilities on a number of tasks.

Riddles (ages 3 through 12 1/2)—The child is given a list of characteristics of a concrete or abstract concept and must determine that concept.

Reading/Decoding (ages 5 through 12 1/2)—The child must identify letters and read words.

Reading/Understanding (ages 7 through 12 1/2)—The child must execute commands that he or she reads in sentences.

Interpretation of Results

Standard scores (mean = 100; standard deviation = 15) are available for the sequential-processing scale, simultaneous-processing scale, achievement scale, and for a mental-processing composite (sequential and simultaneous). In addition, national percentile ranks and sociocultural percentile ranks are also available for each of these four areas. The sociocultural percentile rank allows a child's scores to be compared with the scores of children of similar ethnic and socioeconomic background. Sociocultural data are obtainable for the subtests in the sequential-processing and simultaneous-processing scales (scaled score mean = 10; standard deviation = 3) and for the achievement subtests (standard score mean = 100; standard deviation = 15). A profile sheet is available to provide direct comparisons of the scores as well as to determine discrepancies between the mental-processing and achievement scores. An interpretation manual is available separately and includes research reports and possible uses with exceptional children.

Technical Characteristics

Normative Sample. Two thousand children from twenty-two states were included; stratified sample based on 1980 census; exceptional children were also included. This normative sample overlapped with that used for the Vineland Adaptive Behavior Scales (see Chapter 10).

Reliability.   Split-half reliability coefficients ranged from .86 to .93 (preschool) and from .89 to .97 (elementary). Test-retest coefficients increased with age, ranging from .77 to .95 for preschoolers to .87 to .97 for a sample of children ages 9–12 1/2.

Validity.   Evidence for construct and criterion-related validity is relatively strong. The interpretation manual summarizes more than forty validity studies with a variety of populations.

Review of Relevant Research
The K-ABC received a great deal of attention when it first appeared on the market. Entire issues of journals were devoted to related reviews and research. The following is a discussion of the major issues that have been addressed:

- Some researchers believe the K-ABC has adequate construct validity (Kaufman & McLean, 1986; Majorski, 1984), but others question the theoretical and psychometric validity claims of the test (Hopkins & Hodge, 1984; Sternberg, 1984; Weibe, 1986).
- There are many questions about the simultaneous and sequencing processing components of the K-ABC (Bracken & Howell, 1989; Strommen, 1988). Some researchers question whether the two components can be specified from achievement and from each other (Hall & Goetz, 1984). Das (1984) indicated that the processes are actually measures of nonverbal and verbal abilities. Gridley, Miller, Barke, Fischer, and Smith (1990) found no evidence of the two constructs with a preschool population. Swanson, Bradenburg-Ayres, and Wallace (1989) found no evidence with gifted students.
- A lack of long-term reliability data and predictive validity has been noted (Mehrens, 1984); however, one study reports adequate stability when used with at-risk preschool children (Lyon & Smith, 1987). Another study showed that stability improved with the subject's increasing age (Kamphaus & Reynolds, 1984).
- The K-ABC does not provide an adequate data base from which to propose remediation (Weibe, 1986). It has been suggested that the test's components be interpreted as reading achievement and verbal reasoning to facilitate educational decision making (Dunbar & Keith, 1984).
- It is inconclusive whether weak processes can be trained (Hritcko & Salvia, 1984). Kaufman (1984) opposes the ability-training approach, although others are proponents. Simultaneous processing was reported to be more amenable to change in one study (Lyon & Smith, 1987).
- Further research needs to be done in the area of proper interpretation (Dunbar & Keith, 1984). Profiles must be interpreted cautiously (Hopkins & Hodge, 1984); it must be noted that significant processing differences are common in

the normal population (Chatman, Reynolds, & Willson, 1984). A microcomputer program, *ASSIST,* is available for scoring and is helpful in increasing scoring accuracy and reducing scoring time (Merz, 1984).

- The K-ABC has moderate positive correlations with WISC-R for learning-disabled, mildly retarded, and normal children (Klanderman, Perney, & Kroeschell, 1985; Naglieri, 1985; Smith, Lyon, Hunter, & Boyd, 1988). There is also some indication that the factor structure for learning-disabled (LD) and non-LD students is similar on the K-ABC (Kaufman & McLean, 1986). The K-ABC appears useful in identifying dyslexic readers (Hooper & Hynd, 1986) and other LD children, although a characteristic LD profile was not found (Naglieri, 1985).

- More research is needed to support the K-ABC's claim of being a relatively nondiscriminatory test (Naglieri, 1986). There is some evidence that the reliability of the test is similar for black and white children (Matazow, Kamphaus, Stanton, & Reynolds, 1991) and that the items are not racially biased (Wilson, Nolan, Reynolds, & Kamphaus, 1989). However, Jensen (1986) noted that the reduced difference between black and white scores (compared to the WISC-R) was not the result of greater validity or of a less biased measurement of IQ. In addition, Valencia and Rankin (1988) reported that the K-ABC is not as good a predictor of achievement for Mexican-American students as it is for white students.

- The nonverbal K-ABC subtests adequately differentiate intellectual functioning in school-age deaf children when either pantomime and gestures or American Sign Language are used (Kirby & Porter, 1986); however, caution should be taken when using it with hearing-impaired preschoolers, because the test provides only three subtests (Telzrow, 1984).

- It has been suggested that the test be supplemented with paper-and-pencil tasks in such areas as arithmetic, language, and behavior (Telzrow, 1984). In addition, the Bender-Gestalt has been suggested as a valuable aid to be used with the simultaneous scale (Haddad, 1986).

- English-speaking Mexican-American children score generally higher on the simultaneous than on the sequential scale and show a restricted range of all scores involved with verbal scales (Valencia, 1984).

- The test should be used with caution to identify gifted children (Harrison, 1988); many subtests have low ceilings, there is a lack of complex intellectual content in the mental processing scales, and it has low concurrent predictive validity for general academic achievement (Hessler, 1985). In addition, the factor structure for gifted students is different from that reported for the standardization sample (Swanson et al., 1989).

- The K-ABC is of limited use with preschool children having lower levels of cognitive ability (Bloom et al., 1988). Further, the K-ABC results in lower scores with preschool children than the Wechsler Scale (Wade, Kutsick, & Vance, 1988).

- There are questions concerning the representativeness of the norms used for the K-ABC (Hopkins & Hodges, 1984).

- The factor structure for the K-ABC and the WISC-R is similar. The verbal-comprehension, perceptual-organization, and freedom-from-distractibility factors from the WISC-R corresponded to the achievement, simultaneous-processing, and sequential-processing components from the K-ABC, respectively (Kaufman & McLean, 1986).
- The use of K-ABC subtest patterns for diagnostic purposes should be avoided (Glutting, McGrath, Kamphaus, & McDermott, 1992).
- Students with Down syndrome and Fragile X syndrome scored lower in the sequential processing than simultaneous processing or achievement section (Hodapp et al., 1992).
- The K-ABC was not helpful in differentiating autistic from nonautistic children; further, the use of the simultaneous- and sequential-processing scales was not supported (Stavrou & French, 1992).
- In a review of the K-ABC, Kaufman, Kamphaus, and Kaufman (1985) noted that

    1. The sequential processing component is less reliable than the simultaneous component.
    2. There is a heavy emphasis on visual stimuli, making the test inappropriate for children with visual problems.
    3. The test does not adequately measure verbal reasoning and spontaneous expression.
    4. There are too few manipulative tasks for preschoolers and too few easy items for children ages two to six.

Summary of Research Findings

Much of the research on the K-ABC has focused on its construct validity. Specifically, the meaning of the simultaneous and sequential processing components has been investigated with unclear results. Criterion-related validity is generally good. Research on its use with exceptional students is equivocal. There is evidence that it can be helpful with students with LD and students with hearing impairments. Its use with students with visual impairments and gifted students has been discouraged. Its use with young, preschool children also appears to be limited. The nondiscriminatory nature of the K-ABC has also been debated. More research will undoubtedly shed light on a number of issues.

OVERVIEW: KAUFMAN ASSESSMENT BATTERY FOR CHILDREN

- *Age level*—2 1/2 to 12 1/2 years old
- *Type of administration*—Individual
- *Technical adequacy*—Good standardization, adequate reliability, questionable validity (construct)
- *Scores yielded*—Scaled scores, standard scores, national percentile ranks, sociocultural percentile ranks

■ *Suggested use*—The K-ABC was a much awaited instrument when it was published more than a decade ago. As such, it has received much attention in the professional literature. The technical characteristics of the instrument are acceptable, and the addition of the sociocultural percentile ranks is a useful feature. This addition, in fact, helped give the instrument an early favorable reputation as a nondiscriminatory assessment measure. Questions about this as well as other claims (such as usefulness for diagnosis of LD because of intelligence-achievement comparisons), however, have not been answered adequately. There is also some question about the interpretation of the various processing components. Further research and continued use will hopefully answer many of the questions regarding the interpretation of the K-ABC. It should be noted that another instrument can be used with older individuals. The Kaufman Adolescent and Adult Intelligence Test (KAIT) can be used with persons ages 11 through adulthood. Also available is a short screening test, the Kaufman Brief Intelligence Test (KBIT). The KBIT is discussed later in this chapter.

Stanford-Binet Intelligence Scale–Fourth Edition

The fourth edition of the Stanford-Binet Intelligence Scale (SBIS-4) (Thorndike, Hagen, & Sattler, 1986) retained many of the characteristics of the earlier versions yet made some significant changes. According to the authors, the SBIS-4 was constructed for the following purposes:

1. To help differentiate between students who are mentally retarded and those who have specific learning disabilities
2. To help educators and psychologists understand why a particular student is having difficulty in school
3. To help identify gifted students
4. To study the development of cognitive skills of individuals from ages 2 to adult (p. 2)

The SBIS-4 includes fifteen subtests that fit into a three-level hierarchical model that includes a general intelligence level at the top, three broad factors (crystallized abilities, fluid-analytic abilities, and short-term memory) at the second level, and three narrower factors (verbal reasoning, quantitative reasoning, and abstract-visual reasoning) at the third level (see Figure 9.1 on page 184).

Description of Subtests

Vocabulary (46 items)—This subtest includes fourteen picture-vocabulary items and thirty-two oral-vocabulary items. This subtest is also used to determine the starting point for the other fourteen subtests.

		g	
Crystallized Abilities		**Fluid-Analytic Abilities**	**Short-Term Memory**
Verbal Reasoning	**Quantitative Reasoning**	**Abstract/Visual Reasoning**	
Vocabulary	Quantitative	Pattern Analysis	Bead Memory
Comprehension	Number Series	Copying	Memory for Sentences
Absurdities	Equation Building	Matrices	Memory for Digits
Verbal Relations		Paper Folding and Cutting	Memory for Objects

FIGURE 9.1   Hierarchical Model of the Stanford-Binet Intelligence Scale

Reprinted with permission of THE RIVERSIDE PUBLISHING COMPANY from page 4 of *Stanford-Binet Intelligence Scale: Guide for Administering and Scoring the Fourth Edition* by R. L. Thorndike, E. P. Hagen, and J. M. Sattler. THE RIVERSIDE PUBLISHING COMPANY, 8240 W. Bryn Mawr Avenue, Chicago, IL 60631. Copyright © 1986.

Bead Memory (42 items)—This subtest requires the examinee to look at a picture of beads of various sizes and colors that are arranged in a certain pattern and then reproduce the pattern placing beads on a stick.

Quantitative (34 items)—This subtest measures quantitative skills and concepts.

Memory for Sentences (42 items)—In this subtest, the examiner reads a sentence that must be repeated by the examinee.

Pattern Analysis (36 items)—The examinee must reproduce a cube pattern constructed by the examiner or presented in a picture.

Comprehension (42 items)—This subtest includes identification of body parts and questions requiring verbal reasoning.

Absurdities (32 items)—The examinee must indicate why a picture or parts of a picture are absurd.

Memory for Digits (12 items)—The examinee must listen to a series of digits and then repeat them in the same or in reverse order.

Copying (28 items)—The examinee must either duplicate block patterns or copy geometric figures using a pencil and paper.

Memory for Objects (14 items)—The examinee is shown a series of pictures and then must identify the correct sequence.

Matrices (26 items)—The examinee must complete a series of incomplete matrices.

Number Series (26 items)—The examinee must identify the next number in a series of numbers that is presented following a certain rule.

Paper Folding and Cutting (18 items)—The examiner folds and cuts a piece of paper in a certain way and the examinee must identify from several choices how the paper will look unfolded.

Verbal Relations (18 items)—The examinee must look for similarities and differences in a set of words.

Equation Building (18 items)—The examinee must arrange numbers and mathematical signs to form number sentences.

Interpretation of Results

Standard scores are available for individual subtests (mean = 50; standard deviation = 8). It is also possible to obtain standard scores for Verbal Reasoning, Abstract/Visual Reasoning, Quantitative Reasoning, Short-Term Memory, and Total Test Composite (mean = 100; standard deviation = 16).

Technical Characteristics

Normative Sample. More than five thousand individuals from all fifty states stratified according to ethnic status, geographic region, community size, and sex.

Reliability. Internal consistency coefficients were generally above .90. Test-retest coefficients ranged from .71 (quantitative reasoning) to .91 (total test composite) for a preschool sample and from .51 to .90 for an elementary school sample.

Validity. Data supporting construct validity are presented in the technical manual. Criterion-related validity coefficients with the Wechsler Scales were above .80. The correlation between the total test composite and the K-ABC composite was .89. Criterion-related validity for samples of exceptional students was somewhat lower.

Review of Relevant Research

- The SBIS-4 had adequate validity with LD students; there was some support for the validity of the fluid/crystallized interpretation model as well (Knight, Baker, & Minder, 1990).
- The SBIS-4 is useful for assessing black students classified as behavior disordered or mentally retarded but not LD (Greene, Sapp, & Chissom, 1990).
- Gifted students score considerably lower on the SBIS-4 than on the Wechsler Intelligence Scale for Children–Revised (WISC-R) (Carvajal & Weaver, 1989; Phelps, 1989). In addition, gifted students score lower on the Short Term Memory composite than on the other SBIS-4 composites (Carvajal, 1988).
- Factor analysis of the SBIS-4 does not support the presence of the four composites (Gridley & McIntosh, 1991; Reynolds, Kamphaus, & Rosenthal, 1988)
- Choi and Proctor (1994) analyzed the administration errors on the various subtests of the SBIS-4. They found that Pattern Analysis had the highest number of administration errors with approximately two thirds of the test administrators making some type of error.

- The Full Scale IQs from the SBIS-4 and the Wechsler Preschool and Primary Scale of Intelligence–Revised (WPPSI-R) were similar when administered to young children. The Verbal IQ, however, was approximately five points lower on the WPPSI-R (McCrowell & Nagle, 1994).
- Validity coefficients between the SBIS-4 and the Leiter International Performance Scale (a nonverbal measure of intelligence) was .70. In addition, the SBIS-4 correlated .70 with the Vineland Adaptive Behavior Scales (Atkinson, Bevc, Dickens, & Blackwell, 1992).
- A six-subtest short form of the SBIS-4 accurately approximated the composite standard score for children whose IQ was below 79 (Atkinson, 1991).
- Wilson (1992) argued that the SBIS-4 is poorly suited for the assessment of young children (under 5 years of age) with mild mental retardation and individuals of any age with severe mental retardation.
- The SBIS-4 yielded significantly higher scores than did the WISC-R for students with lower IQs but yielded significantly lower scores for students with higher IQs. The two tests yielded similar scores for students with IQs between 70 and 90 (Prewett & Matavitch, 1992).
- Support for the use of the SBIS-4 verbal comprehension score at ages 2 and 3 and the nonverbal reasoning factor at age 3 was provided (Shanahan & Bradley-Johnson, 1992).
- The SBIS-4 correlated significantly with the Matrix Analogies Test short form (Prewell & Fahrney, 1994).
- Short forms of the SBIS-4, when used with older adolescents and young adults, tend to underestimate the total test score (Nagle & Bell, 1993).
- The SBIS-4 and the K-ABC correlated .70 for a sample of gifted students, although the SBIS-4 yielded higher scores (Hayden, Furlong, & Linnemeyer, 1988). The SBIS-4 also had high correlations with the K-ABC for LD students (Smith, Martin, & Lyon, 1989).
- A nonverbal short form of the SBIS-4 for use with individuals with hearing impairments, speech/language impairments, and limited English proficiency has been developed (Glaub & Kamphaus, 1991).
- The SBIS-4 yielded strong correlations with the K-ABC although there was little support for the theoretical structure of either instrument (Rothlisberg & McIntosh, 1991).
- The SBIS-4 has shown some promise for use with the preschool populations (Krohn & Lamp, 1989; Smith & Bauer, 1989).
- A computer program has been developed to aid in the evaluation of subtest scores (Madle, 1989).
- Glutting (1989) in a review of the SBIS-4 reached the following conclusions:

    1. It should not be used with preschoolers suspected of being in the retarded range.
    2. It provides sufficient ceiling for use with gifted students at any age.
    3. There is reasonable construct validity for the composite (the score that psychologists should interpret).

4. Lack of appropriate factor structure suggests that the four area scores should not be interpreted.
5. Abbreviated forms of the test should be avoided.

• In a survey of school psychologists, Obringer (1988) reported the following advantages of the SBIS-4:

1. It is based on current psychological theory.
2. It has a broad coverage of information-processing capabilities.
3. It includes subtests that are attractive and challenging to examinees.

Its disadvantages included the following:

1. It has factor analyses that do not support the structure of the scale (interpretation of the composite score is the only one that is recommended).
2. Some of its subtests are difficult to administer and score.
3. Its standard age scores for subtests are nontraditional and difficult to evaluate.

Summary of Research Findings

In general, research on the SBIS-4 supports the use of the global score although the validity of the individual area scores has been questioned. There is also research suggesting that the SBIS-4 yields scores different from those of other traditional IQ measures, particularly with gifted students. More research is necessary to clarify its strengths and limitations with preschool children and with different types of exceptional children.

OVERVIEW: STANFORD-BINET INTELLIGENCE SCALE–4

■ *Age level*—2 to adult
■ *Type of administration*—Individual
■ *Technical adequacy*—Good standardization, acceptable reliability and validity
■ *Scores yielded*—Standard scores
■ *Suggested use*—The fourth edition of the SBIS is one of the major individually administered intelligence tests, although many school psychologists still appear to prefer the third edition of the instrument, particularly for young children. The fourth edition, however, is the most appropriate to use. Certainly the earlier versions of the Stanford-Binet have played an important role in the history of intelligence testing. Data indicate that the SBIS-4 (at least the global composite) is an adequate measure of general intelligence. There is some question whether the four individual composites should be used, however. Several studies have been conducted that do not support the presence of the four specific areas. Users should also be aware that the SBIS-4 yields different scores than other widely used instruments with certain populations, such as students who are gifted.

Wechsler Intelligence Scale for Children–Third Edition (Wechsler, 1991)

The WISC-III is a relatively recent revision of the WISC-R, which was one of the most popular, most widely used individual intelligence tests. The WISC-III is one of three scales developed by Wechsler. The others are the Wechsler Preschool and Primary Scale of Intelligence–Revised (used for children 3 to 7 years old) and the Wechsler Adult Intelligence Scale–Revised (used for individuals from age 16 to adult). The WISC-III is used with children from 6 to 16 years old and, therefore, of the three scales is the most used in schools.

The WISC-III, like all of Wechsler's scales, is based on the concept of global intelligence. In other words, intelligence is viewed as a multifaceted concept as opposed to a single entity. Specifically, the WISC-III has both a verbal section and a performance section. Because of the type of information yielded by the WISC-III, as well as the frequency with which this test is administered, it is one of the most widely researched instruments in special education.

Description

The WISC-III has ten subtests and three optional subtests. Six subtests comprise the verbal section and seven comprise the performance section. To avoid the administration of unnecessary items, the subtests have guidelines for discontinuing the testing after the child makes a certain number of consecutive errors. Also, the subtests on the performance section are timed.

Verbal Section

Information (30 items)—This subtest measures the student's knowledge of general information and facts.

Similarities (19 items)—This subtest measures a student's ability to perceive the common element of two terms.

Arithmetic (24 items)—This subtest measures the student's ability to solve problems requiring arithmetic computation and reasoning. This is primarily an oral subtest requiring concentration. Additional items were designed to make it more sensitive to the upper and lower age levels,

Vocabulary (30 items)—In this subtest, the student is told a word and must orally define it. Items range in difficulty.

Comprehension (18 items)—This subtest measures the social, moral, and ethical judgment of the student, who must answer questions such as "What are you supposed to do if you find someone's wallet or purse in a store?" and "Why do cars have seat belts?"

Digit Span—This subtest includes two parts: *Digits Forward* and *Digits Backward*. The student is given a series of digits at a rate of one digit per second. Digits forward requires the student to say them back exactly. Digits backward requires the student to say the numbers in reverse order. There are seven progressively longer series of digits for both sections.

Performance Section

Picture Completion (30 items)—In this subtest, the student is shown a picture in which an important element is missing. The student must either verbalize or point to the missing element. Color artwork has been added to the WISC-III.

Picture Arrangement (14 items)—In this subtest, the student is given a series of pictures that represent a story but are in incorrect order. The task is to sequence the pictures in the correct order. Again, color artwork is used.

Block Design (12 items)—In this subtest, the student must look at pictures of certain designs and reproduce these using red and white blocks. This subtest basically measures visual analysis and synthesis.

Object Assembly (5 items)—This subtest for visual organization and synthesis requires the student to put together five jigsaw puzzles.

Coding—This subtest requires the student to copy geometric symbols that are paired or coded with other symbols within a certain time limit. There are two parts, A for children under age eight, and B for individuals of age eight and older. Figure 9.2 shows an example of the type of task included in the coding subtest. The coding subtest measures visual-motor speed, coordination, and to a certain extent, memory. It is the only subtest (other than the supplementary mazes subtest) on the WISC-III that uses a pencil-and-paper format.

Mazes—This subtest requires the child to use skills in visual planning to complete a number of progressively more difficult mazes.

Symbol Search—In this subtest, the student is required to visually scan a group of symbols to determine if a target symbol is present.

Interpretation of Results

Each subtest raw score is converted to a scaled score with a mean of 10 and a standard deviation of 3. This allows for direct comparisons between subtests and

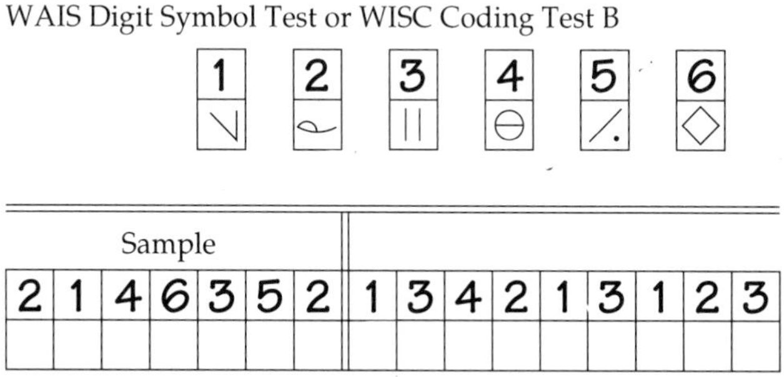

WAIS Digit Symbol Test or WISC Coding Test B

FIGURE 9.2   Tasks Similar to the Coding Subtest from the WISC-III

Courtesy of The Psychological Corporation.

led, in part, to the profile analysis of the WISC-R that has been criticized (see the section on review of relevant research). The WISC-III also yields Full-Scale, Verbal, and Performance IQs, each having a mean of 100 and a standard deviation of 15. Considerable diagnostic emphasis has been placed—perhaps erroneously—on the difference between the Verbal and Performance IQs. In addition to the scoring options that were available for the WISC-R, new user tables are included in the WISC-III. These include tables that allow the interpretation of intersubtest scatter, verbal-performance differences, digits forward–digits backward comparisons, and the significance of subtests scores that differ from the mean of all the subtests. Also included are Index Score Equivalents (mean = 100, SD = 15) for four new factors determined through factor analysis. These are Verbal Comprehension (Information, Similarities, Vocabulary, and Comprehension), Perceptual Organization (Picture Completion, Picture Arrangement, Block Design, and Object Assembly), Freedom from Distractibility (Arithmetic and Digit Span), and Processing Speed (Coding and Symbol Search).

Technical Characteristics

Normative Sample.   The WISC-III used a nationally representative sample (similar to the 1988 census) of twenty-two hundred. Variables considered were geographic region, race/ethnicity, and parent educational level (to determine socioeconomic status). There were an equal number of boys and girls.

Reliability.   Split–half reliability coefficients were determined for all subtests except Coding and Symbol Search (test-retest was computed). These coefficients ranged from approximately .60–.95. The coefficients for the three IQs were all .90 or better, whereas the coefficients for the four factors were in the .80–.95 range.

Validity.   Construct validity of the WISC-III was established using factor analysis and intercorrelations of the subtests and scales. Correlations with the WISC-R are also presented (approximately .60–.80 for subtests, .80–.90 for IQs). Criterion-related validity studies with a number of intelligence and achievement tests are discussed in the manual. In addition, studies reporting WISC-III data for different types of exceptional students are also presented.

Review of Relevant Research
- Confirmatory factor analysis supported the use of the four factors from the WISC-III (Verbal Comprehension, Perceptual Organization, Freedom from Distractibility, and Processing Speed). Further, the Freedom from Distractibility factor appears to measure a component that is important in solving mathematics problems and, therefore, measures more than simply distractibility (Roid, Prifitera, & Weiss, 1993).
- In one review of the WISC-III, Carroll (1993) noted several shortcomings. First, the factorial structure of the WISC-III was not a significant improvement

over earlier versions. Second, there were questionable aspects of the four index scores, particularly Freedom from Distractibility and Processing Speed.

- Kamphaus, Benson, Hutchinson, and Platt (1994) conducted a confirmatory factor analysis on the WISC-III and found general support for the two, three, and four factor conceptualizations, although the clinical importance of the four factor model was unclear.

- Edwards and Edwards (1993) noted that the WISC-III is well constructed with satisfactory reliability, although, as with the WISC-R, its use to plan intervention strategies should be discouraged.

- Bracken, McCallum, and Crain (1993) reported that the WISC-III reliabilities are slightly higher than those from the WISC-R. Similar to a trend found in the WISC-R, reliabilities tend to increase with age for the verbal subtests and decrease with age for the performance subtests.

- Graf and Hinton (1994), in a study of the WISC-R and WISC-III, noted that the WISC-III appears to be more difficult than the WISC-R at the higher IQ ranges and less difficult at the lower IQ ranges.

- Lowered scores have been reported when comparing the WISC-III to the WISC-R in several studies. In the WISC-III test manual, Wechsler (1991) reported WISC-III scores that were approximately two points lower on the verbal section, seven points lower on the performance section, and five points lower for the full scale than the comparable scores on the WISC-R. Also, in a clinical sample of students with learning disabilities and ADHD, the WISC-III was about five points lower on the verbal and performance sections and six points lower overall.

- In a study of a group of children with reading disabilities, Newby, Recht, Caldwell, and Schaefer (1993) reported a five-point decline in verbal IQ when the WISC-III was administered, although there was no decrease in performance IQ from the administration of the WISC-R to the WISC-III.

- Although the WISC-III correlated .81 with the IQ from the SBIS-4, the IQs were considerably lower for the WISC-III. For example, the Full Scale IQ was 9.4 points lower, the Verbal IQ 13.1 points lower and Performance IQ 8.1 points lower than their counterpart scores from the SBIS-4 with a population of low SES students referred for special education (Prewett & Matavitch, 1994).

- Javorsky (1993) used the Kaufman Brief Intelligence Test to predict the WISC-III IQ in a population of psychiatric patients. He also provided a regression equation to help identify the more global WISC-III IQ score from the K-BIT information.

- Dumont and Faro (1993) created a short form for the WISC-III that was accurate in classifying students who had learning disabilities.

- The *Kaufman WISC-III Integrated Interpretive System* (K-WIIS) is a computerized scoring system for the WISC-III (Kaufman, Kaufman, & Dougherty, 1995). This software package allows for the interpretation and integration of WISC-III scores with background and behavioral information to provide a profile of the child's cognitive and intellectual strengths and weaknesses.

- Hishinuma and Yamakawa (1993) reported that both the construct and criterion-related validity of the WISC-III were supported in a population of exceptional students and others who were at risk.
- Maller and Braden (1993) reported that the WISC-III was useful with adolescents who are deaf. They reported results that supported the concurrent validity of the predictor of academic achievement than the performance scale. They cautioned, however, that the administration of the verbal subtests is risky because of the possibility of the results being interpreted as estimates of cognitive ability. They also suggested that the Full-Scale IQ not be used with adolescents who are deaf.
- Students with learning disabilities and ADHD performed lower on the so-called ACID profile (Arithmetic, Coding, Information, Digit Span), and on the Freedom from Distractibility and Processing Speed factors than did subjects from the general standardization sample (Prifitera & Dersh, 1993).
- ADHD children had lower scores on the Freedom from Distractibility and Processing Speed factors than did their peers without ADHD. Interestingly they performed better on the Perceptual Organization factor than did the comparison group (Schwean, Saklofske, Yackulic, & Quinn, 1993). They also reported, however, that the validity of the test with ADHD children was similar to that for those without ADHD based on intersubtest correlations.
- For students with speech and language impairments, the performance section from the WISC-III seems to be a stronger and more consistent measure of nonverbal intelligence than the performance section from the WISC-R (Phelps, Laguori, Nisewaner, & Parker, 1993).
- Stone (1994) suggested that the Processing Speed index on the WISC-III might be a viable score to use to identify children who are gifted.
- Wilkinson (1993) found that subtest scatter, verbal-performance discrepancies, and other types of variability were common in students with IQs above 120.
- The WISC-III correlated positively with the scores from the Key-Math Revised test and the Peabody Picture Vocabulary Test-Revised (Slate, Jones, Graham, & Bower, 1994).

The following information from the previous edition of the WISC-III (the WISC-R) might also be relevant.

- The factor structure of the WISC-R is remarkably similar for LD, emotionally disturbed, and mentally retarded students (Schooler, Beebe, & Koepke, 1978), as well as for children from different ethnic backgrounds (Reschly, 1978; Taylor, Ziegler, & Partenio, 1985; Taylor & Ziegler, 1987). The factor structure for gifted students is not as clear, however (MacMann, Plasket, Barnett, & Siler, 1991).
- Dudley-Marling, Kaufman, and Tarver (1981) reviewed the literature about WISC-R profiles of LD children. They focused on three specific questions that had previously been addressed in the literature: (1) Do LD children have high

Performance IQ–low Verbal IQ? (2) Do LD children exhibit greater subtest scatter than non-LD children? and (3) Do LD children exhibit a characteristic profile? They found that the answers to the first two questions were inconclusive. Regarding the third question, they concluded that "although there may be a characteristic WISC(-R) profile for LD individuals as a group, few individual LD children may actually conform to this pattern. Therefore, differential diagnosis should not be based on patterns of WISC(-R) performance" (p. 317–318). Similarly, Taylor, Ziegler, and Partenio (1984) found an average V–P discrepancy of almost 11 points for a large, nonhandicapped sample. These findings minimize the use of a profile analysis in differentiating LD children from non-LD children.

- Gutkin (1979) looked at subtest scatter as a possible aid in differential diagnosis. He found no significant differences among various special education categories (for example, emotionally disturbed, LD, brain injured). He also found that 40 percent of the non-special education group exhibited as much or more scatter as the special education groups. Similarly, Tabachnick (1979) suggested that subtest scatter should not be used as a means of diagnosing learning disabilities.
- Research has not supported item bias or psychometric bias for the WISC-R (Sandoval, 1979), although mean difference bias has been well documented for ethnic minority students (for example, Reschly & Ross-Reynolds, 1980; Taylor & Partenio, 1983) and children of low socioeconomic status (Reschly, 1979).

Summary of Research Findings

The two previous versions of the WISC-III (WISC and WISC-R) were two of the more widely researched norm-referenced instruments. There is every indication that research will continue on this newest version. To date, much of the research on the WISC-III has focused on issues of construct validity, comparisons of scores with the WISC-R, and its use with different types of exceptional students. In general, there has been overall support for its factor structure although more research is needed. Not surprisingly, the WISC-III yields lower scores than the WISC-R so that the instruments should not be used interchangeably. Scores from the WISC-III might also be lower than those from other intelligence measures (e.g., the Stanford-Binet–4). Research to date also has shown that the WISC-III is useful with different types of students including those with hearing impairments, language disabilities, AD/HD, and those students thought to be at risk.

Although caution should be made about generalizing results of WISC-R research to the WISC-III (Sattler, 1992), it is expected that the relationships between the research from the two instruments will be similar (Edwards & Edwards, 1993). Particular research with the WISC-R that might have relevance for the WISC-III is related to the inappropriate use of subtest scatter and verbal-performance discrepancies in the identification of learning disabilities. Another is the well-documented lack of evidence of psychometric bias for students of different ethnic background. Clearly, these areas need to be pursued with the WISC-III.

OVERVIEW: WESCHLER INTELLIGENCE SCALE FOR CHILDREN–III

- *Age level*—6 to 16 years old
- *Type of administration*—Individual
- *Technical adequacy*—Good standardization, adequate reliability for subtests, good reliability for IQs, and good validity (based primarily on literature)
- *Scores yielded*—Scaled scores, verbal and performance IQs, full-scale IQ, index score equivalents
- *Suggested use*—The WISC-R was the most widely used intelligence test for school-age students and was well constructed and widely researched. It is anticipated that the WISC-III will continue that tradition. The WISC-III measures a number of intellectual skills in both the verbal and performance areas. One additional feature of the WISC-III is that it was normed concurrently with the Weschler Individual Achievement Test (WIAT). (See Chapter 13).

    Results of the WISC-R were overinterpreted and misused. Hopefully, information learned from the WISC-R will be applied to the WISC-III. For example, the IQ from the WISC-R is a fairly good predictor of school performance but should not be used as a measure of intellectual potential. Profiles from the WISC-R (for example, subtest scatter, verbal-performance discrepancies) have also been used incorrectly. Research has indicated that a considerable amount of variation in intratest scores exists within the "normal" population. The use of variability as basis for diagnostic and classification decisions is therefore not advised. Evidence exists that scores on the WISC-III are lower than the scores from other intelligence tests including the WISC-R. Research, to date, has been supportive of the validity and other characteristics of the test although more data are needed.

    In summary, the WISC-III is a well–standardized instrument that can be used confidently to determine an individual's performance in a number of intellectual skill areas. The results should not be overused, however. A book, *Intelligent Testing with the WISC-III* (Kaufman, 1994), is available that provides in-depth analysis of the use of WISC-III data.

Woodcock-Johnson–Revised (Cognitive)

The Woodcock-Johnson Psychoeducational Battery–Revised (WJ-R) (Woodcock & Johnson, 1989) is a revision of the original instrument published in 1977. The WJ-R is a wide-range set of individually administered tests designed to measure cognitive abilities, scholastic aptitude, and achievement. One difference between the WJ and the WJ-R is the omission of the Interest Battery in the revised edition. The WJ-R consists of an Achievement Battery (discussed in Chapter 13) and a Cognitive Battery.

According to the authors, the WJ-R can be used for a variety of purposes, including diagnosis or identification of specific weaknesses, determination of psychoeducational discrepancies, program placement, planning IEPs, guidance, assessing growth, program evaluation, and research. Norms are available for individuals ages 24 months to 95 years. There are also separate norms available for college and university students. There are both "standard" and "supplemental" cognitive batteries.

Description

The cognitive tests included in the WJ-R are based on the Horn–Cattell theory, an extension of the fluid/crystallized model of intelligence. There are seven broad cognitive factors included: long-term retrieval, short-term memory, processing speed, auditory processing, visual processing, comprehension-knowledge, and fluid reasoning. A brief description of the tests in the cognitive battery follows.

Standard Cognitive Battery.   Each of the seven tests in the standard battery measures the seven corresponding cognitive factors noted in the previous discussion.

> *Memory for Names (72 items)*—This is an auditory-visual association task using unfamiliar stimuli.
> *Memory for Sentences (32 items)*—This measures the ability to remember and repeat phrases presented auditorily.
> *Visual Matching (70 items)*—This timed test requires the individual to locate and circle the two identical numbers in a row of six numbers.
> *Incomplete Words (40 items)*—This is an auditory closure task in which words with one or more phonemes missing are presented.
> *Visual Closure (49 items)*—This measures the ability to identify pictures that have been altered (e.g., distortions, missing lines).
> *Picture Vocabulary (58 items)*—This requires the individual to name pictured objects.
> *Analysis-Synthesis (35 items)*—This reasoning task involves the presentation of an incomplete logic puzzle for which the individual must present the missing components.

Supplemental Cognitive Battery.   The supplemental battery consists of fourteen subtests. The first seven, described in the following list, coincide with the seven cognitive factors, consistent with the standard battery. The other seven subtests (Delayed Recall–Memory for Names, Delayed Recall–Visual/Auditory Learning, Numbers Reversed, Sound Patterns, Spatial Relations, Listening Comprehension, Verbal Analogies) are used selectively to probe specific cognitive areas.

> *Visual/Auditory Learning (7 stories)*—Measures the ability to associate new visual symbols with familiar words and then "read" sentences consisting of the verbal symbols.

Memory for Words (27 items)—Requires the individual to repeat a series of unrelated words in the correct sequence.

Cross Out (37 items)—A timed task measuring the ability to scan visual information.

Sound Blending (33 items)—An auditory blending task requiring the individual to say whole words after hearing their parts.

Picture Recognition (30 items)—Requires the individual to recognize a subset of
previously presented pictures within a field of distracting pictures.

Oral Vocabulary (44 items)—Measures the meaning of words using both synonyms and antonyms.

Concept Formation (35 items)—A controlled learning task requiring categorical
reasoning based on principles of logic.

Interpretation of Results

Scoring the WJ-R is somewhat tedious and affords the opportunity for errors. The
conversion tables for each subtest (raw scores to W scores, age equivalents, and
grade equivalents) are presented on the test record itself. This reduces the number
of tables that must be used in the manual. The test booklet includes sections for
summarizing a variety of scores and plotting the scores to provide a visual profile.
A computerized scoring program (Compuscore) also is available for both Apple
and IBM. This procedure is recommended to decrease the likelihood of scoring
errors.

For all tests but Memory for Sentences, which is scored 0, 1, or 2, each item is
scored as either 0 (incorrect) or 1 (correct). The raw scores for each of the twenty-
one tests in the standard and supplemental batteries can be converted into percentile ranks and standard scores (mean = 100; standard deviation = 15). In addition,
those scores are available for a variety of clusters consisting of various combinations of tests from the standard and supplemental batteries. Those clusters
are Broad Cognitive Ability (Extended), Long-term Retrieval, Short-term Memory, Processing Speed, Auditory Processing, Visual Processing, Comprehension-
Knowledge, Fluid Reasoning, Reading Aptitude, Math Aptitude, Written Language Aptitude, Knowledge Aptitude, Oral Language, and Oral Language Aptitude. An Early Development Scale can also be used with children as young as age
two. The subtests from the standard battery for that scale are Memory for Names,
Memory for Sentences, Incomplete Words, Visual Closure, and Picture Vocabulary. All of the seven tests from the standard battery can be combined for a Broad
Cognitive Ability (Standard).

Technical Characteristics

Normative Sample.   More than sixty-three hundred individuals were included.
The subjects were selected by a random stratified procedure. The stratification
variables were census region, community size, gender, race, funding of college or

university, type of college or university, education of adults, occupational stress of adults, and occupation of adults. In general, the similarity of the sample to the 1980 census data for the United States was relatively close (between one and five percent difference).

Reliability.   The split-half procedure was used for all tests with the exception of Visual Matching and Cross Out, for which the test-retest coefficients were calculated. For individual tests, the median coefficient ranged from .69 (Visual Closure) to .91 (Memory for Names) for the standard battery and from .75 (Cross Out) to .93 (Concept Formation) for the supplemental. The coefficients of the cluster scores were generally above .90 with the notable exception of Fluid Reasoning (.81).

Validity.   The authors provide a description of the content validity and report the concurrent validity through the use of studies at three age levels (using relatively small sample sizes). At the 3-year-old level, the Early Development Scale was correlated with the K-ABC, McCarthy Scales General Cognitive Index, and the SBIS-4, in addition to several achievement and basic concept measures. The coefficients with the cognitive measures were in the .60s range and in the .50s with the other measures. For the 9-year-old group, coefficients ranged from .57 (K-ABC) to .69 (WISC-R and SBIS-4) for the Standard Battery. In the 17-year-old age group, the coefficients were approximately .64 for the Standard Battery. Tables are also presented that show the correlations of the eight cognitive factor clusters and the cognitive clusters from other tests. Moderate correlations were found for the Short-term Memory, Comprehension-Knowledge, and Fluid Reasoning clusters with several of the criterion measures. These data in their present form, however, make it difficult to adequately address the issue of validity.

The issue of construct validity was primarily addressed through the use of tables showing the intercorrelations of the tests and clusters, along with results of factor analysis that indicated the two tests making up each cluster do, in fact, load on that specific factor.

Review of Relevant Research
Interestingly, there is a general lack of research that investigates the uses and limitations of the WJ-R. It should be noted that the validity of the cluster scores was of some concern on the original WJ (e.g., Phelps, Rosso, & Falasco, 1984). In addition, there was some indication that students with learning disabilities scored lower on the cognitive section than on other intellectual measures (e.g., Reeve, Hall, & Zakreski, 1979).

Some of the limited research on the WJ-R is summarized below.

- It is possible on the WJ-R to determine if an individual possesses adequate language skills to validate testing in English. This is accomplished by admin-

istering the oral language cluster and using the relative mastery index to
make that decision (Bearden, 1994).

- A graphic scoring system has been developed for the WJ-R to help reduce the
  time and complexity for scoring (McGrew, Murphy, & Knutson, 1994).
- Schrank (1995) noted that the early development tests from the WJ-R are attractive and well organized and particularly appropriate for assessing cognitive and pre-academic skills of young children.

Several books also have been written to aid in the interpretation of the WJ-R.
For example, *The Use and Interpretation of the Woodcock-Johnson–Revised* (Hessler,
1994) provides an in-depth guide for diagnostic purposes. Also available is the
Instructional Guide to the Woodcock-Johnson–Revised (Mather, 1990), which provides
information on how to translate test results into meaningful educational programs.

OVERVIEW: WOODCOCK-JOHNSON–REVISED (COGNITIVE)

- *Age level*—2 through adult
- *Type of administration*—Individual
- *Technical adequacy*—Good standardization, adequate reliability, questionable validity
- *Scores yielded*—Standard scores, percentile ranks (age equivalents and
  grade equivalents also available)
- *Suggested use*—The cognitive battery was developed within a theoretical
  framework (Horn-Cattell), making the interpretation more meaningful.
  Another improvement in the WJ-R is the slightly easier scoring procedures, although a number of tables must still be used, thus increasing the
  possibilities of errors. Clearly, if possible, a computerized scoring program (Compuscore) should be used. Also available for the WJ-R is a com-
  puter-scored test report called *The Report Writer*. This helps to explain a
  subject's performance on any particular measure by defining it from several perspectives. *The Report Writer* was also written to carefully exclude
  certain information that should not be generated by the computer. These
  include clinical hypothesis, qualitative interpretations, and recommendations. One advantageous feature of the WJ-R is the use of continuous-year
  norms. This means that the standardization occurred throughout the year
  for the school-age subjects rather than at one or two times. Thus the scores
  can be compared to individuals of the exact age or grade placement rather
  than to individuals of an average age or grade. This procedure helps
  eliminate the error variance associated with grouping students of similar,
  but not the same, age or grade. It should also be noted that a Spanish
  version of the WJ-R is available.

ADDITIONAL INSTRUMENTS

There are several other less frequently used instruments that provide measures of intelligence. Their more limited use is a result of a variety of reasons including extremely questionable validity (Goodenough-Harris Drawing Test), outdated norms (McCarthy Scale of Children's Abilities), and heavy reliance on one aspect of intelligence (Slosson Intelligence Test–Revised). Other tests are a shorter version of the same comprehensive instrument (Kaufman Brief Intelligence Test) or are similar to a more comprehensive instrument (Slosson Full-Range Intelligence Test). A brief description of these instruments follows.

Goodenough-Harris Drawing Test

- *Age level*—5 to 15 years old
- *Type of administration*—Individual or group
- *Technical adequacy*—Very limited
- *Scores yielded*—Standard scores
- *Suggested use*—The Goodenough-Harris Drawing Test (Harris, 1963) is an instrument that requires the child to draw a picture of a man, a woman, and himself or herself. The quality of the drawings is scored as a measure of "intellectual maturity." Its popularity is due largely to its ease of administration. The scoring, however, is somewhat subjective. This test should not be considered as a measure of intelligence. There are too many factors that could account for low scores. Research indicates that it tends to underestimate the level of a child's actual ability. It should be noted that a revised instrument— Draw-a-Person: A Quantitative Scoring System has been developed (Naglieri, 1988).

Kaufman Brief Intelligence Test

- *Age level*—4 to 90 years old
- *Type of administration*—Individual
- *Technical adequacy*—Good standardization and reliability, adequate validity
- *Scores yielded*—Standard scores, percentile ranks, descriptive categories
- *Suggested use*—The Kaufman Brief Intelligence Test (K-BIT) (Kaufman & Kaufman, 1990) is a brief screening instrument that uses two subtests (Vocabulary and Matrices) from the K-ABC. The vocabulary subtest measures word knowledge and verbal concept formation. Matrices are nonverbal problem solving tasks. The K-BIT appears to have adequate technical characteristics and can be used confidently as a brief screener of verbal and nonverbal intelligence. Prewett (1992) did report that the K-BIT produced lower scores (6–10 points) than the WISC-R, although its relationship to other intelligence tests has not been established.

McCarthy Scales of Children's Abilities

- *Age level*—2 1/2 to 8 1/2 years old
- *Type of administration*—Individual
- *Technical adequacy*—Good standardization, adequate reliability (motor index, low reliability), and validity
- *Scores yielded*—General cognitive index, scaled scores, percentile ranks, mental ages
- *Suggested use*—The McCarthy Scales (McCarthy, 1972) is a well-constructed (although outdated) instrument for use with young children. It includes eighteen subtests that measure Verbal, Quantitative, Memory, Perceptual Performance, and Motor areas. Its limited age range (2 1/2–8 1/2) has both advantages and disadvantages: there are a representative number of items to measure the various areas, but the instrument cannot be used after approximately second grade, which makes direct comparisons of a child's ability difficult after that time. The McCarthy Scales is a potentially useful instrument. It measures a number of areas associated with cognitive abilities of young children. There is some evidence that the McCarthy Scales might be more sensitive to the actual school performance level of students than are other intelligence measures. At this time, the instrument should be used primarily to identify strengths and weaknesses and to a lesser extent to determine eligibility for special education. Drawbacks of the test are its outdated norms and the limitations of the types of scores available. A revised version of the McCarthy Scales is being planned, however.

Slosson Full-Range Intelligence Test

- *Age level*—5 to 21 years
- *Type of administration*—Individual
- *Technical adequacy*—Adequate reliability and validity
- *Score yielded*—Standard scores, percentile ranks, stanines, cognitive-age levels
- *Suggested use*—The Slosson Full-Range Intelligence Test (SFRIT) (Algozzine, Eaves, Vance, & Mann, 1993) was designed to "mirror" the Stanford-Binet. Its advantage is a short administration time (approximately twenty to thirty-five minutes). A Rapid Cognitive Index can be obtained in approximately fifteen minutes. The test has a relatively solid technical base and can be used confidently as a screening instrument.

Slosson Intelligence Test–Revised

- *Age level*—Approximately birth to 27 years old
- *Type of administration*—Individual
- *Technical characteristics*—Adequate standardization, limited reliability, adequate validity
- *Scores yielded*—Mean-age equivalent, total standard score

- *Suggested use*—The Slosson Intelligence Test–Revised (SIT-R) (Slosson, 1991) gives a quick estimate of a person's intelligence. The majority of items are highly verbal, and the scores tend to overestimate a person's IQ as determined from more comprehensive measures. The SIT-R should be used for screening only. It can help to identify students for whom intelligence testing in more depth might be necessary. The inclusion of a total standard score in the revised version allows for more meaningful interpretation than for its predecessors.

Instrument or Technique	Screening and Initial Identification	Informal Determination and Evaluation of Teaching Programs and Strategies	Determination of Current Performance Level and Educational Need	Decisions about Classification and Program Placement	IEP Goals	IEP Objectives	IEP Evaluation	Mild/Moderate	Severe/Profound	Preschool	Elementary Age	Secondary Age	Adult	Special Considerations	Educational Relevance for Exceptional Students
	Prereferral (Suggested Use)	Prereferral (Suggested Use)	Suggested Use	Postreferral	Postreferral			Target Population							
Group Intelligence Tests	X							X		X	X	X	X	Use for screening only; resemble group-achievement tests in format and, to a certain extent, content	limited
Detroit Tests of Learning Aptitude–3			X	X				X			X	X		Some question about its validity; needs further research	adequate
Differential Ability Scales			X	X	X			X		X	X	X		Well constructed; includes both core and diagnostic subtests; good potential for preschool children	useful
Kaufman Assessment Battery for Children			X	X				X		X	X	X		Some question about its construct validity; includes an achievement component	useful
Stanford-Binet Intelligence Scale–4			X	X				X		X	X	X	X	The "grandfather" of intelligence tests; global composite should be used	useful
Wechsler Intelligence Scale for Children–III			X	X				X		X	X	X		Very widely used, well constructed; profile analyses of subtests should be avoided	very useful
Woodcock-Johnson–Revised			X	X				X		X	X	X	X	WJ-R is an improvement over original; more validity data necessary	adequate
Cognitive Levels Test	X		X					X		X	X	X		"Mirrors" the content of the Stanford-Binet	useful
Goodenough-Harris Drawing Test	X							X		X	X			Very limited technical aspects; should not be used as a sole measure of intelligence	very limited

Test										Description	Rating
Kaufman Brief Intelligence Test	X				X		X	X	X	Brief version of the K-ABC; use for screening only	useful
McCarthy Scales of Children's Abilities		X	X		X		X	X		Well constructed but outdated; measures areas that are important to early school success	adequate
Slosson Intelligence Test–Revised	X				X		X	X	X	Use for screening only; easy to administer; revised version an improvement	adequate

10

ASSESSMENT OF
ADAPTIVE BEHAVIOR*

Instruments and Procedures Included

Adaptive Behavior Instruments

Adaptive Behavior Inventory

AAMR Adaptive Behavior Scale–Second Edition:
Residential and Community Edition; School Edition

Assessment of Adaptive Areas

Scales of Independent Behavior

Vineland Adaptive Behavior Scales

Adaptive Behavior Screening Instruments

Adaptive Behavior Inventory for Children

Cain-Levine Social Competency Scale

Camelot Behavioral Checklist

Normative Adaptive Behavior Checklist

TARC Assessment System

*Portions of this chapter were adapted from R. Taylor, "Assessment Instruments," in *Educating Students with Severe or Profound Handicaps* (2nd ed.), edited by L. Sternberg. Austin, TX: Pro-Ed. Copyright © 1988 by Pro-Ed. Reprinted with permission of Pro-Ed.

Sam, an 8-year-old boy, was referred by his teacher to the school psychologist. Sam was new to his present school and seemed to be significantly below his third-grade peers in academic and social skills. Further, he scored 58 on a group-administered intelligence test. His teacher believed that Sam needed some type of additional assistance. After Sam was referred, the school psychologist administered the Wechsler Intelligence Scale for Children-III (WISC-III) and found Sam's IQ to be 65. A further study of Sam's background, however, indicated that he came from a lower socioeconomic family environment and that he had been at four schools in the past three years. The school psychologist, therefore, administered an adaptive-behavior scale to help determine the best placement for Sam.

Joanna, a 12-year-old girl with severe retardation, is enrolled in a private day program for students with physical disabilities. Her teacher believes that Joanna has potential in a number of areas including self-help and communications but is unclear about how to establish sequential objectives in those areas. She is also interested in monitoring Joanna's progress, which must be measured in small steps. The consulting psychologist recommended that an adaptive-behavior scale specifically designed for children with severe disabilities be administered to Joanna as a help in establishing the objectives and in monitoring her progress.

In its broadest sense, adaptive behavior has to do with a person's ability to deal effectively with personal and social demands and expectations. Adaptive behavior, in general, is a difficult concept to define and measure. Although Harrison (1987) reported that adaptive behavior is a multidimensional concept, Witt and Martens (1984) noted that most definitions include such areas as independent functioning and social responsibility.

The two vignettes noted at the beginning of this chapter demonstrate the diverse uses of adaptive-behavior testing. In general, these instruments can be used for three purposes. The specific purpose for an instrument depends largely on its depth, breadth, and technical characteristics, most notably the nature of the standardization sample. Some instruments are used to help make *classification* decisions. The American Association on Mental Retardation (AAMR) definition of mental retardation requires a deficit in adaptive behavior, and these instruments play an important role in those labeling decisions. Tests used for this purpose usually measure a number of areas and are usually standardized on nondisabled populations. Other adaptive-behavior scales are used more for *developing* and *evaluating specific teaching programs*. Tests used for this purpose usually include specific sequential items that cover functional, independent-living skill areas. Some of these tests are standardized on, and used with, individuals with more severe disabilities (e.g., Balthazar Scales of Adaptive Behavior; Balthazar, 1976). Others are standardized on nondisabled individuals and simply include more expanded and detailed items than those instruments used for classification purposes. A final purpose for adaptive-behavior scales is *screening*. Screening in this sense means either identification of those who need further evaluation or the delineation of general program goals. These instruments are not comprehensive enough to be used for classification purposes or for the development of educational programs.

The content of adaptive-behavior instruments will differ depending on the age range for the test. For instance, adaptive behavior for a 3-year-old child primarily includes motor skills, language skills, and self-help skills. On the other hand, adaptive behavior for a 15-year-old might include social skills and prevocational skills (Taylor, 1985).

The technical characteristics of many adaptive-behavior scales have been questioned. Cicchetti and Sparrow (1981) noted, for instance, that many adaptive-behavior scales have deficient reliability and validity estimates and that for many, the standardization sample is small. Similarly, Kamphaus (1987) reported that many of the instruments lacked predictive validity in particular. On the other hand, Harrison (1987), in a review of adaptive-behavior research, concluded that the instruments exhibit adequate reliability and can differentiate individuals with different labels. The format of adaptive-behavior scales has also been scrutinized. Some scales allow for direct observation, whereas others require an interview. These two procedures do not always yield similar information or results.

A discussion of some of the more widely used adaptive behavior instruments follows including a brief overview of several that are used for screening purposes.

ADAPTIVE BEHAVIOR INSTRUMENTS

WHY USE ADAPTIVE BEHAVIOR INSTRUMENTS?

Screening and identification; documentation of educational need; decisions about classification and program placement; development and evaluation of IEPs (largely depending on target population)

WHO SHOULD USE THEM?

Teachers or staff members; school psychologists (often using interview with parent)

Adaptive Behavior Inventory

The Adaptive Behavior Inventory (ABI) (Brown & Leigh, 1986) is an individually administered instrument used with individuals ages 6 through 18. It is designed to be completed by the classroom teacher and is relatively simple to score. The respondent must use a four-point scale to indicate the degree to which the examinee can perform certain behaviors (the items).

The primary use of the ABI is to aid in classification decisions regarding mental retardation and to determine general strengths and weaknesses in various adaptive behavior areas. The ABI does not provide specific information that could be used for educational programming. The ABI includes 150 items (thirty items in each of five areas). There is also a fifty-item ABI–Short Form available for quick screening.

Description

> *Self-Care Skills*—Items in this scale measure areas such as grooming and personal hygiene.
>
> *Communication Skills*—This scale measures writing ability as well as expressive and receptive oral language skills.
>
> *Social Skills*—This scale measures a wide range of skills including responsibility, organizational skills, and leadership ability.
>
> *Academic Skills*—This scale measures both preacademic and academic reading and mathematics skills.
>
> *Occupational Skills*—This includes such areas as job responsibility and supervisory skills.

Interpretation of Results

For each of the five scales, percentile ranks and standard scores (mean = 100; standard deviation = 15) are available. The scales can thus be used independently, although a composite quotient (Total Score) is also available.

Technical Characteristics

Normative Sample.   The ABI was standardized on both a sample of students with mental retardation and a sample of children with normal intelligence. The mental retardation sample included approximately eleven hundred individuals from twenty-four states. The normal intelligence group included approximately thirteen hundred individuals from those same locations.

Reliability.   Internal consistency (coefficient alpha) was generally good for all the age ranges for all five scales (.86–.97). The coefficients for the total score all exceeded .90. Test-retest reliability coefficients for the individual scales and the total score were also above .90. In general, reliability data for the ABI–Short Form were similar.

Validity.   In general, the ABI is lacking evidence of validity. Some concurrent validity data are presented (moderate coefficients) using the AAMD Adaptive Behavior Scale and Vineland Adaptive Behavior Scales as criteria. There is also a discussion by the authors regarding the test's content and construct validity. For example, they note the significant differences in the scores of the individuals in the two standardization samples.

Review of Relevant Research

Although no empirical studies were located, several reviews of the ABI were found; those reviews were, in general, relatively positive.

- Hughes (1988) believed that the test was highly useful for diagnosis and placement decisions because of the inclusion of both mentally retarded and normal samples. Ehly (1989) found the instrument attractive as well as quick and easy to administer.
- Smith (1989) considered the test best used to identify general strengths and weaknesses as well as areas for which further assessment to determine instructional goals could be pursued. He added that the total score was better to report than the individual scale scores.

OVERVIEW: ADAPTIVE BEHAVIOR INVENTORY

- *Age level*—6 through 18
- *Type of administration*—Individual
- *Technical adequacy*—Good reliability, questionable validity
- *Scores yielded*—Percentile ranks, standard scores
- *Suggested use*—The ABI is relatively quick and easy to administer. It is designed for use by the classroom teacher or other professional who is familiar with the student. As with most adaptive behavior tests, the ABI should be used to supplement other assessment information, particularly when being used to assist in classification and placement decisions. The test appears to be reliable, and the use of two sets of norms is a good feature. More evidence of the test's validity would be beneficial.

AAMR Adaptive Behavior Scale–Second Edition: Residential and Community Edition; School Edition

The American Association on Mental Retardation (AAMR) Adaptive Behavior Scales (ABS) were revised in 1993. The new scales are the Residential and Community Edition (AAMR ABS-RC:2) (Nihira, Leland, & Lambert, 1993), designed for use with individuals between the ages of 6 and 79 years who live in residential and community settings, and the School Edition (AAMR ABS-S:2) (Lambert, Leland, & Nihira, 1993), to be used with students ages 6 through 21 years who are receiving services in the public schools. Both scales are used with individuals who have mental retardation, emotional handicaps, and other disabilities. The School Edition is actually a short form of the Residential and Community Edition, with some items deleted from the longer version because of their inappropriateness for use with school-age children receiving services in the public schools. According to the authors, the ABS can be used for identifying persons who may be in need of specialized clinical services; identifying adaptive strengths and weaknesses in individuals under different situations; documenting progress in an intervention program; and stimulating research. It should also be emphasized that a deficit in adaptive behavior and cognitive functioning must be documented before an individual is labeled as having mental retardation. The ABS, in part, was developed for that purpose.

The ABS consists of two parts: Part One deals primarily with personal independence in daily living skills. Part One of the Residential and Community Edition includes seventy-three items that are divided into ten areas or domains and three factors. Part One of the School Edition consists of sixty-seven items that contribute to nine domains and three factors. Part Two, which concerns the measurement of maladaptive behavior, includes eight domains (seven for S:2) and two factors. The RC:2 has forty-one items, and the S:2 contains thirty-seven items. For the most part, items deleted from the RC:2 involved sexual relations (e.g., "exposes body improperly," "has sexual behavior that is socially unacceptable"). For both parts of the ABS, information is collected by one of two methods. The first is first-person assessment. This method is used when the evaluator is thoroughly familiar with the person who is being evaluated. The second method is third-party assessment. In this approach, the evaluator asks another individual (e.g., teacher, parent, or ward attendant) about each item on the scale. This is usually a time-consuming endeavor.

Description

Part One.   This part includes ten domains assessing the degree of independence in daily living skills. Each item in a given domain is scored in one of two ways. For some items, there is a breakdown and description of skills on a dependent–independent continuum. The examiner chooses which behavioral description best fits the individual being evaluated. For the remaining items, a list of behaviors is provided, and the examiner must check all that apply. Descriptions of the ten domains follow.

> *Independent Functioning (24 items)*—Included in this domain are eating, toilet use, cleanliness, appearance, care of clothing, dressing and undressing, travel, and other independent functioning.
>
> *Physical Development (6 items)*—This domain includes items measuring a person's sensory development (vision and hearing) and motor development (gross motor and fine motor skills).
>
> *Economic Activity (6 items)*—Items in this domain measure ability in money handling and budgeting and shopping skills.
>
> *Language Development (10 items)*—This domain includes measures of expression and verbal comprehension plus two items concerning social language development (e.g., conversational behavior).
>
> *Numbers and Time (3 items)*—Items in this domain measure a person's ability to understand and manipulate numbers and to understand time concepts.
>
> *Domestic Activity (6 items)*—This domain includes items measuring skills in cleaning, kitchen activities, and other domestic activities.

Prevocational/Vocational Activity (3 items)—These items measure work and
school habits and job performance.

Self-Direction (5 items)—These items measure an individual's initiative, perseverance, and use of leisure time.

Responsibility (3 items)—These items measure an individual's dependability.

Socialization (7 items)—This domain includes measure of cooperation, consideration for others, and social maturity.

Part Two.   This part was designed specifically to measure the degree of an individual's *maladaptive behavior*. It includes eight domains. For each item in a given
domain, several behaviors are listed. The examiner must determine whether each
behavior occurs frequently (scored as 2), occasionally (scored as 1), or not at all
(scored as 0). Unfortunately, no guidelines are provided that operationally define
"frequently" and "occasionally." The eight behavioral domains are summarized
below.

Social Behavior (7 items)—This domain includes such items as "threatens or
does physical violence" and "reacts poorly to frustration."

Conformity (6 items)—This domain includes questions about impudence, re-
sistance to instructions, and absenteeism.

Trustworthiness (6 items)—These items inquire about the possible presence of
lying, cheating, and stealing behavior.

Stereotyped and Hyperactive Behavior (5 items)—These items measure stereo-
typical and repetitive behaviors, as well as hyperactive tendencies.

Sexual Behavior (4 items)—This domain measures behaviors that relate to physical exposure and/or masturbation (not included in S:2).

Self-Abusive Behavior (3 items)—This domain includes items such as "does
physical violence to self" and "has strange and unacceptable habits."

Social Engagement (4 items)—This domain includes measures of inactivity and
shyness.

Disturbing Interpersonal Behavior (6 items)—This domain measures such behaviors as "reacts poorly to criticism" and "has hypochondriacal tendencies."

Interpretation of Results

Each item on the ABS is scored by the methods previously described. Scores for all
the items in a given domain are added together to obtain a raw score for that
domain. Raw scores for various factors can also be obtained. The domain raw
scores—or attained scores, as they are referred to—can then be transformed into
percentile ranks and standard scores. The standard scores are then plotted on a
Profile/Summary Sheet (see Figure 10.1 on page 212) to provide a visual representation of the individual's adaptive behavior functioning.

One important consideration in using this instrument is that, for the most
part, there are too few items in a given domain to provide adequate information

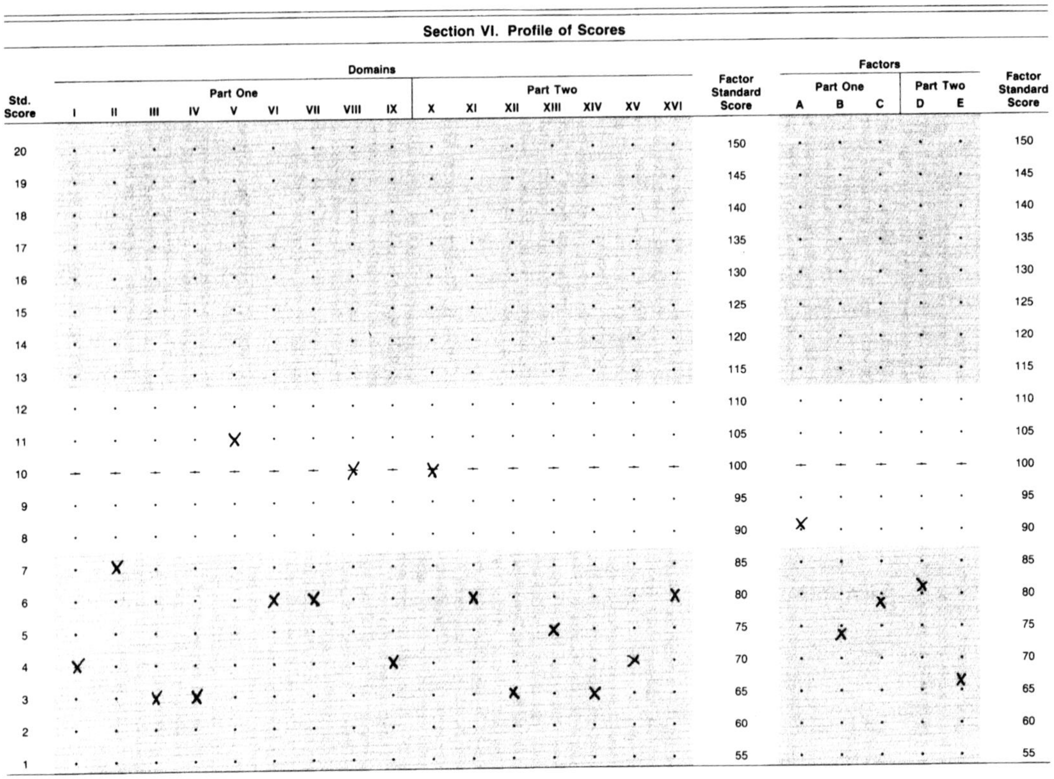

Section VI. Profile of Scores

FIGURE 10.1   **Profile Sheet from the AAMR Adaptive Behavior Scale**

From K. Nihira, H. Leland, and N. Lambert, *AAMR Adaptive Behavior Scale*, second edition. Copyright © 1993 by American Association on Mental Retardation. Additional copies of this form (#6194) are available from Pro-Ed, 8700 Shoal Creek Boulevard, Austin, TX 78757, 512/451-3246.

for specific educational programming. The authors do address this issue, however.

Technical Characteristics

Normative Sample.   The RC:2 sample consisted of more than four thousand persons with developmental disabilities who reside in residential or community settings. The S:2 sample consisted of more than one thousand nondisabled students and more than two thousand students with mental retardation. In both instances, the samples' demographic characteristics are representative of the nation as a whole.

Reliability.   Interrater reliability was established in separate studies by having two staff members or a parent and a staff member independently rate clients or students. In most instances, the coefficients for the various domains approach or exceed .80. Internal consistency reliability coefficients for the RC:2 and S:2 domains generally exceed .80 across ages. Factor score reliability coefficients exceed .90 across most ages. Stability reliability coefficients, for the most part, also exceed .80 for the domains and factors.

Validity.   Validity for each version of the ABS was examined in a number of ways. For content validity, a description is provided of how the items were selected for inclusion on the scale. Item discriminating powers and item difficulties lend empirical support. Criterion-related validity evidence is explained by comparing the results of each ABS version with other adaptive behavior scales. In general, moderate coefficients were reported for Part One and low insignificant coefficients for Part Two. Construct validity for both versions was explored by demonstrating that the scales (1) are developmental in nature; (2) correlate significantly with measures of intelligence; (3) relate significantly to measures of achievement; (4) differentiate among groups of students with varying disabilities (i.e., mental retardation, emotional handicaps, learning disabilities) and those without disabilities; (5) have factor clustors that are supported through factor analytic research; and, (6) have valid items.

Review of Relevant Research
To date, there is no independent research available. The 1993 scales are similar to predecessors, however, in the content measured. Thus, a review of the research conducted on the earlier instruments may be of value.

Research Relevant for the ABS-RC:2
- The ABS was helpful in discriminating among three groups of mentally retarded individuals: institutionalized, deinstitutionalized, and those referred for discharge (Spreat, 1980).
- Part Two has been severely criticized. The standardization data are markedly skewed, with 40 to 50 percent of the sample displaying no inappropriate behavior (McDevitt, McDevitt, & Rosen, 1977). In addition, the severity of the behavior is not considered.
- The feasibility of adapting the scoring system to include the severity of behavior has been demonstrated (Taylor, Warren, & Slocumb, 1979) and subsequent severity weightings have been developed for the items in Part Two (Clements, Bost, Dubois, & Turpin, 1980). Spreat (1982a), however, found that the severity weightings did not improve the predictive efficiency of Part Two.
- Several factor analytic studies have been conducted. Spreat (1982b) reviewed these studies and found that it was difficult to make any definite statements about their findings. It appeared that there were two factors for Part One (self-care and motivational aspects of personality) and two factors for Part Two (maladaptive behavior towards self and maladaptive behavior towards others).
- Administering the ABS using direct observation yielded different results than administering it through retrospective observation (Millham, Chilcutt, & At-

kinson, 1978), although Stack (1984) found that the method of administration made little difference.

- Scores on the ABS differed when teachers and parents supplied the information (Mealor & Richmond, 1980; Heath & Obrzut, 1984). Further, teachers were more likely to rate children as being eligible for special education programs (Ronka & Barnett, 1986).
- Teachers demonstrate a slight preference for using direct observation rather than interviews to obtain information for the ABS, except for those items that were considered extremely maladaptive (Taylor & Ivimey, 1982).
- Computerization of the ABS results made using them more effective (Malone & Christian, 1975).
- In a review of the psychometric properties of the ABS, Spreat (1982b) concluded that Part One has reasonably adequate reliability, although for Part Two the reliability is low enough to warrant caution in the interpretation of its scores. Spreat also noted that the ABS was adequate in discriminating among various groups who have various behavioral characteristics.
- When portions of the ABS were completed by several raters, the score was higher than when the entire test was completed by one rater (Vandergriff, Hester, & Mandra, 1987).
- Operational definitions of "occasionally" and "frequently" for Part Two have been developed that subsequently improved reliability (MacDonald, 1988).

Research Relevant to the ABS–S:2

- The ABS-SE Part Two was useful in identifying behavior-disordered students ages seven to twelve (Cheramie & Edwards, 1990).
- In a review of the ABS-SE, Vallecorsa and Tittle (1985) stated that it had more representative norms and a broader age range than the ABIC. They also noted that it was easier to administer than the Vineland Adaptive Behavior Scales (discussed later in this chapter).
- When scores from the ABS-SE are compared to WISC-R scores, a common factor of verbal comprehension emerges (Huberty, 1986).
- Factor and comparison scores are not affected by gender or ethnic status of the examinee, thus providing additional data to support its validity (Lambert, 1986).

Summary of Research Findings

Most of the research on the ABS explored its psychometric characteristics, particularly its reliability and validity. These studies, in general, supported the use of the ABS to identify groups of individuals according to diagnostic category. In other words, there are significant differences among the scores of differently labeled groups of individuals. As with most adaptive behavior instruments, there has been research on the method of gathering the information and the nature of the informant (usually teacher versus parent). Finally, the reliability of the ABS has been questioned, particularly for Part Two. Part Two, in fact, has been criticized for a number of technical inadequacies although many of these inadequacies have been addressed through alternate scoring methods. It should also be noted that many of these inadequacies were addressed in the revised version. The more limited research on the ABS-SE generally supported its use as an instrument to aid in classification decisions. Clearly, research will need to be conducted to determine if this research will be relevant for the revised edition.

OVERVIEW: AAMR ADAPTIVE BEHAVIOR SCALE–RESIDENTIAL AND COMMUNITY EDITION–SCHOOL EDITION

- *Age level*—6 to 79 years old (RC:2) and 6 to 21 years old (S:2)
- *Type of administration*—Individual
- *Technical adequacy*—Reliability of domains is adequate, reliability of factors is good, validity is adequate for Part One, questionable for Part Two
- *Scores yielded*—Percentile ranks, standard scores
- *Suggested use*—The ABS originally was developed primarily as a result of the AAMR's emphasis on adaptive behavior in its definition of mental retardation. Although no research was located on the ABS-RC:2 or the ABS-S:2, it would appear that the instruments are similar enough to the earlier versions to warrant some generalization. For example, the ABS was successful in identifying groups of individuals according to their diagnostic classification. The ABS, however, had several limitations. Generally speaking, the items were not sensitive enough to be useful for individuals with severe retardation. Technical inadequacies in Part Two, in particular, were criticized. The revised versions have addressed many of the technical limitations of the previous editions, however.

  Overall, the results from the ABS should be used to aid in classification and placement decisions and to identify general areas of programming needs. Important decisions should not be based on the results alone, nor should specific educational plans be developed around the child's adaptive-behavior profile. Obviously, research needs to be conducted to determine the uses and limitations of the two revised versions of the ABS.

Assessment of Adaptive Areas

The Assessment of Adaptive Areas (AAA) (Bryant, Taylor, & Rivera, 1996) is a recategorization of the items from Part One of the AAMR ABS-RC:2 and the AAMR ABS-S:2. The recategorization was conducted to provide scores for the ten adaptive areas noted in the newest AAMR definition of mental retardation (see Chapter 4). According to the AAMR definition, a person must have a deficit in at least two of the following ten adaptive skill areas: communication, self-care, home living, social skills, community use, self-direction, health and safety, functional academics, leisure, and work. The AAA is the only adaptive behavior instrument that provides scores for all of the ten adaptive areas noted in the definition.

Description

Communication (44 items)—This area includes activities related to understanding and expressing information, thoughts, and feelings.

Self-Care (80 items)—These items focus on personal care and well being in areas such as grooming, toileting, dressing, and eating.

Home Living (34 items)—This area measures a person's ability to function successfully within the home setting. Examples include cooking, budgeting, and implementing safety measures.

Social Skills (43 items)—These items measure the ability to develop appropriate interpersonal relationships in a variety of settings.

Community Use (38 items)—This area measures an individual's ability to use community resources, such as grocery stores, medical facilities, churches, and theaters.

Self-Direction (28 items)—These items measure areas such as assertive behavior and self-advocacy.

Health and Safety (11 items)—Included in this area are items about first aid, implementing safety activities, and personal hygiene.

Functional Academics (44 items)—These items measure basic school-related skills that apply to daily living, such as reading warning labels and writing a letter.

Leisure (13 items)—This area measures the individual's involvement in recreational activities.

Work (20 items)—These items measure the individual's ability to secure and maintain employment, including such behaviors as working with peers, accepting criticism, and following instruction.

Interpretation of Results

For each of the ten areas, it is possible to obtain standard scores (mean = 10, standard deviation = 3), percentile ranks, and age equivalents. These derived scores can be obtained using both a comparison group of individuals with mental retardation and individuals without mental retardation. Scores can then be placed on a profile/examiner record form that provides a visual display of the relative strengths and weaknesses of the individual in the ten adaptive skill areas.

Technical Characteristics

Normative Sample. The normative sample for the AAA is the same as the normative sample for the AAMR ABS-RC:2 and the AAMR ABS-S:2. (See description for those instruments in this chapter.)

Reliability. Internal consistency reliability coefficients for each of the ten adaptive skill areas were primarily in the .80s and .90s for the nonretardation sample and in the .90s for the mental retardation sample. In general, reliability coefficients increased with age. Test-retest coefficients were also primarily in the .80s and .90s range.

Validity. Content validity of the instrument was empirically determined by having a panel of experts in the field of mental retardation rate each item on Part One of the AAMR ABS in each of the ten adaptive skill areas. This formed the basis for the reconfiguration and the weighting system used within the AAA. Discriminating powers of the items were also determined and reported in the manual. Results of several criterion-related validity studies are also reported; these correlations with other adaptive behavior scales were in the low to moderate range. These correlations, however, were based on each of the ten adaptive skill areas correlations with the total test score from the other adaptive behavior instruments. A discussion of construct validity is also provided, including data to support the age differentiation of the items (i.e., adaptive performance in each of the ten areas increases with age).

Review of Relevant Research
At the time of the completion of this book, the AAA had just been published. Subsequently, no research other than that provided in the manual is available.

OVERVIEW: ASSESSMENT OF ADAPTIVE AREAS

- *Age level*—6 to 79 years old (when used with the RC:2); 6 to 21 years (when used with the S:2)
- *Type of administration*—Individual
- *Technical adequacy*—Reliability and validity acceptable (more validity data necessary)
- *Scores yielded*—Standard scores, percentile ranks, age equivalents
- *Suggested use*—The AAA was developed specifically to address the adaptive behavior component in the newest AAMR definition of mental retardation. Specifically, it addresses the ten adaptive skill areas that should be evaluated when determining the classification of mental retardation. No other instrument provides scores in the ten specific adaptive areas noted in the AAMR's definition. In order to obtain scores for the AAA, it is necessary to administer Part One of the AAMR ABS-RC:2 or AAMR ABS-S:2. Those scores can then be reconfigured using the AAA scoring form.

Scales of Independent Behavior

The Scales of Independent Behavior (SIB) (Bruininks, Woodcock, Weatherman, & Hill, 1984) is an individually administered instrument designed for use with a wide age range (three months to adult). The SIB uses a structured format in which the interviewer makes a statement (e.g., "Picks up and eats food such as crackers" to which the respondent must indicate if the examinee exhibits that behavior "never or rarely," "about one-fourth of the time," "about three-fourths of the

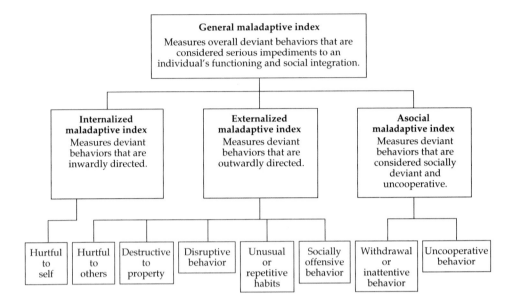

FIGURE 10.2   Problem Behavior: Eight Critical Areas Scored in Three Valid and Useful Indexes

Adapted from R. Bruininks, R. Woodcock, R. Weatherman, and B. Hill, *The Scales of Independent Behavior.* Copyright © 1984 by DLM Teaching Resources, Allen, TX. Used by permission.

time," or "almost always." The SIB consists of fourteen subscales that can be grouped into four larger clusters. In addition, there is a Problem Behavior Scale (Figure 10.2). Finally, there is a short form consisting of thirty-two items, and an Early Development Scale to use with younger children that also consists of thirty-two questions. Also available are a shorter version of the SIB called the *Inventory for Client and Agency Planning* (ICAP) and a related criterion-referenced instrument called the *Checklist of Adaptive Living Skills* (CALS). A correlated curriculum called the *Adaptive Living Skills Curriculum* (ALSC) completes the package.

Description

Motor Skills Cluster

> *Gross Motor (17 items)*—Items range from "Sits alone for thirty seconds with head and back held straight and steady (with support)" to "Takes part in strenuous physical activities on a regular basis that requires strength and endurance."
>
> *Fine Motor (17 items)*—Items range from "Picks up small objects with hand" to "Assembles objects that have at least ten small parts that must be screwed or bolted together."

Social Interaction and Communication Cluster

Social Interaction (16 items)—Ranges from "Reaches for a person whom he or she wants" to "Makes plans with friends to attend activities outside the home without needing permission."

Language Comprehension (16 items)—Includes "Turns head toward speaker when name is called" and "Reads one or more articles in a regular newspaper at least weekly."

Language Expression (17 items)—Ranges from "Makes sounds or gestures to get attention" to "Explains the terms of a written contract, such as an installment purchase agreement."

Personal Living Skills Cluster

Eating (16 items)—Ranges from "Swallows soft foods" to "Plans and prepares meals regularly for self and family."

Toileting (14 items)—Items include "Stays dry for at least three hours" and "Closes the bathroom door when appropriate before using the toilet."

Dressing (18 items)—Includes "Removes socks" and "Selects and buys appropriate size and style of clothing."

Personal Self-Care (15 items)—Ranges from "Holds hands under running water to wash them when placed in front of sink" to "Makes appointments for periodic medical or dental examinations."

Domestic Skills (16 items)—Includes "Places his or her empty dish in or near the sink" and "Cleans refrigerator and throws out food that may be spoiled."

Community Living Skills Cluster

Time and Punctuality (15 items)—Includes "Points to any number from one to five when asked" and "States the time on a clock with hands to the nearest minute."

Money and Value (17 items)—Items range from "Counts from one to five" to "Invests savings to achieve the most favorable conditions and rate of return."

Work Skills (16 items)—Includes "Indicates when a chore or assigned task is finished" and "Prepares a written summary of work experience."

Home/Community Orientation (16 items)—Includes "Finds toys or objects that are always kept in the same place" and "Locates his or her polling center at election time."

Interpretation of Results

A variety of derived scores are available for each of the four clusters as well as Broad Independence (a global score combining the clusters). Scores for those areas include age equivalents, standard scores (mean = 100; standard deviation = 15), percentile ranks, and normal curve equivalents. Because the SIB is a part of the original Woodcock-Johnson Psychoeducational Battery, the types of scores common to that Battery are also available. They include instructional ranges, relative performance indexes, and functioning levels (e.g., moderate deficit). For the Problem Behavior Scale, stanines, maladaptive behavior indices, and an indication of the level of seriousness are available.

Overall, the SIB is easy to administer; the use of suggested starting points and basal and ceiling rules decreases the number of items that must be given. Scoring, however, can be tedious because of the number of tables that must be used. There is an automated computer scoring program, that is available, however.

Technical Characteristics

Normative Sample.   More than seventeen hundred individuals were included. The authors intended to include subjects in the same proportion as the U.S. population regarding gender, community size, race, socioeconomic status, and geographic region.

Reliability.   Split-half reliability coefficients for each subscale for each of thirteen age groups were computed. The resulting coefficients were quite varied, ranging from .00 to .95. The coefficients for the cluster scores were higher and more consistent (generally in the .80–.90 range), although Motor Skills and Community Living Skills yielded lower coefficients (.60s) for some age groups. The Broad Independence was the highest (.95 or higher).

Test-retest coefficients are reported for two specific age groups (6 to 8 and 10 to 11 years). A similar pattern to the split-half coefficients emerged with the subscale coefficients lower and more variable than the clusters (.70s–.90s) and Broad Independence (.87–.96).

Validity.   Criterion-related validity coefficients with the AAMD ABS ranged from approximately .60 to .90. The Problem Behavior Scale demonstrated moderate coefficients with the Revised Problem Behavior Checklist (discussed in Chapter 11). The authors also present arguments supporting its content validity and the results of several studies that demonstrate its construct validity.

Review of Relevant Research
- In one review, Camp (1989) noted that the materials (easel kit) were cumbersome when administering the test.
- In another review, Thomas (1990) felt that the SIB was psychometrically stronger than most of the indirect measures of adaptive behavior.
- Similarly, Heifetz (1989) praised several of the instrument's psychometric properties and concluded that it was a better indirect measure of adaptive behavior than the ABI or AAMD ABS but not as good as the Vineland Adaptive Behavior Scales.
- The SIB Broad Independence score correlated .83 with the Vineland Composite score with a sample of 3- to 7-year-old children (Middleton, Keene, & Brown, 1990).

- Scores on the SIB were used to correctly classify 76 percent of subjects according to their level of retardation (Ilmer, Bruininks, & Hill, 1988).
- Factor analysis of the SIB with both retarded and nonretarded samples yielded a large adaptive or personal independence dimension for both samples (Bruininks, McGrew, & Maruyama, 1988).

Summary of Research Findings
The results of the few studies on the SIB reported in the professional literature have been relatively positive. Overall, the instrument appears to have good validity and can help in making classification decisions.

OVERVIEW: SCALES OF INDEPENDENT BEHAVIOR

- *Age level*—3 months to 44 years
- *Type of administration*—Individual
- *Technical adequacy*—Good standardization, adequate reliability (not for individual subscales), good validity
- *Scores yielded*—Standard scores, age equivalents, percentile ranks, normal curve equivalents, stanines, several descriptive approaches
- *Suggested use*—The SIB appears to be a reasonably valid instrument to aid in classification decisions. The technical characteristics of the instrument indicate that it is more advisable to use the cluster scores or preferably, the Broad Independence score rather than the individual subscale scores. This is particularly true in tests of a young child or an adult for whom subscales would be of little value (e.g., work skills for infants or gross motor skills for adults).

  Several features of the test and related materials are favorable. One is a Spanish version of the SIB that can be purchased from the publisher. The second is the inclusion of the Early Development Scale for a quick estimate of young children's adaptive behavior. The third is the computerized scoring system that is recommended to save time and decrease the possibility of making errors. Finally, the availability of the ICAP, CALS, and ALSC provides a total adaptive behavior package to examiners. It should be noted that the SIB is currently being revised.

Vineland Adaptive Behavior Scales

The Vineland Adaptive Behavior Scales (VABS) (Sparrow, Balla, & Cicchetti, 1984) is a revision and modification of the Vineland Social Maturity Scale (Doll, 1965). Doll made a significant contribution to the overall area of adaptive behavior assessment, and the authors of the VABS incorporated many of his concepts in designing the new instrument. The VABS, however, is a much more comprehensive test than its predecessor.

The VABS, designed for use with individuals from birth to age 18, has three separate editions that can be used individually or in combination. These are the classroom edition, which allows teachers to assess adaptive behavior within the classroom environment, and two interview editions that are administered in a semistructured format with the parents or primary caregiver as the respondent. The Interview Edition–Survey Form is most like the original Vineland and provides an overall measure of an individual's strengths and deficits. The Interview Edition–Expanded Form is more comprehensive and is the edition that has the most relevance for individuals with severe disabilities. Both interview editions measure five domains that are further broken down into twelve subdomains.

Description

Interview Editions. The five areas measured by the interview editions are communication, daily living skills, socialization, motor skills, and maladaptive behavior. There are a total of 574 items on the expanded form and 297 on the survey form.

> *Communication Domain (survey form—67 items, expanded form—133 items)—* There are three subdomains contained in this section. These are (1) the Receptive subdomain, which measures areas such as "beginning to understand" and "listening and attending"; (2) the Expressive subdomain, with areas such as "prespeech sounds" and "articulating"; and (3) the Written subdomain, which measures reading and writing skills.
>
> *Daily Living Skills Domain (survey form—92 items; expanded form—200 items)—* The three subdomains in this section are (1) Personal, which measures areas such as eating and toileting; (2) Domestic, measuring such areas as housecleaning and food preparation; and (3) Community, which includes such areas as safety and understanding money.
>
> *Socialization Domain (survey form—66 items; expanded form—134 items)—*The three subdomains are (1) Interpersonal Relationships (areas such as "recognizing emotions" and "initiating social communication"); (2) Play and Leisure Time (areas such as "playing with toys" and "sharing and cooperating"); and (3) Coping Skills (such as "following rules").
>
> *Motor Skills Domain (survey form—36 items; expanded form—71 items)—*This section includes items divided into gross-motor and fine-motor areas.
>
> *Maladaptive Behavior (36 items—both editions)—*This optional domain allows for the ratings of a number of maladaptive or inappropriate behaviors.

Classroom Edition. This section of the VABS is designed for use by the classroom teacher and is presented in a checklist format. As such, it assumes that the teacher has had the opportunity to observe directly the adaptive behaviors included on the checklist. The Classroom Edition is designed for children ages 3 through 13.

Interpretation of Results

A variety of scores are available from the VABS. These include standard scores, percentile ranks, stanines, and age equivalents. These are available for the domains, subdomains, and a composite of the Communication, Daily Living Skills, Socialization, and Motor Skills domains. One nice feature is a summary report for parents (Figure 10.3 on page 224) that is used to provide meaning to the test scores. A computer program called ASSIST can be used for scoring the VABS Interview Editions.

Technical Characteristics

Normative Sample. A nationally representative sample of more than three thousand individuals was used; approximately 10 percent were receiving some type of special education.

Reliability.   Test-retest of survey form is high (.98–.99); interrater reliability ranged from .62 (socialization) to .78 for motor skills.

Validity.   Concurrent-validity coefficient between survey edition and original Vineland was .55. Authors also provide arguments for its content and construct validity.

Review of Relevant Research

- In a review of the VABS, Kamphaus (1987) summarized several important points:

  1. The VABS is truly a set of scales rather than a single instrument.
  2. The Expanded Form should be used primarily for intervention planning.
  3. There is a general lack of technical data for the Expanded Form. In reality, the norms for this edition were determined through extrapolation of the normative data from the Survey Form.
  4. The Classroom Edition is different from the Interview Editions. It is somewhat lengthy, and teachers often have not had the opportunity to observe some of the behaviors.

- In another review, Sattler (1989a) noted that many of the items require information that might be beyond the informant's knowledge base.
- The VABS and ABS-SE were highly correlated with a sample of autistic students (Perry & Factor, 1989), although the VABS and the ABS yielded significant differences with a group of children with developmental and learning disabilities (Ronka & Barnett, 1986).
- For a group of 3- to 7-year-old children, the most valid scales were Personal Living Skills, Communication Skills, and Community Living Skills (Middleton, Keene, & Brown, 1990).
- Tables have been developed to indicate the differences necessary between VABS scores and scores from a variety of IQ measures to reach statistical significance (Atkinson, 1990a). In addition, tables are available that provide confidence intervals when using the VABS with the same person more than once (Atkinson, 1990b).

The following chart describes more specific areas of adaptive behavior. Although scores such as percentile ranks and stanines are not given for these specific areas, the chart shows the areas in which your child's performance is above average, average, or below average when compared with the national norm group.

			Above Average	Average	Below Average
Communication	Receptive	What your child understands			
	Expressive	What your child says			
	Written	What your child reads and writes			
Daily Living Skills	Personal	How your child eats, dresses, and practices personal hygiene			
	Domestic	What household tasks your child performs			
	Community	How your child uses time, money, the telephone, and job skills			
Socialization	Interpersonal relationships	How your child interacts with others			
	Play and leisure time	How your child plays and uses leisure time			
	Coping skills	How your child demonstrates responsibility and sensitivity to others			
Motor Skills	Gross	How your child uses arms and legs for movement and coordination			
	Fine	How your child uses hands and fingers to manipulate objects			

General summary _____

_____

_____

_____

Recommendations _____

_____

_____

_____

_____

FIGURE 10.3   Portion of Parent Report for the Vineland Adaptive Behavior Scales

From S. Sparrow, D. Cicchetti, and D. Balla, *Vineland Adaptive Behavior Scales*. Copyright © 1984 by American Guidance Service, Circle Pines, MN.

- The VABS is of limited use for moderately to severely retarded individuals (Bensberg & Irons, 1986). These researchers also compared the VABS with the ABS-SE and reported high correlations and that teachers voiced no preference over either of the tests.
- The means and standard deviations vary considerably from age group to age group, making comparisons difficult (Silverstein, 1986a). Cicchetti and Sparrow (1986) argue, however, that that criticism is based on flawed reasoning and invalid statistical arguments.
- There were no differences between black and white children on the VABS (Calnon, 1984).
- The VABS was successful in differentiating between children with learning disabilities and children with mental retardation (Rainwater-Bryant, 1985) and children without disabilities and children with mild personality problems (Sparrow et al., 1986).

Summary of Research Findings

In general, research on the VABS has supported its use. Most of the research has been conducted on the Survey Form, which seems to be measuring similar constructs as many other adaptive behavior tests. There is some question about the appropriateness of the norms for the Expanded Form and the practicality of the Classroom Edition. Several additional tables have been developed to aid in interpretation of the VABS.

OVERVIEW: VINELAND ADAPTIVE BEHAVIOR SCALES

- *Age level*—Birth to 18 years old
- *Type of administration*—Individual
- *Technical adequacy*—Good standardization and test-retest reliability, good validity (Survey Form)
- *Scores yielded*—Standard scores, percentiles, age equivalents, stanines
- *Suggested use*—The VABS is probably the most widely used adaptive behavior instrument. Its standardization and technical aspects are generally good, and it is based on a sound theoretical model. The interview editions use a semistructured interview to gather the information. Users should be familiar with the items and scoring criteria before administering the test. In general, the interview editions are recommended over the classroom edition. The test has its greatest use with students with mild and moderate disabilities, although the expanded form contains many items that are appropriate for individuals with more severe disabilities. The format of the VABS allows its use in making decisions about placement as well as educational programming.

ADAPTIVE BEHAVIOR INSTRUMENTS: FOR SCREENING ONLY

As noted earlier in this chapter, a number of adaptive behavior instruments are used more for screening purposes. These instruments are not as comprehensive as those previously discussed, and the majority are used to get a quick overview of the student's adaptive behavior skills so that general program goals can be determined.

Adaptive Behavior Inventory for Children

- *Age level*—5 to 11 years old
- *Type of administration*—Individual (interview)
- *Technical adequacy*—Adequate reliability, questionable validity
- *Scores yielded*—Scales scores, percentile ranks
- *Suggested use*—The Adaptive Behavior Inventory for Children (ABIC) (Mercer & Lewis, 1977) is actually a part of a larger evaluation instrument, the System of Multicultural Pluralistic Assessment (SOMPA). The SOMPA attempts to measure an individual's ability using three models: the medical model, the social-system model, and the pluralistic (intellectual and learning ability) model. The ABIC has been used primarily as a measure to declassify minority children who have been labeled as having mental retardation. The ABIC focuses on nonschool behaviors, a focus that has certain advantages and disadvantages. It certainly helps to decrease the number of children labeled as having mental retardation; its ability to predict school performance is less certain, however. The ABIC should be used as a screening or classification measure (particularly if one believes in the SOMPA model) and not as an instrument to provide information for making decisions about program development or instruction.

Cain-Levine Social Competency Scale

- *Age level*—5 to 13 years old
- *Type of administration*—Individual
- *Technical adequacy*—Limited standardization (individuals with IQs 25–50), adequate reliability, no validity data
- *Scores yielded*—Percentile ranks
- *Suggested use*—The Cain-Levine (Cain, Levine, & Elzey, 1977) should be used to determine general program objectives for children with moderate mental retardation. The test is not appropriate for individuals with severe or profound retardation. The scoring system is somewhat subjective, although the reliability is adequate. The lack of validity data for the Cain-Levine seriously limits the use of the instrument. Overall, it covers four domains: self-help, initiative, social skills, and communication.

Camelot Behavioral Checklist

- *Age level*—Children and adults (no age range given)
- *Type of administration*—Individual
- *Technical adequacy*—Limited standardization, questionable reliability and validity
- *Scores yielded*—Percentiles, item profiles, and score profiles
- *Suggested use*—The Camelot (Foster, 1974) is best thought of as a screening instrument to determine general areas of program need. A profile sheet offers a visual representation of that information. The scoring system, however, does not allow for sensitive discriminations. The technical adequacy of the Camelot is also somewhat questionable. The test includes ten domains and forty subdomains.

Normative Adaptive Behavior Checklist

- *Age level*—Infancy to age 21
- *Type of administration*—Individual (questionnaire)
- *Scores yielded*—Standard scores, age equivalents
- *Technical adequacy*—Good reliability, adequate validity; standardized on more than six thousand individuals
- *Description and suggested use*—The N-ABC (Adams, 1986) includes more than one hundred items that measure the areas of self-help, home living, independent living, social, sensorimotor, and language and academic skills. It can be used to provide a quick, reliable estimate of a person's adaptive behavior. If a person scores low on the N-ABC, an extended, much longer version, the Comprehensive Test of Adaptive Behavior, can be administered to provide more specific information.

TARC Assessment System

- *Age level*—3 to 16 years old
- *Type of administration*—Individual
- *Technical adequacy*—Limited (standardized on a heterogeneous group of individuals with severe disabilities)
- *Scores yielded*—Raw scores are plotted on profile sheet that yields standard scores
- *Suggested use*—The TARC (Sailor & Mix, 1975) should be used for screening purposes only. The normative aspects of the instrument are limited and, therefore, use of the standard scores should be discouraged. The TARC does offer a quick estimate of an individual's strengths and weaknesses in self-help skills, motor skills, communication skills, and social skills.

Instrument or Technique	Screening and Initial Identification (Prereferral)	Informal Determination (Prereferral)	Determination of Current Performance Level and Educational Need	Evaluation of Teaching Programs and Strategies	Decisions about Classification and Program Placement (Postreferral)	IEP Goals	IEP Objectives	IEP Evaluation	Mild/Moderate	Severe/Profound	Preschool	Elementary Age	Secondary Age	Adult	Special Considerations	Educational Relevance for Exceptional Students
Adaptive Behavior Inventory			X		X	X			X			X	X		Easy to administer and score; there is a shorter version for screening purposes	useful
AAMR Adaptive Behavior Scale–Second Edition: Residential and Community Edition			X		X	X			X	X	X	X	X	X	Technical aspects of Part Two have been questioned; has limited use for more severely retarded individuals	useful
AAMR Adaptive Behavior Scale–Second Edition: School Edition			X		X	X			X		X	X	X		Potentially useful instrument to aid in classification and placement decisions	useful
Assessment of Adaptive Areas			X		X	X			X	X	X	X	X	X	A recategorization of items from the ABS: RC–2 and S:2 that is consistent with the AAMR definition	useful
Scales of Independent Behavior			X		X	X			X	X	X	X	X	X	There is a screening version, criterion-referenced instrument, and a curriculum that is associated with the SIB	useful
Vineland Adaptive Behavior Scales			X		X		X	X	X	X	X	X	X		A useful instrument for the over-all measurement of adaptive behavior	very useful
Adaptive Behavior Inventory for Children					X				X			X			Part of System of Multicultural Pluralistic Assessment; used primarily to "declassify" minority children	adequate
Cain-Levine Social Competency Scale	X								X			X	X		Does not yield specific information for programming; validity data are lacking	limited
Camelot Behavioral Checklist	X		X		X	X			X			X	X	X	Does not yield specific information for programming; limited technical aspects	limited

									Comments	
Normative Adaptive Behavior Checklist	X		X		X		X	X	Can be used in conjunction with the Comprehensive Test of Adaptive Behavior	useful
TARC Assessment System	X		X			X	X	X	Use informally to determine strengths and weaknesses	limited

11

ASSESSMENT OF BEHAVIORAL AND EMOTIONAL STATUS

Instruments and Procedures Included

Classroom and Home Behavior-Rating Scales

Behavior Assessment System for Children

Revised Behavior Problem Checklist

Behavior Rating Profile–2

Child Behavior Checklist

Devereux Behavior Rating Scale–School Form

Behavior Evaluation Scale-2

Burks Behavior Rating Scale

Emotional or Behavior Disorder Scale

School Social Behavior Scales

Walker Problem Behavior Identification Checklist

Social Skills Instruments

Social Skills Rating System

Walker-McConnell Scale of Social Competence and School Adjustment

ADD/ADHD Instruments

Attention Deficit Disorders Evaluation Scale

ADD-H Comprehensive Teacher's Rating Scale (2nd Edition)

Attention Deficit/Hyperactivity Disorder Test

Children's Attention and Adjustment Survey

Conners Rating Scales

Autism Instruments
>   Autism Screening Instrument for Educational Planning–2
>   Childhood Autism Rating Scale
>   Gilliam Autism Rating Scale

Measurement of Emotional Status
>   Projective Methods
>   Self-Concept
>   Inventories and Questionnaires

Wendy had a history of emotional problems. Her parents reported that she would have extreme mood swings. One minute she would be depressed and withdrawn, and the next, elated, happy, and laughing. No environmental effect seemed to be triggering these changes. At other times, she would become extremely aggressive. When she was 5, she seriously injured her 2-year-old brother. At that time she was taken to a psychologist, who attempted to evaluate her emotional state. There was some question as to whether placing Wendy in a school for children with serious emotional disturbance would be the most appropriate thing to do.

Hector is a fifth-grade student who is constantly getting into trouble. Both his teacher and parents describe him as "very active." Recently, Hector has also been getting into trouble for stealing and destroying property. His teacher decided to administer a behavior-rating scale to document the areas in which Hector was having problems and to help set priorities among behavioral goals for him to achieve.

In recent years, there has been increasing interest in the measurement of an individual's emotional and behavioral status. This can be traced to three specific issues. First, the importance and relevance of *social skill development* has become more recognized in the past decade. Second, *autism* was recognized by IDEA as a separate disability area; subsequently, there has been a search for reliable methods of screening and identifying children with this condition. Third, although not officially noted as a disability area under IDEA, *Attention Deficit Disorder (ADD)* and *Attention-Deficit/Hyperactivity Disorder (ADHD)* remain highly visible topics within the field of special education. A number of instruments have been developed to help identify children with ADD and ADHD.

Most instruments that measure emotional and behavioral status involve the *indirect measurement* of emotional status or the *direct measurement* of behavior. Measurement of an individual's emotional state usually requires a great deal of inference and subjectivity on the part of the examiner. On the other hand, standardized measures of classroom behavior usually involve direct observation documented by some type of behavior-rating scale.

BEHAVIOR-RATING SCALES

WHY USE BEHAVIOR-RATING SCALES?

Screening and identification, decisions about classification and program placement; establishment of IEP goals

WHO SHOULD USE THEM?

Teachers, school psychologists

Behavior-rating scales are concerned with documenting observable behavior. Typically, these scales are developed for use by the classroom teacher or some other individual who has an opportunity to observe the examinee. Like inventories and questionnaires (discussed later in this chapter), behavior-rating scales usually include items grouped according to some categorical characteristic. Although there are few similarities across the names of categories in different rating scales, many of the categories tend to measure the same behavioral dimensions (Bullock, Wilson, & Campbell, 1990). Theoretically, the grouping of items leads to a profile of a student's behavior patterns. Behavior-rating scales have been criticized, however, on a number of grounds. For example, the technical adequacy of many scales has been questioned. Also, the educational significance of their data is limited. In this chapter, the discussion of behavior-rating scales will focus on (a) general classroom and home behavior instruments, (b) social skills instruments, (c) ADD/ADHD instruments, and (d) autism instruments.

CLASSROOM AND HOME BEHAVIOR INSTRUMENTS

Behavior Assessment System for Children

The Behavior Assessment System for Children (BASC) (Reynolds & Kamphaus, 1992) is a multidimensional approach for evaluating the behavior of individuals ages four to eighteen. The BASC includes five separate components that can be used individually or in combination. These are the Teacher Rating Scales (TRS), the Parent Rating Scales (PRS), the Self-Report of Personality (SRP), the Structured Developmental History (SDH), and the Student Observation System (SOS). The BASC is considered multidimensional because it measures many different aspects of behavior and personality.

Description

Teacher Rating Scales.   Three separate forms for the TRS are designed for different age levels. These are the preschool form (ages 4 to 5), the child form (ages 5 to 11), and the adolescent form (ages 12 to 18). Each form can be completed in about ten to twenty minutes. Each of the forms has five composites composed of fourteen separate scales. In addition, an overall composite called the Behavioral Symptoms Index is available. A description of each scale, the number of items for the preschool (PS), child (C), and adolescent (A) forms, and a representative item in each scale are presented next. The scales are grouped according to their corresponding composites.

Externalizing Problems

Aggression (PS—12 items, C and A—14)—"Argues when denied own way."
Hyperactivity (PS—10 items, C and A—13)—"Cannot wait to take turns."
Conduct Disorders (PS—0 items, C—10, A—12)—"Has friends who are in trouble."

Internalizing Problems

Anxiety (PS—11 items, C and A—8)—"Says 'I am afraid I will make a mistake.'"
Depression (PS—11 items, C—10 and A—9)—"Says 'I don't have any friends.'"
Somatization (PS—11 items, C and A—8)—"Has headaches."

School Problems

Attention Problems (PS—7 items, C—8, and A—6)—"Gives up easily when learning something new."
Learning Problems (PS—0 items, C and A—9)—"Does not complete tests."

Other Problems

Atypicality (PS and C—14 items, A—11)—"Hears sounds that are not there."
Withdrawal (PS and C—8 items, A—7)—"Avoids other children/adolescents."

Adaptive Skills

Adaptability (PS—8 items, C—6, A—0)—"Objects to change in routine."
Leadership (PS—0 items, C and A—9)—"Attends afterschool activities."
Social Skills (PS—10 items, C—12, A—11)—"Congratulates others when good things happen to them."
Study Skills (PS—0 items, C—12, A—13)—"Asks to make up missed assignments."

Parent Rating Scales.   The PRS also provides for a comprehensive evaluation of the child's adaptive and problem behaviors. It uses the same response format as the TRS and also takes approximately the same amount of time to complete (ten to twenty minutes). Table 11.1 also shows the composites and scales of the PRS component of the BASC. Note that the areas are similar to the TRS with the exception of the School Problem Composite and the Learning Problems and Study Skills Scales, which are not included in the PRS.

TABLE 11.1   Composites and Scales in the TRS and PRS

Composite/Scale	Teacher Rating Scales			Parent Rating Scales		
	Preschool	Child	Adolescent	Preschool	Child	Adolescent
Externalizing Problems	•	•	•	•	•	•
Aggression	•	•	•	•	•	•
Hyperactivity	•	•	•	•	•	•
Conduct Problems		•	•		•	•
Internalizing Problems	•	•	•	•	•	•
Anxiety	•	•	•	•	•	•
Depression	•	•	•	•	•	•
Somatization	•	•	•	•	•	•
School Problems		•	•			
Attention Problems	•	•	•	•	•	•
Learning Problems		•	•			
(Other Problems)						
Atypicality	•	•	•	•	•	•
Withdrawal	•	•	•	•	•	•
Adaptive Skills	•	•	•	•	•	•
Adaptability	•	•		•	•	
Leadership		•	•	•	•	•
Social Skills	•	•	•	•	•	•
Study Skills		•	•			
Behavioral Symptoms Index	•	•	•	•	•	•

Note: Italicized scales compose the Behavioral Symptoms Index.

Self-Report of Personality.   The SRP has two forms for two different age levels: the child form (ages 8 to 11) and the adolescent form (ages 12 to 18). The child form has twelve scales and the adolescent form has fourteen. The items in the SRP are answered as either true or false. There is also a broad composite score called the Emotional Symptoms Index. The composites and corresponding scales as well as a representative item are listed below.

Clinical Maladjustment

Anxiety (C—17 items, A—14)—"I am afraid of a lot of things."
Atypicality (C—14 items, A—17)—"Sometimes voices tell me to do bad things."

Locus of Control (C—16 items, A—13)—"My parents control my life."
Social Stress (C—12 items, A—13)—"Other children are happier than I am."
Somatization (C—0 items, A—11)—"I have fainting spells."

School Maladjustment

Attitude to school (C—9 items, A—10)—"I can hardly wait to quit school."
Attitude to Teachers (C—10 items, A—9)—"My teacher never understands me."
Sensation Seeking (C—0 items, A—14)—"Stealing something from a store is exciting."

Other Problems

Depression (C—17 items, A—13)—"I never have anything to do that is really fun."
Sense of Inadequacy (C—12 items, A—13)—"I am always disappointed in my grades."

Personal Adjustment

Relations with Parents (C—10 items, A—8)—"My mother and father help me if I ask them to."
Interpersonal Relations (C—10 items, A—16)—"People think I am fun to be with."
Self-Esteem (C—6 items, A—8)—"I wish I were different."
Self-Reliance (C—14 items, A—7)—"I am good at showing others how to do things."

Structured Developmental History. The SDH can either be completed directly by a parent using a questionnaire or by an examiner through an interview with the parent or guardian. The SDH allows for an extensive history of developmental and medical factors that could have an effect on the child's current behavior.

Student Observation System. The SOS form allows for the direct observation of the student in a classroom setting. It uses a momentary time sampling procedure (see Chapter 5 for a discussion of this procedure). It allows for the observation of both positive and negative behaviors.

Interpretation of Results

Each item of the TRS and PRS is rated on a four-point scale from "never" to "almost always." These raw scores can then be converted to T-scores (standard score with a mean of 50 and a standard deviation of 10) and percentile ranks. These scores are available for each scale as well as the composite areas noted above (the exception is the Other Problems composite). In addition, a computer scoring program allows the examiner to enter and score the results in five minutes. A behavior profile is available to display the results visually (see Figure 11.1). The SRP provides T-scores and percentile ranks for the Clinical Maladjustment, School Maladjustment, and Personal Adjustment composites as well as each individual scale. In addition, an Emotional Symptoms Index is available that combines the

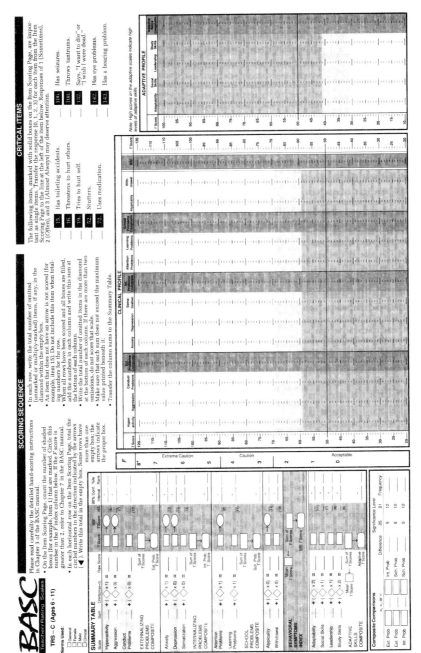

FIGURE 11.1   Summary Page of a TRS

Behavior Assessment System for Children (BASC) by Cecil R. Reynolds and Randy W. Kamphaus. Copyright © 1992 American Guidance Service, Inc., 4201 Woodland Road, Circle Pines, MN 55014–1796. Reproduced with permission of the publisher. All rights reserved.

scores from several scales to give an overall indication of the individual's emotional status. There are also three types of validity scores to determine if the person is "faking bad" or "faking good," or if he or she consistently chooses nonsensical items. The SDH and SOS provide additional information but are not scored in the traditional sense. The authors provide detailed information on the steps to follow in interpreting the results of the TRS, PRS, and SRP.

Technical Characteristics

Normative Sample. The BASC has both general and clinical norms. The general norms included 2,401 individuals for the TRS, 3,483 for the PRS, and 9,461 for the SRP. The subjects were chosen on the basis of geographic region, socioeconomic status, culture, and ethnicity represented in the U.S. census. The clinical norms consisted of 693 for the TRS, 401 for the PRS, and 411 for the SRP. The clinical norms contained individuals receiving special services for emotional or behavioral problems. Geographic and other factors were not controlled. Male and Female norms allow for gender-specific comparisons. These norms are a subset of the general norm sample.

Reliability. The internal consistency reliability coefficients for the TRS scales ranged from a median of .82 (ages 4 and 5) to .90 (ages 12 to 14) for the general norms and .82 to .85 for the clinical norms. Coefficients for the composites were all above .90. Test-retest coefficients for the scales ranged from .83–.92 (Preschool form), .59–.94 (Child form), and .74–.93 (Adolescent form). Coefficients for the composites were generally in the .90s for the Preschool and Child forms and the .80s for the Adolescent form. Interrater reliability was determined for the Preschool level and Child levels. In general, these coefficients were lower than the other types but the authors argue that different observers tend to evaluate a child's behavioral tendencies differently.

Median internal consistency coefficients for the PRS scales ranged .72–.78. Coefficients for the composite ranged from the middle .80s to low .90s for each of the three age levels. Again, coefficients for the clinical norms were somewhat higher. Test-retest correlations for the scales ranged from .41–.92, although the majority were above .70. Composite coefficients ranged from the .70s–.90s. Interrater reliability for the PRS were also lower, although they were acceptable at the Adolescent level.

Internal consistency for the SRP was approximately .80 for all age levels for the general and the clinical samples. Test-retest coefficients were generally in the middle .70s for the scales and middle .80s for the composites.

Validity. Content validity for the TRS, PRS, and SRP was maximized by the authors' careful review of other rating scales, literature on social/emotional assessment, and their background and experience working with students with behavior problems. The BASC went through several item-selection phases as well as factor analyses to determine the final item pool. Construct validity is based on the factor analytic studies that supported the definition of the scales and composites. Criterion validity coefficients provided in the manual show the correlations with other behavior rating scales. In general, these correlations were in the low to moderate range. A fourth type of validity—diagnostic validity—was determined by demonstrating that the BASC differentiated students with and without problems at a moderate level.

Review of Relevant Research

- The BASC Teacher Rating Scale was validated using data from the BASC Student Observation Scale (Lett & Kamphaus, 1992).
- Two advantages of the BASC are the inclusion of a validity scale and separate scales for anxiety and depression. This is different from other behavior-rating scales in which these latter two areas are combined (Kline, 1994).
- The use of the Self Report of Personality is limited for younger children (age eight and younger) because of comprehension difficulties with several items. In addition, the SRP is different from the PRS and TRS in content, format, and structure, thus making cross-source comparisons difficult, particularly in research investigations (Adams & Drabman, 1994).
- The BASC has many strengths and is a psychometrically well-developed instrument, although the SDH and SOS are less technically sound (Hoza, 1994).

Summary of Research Findings

The limited research on the BASC has been somewhat favorable. The BASC appears to be an instrument with many clinical uses, although its value as a research tool might be somewhat limited. In general, the technical characteristics of the instrument have been lauded, and the multiple sources of information have been valued. The TRS and PRS, in particular, seem to have support for their use.

OVERVIEW: BEHAVIOR ASSESSMENT SYSTEM FOR CHILDREN

- ■ *Age level*—4 to 18 years
- ■ *Type of administration*—Individual
- ■ *Technical adequacy*—Good standardization (general norms), limited standardization (clinical norms), varied reliability (depending on component), adequate validity
- ■ *Scores yielded*—T-scores, percentile ranks
- ■ *Suggested use*—The BASC has the potential to be one of the better behavior-rating scales. It has incorporated many positive features of other instruments. For example, it has several components, including a teacher rating scale, a parent rating scale, and a self-report of personality. It also has different forms for different ages and considers the internalizing/externalizing dichotomy of behavior. There is some evidence that the Teacher Rating Scales and the Parent Rating Scales may be more useful than the Self-Report of Personality, the Structured Developmental History, and the Student Observation System. More research will undoubtedly shed more light on the uses and possible limitations of the BASC.

Revised Behavior Problem Checklist

The Revised Behavior Problem Checklist (RBPC) (Quay & Peterson, 1987) includes eighty-nine items designed for use with students from kindergarten through sixth grade. The instrument is designed for use by teachers, and it is easy to administer and score. The examiner indicates whether each of the eighty-nine items (or behavioral characteristics) represents a problem for the child being evaluated.

Description

The eighty-nine items of the RBPC are divided into four major scales and two minor scales. The major scales are Conduct Disorders (twenty-two items), Socialized Aggression (seventeen items), Attention Problems–Immaturity (sixteen items), and Anxiety-Withdrawal (eleven items). The minor scales are Psychotic Behavior (six items) and Motor Excess (five items). For each of the items (for example, "has temper tantrums") the rater must assign the child a score of 0 (does not constitute a problem), 1 (mild problem), or 2 (severe problem).

Interpretation of Results

The scores for each scale are added and then analyzed by looking at a profile that will highlight an individual's behavioral excesses and deficits. It is also possible to compare the scores with "normal" and "clinical" groups. T-scores (standard scores with a mean of 50 and a standard deviation of 10) are available, but the author cautions that more data should be collected before they can be used reliably.

Technical Characteristics

Normative Sample. More than 750 children from four separate samples provided information that was factor analyzed to develop the RBPC. Data regarding the standardization are generally lacking.

Reliability. A number of limited reliability studies have been conducted. Interrater reliability ranged from .52 (Anxiety-Withdrawal) to .85 (Conduct Disorder). Test-retest coefficients ranged from .49 (Social Aggression) to .83 (Attention Problems-Immaturity).

Validity. The construct validity has been carefully established through the use of factor analysis to aid in item selection. The authors also report some concurrent validity data and a discussion of the relationship between dimensions of the RBPC and various diagnostic categories.

Review of Relevant Research

The majority of the literature focuses on the earlier versions of the RBPC. There are considerable similarities in these versions so that these research studies are probably relevant for the RBPC as well. In fact, Heinze (1987) reported high correlations between the BPC and the RBPC. Research on both of these versions is included.

- Four factors have been identified for the BPC: hyperkinetic, shy-inept, depressed, and dyssocial (Arnold, Barneby, & Smeltzer, 1981).
- The BPC can be used effectively with preschool children (Gayton, Thornton, & Bassett, 1982).
- Three dimensions of problem behavior are typically identified to account for the majority of variance in children classified as deviant. These are conduct disorder, anxiety-withdrawal, and immaturity (Von Isser, Quay, & Love, 1980). The same researchers point out that the BPC measures these three areas.
- Students with learning disabilities (LD) scored differently than did non-LD students on items measuring traits such as anxiety, nonparticipation, and poor self-confidence (Cullinan, Epstein, & Lloyd, 1981).
- The conduct-disorder and personality-problem factors best discriminated groups of students with behavioral disorders, educable mental retardation, and LD (Cullinan, Epstein, & Dembinski, 1979). Students with educable mental retardation (EMR), LD, and emotional disturbance all scored high on the immaturity-inadequacy factor (Gajar, 1979).
- The BPC can be used confidently with deaf students (Hirshoren & Schnittjer, 1979).

A few studies located looked at the use of the RBPC. Those are described below.

- The RBPC can effectively discriminate groups of children with behavior disorders from those without disabilities (Quay & Peterson, 1987).
- Only low to moderate correlations were found between two groups of teachers using the RBPC (Simpson, 1989; Simpson & Arnett, 1987).
- Low correlations between mothers' and teachers' ratings were reported (Mattison, Bagnato, & Strickler, 1987; Simpson & Halpin, 1986).
- The Motor Excess Scale was useful in differentiating attention deficit disorders (ADD) with hyperactivity and ADD without hyperactivity (Lahey, Schaughency, Strauss, & Frame, 1984).
- The RBPC was useful in differentiating inattentive preschool children versus those with conduct disorders (Hinshaw, Morrison, & Carta, 1987).
- The RBPC was found to have less than acceptable reliability and was criticized for measuring only negative behaviors (Wilson & Bullock, 1988).
- The lack of national norms is a serious drawback (Lahey & Piacentini, 1985).
- There have been several reviews of the RBPC. Cancelli (1985) noted that the increased number of items in the revised version increased its reliability and that the minor subscales did little to add to its predictive validity. Lahey and Piacentini (1985) stated that the RBPC had excellent construct validity and was "perhaps the most valid of all teacher rating scales in terms of factor structure and related measures of validity." Both reviewers noted that local

norms should be developed, particularly because nationally representative derived scores are not available. Finally, Simpson (1990) noted that the RBPC had relatively low interrater reliability, although overall it is still judged to be one of the better behavior rating scales.

Summary of Research Findings

Research on the RBPC and its earlier versions has primarily investigated the instruments' technical characteristics. The careful analysis of the various behavior factors and the subsequent items chosen for each factor makes a profile analysis appropriate. In general, the construct validity of the instrument has been supported, although the reliability, particularly interrater reliability has been questioned.

OVERVIEW: REVISED BEHAVIOR PROBLEM CHECKLIST

- *Age level*—Kindergarten to grade 6
- *Type of administration*—Individual
- *Technical characteristics*—Adequate reliability (limited interrater), acceptable validity (based on research data)
- *Scores yielded*—Profile analysis, T-scores (used cautiously)
- *Suggested use*—The RBPC is a popular rating scale that is easy to administer and score. A growing body of literature is focused on its technical and interpretive characteristics. The RBPC seems to be a valid measure of classroom behavior problems although, like many behavior rating scales, it has some problems regarding reliability. One concern is the limited standardization sample.

Behavior Rating Profile–2

The Behavior Rating Profile–2 (BRP-2) (Brown & Hammill, 1990) is an ecological approach to assessment, in that the information is obtained from a number of sources. The BRP-2 includes four components: Student Rating Scales—Home, School, and Peer; a Teacher Rating Scale; a Parent Rating Scale; and a Sociogram. This allows for the evaluation of the student in a number of settings and by a number of individuals. The test is individually administered (except for the Sociogram) and is appropriate for children 6 1/2–18 1/2 years old.

Description

Student Rating Scales—The three student rating scales consist of twenty items about school, twenty items about home, and twenty items about peers. This section, which is completed by the student, is presented in a true-false format. Examples include "I can't seem to stay at my desk in school"

(school item); "Other children are always picking on me" (peer item); and "I don't listen when my parents are talking to me" (home item).

Teacher Rating Scale—This scale can be completed by all school personnel who have significant contact with the student. It consists of thirty items that the teacher must categorize as "very much like the student," "like the student," "not like the student," or "not at all like the student." Examples of items are "doesn't follow class rules" and "tattles on classmates."

Parent Rating Scale—This section can be completed by one or both of the parents. It is similar in format to the Teacher Rating Scale. Examples of items include "is verbally aggressive to parents" and "won't share belongings willingly."

Sociogram—This is a method to get peer perceptions into the evaluation. A pair of questions is given to each student in the class. An example is, "Which of the girls and boys in your class would you most like to have as your friend?" and "Which of the girls and boys in your class would you least like to have as your friend?" Each student must provide three names for each question. Using the scoring procedures noted in the manual, the examiner ranks the students according to their acceptance level.

Interpretation of Results

Results from each section can be converted to standard scores with a mean of 10 and a standard deviation of 3. These scores can be plotted on a behavior-rating profile sheet. Percentile ranks are also available.

Technical Characteristics

Normative Sample.   The sample included 2,682 students and 1,452 teachers from twenty-six states. The 1,948 parents involved came from only nineteen states. Demographic information is included in the manual.

Reliability.   Internal consistency was generally acceptable. Most coefficients were above .80. Test-retest coefficients ranged from .78 to .91 with a sample of thirty-six high school students and from .76 to .97 with approximately seventy-five children with emotional and learning problems. In a somewhat larger study (approximately two hundred students, teachers, and parents), test-retest coefficients ranged from .43 to .90 (student), .69 to .96 (parent), and .90 to .96 (teacher). The lowest coefficients were for grades one and two.

Validity.   Concurrent validity was established with the Walker Problem Behavior Checklist, the Behavior Problem Checklist, and the Vineland Social Maturity Scale. The authors state that 86 percent of the coefficients were above their acceptable level of .35. Relatively low coefficients with measures of aptitude and achievement are reported, although the authors argue that this is expected. Arguments supporting content and construct validity are also provided.

Review of Relevant Research

To date, no research has been reported on the BRP-2. The original BRP has received limited attention in the literature. In one review, Posey (1989) noted limitations including response bias and its unidimensionality. Bacon (1989) noted that no interrater reliability was given.

In one empirical study, Ellers, Ellers, and Bradley-Johnson (1989) found that the teacher form had adequate reliability for both screening and eligibility decisions for grades 1 through 12. They reported that the parent form was suitable for screening for grades 3 through 12 and eligibility for grades 3 through 6 and 11 through 12. They also found that the student form was not reliable enough for use at any age. These data can be generalized to the BRP-2 with some degree of confidence given the slight changes in the revised edition.

OVERVIEW: BEHAVIOR RATING PROFILE–2

- *Age level*—6 1/2–18 1/2 years old
- *Type of administration*—Individual (except for sociogram); small group possible
- *Technical characteristics*—Adequate reliability (except for grades 1 and 2, and for student form), questionable validity
- *Scores yielded*—Standard scores, percentile ranks
- *Suggested use*—The BRP-2 measures a student's behavior in a number of settings and with information from a number of individuals. This yields information that, for instance, will help to determine if a student's behavior problem occurs only at home or only at school. Unfortunately, it is difficult to determine whether a difference in behavior is really a difference or only the way in which the behavior is perceived, because more than one person is rating. (What if, for instance, two teachers and the parents rate the student as average, and one other teacher indicates that a problem exists. Does the student behave differently in that one teacher's class or does that particular teacher have different standards and expectations?) Perhaps using multiple raters in each setting would be the procedure to follow. Alternatively, more interrater-reliability studies might allow examiners to interpret the results more confidently. It does appear to be limited for younger children and the student form has questionable relevance at all age levels.

  In summary, the BRP-2 is a potentially useful tool to determine how a student behaves in different settings, and how different individuals perceive that behavior. However, definitive diagnostic decisions should not be based solely on the BRP-2. Clearly, more research should be conducted on the BRP-2.

Child Behavior Checklist

The Child Behavior Checklist (CBCL) (Achenbach, 1991a) is designed to be used by parents to rate the behavioral competencies and behavioral problems of their child. The CBCL is designed to be used in conjunction with the 1991 Child Behavior Profile for ages 4 to 18, which provides the interpretive guidelines for the information obtained from the CBCL. There are also supplemental instruments or components called the Teacher Report Form, Direct Observation Form, and a Youth Self-Report that together provide a comprehensive behavior rating system. A brief description of the components follows.

Description

Child Behavior Checklist and 1991 Child Behavior Profile.   The CBCL includes items that measure social competence in areas such as involvement with social organizations and relationships with friends. Additional items focus on behavior problems. Results of the CBCL are placed on the profile, which consists of three social competency scales and a number of behavior-problem scales identified through factor analysis. There are separate profiles (with differing scales) for both boys and girls for two separate age ranges (4–11 and 12–18). In general, the various factors or scales can be classified as internalizing (withdrawn, somatic complaints, and anxious/depressed) and externalizing (delinquent behavior, aggressive behavior). There are four other scales: social problems, thought problems, attention problems, and sex problems (for 6 to 11 years only).

There is also a CBCL and 1992 profile for ages 2 to 3 (Achenbach, 1992) that includes ninety-nine items, fifty-nine of which have counterparts on the CBCL for ages four through eighteen. The scales for the CBCL/2-3 are internalizing (anxious/depressed and withdrawn), externalizing (aggressive behavior and destructive behavior), sleep problems, and somatic problems.

Teacher Report Form.   This component is used with the 1991 Child Behavior Profile for ages 5 five to 18 (Achenbach, 1991b) and has separate forms for boys and girls ages 5 through 11 and 12 through 18. There are items that allow the rating of behavior problems, plus an item on academic performance and an item on adaptive functioning.

Direct Observation Form.   The Direct Observation Form (Achenbach, 1986) is somewhat unique; it requires the evaluator to observe the child in ten-minute time samples and then respond to ninety-six items that yield a behavior problem score and an on-task score. The revised version provides more detailed scoring and item definitions than the original.

Youth Self-Report.   The YSR and 1991 profile for ages 11 through 18 (Achenbach, 1991C) is used with the 1991 Child Behavior Profiles for ages 4 through 18 and 5 through 18 (Achenbach, 1991a & b) and requires the individual to rate him-

or herself. There are several general questions (for example, "Please list any jobs or chores that you have") and other items (for example, "I show off or clown") that must be rated "not true," "sometimes true," or "very true." Essentially, this section is the same as the CBCL, with the wording changed to reflect the first person. Sixteen items from the CBCL have been replaced with socially desirable items endorsed by most youth. This can be completed by students with at least a fifth-grade-level reading ability.

Interpretation of Results

As noted previously, results of the CBCL and other components are interpreted through the use of the various profiles. The profile shown in Figure 11.2 shows the "normal range" of performance that is based on the T-scores (mean = 50; standard deviation = 10) yielded. Profiles are also interpreted as "borderline" or "clinical." A computer scoring program for the profile is also available and provides a visual graph.

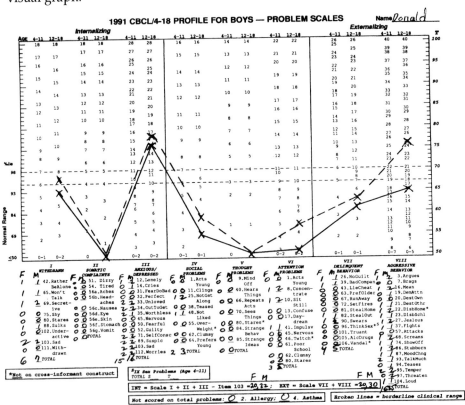

FIGURE 11.2   Example of CBCL and Revised Behavior Profile for Boys

From T. M. Achenbach, *Child Behavior Checklist.* Copyright © 1991 by T. M. Achenbach. Reproduced by permission.

Technical Characteristics

Normative Sample.   The CBCL was normed on 2,368 children. Scales were devised from parents' ratings of 4,455 clinically referred children.

Reliability.   Interrater reliabilities were primarily in the .90s for the CBCL and from the .70s to the .90s for the Direct Observation Form. Test-retest coefficients were in the .80s–.90s for the Teacher Report Form.

Validity.   Results of several validity studies are reported in the manual. These generally demonstrate moderate correlations with other behavior-rating scales and the instruments' ability to identify children who have been referred for mental health services.

Review of Relevant Research

- More reliable information can be obtained by adding the Teacher Rating Form to the overall Child Behavior Profile when screening for behavior problems (Edelbrock & Achenbach, 1984).
- The CBCL did not correlate highly with risk factors typically associated with childhood psychiatric problems (Mooney, Thompson, & Nelson, 1987).
- There was generally low agreement between teachers and parents using the CBCL, thus indicating the need for a multiple-rater system (Garrison & Earls, 1985).
- The Direct Observation Form provides valid and reliable information with a minimum of training (Reed & Edelbrock, 1983).
- Elliot and Busse (1990) felt that the Youth Self-Report was useful but not for classification decisions. They also pointed out that whereas the Teacher Form was not user-friendly, it was psychometrically superior to most behavior-rating scales.
- The CBCL correlated highly with the RBPC (Heinze, 1987).
- The CBCL scores were dissimilar when administered to both parents. There is a need for separate norms for mothers and fathers (Leblanc & Reynolds, 1989).
- The CBCL has good internal consistency and construct validity in relation to widely accepted indices of school functioning (Pryor, Wilkinson, Harris & Travato, 1989).
- Christenson (1990), in a review of the CBCL, highly recommended both the Teacher and Self-Report forms. She noted that the manuals were well written, were reliable and valid, and were based on ongoing research.
- The CBCL can be used to help identify individuals with adaptive behavior deficits (Pearson & Lachar, 1994).
- Interpretive guidelines for the CBCL are limited (Kline, 1994).

Summary of Research Findings

The majority of published research on the CBCL has focused on establishing the validity and reliability of its various components. In general, the technical characteristics of the CBCL have been favorable. There are also many articles that describe and review the CBCL. A bibliography that includes numerous articles in which the CBCL has been used is available (Achenbach & Brown, 1991).

OVERVIEW: CHILD BEHAVIOR CHECKLIST

- *Age level*—2 to 16 years old
- *Type of administration*—Individual
- *Technical adequacy*—Generally good reliability and validity
- *Scores yielded*—T-scores (type of standard score); results are placed on the Child Behavior Profile
- *Suggested use*—Overall, the CBCL is one of the better behavior-rating scales available. Items were carefully selected and statistically validated. The idea of separate profiles (with different scales included) for boys and girls at different age levels is an excellent one. In addition, the use of separate forms that allow multiple ratings provides potentially important information. The CBCL and its associated components are continually updated through ongoing research by the author. This is advantageous, but it requires test users to keep up with the latest versions of the latest instruments. Overall, the CBCL can be used confidently to document the behavioral status of students in a variety of areas.

The Devereux Behavior Rating Scale–School Form

The Devereux Behavior Rating Scale–School Form (DBRS-SF) (Naglieri, LeBuffe, & Pfeiffer, 1993) is the most recent revision of the Devereux Behavior Rating Scales that date to the 1960s. According to the authors, the DBRS-SF can be used for a variety of purposes, including the identification of individuals who need more in-depth behavioral evaluation and the determination of which specific aspects of behavior might be more atypical for an individual than for others. The instrument can also be used to identify problem behaviors and to monitor and evaluate behavioral changes over time. The DBRS-SF actually contains two levels or versions corresponding to the age groups 5 to 12 years and 12 to 18 years. Although some of the items were selected from previous Devereux Scales, the 1993 revision is considerably different from its predecessors. For each age level of the DBRS-SF there are four subscales (each with ten items) that correspond to the criteria listed in PL 94-142 regarding the identification of serious emotional disturbance.

Description of Scales

Interpersonal Problems—This includes ten items such as "annoy others?" (5–12 years) and "disregard the feelings of others?" (13–18 years).

Inappropriate Behaviors/Feelings—This includes items such as "become very upset or emotional if he/she did not get what he/she wants?" (5–12 years) and "failed to control his/her anger?" (13–18 years).

Depression Subscale—Items include "fail to participate in activities?" (5–12 years) and "appear discouraged or depressed?" (13–18 years).

Physical symptoms/fears—Items include "say that others were picking on him/her?" (5–12 years) and "say that people picked on or did not like him or her?" (13–18 years).

Interpretation of Results

For each of the forty items on the DBRS-SF the informant is asked to rate the student using a five-point scale (from "never" to "very frequently"). Each item is preceded by the phrase "During the past four weeks how often did the child...?" Raw scores are totaled for each subscale and are converted to a standard score with a mean of 10 and a standard deviation of 3. These conversions are available on the basis of the rater (parent or teacher), age group (5 to 12 or 13 to 18) and the individual's gender. It is also possible to obtain a total standard score and percentile rank for the combination of the four subscales. The standard scores can then be classified as being normal, borderline, significant, or very significant. The authors also provide a method to identify problem behaviors that occur in a specific area or areas. In other words, it might be possible for the individual to receive scores in the average range for total and subscale scores, yet have a specific pattern or problems in a certain area. Tables are provided to determine if specific items should be considered significant.

Technical Characteristics

Normative Sample. The DBRS-SF included 3,153 children and adolescents in its standardization sample. The authors detail the procedures used to ensure a representative sample on the basis of age, gender, geographic region, race, ethnicity, socioeconomic status, community size, and educational placement.

Reliability. Internal reliability of the subscales were generally in the .80s range, with slightly lower coefficients for ages 13 to 18. The internal reliability coefficient for the total scale was .94 and .95 for ages 13 to 18 and 5 to 12, respectively. In general the internal reliability coefficients were higher for teacher ratings than for parent ratings. Test-retest reliability was determined at twenty-four-hour, two-week, and four-week intervals. Not surprisingly, the coefficients were higher given a shorter interval between tests. For example, total scale coefficients decreased from .75 at twenty-four hours to .65 for two weeks to .52 for four weeks. Interrater reliability studies were conducted that resulted in total scale coefficients of .40 between teacher and residential counselor and .53 between teacher and a teacher's aide. Intrarater reliability was also determined in two studies in which a teacher and residential counselor each separately rated the individual two times. Those total scale coefficients were .78 for the teacher and .57 for the residential counselor. For the most part, the subscale coefficients for intra- and interrater reliability were similar to the total scale coefficients.

Validity.   Criterion-related validity was determined through the use of six separate studies that investigated the accuracy of the DBRS-SF in differentiating between individuals with serious emotional disturbance and those without. For the 5 to 12 age range, the average percentage of total correct identification was 75.3 percent. The average percentage for ages 13 to 18 was 77.5 percent. Arguments for both content and construct validity are also reported in the test manual.

Review of Relevant Research
Little research was found on the DBRS-SF although previous versions have been widely researched. In one study of the DBRS-SF, Naglier, Bardos, and LeBuffe (1995) found that it was able to correctly identify approximately 75 percent of those students with and without serious emotional disturbance. The following provides a sample of studies from previous editions although they should be interpreted cautiously because of the differences in the new scale.

- The DESB is valid and reliable, although teachers may vary in their use of the instruments (Finkelman, Ferrerase, & Garmezy, 1989).
- The DESB is a valid and reliable measure of inappropriate behavior for visually impaired children (Ross & Gallagher, 1976).
- The reliability of the DESB is satisfactory (Schaefer, Baker, & Zawel, 1975). The researchers identified three factors: (1) classroom-management problem, (2) self-reliant learner, and (3) seeks teacher approval.
- The DESB was not as accurate as the Behavior Problem Checklist in identifying children as aggressive, hyperactive, or withdrawn (Proger, Mann, Green, Bayuk, & Burger, 1975).
- In a longitudinal study of six hundred children, eight profile patterns were identified. These profiles roughly corresponded to eight achievement levels (reported in Spivack & Swift, 1973).
- In studying the item validity of the DESB, Willis, Smithy, and Holliday (1979) suggested that the instrument is much more effective in identifying students with severe rather than mild problems. They also suggested a thirty-six item instrument that eliminates four scales (Irrelevant-Responsiveness, Impatience, Disrespect-Defiance, and External Blame).

OVERVIEW: DEVEREUX BEHAVIOR RATING SCALE–SCHOOL FORM

- *Age level*—5 through 18 (2 forms)
- *Type of administration*—Individual
- *Technical adequacy*—Good standardization sample, good reliability (teacher), adequate reliability (parent), adequate validity

- *Scores yielded*—Standard scores, descriptive profiles
- *Suggested use*—The DBRS-SF is the newest revision of a series of tests originally published by the Devereux Foundation. There are two separate forms based on age level. The items and factors are consistent with the diagnostic criteria included in the definition of emotional disturbance noted in PL 94-142. The newest revision appears more technically sound than earlier versions and can be administered in a relatively short period of time. A more lengthy instrument, the Devereux Scales of Mental Disorders, is also available.

ADDITIONAL CLASSROOM/HOME BEHAVIOR INSTRUMENTS

In addition to the instruments just described several others are worthy of note. These include the *Behavior Evaluation Scale–2*, a revision of a quickly administered instrument, the *Burks Behavior Rating Scales*, which are somewhat dated yet still in use in many schools, the *Emotional or Behavior Disorder Scale*, designed to measure emotional and behavior problems based on the most recent definition, and the *School Social Behavior Scales*, which include a measure of both social competency and problem behaviors. Finally, the *Walker Problem Behavior Identification Checklist* has received a lot of use, primarily as a screening test.

The Behavior Evaluation Scale–2

- *Age level*—Kindergarten through grade 12
- *Type of administration*—Individual
- *Technical adequacy*—Adequate standardization, reliability, and validity
- *Scores yielded*—Standard scores for subscales and total, percentile ranks
- *Suggested use*—The Behavior Evaluation Scale–2 (BES-2) (McCarney, Jackson, & Leigh, 1990) can be administered in approximately fifteen to twenty minutes. It includes seventy-six items broken down into the areas of learning problems, interpersonal difficulties, inappropriate behaviors, unhappiness/depression, physical symptoms/fears, and a total score. It should be used in conjunction with other instruments to make important decisions, although it is appropriate for screening purposes. It is also easy for classroom use. Olmi (1994) concurred with these recommendations, noting that the BES-2 was a quickly administered instrument that would be helpful in screening or in assisting in identification with children with behavior or emotional problems.

Burks Behavior Rating Scales

- *Age level*—Grades 1 to 8 (preschool version ages 3 to 6)
- *Type of administration*—Individual

- *Technical characteristics*—Inadequate standardization, limited reliability and validity
- *Scores yielded*—Raw scores interpreted as "not significant," "significant," and "very significant"
- Suggested use—The Burks Behavior Rating Scales (BBRS) (Burks, 1977) is used to identify patterns of inappropriate behaviors. The BBRS consists of 110 items divided into 19 behavior categories or scales. In general, the behavior categories tend to be more psychiatric in nature and are of limited use in the classroom. Although the author suggested that it can be used to predict students who will or will not do well in special education, diagnostic decisions should not be made using this instrument. The technical characteristics, particularly the standardization group, are limited. The scoring system and typical profiles mentioned in the manual are overly simplified and subject to misinterpretation. The use of the BBRS should be limited to an initial screening of students, but even for this purpose more relevant instruments are available.

The Emotional or Behavior Disorder Scale

- *Age level*—4 1/2 to 21 years
- *Type of administration*—Individual
- *Technical adequacy*—Good normative sample, adequate reliability and validity
- *Scores yielded*—Standard scores, percentiles
- *Suggested use*—The Emotional or Behavior Disorder Scale (EBDS) (McCarney, 1994) was designed to meet the criteria specified in the new behavior disorder definition by the same name (see Chapter 4 for a discussion of this definition). The subscales included are Academic Progress, Social Relationships, Personal Adjustment, and Vocational, although the vocational component of the EBDS is sold separately and designed for use for students age 15 or older. School and home versions of the scale each can be administered in approximately fifteen to twenty minutes. One nice feature of the EBDS is an intervention manual that includes more than four hundred strategies, goals, and objectives for students with EBD. The EBDS can be used in conjunction with other information to meet the criteria for emotional and behavior disorders.

School Social Behavior Scales

- *Age Level*—Kindergarten through grade 12
- *Type of administration*—Individual
- *Technical adequacy*—Adequate normative sample, good reliability, adequate validity
- *Scores yielded*—Standard scores, percentile ranks
- *Suggested use*—The School Social Behavior Scales (SSBS) (Merrell, 1994) includes ratings of both social skills and problem behaviors. It is quick to administer (five to ten minutes) and consists of thirty-two items that measure

Social Competence and thirty-three items that measure Antisocial Behavior. Subscales of the Social Competence area are interpersonal skills, self-management skills, and academic skills. The three subscales from the Antisocial Behavior area are hostile-irritable, antisocial-aggressive, and disruptive-demanding. The author suggests that the SSBS can be used confidently as a screening instrument or as a part of a larger assessment battery to determine program eligibility and to develop intervention programs. Merrell (1994) reported that the SSBS had good internal reliability and moderate correlations with the Child Behavior Checklist.

The Walker Problem Behavior Identification Checklist

- *Age level*—Preschool to grade 6
- *Type of administration*—Individual
- *Technical characteristics*—Adequate reliability (for screening), questionable validity
- *Scores yielded*—T-scores, profile index
- *Suggested use*—The Walker Problem Behavior Identification Checklist (WPBIC) (Walker, 1983) is a list of fifty behaviors that are typically observed in the classroom. These fifty items are broken down into five scales: Acting Out, Withdrawal, Distractibility, Disturbed Peer Relations, and Immaturity. The WPBIC should be considered a quick screening instrument; its checklist format makes it easy to administer and score (see Figure 11.3 on page 254). It can be helpful in identifying areas for which evaluation and more depth may be necessary. The validity of the instrument has not been established adequately, and there is a lack of research information on the test. These limitations should caution overgeneralization of the results.

SOCIAL SKILLS INSTRUMENTS

One criticism of many behavior rating scales is that they focus more on maladaptive or problem behaviors instead of prosocial behaviors. With the acknowledged importance of social skill deficits in children with disabilities, it is not surprising that instruments have been developed that focus more on social competence and social skills. Two examples are the *Social Skills Rating System* and *The Walker-McConnell Scale of Social Competence and School Adjustment*.

Social Skills Rating System

The Social Skills Rating System (SSRS) (Gresham & Elliot, 1990) is a multirater assessment battery of social behaviors that can affect teacher–student relations, peer acceptance, and academic performance. There are teacher, parent, and student forms, each of which elicit information about the student from various viewpoints. The Teacher and Parent Forms are available for three levels: preschool,

	Scale				
	1	2	3	4	5
10. Is overactive, restless, and/or continually shifting body positions.			2		
11. Apologizes repeatedly for himself and/or his behavior.					2
12. Distorts the truth by making statements contrary to fact.	1				
13. Underachieving: performs below his demonstrated ability level.				1	
14. Disturbs other children: teasing, provoking fights, interrupting others.				2	
15. Tries to avoid calling attention to himself.		1			
16. Makes distrustful or suspicious remarks about actions of others toward him.	2				
17. Reacts to stressful situations or changes in routine with general body aches, head or stomach aches, nausea.					3
18. Argues and must have the last word in verbal exchanges.	1				
19. Approaches new tasks and situations with an "I can't do it" response.				1	
20. Has nervous tics: muscle-twitching, eye-blinking, nail-biting, hand-wringing.					3

FIGURE 11.3   Excerpt from the Walker Problem Behavior Identification Checklist

From H. Walker, *Walker Problem Behavior Identification Checklist*. Copyright © 1983, 1976, 1970 by Western Psychological Services, Los Angeles, CA. Reprinted by permission.

K–6, and 7–12, whereas the Student Rating Form is available for grades 3–6 and 7–12. Unlike many other behavior-rating scales, the SSRS focuses on positive behaviors as opposed to maladaptive behaviors. It does, however, include a brief assessment of problem behaviors as well. According to the authors, the SSRS can be used for a variety of purposes, including (1) identifying students at risk for social behavior problems; (2) differentiating mildly handicapped students from nonhandicapped students; (3) categorizing behavior difficulties; (4) selecting behaviors for school and home interventions; and (5) guiding the selection of intervention strategies. The information can also be used to assist in writing IEPs.

Description
In addition to the three rating scales at three different age levels, three specific areas are measured: social skills, problem behaviors, and academic competence.

The various forms and the corresponding areas that they measure are noted in the following section.

Preschool Level: Teacher Form
 Social Skills (30 items)
 Problem Behaviors (10 items)
Preschool Level: Parent Form
 Social Skills (39 items)
 Problem Behaviors (10 items)
Elementary Level: Student Form
 Social Skills (34 items)
Elementary Level: Teacher Form
 Social Skills (30 items)
 Problem Behavior (18 items)
 Academic Competence (9 items)
Elementary Level: Parent Form
 Social Skills (38 items)
 Problem Behaviors (17 items)
Secondary Level: Student Form
 Social Skills (39 items)
Secondary Level: Teacher Form
 Social Skills (30 items)
 Problem Behaviors (12 items)
 Academic Competence (9 items)
Secondary Level: Parent Form
 Social Skills (40 items)
 Problem Behaviors (12 items)

Interpretation of Results

Each rater responds to items such as "has temper tantrums" or "participates in group activities" using a 0 (never), 1 (sometimes), or 2 (very often) scale. In addition, the Parent and Teacher Forms include a separate rating on how important each behavior is to the rater (0—not important, 1—important, 2—critical). This information is used to prepare the intervention program for the individual student.

A variety of scoring options are available for the SSRS. In addition to percentile ranks and standard scores (mean = 100; standard deviation = 15), the behavior level can also be determined. The behavior level is simply a descriptive category that might be used to help identify areas for intervention.

Technical Characteristics

Normative Sample.   The Student Rating Form was standardized using more than four thousand children stratified by gender, race, region, and community size. The Teacher Rating Scale included 259 teachers' ratings of 1,335 children. The

Parent Form used approximately one thousand parents and was based on a volunteer sample. The authors note some limitation in the parent and teacher samples compared to the U.S. population; for example, the parent sample was better educated than the population as a whole.

Reliability.   Internal consistency coefficients for the social skills area ranged from .93 to .94 for the Teacher Form, .87 to .90 for the Parent Form, and were .83 for the Student Form. For the problem behavior area, the internal consistency coefficients ranged from .82 to .88 for the Teacher Form and .73 to .87 for the Parent Form. The coefficients for academic competence were .95. Test-retest coefficients for the Teacher Form were .85 for social skills, .84 for problem behaviors, and .93 for academic competence. Coefficients for the Parent Form for social skills were .87 and for problem behavior .65. For the Student Form, the coefficient for social skills was .68.

Validity.   The authors provide an argument for the assurance of content and social validity (the social significance of the behavior selected for intervention) and provide criterion-related validity coefficients. For the Teacher Form, coefficients for the social skills section with a variety of other rating scales ranged from .64 to .70. The correlations for the problem behavior area were somewhat lower, ranging from .55 to .81. The coefficients for the academic competence area ranged from .59 to .67. For the Parent Form, the coefficients with the CBCL ranged from .37 to .58 for the social skills area and .52 to .70 for the problem behavior area. The Student Form was also correlated with the CBCL (Youth Self-Report Form) and correlations ranged from .23 to .33. A correlation study with a self-concept scale also yielded a low coefficient of .30. The authors spend a considerable amount of time discussing and presenting data to support the construct validity of the instrument. This includes intercorrelations of the scales as well as factor analysis results. In addition, convergent and discriminate validity data are reported.

Review of Relevant Research
Limited research was located on the SSRS. In one study, Bramlett, Smith, and Edmonds (1994) found that the instrument could differentiate between students with and without disabilities, but was not able to discriminate between those with learning disabilities and those with mental retardation.

OVERVIEW: SOCIAL SKILLS RATING SYSTEM

- *Age level*—Preschool through secondary level
- *Type of administration*—Multiple raters (student, parent, teacher)
- *Scores yielded*—Behavior level, standard score, percentile rank
- *Technical adequacy*—Adequate standardization (Student Form), limited standardization (Teacher and Parent Forms); adequate reliability, questionable validity

- *Suggested use*—The SSRS allows for multiple ratings that can provide important diagnostic information. The SSRS was built on a solid theoretical framework and does have the advantage of looking primarily at the pro-social behaviors as opposed to maladaptive behaviors. An important aspect of the SSRS is the inclusion of an Assessment Intervention Record that allows the development of specific intervention programs based on data obtained on the SSRS. This provides a convenient record to list social skill strengths, social skill performance deficits, social skill acquisition deficits, and problem behaviors. In addition, the record provides a table that links the assessment needs with specific intervention suggestions. The test manual, in fact, devotes a chapter to discussing the development of intervention plans. Although the information presented is cursory, it does emphasize the importance of linking the assessment to a program of intervention strategies. It should be noted that the preschool version of the SSRS is somewhat limited due to the small standardization sample. Clearly, research needs to be conducted on the SSRS, primarily to discover the validity of the instrument. Hopefully, such data will support its use. Its several positive features (multiple ratings, consideration of importance of social behaviors, and assessment-intervention record) make it a viable alternative to other behavior rating scales.

Walker-McConnell Scale of Social Competence and School Adjustment

The Walker-McConnell Scale (W-M Scale) (Walker & McConnell, 1995) was designed to identify children with social skill deficits. The instrument is a rapid measure requiring only approximately five minutes to complete. There are three subscales to the W-M Scale: Teacher-Preferred Social Behavior, Peer-Preferred Social Behavior, and School Adjustment Behavior. The instrument is designed to be administered or completed by teachers who have had the opportunity to observe the student for at least two months. Although no age range is noted in the manual, norms are provided for children from kindergarten through grade 6. There is also an adolescent form for the instrument that is used with older students.

Description
  Teacher Preferred Social Behavior (16 items)—Examples include "accepts constructive criticism from peers without becoming angry" and "controls temper."
  Peer Preferred Social Behavior (17 items)—Examples include "plays or talks with peers for extended periods of time" and "plays games and activities at recess skillfully."
  School Adjustment Behavior (10 items)—These items, which measure adaptive social behavioral competencies, include "displays independent study skills" and "uses free time appropriately."

Interpretation of Results

The W-M Scale is completed using a likert-type scale (1 = never, 5 = frequently). The raw score for the total scale is converted to a standard score with a mean of 100 and a standard deviation of 15. In addition, percentile ranks and standard scores for the subscales (mean = 10, standard deviation = 3) are also available. According to the authors, any individual who scores 1 to 1 1/2 standard deviation units below the mean should be considered for further evaluation. They also briefly describe a method of using profile analysis to interpret the results. While the authors also mention that individual items could be used for writing objectives for IEPs, this practice has been questioned by reviewers (Worthington & Harrison, 1990).

Technical Characteristics

Normative sample.   Approximately eighteen hundred individuals were included in the standardization sample. In general, information about the sample is somewhat limited in the manual, although the authors do provide a description of some of the sample characteristics. Information such as socioeconomic status and the intellectual level of the students is not given.

Reliability.   Test-retest reliability ranged from .67 to .97 for the subscales and total score. Internal consistency reliability coefficients were high and all exceeded .90. Interrater reliability coefficients ranged considerably (from .11 to .74). The Teacher-Preferred Social Behavior subscale had the lowest interrater reliability.

Validity.   The authors describe the rationale for choosing the items that were initially used in the development of the instrument. They also discuss preliminary studies that were used to determine the final items used in the W-M Scale. Evidence of construct validity was provided through the use of confirmatory factor analysis, as well as by the results of studies that differentiated students of known different behavioral status. The concurrent validity of the W-M Scale was established using the Walker Problem Behavior Identification Checklist and the Social Skills Rating System and a self-concept scale. Coefficients were moderate, with most in the .70 range. No evidence of predictive validity was presented.

Review of Relevant Research

A limited number of empirical studies were found in the professional literature. Merrell (1989) reported that the W-M Scale had moderate to high correlations with the Teachers Self-Control Rating Scales. Similarly, Webber, Scheuermann, and Wheeler (1992) reported significant correlations between the W-M Scale and two other teacher rating scales. There is also some evidence that the instrument is more appropriate for younger elementary-aged students than with older students (Tur-Kaspa & Bryan, 1995). The W-M Scale has been reviewed on several occasions. Worthington and Harrison (1990) reported that the W-M Scale was brief, easily administered, and provided important information about the child's interpersonal social skills. They further noted that the technical characteristics of the instrument were good, although the standardization sample was not adequately described. Lewis (1991) also noted the brevity of administration time and pointed out that the instrument was good for identifying withdrawn, and not just acting out, students.

OVERVIEW: WALKER-MCCONNELL SCALE OF SOCIAL COMPETENCE AND SCHOOL ADJUSTMENT

- *Age level*—Kindergarten through grade 6 (adolescent form available)
- *Type of administration*—Teacher rating (individual student)
- *Technical adequacy*—Limited standardization (poorly described), good reliability, adequate validity
- *Scores yielded*—Standard scores, percentile ranks
- *Suggested use*—The W-M Scale appears to be a reliable, relatively valid yet quick measure of social skill development in elementary-age students. Its use as a screening instrument appears to be justified, and its short administration time (five minutes) will allow its use in combination with other measures. The W-M Scale is based on a sound theoretical framework. Its use to make comprehensive diagnostic decisions should be avoided, however. Further studies that focus on the predictive validity of the instrument should be forthcoming.

ADD/ADHD INSTRUMENTS

Although not recognized as separate disability areas in the Individuals with Disabilities Education Act, Attention Deficit Disorder and Attention Deficit-Hyperactivity Disorder have been receiving increasing interest. Similarly, in recent years new instruments designed to measure these areas have been published. Among these are the *Attention Deficit Disorder Evaluation Scale,* the *ADD-H Comprehensive Teacher's Rating Scale,* the *Attention Deficit/Hyperactivity Disorder Test,* and the *Children's Attention and Adjustment Survey.* In addition, the *Connors Rating Scales,* originally developed to measure hyperactivity, have also received new attention.

Attention Deficit Disorders Evaluation Scale

- *Age level*—4 1/2 to 20 years
- *Type of administration*—Individual
- *Technical adequacy*—Good normative sample (school version), adequate normative sample (home version), good reliability, adequate validity
- *Scores yielded*—Standard scores and percentile ranks; a profile analysis is also available

- *Suggested use*—The Attention Deficit Disorders Evaluation Scale (ADDES) (McCarney, 1989) was developed to help identify individuals with attention deficit disorder (with and without hyperactivity). The scale was designed based on the American Psychiatric Association's (APA) Diagnostic and Statistical Manual III-R (DSM III-R) criteria. Subsequently, three subscales measure inattention, impulsiveness, and hyperactivity. Both a school version and a home version are available, and each can be completed in approximately fifteen to twenty minutes. In addition to the scale itself, an Attention Deficit Disorders Intervention Manual also coincides with the behaviors noted in the school version of the test. A parent guide to attention deficit disorders provides suggestions for interventions based on the behavior noted in the home version. A computerized program is also available for both the scale and intervention manual. In a review of the ADDES, Silverthorne (1994) noted several positive features, including the ease of administration and scoring, and its construction on the basis of ADD criteria established by the APA. She also pointed out that factor analytic studies have indicated the presence of only two factors—inattention-disorganization and motor hyperactivity-impulsivity.

ADD-H Comprehensive Teacher's Rating Scale (Second Edition)

- *Age level*—Kindergarten through grade 8
- *Type of administration*—Individual
- *Technical adequacy*—Adequate normative sample, adequate reliability, questionable validity
- *Scores yielded*—Percentile ranks and a visual profile
- *Suggested use*—The ADD-H Comprehensive Teacher's Rating Scale (ACTeRS) (Ullmann, Sleator, and Sprague, 1991) is a brief checklist of twenty-four items that measures the areas of attention, hyperactivity, social skills, and oppositional behavior. The authors recommend that the scale be administered by teachers because the majority of the items on the scale would be demonstrated in the classroom. The ACTeRS is probably best used as a quick screening device, although it might be used with other information to help identify a student as having either ADD or ADD-H. Computerized scoring is also available for the ACTeRS.

Attention Deficit/Hyperactivity Disorder Test

- *Age Level*—3 to 23
- *Type of administration*—Individual
- *Technical adequacy*—Good normative sample, good reliability, adequate validity
- *Scores yielded*—Standard scores and percentile ranks

- *Suggested use*—The Attention Deficit/Hyperactivity Disorder Test (ADHDT) (Gilliam, 1995a) is a recent addition to the available instruments to evaluate ADD and ADHD. The items were selected based on the diagnostic criteria for ADHD found in the DSM-IV and contains thirty-six items measuring the areas of hyperactivity, impulsivity, and inattention. The instrument is basically used as a screening measure and can be completed by teachers, parents, as well as others who are knowledgeable about the child.

The Children's Attention and Adjustment Survey

- *Age level*—5 to 13
- *Type of administration*—Individual
- *Technical adequacy*—Adequate normative sample, reliability, and validity
- *Scores yielded*—Standard scores and percentiles
- *Suggested use*—The Children's Attention and Adjustment Survey (CAAS) (Lambert, Hartsough, & Sandoval, 1990) is a short checklist of behaviors related to attention problems and hyperactivity. Specifically, the CAAS provides information regarding four areas: inattentiveness, impulsivity, hyperactivity, and conduct problems and aggressiveness. Similar to other instruments, there is both a home form and a school form. Each form consists of thirty-one items and can be administered in approximately five to ten minutes. Similar to the ADDES, the behaviors were chosen based on the criteria established in the DSM III-R.

Connors Rating Scales

- *Age level*—Teacher Rating Scales, 3 to 17 years, 4 to 12 years (depending on version); Parent Rating Scales, 23 to 17 years, 6 to 14 years (depending on version)
- *Type of administration*—Individual
- *Technical adequacy*—Varied, depending on type and form of scale used. The Connors Teacher Rating Scale with thirty-nine items (CTRS-39) is preferable for teacher use and the Connors Parent Rating Scale-93 (CPRS-93) is recommended for parent use. These have more items and are based on a more representative standardization sample.
- *Suggested use*—The Connors Rating Scales have been used in the schools for years. Although they were originally designed to identify children with hyperactivity, they are now used to identify children with other types of problems, including ADD. The CTRS-39 includes six scales: Hyperactivity, Conduct Problems, Emotional Overindulgence, Anxious/Passive, Asocial, and Daydream–Attendance Problem. The CPRS-93 includes eight scales: Conduct Disorder, Fearful Anxious, Restless Disorganized, Learning Problem-Immature, Psychosomatic, Obsessional, Antisocial, and Hyperactive Immature. Although the Connors Rating Scales have been in existence for a longer period

of time, there are probably more technically adequate instruments designed for both parents and teachers to identify children with ADD and ADHD. A brief version of both the teacher and parents scales is called the Abbreviated Symptoms Questionnaire. Again, those who use the Connors Rating Scales should be familiar with the various forms available as well as some of the uses and limitations of each.

AUTISM INSTRUMENTS

With the passage of Public Law 101-476 (IDEA), traumatic brain injury and autism became new categories of disability. The result has been an increase in the number of assessment instruments designed to identify individuals who have autism. These include the *Autism Screening Instrument and Educational Planning-2*, the *Childhood Autism Rating Scale*, and the *Gilliam Autism Rating Scale*.

Autism Screening Instrument for Educational Planning–2

- *Age level*—18 months through adulthood
- *Type of administration*—Individual
- *Technical adequacy*—Adequate normative sample, reliability, and validity
- *Scores yielded*—Standard scores and percentiles; summary booklet profile
- *Suggested use*—The Autism Screening Instrument for Education Planning-2 (ASIEP-2) (Krug, Arick, & Almond, 1993) is a revision of a popular autism screening instrument that includes subtests measuring five areas. Those five areas are a sample of vocal behavior, assessment of interaction, assessment of communication, determination of learning rate, and a behavioral checklist measuring sensory, relating, body concept, language, and social self-help skills. Not all five areas are necessarily administered for each individual; guidelines are provided to assist the examiner in making that decision. In general, the authors provide evidence that the battery is helpful in distinguishing among groups of subjects with a variety of disabilities including autism. One potential drawback is the amount of time (1 1/2–2 hours) that is necessary to obtain basic screening information. It should be noted, however, that this instrument yields more in-depth information than that obtained from other types of screening instruments.

Childhood Autism Rating Scale

- *Age level*—2 years and up
- *Type of administration*—Individual
- *Technical adequacy*—Adequate normative sample, reliability, and validity
- *Scores yielded*—A diagnostic categorization system is provided based on the individual's raw score on the fifteen items

- *Suggested use*—The Childhood Autism Rating Scale (CARS) (Schopler, Reichler, & Renner, 1988) was originally developed as a means of evaluating children for a statewide program called Treatment and Education of Autistic and Related Communication Handicapped Children (TEACCH). There are fifteen items or areas in which the examiner must rate the individuals on a seven-point scale from 1 (within normal limits for that age) to 4 (severely abnormal for that age). The areas covered are Relating to People, Imitation, Emotional Response, Body Use, Object Use, Adaptation to Change, Visual Response, Listening Response, Taste, Smell and Touch Response, Fear or Nervousness, Verbal Communication, Nonverbal Communication, Activity Level, Level and Consistency of Intellectual Response, and General Impressions.

Gilliam Autism Rating Scale

- *Age level*—3 through 22 years
- *Type of administration*—Individual
- *Technical adequacy*—Adequate normative sample, good reliability and validity
- *Scores yielded*—Standard scores and percentiles
- *Suggested use*—The Gilliam Autism Rating Scale (GARS) (Gilliam, 1995b) was designed for use by teachers, parents, and other professionals. The GARS was based on the information on autism provided, in part, from the DSM-IV manual of the American Psychiatric Association and by the Autism Society of America. The items are grouped in areas related to stereotyped behaviors, communication, social interaction, and developmental disturbances (the first three form the core subtests). The instrument is extremely quick to administer, requiring only five to ten minutes to complete. The author provides evidence that the GARS discriminates between individuals with autism and those with other severe behavioral and cognitive problems.

MEASUREMENT OF EMOTIONAL STATUS

WHY USE MEASURES OF EMOTIONAL STATUS?

Determination of personality characteristics, self-concept, and general emotional status; frequently used in non-school settings for individuals with emotional problems

WHO SHOULD USE THEM?

Psychologists

Ironically, many examiners try to infer a child's emotional state by "analyzing" the observable behavior. For instance, "Because Susan is sitting alone in the back of the classroom, she has a poor self-concept"; or "Because Billy hit his sister, he is having problems with sibling rivalry." Inferences of this type should be avoided; they usually result in some kind of misinterpretation.

Several types of instruments have been used historically to measure emotional status. Most of these procedures are administered only by trained psychologists and psychiatrists. Their relevance to special education is questionable. These instruments include projective tests, measures of self-concept, and objective inventories.

Projective Methods

Projective methods grew out of psychoanalytic and Gestalt psychology. The concept is simple. When presented with an ambiguous stimulus, an individual will "project" his "way of seeing life, his meanings, significances, patterns and especially his feelings" (Frank, 1939). Theoretically, the ambiguous stimulus will break down the individual's defense mechanisms; further, the more ambiguous the stimulus, the deeper the penetration into the personality (Haley, 1963). Thus, an ink blot, hypothetically, will penetrate more deeply into the personality than a picture of people engaging in some activity.

The appropriateness of projective testing has been seriously questioned. O'Leary and Johnson (1979) noted, for example, that the Society for Projective Techniques and Personality Assessment dropped the words *Projective Techniques* from their title in 1970. Similarly, that organization's journal also deleted the same words from its title. The use of projective tests in special education particularly has been challenged for a number of reasons. As a general rule, projective tests lack reliability and validity. The subjective way in which they are scored tends to lower their reliability. Because the tests measure abstract hypothetical constructs, validity is difficult to establish. For example, Motta, Little, and Tobin (1993) reviewed several studies using human figure drawing projective techniques and found little support for their validity or use to assess personality or behavior.

Even though projective tests have been criticized by many, they are still used in the school and are frequently defended. Sarbaugh (1983) stated, for example, that because of the unique nature of projective instruments, traditional standards of technical adequacy are not important, although others (for example, Peterson & Batche, 1983) take the opposite view. In fact, professionals' views about projectives are generally mixed. In one survey of school psychologists, 63 percent said that projectives would not be important in schools in the future, while 37 percent said that they had their role.

Another problem with projective tests is insufficient standardization or an insufficient normative group. Many times, in fact, norms are not used—the results are interpreted completely subjectively. This is particularly true if the examiner is highly experienced in projective techniques. It can, however, result in a type of "reverse projection." Consider this hypothetical situation:

EXAMINER: (shows examinee a card with an ink blot) Tell me what you see.

EXAMINEE: A bat.

EXAMINER: Anything else?

EXAMINEE: Just a bat, an angry bat.

After several interactions about various ink blots, the examiner determines that the examinee is "a hostile, impulsive person with hyperactive tendencies." In reality, the examiner's own response has been "projected"—the examinee's response was the stimulus! The message, clearly, is to avoid subjective interpretation of the response.

A number of projective tests are still used in special education. Many of these (for example, the Rorschach Ink Blot Test, the Thematic Apperception Test, the Tasks of Emotional Development) are administered by trained psychologists. Other tests (such as sentence-completion tests, the Human Figure Drawing Test, and the projective adaptation of the Bender-Gestalt) are sometimes administered by teachers and diagnosticians as well; this practice, however, is discouraged. The following is a brief discussion of several projective tests.

Rorschach Ink Blot Test (Rorschach, 1932)

The Rorschach Ink Blot Test is the test that typically comes to mind when the term *projective test* is mentioned. The test consists of ten ink blots that are presented one at a time to the individual. Examinees simply state what they see in each blot. A number of different scoring systems were devised for the Rorschach (for example, Beck, Beck, Levitt, & Molish, 1961; Klopfer & Kelly, 1942). In general, the examiner considers the content of the response, the part of the ink blot that was used, and the determinants (for example, the blot's shape or color) that led to the response. Diagnostic interpretation of Rorschach is based on clinical data. (For example, 75 percent of schizophrenic subjects have a certain pattern. An individual who takes the test and has that pattern will more than likely be considered schizophrenic on the basis of the results.)

Thematic Apperception Test (Murray, 1943)

The Thematic Apperception Test (TAT) uses a series of thirty-one pictures as stimuli to elicit projected stories. The examiner looks for themes in the stories, particularly themes related to the main character. Although quantitative scoring systems have been devised for the TAT, its interpretation is largely subjective.

Children's Apperception Test
(Bellak, Bellak, & Haworth, 1974)

In the Children's Apperception Test (CAT), as in the TAT, cards with pictures on them are used as stimuli. The CAT consists of two sets of cards: One set of ten cards has pictures of animals involved in a variety of situations. (Younger children supposedly identify more with animals than with humans.) The other set of ten cards has pictures of humans. (This set can be used with older children.)

Education Apperception Test (Thompson & Sones, 1973)

The Education Apperception Test (EAT) consists of eighteen pictures of children engaged in school-related activities. The test supposedly measures a child's emotions in four areas: reaction toward learning, reaction toward authority, peer relations, and home attitude toward school. As with the other apperception tests, the primary scoring procedure for this test is the interpretation of the stories.

Tasks of Emotional Development (Cohen & Weil, 1971)

The Tasks of Emotional Development (TED) consists of thirteen photographs that are associated with specific areas of emotional development in children and adolescents. Those areas, as designated by the authors, are

1. Socialization within the peer group
2. Establishment of trust in people
3. Acceptance and control of aggressive feelings toward peers
4. Establishment of positive attitudes toward academic learning
5. Establishment of a conscience with respect to the property of others
6. Separation from the mother figure
7. Identification with the same-sex parent
8. Acceptance of siblings
9. Acceptance of limits from adults
10. Acceptance of affection between parents (the resolution of the Oedipal conflict)
11. Establishment of positive attitudes toward orderliness and cleanliness (the ability to control drives)
12. Establishment of a positive self-concept
13. Establishment of positive heterosexual socialization

Unlike other projective-story tests, the TED attempts to make the stimulus resemble the person being tested. For this reason, the set of pictures for each of the areas comes in multiple versions showing males and females of different ages. The examiner uses the picture version (for example, adolescent male) that is most similar to the subject.

Sentence Completions

Two tests for this popular technique are the Rohde Sentence Completion Test (Rohde, 1957) and the Rotter Incomplete Sentences Blank (Rotter & Rafferty,

1950). In these tests, based on a popular projective technique, the examinee must fill in incomplete sentences by writing anything that comes to mind.

Hutt Adaptation of the Bender-Gestalt Test (Hutt, 1977)

This adaptation uses the Bender Visual Motor Gestalt Test (see Appendix A) as a projective instrument. Types of errors made and the approach taken in copying the geometric forms are interpreted in terms of personality characteristics. For example, if a person places the figures compactly on one section of the paper, it might be indicative of depression or rigidity.

Human Figure Drawing Test (Koppitz, 1968)

This popular test is one of many instruments designed to use a child's drawing of a human figure as a projective measure. The HFDT is scored according to thirty emotional "indicators" identified by Koppitz. Unfortunately, many unqualified individuals have administered this test and attempted to interpret the results of children's drawings.

Kinetic Drawing System for Family and School (Knoff & Prout, 1985)

This instrument is a combination of the older Kinetic Family Drawing and the Kinetic School Drawing. It is designed for ages 5 to 10 and includes five diagnostic categories.

Self-Report and Projective Inventory (Ziffer & Shapiro, 1995)

There are actually two editions of the Self-Report and Projective Inventory (SRPI): the child (CSRPI) and adolescent (ASRPI) versions. The CSRPI is designed for children ages 5 to 12 and the ASRPI designed for students ages 12 to 18. Each has a similar structure, although the actual materials included for each level are slightly different. As noted in the title, the instrument combines both self-report and projective components. According to the authors, the test can be used for a variety of purposes, such as to help in school counseling, diagnostic assessment, child therapy, and treatment planning. Included in the SRPI are coloring and drawing tasks, which allow for nonverbal expression, self-report items in areas such as perceived competence and self-description, sentence completion items, and projective story cards. The instrument takes approximately an hour and a half to administer and should be used in conjunction with other information to make decisions.

Draw-a-Person: Screening Procedure for Emotional Disturbance (Naglieri, McNeish, & Bardos, 1994)

The Draw-a-Person Screening Procedure (DAP:SPED) is a screening instrument based on the interpretation of the child's drawing of a man, a woman, and him or herself. It is designed for ages 5 to 17 and can be either group or individually administered. The DAP:SPED, unlike most other DAP measures, is based on a representative standardization sample and includes reliability and validity data.

Summary of Projective Techniques

Theoretically, projective tests are able to measure some underlying emotional characteristic of an individual that he or she cannot or will not verbalize. By using ambiguous stimuli, the individual "projects" his feelings and needs. Unfortunately, evaluating the responses usually requires a great deal of subjective interpretation by the examiner. The use of projective testing should be limited to those examiners who have been trained specifically in projective techniques.

Regardless of the examiner, however, it should be questioned whether projective tests have any relevance at all in the field of special education. Research, in general, has not supported the validity of these instruments. Commonly used projective tests such as the Human Figure Drawing and the Bender-Gestalt have been found, for instance, to add little in the identification and evaluation of children with behavior problems (studies include Dieffenbach, 1977; Trahan & Strickland, 1979). O'Leary and Johnson (1979) summarized the state of the art for projective testing almost two decades ago:

> The data are simply not compelling enough to suggest that projective methods be used for clinical purposes. With a few exceptions, the validity coefficients are either inconsistent or so small as to preclude their use in routine clinical work. Most projective methods require substantial time to administer and score and, as important, they require many hours to learn. Since information gathered on projective techniques can generally be obtained from simpler and less expensive methods, it is incumbent upon advocates of projective methodologies to demonstrate their clinical utility in terms of costs in time and training as well as predictive validity. (pp. 218–219)

Measure of Self-Concept

One area that is assessed frequently is a student's self-concept. Because this is a difficult construct to define, most of the instruments in this area are of questionable validity. Many self-concept instruments use a system of self-evaluation and self-report. In other words, the subject reads a statement such as "I am an unhappy person" and must agree or disagree with that statement. Other self-concept scales are nonverbal, and still others are completed by someone other than the subject. One problem with most self-concept scales is that the positive or negative intent of the items is fairly obvious. Many children will answer the way they think others expect them to respond. Brief descriptions of several measures of self-concept follow.

Inferred Self-Concept Scale

Age level—Grades 1 to 6

Areas measured—General self-concept

Administration and scoring—The Inferred Self-Concept Scale (McDaniel, 1973) has thirty items. For each item, teachers or counselors must rate the subject on a scale of 1 (seldom) to 5 (always).

Reading required—No

Technical adequacy—Very limited

Martinek-Zaichkowsky Self-Concept Scale for Children

Age level—Grades 1 to 8

Areas measured—

Satisfaction and happiness

Home and family relationships and circumstances

Ability in games, recreation, and sports

Personal traits and emotional tendencies

Behavioral, personal, and social characteristics in school

Administration and scoring—In the Martinek-Zaichkowsky Self-Concept Scale for Children (Martinek & Zaichkowsky, 1977) the subject is shown twenty-five pairs of pictures and must state, for each pair, which picture he or she identifies with more.

Reading required—No

Technical adequacy—Adequate reliability, limited validity

Piers-Harris Children's Self-Concept Scale

Age level—Grades 4 to 12

Areas measured—

Behavior

Intellectual and School Status

Physical Appearance and Attributes

Anxiety

Popularity

Happiness and Satisfaction

Lie Scale

Administration and scoring—The Piers-Harris Children's Self-Concept Scale (Piers & Harris, 1984) includes eighty statements. The subject must read each statement (for example, "I am a good person") and score it yes or no.

Reading required—Yes (approximately third-grade level)

Technical adequacy—Adequate reliability, limited validity

Self-Esteem Index

Age level—7 to 18 years

Areas measured—

Academic competence (self-esteem in school)

Family acceptance (self-esteem at home)

Peer popularity (relationships outside the family unit)

Personal security (physical appearance and personal attributes)

Administration and scoring—The Self-Esteem Index (Brown & Alexander, 1991) is administered to individuals or groups. It includes a self-report format using a four-point likert scale.

Reading required—Yes

Technical adequacy—Adequate reliability and validity

Student Self-Concept Scale

Age level—Grades 3 to 12

Areas measured—

Academic

Social

Self-image

Lie Scale

Note: The first three self-concept areas are measured along three dimensions: self-confidence, importance, and outcome confidence.

Administration and scoring—The Student Self-Concept Scale (SSCS) (Gresham, Elliott, & Evans-Fernandez, 1993) uses a self-report rating format and is based on Bandura's theory of self-efficacy. The SSCS can be either administered individually or in a group and consists of seventy-two items. Standard scores with a mean of 100 and a standard deviation of 15 are available for six subscales and two composites.

Reading required—Yes

Technical adequacy—Good reliability and validity

Tennessee Self-Concept Scale

Age level—12 and older

Areas measured—

Counseling form—Self-criticism; self-esteem (nine areas, including identity, moral-ethical self)

Clinical and research form—Above areas; plus fifteen others, including response bias, net conflict, total conflict, empirical scales, and deviant signs

Administration and scoring—The Tennessee Self-Concept Scale (Fitts, 1984) has one hundred items. The subject must rate each item on a scale of 1 (false) to 5 (true).

Reading required—Yes (approximately sixth-grade level)
Technical adequacy—Adequate reliability, limited validity

INVENTORIES AND QUESTIONNAIRES

The intent of inventories and questionnaires is to measure objectively the emotional and personality characteristics of individuals. Most of these instruments are designed for adolescents and adults. One notable exception is the Personality Inventory for Children (PIC) discussed in the following section. They usually include a large number of items that purportedly measure several personality traits or characteristics. (A group of items referring to a given trait is usually referred to as a scale for that trait.) Many times, these items are in the form of a behavioral description (such as "I sometimes hear strange voices") that the examinee must label as true or false. This self-report technique is used in the majority of these instruments, although some of them require a familiar person (such as a parent) to complete the items about the examinee.

In addition to the personality scales themselves, these instruments usually include some type of validity scale to help determine if the examinee is "telling the truth." In general, however, both the reliability and the validity of these instruments have been questioned. Many inventories have also been criticized because the various areas identified for a profile analysis overlap in content. For these and several other reasons, the use of these instruments as tools in the process of education is limited. A discussion of the PIC follows, in addition to a brief description of three other popular personality inventories.

Personality Inventory for Children

The Personality Inventory for Children (PIC) (Wirt, Lachar, Klinedinst, & Seat, 1984) is one of the few inventories designed specifically for evaluating children. It is often thought of as a downward extension of the popular Minnesota Multiphasic Personality Inventory (MMPI) and is appropriate for children ages 3 to 16 years.

Description
The PIC includes six hundred items grouped into thirty scales. Of these thirty scales, thirteen are considered the "profile scales" that have the most clinical relevance. Three validity scales help determine if truthful responses are being given. The remaining scales are called experimental. The items are completed in a true-false format by the child's parent. An example of an item in each of the thirteen profile scales follow. The first three scales are known as the cognitive triad, because they measure characteristics related to the child's cognitive ability.

Adjustment (74 items)—"My child loves to make fun of others."
Achievement (31 items)—"My child could do better in school if he (she) tried."
Intellectual Screening (35 items)—"My child learned to count things by age six."
Development (25 items)—"My child could eat with a fork before the age of four
     years."
Somatic Concern (40 items)—"My child seldom has back pains."
Depression (46 items)—"Others often remark how moody my child is."
Family Relations (35 items)—"During the past few years we have moved of-
     ten."
Delinquency (47 items)—"I have heard that my child drinks alcohol."
Withdrawal (25 items)—"Often my child takes walks alone."
Anxiety (30 items) —"My child is afraid of animals."
Psychosis (40 items)—"My child gets lost easily."
Hyperactivity (36 items)—"My child will do anything on a dare."
Social Skills (30 items)—"My child tends to be pretty stubborn."

Interpretation of Results

Scores from the PIC can be transformed into T-scores and plotted on a visual profile (Figure 11.4).

Technical Characteristics

Normative sample.   The sample included 2,390 individuals ages 6 to 16. Information in the manual describes age, gender, and education and occupation of the
parents. A separate preschool sample of 192 children was also used.

Reliability.   Test-retest coefficients from several studies with clinical and normal
samples averaged in the .71–.89 range. Internal consistency ranged from .57 (intellectual screening) to .86 (depression). Interrater reliability was somewhat lower,
ranging from .34 to .68 for a normal sample and .21 to .79 for a clinical sample.

Validity.   The authors attempted to maximize the validity of the PIC through
careful, empirically based item selection.

Review of Relevant Research

The PIC has been reviewed extensively. On the one hand, Achenbach (1981) criticized the PIC, arguing that it was based on outdated personality theories and was
subject to respondent bias. Similarly, DeMoor-Peal and Handal (1983) criticized
the PIC, most notably with preschool children because of the small normative
sample. On the other hand, Dreger (1982) felt that the PIC was a good child-per-
sonality inventory with sound empirical support. Lachar and LaCombe (1983)
also noted the technical adequacy of the PIC, and Knoff (1989) reported that the
PIC had enormous potential but needed a stratified national restandardization.

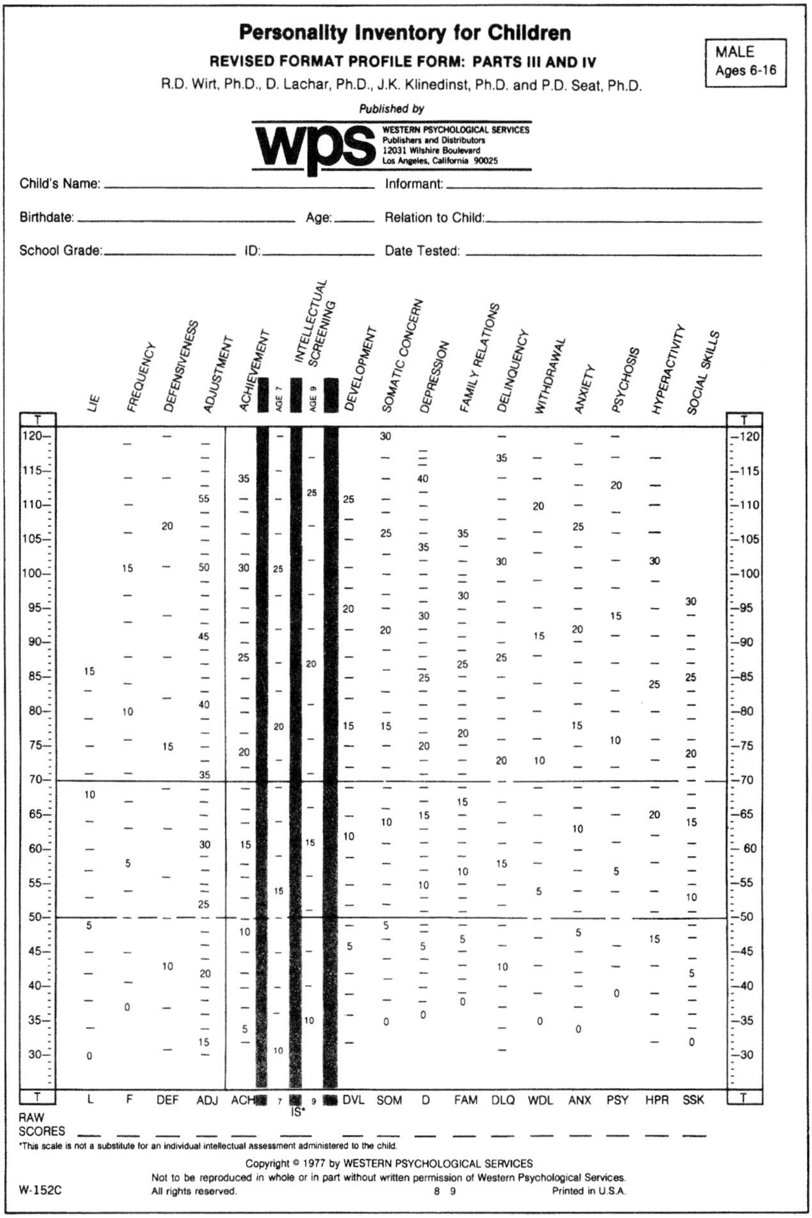

Personality Inventory for Children

REVISED FORMAT PROFILE FORM: PARTS III AND IV

R.D. Wirt, Ph.D., D. Lachar, Ph.D., J.K. Klinedinst, Ph.D. and P.D. Seat, Ph.D.

Published by

WPS WESTERN PSYCHOLOGICAL SERVICES
Publishers and Distributors
12031 Wilshire Boulevard
Los Angeles, California 90025

MALE
Ages 6-16

Child's Name: _____ Informant: _____

Birthdate: _____ Age: _____ Relation to Child: _____

School Grade: _____ ID: _____ Date Tested: _____

*This scale is not a substitute for an individual intellectual assessment administered to the child.

W-152C

FIGURE 11.4   Example of a Profile from the Personality Inventory for Children

From R. Wirt, D. Lachar, J. Klinedinst, and P. Seat, *Personality Inventory for Children.* Copyright © 1977 by Western Psychological Services, Los Angeles, CA. Reprinted with permission.

The PIC has been used in a number of research studies as a measure of personality status. The following studies, however, are representative of those that focus on its technical characteristics and clinical utility.

- The PIC can be used to help identify individuals with adaptive behavior deficits (Pearson & Lachar, 1994).
- The validity of the PIC does not appear to be affected by either race or gender variables, although it was affected at certain ages (Kline & Lachar, 1992).
- Parents are effective informants on the PIC (Keenan & Lachar, 1988).
- Some researchers have noted high correlations between PIC results and intelligence (Keenan & Lachar, 1985), whereas others have reported low correlations (Beck & Spruill, 1987).
- Because of the possibility of faking responses, profiles on the PIC cannot be considered valid all the time (McVaughn & Grow, 1984).
- Students with learning disabilities and behavior disorders were differentiated on the PIC (Goh, 1984). It also discriminated children with emotional disturbance with learning problems from those with emotional disturbance without learning problems, and children with learning disabilities with emotional problems from underachieving children with emotional disturbance (Forbes, 1987).
- The PIC was effective in screening intelligence in a preschool population (Durrant & Porter, 1989).
- The PIC differentiated between children with conduct disorders and those with emotional disturbance (Kelly, 1988). Also, Clarke, Kehle, and Bullock (1988) reported that children with learning disability, mental retardation, and emotional disturbance all had elevated scores in cognitive deficits and maladaptive behavior. They noted that the *degree* of elevation discriminated group status.

OVERVIEW: PERSONALITY INVENTORY FOR CHILDREN

- *Age level*—3 to 16 years old
- *Type of administration*—Individual (group possible)
- *Technical adequacy*—Limited standardization for preschool population, questionable interrater reliability, adequate validity
- *Scores yielded*—T-scores, visual profile
- *Suggested use*—The PIC is one of the few available personality inventories designed for children. One must be aware of the possible bias of the respondents (as with any instrument that requires third-party information). The test is more a clinical instrument than an educational instrument; the results will be used more for classification purposes than educational programming. Caution should be taken when using the PIC with a preschool population.

California Psychological Inventory (Gough, 1969)

The California Psychological Inventory (CPI) is a popular instrument used with individuals thirteen years of age and older. The test consists of 480 true-false items (of which approximately 200 also appear in the Minnesota Multiphasic Personality Inventory). The CPI is organized into fifteen personality scales and three validity scales. The personality scales are Dominance; Capacity for Status; Sociability; Social Pressure; Self-Acceptance; Sense of Well-Being; Responsibility; Socialization; Self-Control; Tolerance; Achievement via Conformity; Achievement via Independence; Intellectual Efficiency; Psychological-Mindedness; and Femininity. The validity scales are Well-being; Good Impression; and Community. Researchers have generally supported the use of the CPI, even though there is some redundancy among the scales (Lanyon & Goodstein, 1971).

The Minnesota Multiphasic Personality Inventory–2 (Butcher, Dahlstrom, Gramm, & Kaemmer, 1989

The Minnesota Multiphasic Personality Inventory–2 (MMPI-2) is the most recent revision of the extremely popular, widely uses MMPI that has been in existence for more than fifty years. The instrument is designed for individuals sixteen years of age and older. The MMPI-2 consists of 704 items, 550 of which were from the original version. The items are designed to be answered in a true-false format, and there are scores for ten clinical scales, three validity scales, and seven additional scales. Generally, the *pattern* of scores is used in interpretation. The clinical scales include Hypochondriasis; Depression; Hysteria; Psychopathic Deviate; Masculinity-Femininity; Paranoia; Psychoasthenia; Schizophrenia; and Hypomania. The three validity scales are Lie; Infrequency; and Defensiveness. The additional scales include an Anxiety scale, a Repression scale, an Ego-Strength scale, and an Alcoholism scale in addition to three scales that focus on variable response, inconsistency, and unusual responding.

Duckworth (1991) noted that the MMPI-2 had many positive features, including updated items and additional validity scales. She also noted that the new norms were an improvement over the original MMPI, although there were still some concerns with the representativeness of the norms. She also pointed out that the differences between the MMPI and the earlier versions may lead to a tendency for individuals familiar with the original MMPI to misinterpret the results of the revised edition.

Sixteen Personality Factor Questionnaire (Cattell, Eber, & Tatsuoka, 1970)

Usually referred to as the 16PF, the Sixteen Personality Factor Questionnaire is designed for use with individuals 16 years of age and older. The test was designed on the basis of years of factor-analytic studies by Cattell. Its scores supposedly measure sixteen primary factors: Reserved versus Outgoing; Less Intelligent versus More Intelligent; Affected by Feelings versus Emotionally Stable; Humble versus Assertive; Sober versus Happy-go-lucky; Expedient versus Conscientious; Shy versus Venturesome; Tough-minded versus Tender-minded; Trusting versus Suspicious; Practical versus Imaginative; Forthright versus Shrewd; Self-Assured versus Apprehensive; Conservative versus Experimenting; Group-Dependent versus Self-Sufficient; Undisciplined Self-Conflict versus Controlled; and Relaxed versus Tense. The test also includes scores for six second-order factors: Introversion versus Extraversion; Low Anxiety versus High Anxiety; Tender-minded Emotionality versus Tough Poise; Subduedness versus Independence; Naturalness versus Discreetness; and Cool Realism versus Prodigal Subjectivity.

Although the 16PF has several forms, these forms should not be considered interchangeable (Bouchard, 1972). In general, this instrument lacks validity data.

Summary of Inventories and Questionnaires
Inventories and questionnaires generally lack supportive data that would establish their reliability and validity. The use of these instruments in special education is questionable and is typically limited to providing information to help make classification and placement decisions. Most of these instruments are designed for use with adolescents and adults. The notable exception is the PIC, which has received some attention in special education.

Instrument or Technique	Screening and Initial Identification	Informal Determination and Evaluation of Teaching Programs and Strategies	Determination of Current Performance Level and Educational Need	Decisions about Classification and Program Placement	IEP Goals	IEP Objectives	IEP Evaluation	Mild/Moderate	Severe/Profound	Preschool	Elementary Age	Secondary Age	Adult	Special Considerations	Educational Relevance for Exceptional Students
	Prereferral / Suggested Use			Postreferral				Target Population							
Behavior Assessment System for Children	X		X	X	X			X			X	X		Includes several components involving input from multiple sources	useful
Revised Behavior Problem Checklist	X		X		X			X			X			Adequate technical aspects; has some empirical support in the literature	useful
Behavior Rating Profile–2	X		X		X			X			X			Student is evaluated by several of individuals in various settings; validity data are lacking	adequate
Child Behavior Checklist	X		X	X	X			X			X	X		Has separate forms for multiple raters; different profiles for boys and girls	useful
Devereux Behavior Rating Scales–School Form	X		X					X			X	X		Based on diagnostic criteria from the P.L. 94-142 definition of emotional disturbance	adequate/ useful
Social Skills Rating System	X		X		X			X		X	X	X		Assessment-intervention record is a nice feature; preschool version limited	useful
Walker–McConnell Scale	X							X			X			A valid screening instrument that can be quickly administered	useful
ADD/ADHD Instruments	X							X		X	X	X		Many are checklists based on the diagnostic criteria of ADD/ADHD from the DSM-4	adequate
Autism Instruments					X			X	X	X	X	X	X	These are primarily screening instruments based on the diagnostic criteria of autism	adequate
Projective Techniques		X						X			X	X	X	Losing popularity in special education; little evidence of reliability or validity for most of these instruments	very limited

Instrument or Technique	Suggested Use							Target Population						Special Considerations	Educational Relevance for Exceptional Students
	Prereferral			Postreferral											
	Screening and Initial Identification	Informal Determination and Evaluation of Teaching Programs and Strategies	Determination of Current Performance Level and Educational Need	Decisions about Classification and Program Placement	IEP Goals	IEP Objectives	IEP Evaluation	Mild/Moderate	Severe/Profound	Preschool	Elementary Age	Secondary Age	Adult		
Self-Concept Scales	X							X			X	X	X	Most lack validity data; many use a self-report system to obtain the scores	limited
Inventories and Questionnaires				X				X			X	X	X	Most have limited technical aspects; most are designed for adolescents and adults	limited
Personality Inventory for Children				X						X	X	X		One of the few personality inventories for children	adequate

12

ASSESSMENT OF
ORAL LANGUAGE

Instruments and Procedures Included

Informal Assessment of Language Skills
Language Sampling
Formal Language Tests
Comprehensive Receptive and Expressive Vocabulary Test
Peabody Picture Vocabulary Test–Revised
Test of Adolescent and Adult Language–3
Test of Language Competence
Tests of Language Development–2
Tests for Speech and Language Clinicians

Bobby is a sixth-grade student who has been making little progress in his weak areas of reading and spelling. Bobby typically does not follow directions, writes slowly, and uses incorrect grammar when responding to the resource-room teacher. After reviewing Bobby's records, the teacher noted that he had been given a number of tests but that none of the tests measured his ability to process and produce language. She therefore decided to administer a language test to Bobby to provide information that might be incorporated into his educational program.

Although there are many definitions of language, it is generally agreed that communication is its primary function. Bryen (1982) stated that language is "a rule-governed symbol system that is capable of representing one's understanding of the world." Language is usually thought of as the use of spoken or written symbols, although manual symbols should also be considered. In education, language, as a way in which we receive and express information, is important for success in virtually all areas of academic life. Reading, writing, spelling, and following directions are just a few of the areas in which language plays an important part. In special education, language assessment is an important area.

Structurally, language can be viewed as having five components: phonology, morphology, syntax, semantics, and pragmatics. Each of these five components involves both reception (or processing) and expression (or production) (see Figure 12.1). *Phonology* involves the use of phonemes, the smallest significant units of sound that are combined into words, or with words, to create meaning. For example, the word "goes" comprises three phonemes: /g/, /o/, /z/. The assessment of phonology involves both the aural discrimination of speech sounds and the articulation of speech sounds. Examples of instruments that measure these areas are the Auditory Discrimination Test (Wepman & Reynolds, 1986) and the Goldman-Fristoe Test of Articulation (Goldman & Fristoe, 1986).

Morphology is concerned with how phonemes are put together to give meaning. A morpheme is the smallest combination of sounds that has a meaning. For instance, the word "displacement" has three morphemes: (dis), (place), (ment). Most assessment instruments measure morphology and syntax together because they are both concerned with grammar; one exception is the Test for Examining Expressive Morphology (Shipley, Stone, & Sue, 1983).

Syntax involves the relational meanings of language—that is, how words are put together to form sentences. Assessment of syntax involves the measurement of the understanding of the meaning of sentences and the ability to formulate sentences. For the most part, syntax measures are designed for younger children. Examples are the Tests of Auditory Comprehension of Language–Revised (Carrow-Woolfolk, 1985), the Developmental Sentence Analysis (Lee, 1974), and the Carrow Elicited Language Inventory (Carrow, 1994).

Semantics refers to the meaning of words. The assessment of semantics skills usually involves the measurement of a person's receptive and expressive vocabu-

Components of Language

Mode of Language	Phonology	Morphology	Syntax	Semantics	Pragmatics
Receptive					
Expressive					

FIGURE 12.1   Model of Language

lary skills. Receptive vocabulary can be measured using instruments such as the Peabody Picture Vocabulary Test–Revised (discussed later in this chapter). Expressive vocabulary measures are included on tests such as the Kaufman Assessment Battery for Children (K-ABC) and Wechsler Intelligence Scale for Children–III (WISC-III). There are also quick measures of semantics such as the Receptive One Word Vocabulary Test (Gardner, 1990a) and the Expressive One Word Vocabulary Test (Gardner, 1990b). The Comprehensive Receptive and Expressive Vocabulary Test (CREVT), discussed later in this chapter, includes the assessment of both receptive and expressive semantics.

Pragmatics refers to the use of language within the communicative context. In a certain sense, pragmatics deals with the most important function of language, that of communication. Although all the other components of language must be intact before communication can occur, it is possible that an individual might have all the necessary skills in the areas of phonology, morphology and syntax, and semantics, yet still have difficulty communicating with others. This is particularly true with older students. The *assessment* of pragmatics is a relatively new practice. The Test of Pragmatic Skills (discussed later in this chapter) is one example of the interest in this area.

The overall area of language assessment is a complex process for a number of reasons. As previously discussed, a number of language components are involved. There is also the issue of the processing/production dichotomy, and the fact that language can be transmitted and understood in oral and written form (not to mention manual and other forms). Still further, there is the question of whether or not language tests accurately measure the language skills that an individual actually uses. As a result, informal assessment of language is important; in addition, there are many types of formal tests available. Many of the tests are designed to be used by different professionals for different reasons.

The discussion that follows will focus on informal oral language sampling and the formal oral language tests typically used by special educators. Also included will be a brief discussion of specific language tests that are used more by speech and language clinicians.

INFORMAL ASSESSMENT OF LANGUAGE SKILLS

WHY USE INFORMAL LANGUAGE SKILLS ASSESSMENT?

Screening and identification of language problems; informal determination of objectives and teaching strategies; analysis of spontaneous use of language

WHO SHOULD USE IT?

Teachers; speech and language clinicians

During the past forty years, the increase in knowledge of language development has resulted in many changes in language assessment with increasing emphasis on evaluating in a naturalistic, interactive context (Lund & Duchan, 1988). In fact, the dynamic assessment technique that involves mediated learning (discussed in Chapter 9) has been successfully applied to language assessment (Pena, Quinn, & Iglesias, 1992). Because formal language testing usually occurs in a contrived situation (sometimes requiring the student to imitate language skills), it is possible that many individuals may be able to exhibit certain language skills that they do not produce spontaneously. Conversely, it is possible that they may fail to exhibit certain skills that they might be able to perform within a naturalistic context (e.g., Bloom & Lahey, 1978).

One approach that can be used to evaluate the spontaneous use of language in a naturalistic setting is *language sampling*. This usually involves eliciting (taping, transcribing) and analyzing an individual's language. Language sampling actually refers to a set of possible procedures for gathering information ranging from a spontaneous unstructured sample to a highly structured sample.

Eliciting the Sample

In general, the procedures for obtaining a language sample include (1) a spontaneous sample taken during free play or a conversation; (2) an elicited sample asking the child to tell or retell a story; (3) an elicited imitative sample requiring the child to respond to questions, pictures, or activities that are specifically designed to elicit certain language structures; and/or (4) an imitative language sample asking the child to repeat sentences produced by the examiner.

Each procedure for obtaining a language sample provides different types of evaluation information on the child's language abilities. The decision to use one procedure over another is dependent upon the child who is being evaluated and the behaviors to be examined. As noted previously, however, the most meaningful information regarding the individual's actual use of language will be gathered from the spontaneous procedure. If this is the procedure chosen, it is important that the sample represent the highest level of language of which the student is capable (Smiley, 1991a). Provided below are suggestions for obtaining a language sample regardless of the procedures (Florida Department of Education, 1989):

1. Use a high-quality recorder to assure a good playback. The tape recorder should have a quality microphone that will result in a quality sample. The speakers are also important during playback. For purposes of transcription, a recorder with a counter will be invaluable as you will find you need to stop many times, rewind a short distance, and listen again.

2. Use appropriate stimulus materials (e.g., toys, pictures) based on the interests, intellectual level, and disabilities of the child.

3. Present the stimulus material to the child and ask questions about the material that require more than one- or two-word responses from the child. Try to elicit

complete sentences from the child and set a conversational climate conducive to eliciting responses from the child.

4. Try to elicit different grammmatical forms such as past tense, plural, and so on, if possible. Encourage this by using them in your own speech. For example, ask, "What will he do next?" "What did he say then?"

5. Repeat what the child says, if possible. This will aid you later in transcribing the tape. This should be done so that the child is unaware of it. If the repeating becomes distracting, discontinue. For example:

> *CHILD:*   He don't goes in.
>
> *EXAMINER:*   He don't goes in? Why not?
>
> *CHILD:*   He too big.
>
> *EXAMINER:*   He too big. Yes, he is.

6. Take notes while the child is talking, including attempts to write out some of the utterances. These notes help when you go back and transcribe the tape. Also, this gives you a good idea of the number of utterances obtained from the child.

7. Transcribe the tape as soon as possible after the session so that you can make use of your own recall of the sample.

Analyzing the Sample

Once the language sample has been obtained from the child, the examiner needs to determine the level of analysis of the sample. This analysis includes (1) form, including phonology, morphology, and syntax; (2) content, including vocabulary; and (3) use, including pragmatics. In addition, the use of any nonstandard dialect should be noted. The specific guidelines to follow are beyond the scope of this discussion. However, Smiley (1991a; 1991b) provided teacher-oriented suggestions for the analysis of both the quantitative and qualitative aspects of language sampling. For example, she noted that the following information should be included, at least when morphology and simple syntax are analyzed:

1. Plural markers, both regular and irregular
2. Past tense markers, both regular and irregular
3. Third person singular markers, both regular and irregular
4. Articles (a, an, the)
5. Copula (linking verb) and auxiliary (helping verb)
6. Modal auxiliaries and emphatic auxiliary
7. Pronouns
8. Prepositions
9. Comparative and superlative markers

In addition, Smiley provides examples and suggestions for analysis. Interested readers are encouraged to read the two articles designed for a teacher audience.

FORMAL LANGUAGE TESTS

WHY USE FORMAL LANGUAGE TESTS?

Screening and identification of language problems; informal determination of objectives and teaching strategies; establishment of IEP goals.

WHO SHOULD USE THEM?

Teachers; speech and language clinicians

Comprehensive Receptive and Expressive Vocabulary Test

The Comprehensive Receptive and Expressive Vocabulary Test (CREVT) (Wallace & Hammill, 1994) is an individually administered test of both expressive and receptive oral vocabulary. It has two equivalent forms that can be used for students ages four through seventeen. The authors note four distinctive features of the CREVT. First, both receptive and expressive vocabulary skills are measured; second, those areas are both measured based on the same normative sample. Third, both the receptive and expressive vocabulary items pertain to the same ten categories of words. Fourth, the authors note that the CREVT uses color photographs in the receptive vocabulary subtest unlike other measures that use black-and-white drawings.

The four primary uses of the CREVT are: "(a) to identify students who are significantly below their peers in oral vocabulary proficiency, (b) to determine any discrepancy between receptive and expressive oral vocabulary skills, (c) to document progress in oral vocabulary development as a consequence of special intervention programs, and (d) to measure oral vocabulary in research studies" (Wallace & Hammill, 1994; p. 5).

Description of Subtests

Subtest 1

Receptive Vocabulary (61 items)—In this subtest the student is shown ten plates (e.g., one with animals, one with modes of transportation), each of which has six pictures. The examiner then says a series of stimulus words one at a time. After each word, the student must select the correct choice from one of the six pictures. As noted, each of the ten plates represents a different category of vocabulary words. In this subtest, all students begin with the first item and continue until two items in a row are missed (at which point the testing is discontinued).

Subtest 2

Expressive Vocabulary (25 items)—This subtest requires the student to provide an oral definition for words that are stated by the examiner. ("What does

_____ mean?") The words used in this subtest are based on the same categories used in the Receptive Vocabulary subtest. The basal for this subtest is three in a row correct and the ceiling is three in a row incorrect. This subtest is not administered to children under age 5.

Interpretation of Results

Raw scores from the Receptive Vocabulary and Expressive Vocabulary subtests are converted into standard scores (mean = 100; standard deviation = 15), percentile ranks, and age equivalents. It is also possible to obtain a standard score for a composite of the two subtests called General Vocabulary. A table is presented in the test manual that also allows the conversion of the CREVT scores to stanines, T-scores, and national curve equivalents.

Technical Characteristics

Normative Sample. The normative sample consisted of 1,920 students from thirty-three states. The percentage in the sample compared favorably to the percentage of the school-age population based on the 1990 census data regarding gender, residence, ethnicity, and geographic area, and on the U.S. Department of Education data regarding disability status.

Reliability. The average internal reliability (coefficient alpha) was above .90 for both subtests and the General Vocabulary. The standard errors of measurement were relatively high with the average being five for both the receptive and expressive subtests. Alternate-form reliabilities were in the .80s and .90s and increased with age. Test-retest reliability was determined in a kindergarten and a twelfth-grade sample for the three scores from the two forms. Coefficients were generally in the .80s. Finally, interscorer reliability was reported at .99.

Validity. The authors provide detailed argument regarding the choice of items and the format of the test in a discussion of content validity. They also provide the information regarding the item's discriminating powers. Criterion-related validity was established by correlating the CREVT scores with a number of tests of receptive and expressive language. These correlations were generally in the moderate range although the range of coefficients was wide.

Construct validity was reported by providing data indicating that scores improved with age and high intercorrelations among the subtests. Also reported are the scores from three groups of students with different disabilities showing test performance consistent with the expected language performance of the three groups (mental retardation, learning disability, speech and language problems).

Review of Relevant Research

No research was located on the CREVT. Information related to the clinical use of the instrument for the diagnosis and classification, particularly of language problems, should be forthcoming.

OVERVIEW: COMPREHENSIVE RECEPTIVE AND EXPRESSIVE VOCABULARY TEST

- *Age level*—4 through 17
- *Type of administration*—Individual
- *Technical adequacy*—Adequate standardization, good reliability, adequate validity
- *Scores yielded*—Standard scores, percentile ranks, and age equivalents
- *Suggested use*—The CREVT is a potentially valuable instrument that provides scores for both expressive and receptive oral vocabulary based on the same normative sample. The technical characteristics appear to be adequate enough to confidently make decisions regarding a person's vocabulary skills. The receptive portion is also colorful and would be appropriate for younger children. More evidence of validity would be helpful.

Peabody Picture Vocabulary Test–Revised

The Peabody Picture Vocabulary Test–Revised (PPVT-R) (Dunn & Dunn, 1981) is an extremely popular individually administered instrument that measures an individual's receptive language ability (semantics: receptive). According to the authors, the PPVT-R can be considered both an achievement test and a scholastic-aptitude test for individuals from standard-English-speaking environments. The original 1965 edition of the PPVT was frequently used—actually, misused—as an intelligence measure, primarily because it included a table to transform raw scores to IQs. The authors do point out, however, that the test is not a comprehensive measure of general intelligence. In the manual, the authors also mention several school, clinical, vocational, and research uses for the PPVT-R. The test is both easy and quick to administer. It has two forms (L and M) that can be used with individuals from ages 2 1/2 to 40.

Description
The PPVT-R is included in an easel kit. On each plate four pictures are shown. The vocabulary word is stated, and the examinee must indicate the correct picture either verbally or by pointing. Figure 12.2 shows an example for the word *giant*.

Interpretation of Results
The PPVT-R offers four types of derived scores: standard-score equivalents, percentile ranks, stanines, and age equivalents. The standard-score equivalents and the age equivalents take the place of the intelligence quotient and the mental ages that were yielded by the 1965 PPVT. The standard-score equivalent is based on a mean of 100 and a standard deviation of 15. The authors also mention that the standard error of measurement (approximately 7 for the standard-score equivalent) should also be considered in the overall interpretation of the score.

FIGURE 12.2   Example from the Peabody Picture Vocabulary Test–Revised

From L. Dunn and L. Dunn. *Peabody Vocabulary Test–Revised.* Copyright © 1981 by American Guidance Service, Circle Pines, MN. Reprinted with Permission.

Technical Characteristics

Normative Sample.   The population included 4,200 subjects 2 1/2–18 years old in a representative sample and 828 subjects 19–40 years old in a less representative sample.

Reliability.   Split-half coefficients were .84 for Form L and .81 for Form M. Alternate-form coefficients ranged from .77 to .79.

Validity.   A discussion of content and construct validity is included in the manual. No criterion-related validity data are presented, although an extensive review of the 1965 edition of the PPVT is included.

Review of Relevant Research

- The PPVT-R yields lower scores than the PPVT for educable mentally retarded (EMR) students (Bracken & Prasse, 1981) and for gifted students (Pedriana & Bracken, 1982), as well as for preschool children (Naglieri & Naglieri, 1981).
- The relationship of the PPVT-R with a variety of intelligence measures is unclear. The instrument produced significantly higher scores than did the Cognitive Levels Test with college students (Overton & Apperson, 1989) although it had considerably lower scores than the SB-IV for referred students (Hunter,

Ballash, & Chen, 1992). With younger children, the PPVT-R should not be used to predict WPPSI-R scores (Carvajal, Parks, Logan, & Page, 1992).

- The PPVT-R yielded significantly different scores for boys and girls (Smith, Edmonds, & Smith, 1989).
- The PPVT-R is a useful measure of receptive language of EMR students (Prasse & Bracken, 1981). Its effectiveness in screening for gifted students is limited, however (Wright, 1983).
- The alternate-form reliability is adequate for most preschool children (Bracken & Prasse, 1983). Black preschoolers, however, systematically obtained higher scores on Form M than on Form L (McCallum & Bracken, 1981). The alternate form reliability coefficient was only .65 for students with learning disabilities (LD) in one study (Breen, 1983). Also, Worthing, Phye, and Nunn (1984) found that the two forms were not equivalent for older special education students.
- Correlations reported between the PPVT-R and both the Peabody Individual Achievement Test (.53) and the McCarthy Scale GCI (.78) were similar to correlations reported between the PPVT and those tests (Naglieri, 1981).
- The PPVT-R has adequate test-retest reliability for bilingual children (Scruggs, Mastropieri, & Argulewicz, 1983) although its use with Hispanic students has been questioned (Sattler & Altes, 1984).
- The PPVT-R correlated significantly with the Wide Range Achievement Test–Revised (WRAT-R) and the Wechsler Intelligence Scale for Children–Revised (WISC-R), suggesting that it could be used to screen underachievers (Smith, Smith, & Dobbs, 1991).
- Vance and Stone (1990) found that while the PPVT-R's manual and technical supplement provided much useful information, further research was necessary on its validity with young children.

Summary of Research Findings

Most research studies on the PPVT-R have compared the revised test with the 1965 edition (which was discussed in hundreds of articles). The results suggest that the two instruments yield similar correlations with various criterion measures. The PPVT-R, however, yields *lower* scores than the 1965 PPVT. There is also some evidence that the two forms (L and M) might not be equivalent. The PPVT-R has also been found to have moderate correlations with a variety of criterion measures including intelligence and achievement tests.

OVERVIEW: PEABODY PICTURE VOCABULARY TEST–REVISED

- *Age level*—2 1/2 to 40 years old
- *Type of administration*—Individual
- *Technical adequacy*—Limited standardization for individuals 19–40 years of age, adequate reliability, limited validity data

- *Scores yielded*—Standard scores, percentile ranks, stanines, age equivalents
- *Suggested use*—For years, the 1965 edition of the PPVT was used inappropriately as an intelligence measure. In the PPVT-R, the authors carefully excluded the IQ transformation table. The PPVT-R seems to be a reasonable measure of receptive vocabulary, but its use as a basis for serious educational decisions should be avoided. The PPVT-R can be used with individuals with speech, and (to a certain extent) motor disabilities. Until its psychometric properties have been more extensively investigated, it should be used primarily as a screening instrument.

Test of Adolescent and Adult Language–3

The Test of Adolescent and Adult Language–3 (TOAL-3) (Hammill, Brown, Larsen, & Weiderholt, 1994) is an individually administered instrument designed for use with students ages 12 through 25. The third edition extended the norms to include young adults ages 18 to 24 enrolled in postsecondary programs. Portions of the test can also be group administered. According to the authors, the TOAL-3 can be used

> (a) to identify adolescents and adults whose scores are significantly below those of their peers who might need interventions designed to improve language proficiency; (b) to determine areas of relative strength and weakness across language abilities; (c) to document progress in language development as a consequence of intervention programs; and (d) to serve as a measure for research efforts designed to investigate language characteristics of adolescents and adults. (p. 3)

The TOAL-3 is one of the few tests available for measuring language skills in older students.

Description
The TOAL-3 is designed to measure the areas of semantics and syntax, both receptively and expressively, as well as in spoken and written form. This design results in eight subtests (see Table 12.1 on page 290).

> Listening/Vocabulary (35 items)—In this subtest, the examiner says a word and the student must choose from four pictures the one that represents its meaning.
>
> Listening/Grammar (35 items)—In this subtest, the examiner reads three sentences, two of which have essentially the same meaning. The student must indicate the two sentences that are similar in meaning. For example, "(a) He is not someone I know, (b) I know someone who knows him, and (c) Someone who knows him knows me."

TABLE 12.1   The Relationship of the TOAL-3 Subtests to the Dimensions in the Test Model

TOAL-3 Subtest	Dimensions		
	Form	System	Feature
Listening/Vocabulary	Spoken	Receptive	Vocabulary
Listening/Grammar	Spoken	Receptive	Grammar
Speaking/Vocabulary	Spoken	Expressive	Vocabulary
Speaking/Grammar	Spoken	Expressive	Grammar
Reading/Vocabulary	Written	Receptive	Vocabulary
Reading/Grammar	Written	Receptive	Grammar
Writing/Vocabulary	Written	Expressive	Vocabulary
Writing/Grammar	Written	Expressive	Grammar

From D. Hammill, V. Brown, S. Larsen, and J. L. Wiederholt. *The Test of Adolescent and Adult Language–3* (Austin, TX: Pro-Ed, Inc., 1994). Copyright ©1994 by D. Hammill, V. Brown, S. Larsen, and J. L. Wiederholt. Reprinted with permission.

Speaking/Vocabulary (25 items)—In this subtest, the examiner says a word to the student who, in turn, must make up a sentence using that word.

Speaking/Grammar (30 items)—In this subtest, the examiner reads a sentence and the student must repeat it verbatim.

Reading/Vocabulary (30 items)—In this subtest, the student is given three stimulus words that are similar in some way. The student is then given four words and is asked to choose two of these words that are similar to the stimulus words. For instance, if the stimulus words were "duke, earl, emperor," the choices might be "knight, military, dazzle, noble."

Reading/Grammar (25 items)—This subtest is similar to the listening/grammar subtest except that the student reads five sentences and chooses the two that mean almost the same thing. For example, "(a) She belonged to the cat, (b) Whose cat was it? (c) It was her cat, (d) The cat was hers, and (e) That is my cat."

Writing/Vocabulary (30 items)—In this subtest, the student is given a stimulus word and asked to write a sentence using that word.

Writing/Grammar (30 items)—In this subtest, the student is given a series of sentences and asked to combine them into one sentence. For instance, "She has two dogs," "One dog is a collie," "One dog is a spaniel," "They perform different duties on the farm."

Interpretation of Results

Two types of derived scores, subtest and composite, are available. Subtest scores are scaled with a mean of 10 and a standard deviation of 3. The composite scores are obtained by combining certain subtests to form ten areas: listening, speaking, reading, writing, spoken language, written language, vocabulary, grammar, receptive language, and expressive language. Two to four subtests are combined to form each area. Composite scores (or quotients) are based on a mean of 100 and a standard deviation of 15. An overall General Language Quotient has the same mean and standard deviation. It is somewhat questionable if the combination of only two subtests adequately measures the general areas of reading, writing, speaking, and listening. A profile sheet is available for both the subtest scores and the composite scores.

Technical Characteristics

Normative Sample.   A total of 3,056 students comprised the norms; of these, all but 587 (representing the age group 18 to 24 years) were from previous additions of the TOAL. The ethnicity, race, gender, place of residence, and geographic location of the sample were similar to the total U.S. population in 1990.

Reliability.   Median internal reliability coefficients were generally .90 or above for subtests and composites. (Exceptions were the speaking subtests in the .80s). Average test-retest coefficients ranged from .80 to .87 for the subtests and .83 to .86 for the composites.

Validity.   Discussions regarding the test's content and construct validity are in the manual. The criterion-related validity coefficients with a wide variety of measures were primarily in the moderate range.

Review of Relevant Research
Research on the TOAL-3 is limited primarily to the validity studies mentioned in the test manual. There is a need for further research on the TOAL-3, particularly with students with learning or language disabilities.

OVERVIEW: TEST OF ADOLESCENT AND ADULT LANGUAGE–3

- *Age level*—12 through 24 years old
- *Type of administration*—Individual; some portions can be group administered
- *Technical adequacy*—Adequate reliability, questionable validity
- *Scores yielded*—Subtest standard scores, composite quotients
- *Suggested use*—The TOAL-3 is one of the few instruments that measures the language ability of older students. It is therefore a much-needed and potentially useful instrument. The validity of the TOAL-3 is not established adequately and research in this area is necessary. Whether it is meaningful to put a few subtests together to form a general composite score has been questioned. The inclusion of both oral and written language tasks is a positive feature, particularly for the age range for which the test is intended.

Test of Language Competence

The Test of Language Competence (TLC) (Wiig & Secord, 1985) was designed to identify individuals ages 9 to 19 who have language disabilities. The test focuses on the areas of semantics, syntax, and pragmatics. The test is individually administered and takes about an hour to give. There are four subtests; the examiner can discontinue each subtest when the examinee fails to make *any* response for three consecutive items.

Description of Subtests

Understanding Ambiguous Sentences (13 items)—In this subtest, the examinee is read a sentence that could mean more than one thing and is asked to identify the two meanings. For example, "the elephant was ready to lift" could mean either the elephant was ready to lift something or the elephant was ready to be lifted.

Making Inferences (12 items)—In this subtest, the examinee is read related statements and asked to make inferences. For example, the examinee is read:

Mother was happy to have the turkey and all the trimmings in the house.

The family was disappointed when they had to eat at a restaurant on Thanksgiving day.

The examinee must then indicate which two of the four sentences might be the reason that they had to go to a restaurant:

A. The mother got sick with the flu.
B. Mother forgot to buy the turkey.
C. Most people think Thanksgiving dinner is always better at a restaurant.
D. Mother burned the turkey by cooking it too long.

Recreating Sentences (13 items)—In this subtest, the examinee is shown a picture and given three words. He or she must make up a sentence about the picture that uses the three words. For example, the words for Figure 12.3 are "sit," "painted," and "because."

Understanding Metaphoric Expression (12 items)—In this subtest, the examinee is told about a situation that includes a metaphoric expression. For example, "The situation is two boys talking at a dog show. One of them said 'He is crazy about that pet.'" The examinee must first tell what the statement means and must then indicate from four choices the one that represents its meaning.

Interpretation of Results

Standard scores, percentile ranks, age equivalents, and stanines are available for both subtests (mean = 10; standard deviation = 3) and total test (mean = 100; standard deviation = 15). In addition, the authors provide goals and objectives for

sit   painted   because

FIGURE 12.3   Example from the Recreating Sentences Subtest from the Test of Language Competence

From E. Wiig and W. Secord, *Test of Language Competence*. Copyright © 1985 by The Psychological Corporation. Reproduced by permission. All rights reserved.

each subtest that could be used for the development of IEPs. Guidelines are also provided for extension testing that uses an error analysis approach.

Technical Characteristics

Normative Sample.   A representative sample of 1,796 students between the ages of 9 and 19 from thirteen states was used.

Reliability.   Internal consistency coefficients ranged from .75 to .82 for the total test; coefficients were somewhat lower for the individual subtests. Test-retest coefficients were .78 for the total test and ranged from .34 (Recreating Sentences) to .73 (Understanding Metaphoric Expressions) for the subtests.

Validity.   Data from factor analysis and intercorrelations are presented to demonstrate its construct validity. Moderate correlations with the TOAL, WISC-R, and the Educational Abilities Series with students with language-learning disability

(LLD) and students without LLD are reported. Evidence of predictive validity is also reported.

Review of Relevant Research
No research other than that reported in the *Technical Manual* was located.

OVERVIEW: TEST OF LANGUAGE COMPETENCE

- *Age level*—9 to 19 years old
- *Type of administration*—Individual
- *Technical adequacy*—Limited reliability, adequate validity
- *Scores yielded*—Standard scores, percentile ranks, age equivalents, stanines
- *Suggested use*—The TLC focuses on language usage and is designed on a solid research base suggesting that individuals with language-learning disabilities demonstrate deficits in the use of cognitive and linguistic strategies. The format of the test is unique and interesting and requires the application of linguistic rules. Research is needed to demonstrate that the TLC can efficiently differentiate individuals with and without learning disabilities.

Tests of Language Development–2

The Tests of Language Development–2 (TOLD-2) (Newcomer & Hammill, 1988) consist of a primary edition (TOLD-2 Primary) and an intermediate edition (TOLD-2 Intermediate). According to the authors, the TOLD-2 can be used to identify children who have language disorders and to profile individual strengths and weaknesses in basic language abilities. They add that the test is based on a sound theoretical model. The TOLD-2 Primary, for example, follows the model used by its predecessor, the Test of Language Development–Primary (see Table 12.2). This model includes semantics, syntax, and phonology through both the receptive and expressive channels. The TOLD-2 Intermediate measures both semantics and syntax.

Description

TOLD-2 Primary.   The primary edition of the TOLD-2 is designed for use with children ages four to eight. It includes five subtests that measure syntax and semantics and two optional subtests that measure phonology. The subtests and what they measure follow.

> *Picture Vocabulary*—understanding words
> *Oral Vocabulary*—defining words
> *Grammatic Understanding*—understanding sentence structure

TABLE 12.2   Theoretical Model for the Test of Language Development–2 Primary

Linguistic Features	Linguistic Systems	
	Listening (Receptive Skills)	**Speaking (Expressive Skills)**
Semantics	Picture Vocabulary	Oral Vocabulary
Syntax	Grammatic Understanding	Sentence Imitation Grammatic Completion
Phonology	Word Discrimination	Word Articulation

From P. Newcomer and D. Hammill, *Test of Language Development–2.* Copyright © 1988 Pro-Ed, Inc., Austin, TX. Reprinted with permission.

> *Sentence Imitation*—generating proper sentences
> *Grammatic Completion*—using acceptable morphological forms
> *Word Discrimination (supplemental)*—noticing sound differences
> *Word Articulation (supplemental)*—saying words correctly

TOLD-2 Intermediate.   The intermediate version of the TOLD-2 is designed for use with children ages 8 1/2 to 12. The six subtests and what they measure follow.

> *Sentence Combining*—constructing sentences
> *Vocabulary*—understanding word relationships
> *Word Ordering*—constructing sentences
> *Generals*—knowing abstract relationships
> *Grammatic Comprehension*—recognizing grammatical sentences
> *Malapropisms*—correcting ridiculous sentences

Interpretation of Scores

The TOLD-2 yields several derived scores. These include language ages, percentiles, and standard scores for the individual subtests. The standard scores have a mean of 10 and a standard deviation of 3. In addition, the subtests can be grouped into the following composites: syntax, semantics, speaking, listening, phonology (primary edition only), and overall spoken language. Each of these composites yields quotients with a mean of 100 and a standard deviation of 15. A summary sheet and profile chart are also available that display the scores visually.

Technical Characteristics

Normative Sample.   The primary edition was standardized on approximately twenty-five hundred children from twenty-nine states; the intermediate edition used more than twelve hundred children from twenty-one states. The characteristics of the samples were similar to the national population in 1985.

Reliability.   Internal consistency and test-retest coefficients for both editions were generally acceptable.

Validity.   The manual presents evidence to support both editions' content and construct validity. Concurrent validity data with a variety of criterion measures are also presented.

Review of Relevant Research
The limited literature to date primarily addresses the TOLD and the TOLD-P, predecessors of the TOLD-2 Primary. All three of the tests are similar in format, however. The one study located on the TOLD-2 indicated that both the primary and intermediate forms had adequate reliability with the exception of the 8-year-old level (Fodness, McNeilly, & Bradley-Johnson, 1991). A list of research on previous editions follows.

- The TOLD is a reliable and valid measure when used with a language-impaired population (Newcomer & Hammill, 1978).
- Total scores from the TOLD successfully discriminated group status for normal-reading, reading-disabled, and language-delayed children. The Sentence Imitation subtest was the best discriminator (Wong & Roadhouse, 1978).
- On the TOLD, LD students showed a deficit in oral language (Newcomer & Magee, 1977).
- A table has been developed to help determine statistically significant differences among subtests on the TOLD-P (Reynolds, 1983).

Summary of Research Findings
The research on the TOLD, though limited, suggests that it is a useful instrument for children with learning disabilities and language disorders. Further research is needed in this area, however, particularly with the TOLD-2.

OVERVIEW: TESTS OF LANGUAGE DEVELOPMENT–2

- *Age level*—4 to 8 years (primary); 8 1/2 to 12 years (intermediate)
- *Type of administration*—Individual
- *Technical adequacy*—Acceptable reliability and validity
- *Scores yielded*—Standard scores, percentile ranks, age equivalents
- *Suggested use*—The TOLD-2 editions are similar to their predecessors, the TOLD Primary and the TOLD Intermediate. Both tests measure a number of language areas in both the receptive and expressive channels. This model allows for a profile of a child's strengths and weaknesses in language, using the same comparison group. The value of the tests depends on the extent to which the subtests actually measure the various language

components. Although the au[...]
gest research base of any curre[...]
published in the professional [...]
has supported its validity and [...]

TESTS FOR SPEECH AND LANGUAGE CLI[...]

WHY USE SPECIALIZED LANGUA[...]

Identification; determination of goals a[...]

WHO SHOULD USE THEM?

Speech and language clinicians

Some tests, although useful to the special educator, are typically administered by speech and language clinicians. These tests focus on various aspects of language and are typically used to identify individuals that might have a language disorder in one or more areas. Many of these tests emphasize pragmatic skills, which have received so much attention. It is recommended that the manuals and test materials be consulted for more information about these tests.

Clinical Evaluation of Language Fundamentals–Revised

The Clinical Evaluation of Language Fundamentals–Revised (CELF-R) (Semel & Wiig, 1987) is a revised edition of the Clinical Evaluation of Language Functions (CELF). The CELF-R, in addition to the name change, revised several subtests from the CELF, added and deleted others, and provides more interpretative guidelines. The CELF-R provides an evaluation of both language processing and production for students from kindergarten through grade 12. The eleven subtests are Formulated Sentences, Listening to Paragraphs, Semantic Relationships, Word Structure, Sentence Structure, Sentence Assembly, Oral Directions, Recalling Sentences, Word Associations, Word Classes, and Linguistic Concepts.

The test can be administered in approximately an hour and can provide standard scores, age equivalents, and percentile ranks. There is also an intervention program called the Clinical Language Intervention Program (CLIP) that can be used with both the CELF and the CELF-R.

Language Processing Test

The Language Processing Test (LPT) (Richard & Hanner, 1985) was designed to measure an individual's ability to attach meaning to language and to effectively formulate a response. Norms are available for individuals ages 5 to 12, although

e that the LPT can be used with older individuals for more infor-
s. The authors further indicated the types of behaviors that might be
in individuals whose language problems might be identified through
of the LPT. These include word-retrieval problems, inappropriate word
ge, neutral or nonspecific word usage (for example, thingamajig), inability to
orrect recognized errors, seemingly poor memory, avoidance or no response, repeating what has been asked, and pausing.

There are six subtests on the LPT: (1) Associations, (2) Categorization, (3)
Similarities, (4) Differences, (5) Multiple Meanings, and (6) Attributes. There are
also two pretests called Labeling and Stating Functions. Age equivalents, percentile ranks, and standard scores are available for interpretation purposes. Guyette
(1989) suggested that the LPT should be used as a clinical instrument rather than
a test whose scores are interpreted rigidly.

Test of Pragmatic Skills

The Test of Pragmatic Skills (TPS) (Shulman, 1986) is used with children ages
three to eight and assesses their use of language for conversational intent. The TPS
format is somewhat unique. It consists of four guided-play interactions, or tasks,
that serve as a basis through which pragmatic behaviors are elicited and recorded.
The TPS was designed to provide information on ten categories of communicative
intentions. Those are: Requesting Information, Requesting Actions, Rejection/De-
nial, Naming/Labeling, Answering/Responding, Informing, Reasoning, Sum-
moning/Calling, Greeting, and Closing Conversation. The author specifically
states that the test focuses only on pragmatics and that other tests should be used
to identify semantic and syntax problems. Although the TPS format is unique,
some question remains as to whether or not it provides any more information
than might be gathered in a thorough language sample (Fujiki, 1989).

For each of the four tasks, the examiner makes probes or statements to which
the examinee responds.

Playing with puppets—10 probes
Playing with pencil and paper—7 probes
Playing with telephones—9 probes
Playing with blocks—8 probes

Each of the tasks and subsequent probes are intended to measure up to eight
of the ten conversational intentions previously listed. The examinee is rated as a 0
(no response) to a 5 (contextually appropriate response with extensive elabora-
tion) for each of the responses to the probes. Normative data based on 650 children are available in the form of percentile ranks.

Test of Problem Solving

The Test of Problem Solving (TOPS) (Zachman, Jorgensen, Huisingh, & Barrett,
1984) is designed for use with children ages 6 to 12. It assesses their ability to

verbalize reasons, solutions, and justifications in an appropriate manner. According to the authors, the TOPS is an expressive test that is used to determine a child's thinking and reasoning ability related to events of everyday living. The test includes five subtests: (1) Explaining Inferences, (2) Determining Causes, (3) Negative Why Questions, (4) Determining Solutions, and (5) Avoiding Problems. As in the LPT, the authors feel that the test can be used informally for individuals outside the intended age range. Three types of scores are available for the TOPS: age equivalents, percentile ranks, and standard scores. In a study designed to evaluate speech-language clinicians' impressions of the TOPS, it was concluded that the content validity of the instrument is questionable (Bernhardt, 1990).

Test of Word Finding

The Test of Word Finding (TWF) (German, 1986) is designed to measure the word-finding ability of elementary school–age children. There are two forms, the primary form for grades 1 and 2 and the intermediate form for grades 3 to 6. Norms are provided for children ages 6 1/2 to 12. The author states that prior to the development of the TWF, the identification of children with this expressive language disorder was done informally.

There are six sections to the TWF: (1) Picture Naming: Nouns, (2) Sentence Completion Naming, (3) Description Naming, (4) Picture Naming: Verbs, (5) Picture Naming: Categories, and (6) a Comprehension section. This last section is given after the five other sections and involves only the items that are missed on those sections. The TWF provides percentile ranks and standard scores for both age and grade comparisons. There is also considerable information in the manual about the types of word-finding skills that can be identified. Although the TWF appears to be a reliable, technically sound instrument, there has been some question about how useful the test results actually are for classification or instructional decisions (Drum, 1989).

Instrument or Technique	Suggested Use — Prereferral: Screening and Initial Identification	Suggested Use — Prereferral: Informal Determination and Evaluation of Teaching Programs and Strategies	Determination of Current Performance Level and Educational Need	Postreferral: Decisions about Classification and Program Placement	IEP Goals	IEP Objectives	IEP Evaluation	Target Population: Mild/Moderate	Severe/Profound	Preschool	Elementary Age	Secondary Age	Adult	Special Considerations	Educational Relevance for Exceptional Students
Language Sampling	X	X			X			X		X	X	X	X	Productive means to determine individual's actual spontaneous use of language	very useful
Comprehensive Receptive and Expressive Vocabulary Test	X		X					X		X	X	X		Includes a measure of both receptive and expressive semantics using the same norms	useful
Peabody Picture Vocabulary Test-Revised	X		X					X		X	X	X	X	Can be used with individuals with speech and motor handicaps	useful
Test of Adolescent Language–3	X	X	X		X			X				X		One of a few tests designed to measure language abilities of older students	adequate
Test of Language Competence	X	X	X					X			X	X		Focuses on language usage in older students	useful
Tests of Language Development–2	X	X	X		X			X		X	X	X		Measures a variety of language skills; has a primary and intermediate form	adequate
Clinical Evaluation of Language Fundamentals	X	X	X		X			X			X	X		Measures language processing and production	useful
Language-Processing Test	X	X						X			X			Used to identify children with language processing problems	adequate
Test of Pragmatic Skills	X	X								X	X			One of the few tests designed to measure pragmatics	adequate

Test of Problem Solving	X	X						X			X		Measures the use of language related to events of everyday living	adequate
Test of Word Finding	X							X			X		Tests for expressive language problems	adequate

Part **IV**

ASSESSMENT OF ACHIEVEMENT

As noted in Part III, one major focus of educational and psychological assessment is the evaluation of an individual's abilities. Another major focus of assessment is the measurement of achievement. This usually involves the basic skill areas of reading, arithmetic, and written expression (including spelling). They are sometimes evaluated together with a general achievement test, at other times they are evaluated separately with a variety of instruments and techniques.

The assessment of achievement is extremely important in making appropriate educational decisions. Evaluation in this area is necessary to document that an educational need exists (a requirement of Public Law 101-476 IDEA) and to help make eligibility decisions (e.g., aptitude/achievement discrepancies for learning disabilities). More importantly, information in this area is used to assist in establishing relevant goals and objectives and to monitor progress in relation to those goals and objectives. The use of the instruments and procedures discussed in this section (along with the techniques discussed in Part II) are primarily the responsibility of the teacher.

As in Part III, both formal and informal tests will be discussed and information provided describing how each type fits into the overall assessment process; the same format will be used to describe the tests. That includes the following elements:

1. A summary matrix that presents information about specific instruments and techniques in a format that allows easy comparison of the instruments for suggested use and target population. The matrix also includes a statement of any special considerations of which a user should be aware. In addition, for each instrument, the matrix gives the educational relevance for exceptional students. The matrices are directly related to the assessment model proposed in Chapter 2.

2. A thorough review of relevant research for each norm-referenced instrument. The review emphasizes use of the test with exceptional students.
3. An overview box for each test. The overview summarizes the age range, technical adequacy (for norm-referenced tests), and suggested use for each instrument.

AFTER READING PART IV YOU SHOULD BE ABLE TO:

- Identify strengths and weaknesses of the major general achievement tests.
- Identify strengths and weaknesses of individual- and group-administered reading tests.
- Identify a variety of informal methods of assessing reading.
- Identify strengths and weaknesses of individual- and group-administered arithmetic tests (formal and informal).
- Identify strengths and weaknesses of spelling instruments (formal and informal).
- Identify strengths and weaknesses of tests for written expression.
- Identify strengths of written language sampling.

13

ASSESSMENT OF GENERAL ACHIEVEMENT

Instruments and Procedures Included

Norm-Referenced Tests
Group-Administered Tests
Individually Administered Tests
Diagnostic Achievement Battery–2
Diagnostic Achievement Test for Adolescents–2
Kaufman Test of Educational Achievement
Peabody Individual Achievement Test–Revised
Wechsler Individual Achievement Test
Wide Range Achievement Test–3
Woodcock-Johnson–Revised (Achievement)
Additional Instruments

Criterion-Referenced Instruments
The Brigance Inventories
Multilevel Academic Survey Test
Mastery: An Evaluation Tool

Mr. Segerson is a sixth-grade teacher in a rural school district. As part of his duties he is required to administer a group achievement test at the end of the year to document the academic level of each of his students. In the most recent testing, two of his students scored extremely low in reading and mathematics. He referred the two students to the learning-disabilities specialist, who scheduled them for in-depth academic testing. The first step was to administer an individual achievement test. After it was determined that one of the students was eligible for special education, portions of a criterion-referenced inventory was given in his deficient areas to help determine objectives for his IEP.

Probably all individuals have taken some kind of achievement test during their years as students. Typically, group achievement tests are administered annually or semiannually to document both the level of academic ability and the progress of individuals in specific academic areas. Individual achievement tests are sometimes administered to yield more specific academic information and to allow the examiner to observe the student's approach to the individual tasks. Many students perform quite differently on group and individual achievement tests, although individual achievement tests are usually required for students who receive special education services. Criterion-referenced inventories are also used to gather more specific information about certain academic areas.

An extremely important issue in achievement testing is content validity. It is absolutely necessary that an achievement test measure the curriculum to which a student is exposed. This requires that the "appropriate" achievement test be carefully selected. In other words, the content of an achievement test must be appropriate and complete in relation to the behaviors (curriculum) being measured. This can best be achieved by choosing valid instruments that measure the content a student has been taught. This is also one of the reasons that curriculum-based assessment has become so widespread.

Although most norm-referenced achievement tests are not really thought of as screening tests, many are used for this purpose. In fact, most achievement tests are used to gather some basic, preliminary information before more in-depth academic assessment is pursued. Some individually-administered achievement tests are also used to document that an educational deficit exists in order to meet that requirement of P.L. 94-142 and P.L. 101-476.

NORM-REFERENCED TESTS

Group-Administered Tests

WHY USE GROUP-ADMINISTERED TESTS?

Screening and identification of students needing further academic testing; informal determination of objectives

WHO SHOULD USE THEM?

Teachers

Group achievement tests usually have different levels for different grades in school. Tests that measure achievement in the elementary grades typically include items related to the basic skill areas of reading, spelling, and arithmetic. The levels for older students are concerned not only with basic skills, but also with content areas such as science and social studies. Therefore, it is important to note that not all of the areas measured by each test are used with students of all ages; certain areas are relevant and designed for students at specific grades. A brief description of the most commonly used group achievement tests follows.

California Achievement Tests

Age range—Kindergarten through grade 12

Standardization—Stratified sample of approximately 225,000

Technical adequacy—Acceptable

Areas measured—Seven major areas are measured: Reading, Spelling, Language, Mathematics, Study Skills, Science, Social Studies

Types of scores obtained—Grade equivalents, stanines, percentile ranks, scaled scores, normal curve equivalents

Special features—The California Achievement Tests (CAT) (CTB/McGraw-Hill, 1993) include a locater test that is used to identify the level of test that is most appropriate to give to an individual. Its value for group administration to exceptional students is questionable, however, due to the heterogeneity of the population. There is a Survey Battery that includes norm-referenced information and a Complete Battery that also includes criterion-referenced objectives.

Iowa Test of Basic Skills

Age range—Kindergarten through grade 9

Standardization—Stratified sample of more than 150,000 students (concurrently with the Tests of Achievement and Proficiency)

Technical adequacy—Good

Areas measured—The Iowa Test of Basic Skills (ITBS) (Hoover, Hieronymus, Frisbie, & Dunbar, 1993) has ten levels. The following are the areas measured: Listening, Writing, Vocabulary, Word Analysis, Reading Comprehension, Language Skills, Mathematics Skills, Social Studies, Science, and Sources of Information (e.g., map reading, using the encyclopedia)

Types of scores obtained—Percentile ranks, national stanines, standard scores, grade equivalents, normal curve equivalents

Special features—The ITBS includes both norm-referenced and criterion-referenced information. It was standardized concurrently with the Cognitive Abilities Test (a group-administered intelligence test). Administration of these two tests allows comparisons based on the same normative sample.

Metropolitan Achievement Tests

Age range—Kindergarten through grade 12

Standardization—Stratified sample of almost two hundred thousand

Technical adequacy—Good

Areas measured—The Metropolitan Achievement Tests—Seventh Edition (MAT-7) (Balow, Farr, & Hogan, 1992) include fourteen levels that measure the areas of reading, mathematics, language, science, and social studies. There is also a subtest called Research Skills/Thinking Skills.

Types of scores obtained—Scaled scores, percentile ranks, stanines, grade equivalents, normal-curve equivalents, functional reading levels, proficiency statements, and content cluster performance categories.

Special features—The MAT-7 is a major revision of an old standby that takes between approximately one-and-one-half to four hours to administer, depending on the level. It provides a complete battery of norm-referenced and criterion-referenced information.

SRA Achievement Series

Age level—Kindergarten through grade 12

Standardization—Stratified sample of approximately two hundred thousand

Technical adequacy—Good

Areas measured—Reading, Mathematics, Language Arts, Reference Materials, Social Studies, and Science

Types of scores obtained—Grade equivalents, percentiles, stanines, standard scores (two types: normal-curve equivalents and growth-scale values)

Special features—The SRA Achievement Series (Naslund, Thorpe, & Lefever, 1981) was standardized concurrently with the Educational Ability Series. This theoretically allows aptitude–achievement comparisons using the same normative sample. There are also six types of computer-printed report forms.

Stanford Achievement Test and Stanford Test of Academic Skills

Age range—

Stanford Achievement Test (SAT): Grade 1 through grade 9

Test of Academic Skills: Grades 9 through 13 (community college)

Standardization—Stratified sample of almost two hundred thousand

Technical characteristics—Good

Areas measured—The SAT (Psychological Corporation, 1992a) includes more than twenty subtests that measure the general areas of vocabulary, reading, study skills, mathematics, spelling, language, social science, science, and listening skills.

Areas measured—The Stanford Test of Academic Skills measures the following areas for grades 9 through 13:

Reading Vocabulary, Reading Comprehension
Language/English, Study Skills, Spelling
Mathematics Applications, Science, Social Science

Types of scores obtained—Percentile ranks, stanines, grade equivalents, and standard scores

Special features—In addition to these Stanford tests, another, the Stanford Early School Achievement Test, is used with children in kindergarten and first grade. It should be noted that the SAT also has both an edition for use with blind or partially sighted students and one for students with hearing impairments.

Tests of Achievement and Proficiency

Age range—High school (grades 9 through 12)

Standardization—Stratified sample of more than 150,000 (concurrently with the ITBS)

Technical adequacy—Acceptable

Areas measured—For grades 9 through 12 the following areas are measured: Reading Comprehension, Written Expression, Vocabulary, Mathematics, Social Studies, Science, and Information Processing (e.g., reading maps).

Types of scores obtained—National percentiles, national stanines, standard scores, grade equivalents, and normal curve equivalents.

Special features—The Tests of Achievement and Proficiency (TAP) (Scannell, Haugh, Lloyd, & Risinger 1993) are an upward extension of the Iowa Test of Basic Skills. This instrument was standardized concurrently with the Iowa Test and the Cognitive Abilities Test.

INDIVIDUALLY ADMINISTERED TESTS

WHY USE INDIVIDUALLY ADMINISTERED TESTS?

Screening and identification of students needing further academic testing; documentation of educational need; establishment of IEP goals

WHO SHOULD USE THEM?

Teachers; diagnosticians; school psychologists

Until the 1980s, only two individually administered norm-referenced tests were specifically designed to measure overall academic achievement. Those two tests, the Peabody Individual Achievement Test and the Wide Range Achievement Test, were frequently used and constantly scrutinized. Other tests were developed, and the two "old standbys" were revised. Descriptions of several of these instruments follow.

Diagnostic Achievement Battery–2

The Diagnostic Achievement Battery–2 (DAB-2) (Newcomer, 1990) is an individually administered group of subtests used to measure a number of academic areas. According to the author, the DAB-2 is intended to address four purposes: the identification of students who are having difficulties in the areas of spoken language, written language, and mathematics; the determination of an individual's strengths and weaknesses; the documentation of student progress; and the possible use as a measurement device for research studies regarding academic achievement. The DAB-2 includes twelve subtests that are grouped together in various combinations to provide a number of composite areas. The model followed includes composite scores in spoken language, including the areas of listening and speaking; written language, including the areas of reading and written language generation; and mathematics (Figure 13.1). The test is designed for students ages 6 to 14.

Description
As noted previously, there are twelve subtests in the DAB-2. A brief description of each follows.

Listening

Story Comprehension (35 items)—The student is required to listen to brief stories and then answer several questions about each story. This subtest is essentially a measure of listening comprehension.

Characteristics (35 items)—Requires the student to give true-false answers to questions such as "all trees are maples" and "all nails are metal."

Speaking

Synonyms (25 items)—The examiner says a word, and the student must supply another word that has the same meaning.

Grammatic Completion (27 items)—The student is given an incomplete statement such as, "I lost one tooth and you lost one tooth. We lost two _____," and is asked to supply the missing answer.

Reading

Alphabet/Word Knowledge (65 items)—This subtest measures visual discrimination skills, letter recognition, and beginning sounds at the beginning of the subtest and word recognition for the majority of the subtest.

Reading Comprehension (45 items)—This subtest includes a series of eight progressively more difficult passages that the student must read and subsequently answer questions asked by the examiner.

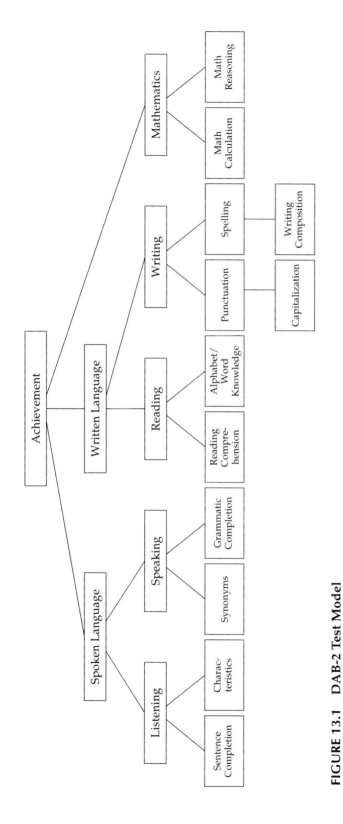

FIGURE 13.1   DAB-2 Test Model

From: P. Newcomer. *Diagnostic Achievement Battery–2.* Copyright © 1990 by Pro-Ed, Austin, TX. Reprinted with permission.

Writing

Capitalization (30 items)—The student is provided a series of sentences that have no capitalization (Figure 13.2). The student must rewrite the sentences, editing appropriate capital letters.

Punctuation (20 items)—The same sentences used in punctuation are used in this subtest. The student must also add the appropriate punctuation to the sentences.

Spelling (20 items)—The words are orally read by the examiner and written by the student.

Writing Composition (see description of subtest)—The student looks at three pictures that depict a car race. The student is instructed to write a story about the picture that has a beginning, middle, and end. The examiner simply counts the number of words with seven or more letters and evaluates the thematic content to determine the raw score.

Mathematics

Mathematics Reasoning (30 items)—This subtest uses pictures at the lower levels in which the majority of the problems are presented orally and the student points to the correct response. The last half of the subtest includes orally presented problems that the student must solve without the use of visual cues or pencil and paper.

Mathematics Calculation (36 items)—This subtest is a series of progressively more difficult math computation problems. The student has fifteen minutes to complete as many as possible.

Interpretation of Results

Each of the twelve subtests yields grade equivalents, percentile ranks, and standard scores (mean = 10; standard deviation = 3). Further, the subtests are combined as noted above into composites that yield quotients with a mean of 100 and a standard deviation of 15. The five quotients are listening, speaking, reading, writing, and math. In addition, the listening and speaking areas can be combined to form a spoken language quotient, and the reading and writing areas can be combined to form a written language quotient. Finally, all of the subtests can be combined to provide a total achievement quotient. All of the quotients have a mean of 100 and a standard deviation of 15. There is a computerized scoring program as well.

Technical Characteristics

Normative Sample.   The sample consisted of 2,623 children from forty states. The sample was stratified according to gender, type of residence, race, ethnicity, and geographic region. According to the author, the percentage of individuals included in the standardization sample was similar to the U.S. population in 1985.

Practice Item: the dog is big

1. the man is tall
2. we ate breakfast
3. today is monday
4. where are evans shoes
5. his name is mr a w parker
6. katie lives on main street
7. didnt alan mail the letter
8. christmas comes in december
9. jeffs mother came from canada
10. joan and angela got home at 230 am
11. yes elaine there is a santa claus
12. no she said i dont want to go
13. they sailed around the cape of good hope
14. steve was born on july 6 1985 wasnt he
15. stop the wedding the brides father shouted
16. mickey mouse is my favorite cartoon character
17. the largest dolphins live in the pacific ocean
18. the italian german and russian all spoke english
19. marilyn was elected president of harvard college
20. she works for a good newspaper the daily chronicle
21. isnt your brothers house in philadelphia pennsylvania
22. the teacher asked what have you children been doing
23. there were thirty five ducks swimming in the farmers pond
24. did you read william shakespeares midsummer nights dream
25. among her children were four females sandy kathy dale and marge
26. watch your step jean shouted to the crowd as she waved the sword
27. the chimp after climbing to the top of the oak tree threw an orange at barbara
28. sol and his brothers all six of them played baseball for the new york tigers
29. ednas powerful backhand carried her to the wimbledon championship didn't it
30. marjorie and allen dressed as peter pan and tinker bell for the halloween party

FIGURE 13.2   Capitalization Subtest from the Diagnostic Achievement Battery–2

From: P. Newcomer. *Diagnostic Achievement Battery–2.* Copyright © 1990 by Pro-Ed, Austin, TX. Reprinted with permission.

Reliability.   The internal consistency reliability was computed using a sample of 450 children for both the individual subtests and the composites. For the most part, the reliability coefficients exceeded .80 and the majority exceeded .90. Synonyms and Spelling had the lowest coefficients. Test-retest coefficients ranged from .80 (Mathematical Reasoning) to .99 (Alphabet/Word Knowledge) for individual subtests and .92 (Mathematics) to .99 (Writing and Written Language) for the composites. These data were based on a limited sample of thirty-four children, however.

Validity.   Criterion-related validity was determined by comparing scores from the DAB-2 with scores from seven other tests. Unfortunately, only twenty-five third-graders and twenty-one sixth-graders were included in the analysis. The coefficients ranged from .37 (Written Vocabulary) to .81 (Spelling) for individual subtests and from .46 (Speaking) to .73 (Reading) for the composites. Another study, using forty-five students, reported coefficients ranging from .36 to .78 with two additional tests. Also, the author provides a theoretical argument supporting the construct validity of the DAB-2.

Review of Relevant Research
No research articles investigating the DAB-2 or the original DAB were located in the professional literature. There is a definite need for research on this test to determine its potential uses and limitations. Deni (1985) reviewed the DAB and determined that it was a useful tool for screening and evaluating achievement, although the written subtests were limited with younger children. Lewandowski (1985) also gave the DAB a positive review, noting that it was carefully designed.

OVERVIEW: DIAGNOSTIC ACHIEVEMENT BATTERY–2

- *Age level*—6 to 14 years old
- *Type of administration*—Individual; some small group
- *Technical adequacy*—Adequate standardization; adequate reliability and validity, particularly for composite scores; technical data based on limited samples
- *Scores yielded*—Percentiles, standard scores
- *Suggested use*—The DAB-2 is a potentially useful instrument to determine individual strengths and weaknesses in a number of academic areas. As with most tests, the composite scores are more stable than the individual subtest scores and should be used for important educational decisions. Research on the DAB-2 is needed before its full potential can be determined. A computerized scoring program (PROSCORE) is available.

Diagnostic Achievement Test for Adolescents–2

The Diagnostic Achievement Test for Adolescents (DATA-2) (Newcomer & Bryant, 1993) is an individually administered instrument designed to evaluate the overall achievement areas for individuals ages twelve through eighteen. According to the authors, the DATA-2 can be used for four purposes: (1) to identify students who are significantly below their peers in academic areas, (2) to identify strengths and weaknesses, (3) to document student progress and, (4) to serve as a measurement device for research studies. These purposes are essentially the same as those noted by the author of the DAB-2. The DATA-2 has thirteen subtests and takes between one and two hours to administer. Basal and ceiling guidelines are used in the DATA-2 in an attempt to decrease the testing time as much as possible.

Description

Receptive Vocabulary (35 items)—This requires the student to listen to pairs of words (e.g., "evil-bad," "sweet-sour," "walk-saw") and to indicate whether the pair are the opposite, the same, or neither.

Receptive Grammar (35 items)—This subtest requires the student to indicate if pairs of sentences are grammatically correct (C) or incorrect (I). For example, "The three balls is round" (I) and "Can you roll them?" (C).

Expressive Grammar (30 items)—This is an imitation task that requires the student to repeat an orally presented sentence ("Before lunch, it will be necessary to finish the work").

Expressive Vocabulary (30 items)—The student must use a vocabulary word in a sentence to demonstrate comprehension of the word meaning.

Word Identification (45 items)—This requires the individual to correctly pronounce words such as "transfusion" and "bucolic."

Reading Comprehension (42 items)—This consists of seven short stories that the student reads and six comprehension questions asked about each reading passage.

Mathematics Calculation (45 items)—This includes mathematical problems that must be completed. Pencil and paper are provided to the student.

Mathematics Problem Solving (45 items)—In this subtest, the examiner reads mathematical story problems to the student, who must provide the correct answer. The students may also read the items as the examiner reads them. Again, pencil and paper are provided to the student.

Spelling (45 items)—This requires the student to write the correct spelling of words ranging from "banquet" to "derelict."

Writing Composition—The student is shown three pictures and is instructed to write a story based on those pictures. This test is scored simply by counting the number of words containing seven or more letters. That number becomes the raw score.

Science (supplemental 45 items)—The student is read questions such as "what are Earth, Pluto, and Mars?" and "what instrument is used to detect earthquakes?" The student must provide an oral response.

Social Studies (supplemental 45 items)—This subtest uses the same format as science with questions such as "who invented the telephone?" and "what is the formal indictment of a President called?"

Reference Skills (supplemental)—This subtest has six sections. These sections are guide words, alphabetizing, encyclopedia skills, dictionary skills, library catalog skills, and table of contents. Figure 13.3 shows a portion of this subtest.

Interpretation of Results

A variety of scores are available for the DATA-2. These include percentile ranks and standard scores for individual subtests (standard score mean = 10, standard deviation = 3). Several composite scores are also available. These composites (Listening, Speaking, Reading, Mathematics, Writing, Spoken Language Quotient, and Written Language Quotient) are combinations of various subtests and also are reported as standard scores with a mean of 10 and standard deviation of 3. Also available is an Achievement Screener (Word Identification, Math Computation, and Spelling) and Total Achievement, which is combination of all of the subtests. These are also reported as quotients (standard scores with a mean of 100 and a standard deviation of 15). A computerized scoring system—the DATA-2 PROSCORE—is available. Examples of the printouts are provided in the manual.

Technical Characteristics

Normative Sample. More than two thousand children residing in nineteen states were included in the standardization. The demographic characteristics of gender, residence, race, geographic area, and ethnicity were considered, and the percentages of individuals in the standardization sample were similar to the 1990 total U.S. percentages.

Reliability. Internal consistency was determined using coefficient alpha using a sample of 350 students. All coefficients for the individual subtests were above .90 with the exception of Receptive Grammar (.84). The composite coefficients ranged from .93 to .98. No test-retest reliability was reported, although the authors do provide a table of standard error of measurements. The subtests each had a SEM of 1. The composites had SEMs ranging from 2 to 4 (based on a mean of 100 and a standard deviation of 15).

Validity. The authors provide a brief discussion of their attempt to ensure content validity at the point of test construction. Regarding criterion-related validity, 234 children from the original DATA's normative sample who had been administered other achievement tests were included in a variety of studies. These 234 children had been administered one of five achievement tests or diagnostic academic

---

Guide Words

Directions: Imagine that the words listed below are guide words found at the top of a dictionary page. The page number between each set of words represents the page on which the guide words are found. Using the guide words as a source, write the number of the page that would contain each word.

rabble	625	radiance
radical	626	rampant
rampart	627	ransack
ransom	628	rare
rarefied	629	rate
ratify	630	reach
ready	631	reasonable

Practice: rant _____

1. radian _____
2. rayless _____
3. rabies _____
4. rarely _____

5. rancorous _____
6. rampion _____
7. rearwards _____

Alphabetizing

Directions: Below are sets of four words each. You are to put the four words in alphabetical order by placing a 1, 2, 3, or 4 next to each word, depending on which word comes first, second, third, or fourth.

Practice:

_____ coerce
_____ cognitive
_____ codger
_____ coffee

Set 1:

_____ revealment
_____ retreat
_____ revel
_____ retrograde

Set 2:

_____ committee
_____ commode
_____ commital
_____ commixture

FIGURE 13.3   Portion of Reference Skills Subtest from the Diagnostic Achievement Test for Adolescents

From: P. Newcomer and Bryant. *Diagnostic Achievement Test for Adolescents.* Copyright © 1986 by Pro-Ed, Austin, TX. Reprinted with permission.

tests. There is a wide range of correlations mostly in the moderate range. The authors note that 86 percent of the correlation coefficients were at or exceeded .35 although this is relatively low for a validity coefficient. Evidence for construct validity was also presented, including data that showed the interrelationships among the subtests and composites and correlations with various aptitude measures.

Review of Relevant Research

Although no empirical studies were located in the professional literature, several reviews of the original DATA were found. The reviewers were generally supportive of the DATA, although several questioned the test's technical characteristics. For example, Kamphaus (1989) noted that the DATA had several appealing features but the standardization was inadequate. Similarly, Ysseldyke (1989) noted that although the DATA was the only individually administered achievement test that measures reading, mathematics, spelling, social studies, as well as science and use of references, the standardization procedures were insufficiently described. Conversely, Stuempfig (1987) felt that the test was well constructed and had adequate reliability and validity. Stuempfig noted, however, that the DATA was more a survey instrument of general achievement than a diagnostic test to pinpoint specific learning problems. It should be noted that the DATA-2 improved both its standardization and the description of the normative sample.

OVERVIEW: DIAGNOSTIC ACHIEVEMENT TEST FOR ADOLESCENTS–2

- *Age level*—12 years through 18 years old
- *Type of administration*—Individual
- *Technical adequacy*—Adequate standardization, reliability, and validity
- *Scores yielded*—Standard score and percentile ranks for subtests, composites, the achievement screener, and total achievement
- *Suggested use*—The DATA-2 is the only individually administered achievement test designed specifically for adolescents. Therefore, for that age range it includes more appropriate items than many of the other achievement tests that attempt to cover a wide age range—usually from kindergarten to high school. The use of the reference skills subtest is unique; more research, however, is necessary to determine its true utility. The criticism that was aimed at the DATA of the lack of appropriate description regarding the standardization sample has been addressed in the revision. The test is best thought of as a general achievement test. Until further validity data are generated, the use of individual subtest scores should probably be discouraged. Users should also look carefully at the subtests that determine the composites for interpretive purposes. For example, the Written Language Quotient is composed of Word Identification and Reading Comprehension in addition to Spelling and Writing Composition.

Kaufman Test of Educational Achievement

The Kaufman Test of Educational Achievement (K-TEA) (Kaufman & Kaufman, 1985) is an individually administered instrument designed to measure achievement areas of students in grades 1 through 12. There are two forms of the K-TEA, a comprehensive form that measures five areas and a brief form that measures only three. This description focuses on the comprehensive form. The time requirements for administration range from approximately twenty to thirty minutes for first-grade students to approximately one hour for secondary-level students. The authors cite eleven purposes for which the K-TEA would be appropriate, including the identification of individual strengths and weaknesses, the determination of the types of academic errors made, program planning, and making program decisions. The K-TEA is presented in an easel-type format that makes administration easy. The directions are clear and the manual is comprehensive and easily understood.

Description
Five subtests are included in the comprehensive form of the K-TEA. The brief form consists of three subtests (reading, spelling, mathematics) that measure a combination of these five areas.

> *Mathematics Applications (60 items)*—The student is required to answer different types of conceptual and reasoning questions. The items are presented orally, although the student has a visual stimulus (for example, table, graph, or word problem) to act as a cue. In addition, the student can use pencil and paper to aid in computations.
>
> *Reading Decoding (60 items)*—This subtest includes items ranging from letter identification to word identification and pronunciation.
>
> *Spelling (50 items)*—The student must write the correct spelling of words of increasing difficulty dictated by the examiner.
>
> *Reading Comprehension (50 items)*—The majority of items require the student to read a passage and subsequent questions and respond orally to the questions. One interesting feature is the inclusion of eight items at the beginning of the subtest that require the student to respond gesturally, such as "make a fist." Five items at the end of the subtest require the student to respond orally to commands presented in printed sentences.
>
> *Mathematics Computation (60 items)*—The student must solve traditional addition, subtraction, multiplication, and division problems as well as fractions, algebraic formulae, and other more complex types of problems.

Interpretation of Results
The K-TEA provides a variety of interpretative guidelines to help the examiner get the most out of the test results. Each subtest yields standard scores (mean = 100; standard deviation = 15) based on both age and grade norms. In addition, the two reading subtests and the two mathematics subtests can be combined to form a reading and mathematics composite score, respectively. Finally, all five subtests can be combined to provide a battery composite score. All of the composite scores also have a mean of 100 and a standard deviation of 15. Tables aid in transforming the standard scores into age or grade equivalents, percentile ranks, and stanines.

The authors also provide tables that allow additional interpretation of the results. For instance, it is possible to determine when a specific subtest standard score differs significantly from the average of all the subtest standard scores. This information is important in determining student strengths and weaknesses. Another notable feature is the error analysis guidelines. These provide a classification system for the type of errors made on each subtest as well as normative data that indicate whether or not the number of different types of errors are considered significant depending on the age of the examinee. Figure 13.4 shows the types of errors noted for the Mathematics Application subtest.

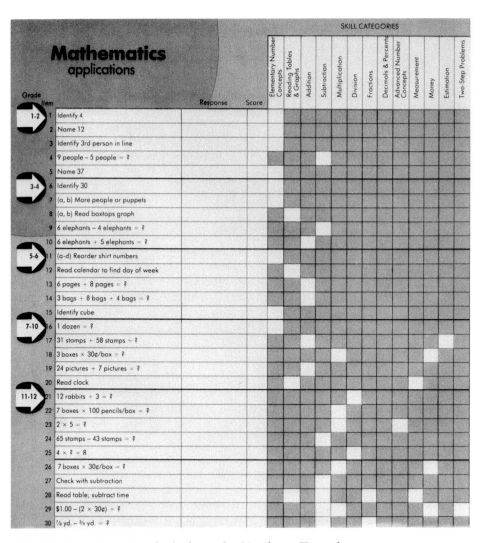

FIGURE 13.4   Error Analysis from the Kaufman Test of Educational Achievement

From A. Kaufman and N. Kaufman, *Kaufman Test of Educational Achievement.* Copyright © 1985 by American Guidance Service, Circle Pines, MN. Reprinted with permission.

Technical Characteristics

Normative Sample.   The K-TEA was involved in two separate standardizations (spring and fall) to provide more specific comparative information based on the time of year that a student is tested. The spring standardization included more than fourteen hundred students from fifteen states. The fall standardization included more than one thousand students from sixteen states. Sampling was based on census reports from 1983–1984 considering geographic region, socioeconomic background, and ethnic group.

Reliability.   Split-half reliability coefficients were determined for both subtest and composite scores. In general, these coefficients were greater than .90, with a few in the .80 range. The test-retest coefficients were computed in two separate studies. In the first study (grades 1 to 6), the coefficients ranged from .83 (Mathematics Computation) to .95 (Spelling). In the second study (grades seven to twelve), the coefficients ranged from .90 (Reading Comprehension) to .96 (Spelling). For both samples, the battery composite yielded a .97 coefficient. Data correlating the Brief form with the Comprehensive form are also reported with the majority above .80.

Validity.   The authors detail the steps followed in ensuring the content validity of the test (for example, item selection) and provide empirical support. They also present data supporting construct validity. Concurrent validity was established by reporting correlational data with the Wide Range Achievement Test and Peabody Individual Achievement Test, the Kaufman Assessment Battery for Children, the Peabody Picture Vocabulary Test–Revised, and a number of group achievement tests. More data using more appropriate criterion measures are necessary.

Review of Relevant Research

Interestingly, relatively little research related to the K-TEA has appeared in the professional literature. One study indicated that the K-TEA yielded scores that were 5–9 points higher than the popular Wide Range Achievement Test–Revised (WRAT-R) (Webster, Hewett, & Crumbacker, 1989). In another, McGhee (1986) found some overlap in the subtests in a group of underachieving students. The relationship of the K-TEA with various intelligence tests has also been investigated. Prewett and Farhney (1994) reported that the K-TEA brief form correlated .59 (Spelling) and .65 (Reading and Mathematics) with the Stanford Binet–IV and were also 4 to 7 points lower. Similarly, Prewett and McCaffery (1993) reported significant correlations between the Kaufman Brief Intelligence Test and the K-TEA. One interesting finding was the indication that the reliability coefficients are actually higher than those reported in the test manual (Shull-Senn, Weatherly, Morgan, & Bradley-Johnson, 1995).

The K-TEA has also received several favorable reviews. Henson and Bennett (1986) noted that it is easy to administer, has a well-written manual, and has a good empirical and normative base. Similarly, Worthington (1987) agreed that the

K-TEA had good technical characteristics and allowed the maximum analysis of an individual's academic strengths and weaknesses. Miller (1990) noted that the K-TEA should not be used for academically delayed first-grade students but that the instrument had unique features and good psychometric properties that allowed its use for students of other ages. Sattler (1989b) also noted that the K-TEA had good norms and technical characteristics.

OVERVIEW: KAUFMAN TEST OF EDUCATIONAL ACHIEVEMENT

- *Age level*—6 to 18 years old (grades 1 to 12)
- *Type of administration*—Individual
- *Technical characteristics*—Good reliability, acceptable validity
- *Scores yielded*—Standard scores, percentile ranks, age and grade equivalents, stanines, error analysis guidelines
- *Suggested use*—The K-TEA is a technically sound, well-constructed general achievement test. It is relatively easy to administer and score. For the most part, the K-TEA measures achievement in a similar fashion to classroom demands (for example, written spelling and math computation). The error analysis guidelines are a helpful addition and should serve as a constant reminder of the importance of error analysis on any norm-referenced test. In summary, the K-TEA has the potential to be one of the better general achievement tests. More research on the instrument is needed before more definitive statements can be made. The limited data indicate that the test might yield slightly elevated scores compared to other tests. It should be noted that the K-TEA is currently being revised.

Peabody Individual Achievement Test-Revised

The Peabody Individual Achievement Test-Revised (PIAT-R) (Dunn & Markwardt, 1988) is designed for use with students from kindergarten through grade twelve. The PIAT-R retained many features from the original PIAT including quick administration and scoring, use of demonstration and training exercises, and the use of easels for test administration. It also retained the PIAT format that includes a visual, multiple-choice stimulus that requires a verbal or motor (pointing) response for the Spelling, Mathematics, and Reading Comprehension subtests. The optional response requirements makes the test attractive to use with individuals with speech or motor problems. The PIAT-R consists of five subtests: General Information, Reading Recognition, Reading Comprehension, Mathematics, and Spelling as well as an optional subtest of Written Expression. The five subtests were retained from the original PIAT although the item content was updated and approximately 20 percent of the items are new. The Written Expression subtest is a new addition.

Description

General Information (100 items)—This is the only subtest that is given entirely verbally and requires only a verbal response. Questions are asked on subjects ranging from science and social studies to fine arts and sports.

Reading Recognition (100 items)—This subtest includes items ranging from matching letters of the alphabet to orally reading words of increasing difficulty.

Reading Comprehension (82 items)—This subtest requires the student to silently read a sentence on one page and then to choose which one of four pictures presented on another page best represents the meaning of the sentence.

Mathematics (100 items)—This subtest ranges from matching and recognizing numbers to solving geometry and trigonometry problems (the student must indicate which of four choices is the correct answer).

Spelling (100 items)—This subtest includes items that require the identification of a letter that is presented with three other objects, items that require the identification of one specific letter or word from four choices, and items that require the correct spelling of a word from four choices.

Written Expression (optional)—This subtest has two levels. Level I, designed for kindergarten through grade two, requires the student to copy letters and words, write his or her name, and write letters and words from dictation. Level II requires the student to write a story about one of two pictures. The story is scored according to criteria such as sentence construction and the use of metaphors.

Interpretation of Results

Raw scores from the PIAT-R can be transformed into a variety of derived scores. Standard scores (mean = 100, standard deviation = 15), percentile ranks, grade equivalents, stanines, normal curve equivalents, and age equivalents are available for each of the five subtests. Total Score (combination of the five subtests) and Total Reading (combination of Reading Recognition and Reading Comprehension) are also available. Scores from the optional subtest (Written Expression) are not included in the total score but rather are reported in terms of stanines within grades and developmental scaled scores. The optional subtest is also considerably more difficult to score.

Technical Characteristics

Normative Sample.   The PIAT-R used a stratified sample of more than fifteen hundred students from kindergarten through grade 12. The stratification variables were geographic region, gender, socioeconomic status, and ethnic background. The sample was similar to the breakdown of census data, although there were some minor deviations for the earlier and later age groups.

Reliability.   Reliability coefficients were calculated for each subtest for each age group in the standardization sample. Split-half coefficients and internal consistency coefficients were good; the vast majority exceeded .90. Test-retest coefficients were somewhat lower, although approximately two thirds of the coefficients also exceeded .90. Coefficients for the Written Expression subtest were calculated and reported separately. The internal consistency coefficients were considerably lower than those of the other five subtests. Interrater reliability was also calculated in the .50s.

Validity.   In general, validity data on the PIAT-R are lacking. The manual includes a discussion regarding its content validity, and criterion-related validity data are provided. The criterion measure used, however, is the Peabody Picture Vocabulary Test–Revised, a measure of receptive vocabulary only.

Review of Relevant Research
Surprisingly, very little research has appeared in the professional literature that investigates the PIAT-R. In one study, Robertson, Rengel, and Wang (1989) attempted to refine the Written Expression subtest by adding age-related weights to the scoring system, but found that it did not improve the instrument. Costenbader and Adams (1991) reviewed the PIAT-R and noted the low reliability of the Written Expression Subtest. They also cautioned against its use for ages 5 and 9 and grades 9 and 12 because of norming limitations. Below is a sampling of some of the findings on the PIAT. Although the format of the PIAT and PIAT-R are similar, some caution should be taken in generalizing the research findings from one test to the other.

- The PIAT is not discriminatory against lower socioeconomic or minority-group children (Rodriguez, 1989).
- Validity coefficients between the PIAT and Woodcock Reading Mastery Tests decreased as the age of the subjects increased (Eaves, Darch, & Haynes, 1989).
- The PIAT is a good test to use with secondary-school learning-disabled students (Stonebumer & Brown, 1979) and intellectually advanced preschoolers (Shorr, Jackson, & Robinson, 1980).
- The reliability of the PIAT subtests with emotionally disturbed children is generally lower than the reliabilities reported in the manual (Dean, 1979).
- An alternate method of interpreting the scores has been suggested in which the standard score of a subtest is compared to the mean of the standard score of all the subtests. Statistical tables to facilitate this pattern analysis are available for the original PIAT (Naglieri & Kamphaus, 1981; Reynolds & Gutkin, 1980; Silverstein, 1981). It is anticipated that similar tables will be available for the PIAT-R.
- The overall PIAT has adequate validity with mentally retarded students (Burns, Peterson, & Bauer, 1974; Ysseldyke, Sabatino, & Lamanna, 1973). However, a more suitable reading-vocabulary measure should be substituted

for Reading Comprehension, since that subtest and the Reading Recognition subtest measure the same thing in nonreaders (Baum, 1975; Burns, 1975). Also, the validity of the Spelling subtest with mentally retarded students is limited (Ysseldyke, Sabatino, & Lamanna, 1973).

- There is evidence that the PIAT measures two factors: a verbal comprehension and reasoning skills factor and an acquired practical knowledge factor (Reynolds, 1979).
- The Mathematics subtest can and should be approached using a diagnostic-testing or error-analysis framework. An error-analysis matrix has been developed to facilitate this process (Algozzine & McGraw, 1980).

Summary of Research Findings

Because of the similarity in format, research on the PIAT might be generalized to the PIAT-R, although this should be done with some degree of caution. In general, there is some evidence that the PIAT can be used reliably with gifted students or students with learning disabilities, although its reliability with students with emotional problems has been questioned. The PIAT also was found useful with students with mild retardation. Alternate interpretation models have been suggested by researchers. Research on the PIAT-R is necessary.

OVERVIEW: PEABODY INDIVIDUAL ACHIEVEMENT TEST–REVISED

- *Age level*—Kindergarten through grade 12
- *Type of administration*—Individual
- *Technical adequacy*—Good standardization; limited validity; adequate reliability
- *Scores yielded*—Age and grade equivalents, percentile ranks, standard scores, stanines, normal curve equivalents
- *Suggested use*—The PIAT-R is a well-standardized general achievement test designed for kindergarten through grade 12. Its appropriateness with special education students largely depends on the nature of the disability. For students with language or motor impairments, it would be the more appropriate general-achievement test. On the other hand, its use with students with visual or visual-perceptual problems is limited. You must keep in mind the nature of the tasks presented on the PIAT-R. The mathematic and spelling subtests, in particular, measure different aspects of those skills than are measured in typical classroom activities. The addition of the written expression subtest may prove helpful, although Lazarus, McKenna, and Lynch (1990) noted that informal interpretation of the writing samples is probably the best procedure to follow. The PIAT-R is currently being restandardized.

Wechsler Individual Achievement Test

The Wechsler Individual Achievement Test (WIAT) (Psychological Corporation, 1992b) is an individually administered test that was developed and normed concurrently with the Wechsler Intelligence Scale for Children–III (WISC-III). It also shares a linking sample with the Wechsler Preschool and Primary Scale of Intelligence–Revised (WPPSI-R) and the Wechsler Adult Intelligence Scale–Revised (WAIS-R). As a result, an individual can be compared in the areas of intelligence and achievement to the same standardization sample. The instrument was also designed to measure the areas of achievement in which a student with a learning disability must show some discrepancy. Those are oral expression, listening comprehension, written expression, basic reading skills, reading comprehension, mathematics calculation, and mathematics reasoning. The WIAT subtests reflect these seven areas and also include an additional subtest that measures the area of spelling.

Description

> *Basic Reading (55 items)*—This subtest measures basic word reading ability primarily through sight recognition.
>
> *Mathematics Reasoning (50 items)*—This requires the student to respond by speaking, pointing, or writing to a variety of tasks that require knowledge of mathematic concepts.
>
> *Spelling (50 items)*—This written spelling subtest requires the student to spell words that are dictated by the examiner.
>
> *Reading Comprehension (38 items)*—This subtest requires the student to read short passages and then respond orally to comprehension questions.
>
> *Numerical Operations (40 items)*—This subtest requires the student to perform basic mathematical calculations in addition, subtraction, multiplication, and division.
>
> *Listening Comprehension (36 items)*—The student is required to respond verbally to comprehension questions about passages read by the examiner. The earlier portions of this subtest require the student to point to the correct response after the examiner presents a word orally.
>
> *Oral Expression (40 items)*—The student must describe scenes orally, explain steps involved in completing a process, and provide directions.
>
> *Written Expression (Passages scored on six criteria)*—This subtest requires the student to write a passage about a certain topic (two possible) for fifteen minutes. It is administered to students in grades 3 through 12.

Interpretation of Scores

Derived scores are available for each subtest, as well as a composite for Reading, Mathematics, Language, and Writing. A Total Composite Score that includes all of the subtests is also available. Standard scores, age and grade equivalents, percentiles, stanines, and normal curve equivalents are reported. Tables are available to compare students by their age or grade. One noteworthy feature of the WIAT is the tables that allow the determination of ability (aptitude)–achievement discrepancies that most states require for the determination of a learning disability. In fact, two different methods of determining a significant discrepancy are discussed in the manual with appropriate tables presented for the examiner's use.

Technical Characteristics

Normative Sample.   The WIAT went through several stages of development to determine the final normative sample. The final sample included 4,252 students from age 5 through 19 (kindergarten through grade 12). The sample was stratified according to age, grade, gender, ethnicity, geographic region, and the educational level of the parents. Data from the 1988 U.S. census were used to determination the stratification.

Reliability.   Internal consistency reliability was determined using the split-half procedure and were generally in the .80s for the subtests and .90 or above for the composite scores. Test-retest reliability was determined using a subtest of 367 students from five grade levels. The coefficients ranged from .68 to (Oral Expression) to .94 (Basic Reading and Spelling) for the subtests, and from .78 (Language) to .94 (Writing) for the composites. Interscorer reliability was also determined for a limited number of subtests. In general, these were high with the exception of Written Expression, which was .79 and .89, depending on the storyline used by the subject.

Validity.   Content validity was determined by a review from a panel of experts. Criterion-related validity was determined by correlating the WIAT with several other measures of achievement, including the Kaufman Test of Educational Achievement, the Wide Range Achievement Test–Revised, and the Woodcock-Johnson–Revised achievement test. Correlations were generally in the .70s and .80s. The WIAT was also correlated with group-administered achievement tests with the correlations primarily in the .70s range. Evidence of construct validity is also presented in the manual through the use of intercorrelations of subtests within each composite as well as a multitrait–multimethod analysis.

Review of Relevant Research
Interestingly, only a few studies were located that looked at the technical characteristics of the WIAT. Slate (1994) reported higher correlations between the WIAT and the WISC-III than are noted in the WIAT manual. He suggested that the regression formula model be applied carefully when determining aptitude-achievement discrepancies. In a series of studies, Flanagan and Alfonso (1993a, 1993b) provided tables that allow for the determination of statistically significant differences between WISC-III Verbal IQs/Performance IQs and WIAT scores. Cohen (1993), in a comprehensive review, noted that the test might be limited for gifted students and those with mental retardation because of ceiling and floor effects. She also noted that information about subject characteristics in the linking sample

(those who were administered the WISC-III) is limited, and the internal consistency reliability coefficients for some of the subjects suggests that they should be used for screening purposes only.

OVERVIEW: WECHSLER INDIVIDUAL ACHIEVEMENT TEST

- *Age level*—5 to 19 years
- *Type of administration*—Individual
- *Technical adequacy*—Good standardization, adequate reliability (limited for some subtests), adequate validity
- *Scores yielded*—Standard scores, age and grade equivalents, percentiles, stanines, normal curve equivalents
- *Suggested use*—The WIAT is a well-constructed instrument that was designed, in part, to help identify students with learning disabilities. In general, the WIAT's technical adequacy is good although the reliabilities of some of the subtests are too low to be used for diagnostic purposes. In addition, several of the subtests (e.g., Listening Comprehension, Oral Expression) appear to measure areas other than those they purport to measure. As a result, composite scores should be used, particularly for diagnostic use. The major feature of the WIAT is the "linking sample" with the WISC-III that allows the determination of an aptitude-achievement discrepancy based on the same normative group.

Wide Range Achievement Test–Revised–3

The WRAT-3 (Wilkinson, 1993) is an individually administered general achievement test that measures word recognition and pronunciation, written spelling, and arithmetic computation. The WRAT-3 is a popular, widely used instrument that takes a relatively short time to administer and score. It is designed for use with individuals ages 5 to 75. There are also two alternate forms of the test. These two forms are color-coded and printed in either blue or tan. The author states that the WRAT-3 can be used to "measure the codes which are needed to learn the basic skills of reading, spelling, and arithmetic." He also states that the test can be used in conjunction with an intelligence test with the same mean and standard deviation to determine the presence of a learning disability.

Description

> *Spelling (40 items)*—This section requires the person to spell dictated words that range in complexity from *go, cat,* and *boy* to *iridescence, boutonniere,* and *mnemonic.* This part of the test is discontinued when and if the person misspells ten consecutive words. If fewer than six successes are obtained, the prespelling section (15 items) is administered. This includes the copy-

ing of geometric symbols and the printing or writing of the person's name as well as certain letters of the alphabet.

Reading (42 items)—This section includes words that are read aloud by the person taking the test. The words range in difficulty from *in, cat,* and *book* to *assuage, disingenous,* and *terpsichorean.* The prereading section (15 items) is administered if the person does not read at least six words correctly. This includes the identification and naming of several letters of the alphabet.

Arithmetic (40 items)—This section includes computation problems that are printed on the test form. The person is given fifteen minutes to complete the problems. If fewer than six problems are answered correctly, the pre-arithmetic part (15 items), which includes counting, reading digits, understanding numerical concepts, and orally adding and subtracting, is administered.

Interpretation of Results

Scores from the WRAT-3 can be transformed into absolute scores and standard scores. The absolute score is useful when the examiner is interested in using cut-off scores or in comparing pre- and posttesting levels. The standard score (mean = 100 standard deviation = 15) is probably the most appropriate score to use for comparison purposes.

Grade equivalents are printed on the test form and give a rough idea of the individual's grade level in reading, arithmetic, and spelling. The author warns users that this is not a statistical score and provides only an indication of whether a student scores at the beginning, middle, or end of a certain grade. Tables in the manual do provide more specific information about grade equivalents, although the scores should not be compared to give an indication of how many months' improvement a student supposedly has made. Grade scores do not take into consideration instructional differences, school expectations, or the age of persons taking the test. A table is also available that allows for the conversion of the standard score to percentiles and normal curve equivalents.

Technical Characteristics

Normative Sample. The sample included 4,433 individuals. The sample was stratified according to age, gender, geographic region, ethnicity, and SES.

Reliability. Test-retest coefficients were greater than .90 (determined for six- to sixteen-year-olds). Internal reliability coefficients in the .80s and .90s for most age groups were reported. Alternate-form reliability coefficients were .89 for arithmetic, .92 for reading, and .93 for spelling.

Validity. The authors provide arguments for the test's content and construct validity. Criterion-related validity coefficients with a number of group achievement tests were moderate.

Review of Relevant Research

Most of the information found in the professional literature focuses on previous editions of the test. The items on the WRAT have essentially remained the same through several editions. The norms, however, have been updated in each edition. As noted earlier, there have been some changes in format. For example, the WRAT-R included two levels, whereas the WRAT-3 includes only one, but with two forms. In general, the research on previous editions of the WRAT might have some relevance. Some of the research on the earlier versions on the WRAT is noted below.

- Correlations between the WRAT-R and the WISC-R were similar to those of the WRAT and the WISC-R (Smith & Smith, 1986).
- The WRAT-R standard scores were significantly lower than the WRAT standard scores (8 to 11 points) (Spruill & Beck, 1986).
- The same edition of the WRAT should be used in test-retest situations, an opinion based on a comparison of the norms of the 1976 and 1978 editions (Silverstein, 1980), and of the 1965 and 1978 editions (Sattler & Feldman, 1981).
- The WRAT is a valid instrument to use with a visually handicapped population (Alford, Moore, & Simon, 1980).
- The WRAT does not accurately identify young underachievers and should be used with caution as a screening or diagnostic device with this population (Grossman, 1981).
- Moderate to high correlations have been reported between scores on the PIAT and WRAT with learning-disabled (LD) students. The PIAT, however, yields significantly higher math scores for older LD students (approximately fourth grade and up). This difference is presumably due to the written worksheet format of the WRAT (Harmer & Williams, 1978; Scull & Brand, 1980).
- The WRAT and the PIAT should not be used interchangeably for educable mentally retarded (EMR) or LD students. Significant differences were noted for both elementary and secondary students (Lindsey & Armstrong, 1984).
- The 1976 and 1978 editions yielded significant differences in the spelling and reading grade equivalents for LD students. The two editions had no significant differences in standard scores, suggesting their use as derived scores in preference to grade equivalents (Breen & Prasse, 1982).
- Test-retest reliabilities with emotionally disturbed and slow-learning children are generally high (.87 to .98) (Woodward, Santa-Barbara, & Roberts, 1975).
- The norms on the WRAT tend to underestimate the true achievement level of individuals (Silverstein, 1978). This finding was based on a large national representative sample.
- The WRAT does meet the minimum reliability and validity requirements with Mexican-American children (Mishra, 1981).
- The appropriateness of the WRAT-R with lower socioeconomic and minority children has been reported (Rodriguez, 1989).

Summary of Research Findings

There has been surprisingly little research conducted on the WRAT-3. As noted from the summarization of the previous literature, little has also been conducted on the WRAT-R. In one study, Vance, Mayes, Fuller, and Abdullah (1994) reported significant positive correlations between the WRAT-3 and the WISC-III for a sample of children who were receiving special education services. Overall, the research on the various editions of the WRAT have shown that they have a moderate correlation with intelligence tests scores and that the various editions should not be used interchangeably. There is also some evidence that the various editions of the WRAT should not be used interchangeably with other achievement measures.

OVERVIEW: WIDE RANGE ACHIEVEMENT TEST–3

- *Age level*—5 to 74 years
- *Type of administration*—Individual
- *Technical adequacy*—Acceptable reliability, questionable validity
- *Scores yielded*—Standard scores, percentiles, grade equivalents, normal curve equivalents, absolute scores
- *Suggested use*—The WRAT-3 is a quick and easily administered achievement test. This is perhaps the primary advantage of the test. The weaknesses of the WRAT-3 are numerous. It has been criticized for its lack of a reading comprehension component, although the author stated that he intentionally designed the test to eliminate the effects of comprehension. Overall, the lack of validity has been a common criticism. There is also some evidence that earlier editions of the WRAT are not appropriate for use with younger children; previous research has indicated that it provides inflated scores for children approximately 5 to 7 years old. In summary, the WRAT-3 should be used for screening purposes only to identify individuals who need more in-depth testing. An analysis of the types of errors might be helpful.

Woodcock-Johnson–Revised (Achievement)

A general description of the Woodcock-Johnson–Revised (WJ-R) (Woodcock and Johnson, 1989) can be found in Chapter 9 in the section that focuses on the cognitive battery. This discussion will address the achievement battery of the WJ-R. There are two forms for the achievement tests (A and B). Both the achievement and cognitive tests contain standard and supplemental batteries. There are nine tests in the standard achievement battery and five tests in the supplemental achievement battery.

Description

Standard Achievement Battery

Letter Word Identification (57 items)—This measures the individual's skill in identifying isolated letters and words.

Passage Comprehension (43 items)—This uses a modified cloze procedure to evaluate a person's comprehension and vocabulary skills.

Calculation (58 items)—This uses a traditional format in which problems of varying difficulty are presented in the subject's response booklet.

Applied Problems (60 items)—This requires the subject to solve and analyze practical mathematical problems. This subtest requires decision making regarding the most appropriate mathematical operations to use.

Dictation (56 items)—This requires the subject to provide written responses to a variety of questions measuring spelling, punctuation, capitalization, and so on.

Writing Samples (30 items)—The subject is required to provide written sentences that are evaluated as to the quality of expression.

Science (49 items)—The subject orally responds to questions regarding the biological and physical sciences.

Social Studies (49 items)—This requires oral responses to questions related to history, geography, government, and economics.

Humanities (45 items)—The subject answers questions about art, music, and literature.

Supplemental Achievement Battery

Word Attack (30 items)—This measures the individual's ability to apply phonic and instructional analysis skills using nonsense words.

Reading Vocabulary (69 items)—This measures the individual's knowledge of both synonyms and antonyms.

Quantitative Concepts (48 items)—This measures mathematical concepts and vocabulary but does not require calculation or application decisions.

Proofing (36 items)—This requires the subject to identify a mistake in a type-written passage and indicate how it should be corrected. The mistakes might be incorrect punctuation or capitalization, inappropriate word usage, or misspelling.

Writing Fluency (43 items)—This timed subtest measures the individual's ability to formulate and write simple sentences quickly.

NOTE: Four other measures (Punctuation and Capitalization, Spelling, Usage, and Handwriting) can be obtained with the administration of Dictation and Writing Samples from the Standard Battery and Proofing from the Supplemental Battery.

Interpretation of Results

For all tests but Writing Samples, each item is scored either 0 or 1. (Writing Samples is scored 0, 1, or 2.) Through a series of transformations, the raw scores can be converted to percentile ranks or standard scores (mean = 100; SD = 15). The WJ-R also provides a Relative Mastery Index (RMI), a score that is presented as a fraction with a constant denominator of 90. This score indicates the percentage of material that the examinee has mastered that a reference group (by either age or grade) has mastered at 90 percent. For example, if a 10 1/2-year-old boy received a RMI of 62/90 in calculation, it would indicate that he has mastered 62 percent of the content in that area compared to 90 percent for the average child of the same age. All of these scores (standard scores, percentile ranks, RMIs) are also available for standard-battery clusters of broad reading, broad mathematics, broad written language, broad knowledge, and skills.

Technical Characteristics

Normative Sample.   See description of WJ-R–Cognitive in Chapter 9.

Reliability.   For the standard battery, the median internal consistency coefficients ranged from .87 to .93 for the individual tests. The knowledge tests had slightly lower coefficients, as did the supplemental tests (ranging from .76 to .93). For the cluster scores, the median coefficients ranged from .94 to .96 for the Standard Battery and .91 to .96 for the Supplemental Battery.

Validity.   According to the authors, content validity was maximized through careful item design that closely parallels the academic demands of the classroom (i.e., open-ended or open response as opposed to multiple choice). The concurrent validity was determined through a series of studies conducted at three different age groups: three, nine, and seventeen. In general, the sample sizes for the studies were small, ranging from approximately fifty to seventy. At the 3-year-old level, the Knowledge cluster and Skills cluster were correlated with a variety of criterion measures with correlations ranging from .29 to .72 for the Knowledge cluster and .10 to .63 for the skills cluster. The majority of the coefficients were in the .50s and .60s. For the 9-year-old group, correlations for the Broad Reading, Broad Math, Broad Written Language, and Knowledge clusters were generally in the .60s to .80s range. The correlations for the 17-year-old group were appreciably smaller, particularly in the area of reading. The author also provides evidence of the construct validity of the achievement battery through tables showing the intercorrelation of the various tests at different age levels.

Review of Relevant Research
There has been little research on the achievement battery of the WJ-R. There is some evidence that the reliability coefficients are lower than those reported in the manual (Shull-Senn, Weatherly, Morgan, & Bradley-Johnson, 1995). Mather (1989) found that the writing tests on the WJ-R had relatively high correlation coefficients with other standardized writing tests such as the Test of Written Language. Also, Taylor (1990), in a review of the achievement battery, noted the favorable addition of the writing tests to the WJ-R.

OVERVIEW: WOODCOCK-JOHNSON–REVISED (ACHIEVEMENT)

- *Age level*—2 years to adult
- *Type of administration*—Individual
- *Technical adequacy*—Good standardization, adequate reliability and validity
- *Scores yielded*—Standard scores, percentile ranks, relative mastery index (age and grade equivalents also available)
- *Suggested use*—The WJ-R Achievement Battery is a comprehensive, wide-range set of tests that measure a variety of areas. The WJ-R is a substantially different instrument from the original WJ. Users of the WJ-R should *not* consider the two instruments interchangeable. In addition, users should make note of the administration differences related to the basal and ceiling items.

    Several changes and improvements in the WJ-R are worthy of mention. First, more tests are available with the inclusion of standard and supplemental batteries. This also means that additional planning must be done to determine which tests to administer to an individual. A second change is a much-welcomed addition of actual writing samples to the Written Language cluster.

    Another improvement in the WJ-R is the slightly easier scoring procedures, although a number of tables must still be used, thus increasing the possibilities of errors. Clearly, if possible, the computerized scoring program (Compuscore) should be used. In addition, an Early Development scale (six subtests) can be used for preschool testing programs in light of P.L. 99-457. If both the achievement and cognitive batteries are administered, it is possible to calculate aptitude and achievement discrepancies in the areas of Oral Language, Reading, Mathematics, Written Language, and Knowledge.

ADDITIONAL INDIVIDUALLY ADMINISTERED INSTRUMENTS

In addition to the instruments previously described, several others deserve mention. These tests are less frequently used, and for the most part should be used primarily for screening. This list includes the Basic Achievement Skills Individual Screener, the Quick-Score Achievement Test, and the Norris Educational Achievement Test.

Basic Achievement Skills Individual Screener

- *Age level*—6 to 18 years
- *Type of administration*—Individual
- *Technical adequacy*—Adequate reliability, limited validity

- *Scores yielded*—Standard scores, percentiles, age and grade equivalents
- *Suggested use*—The Basic Achievement Skills Individual Screener (BASIS) (Psychological Corporation, 1983) is designed essentially as a first step in documenting the performance of students in the basic skill areas. It can be administered in less than an hour and provides information in the areas of reading, mathematics, spelling, and writing (an optional area). Although the mathematics and spelling areas are measured in a traditional fashion, the reading area incorporates a cloze procedure and might not provide a true picture of a student's comprehension skills (see Figure 13.5). The writing section

The Peanut Hunt

My friends and I went on a peanut hunt. My sister helped us. She hid the peanuts in the long grass in the park. Then she said, "Ready!' We had to __________ for the peanuts. It was hard. The peanuts were very little. We could not __________ them.

At last, I found two peanuts. My friend found five. It was fun after the game was over too. We put all our peanuts together. Then we got to __________ them.

FIGURE 13.5 Example of Cloze Procedure from BASIS

From the *Basic Achievement Skills Individual Screener.* Copyright © 1983 by the Psychological Corporation. Reproduced by permission.

provides little educationally relevant information. There is also some question about whether there are a sufficient number of items, particularly for older students. The BASIS was intended as a screening instrument and should not be used for any type of diagnostic purposes.

Quick-Score Achievement Test

- *Age level*—7 to 17 years
- *Type of administration*—Individual
- *Technical adequacy*—Adequate reliability, limited validity
- *Scores yielded*—Standard scores, General Achievement Quotient
- *Suggested use*—The Quick-Score Achievement Test (QSAT) (Hammill, Ammer, Cronin, Mandlebaum, & Quinby, 1987) is an individually administered test that measures the areas of writing, arithmetic, reading, and facts. It is easy to administer and score although there is limited technical data, particularly related to validity. It is probably best used as a screening instrument because of the lack of reading comprehension and math operations components.

Norris Educational Achievement Test

- *Age level*—4 years through 17 years
- *Type of administration*—Individual
- *Technical adequacy*—Good standardization, adequate reliability and validity
- *Scores yielded*—Standard scores, percentiles, stanines
- *Suggested use*—The Norris Educational Achievement Test (NEAT) (Switzer & Gruber, 1991) combines the areas of readiness testing and achievement testing. For children 4 to 6 years old, there are subtests in the areas of fine motor coordination, math concepts, and letters. The achievement tests are word recognition, spelling, and arithmetic. There are also supplemental achievement tests in the areas of oral reading and comprehension and written language. One interesting feature is a set of tables that allows for the documentation of discrepancies between IQ (from the Weschler Series and Stanford Binet) and the NEAT scores. The basic portion of the test can be administered in approximately thirty minutes, although the supplemental achievement tests should be used for more in-depth diagnostic use.

CRITERION-REFERENCED INSTRUMENTS

WHY USE CRITERION-REFERENCED INSTRUMENTS?

Establishment of IEP goals and objectives; monitoring educational progress

WHO SHOULD USE THEM?

Teachers

Inventories and criterion-referenced tests that measure academic skills are crucial tools for both pre- and postreferral assessment, particularly for students with mild disabilities. Frequently, the use of these instruments (in conjunction with informal techniques) is all that is necessary to evaluate students. Even if a student goes through the formal assessment process, these instruments, typically, are the ones that yield the most functional educational data for instructional purposes. Information from these instruments, for instance, is extremely helpful in developing IEPs. These instruments, usually described as *multicomponent*, are also comprehensive, so that only selected portions are administered.

Multicomponent Instrument: The Brigance Inventories

Over the past two decades, a number of inventories developed by Albert Brigance and published by Curriculum Associates have received widespread attention. These inventories consist of lists of skill sequences that cover a large number of areas. For each skill sequence, an objective is provided (see Figure 13.6 on page 338) that can be used for an IEP or as an informal teaching objective. There is, in fact, a computer program available for the Brigance Inventories called the *Talley Goals and Objectives Writer* (Talley, 1985).

Appropriate use of the Brigance Inventories requires that the teacher or test administrator carefully select those skill sequences that are relevant for a given student. Under no circumstances should any inventory be given in its entirety. Many people unfortunately have assumed that "because this is a test, I'll administer it." This has led to criticism of the inventories because of inappropriate use. In reality, the inventories are not really tests in a literal sense. Robinson and Kovacevich (1984), in reviewing the Brigance inventories, noted that they could best be described as "an item pool waiting for a test to happen." They go on to say that if the user realizes the inventories' intentions and limitations, important information can be gathered.

The Brigance Inventories are often referred to by their color rather than their name. These are yellow (Inventory of Early Development–Revised)—discussed in Chapter 15—blue (Inventory of Basic Skills), green (Comprehensive Inventory of Basic Skills), and red (Inventory of Essential Skills).

Brigance Inventory of Basic Skills (Blue)

The Brigance Inventory of Basic Skills (Brigance, 1977) is a comprehensive instrument that measures basic readiness skills as well as academic skills through grade six. The inventory specifically measures four major content areas: Readiness; Reading; Language Arts; and Mathematics. The inventory is primarily used to establish educational objectives and monitor progress toward these objectives. The test format allows the easy identification of behavioral objectives associated with the various items. The Brigance Inventory of Basic Skills is one of a group of four inventories designed for use with children from birth through grade twelve.

NUMBER OF SYLLABLES AUDITORILY

Skill: Can tell the number of syllables in a word auditorily.

Directions: Pronounce the words in the lists below, one at a time. Pause for the student to indicate the number of syllables.

>**Say:** *I'm going to say some words. Listen carefully and tell me how many syllables you hear in each word.*

List for Testing One-Syllable Words

1. *ring* (1)
2. *sounded* (2)
3. *tested* (2)
4. *sand* (1)
5. *must* (1)
6. *inform* (2)

List for Testing Two-Syllable Words

1. *refund* (2)
2. *shown* (1)
3. *understand* (3)
4. *friendly* (2)
5. *pretend* (2)
6. *referring* (3)

List for Testing Three-Syllable Words

1. *understanding* (4)
2. *labor* (2)
3. *innocent* (3)
4. *comprehend* (3)
5. *volcano* (3)
6. *public* (2)

Objective: When a word is pronounced by the examiner, the student will verbally indicate the number of syllables the word contains with 100 percent accuracy for _____ (quantity) syllable words.

Discontinue: If the student does not respond correctly to the three words being tested on any list. Disregard incorrect responses on other words in the lists.

Time: 10 seconds per response.

Accuracy: 3/3 for each list. In each list, the student must respond correctly only for the words containing the number of syllables being tested in that list. Disregard incorrect responses on other words. For example, in the first list, score only for correct responses on the words *ring, sand,* and *must.*

FIGURE 13.6   Example of an Objective Provided by the Brigance Inventories

From A. Brigance, *BRIGANCE® Inventory of Basic Skills.* Copyright © 1977 by Curriculum Associates, Inc. Reprinted with permission. BRIGANCE® is a registered trademark of Curriculum Associates, Inc.

Description. The four content areas of this test include 141 skill sequences. These skill sequences are essentially identifiable abilities for which sequential test items are available. For example, the skill sequence gross motor coordination includes "walks line," "jumps on both feet," "hops on right foot," "hops on left foot," and "steps." The examiner chooses the skill sequences to be administered.

> *Readiness*—This content area includes twenty-four skill sequences, among them, color recognition; body image; verbal directions; alphabet; and recognition of lowercase and uppercase letters.
>
> *Reading*—This content area is further broken down into four components: word recognition (six skill sequences); reading (including comprehension level and oral reading level); word analysis (nineteen skill sequences); and vocabulary (five skill sequences).
>
> *Language Arts*—This content area is also divided into four components: handwriting (three skill sequences); grammar mechanics (three skill sequences); spelling (five skill sequences); and reference skills (nine skill sequences).
>
> *Mathematics*—This content area is divided into five components: estimated grade level; numbers; operations; measurement (including money, time, calendar, and liquid measurement); and geometry. In all, it includes sixty-four skill sequences.

Interpretation of Results. As previously mentioned, the primary reason for using the Inventory of Basic Skills is to identify appropriate objectives for a student. The inventory is designed to facilitate this purpose. Each skill sequence is associated with a stated behavioral objective, so that objectives can be directly determined from a child's performance on the inventory. Figure 13.7 on page 340 shows an example of the suggested procedures in using this as well as the other Brigance Inventories.

OVERVIEW: BRIGANCE INVENTORY OF BASIC SKILLS

- *Age level*—Kindergarten to grade 6
- *Suggested use*—The Brigance Inventory of Basic Skills is used with children from kindergarten through grade 6. It covers the basic areas of readiness skills, reading, language arts, and math. It is quickly becoming (along with the other Brigance Inventories) one of the more popular multicomponent instruments. Many school systems have, in fact, adopted the Brigance as a primary instrument used in developing IEPs. The format of the test also allows for its use in monitoring progress within the various skill areas. The inventory is comprehensive and is not designed to be used in its entirety; rather, the examiner must identify those areas in need of evaluation and instruction for each individual. This could be a disadvantage if the examiner is not familiar with the student. For this reason, the

MODEL OF FORMAT FOR AN ASSESSMENT PROCEDURE WITH A CHILD PAGE

1. **SKILL:** A general statement of the skill being assessed. When appropriate, the skill sequence in the *Developmental Record Book* is also listed.

2. **DEVELOPMENTAL AGE NOTATION:** The numbers preceding a sequence indicate the year and month the child usually begins to learn or master that skill. Those following indicate when mastery is usually accomplished. Example: for [4-7], read 4 years and 7 months developmental age.

   In addition, the developmental ages are explained or discussed in a separate note where necessary.

3. **DEVELOPMENTAL RECORD BOOK:** The page on which this skill is listed in the *Developmental Record Book.*

4. **ASSESSMENT METHODS:** The means recommended for assessing.

5. **MATERIALS:** Materials which are needed for the assessment.

6. **DISCONTINUE:** Indicates the number of items the child may fail before you discontinue the assessment of skills in this sequence.

7. **TIME:** Time limits suggested for the child's response.

8. **ACCURACY:** Explanation of scoring criteria.

9. **DIRECTIONS:** The recommended directions for assessing the skills sequence. Recommended phrasing of instructions or questions is clearly labeled, indented and printed in bold face type.

10. **OBJECTIVE:** The objective for the skills being assessed is stated, and is a valuable resource for developing individualized education programs (IEP's).

NOTES ON CHILD PAGE:

a. You have the publisher's permission to reproduce the child pages in the *Inventory* for non-profit educational purposes.

b. Some child pages have been designed for copying and cutting so you can present items individually.

c. Screen part of the page if the child finds a whole page visually confusing.

d. You may cover the child's page with acetate to prevent soiling and to make it possible to use an acetate marker.

e. All child pages are designated with a "C" preceding the number, which corresponds to the facing examiner page.

11. **REFERENCES:** the numbers listed correspond to the sources used to establish and validate the skill sequences and developmental ages. References are found in the *Bibliography* on page 246-7.

12. **NOTES:** Helpful notes on observations, resources or diagnosing are listed here.

13. Examiner's page number.

14. Skill assessed.

15. The first letter, "I," indicates the section, where all basic reading skills are located.

16. This number indicates the ninth of the skills sequenced in the basic reading section of the *Inventory.*

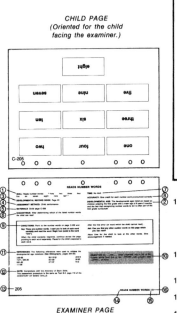

FIGURE 13.7   Format for the Brigance Inventories

From A. Brigance, *BRIGANCE® Inventory of Basic Skills.* Copyright © 1977 by Curriculum Associates. Reprinted with permission. BRIGANCE® is a registered trademark of Curriculum Associates, Inc.

Brigance is usually administered by the teacher. It should also be noted that this inventory, like all the Brigance Inventories, is somewhat cumbersome to administer.

Brigance Inventory of Essential Skills (Red)

The Brigance Inventory of Essential Skills (Brigance, 1981) is designed for use with students in grades four to twelve. The inventory basically measures those minimal competencies commonly accepted as important in lifetime experiences. As such, it is one of the few instruments that includes measures of functional academics at the secondary level. Like the Brigance Inventory of Basic Skills, this inventory is used primarily to establish and monitor educational or prevocational objectives.

Description

The Inventory of Essential Skills includes 26 content areas, with a total of 181 skill sequences. Ten informal rating scales are also included.

Word Recognition Grade Placement—This content area assesses the approximate grade level of the student's word-recognition ability.

Oral Reading—This content area includes five skill sequences that give the student's approximate grade level for oral reading skills.

Reading Comprehension—This content area has nine skill sequences that measure the student's grade level in reading comprehension.

Functional Word Recognition—This content area includes six skill sequences, for example, basic sight vocabulary, warning/safety signs, and informational signs.

Word Analysis—This content area includes nine skill sequences, for example, common endings of rhyming words, suffixes and prefixes, and syllabication concepts.

Reference Skills—This content area includes five skill sequences, for example, uses dictionary and uses library card catalogues.

Schedules and Graphs—The three skill sequences for this content area are reads class schedule, reads television schedules, and identifies and interprets graphs.

Writing—This content area includes seven skill sequences, for example, writing manuscript and cursive letters, capitalization, and punctuation.

Forms—The two skill sequences for this content area are school information form and computer-based form. These measure the individual's ability to correctly fill out blank forms.

Spelling—This content area includes eight skill sequences, for example, spelling number words, days of the week, and months of the year.

Math Grade Placement—This content area gives grade levels for computation and math comprehension.

Numbers—This content area has four skill sequences, including writes numerals as dictated and rounds off numerals.

Number Facts—This content area measures a student's knowledge of addition, subtraction, multiplication, and division facts.

Computation of Whole Numbers—This content area has six skill sequences, including subtraction of whole numbers, division of whole numbers, and computes averages.

Fractions—This content area includes nine skill sequences related to the comprehension and computation of fractions.

Decimals—This content area includes six skill sequences related to the knowledge and understanding of decimals.

Percents—This content area includes four skill sequences that require conversion of fractions and decimals into percentages.

Measurement—This content area includes fifteen skill sequences, for example, conversion to units of time, understanding of a calendar and a ruler, and conversion to units of measurement.

Metrics—This content area includes sixteen skill sequences measuring the understanding of and ability to apply the metric system.

Math Vocabulary—The three skill sequences of this content area are basic mathematics vocabulary, computational vocabulary, and basic geometric shapes and concepts.

Health and Safety—This content area includes four skill sequences. Examples are medical vocabulary, medicine labels, and warning labels. Two rating scales are also included: health practices and attitude rating scale and self-concept scale.

Vocational—This content area includes twenty-three skill sequences, for example, employment signs and simple application for employment. Five rating scales are also included, among them, job-interview rating scale and attitude rating scale.

Money and Finance—This content area includes eleven skill sequences, for example, banking and credit vocabulary, computing interest on loans, and comprehending monthly credit statement.

Travel and Transportation—This content area includes nine skill sequences, for example, application for driver's instruction permit, mileage table, and road maps. A rating scale, auto safety, is also included.

Food and Clothing—This content area includes ten skill sequences, for example, food preparation vocabulary, quantity at the best price, and clothing labels.

Oral Communication and Telephone Skills—This content area has five skill sequences, including listening skills and telephone book. Two rating scales are also included: speaking skills and listening skills.

Interpretation of Results

The Inventory of Essential Skills primarily yields information related to behavioral objectives, although grade-placement approximations are given in a number of areas. Results from the inventory are often used in secondary-level special education classrooms to identify and help develop prevocational and other survival skills necessary after high school.

The information from the ten rating scales can be used to identify "specific traits, behavior attitudes, and skills that may need to be changed or improved in order to help a student achieve optimal adjustment and success" (p. 373). These scales should be used with caution, because no validity data exist to support their use. They are, in fact, more similar to checklists than rating scales.

OVERVIEW: BRIGANCE INVENTORY OF ESSENTIAL SKILLS

- *Age level*—grades 4 to 12
- *Suggested use*—The Inventory of Essential Skills is designed for use with students in grades four to twelve. The inventory emphasizes minimal competencies and includes measures of "functional academics." This instrument is, in fact, one of the few that includes items for the secondary-

level special education student and is a popular instrument for IEP development for older students. Objectives from the Essential Skills Inventory also have been correlated with instructional materials from the Janus Company, although no research is available to support or refute their effectiveness. This test, like all Brigance Inventories, should not be administered in its entirety. Rather, the skill sequences should be carefully chosen by the teacher or other examiner who is familiar with the student to be evaluated.

Brigance Comprehensive Inventory of Basic Skills (Green)

The Brigance Comprehensive Inventory of Basic Skills (Brigance, 1982) is designed for students from kindergarten through grade nine. This inventory essentially includes skill sequences found on the Inventory of Basic Skills and the Inventory of Essential Skills. In all, 22 content areas are measured, with 185 total skill sequences. Because the content areas of this Inventory have been described in the discussion of the two preceding instruments, a limited description follows.

> *Readiness* (31 skill sequences)
> *Speech* (5 skill sequences)
> *Word Recognition and Grade Placement* (2 skill sequences)
> *Oral Reading* (7 skill sequences)
> *Reading Comprehension* (14 skill sequences)
> *Listening* (6 skill sequences)
> *Functional Word Recognition* (9 skill sequences)
> *Word Analysis* (17 skill sequences)
> *Reference Skills* (8 skill sequences)
> *Graphs and Maps* (5 skill sequences)
> *Spelling* (9 skill sequences)
> *Writing* (9 skill sequences)
> *Math Grade Placement* (2 skill sequences)
> *Numbers* (4 skill sequences)
> *Number Facts* (4 skill sequences)
> *Computation of Whole Numbers* (6 skill sequences)
> *Fractions and Mixed Numbers* (10 skill sequences)
> *Decimals* (6 skill sequences)
> *Percents* (4 skill sequences)
> *Measurement* (18 skill sequences)
> *Metrics* (7 skill sequences)
> *Mathematical Vocabulary* (4 skill sequences)

Interpretation of Results

This inventory is scored in the same manner as the previously discussed Brigance Inventories.

OVERVIEW: BRIGANCE COMPREHENSIVE INVENTORY OF BASIC SKILLS

- *Age level*—Kindergarten to grade 9
- *Suggested use* —The Brigance Comprehensive Inventory of Basic Skills is essentially a combination of parts from the Inventory of Basic Skills and the Inventory of Essential Skills. The instrument covers skills usually taught from kindergarten through middle school. If you are interested in testing students in the late elementary or early secondary grades, this inventory might be the one of choice, and it might give the continuity missing in the other two instruments. If you are interested in testing students in the early elementary or later secondary grades, the other Brigance Inventories would be more appropriate.

Multilevel Academic Survey Test–Curriculum Level

The Multilevel Academic Survey Test (MAST) (Howell, Zucker, & Morehead, 1985) actually comprises two different types of tests. The first, a *grade-level test,* is a norm-referenced measure of reading and mathematics designed for students from kindergarten to grade 8. The *curriculum-level test* is intended to complement the grade-level test by providing specific information regarding content-skill deficits. Used together, the two provide comparative and curricular information. Much of the information in the MAST evolved from the authors' previous assessment instrument, the Multilevel Academic Skills Inventory (MASI) described by Taylor (1984).

Description

Reading—This section includes eight levels of graded passages that are read aloud by the student to determine decoding skills. The comprehension part also involves graded passages that the student must read silently and then answer questions about. A series of passages that use the maze procedure is also included.

Mathematics—Included in this section are computation items related to whole numbers, fractions, decimals, ratios, and proportions, as well as a problem-solving test that uses a multiple-choice format.

Interpretation of Results

The curriculum-level test from the MAST provides specific information for teaching purposes. A decision/activity analysis tree on the record form indicates when a student needs additional testing, instruction, or progression into more difficult content areas.

OVERVIEW: MULTILEVEL ACADEMIC SURVEY TEST

- *Age level*—Kindergarten to grade 8
- *Suggested use*—The MAST is a comprehensive assessment instrument that provides both norm-referenced and criterion-referenced information. The curriculum-level test provides the more specific information for teaching purposes. The grade-level test, however, can be used initially to determine the appropriate starting point in the curriculum-level test. Issacson (1990), in a review of the instrument, noted that the MAST had many desirable features.

Mastery: An Evaluation Tool

Mastery: An Evaluation Tool (Science Research Associates, 1980) is a series of criterion-referenced tests in mathematics and reading. The Mastery program is designed for students from kindergarten through grade 9. Objectives have been identified for both reading and mathematics.

Description

There are 175 math objectives for kindergarten to second grade; 352 mathematical objectives for grades 3 to 8; 162 reading objectives for kindergarten to second grade; and 140 reading objectives for grades 3 to 9. For each objective, three test items have been developed. For mastery of a specific objective, the criterion is correct answers to all three items. Two options are available for users: custom tests and catalog tests. Custom tests allow you to select the objectives to be measured. The catalog tests include preselected objectives that are most commonly taught at each grade level.

OVERVIEW: MASTERY: AN EVALUATION TOOL

- *Age level*—Kindergarten to grade 9
- *Suggested use*—Mastery: An Evaluation Tool includes criterion-referenced tests of reading and math objectives for curricula in kindergarten through grade nine. The system was designed more for monitoring and documenting progress than for specific educational programming. The custom tests are an attractive feature because they give the teacher or examiner some degree of latitude in determining the content of the test. The system is expensive, however, and its equivalent could be developed in a teacher-made test format. Mastery: An Evaluation Tool can be used with Diagnosis: An Instructional Aid (discussed in the next two chapters) to give a comprehensive evaluation package.

Instrument or Technique	Suggested Use — Prereferral: Screening and Initial Identification	Informal Determination and Evaluation of Teaching Programs and Strategies	Determination of Current Performance Level and Educational Need	Postreferral: Decisions about Classification and Program Placement	IEP Goals	IEP Objectives	IEP Evaluation	Target Population: Mild/Moderate	Severe/Profound	Preschool	Elementary Age	Secondary Age	Adult	Special Considerations	Educational Relevance for Exceptional Students
Group Achievement Tests	X							X			X	X		Stanford and Metropolitan have good technical characteristics; good for initial screening	adequate/useful
Diagnostic Achievement Battery-2	X	X	X		X			X			X	X		Provides a profile of strengths and weaknesses; composite scores most useful	adequate
Diagnostic Achievement Test for Adolescents-2	X	X	X		X			X				X		The only achievement test designed specifically for adolescents	adequate
Kaufman Test of Educational Achievement	X	X	X		X			X			X	X		Good technical aspects; error analysis helpful; overall one of the better achievement tests	very useful
Peabody Individual Achievement Test-Revised	X	X	X		X			X			X	X		Adequate technical aspects; revised version has optional written subtest; unique format	useful
Wechsler Individual Achievement Test	X	X	X		X			X			X	X		Has a linking sample with WISC-III. Subtests are consistent with definition of learning disability	useful
Wide Range Achievement Test-3	X	X	X		X					X	X	X	X	Results often overused; best used as a screening measure	adequate
Woodcock-Johnson–Revised (Achievement)	X	X	X					X		X	X	X	X	Part of WJ Battery that also includes a cognitive section	useful
Basic Academic Skills Individual Screener	X							X			X	X		Should be used for screening only; writing section probably not helpful	adequate

Test											Comments	Rating
Norris Educational Achievement Test	X	X	X		X			X	X		Supplemental tests should also be used for diagnostic purposes	adequate/useful
Quick-Score Achievement Test	X						X	X			Use for screening only; easy to administer and score	adequate
Brigance Inventory of Basic Skills		X	X	X	X	X	X				Includes objectives for each skill measured; used in IEP development	useful
Brigance Inventory of Essential Skills		X	X	X	X	X		X			Same as above	useful
Brigance Comprehensive Inventory of Basic Skills		X	X	X	X	X	X	X			Most appropriate for students in later elementary grades	useful
Multilevel Academic Survey Test	X	X	X	X		X	X				Includes both a grade level and curriculum level	useful
Mastery: An Evaluation Tool	X	X	X		X		X	X			Used for screening and monitoring progress	adequate

14

ASSESSMENT OF READING

Instruments and Procedures Included

Informal Assessment Procedures
    Diagnosis: An Instructional Aid in Reading
    Informal Reading Inventories
    Cloze and Maze Procedures
    Reading Diagnosis Sheet

Diagnostic Reading Tests
    Gray Oral Reading Tests–Diagnostic
    Stanford Diagnostic Reading Test
    Test of Reading Comprehension–3
    Woodcock Reading Mastery Tests–Revised
    Durrell Analysis of Reading Difficulty
    Diagnostic Reading Scales

Oral Reading Tests
    Gray Oral Reading Test–3
    Gilmore Oral Reading Test

Dexter is a 9-year-old boy in the third grade. His teacher has noted that he constantly falls behind on reading assignments, reads very slowly, often sounds out the words orally, and has difficulty remembering what he reads. Dexter was tested to determine which area or areas within the reading process were causing him difficulty.

One certainly cannot minimize the importance of reading to the overall success of the student during the school years. Reading affects virtually all areas of an individual's life. It certainly is not surprising that so much attention is paid to the assessment and subsequent remediation of reading. Reading involves the components of recognition, analysis, and comprehension. Ekwall and Shanker (1988) provided a cohesive framework for the components of reading and its subsequent evaluation or assessment. Figure 14.1 provides a schematic of that framework. Within this model, the overall process of reading is broken down into two subareas: (1) recognition and analysis of words and (2) understanding words and ideas. This roughly is equivalent to word recognition and reading comprehension. Word recognition can further be broken down into sight word identification and word-analysis skills. Sight word identification involves the immediate identification of a word even though the individual might not understand its meaning. Word-analysis skills are used when a reader does not instantly recognize the word and therefore must use a variety of word attack skills to attempt to read it. As noted in Figure 14.1, word attack involves the configuration or the shape of the word, context cues that a person receives from the way a word is used in the sentence, phonetic analysis, structural analysis (ability to derive meaning from word parts), and dictionary skills, such as alphabetizing and using guide words.

The other main area of reading involves the understanding of words and ideas. According to Ekwall and Shanker, this involves (1) vocabulary development or the understanding of the meaning of words and (2) other comprehension skills or the student's ability to make sense from written material. As noted, this involves such things as literal comprehension (e.g., understanding and remembering the facts presented in a passage) and inferential comprehension (e.g., the ability to understand what might happen next in a passage).

READING ASSESSMENT

As in most areas, the evaluation of the reading process can be done either informally or formally. Parker (1992) did note, however, an increased need for the use of informal tests and teacher observation of reading behavior. Information from these sources can be combined with results from criterion-referenced or teacher-made tests to assist in reading diagnosis. One advantage of informal reading assessment is that it provides more of an opportunity to understand the *reading process* rather than simply to analyze the *reading product*. The areas of informal reading assessment that will be discussed in this chapter include criterion-refer-

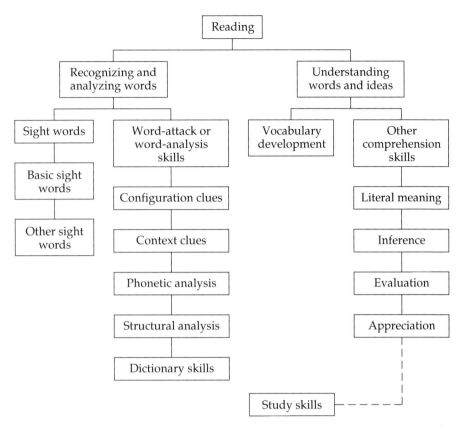

FIGURE 14.1   **Components of the Reading Process**

From Eldon E. Ekwall and James L. Shanker, *Diagnosis and Remediation of the Disabled Reader* (3rd ed.). Copyright © 1988, Allyn & Bacon. Reprinted with permission.

enced and informal reading inventories as well as other informal techniques such as the cloze procedure and the maze procedure. For information on error analysis, Chapter 6 and on portfolio assessment see Chapter 8.

Those instruments considered more formal tests are usually called diagnostic reading tests, although the term diagnostic is somewhat a misnomer. The reasons for administering the test is not to diagnose a problem in a traditional sense but to gather specific information about where a problem might exist and how to remediate it. Many of these diagnostic academic tests actually magnify a particular area to determine an individual's strengths and weaknesses. In other words, although these tests are norm-referenced, their primary objective is frequently to obtain important information for remediation and not to compare the student's performance to others. Most diagnostic reading tests measure such areas as oral reading recognition, reading rate, comprehension, word attack skills, and vocabulary, although not all tests measure all of these areas.

Another type of formal test is the oral reading test. These instruments provide documentation of the child's overall reading ability considering such areas as speed and accuracy. Some also include measures of comprehension areas.

INFORMAL ASSESSMENT PROCEDURES

WHY USE INFORMAL DIAGNOSTIC PROCEDURES?

Identification of areas for further evaluation or remediation; informal determination of objectives and teaching strategies; development and evaluation of IEPs

WHO SHOULD USE THEM?

Teachers

Diagnosis: An Instructional Aid in Reading

Diagnosis: An Instructional Aid in Reading (Shub, Carlin, Friedman, Kaplan, & Katien, 1973) is a comprehensive reading skills program for students in grades 1 to 6. The system is composed of three components: Survey Tests, Probes, and Prescription Guides. The Survey Tests measure general strengths and weaknesses and act as a screening instrument. Alternative forms are available for posttesting. The Probes are a series of specific criterion-referenced measures designed to identify specific learning objectives. In the Prescription Guides, materials for remediation (from workbooks, textbooks, and other resources) are correlated with each learning objective. The program has two levels: A and B.

Description

Level A—This level is designed for students in grades 1–4. It covers phonetic analysis, comprehension, vocabulary, and uses of sources (for example, dictionary use).

Level B—This level is designed for students in grades 3–6. It covers phonetic analysis, structural analysis, comprehension, vocabulary, and study skills.

Interpretation of Results

This instrument yields instructional objectives and suggested curriculum materials.

OVERVIEW: DIAGNOSIS: AN INSTRUCTIONAL AID IN READING

- *Age level*—Grades 1 to 6
- *Suggested use*—Diagnosis: An Instructional Aid in Reading is a comprehensive assessment package that includes screening, in-depth testing, and specific suggestions for remediation

---

Informal Reading Inventories

Informal reading inventories (IRIs), like many other informal assessment procedures, are sometimes developed and sold commercially. When a teacher or other test user develops an IRI, it is usually necessary to select representative passages from various levels of a student's reading program and generate comprehension questions related to those passages. Newcomer (1985) found, however, that teachers frequently had difficulty selecting representative passages, partly as a function of variations of reading levels within the same text. She also noted that teachers often have problems formulating the comprehension questions. As a result, commercially-prepared IRIs are relatively popular.

Although IRIs differ from one another in format and content, most contain graded reading passages that yield a measure of word recognition and comprehension skills. Most commercially prepared IRIs construct the reading passages from existing word lists. Among the more popular commercially prepared IRIs are the Analytical Reading Inventory (Woods & Moe, 1989), the Basic Reading Inventory (Johns, 1988), the Classroom Reading Inventory (Silvaroli, 1989), the Informal Reading Inventory (Burns & Roe, 1989), and the Ekwall Reading Inventory (Ekwall, 1986). Table 14.1 on page 354 shows a comparison of four of these IRIs. The term *graded* refers to the approximate grade level associated with the passages. Typically, three levels of reading are determined from an IRI. The *independent* level is identified as the level at which the student can read alone without any help from another person. The *instructional* level is the teaching level where the student can read relatively comfortably but finds it challenging. The *frustration* level is the level at which the student finds the material difficult and frustrating. In some IRIs, the *listening comprehension* level is also determined. That is the level at which the student can comfortably understand material that is read to him or her. As in criterion-referenced tests, criteria are established that indicate how much of the material the student must read correctly (oral reading) and understand (comprehension) to be placed at the various reading levels. Although the criteria for these reading levels vary for different IRIs, there is at least some agreement on some general guidelines. One widely accepted criteria for reading levels are those proposed by Betts (1946) more than fifty years ago. He indicated that recognition of 99, 95, and 90 percent of the words at a specific grade level corresponds to the independent, instructional, and frustration levels. The criteria for *comprehension* for the three levels were 90, 75, and 50 percent, respectively. Several

TABLE 14.1 A Comparison of Four Commonly Used Informal Reading Inventories

Inventory	Grade levels	Forms of inventory	Length of passages	Source of passages	Use of pictures	Use of purpose-setting questions	Number of comprehension questions per passage	Types of comprehension questions	Criteria for instructional level	Time needed for administration
Analytic Reading Inventory (ARI)	Primer to 9th, 1st–9th for science and social studies	3 equivalent narrative forms; 1 social studies and 1 science form	varies: 50 words to 352 words	Written for inventory. Some science and social studies passages from textbooks	No	Discourages discussion before reading, but allows examiner discretion	6 for levels primer–2nd; 8 for levels 3rd–9th	main idea factual terminology cause/effect inferential conclusion	95% for word recognition; 75% comprehension	not stated
Basic Reading Inventory (BRI)	Preprimer to 8th	3 forms; A for oral, B for silent, C as needed	50 words at preprimer; 100 words primer to 8th grade	Revised from earlier editions; original source not stated	No	Uses prediction from titles	10 for all levels	main idea fact inference evaluation vocabulary	95% for word recognition (only "significant" miscues counted); 75% comprehension	not stated
Classroom Reading Inventory (CRI)	Preprimer to 8th	4 forms in all; A and B for students in grades 1–6; C for junior high students; D for high school and adults	Varies; 24 words to 157 words	Written for inventory based on readability	Yes	Yes	5 for all levels	factual inferential vocabulary	95% for word recognition; 75% comprehension	12 minutes
Informal Reading Inventory by Burns & Roe (IRI-BR)	Preprimer to 12th	4 forms; all interchangeable	Varies; 60 words to 220 words	Primarily from graded materials in basal readers and literature books	No	Yes	8 for all levels	main idea detail inference sequence cause/effect vocabulary	85% word recognition for grades 1 and 2; 95% word recognition for grades 3 and above; 75% comprehension	40–50 minutes

From J. Pikulski, Informal Reading Inventories. *Reading Teacher, 43*, 515. Copyright © 1990 by The Reading Teacher. Reprinted with permission.

critics, such as Powell (1972) and Spache (1964), however, argued that these levels were too stringent.

Several researchers have compared the strengths and weaknesses of various IRIs and noted certain limitations. Elliott and Piersel (1982), for example, stated that IRIs are not rigorously constructed and are more prone to measurement error than standardized reading tests. In addition, the usefulness of the comprehension measures has been questioned (Dufflemeyer, Robinson, & Squier, 1989), particularly related to main ideas (Dufflemeyer & Dufflemeyer, 1989).

Newcomer (1985) also noted a general lack of reliability and validity data for most IRIs and that different IRIs do not necessarily yield similar results when administered to the same student. She found, in fact, that in more than 50 percent of the students tested, the two tests (Classroom Reading Inventory and Ekwall Reading Inventory) identified different instructional levels. In a comparison of the Analytic Reading Inventory (ARI), Basic Reading Inventory (BRI), Classroom Reading Inventory (CRI), and Informal Reading Inventory (IRI), Pikulski (1990) made the following recommendations:

ARI—Use when longer passages are preferred to sample reading ability
BRI—Use when information about use and interpretation of IRIs is desired
CRI—Use when quick, less complete evaluation is preferred
IRI—Use for older students (forms available above ninth grade)

Other Informal Techniques

A number of other informal techniques are available. Examples are the *cloze* and *maze* procedures and the *Reading Diagnosis Sheet.*

Cloze Procedure

The cloze procedure consists of a reading passage (usually 250–300 words) in which certain words are deleted (usually every fifth or tenth). This *fixed ratio* approach of choosing the deleted words has been criticized, although Jonz (1990) found that such an approach was not erratic in choosing deleted words with similar linguistic and content characteristics.

In the cloze procedure, the student must read the passage and provide the missing words by analyzing the content and its structure. This procedure measures the reader's ability to interpret written passages and it requires the student to use both comprehension skills and knowledge of linguistic structure. The percentage of correct responses can be determined and can serve as a rough indication of the reading level of the student.

Rankin and Culhane (1969), for example, developed criterion levels for the cloze procedure. They suggested, for instance, that the instructional reading level was the level at which a student could correctly replace 41 percent to 61 percent of the missing words. For a student who read a cloze passage from a third-grade text and correctly replaced 50 percent of the words, the instructional reading level would be the third grade, according to this criteria. If, however, the student cor-

Sir Walter Raleigh

Four hundred years ago, when Elizabeth I was Queen of England, a young man *called* (named) Walter Raleigh once saw *her* (her) crossing a street. It *was* (was) raining hard and the *streets* (streets) were muddy. He took *down* (off) his rich velvet cape *then* (and) threw it down in *front* (front) of the Queen, so *when* (that) she could step on *it* (it) as on a carpet. *The* (The) Queen was so pleased *when* (that) she made Walter Raleigh *the* (a) knight. From then on, *he* (he) was called Sir Walter *Raleigh* (Raleigh,) and he became one *of* (of) the Queen's special friends.

Sir (Sir) Walter Raleigh was very *very* (much) interested in the new *city* (country) of America. He sent *many* (some) Englishmen to the American *city* (Coast) to found a colony, *then* (which) he named Virginia. They *took* (brought) back potatoes and tobacco *for* (to) England, and Sir Walter *Raleigh* (Raleigh) learned how to smoke *like* (as) the Indians did.

The *dumb* (English) people did not know *about* (about) tobacco and they didn't *know* (know) how to smoke. One *time* (day) while he was smoking *a* (his) pipe, a servant saw *much* (the) smoke coming out of *his* (his) master's mouth and thought *Walter* (he) was on fire. He *went* (ran) for a bucket of *water* (water) and dumped it on *his* (his) master's head.

FIGURE 14.2   Example of the Cloze Procedure

From William H. Rupley and Timothy R. Blair, *Reading Diagnosis and Remediation,* 1979, p. 116. Copyright © 1979 by Houghton Mifflin Company, Boston, MA. Reprinted with permission.

rectly replaced only 30 percent of the words, an easier passage would be needed to establish the reading level. Figure 14.2 gives an example of a cloze passage. In this example, the student correctly replaced approximately 45 percent of the words (sixteen out of thirty-six).

The cloze procedure can also be used to evaluate spelling. For example, the student might be given a series of sentences such as "I hope mother doesn't b___n the food" and asked to supply the missing letters. Obviously the child's reading ability might also affect the results.

Maze Procedure

Another technique used to measure a student's reading comprehension and knowledge of linguistic structure is the maze procedure. This procedure is similar to the cloze method, except that vertically presented choices are given instead of blanks. The following sentence is an example of the maze procedure:

On Tuesday, John went to the
$$\begin{array}{l}\text{store}\\ \text{corn}\\ \text{on}\end{array}$$

Parker, Hasbrouck, and Tindal (1992) reviewed twenty years of research on the maze procedure and reported overall support of the technique. They did note that more research is needed on the reliability of the maze procedure.

Both the cloze and the maze procedures are examples of informal adaptations of curriculum materials into assessment devices. As with the criterion-referenced tests previously discussed, however, it is necessary for the teacher to establish criteria that reflect not only the curriculum and objectives for their students, but also the learning abilities of these students. The criteria that others have established as standards may be too strict or too lenient. Pikulski and Pikulski (1977) found, for instance, that in a study of regular fifth graders, the maze and cloze scores were higher than teachers' judgments of the students' reading abilities. On the other hand, Jenkins and Jewell (1993) reported that results from a maze procedure correlated higher with reading achievement test scores than did oral reading ability.

Reading Diagnosis Sheet

Another informal procedure for reading evaluation is offered by Ekwall (1981). He developed a *Reading Diagnosis Sheet* (see Figure 14.3 on page 358) that breaks down the reading process into twenty-eight areas. Ekwall gives information on how to recognize a problem in each of the twenty-eight areas and provides a discussion of possible causes for the problem. He also offers recommendations for remediation.

One approach that has been used to measure reading comprehension is the *think aloud* procedure. According to Meyers and Lytle (1986), this involves having the student read a passage (a sentence or clause at a time), and tell what he or she is thinking about or what might happen next. This procedure has been used primarily with older students but recently has been tried with younger children.

DIAGNOSTIC READING TESTS

WHY USE DIAGNOSTIC READING TESTS?

Screening and identification; informal determination of objectives and teaching strategies; documentation of educational need; establishment of IEP goals

WHO SHOULD USE THEM?

Teachers; diagnostic specialists

Name _____   Teacher_____

Grade _____   School _____

	28	27	26	25	24	23	22	21	20	19	18	17	16	15	14	13	12	11	10	9	8	7	6	5	4	3	2	1
1st Check																												
2nd Check																												
3rd Check																												

Column labels (28 → 1):

28. Inability to locate information
27. Undeveloped dictionary skill
26. Written recall limited by spelling ability
25. Inability to adjust reading rate to difficulty of material
24. Inability to skim
23. Voicing lip movement
22. High rate at expense of accuracy
21. Low rate of speed
20. Response poorly organized
19. Unaided recall scanty
18. Fails to comprehend
17. Contractions not known
16. Unable to use context clues
15. Lacks desirable structural analysis
14. Blends, digraphs or dipthongs not known
13. Vowel sounds not known
12. Consonant sounds not known
11. Guesses at words
10. Sight vocabulary not up to grade level
9. Basic sight words not known
8. Substitutions
7. Insertions
6. Inversions or reversals
5. Repetitions
4. Omissions
3. Poor pronunciation
2. Incorrect phrasing
1. Word-by-word reading

Other related abilities	Silent reading	Oral silent difficulties	Oral reading

The items listed above represent the most common difficulties encountered by pupils in the reading program. Following each numbered item are spaces for notation of that specific difficulty. This may be done at intervals of several months. One might use a check to indicate difficulty recognized or the letters on the right to represent an even more accurate appraisal:

D – Difficulty recognized
P – Pupil progressing
N – No longer has difficulty

FIGURE 14.3   The Reading Diagnosis Sheet

From Eldon Ekwall, *Locating and Correcting Reading Difficulties*, 3rd ed. Columbus, Ohio: Charles E. Merrill, 1981, p. 5. Copyright © 1981 by Bell and Howell Company. Reprinted with permission.

Gray Oral Reading Test–Diagnostic

The Gray Oral Reading Test–Diagnostic (GORT-D) (Bryant & Wiederholt, 1991) is an individually administered set of reading tasks designed for children ages 5 1/2 through 12. There are two forms of the GORT-D, A and B, each of which can be administered in approximately fifty to ninety minutes. Seven subtests are included in the instrument; each subtest has designated entry points, basals, and ceilings.

Description

Paragraph Reading (9 stories)—In this subtest, students are scored according to rate (time in seconds), accuracy, number of mistakes made in oral reading, as well as responses to comprehension questions.

Decoding (15 subtests)—The student is shown a letter followed by a space and more letters (e.g., C_____AL). The child must sound out and blend the sounds to form a word. This particular subtest uses nonsense words.

Word Attack (8 items)—In this subtest, the student is shown a word such as "potato" and is asked to identify as many small words that are in the bigger word as they can (e.g., pot, at, to, and tat).

Word Identification (30 items)—For each item, a series of four words is presented. The student must correctly read each of the four words and indicate which two words go together. For example, "if, car, train, and goat" must all be read correctly and the student must indicate that car and train go together.

Morphemic Analysis (36 items)—This subtest is broken down into three sections. In section 1, *Inflectional Ending*, the student is shown a sentence in which a word is missing and is asked to choose one of four responses that best fits the sentence. In the second section, *Contractions*, the student must look at a series of contractions and indicate the two words that make up the contraction. For example, the student is shown "here's" and must indicate that it is the contraction of "here is." In the last section, *Compound Words*, the student is shown sentences where part of the compound word is missing and the student must complete the compound word. For example, the student is shown "I must finish my home_____ before I can play" and must indicate the correct missing word.

Contextual Analysis (30 items)—The student is again shown series of sentences in which a word is missing, however, this time the missing word has its beginning letter or letters shown to act as a contextual cue for the student.

Word Ordering (25 items)—The student is given a series of words out of order and must put them together in the correct order to make a good sentence. For example, "big Tom is" could be placed together to form "Tom is big" or "Is Tom big?"

Interpretation of Scores

The raw scores from the GORT-D can be transformed into percentiles, subtest standard scores (mean of 10, standard deviation of 3), composite quotients (mean of 100, standard deviation of 15), and grade equivalents. The use of grade equivalents, however, is discouraged by the authors. The composite quotients available are for Total Reading (TRQ), which is a combination of all the subtests; Meaning Cues (paragraph reading, word identification); Graphic Phonemic Cues (decoding, word attack); and Function Cues (morphemic analysis, contextual analysis, and word ordering). A profile sheet is available to visually plot the scores from all the subtests as well as the individual quotients.

Technical Characteristics

Normative Sample.   The GORT-D was standardized on 831 students from thirteen states. Demographic characteristics related to gender, geographic region, race, ethnicity, and type of residence was controlled to approximate that of the 1985 U.S. population.

Reliability.   Internal consistency reliability coefficients ranged from .88 to .96 for individual subtests and .96 to .99 for composites. Other than the one correlation of .88, all coefficients were above .90. Test-retest reliability using alternate forms was also determined. This procedure allows for the determination of both alternate form and stability estimates. The alternate-form coefficients for composites ranged from .75 (Function Cues) to .89 (Meaning Cues). Stability coefficients ranged from .75 (Function Cues) to .92 (Meaning Cues).

Validity.   The authors provide a discussion for the content validity of the instrument and provide data related to construct validity such as age differentiation (scores increasing with age) and intercorrelation among the GORT-D subtest scores. Criterion-related validity was established in a study of 67 students. Correlations between the TRQ of the GORT-D and the reading quotient for the Diagnostic Achievement Battery–2 (DAB-2) was .84, and was .42 for the TRQ of the GORT-D and the total score from the GORT-R.

Review of Relevant Research
No information in the professional literature was located.

OVERVIEW: GRAY ORAL READING TEST–DIAGNOSTIC

- *Age level*—5-1/2 through age 12
- *Type of administration*—Individual
- *Technical adequacy*—Adequate reliability; questionable validity
- *Scores yielded*—Standard scores (total, composite, subtest); percentiles; grade equivalents
- *Suggested use*—The GORT-D covers the main areas of oral reading and comprehension, although it contains a large number of structural analysis tasks as well. The theoretical rationale of the various composite scores is sound, although research on the reliability and validity of those scores should be pursued. One should be aware of the large percentage of "nontraditional" reading subtests that make up the Total Reading Score. This is not an indictment of the test; rather it is a caution that the total score might not reflect the student's classroom performance on traditional classroom measures.

Stanford Diagnostic Reading Test

The Stanford Diagnostic Reading Test (SDRT) (Karlsen & Gardner, 1985) is a group-administered and individually administered instrument designed to measure a student's strengths and weaknesses in reading. It is used with students from the end of first grade through junior college. The authors suggest that the results from the SDRT can be used to help in grouping students and in developing appropriate instructional strategies. The SDRT places special emphasis on the low-achieving student, and it contains more easy items than many reading-achievement tests. The SDRT measures four major components of reading: vocabulary, decoding, comprehension, and rate. The SDRT has four levels, each designed for different age ranges:

> *Red Level*—Used with students at the end of grade 1, grade 2, and low-achieving students in grade 3
> *Green Level*—Used with students in grades 3 and 4 and low-achieving students in grade 5
> *Brown Level*—Used with students from grades 5 through 8 and with low-achieving high-school students
> *Blue Level* (sometimes referred to as the SDRT Level III)—Designed for use with students from grades 9 through 12 and also with community college students

For each level, several tests are given that measure performance in such areas as auditory vocabulary, auditory discrimination, comprehension, reading rate, and phonetic and structural analysis. Each level has two forms: A and B.

Description

Red Level. The Red Level includes five tests that generally measure decoding, vocabulary, and comprehension:

> *Auditory Vocabulary (36 items)*—This test requires a student to recognize the meaning of words found in the primary-grade curriculum.
> *Auditory Discrimination (30 items)*—This test requires a student to identify the similarities and differences among consonant sounds and among vowel sounds.
> *Phonetic Analysis (40 items)*—This test requires a student to identify consonant and vowel sounds by their common spellings.
> *Word Reading (42 items)*—This test requires a student to identify words commonly seen in primary-grade reading materials.
> *Reading Comprehension (48 items)*—This test measures a child's understanding of sentences and paragraphs.

Green Level. The Green Level also includes five tests:

Auditory Vocabulary (40 items)
Auditory Discrimination (30 items)
Phonetic Analysis (30 items)
Structural Analysis (48 items)—This test requires a student to divide two-syllable words into their component parts and to blend sounds to form words.
Reading Comprehension (48 items)—This test includes a measure of both literal and inferential understanding of passages.

Brown Level.   The Brown Level includes five tests that measure all four aspects of reading (decoding, vocabulary, comprehension, and rate):

Auditory Vocabulary (40 items)
Reading Comprehension (60 items)—This test includes both literal and inferential comprehension.
Phonetic Analysis (30 items)
Structural Analysis (78 items)—This test measures word division and blending of three-syllable words.
Reading Rate (33 items)—This test measures the student's ability to combine speed and comprehension in reading easy material.

Blue Level.   The Blue Level includes seven tests. The formats of tests 1, 4, and 5 (Reading Comprehension, Phonetic Analysis, and Structural Analysis) have been discussed under the previous levels. The remaining tests are these:

Vocabulary (30 items)—This test requires the student to recognize the meaning of words in context.
Word Parts (30 items)—This test requires the student to demonstrate the understanding of affixes, root words, and word roots.
Scanning and Skimming (32 items)—This test requires the student to recall information after quickly reading a passage.
Fast Reading (30 items)—This test includes a five hundred-word passage presented in a modified cloze procedure and requires the student to demonstrate both speed and comprehension.

Interpretation of Results
The SDRT can be either hand scored or machine scored. The raw scores from each test can be transformed into a number of norm-referenced scores. The manual for each level includes tables for percentile ranks, stanines, grade equivalents, and scaled scores. Computer scoring can also provide stanines and percentile ranks compared to both local and national norms. In fact, the computer scoring profile provides much valuable information (Figure 14.4). The SDRT also includes progress indicators, which are essentially cutoff points, determined by the authors, that document whether a student has demonstrated competence in various reading skills. The authors suggest that the cut-off points be used only as guides and

THE PSYCHOLOGICAL CORPORATION

SDRT

STANFORD DIAGNOSTIC READING TEST
3rd EDITION © HARCOURT BRACE JOVANOVICH, INC.

TEACHER SUSAN NORRIS
SCHOOL NORTHWESTERN
SYSTEM MIDDLEBURG
TEST DATE 9/84

GRADE 10
LEVEL BLUE FORM G
NORMS GRADE 10 FALL

CLASS SUMMARY PAGE 1

WITH

INSTRUCTIONAL PLACEMENT REPORT COPY 1

SUBTESTS AND TOTALS	MEAN RS	SS OF MN RS	MEAN NCE	GE OF MN RS	PR-S OF MN RS		SKILLS ANALYSIS SUMMARY		N +	%+	N -	%-
TOTAL VOCABULARY	37.6	681	36.92	7.8	26	4	** RAW SCORE/ ITEMS ATTEMPTED	READING COMPREHENSION				
TOTAL DECODING	40.4	650	39.52	6.0	27	4		LITERAL	17	68	8	32
TOTAL RATE	38.6	705	47.42	9.8	46	5		INFERENTIAL	20	80	5	20
READING COMPREHENSION	40.8	669	38.05	6.9	26	4		TEXTUAL	18	72	7	28
								FUNCTIONAL	20	80	5	20
								RECREATIONAL	14	56	11	44
VOCABULARY	21.3	669	37.84	7.5	23	4	VOCABULARY				
WORD PARTS	16.3	673	38.36	7.8	27	4		READING & LITERATURE	17	68	8	32
PHONETIC ANALYSIS	18.5	606	39.36	3.9	29	4		MATH & SCIENCE	16	64	9	36
STRUCTURAL ANALYSIS	21.9	677	39.36	6.8	24	4		SOCIAL STUDIES & THE ARTS	14	56	11	44
SCANNING AND SKIMMING	15.6	679	35.39	7.8	27	4	WORD PARTS				
FAST READING **(RS/IA)	23/26	745	60.24	12.4	69	6		AFFIXES	16	64	9	36
								ROOTS	16	64	9	36
SDRT TOTAL	157.3	661	39.22	7.3	29	4	PHONETIC ANALYSIS				
							CONSONANTS	17	68	8	32
							SINGLE CONSONANTS	18	72	7	28
							CONSONANT DIGRAPHS	17	68	8	32
							VOWELS	18	72	7	28
							SHORT VOWELS	18	72	7	28
							LONG VOWELS	19	76	6	24
							OTHER VOWELS	21	84	4	16

PROGRESS INDICATORS

GROUP 1 REMEDIAL	GROUP 2 DECODING	GROUP 3 VOCABULARY	GROUP 4 COMPREHENSION
NUMBER 0	NUMBER 13	NUMBER 4	NUMBER 2
PERCENT .0%	PERCENT 52.0%	PERCENT 16.0%	PERCENT 8.0%

STRUCTURAL ANALYSIS

	N+	%+	N-	%-
AFFIXES	20	80	5	20
SYLLABLES	18	72	7	28

SCANNING & SKIMMING

SCANNING	15	60	10	40
SKIMMING	17	68	8	32

GROUP 5 RATE	GROUP 6 DEVELOPMENTAL	GROUP 7 ENRICHMENT	GROUP 8 UNCLASSIFIED
NUMBER 2	NUMBER 4	NUMBER 0	NUMBER 0
PERCENT 8.0%	PERCENT 16.0%	PERCENT .0%	PERCENT .0%

MN = MEAN RS = RAW SCORE PR = PERCENTILE RANK S = STANINE
NCE = NORMAL CURVE EQUIVALENT TNT = TEST NOT TAKEN
SS = SCALED SCORE GE = GRADE EQUIVALENT

PROCESS NO 01-004112-002 CONTINUED...

Copyright © 1984 by Harcourt Brace Jovanovich, Inc.
Simulated data.

This report can be used to:

- Determine performance on objectives for a class
- Determine performance on objectives for a school/ system
- Determine overall achievement for a class
- Determine overall achievement for a school/ system
- Identify reading needs for a class
- Identify reading needs for a school/system
- Report results to the public
- Compare groups of students
- Evaluate curriculum
- Evaluate Chapter 1 programs (Measure Growth).

FIGURE 14.4 Computer Scoring Profile from the Stanford Diagnostic Reading Test

From B. Karlsen, R. Madden, and E. Gardner, *Stanford Diagnostic Reading Test*, 3rd ed. Copyright © 1984 by the Psychological Corporation. Reprinted with permission.

that they may need to be modified according to the individual's instructional program. Also included with the SDRT is an instructional-placement report that summarizes the results of an entire class by using the scores that are viewed as the most relevant.

Technical Characteristics

Normative Sample. A nationally stratified sample of more than thirty thousand was used.

Reliability. Internal reliability coefficients were generally above .80; many were .90 or above.

Validity. A discussion of content validity can be found in the manual. Construct and criterion-related data are available from the Psychological Corporation.

Review of Relevant Research

Although the SDRT has not been studied extensively, Lewandowski and Martens (1990) reviewed the test and noted that it was useful as a screening instrument. They did point out, however, that some of the subtests were inappropriately named and found little rationale presented for its theoretical base.

OVERVIEW: STANFORD DIAGNOSTIC READING TEST

- *Age level*—Grade 1 through community college
- *Type of administration*—Group
- *Technical adequacy*—Good
- *Scores yielded*—Percentile ranks, stanines, grade equivalents, scaled scores, progress indicators
- *Suggested use*—The SDRT is a well-constructed diagnostic reading test. Its standardization sample was representative and the reliability and the validity good. It can therefore be used as a reasonable measure of vocabulary, decoding skills, comprehension, and reading rate, particularly for screening purposes. It gives more normative information but less informal information (for example, error analysis) than other diagnostic reading tests.

Test of Reading Comprehension–3

The Test of Reading Comprehension (TORC-3) (Brown, Hammill, & Wiederholt, 1995) is an individually administered instrument designed for students between the ages of seven and eighteen. It can also be used with small groups of students. The test measures the comprehension of *silent* reading; therefore, individuals who have articulation or other oral-reading problems are not penalized. Four uses are specifically mentioned in the manual (1995; p.4):

1. *To identify students whose scores are significantly below those of their peers and who might need interventions designed to improve reading comprehension*

2. *To determine areas of relative strength and weakness across reading comprehension abilities*

3. *To document overall progress in reading development as a consequence of intervention programs*

4. *To serve as a measure for research efforts designed to investigate reading comprehension*

Description

Eight subtests are included in the TORC-3. Subtests 1–4 are called the General Reading Comprehension Core. Subtests 4–8 are called Diagnostic Supplements.

> *General Vocabulary (25 items)*—This subtest measures the student's conceptual understanding of sets of vocabulary items. For instance, the words *sausage, pancake,* and *hamburger* are given as stimulus items. The student must choose which two of a group of four—such as *tortilla, salad, salute, fragrant*—are most like the stimulus words.
>
> *Syntactic Similarities (20 items)*—This subtest measures the child's understanding of syntactically different sentences. For instance, the following sentences are shown to the student: "A. We ran yesterday, B. We run daily, C. We will run tomorrow, D. We run, and E. We run every day." The student must indicate which two sentences have the same meaning.
>
> *Paragraph Reading (30 items)*—Six paragraphs are read silently, and five multiple choice questions are answered from each.
>
> *Sentence Sequencing (10 items)*—Five sentences are presented to the reader. The task is to sequence the sentences to make a meaningful story.
>
> *Content-Area Vocabularies (3 subtests: Mathematics, Social Studies, and Science) (75 items)*—These three subtests use the same format as subtest 1. The vocabulary tests, however, are associated with mathematics, social studies, and science content.
>
> *Reading the Directions of Schoolwork (25 items)*—This subtest is used for younger or remedial readers. The student must read and follow simple directions.

Interpretation of Results

Raw scores from the TORC-3 can be transformed into standard scores, age and grade equivalents, percentile ranks, and a Reading Comprehension Quotient (RCQ). The standard scores for all subtests have a mean of 10 and a standard deviation of 3. The RCQ is based on the total standard scores of the Reading Comprehension Core and has a mean of 100 and a standard deviation of 15.

Technical Characteristics

Normative Sample.   The sample included 1,962 subjects from nineteen states. Information regarding gender, age, grade level, and geographic region is included in the manual.

Reliability.   Internal consistency is good; coefficients were generally above .90. Test-retest consistency ranged from .79 to .87 (based on a limited sample).

Validity.   Data from several concurrent validity studies are presented in the manual. The median correlations ranged from .45 to .65; information related to both content and construct validity is also provided in the manual.

Review of Relevant Research

No studies on the TORC-3 were located; the format of the instrument is similar enough to its predecessor, the TORC, that research on that test might be relevant. In one study, Brown and Sherbenou (1981) found that the TORC results correlated between .40 and .66 with teachers' evaluations of the students' reading abilities. In another, Eaves and Simpson (1986) provided a table that allows an examiner to determine statistically significant differences between subtest scores for a more precise analysis of intraindividual strengths and weaknesses. There also have been several reviews of the revised TORC. Poteet (1989) suggested that potential users should become familiar with the theoretical rationale of the TORC to determine if this matches the curricular demands. Tierney (1989) questioned the limitation or narrowness of the TORC in measuring traditional reading comprehension. On the other hand, Misulis (1989) pointed out that the TORC is interesting, unique, and represents a valuable contribution to the reading profession.

OVERVIEW: TEST OF READING COMPREHENSION-3

- *Age level*—7 to 18 years
- *Type of administration*—Individual (small group is possible)
- *Technical adequacy*—Adequate standardization, good reliability, questionable validity
- *Scores yielded*—Scaled scores, percentile ranks, Reading Comprehension Quotient
- *Suggested use*—The TORC-3 is theoretically a measure of silent reading comprehension. Only a small part of the test actually focuses on traditional comprehension measures (that is, on reading a passage and answering questions about the content). Most of the test is concerned with vocabulary and syntax. This is not necessarily a criticism of the test, although you should be aware of the test's content if you use the results exclusively to assess a student's comprehension. The TORC-3 is most appropriate for students ages 8 to 14.

Woodcock Reading Mastery Tests–Revised

The Woodcock Reading Mastery Tests–Revised (WRMT-R) (Woodcock, 1987) includes six individually administered tests and a two-part supplementary checklist designed for individuals ages 5 to 75 and older. There are two forms of the test—form G contains all six tests and the supplementary checklist, whereas form H contains only four tests. According to the author, the WRMT-R can be used for a variety of reasons including diagnosis of reading problems, program planning, and program evaluation. The tests are designed for both criterion-referenced and norm-referenced purposes, although their use as a criterion-referenced tool is somewhat limited.

Description

Visual-Auditory Learning (Form G only; 133 items)—This subtest requires the examinee to associate new visual symbols with familiar words and then translate sentences using those new symbols.

Letter Identification (Form G only; 51 items)—This subtest requires the student to identify lower- and uppercase letters presented in common styles (such as cursive) and uncommon styles (such as special typestyles).

Word Identification (106 items)—This subtest includes words arranged sequentially according to level of difficulty. The examinee simply has to read the word.

Word Attack (45 Items)—This subtest measures the ability to pronounce nonsense words (for example, "gnouthe") through the use of structural and phonetic analysis.

Word Comprehension (146 items)—This test is comprised of three separate subtests. *Antonyms (34 items)* requires the examinee to say a word that is opposite of a vocabulary word. *Synonyms (33 items)* requires the examinee to say a word that means the same thing as a vocabulary word. *Analogies (79 items)* requires the person to read a pair of analogous words (for example, cowboy-horse) and then complete a second analogy (for example, pilot-_____).

Passage Comprehension (68 items)—This subtest uses a modified cloze procedure. The examinee must read a passage in which a key word is missing and must identify the missing word.

Supplementary Letter Checklist (Form G only; 63 items)—This checklist includes both *capital letter (27 items)* and *lowercase letter (36 items)* sublists. These letters are presented in the sans serif typestyle that is common in many beginning reading programs.

Interpretation of Results

The subtests of the WRMT-R can provide specific information about the examinee or can be combined into various clusters for interpretation. Age equivalents, grade equivalents, percentile ranks, and standard scores (mean = 100; standard deviation = 15) are available in the following areas; Readiness (Visual-Auditory Learning and Letter Identification); Basic Skills (Word Identification and Word Attack); Reading Comprehension (Word Comprehension and Passage Comprehension); Total Reading-Full Scale (Word Identification, Word Attack, Word Comprehension, and Passage Comprehension); and Total Reading-Short Scale (Word Identification and Passage Comprehension). A Relative Performance Index (RPI) is also available that gives an indication of the relative mastery of content at a specific grade level. Scoring of the WRMT-R, although easier than its predecessor, is still rather cumbersome. Several interesting and potentially valuable additions are a word-attack error inventory and tables that allow for the determination of aptitude-achievement discrepancies. Scores can also be placed on a diagnostic profile, a percentile rank profile, and an instructional level profile. The diagnostic profile allows the interpretation of scores from other tests as well as the WRMT-R.

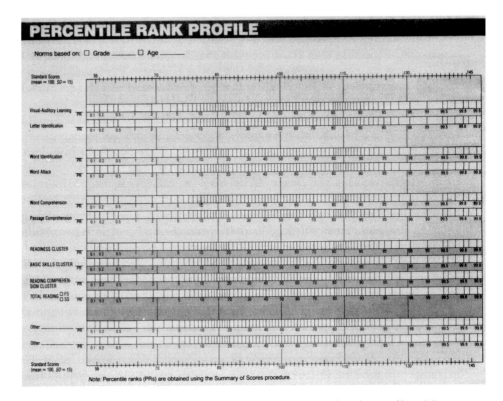

FIGURE 14.5   Percentile Rank Profile from the Woodcock Reading Mastery Tests–Revised

From R. Woodcock, *Woodcock Reading Mastery Tests–Revised.* Copyright © 1987 by American Guidance Service. Reprinted with permission.

Figure 14.5 shows the percentile rank profile. Eaves, Campbell-Whatley, Dunn, Reilly, and Tate-Braxton (1995) also developed a set of tables that allow a comparison of the standard scores taking into account each subtest's reliability.

Technical Characteristics

Normative Sample.   More than six thousand subjects were used in the standardization. The kindergarten to grade twelve population was four thousand of the total. The sample was stratified according to geographic region, race, occupation (for adult subjects), and community type.

Reliability.   Split-half coefficients were above .90 for all subtests and clusters. A coefficient of .99 was reported for the total reading.

Validity.   Concurrent validity coefficients with the reading tests from the Woodcock-Johnson Psychoeducational Battery ranged from .25 to .91. Total reading scores from one test correlated .85 or above with total reading from the other test. Arguments for the test's content and construct validity are also reported in the manual.

Review of Relevant Research

Surprisingly, little research on the WRMT-R was found. Reviews and critiques of the instrument have appeared in the reading literature, however. Cooter (1988) concluded that it was a substantial improvement over the 1973 WRMT, although it still evaluated the reading process in fragments rather than holistically. Lewandowski and Martens (1990) noted several problems, including the lack of information related to the validity of the profiles and lack of alternate form reliability data. Jaeger (1989) questioned the diagnostic and instructional planning value of the instrument, suggesting that it should be used to develop tentative hypotheses that should be confirmed through more extensive assessment. Eaves (1990) reported that the validity for the WRMT-R is weak (primarily because there are so little data) and that more research needs to be conducted in this area.

Because of the similarity between the WRMT-R and its predecessor, some of the research on the WRMT has relevance as well.

- Learning-disabled and non-learning-disabled students performed similarly on the WRMT. The reliability of scores for the two groups was high (McCollough & Zaremba, 1979).
- The WRMT has a unique format that might be helpful in evaluating learning-disabled students (Coleman & Harmer, 1982).
- The word-identification test is the most accurate single predictor of the total reading scores for adolescent learning-disabled students (Williamson, 1976).
- The WRMT is a valid instrument for slow-learning and underachieving individuals (Haines, 1977).
- For a group of reading-disabled students, the word identification test yielded scores approximately one year lower than did sight-vocabulary tests from other reading instruments (Memory, Powell, & Calloway, 1980).
- The analogy format of the word comprehension test has been challenged (Laffey & Kelly, 1979).

Summary of Research Findings

The limited research on the original WRMT suggests that it is a reasonably valid instrument with a variety of students, including those with learning disabilities. The format of the test has been questioned, however. Research on the WRMT-R is needed to substantiate prior findings and explore further issues related to its potential uses and limitations. Reviews of the WRMT-R also note the need for additional technical data.

OVERVIEW: WOODCOCK READING MASTERY TESTS–REVISED

- *Age level*—Ages 5 to 75 and older
- *Type of administration*—Individual
- *Technical adequacy*—Adequate standardization, good but limited reliability (only split-half), somewhat limited validity
- *Scores yielded*—Standard scores, percentile ranks, age and grade equivalents, relative performance index
- *Suggested use*—The WRMT-R is probably the most popular norm-referenced diagnostic reading test used in special education. The tests are easy to administer and cover a number of abilities. The WRMT-R, however, is tedious to score, requiring the use of multiple tables that could lead to scoring errors. It is important that examiners practice the scoring several times before administering it in a real test situation. The meaning and interpretation of the visual-auditory learning subtest and the aptitude-achievement discrepancy tables need to be established. The error inventory is a nice addition. In summary, it appears that the WRMT-R has improved many of the shortcomings of the original test. It should be noted that the WRMT-R is currently being restandardized.

OTHER DIAGNOSTIC READING TESTS

In addition to the previously discussed norm-referenced reading tests, two others deserve mention. These two, the Durrell Analysis of Reading Difficulty and the Diagnostic Reading Scales, are best used informally and are often administered by reading specialists.

Durrell Analysis of Reading Difficulty

Age level—Preprimary through grade 6

Type of administration—Individual

Technical adequacy—Adequate standardization, questionable reliability and validity

Scores yielded—Independent, instructional, capacity reading levels, informal checklist

Description—The DARD (Durrell & Catterson, 1980) includes nine subtests ranging from oral and silent reading to listening comprehension, visual memory of words, and sounds in isolation. The strength of the DARD is its use as an informal instrument. The checklist of instructional needs can be a helpful tool to analyze errors. It does, however, require the examiner to have a certain amount of knowledge in the area of reading. The reading levels yielded should be used as rough estimates only. The DARD should probably be used by experienced reading teachers to maximize its potential diagnostic ability. There is limited information on its use with exceptional students.

Diagnostic Reading Scales

Age level—Grade 1 through grade 8

Type of administration—Individual

Technical adequacy—Adequate (based on limited data)

Scores yielded—Error analysis; instructional, independent, and potential reading levels

Description—The DRS (Spache, 1981) includes word lists and reading passages that measure oral reading and comprehension. There are also measures of word analysis and phonics. The reading levels determined from the DRS should be used as estimates only. There is also evidence that the reading levels determined from the 1981 edition and the 1972 edition are markedly different. Thus, the various editions should not be used interchangeably. One special feature of the DRS is the section focusing on concerns in administering the test to children who speak non-standard-English dialects. (No information is included regarding exceptional students, however.) In addition, the error analysis can be helpful for experienced reading teachers.

ORAL READING TESTS

WHY USE ORAL READING TESTS?

Screening and identification; informal determination of objectives and teaching strategies; documentation of educational need; establishment of IEP goals

WHO SHOULD USE THEM?

Teachers; diagnostic specialists

Oral reading tests measure a student's rate and accuracy of reading and, in some cases, the comprehension of orally read material. Most oral reading tests use graded passages to determine the level of reading and to identify the types of errors made. The two most common oral reading tests are the Gray and the Gilmore. A brief discussion of each follows.

Gray Oral Reading Test–3

(Wiederholt & Bryant, 1992)

> *Age level*—7 to 18 years
>
> *Alternate forms*—This test has two forms.
>
> *Technical adequacy*—Normed on 1,485 students from eighteen states. Evidence for content, criterion-related and construct validity, as well as alternate-form and internal reliability, is reported in the manual.
>
> *Areas measured*—Rate (how long it takes the student to read a passage) and deviations from print (how many and what types of errors are made)
>
> *Types of scores*—Standard scores, percentile ranks, grade equivalents, miscue analysis
>
> *Suggested use*—The error analysis yields the most important information, although an examiner with a strong diagnostic reading background would get the most usable information from the test.

The GORT–Revised (Wiederholt & Bryant, 1986) had technical characteristics that were a considerable improvement over the original GORT (Hickman, 1989). It appears that the GORT-3 is even more improved.

Gilmore Oral Reading Test

(Gilmore & Gilmore, 1968)

> *Age level*—Grades 1 to 8
>
> *Alternate forms*—Two forms, C and D, are available.
>
> *Technical adequacy*—Normed on more than twenty-two hundred children. Alternate form reliability coefficients were moderate at best; no validity data mentioned.
>
> *Areas measured*—Accuracy (number and type of errors), comprehension, reading rate
>
> *Types of scores*—Performance ratings (poor through superior), grade scores (based on accuracy)
>
> *Suggested use*—Clearly, the informal use (error analysis) is the primary advantage of this instrument. Normative use is discouraged.

Instrument or Technique	Screening and Initial Identification (Prereferral)	Informal Determination of Teaching Programs and Strategies (Prereferral)	Determination of Current Performance Level and Educational Need (Prereferral)	Decisions about Classification and Program Placement (Postreferral)	IEP Goals (Postreferral)	IEP Objectives (Postreferral)	IEP Evaluation (Postreferral)	Mild/Moderate	Severe/Profound	Preschool	Elementary Age	Secondary Age	Adult	Special Considerations	Educational Relevance for Exceptional Students
Diagnosis: An Instructional Aid in Reading	X	X	X		X	X	X	X			X			Test items are correlated with instructional materials	useful
Informal Reading Inventories	X	X	X		X			X			X	X		Most measure word recognition and comprehension skills	useful
Cloze Procedure	X	X						X			X	X		The reading levels that are determined should be used only as guidelines	adequate
Maze Procedure	X	X						X			X	X		The reading levels that are determined should be used only as guidelines	adequate
Reading Diagnosis Sheet	X	X						X			X	X		This procedure is included in a book that also suggests remedial strategies	useful
Gray Oral Reading Test–Diagnostic	X		X		X			X			X			Includes a number of "nontraditional" reading tasks	useful
Stanford Diagnostic Reading Test	X		X		X			X			X	X		Well constructed; can be group administered; does not give specific instructional information	useful
Test of Reading Comprehension-3	X				X			X			X	X		Heavily weighted toward vocabulary and syntax	adequate

Instrument or Technique	Suggested Use							Target Population						Special Considerations	Educational Relevance for Exceptional Students
	Prereferral			Postreferral											
	Screening and Initial Identification	Informal Determination and Evaluation of Teaching Programs and Strategies	Determination of Current Performance Level and Educational Need	Decisions about Classification and Program Placement	IEP Goals	IEP Objectives	IEP Evaluation	Mild/Moderate	Severe/Profound	Preschool	Elementary Age	Secondary Age	Adult		
Woodcock Reading Mastery Tests–Revised	X		X		X			X			X	X		Earlier version widely used; some improvements in revision; tedious scoring system	adequate
Durrell Analysis of Reading Difficulty		X	X		X			X			X			Normative data are limited; should be used informally	adequate
Diagnostic Reading Scales		X	X		X			X			X			Best used informally; error analysis could be helpful	adequate
Gray Oral Reading Test-3	X	X						X			X	X		Error analysis yields the most information	adequate
Gilmore Oral Reading Test	X	X						X			X			Limited technical aspects; should be used informally	limited

15

ASSESSMENT OF MATHEMATICS

Instruments and Procedures Included

Diagnostic Mathematics Tests
   Key Math–Revised
   Stanford Diagnostic Mathematics Test
   Test of Mathematical Abilities–2

Criterion-Referenced Mathematics Instruments
   Diagnosis: An Instructional Aid in Mathematics
   Diagnostic Test of Arithmetic Strategies
   Enright Inventory of Basic Arithmetic Skills
   Mathematics Concept Inventory

Informal Assessment

Albert is a fourth-grade student who has always been "scared of numbers." He often confuses the mathematics signs and will add instead of subtract or subtract instead of multiply. He also has great difficulty with time and number concepts. He still has problems reading and understanding a clock. His teacher believed that a sequential list of objectives in the deficient mathematics areas would be beneficial. Albert was referred for testing to evaluate his overall mathematics ability and to identify appropriate educational objectives.

Less attention is given to the assessment of mathematics than of reading. Evaluation of mathematics is important, however, and should be included when conducting a comprehensive basic skill assessment. A look at the general achievement tests discussed in Chapter 13 will reveal that subtests that measure mathematics are included in virtually every instrument.

Mathematics assessment usually involves the areas of mathematical concepts, computation, application, and problem solving. _Mathematical concepts_ focuses on basic information such as the understanding of numeration, mathematical operations, number concepts, and place value. _Computation_ involves such areas as addition, subtraction, multiplication, and division of whole numbers, fractions, and decimals. _Application_ includes such areas as measurement skills, money skills, and time concepts, whereas _problem solving_ involves the ability to (1) determine how to solve a given problem (frequently a word problem) and (2) perform the necessary operation(s) to determine the correct answer.

Norm-referenced tests for the mathematical areas are sometimes referred to as _diagnostic_ tests. Similar to diagnostic reading tests, however, these instruments are used to determine strengths and weaknesses and to identify areas for remediation rather than "diagnosing" in a traditional sense. Criterion-referenced instruments in the area of mathematics are used to identify more specific information that might be incorporated into an IEP.

It is also crucial to consider the use of the error analysis procedures that were discussed in Chapter 6. The ease of obtaining written products in error analysis adds to its benefits. Many of the tests presented in this chapter, particularly the criterion-referenced instruments, are based on an error analysis approach.

DIAGNOSTIC MATHEMATICS TESTS

WHY USE DIAGNOSTIC MATHEMATICS TESTS?

Screening and identification; informal determination of objectives and teaching strategies; documentation of educational need; establishment of IEP goals

WHO SHOULD USE THEM?

Teachers; diagnostic specialists

Key Math–Revised

The Key Math–Revised (Key Math–R) (Connolly, 1988) is the most recent edition of the popular Key Math Diagnostic Arithmetic Test. The Key Math–R, like its predecessor, is contained in an easel kit; most of the items are presented orally by the examiner, using colored plates as a visual stimulus. The Key Math–R has two forms, A and B, and has extended the age range of the test from kindergarten through grade 7 to kindergarten through grade 9.

Description
The Key Math–R contains thirteen subtests that measure the general areas of basic concepts, operations, and applications. Items within each subtest can be clustered into domains. The subtests and their respective domains are listed next.

Basic Concepts

Numeration (24 items)—Numbers 0–9, numbers 0–99, numbers 0–999, multi-digit numbers

Rational Numbers (18 items)—Fractions, decimals, percents

Geometry (24 items)—Spatial/attribute relations, two–dimensional shapes, co-ordinates/transformations, three–dimensional shapes

Operations

Addition (18 items)—Models and basic facts, algorithms: whole numbers, adding rational numbers

Subtraction (18 items)—Models and basic facts, algorithms: whole numbers, subtracting rational numbers

Multiplication (18 items)—Models and basic facts, algorithms: whole numbers, multiplying rational numbers

Division (18 items)—Models and basic facts, algorithms: whole numbers, dividing rational numbers

Mental Computation (18 items)—Computation chains, whole numbers, rational numbers

Applications

Measures (24 items)—Comparisons, nonstandard units, standard units: length, area, standard units: weight, capacity

Time and Money (24 items)—Identifying passage of time, using clocks and clock units, monetary amounts to $1, monetary amounts to $100

Estimation (18 items)—Whole and rational numbers, measurement, computation

Interpreting Data (18 items)—Charts and tables, graphs, probability and statistics

Problem Solving (18 items)—Solving routine problems, understanding nonroutine problems, solving nonroutine problems.

Interpretation of Results

Four levels of diagnostic information are available: total test, area, subtest, and domain. Domain-related information provides insight into the student's specific strengths and weaknesses. Standard scores (mean = 100; standard deviation = 15), grade and age equivalents, percentile ranks, and stanines are available for the three area composites and the total test. Standard scores (mean = 10; standard deviation = 3), percentile ranks, and stanines are available for the subtests. A computer software package is also available that provides a scoring summary and a score profile.

Technical Characteristics

Normative Sample.   Approximately eighteen hundred students were included. The sample was stratified by geographic region, grade, gender, socioeconomic status, and racial and ethnic background. Separate fall and spring norms are available.

Reliability. Alternate-form coefficients are reported. Total score was the only acceptable coefficient. Area and subtest coefficients were below .85. Split-half coefficients were acceptable for the total test and for the areas after approximately grade two.

Validity. Few validity data are presented. A brief discussion of content validity is included in the manual.

Review of Relevant Research
Surprisingly, little research was located on the revised version. The Key Math–R is similar to the original Key Math in format. Therefore, the research on the original might be relevant.

- The Key Math is a useful instrument with learning disabled students, for several reasons: (1) It measures current curricula; (2) it requires neither reading nor writing; (3) it offers a simplified visual presentation; and (4) it allows the examiner to observe the child during the testing (Tinney, 1975).
- The Key Math is a good test to use with adolescent learning-disabled students. The test discriminated between learning-disabled and non-learning-disabled students. Further, the learning-disabled students demonstrated a specific pattern of computational errors (Greenstein & Strain, 1977).
- The Key Math has moderate predictive validity. It correlated .67 with Metropolitan Achievement Test scores obtained one year later (Kratchowill & Demuth, 1976).
- The Key Math should be used as a screening test rather than as a diagnostic test with mentally retarded students. While the difficulty level of the basal items was generally acceptable (except for multiplication and missing elements), the children tended to reach the ceiling rapidly (Goodstein, Kahn, & Cawley, 1976).
- The Key Math and Wide Range Achievement Test arithmetic sections yielded comparable scores for educable mentally retarded students. Therefore, you must weigh the additional diagnostic features of the Key Math against the shorter administration time of the WRAT when you select either of these instruments (Powers & Pace, 1976).
- Because of the relatively low reliabilities of the individual subtests, the standard error of measurement for each should be plotted on the diagnostic record (Van Etten & Watson, 1978).

Summary of Research Finding
Surprisingly, few studies have been reported for a test that was as widely used as the Key Math. The available research suggests that the Key Math is a potentially

useful instrument for students with learning disabilities (LD), although its use with students with mental retardation is limited. Students with LD tend to have a specific pattern with a relatively high number of computation errors. Several studies have also noted the technical inadequacies of the Key Math. Research on the Key Math–R should indicate whether these findings will be true for the newer edition as well. Bachor (1990) did note that the Key Math–R was a substantial improvement over its predecessor. Rivera, Taylor, and Bryant (1995) evaluated the Key Math–R in relation to the National Council of Teachers of Mathematics *Curriculum and Evaluation Standards.* They reported that it met several of the standards with younger students but not for those in grade 5 or higher.

OVERVIEW: KEY MATH–REVISED

- *Age level*—Kindergarten to grade 9
- *Type of administration*—Individual
- *Technical adequacy*—Adequate reliability (total score); limited validity.
- *Scores yielded*—Standard scores, age and grade equivalents, percentile ranks, stanines.
- *Suggested use*—The Key Math–R should be used either informally as a criterion-referenced test, or normatively as a screening device. Users of the Key Math–R must keep in mind the visual (and largely nonwritten) format of the test. This has its advantages and disadvantages. It might be appropriate to measure the mathematical skills of a student with writing problems. On the other hand, the format requires skills that are dissimilar to the majority of skills required of students during classroom activities. To date, validity data are limited. It should be noted that the Key Math–R is currently being restandardized.

Stanford Diagnostic Mathematics Test

The Stanford Diagnostic Mathematics Test (SDMT) (Beatty, Madden, Gardner, & Karlsen, 1985) is a group-administered or individually administered instrument designed to measure basic mathematic concepts and skills from grade 1 through grade 12. The SDMT is divided into four levels.

Red Level—Designed for mathematics concepts usually taught in the first and second grade and is used with children at the end of first grade, second grade, third grade, and students in the fourth grade having problems in the mathematics area. Also included is a practice test that familiarizes the student with general test-taking skills.

Green Level—Measures those concepts and skills usually taught in grades 3 and 4 and is used with students in grades 4 and 5 and some students in grade 6.

Brown Level—Covers those skills usually taught by the end of the sixth grade and is used with sixth and seventh graders and lower-achieving eighth-grade and high-school students.

Blue Level—Overlaps some of the content of the Brown Level and includes mathematics information usually taught by the end of the eighth grade. This level is used with students in grades 8 to 12 and with community college students.

Each level contains three tests that measure a student's knowledge in the following areas: Number Systems and Numeration, Computation, and Applications. The tests themselves are used as diagnostic instruments to determine a student's strengths and weaknesses in math.

Description

Red Level

Number System and Numeration (30 items)—This test measures the child's knowledge of whole numbers, decimal-place value, and operations and properties.

Computation (30 items)—This test includes addition facts, addition with no renaming, subtraction facts, and subtraction with no renaming.

Applications (30 items)—This test includes items measuring problem solving, reading and interpreting graphs, and geometry and measurement.

Green Level

Number System and Numeration (33 items)—This subtest covers whole numbers, decimal-place value, rational numbers and numeration, and operations and properties.

Computation (45 items)—This test includes addition, subtraction, multiplication, and division of whole numbers.

Application (30 items)—This test covers problem solving, reading and interpreting tables and graphs, and geometry and measurement.

Brown Level

Number System and Numeration (36 items)—This test includes items in the areas of whole numbers and decimal place value, rational numbers and numeration, and operations and properties.

Computation (45 items)—This test includes items measuring addition, subtraction, multiplication, and division of whole numbers, fractions, and decimals, as well as equations.

Application (33 items)—This test involves problem solving, reading and interpreting tables and graphs, and geometry and measurement.

Blue Level

Number System and Numeration (36 items)—This test measures whole numbers and decimal place value, rational numbers and numeration, and operations and properties.

Computation (48 items)—This test includes items measuring the addition, subtraction, multiplication, and division of whole numbers, fractions, and decimals; the calculation of percentages; and equations.

Application (33 items)—This test involves problem solving, reading and interpreting tables and graphs, and geometry and measurement.

Interpretation of Results

Raw scores from the SDMT can be transformed into a number of norm-referenced measures. Tables for percentile ranks, stanines, grade equivalents, and scaled scores can be found in the manuals for each level. Like the SDRT, computer scoring can also provide percentiles and stanines compared to both local and national norms. In addition to these, the SDMT offers a progress-indicator (Pi) score that, essentially, is a cutoff point. Its purpose is to help teachers identify students who have reached the level of competence necessary to achieve success in the instructional goals of the individual classroom. Each test can be either hand scored or machine scored. Each level includes an instructional-placement report that summarizes the results for an entire class. The authors also endorse a three-step test-plan-teach process and provide services and materials to facilitate this process (see Figure 15.1 on page 382).

Technical Characteristics

Normative Sample.   A large, stratified, nationally representative sample was used.

Reliability.   Internal consistency was generally good; coefficients were mostly above .90.

Validity.   Information related to content and concurrent validity is available from the Psychological Corporation.

Review of Relevant Research

The SDMT has not been studied extensively. Two reviewers of the 1976 SDMT had different opinions about the diagnostic utility of the instrument. Sowder (1978) indicated that it gave a "not too specific" indication of strengths and weaknesses and that it should be used for comparison rather than for educational programming. Lappan (1978), on the other hand, considered it adequate to identify strengths and weaknesses and to group students for instructional purposes. The format and items of the 1976 and the 1985 versions are similar.

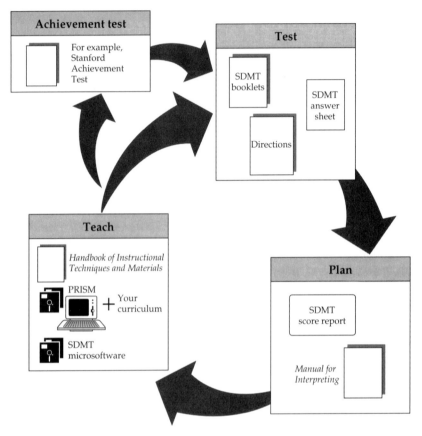

FIGURE 15.1   Three-Step Process Recommended for Users of the Stanford Diagnostic Mathematics Test

OVERVIEW: STANFORD DIAGNOSTIC MATHEMATICS TEST

- *Age levels*—Grades 1 through 12, plus community college
- *Type of administration*—Group
- *Technical adequacy*—Good
- *Scores yielded*—Percentile ranks, stanines, grade equivalent, scaled scores, progress indicator
- *Suggested use*—The SDMT is a well-constructed test. It can be used to identify general strengths and weaknesses in the areas of number concepts, computation, and application. The SDMT is more appropriate as a general comparative test than as a specific test to determine instructional goals and objectives.

Test of Mathematical Abilities–2

The Test of Mathematical Abilities–2 (TOMA-2) (Brown, Cronin, & McEntire, 1994) includes five subtests that provide standardized information about two major skill areas—story problems and computation—and related information about attitude, vocabulary, and the general application of information. It is a norm-referenced test designed for use with students ages 8 through 18. The subtests may be either group or individually administered. Administration takes approximately one hour to two hours, although no time limits are imposed.

Description

Vocabulary (25 items)—This subtest lists math-related vocabulary words which the subject must briefly define in writing.

Computation (25 items)—This subtest is a paper-and-pencil test of math computation. Problems are arranged in order of difficulty.

General Information (30 items)—This is an orally administered subtest of general mathematical knowledge. It requires some subjectivity in the scoring.

Story Problems (25 items)—This subtest includes problems that the subject must read and complete. Nonreaders' scores should not be included, although the problems can be read aloud as part of a separate diagnostic analysis.

Attitude toward Math (15 items)—This optional subtest requires the subject to decide what he or she thinks of each math-related sentence. The student indicates "agree," "disagree," or "don't know." Sentences are usually read to the subject, but good readers may proceed independently.

Interpretation of Results

The TOMA-2 provides standard scores for all subtests, as well as percentiles and a Total Math Quotient that incorporates standard scores for the first four subtests. The manual includes suggestions for proper interpretation and use, as well as a list of resources for further assessment and programming of mathematical difficulties.

Technical Characteristics

Normative Sample.   The sample included 2,082 students residing in twenty-six states. The characteristics of the sample compare favorably with those of the general U.S. population. Eleven percent of the sample were students with disabilities.

Reliability.   Coefficient alpha for all subtests showed adequate internal consistency ranging from .84 (Attitude toward Math) to .97 (Math Quotient). Test-retest reliability was not as strong among subtests with coefficients ranging from .70 to .85. (Total Score yielded .92).

Validity.   Criterion-related validity was demonstrated through correlations with the SRA achievement series, Peabody Individual Achievement Test (PIAT), Wide

Range Achievement Test (WRAT), and the Key Math. Correlations were generally in the moderate range. A discussion of content validity is also presented in the manual.

Review of Relevant Research

No empirical studies on the TOMA-2 or its predecessor, the TOMA, were located. Howell (1990) in a review of the TOMA noted, "The TOMA seems more notable for what it attempts to do than for what it actually does. For example, while a major strength of the test is its innovative conceptualization of mathematics, a major weakness is the attempt to validate this conceptualization through correlations with more typical measures" (p. 216).

OVERVIEW: TEST OF MATHEMATICAL ABILITIES–2

- *Age level*—8-1/2 through 18 years
- *Type of administration*—Individual or small group (individual recommended)
- *Technical adequacy*—Adequate standardization, questionable reliability and validity
- *Scores yielded*—Standard scores, percentiles, and an overall quotient
- *Suggested use*—Properly used, the TOMA-2 can be a useful tool to diagnose mathematical abilities and disabilities, but results should be followed by additional study of mathematical abilities (such as testing, observation, interview). The scores do not provide a sufficient basis for planning instructional programs on IEPs. Individual subtests are not appropriate for certain subjects (such as nonreaders, deaf) and should be eliminated from their assessments. Further validity data are necessary before its potential use can be determined.

CRITERION-REFERENCED MATHEMATICS INSTRUMENTS

WHY USE CRITERION-REFERENCED MATHEMATICS INSTRUMENTS?

Identification of areas for further evaluation or remediation; informal determination of objectives and teaching strategies; development and evaluation of IEPs

WHO SHOULD USE THEM?

Teachers

Diagnosis: An Instructional Aid in Mathematics

Diagnosis: An Instructional Aid in Mathematics (Guzaitis, Carlin, & Juda, 1972) is designed to pinpoint strengths and weaknesses in mathematics. The instrument is also used to identify instructional objectives and appropriate instructional materials. Two levels are included: Level A (kindergarten through grade 3) and Level B (grades 3 through 6). Each level has three major components: Survey Tests, Probes, and a Prescriptive Guide.

Description

> *Survey Tests*—The survey tests serve as a screening device to determine general strengths and weaknesses in mathematical abilities. In addition, they identify specific areas that need further assessment.
>
> *Probes*—This component consists of thirty-two probes, or individual criterion-referenced tests. Each probe measures a specific area (for example, addition, division, problem solving), and each item in a probe is correlated with an instructional objective.
>
> *Prescription Guide*—This component correlates the instructional objective with appropriate sections of available mathematical curricula.

Interpretation of Results

The interpretive value of Diagnosis: An Instructional Aid in Mathematics is in the careful selection of appropriate instructional objectives and concomitant suggested curriculum materials.

OVERVIEW: DIAGNOSIS: AN INSTRUCTIONAL AID IN MATHEMATICS

- *Age level*—Kindergarten to grade 6
- *Suggested use*—Diagnosis: An Instructional Aid in Mathematics is a comprehensive diagnostic-prescriptive instrument that offers the teacher a model from screening through instruction and remediation. The survey tests serve as screening devices, the probes are a series of criterion-referenced tests, and the prescription guide offers alternative methods and materials for teaching the identified instructional objectives.

Diagnostic Test of Arithmetic Strategies

The Diagnostic Test of Arithmetic Strategies (DTAS) (Ginsberg & Mathews, 1984) is used to evaluate the types of procedures that elementary school students use when they perform arithmetic calculations in addition, subtraction, multiplication, and division. In addition to measuring computation skills, the DTAS focuses on the strategies, both successful and unsuccessful, that are used by the student in making their responses. According to the authors, the DTAS can be used to:

1. Identify specific strengths and weaknesses in the area of calculation
2. Provide appropriate instructional practices related to calculation skills
3. Document progress
4. Serve as a measure in research projects

For each of the four areas of calculation (addition, subtraction, multiplication, and division), four types of information are gathered. A description of the four areas related to addition calculation follows.

Description

Setting Up the Problem—In this section, the student is told that he or she will hear some addition problems (can be reworded to adding problems or plus problems) and is asked to write them down as neatly as possible with one number on top and the other number on the bottom. For this particular section, the student is not required to solve the problems.

Written Calculation (Number Facts)—In this section, the student is shown a series of simple one-digit addition facts, such as 3 + 2, and is told to look at the problem and provide a verbal response as quickly as possible.

Written Calculation (Calculation)—For this section, the student is shown addition problems, and is told to both solve the problems on the answer sheet and to tell the examiner out loud what they are doing. This allows the examiner to determine how the student is approaching the problem.

Informal Skills—In this section, the student is read addition problems and again is asked to both solve the problems, and to talk out loud about how he or she is solving each problem.

Interpretation of Results

A scoring sheet is available for each of the four computation areas. Figure 15.2 shows an example of the addition scoring sheet. For the first section, Setting up the Problem, a checklist measures areas such as alignment and writing the numbers and numerals correctly. For Number Facts, the checklist has space available to record any observations noted during the test administration. For Written Calculation, the checklist includes different types of errors that could possibly be made based on the type of problem administered. The section on Informal Skills allows the examiner to look specifically at the student's strategies for solving the problem. Most importantly, in the test manual the authors provide a good description and discussion of remediation techniques for use with the informal results gathered from the DTAS.

DTAS
DIAGNOSTIC TEST OF
ARITHMETIC STRATEGIES
Herbert P. Ginsburg and Steven C. Mathews

ADDITION
SCORING SHEET

Name __Debbie B. G.__   ☑ Female   ☐ Male

	Year	Month	Day
Date Tested	81	14	
Date of Birth	75	8	
Age	6	6	

School __Harley__   Grade __2__

Examiner's Name __Mr. Schneiderman__

Examiner's Title __School Psychologist__

Other Test Results

Test	Date	Standard Score Results
WISC	1-79	115

Additional Information

Very cold in testing room but child seemed well motivated

Testing Conditions	Interfering	Not Interfering
Student Motivation		✓
Distractions		✓
Noise Level		✓
Temperature	✓	

SECTION I: SETTING UP THE PROBLEM

Problems

	1	2	3	4	5	6
1. Numerals						
A. Writes at least one numeral incorrectly	✓	_	_	✓	_	_
B. Writes all numerals correctly	_	✓	✓	_	_	
2. Numbers						
C. Writes at least one number as it sounds	✓	✓	✓	✓	_	
D. Reversal or other mistake	_	_	_	_	_	
E. Writes all numbers correctly	_	_	_	_	_	
3. Alignment						
F. Aligns to left	_	✓	_	✓	_	_
G. Sloppy alignment	✓	_	✓	_	_	_
H. Other, including horizontal alignment or failure to draw line	_	_	_	_	_	_
I. Aligns correctly	_	_	_	_	_	_

SECTION II PART A: NUMBER FACTS

Problems

	1	2	3	4
Answer Correct (circle)	⓾	⑨	11	17
Answer Incorrect (write in)	_	_	10	25
Time (in seconds) or	_	_	_	_
Slow (4 seconds or over)	✓	✓	✓	_
Fast (3 seconds or less)	_	_	_	✓

NOTES: (Observed finger counting, whispering, etc.)

Debbie counted on the first three problems and made a minor error to get the wrong answer on problem 3. She answered quickly and seemed to guess on Problem 4

FIGURE 15.2   Addition Scoring Sheet

From Herbert P. Ginsburg and Steven C. Mathews, *Diagnostic Test of Arithmetic Strategies*, 1984. Copyright © 1984 by Herbert P. Ginsburg and Steven C. Mathews. Additional copies of this form available from Pro-Ed, 5341 Industrial Oaks Blvd., Austin, TX 78735.

Continued

FIGURE 15.2   *Continued*

SECTION IIB: WRITTEN CALCULATION

	Problems 5	6	7	8	9	10	11	12	13	14	15	16
1. Answer												
Correct (circle)	(39)	(27)	(46)	(72)	126	135	42	64	643	730	36	36
Incorrect (write in)	—	—	—	—	*136*	*145*	*312*	*54*	*533*	*620*	*30*	*33*
2. Standard school method	✔	✔	✔	✔	✔	✔	—	—	—	—	—	—
3. Informal method	—	—	—	—	—	—	—	—	—	—	—	—
4. Number fact error	—	—	—	—	✔	✔	—	—	—	—	—	—
5. Bugs												
A. Addition like multiplication	—	—										
B. Zero makes zero			—	—								
C. Add from left to right					—	—						
D. No carry: All digits on bottom							✔	✔	—	—		
E. No carry: Vanishing digit							—	—	✔	✔		
F. Carries wrong digit							—	—	—	—		
G. Wrong operation							—	—	—	—		
H. Add individual digits							—	—	—	—		
I. Other							—	—	—	—		
6. Slips												
A. Skips numbers	—	—	—	—	—	—	—	—	—	—	✔	
B. Adds twice	—	—	—	—	—	—	—	—	—	—	—	✔
C. Other	—	—	—	—	—	—	—	—	—	—	—	—

Notes: *Debbie started out by doing the standard school method on problems 5-8 which do not involve carrying. When carrying was introduced, she obviously did not know how to deal with it and either put all digits on the bottom or ignored the numbers to be carried. On the last two problems, she was sloppy, making two slips.*

SECTION III: INFORMAL SKILLS

	Problems 1	2	3	4
Answer Correct (circle)	(27)	(55)	(69)	(41)
Answer Incorrect (write in)				
Strategy				
A. Counting: from large number, fingers, tallies	✔	✔	—	—
Prompted	✔		—	—
B. Simplification: converting into simpler form	—	—	✔	✔
Prompted	—	—	—	—
C. Imaginary column addition	—	—	—	—
D. Other	—	—	—	—
Prompted	—	—	—	—
E. No response; didn't know; guess	✔	—	—	—

INTERPRETATIONS AND RECOMMENDATIONS

Debbie occasionally reverses numerals. She writes numbers as they sound and aligns from left to right. She also does not know how to do carrying & is sloppy. Positively, she can do column addition without carrying & her mental addition is very good: after 1 prompt she was successful on all problems. I recommend intensive individual instr., with emphasis on neatness, carrying, & use of manipulables.

OVERVIEW: DIAGNOSTIC TEST OF ARITHMETIC STRATEGIES

- *Age level*—Elementary school age
- *Suggested use*—The Diagnostic Test of Arithmetic Strategies allows the examiner to observe a student performing a variety of calculation skills using a "think aloud method." Perhaps more important than accuracy is the type of correct or incorrect strategy used to solve the computation problems that can be ultimately translated into remedial suggestions. The error analysis method used in the written computation section is helpful although not as in-depth as other instruments and procedures (for example, the Enright Inventory of Basic Arithmetic Skills). The DTAS should be used when a teacher is concerned with the type of error pattern the student is making or the type of incorrect strategy the student uses that leads to a certain type of error pattern.

Enright Diagnostic Inventory of Basic Arithmetic Skills

The Enright Diagnostic Inventory of Basic Arithmetic Skills (Enright, 1983) is designed for elementary-, middle-, and junior-high-school students who have specific problems with mathematics. The inventory consists of thirteen sections, including basic computation (adding, subtracting, multiplying, dividing) with whole numbers, fractions, and decimals, as well as conversions of fractions. Items in the inventory are based on a task analysis of each computational skill area. The inventory can be either individually or group-administered. It includes three types of tests: basic facts, wide-range placement, and skill placement.

Description

Basic Facts—This section includes two forms that each measure basic arithmetic facts in the areas of addition, subtraction, multiplication, and division.

Wide-Range Placement—This section includes two forms that each include two items from each of the thirteen computation sections. This can be administered to determine a starting place for the more in-depth skill placement test.

Skill Placement—This section includes thirteen tests, each with two forms, that measure the computation sections. A total of 144 skill sequences are included. A brief description follows.

Addition of Whole Numbers—Twelve skill sequences ranging from "two-digit numbers with sum less than ten" to "two three-digit numbers, regrouping ones and tens."

Subtraction of Whole Numbers—Fifteen sequences ranging from "one-digit number from a one-digit number" to "three-digit number from a three-digit number with zeros in the ones and tens places."

Multiplication of Whole Numbers—Eighteen sequences ranging from "two one-digit numbers" to "three-digit number with zero in the tens place by a two-digit number."

Division of Whole Numbers—Twenty-two sequences ranging from "one-digit number by a one-digit number with no remainder" to "five-digit number by a three-digit number with remainder."

Conversion of Fractions—Eight sequences ranging from "improper fraction to a whole number" to "three fractions to the lowest common denominator (LCD) with the LCD not included."

Addition of Fractions—Ten sequences ranging from "two like fractions" (in horizontal form) to "two mixed numbers."

Subtraction of Fractions—Nine sequences ranging from "fraction from a like fraction" to "mixed number from a mixed number, with regrouping (in horizontal form)."

Multiplication of Fractions—Six sequences ranging from "fraction by a like fraction" to "mixed number by a mixed number."

Division of Fractions—Six sequences ranging from "fraction by a like fraction" to "mixed number by a mixed number."

Addition of Decimals—Eleven sequences ranging from "two tenths decimals with no regrouping" to "two mixed decimals with regrouping (in horizontal form)."

Subtraction of Decimals—Eleven sequences ranging from "tenths decimal from a tenths decimal with no regrouping" to "mixed decimal from a mixed decimal, with regrouping."

Multiplication of Decimals—Six sequences ranging from "whole number times a tenths decimal" to "mixed number times a mixed number with regrouping."

Division of Decimals—Ten sequences ranging from "tenths decimal by a one-digit number with no regrouping" to "mixed number by a mixed number."

Interpretation of Results

According to the author, the Inventory of Basic Arithmetic Skills provides three types of information. First, it provides specific information on which computational skills the student has mastered. A criterion level of 80 percent (four out of five items for each of the skills) is suggested for assuming mastery. Second, each of the 144 skill areas are correlated with the grade levels in which they are taught in five separate basal mathematics series. Finally, a valuable feature is the inclusion of guidelines to perform an error analysis. The author identified 233 discrete error patterns that could be grouped together into seven error clusters: regrouping, process substitution, omission, directional, placement, attention to sign, and guessing. Figure 15.3 shows an example of some of the process-substitution error patterns.

Process substitution 76:
(Doesn't find LCD.) Copies denominator of first fraction as numerator, and copies denominator of second fraction as denominator.

$$4\tfrac{1}{4} \ \text{(first)}$$
$$+2\tfrac{3}{5} \ \text{(second)}$$
$$6\tfrac{4}{5}$$

Process substitution 77: Adds numerators, and copies larger denominator.

$$\tfrac{2}{5} \searrow 3$$
$$+\tfrac{1}{10} \ \text{(larger)}$$
$$\tfrac{3}{10}$$

Process substitution 78:
(Doesn't find LCD.) Adds numerators, and copies denominator of second fraction.

$$\tfrac{2}{5} \searrow 4$$
$$+\tfrac{2}{3} \ \text{(second)}$$
$$\tfrac{4}{3}$$

Process substitution 79:
Subtracts denominators.

$$\tfrac{3}{4} \searrow 0$$
$$-\tfrac{1}{4}$$
$$\tfrac{2}{0}$$

Process substitution 80:
Multiplies numerators, but keeps common denominator.

$$\tfrac{3}{4} \overset{\times}{\searrow} 3$$
$$-\tfrac{1}{4}$$
$$\tfrac{3}{4}$$

Process substitution 81:
Subtracts numerators and multiplies denominators.

$$\tfrac{3}{4} \searrow 2$$
$$-\tfrac{1}{2} \overset{\times}{\searrow} 8$$
$$\tfrac{2}{8}$$

Process substitution 82:
(Doesn't find LCD.) Ignores numerators, and writes difference of denominators as whole number.

$$\tfrac{③}{4}$$
$$-\tfrac{①}{2} \searrow 2$$
$$2$$

Process substitution 83:
(Doesn't find LCD.) Multiplies numerators, and subtracts denominators.

$$\tfrac{3}{4} \overset{\times}{\searrow} 3$$
$$-\tfrac{1}{2} \searrow 2$$
$$\tfrac{3}{2}$$

Process substitution 84:
(Doesn't find LCD.) Subtracts numerators, and subtracts denominators.

$$\tfrac{3}{4} \searrow 2$$
$$-\tfrac{1}{2} \searrow 2$$
$$\tfrac{2}{2}$$

Process substitution 85:
Writes product of numerator and denominator of first fraction as numerator, and writes product of numerator and denominator of second fraction as denominator.

$$\text{(first)} \quad \tfrac{3}{4} \overset{\times}{\searrow} 12$$
$$\text{(second)} \quad -\tfrac{1}{2} \overset{\times}{\searrow} 2$$
$$\tfrac{12}{2}$$

Process substitution 86:
(Doesn't find LCD. Doesn't convert mixed numbers to improper fractions.) Subtracts whole numbers, subtracts numerators, and multiplies denominators.

$$7\tfrac{1}{2} - 2\tfrac{3}{4} = 5\tfrac{2}{8}$$

Process substitution 87:
(Doesn't find LCD.) Subtracts numerators, subtracts denominators, and writes differences as whole number.

$$\tfrac{3}{9} \searrow 2$$
$$-\tfrac{1}{6} \searrow 3$$
$$23$$

FIGURE 15.3   Example of Error Patterns from the Enright® Diagnostic Inventory of Basic Arithmetic Skills

From B. Enright, ENRIGHT® *Diagnostic Inventory of Basic Arithmetic Skills.* Copyright © 1983 by Curriculum Associates, Inc. Reprinted with permission. ENRIGHT® is a registered trademark of Curriculum Associates, Inc.

OVERVIEW: ENRIGHT INVENTORY OF BASIC ARITHMETIC SKILLS

- *Age level*—Elementary to junior high
- *Suggested use*—The Enright Inventory of Basic Arithmetic Skills is a comprehensive, well-constructed instrument. The inventory includes items related to basic computation of whole numbers, fractions, and decimals. The skill areas are sequential, so that information from the test can be used to identify appropriate objectives for an IEP. The error analysis also yields information important in choosing teaching strategies. Individual progress report sheets and class record sheets are available to summarize and clarify the test data. Although the level and detail of information provided by this instrument might not be necessary for the average student, it is quite appropriate for those for whom more complete information is warranted (Smith, 1989).

Mathematics Concept Inventory

The Mathematics Concept Inventory (MCI) (Cawley, Fitzmaurice, Goodstein, Lepore, Sedlak, & Althaus, 1977) is a comprehensive assessment device that is a part of Project MATH. Also included in Project MATH is a multiple-option curriculum that contains prescriptive guides and activity books. The MCI can be used as a measure to determine appropriate objectives and subsequent teaching strategies and as a method of monitoring progress towards reaching the objectives.

Description
The MCI has four levels. Level 1 (58 items) includes content usually covered from prekindergarten through grade one. Level 2 (63 items) is appropriate for grades 1 and 2. Levels 3 (60 items) and 4 (59 items) can be used to measure concepts and skills taught in grades 2.5–4 and grades 5–6, respectively.

Interpretation of Results
Each item for each level is associated with a strand, an area, a concept, and the prescriptive guides to teach the item. Figure 15.4 shows an example of the student page and examiner page for an item from Level 3. For that item, the administration guide would also indicate the appropriate prescriptive guides and learning activities to use to develop that skill. A class record and individual progress records are also available to summarize data from the MCI.

Look at the four multiplication examples on the card. Point to the correct answer for each problem. (Learner may use scratch paper.)

312	946	321	1358	453	1259	542	3252
×3	926	×4	1284	×3	1269	×6	3052
	1036		1248		1349		3042
	936		1344		1359		3242

Answers

936	1284
No Regrouping	Regrouping 100s to 1000

1359	3252
Regrouping 10s and 100s	Regrouping All

Strand—NUMBERS
Area—MULTIPLICATION
Concept—ONE-DIGIT MULTIPLIER

FIGURE 15.4   Example from the Mathematics Concept Inventory: Project Math

From J. Cawley, A. Fitzmaurice, H. Goodstein, A. Lepore, R. Sedlak, and V. Althaus, *Mathematics Concept Inventory: Project Math.* Copyright © 1977 by Educational Development Corp., Tulsa, OK. Reprinted with permission.

OVERVIEW: MATHEMATICS CONCEPT INVENTORY

■ *Age level*—Prekindergarten to grade 6
■ *Suggested use*—The MCI is part of a comprehensive program called Project MATH. Its 240 items cover material normally taught from prekindergarten through grade 6. Each item is associated with both a general and a specific mathematics area, and also with curriculum materials appropriate for that skill. As in any test of this type, content validity is of the utmost importance.

INFORMAL ASSESSMENT

WHY USE INFORMAL ASSESSMENT?

Determination and evaluation of teaching strategies; gathering of prereferral information; development and evaluation of IEPs.

WHO SHOULD USE IT?

Teachers

The area of mathematics can be easily assessed using various informal techniques. The sequential nature of most arithmetic skills (particularly computation) allows for the use of both criterion-referenced testing (discussed in Chapter 6) and curriculum-based assessment (discussed in Chapter 7). These approaches can help determine which skills to target for teaching and remediation. Also, because the student usually creates a written product when computing or solving math problems, error analysis can offer important insight about the correct and incorrect strategies the student uses. This information can then be translated into instructional recommendations. As noted in Chapter 6, a nine-step error analysis model can be used to obtain valuable information for assessment and remediation (Enright, Gable, & Hendrickson, 1988). Those steps are:

1. Obtain samples.
2. Interview the student (i.e., "think aloud").
3. Analyze errors and identify error patterns.
4. Select primary error pattern and show the precise error to the student.
5. Demonstrate a correct computational procedure as part of the corrective feedback mechanism.
6. Select a corrective strategy.
7. Introduce appropriate practice.
8. Identify and apply normative standards.
9. Evaluate performance.

The area of mathematics also is one in which speed, as well as accuracy, is frequently a concern. For example, a teacher might be interested in increasing the speed with which a student can recognize or produce the correct answers to basic number facts (e.g., $12 - 8 = $ _____ ; $9 + 6 = $ _____). Again, criterion-referenced tests can be developed to incorporate both speed and accuracy. One interesting method for approaching this task is a computerized test called the Chronometric Analysis of Math Strategies (Hasselbring & Goin, 1985). This procedure analyzes the response latencies for a student for all the basic facts in addition, subtraction, multiplication, and division. It then selects problems for practice based on the student's performance.

Clearly, informal assessment strategies, particularly when used in combination, can provide valuable information for the teacher. Enright (1992) suggested that a student summary sheet (see Figure 15.5) be used to help guide the teacher when conducting an informal assessment. This form requires the teacher to evaluate the errors in the areas of concern and to identify the specific skills to target for remediation. King-Sears describes the use of the **APPLY** mnemonic (discussed in Chapter 7) as it relates to the assessment of math word problems. Note that this approach combines curriculum-based assessment with error analysis.

Name _____ Date _____

A. Area of Concern (circle one or two)

  I. Readiness

  II. Number Facts

  III. Whole Number Operations

  IV. Fractions

  V. Decimals

  VI. Problem Solving

B. Specific Skills to Remediate

  1.

  2.

  3.

  4.

  5.

C. Types of Errors

COMPUTATION

  1. Careless

  2. Number facts

  3. Regrouping

  4. Process substitution

  5. Directional

  6. Omission

  7. Placement

  8. Attention to sign

  9. Guessing

PROBLEM SOLVING

  1. Ignores question

  2. Uses extraneous data

  3. Leaves out facts

  4. Acts without a plan

  5. Selects wrong operation

  6. Doesn't check work

FIGURE 15.5   Student Summary Sheet for Basic Mathematics

From B. Enright, Basic Mathematics. In J. S. Choate, B. E. Enright, L. J. Miller, J. A. Poteet, and T A. Rakes, *Curriculum-Based Assessment and Programming* (3rd ed.). Copyright © 1995 by Allyn & Bacon. Reprinted by permission.

1. *Analyze the curriculum.*

Mr. Huston is a teacher of students with mild and moderate disabilities in grades 4 through 6. Because there is a range of present levels of performance in his resource room class (that is, he manages instruction for students who are working toward mastery of curriculum objectives at their respective grade *level, and each student is starting at a different point), mathematics is indi-vidualized for each student (shown in <u>underlined</u> portion of the behavioral objective). The instructional objective is: "Given a word problem that includes computations and reasoning with <u>addition and regrouping,</u> the student will earn 10 points for each problem solved according to the checklist of points earned."*

2. Prepare *items to meet the objectives.*

Mr. Huston has developed a large sampling of word problems that include computational skills appropriate for his students (whose present level of per-formance ranges from 2nd to 4th grade, although they are chronologically in grades 4 to 6). On entering the classroom, students are instructed to select the word problem on a transparency for their group and solve the problem (a timesaver to prepare in advance to both relieve the teacher of writing problems on the board each assessment session and providing a reusable set of materi-als).

3. Probe *frequently.*

Two days each week, the transparencies provide "start up" activities that stu-dents are expected to complete at the beginning of class. Mr. Huston collects the students' work at the end of 2 minutes (while he is taking attendance and conducting other class-keeping responsibilities).

Student work is scored on a 10-point scale, much like the evaluation criteria used by Montague, Bos, and Doucette (1991). The teacher's objective for each student can be individualized according to each youngster's instructional level in mathematics. One example of a behavioral objective is: "Given a word problem involving <u>fractional computations,</u> the student will write the correct answer by:

1. *Writing how they got the answer by describing the strategy they used—5 points possible,*
2. *Showing the computation itself on the paper—3 points possible, and*
3. *Writing the correct answer—2 points possible."*

A total of 10 points is possible per word problem.

Because Mr. Huston uses word problem transparencies at the beginning of class at least 2 days a week, he has the option of using other types of problems to begin class the other days of the week. He orients students to math instruc-tion by having a set task for them to complete when they enter the classroom and begins instructional periods by discussing the problems and how students solve their problems.

4. **Load** *data using a graph format.*

Students graph their performance on a 10-point scale, which represents the total number of possible points.

5. **Yield** *to results—revisions and decisions.*

Mr. Huston and his students are able to conduct error analysis of specific problem areas. For Mr. Huston, this helps him to target key reteaching areas for the class, a group within the class, or individuals. Furthermore, he may enlist support from students in the class to work with each other when reteaching is necessary. (King-Sears, 1994; pp. 106–107)

Instrument or Technique	Suggested Use — Prereferral				Suggested Use — Postreferral			Target Population						Special Considerations	Educational Relevance for Exceptional Students
	Screening and Initial Identification	Informal Determination and Evaluation of Teaching Programs and Strategies	Determination of Current Performance Level and Educational Need	Decisions about Classification and Program Placement	IEP Goals	IEP Objectives	IEP Evaluation	Mild/Moderate	Severe/Profound	Preschool	Elementary Age	Secondary Age	Adult		
Key Math–Revised	X	X	X		X			X			X			A revised version of a popular test; the format should be considered in its interpretation	adequate
Stanford Diagnostic Mathematics Test	X		X		X			X			X	X		Good technical aspects; computer scoring available	useful
Test of Mathematical Abilities-2	X	X	X		X			X			X	X		Has sections on attitude toward math and math vocabulary	adequate
Diagnosis: An Instructional Aid in Mathematics	X	X	X		X	X	X	X			X			Can be used for screening and programming; test items are correlated with instructional materials	very useful
Diagnostic Test of Arithmetic Strategies	X	X	X		X	X	X	X			X			Focuses on the correct and incorrect strategies; incorporates "think-aloud" technique	useful
Enright Diagnostic Inventory of Basic Arithmetic Skills	X	X	X		X	X	X	X			X			Used to determine specific math objectives; error analysis is recommended	very useful
Mathematics Concept Inventory	X	X	X		X	X	X	X			X			Includes curriculum materials for each of the 240 items	adequate
Informal Assessment	X	X	X					X			X	X		Includes the error analysis procedures discussed in Chapter 6	very useful

16

ASSESSMENT OF WRITTEN EXPRESSION

Instruments and Procedures Included

Written Expression and Language Tests
 Test of Written Expression
 Test of Written Language–2

Additional Instruments
 Test of Early Written Language
 Test of Written English
 Writing Process Test
 Written Language Assessment

Diagnostic Spelling Tests
 Test of Written Spelling–3
 Spellmaster Assessment and Teaching System

Informal Assessment

Ellen is a fifth-grade student who, according to her teacher, Mr. Garcia, "just doesn't like to write." Her writing samples typically included numerous problems in spelling, punctuation, and capitalization. In addition, she tends to write short passages. Mr. Garcia is concerned that when Ellen goes to middle school she will be having more trouble because of the increased writing demands. He performed an error analysis on Ellen's writing samples and found several consistent patterns in spelling and mechanics. She was also administered a criterion-referenced spelling inventory and a more formal test of written language to further pinpoint her problems in these areas.

Sarah is in the sixth grade in a private school. Her spelling ability is weak and she frequently avoids any tasks requiring her to spell. Her teacher and parents have noted that when she does spell, she does so phonetically (for example, "posishun" for "position"). Often she will spell difficult words correctly and misspell much easier words. Further diagnostic testing in spelling was recommended.

As noted in Chapter 12, the primary function of language is communication. This is true for written language as well as oral language. Clearly, the ability to express oneself in writing is a necessary skill related to school success. Although experts disagree as to the number of components of written expression, the general consensus is that there are at least five major components. Those are handwriting, spelling, mechanics, usage, and ideation (Poteet, 1992). *Handwriting* is the visible product of written expression; if handwriting is not readable then the goal of written expression, namely communication, is affected. Similarly, *spelling* is an important component of the communication process. As Poteet (1992) noted, "when reading incorrectly spelled words, our attention is diverted from the message of the communication to decoding what was written." *Mechanics* refers to the rules of language, such as capitalization, punctuation, and abbreviation, whereas *usage* refers to how the various areas of written language are chosen and combined for

TABLE 16.1   Elements of "Usage" of Written Expression

Element	Usage
Words	When words are used correctly, the writing flows smoothly and is easy to understand.
Phrases	Phrases are groups of words that belong together logically but cannot function as sentences because they do not contain a subject and predicate. The correct use and placement of phrases within sentences aid comprehension of the writing.
Clauses	Clauses have a subject and a predicate. They increase the maturity level of the writing, and they help the writer focus on the precise intent of the communication.
Sentences	A sentence is a logically related group of words containing a subject and predicate. It expresses a complete thought and can function independently of other groups of words to be understood. The sentence must be properly constructed for the writing to be clear to the reader.
Paragraphs	A paragraph is a group of related sentences, usually about one topic, often set off by an indent. Correct structure and transition between paragraphs makes the writing flow smoothly and easy to understand.

TABLE 16.2   Elements of "Ideation" in Written Expression

Element	Ideation
Fluency	An appropriate number of words must be written to clearly express the writer's intent. Otherwise, the reader is left with a sense of emptiness. However, superfluous words detract from the clarity of the writing. The number of words written varies with the type of writing, but generally it increases with the age of the writer (Poteet, 1979).
Four Levels of Writing Maturity	1. Level 1, *naming,* is characterized by the writer simply naming objects or people. A beginning narrative might be "There is a boy, a girl, a cat, a dog, and a house." 2. Level 2, *description,* simply describes something. An example might be "The boy is running. The dog is barking. It is raining." 3. Level 3, *plot,* is a good story with a beginning, middle, and end. A more sophisticated story would present a conflict, problem, or complication that is resolved (Newcomer, Barenbaum, & Nodine, 1988). 4. Level 4, *issue,* is the most mature level of writing. The main purpose is the discussion of some issue, which can be social, personal, political, or philosophical.
Word Choice	The competent writer will choose words carefully to achieve the major purpose of the writing. Trite and mundane expressions will be avoided; words that create excitement, anticipation, and awareness of physical senses and emotions will be used.
Style	Probably the most personal of all elements of written expression, style is how the writer puts it all together. Although there are guidelines for improving the overall quality of the writing, it is the personal approach taken by the writer that ultimately establishes the style. The writing must be comprehensible, well organized, and well developed. Style is the personal trademark of the writer.

From J. Poteet, Written Expression. In J. S. Choate, B. E. Enright, L. J. Miller, J. A. Poteet, and T. A. Rakes, *Curriculum-Based Assessment and Programming* (3rd ed.). Copyright © 1995 by Allyn and Bacon. Reprinted by permission.

written expressive purposes. Table 16.1 shows the elements of usage that are included in the area of written expression. *Ideation* involves the ideas related to the writer's purpose and intent. Table 16.2 shows the various elements of ideation included in written expression. These elements are manipulated based on the intent of the writer. For example, ideation would be different if a person were writing a business letter than if the person were writing a short story or a poem.

Procedures for assessing the five components of written expression include informal techniques such as the analysis of writing samples as well as the use of more formal tests that measure the various components of written language. Also available are both formal and informal diagnostic spelling tests that focus on only one component of the writing process.

WRITTEN EXPRESSION AND LANGUAGE TESTS

WHY USE TESTS OF WRITTEN EXPRESSION AND LANGUAGE?

Screening and identification; informal determination of objectives and teaching strategies; documentation of educational need; establishment of IEP goals

WHO SHOULD USE THEM?

Teachers; diagnostic specialists

Test of Written Expression

The Test of Written Expression (TOWE) (McGhee, Bryant, Larsen, & Rivera, 1995) is an individually-administered instrument that measures the six areas of ideation, semantics, syntax, spelling, capitalization, and punctuation (small-group administration is possible). The TOWE is designed for use with students from ages 6 1/2 years through 14 years, 11 months. According to the TOWE authors, the test can be used to identify students who have writing problems and to discover their writing strengths and weaknesses. It can also be used to help evaluate a student's progress and can be used by researchers who are interested in studying the area of written expression. The test includes two major sections: the *Items* section (76 items) and the *Essay* section. Some items measure more than one of the six skill areas. A list of skills and item examples follows.

Description of Items Section
(Note: Directions are presented orally)

> *Ideation (8 items)*—Mary is writing instructions on how to boil an egg. She wrote, "First you put water in a pot then you put the pot on the stove and turn on the burner." What did Mary forget to write in her directions?
>
> *Semantics (44 items)*—Write the word that completes this sentence, "The opposite of southern is _____."
>
> *Syntax (48 items)*—Write the preposition in this sentence: "The beautiful flowers flourished under the elm tree."
>
> *Capitalization (41 items)*—Write the following sentence: "The girl scout leader introduced the group's newest member, P. J. Winters." (Also score for spelling and punctuation.)
>
> *Punctuation (42 items)*—See capitalization example.
>
> *Spelling (60 items)*—See capitalization example.

Description of Essay Section
The second component of the TOWE requires the student to write an essay based on a story in which the beginning is provided. In other words, the student must

continue writing the story to its conclusion. The essay also is scored using criteria that represent the six skill areas previously noted. There is a possibility of 30 points on the essay portion.

Interpretation of Results

Raw scores are determined for both the Items section and the Essay section (the Items section uses basal and ceiling rules for ease of administration). As noted previously, a total possible score of 76 and 30 are available for those two sections, respectively. Each raw score can then be converted into a standard score (mean =100, standard deviation =15), percentile rank, and age equivalent. An overall descriptive rating for the student's performance on each section (e.g., poor, below average, average) is also available. These normative data can be displayed on a visual profile provided in the test protocol (see Figure 16.1 on page 404). Finally, an informal analysis of the Items section can be conducted through the use of forms provided that allow the plotting of the person's performance in the six skill areas. These data are presented in terms of percentage of correct responses for each skill area.

Technical Characteristics

Normative Sample.   The TOWE was standardized on 1,355 students from twenty states. The percentage of students in the sample was similar to the percentage of the school-age population (based on the 1990 census) regarding race, ethnicity, gender, geographic region, and residence (there was a slight underrepresentation of urban students and overrepresentation of rural students).

Reliability.   The average internal consistency reliability coefficients were .92 and .90 for the Items and Essay sections, respectively. The reliability tended to increase slightly as a function of age. Test-retest reliability was determined using a relatively small sample and resulted in coefficients of .73 for the Items section and .78 for the Essay section. The authors do provide a method of determining the variance attributable to only test-retest reliability after other sources of error variance have been extracted. Those adjusted coefficients are .83 for the Items and .99 for the Essay. Interscorer reliability was also determined by having two examiners score the TOWE. The resulting coefficients were .98 for the Items and .89 for the Essay.

Validity.   Criterion-related validity coefficients were computed using a number of measures of written language, including other test results and ratings of written language. The median coefficients reported were .68 for the Items section and .61 for the Essay section. The authors also provide an argument for both content and construct validity. In the latter area, data indicating age differentiation and the relationship of the TOWE to general tests of mental ability and achievement are provided.

TOWE

Test of Written Expression
PROFILE/EXAMINER RECORD FORM

Section I. Identifying Information

Name _____ Male ___ Female ___
Year Month Day
Date of Testing   ___ ___ ___
Date of Birth   ___ ___ ___
Chronological Age   ___ ___ ___
School _____ Grade _____
Examiner's Name _____
Examiner's Title _____

Section II. Record of TOWE Scores

Score	Raw Score	Std. Score	Grade Equiv.	%ile Rank	Rating
Items	___	___	___	___	___
Essay	___	___	___	___	___

Section III. Record of Other Test Scores

Test Name	Adm. Date	Score	TOWE Equiv.
1.			
2.			
3.			
4.			

Section IV. Profile of Test Scores

Std. Score	Items	Essay	1	2	3	4	Std. Score
150	•	•	•	•	•	•	150
145	•	•	•	•	•	•	145
140	•	•	•	•	•	•	140
135	•	•	•	•	•	•	135
130	•	•	•	•	•	•	130
125	•	•	•	•	•	•	125
120	•	•	•	•	•	•	120
115	•	•	•	•	•	•	115
110	•	•	•	•	•	•	110
105	•	•	•	•	•	•	105
100	•	•	•	•	•	•	100
95	•	•	•	•	•	•	95
90	•	•	•	•	•	•	90
85	•	•	•	•	•	•	85
80	•	•	•	•	•	•	80
75	•	•	•	•	•	•	75
70	•	•	•	•	•	•	70
65	•	•	•	•	•	•	65
60	•	•	•	•	•	•	60
55	•	•	•	•	•	•	55

Section V. Comments/Recommendations

FIGURE 16.1   TOWE Profile/Examiner Record Form

From R. McGhee, B. Bryant, S. Larsen, and D. Rivera, (Austin, TX: Pro-Ed, Inc., 1995). Copyright 1995 by Pro-Ed, Inc.

Review of Relevant Research
The TOWE is recently published and to date no research has appeared in the professional literature.

OVERVIEW: TEST OF WRITTEN EXPRESSION

- *Age level*—6 1/2 to 15 years
- *Type of administration*—Individual (small group possible)

- *Technical adequacy*—Good reliability, adequate standardization and validity
- *Scores yielded*—Standard scores, percentile ranks, age equivalents
- *Suggested use*—The TOWE is a welcome addition to the limited number of instruments measuring written language and written expression. The test measures the areas of ideation, semantics, syntax, spelling, capitalization, and punctuation. Research should be conducted to provide additional information regarding its validity.

Test of Written Language–2

The Test of Written Language–2 (TOWL-2) (Hammill & Larsen, 1988) was developed to identify students who have problems with written expression, to indicate strengths and weaknesses in written language skills, to document progress, and to aid in research studies related to the writing process. The TOWL-2 can be either individually or group administered and is designed to be used with students ages 7 1/2 through 18. The authors divide the area of written language into three components: conventional, linguistic, and cognitive. They also refer to two formats or methods of eliciting writing samples: contrived and spontaneous. The ten subtests on the TOWL-2 measure the various components in the authors' model (see Table 16.3). Two equivalent forms—A and B—are available.

Description
There are ten subtests on the TOWL-2. The first five are considered contrived, and the second five are considered spontaneous. Although the contrived subtests are administered before the spontaneous ones, the student first writes a story using the picture depicted in Figure 16.2 on page 406. This story is the basis for the five spontaneous subtests, which can be scored at a later time.

TABLE 16.3   Component and Format Characteristics of the TOWL-2 Subtests

	Formats	
Components	**Contrived**	**Spontaneous**
Conventional	Style	Contextual Style
	Spelling	Spontaneous Spelling
Linguistic	Sentence-Combining	Syntactic Maturity
	Vocabulary	Contextual Vocabulary
Conceptual	Logical Sentences	Thematic Maturity

From D. Hammill and S. Larsen. *Test of Written Language–2.* Copyright © 1988 by Pro-Ed, Austin, TX. Reprinted with permission.

FIGURE 16.2   Stimulus for the Spontaneous Writing Sample from the Test of Written Language–2

From D. Hammill and S. Larsen. *Test of Written Language–2*. Copyright © 1988 by Pro-Ed, Austin, TX. Reprinted with permission.

Contrived Subtests

Vocabulary (30 items)—This requires the student to write a sentence using a word (e.g., night, umbrage) supplied by the examiner.

Spelling (25 items)—This subtest is scored along with subtest 3, Style.

Style (25 items)—The student is read a series of sentences that must be written with correct spelling, punctuation, and capitalization. Performance on this subtest also results in a score for subtest 2, Spelling.

Logical Sentences (25 items)—The student is given sentences that do not make sense and is told to rewrite them so that they do. For example, "John blinked his nose" should be written as "John blinked his eye" or "John blew his nose."

Sentence Combining (25 items)—The student is given several individual sentences and must combine them to make one sentence.

Spontaneous Subtests

Thematic Maturity—The student's freely written story is scored using thirty criteria such as "Does the student write in paragraphs?" and "Is time set for the story?"

Contextual Vocabulary—The raw score for this subtest is simply the number of words in the story that contain seven or more letters.

Syntactic Maturity—The raw score for this subtest is the number of words in the story that are used grammatically correctly. Unacceptable grammar, such as problems in case, tense, or number agreement, is not scored.

Contextual Spelling—The raw score is the number of words that are spelled correctly in the story.

Contextual Style—The student's punctuation and capitalization usage is scored using thirty-four criteria.

Interpretation of Results

The TOWL-2 includes standard scores and percentile ranks for subtests and three composites: Contrived Writing (first five subtests), Spontaneous Writing (last five subtests), and Overall Written Language (all ten subtests). The standard scores for the subtests have a mean of 10 and a standard deviation of 3. The composite standard scores have a mean of 100 and a standard deviation of 15. All data are placed on a summary-and-profile sheet that presents a visual display of the scores from all ten subtests.

Technical Characteristics

Normative Sample. Approximately twenty-two hundred subjects from nineteen states were included in the sample. Race, geographic region, ethnicity, gender, and urban or rural residence were considered in the selection of subjects.

Reliability. Interscorer reliability was determined using two examiners' scoring of 20 protocols. Coefficients ranged from .91 (Logical Sentences) to .99 (Vocabulary and Spelling). Internal consistency coefficients for the subtests ranged from .74 (Sentence Combining—Form A; Contextual Style—Form B) to .96 (Contextual Spelling—Form A). Coefficients for the composites and total score were well above .90. Test-retest coefficients using the alternate forms were moderate to strong.

Validity. A discussion of the test's content and construct validity is provided in the manual. Concurrent validity coefficients with the SRA Language Arts area were low to moderate for the subtests. The coefficients for the contrived and spontaneous composites were .70 and .39, respectively, and the Overall Written Language score produced a coefficient of .62.

Review of Relevant Research

No research on the TOWL-2 was found in the literature. One study on the original TOWL (which was considerably different from the TOWL-2) by Poplin, Gray, Larsen, Banikowski, and Mehring (1980), found that students with learning disabilities score lower than students without learning disabilities on most subtests, particularly in the areas of spelling, punctuation, and word usage. In a review of the TOWL-2, Poteet (1990) noted that although the revision was a vast improvement over the original instrument, further research investigating the constructs and psychological properties of the TOWL-2 should be conducted.

OVERVIEW: TEST OF WRITTEN LANGUAGE–2

- *Age level*—7 1/2 to 18 years
- *Technical adequacy*—Adequate reliability, questionable validity
- *Scores yielded*—Standard scores and percentile ranks (subtests and composites)
- *Suggested use*—The capacity to use written language is, unfortunately, often overlooked in educational assessment. The TOWL-2 was developed to offer the special educator a measure in that area. The TOWL-2 measures several components of written language and appears to be a considerable improvement over its predecessor. The validity of this instrument, however, particularly of the spontaneous subtests, needs to be established before important decisions are based on the scores.

ADDITIONAL WRITTEN LANGUAGE INSTRUMENTS

In addition to the previously described instruments, others are available, both norm-referenced and criterion-referenced, that directly measure written expression through the use of writing samples. These are the *Test of Written English, Writing Process Test,* and the *Written Language Assessment.* Another instrument, the *Test of Early Written Language,* measures the emerging skills of young children.

Test of Early Written Language

- *Age level*—3 to 7 years
- *Type of administration*—Individual
- *Technical adequacy*—Adequate standardization and reliability, more validity data needed
- *Scores yielded*—Standard scores, percentiles

- *Suggested use*—The Test of Early Written Language (TEWL) (Hresko, 1988) focuses on the emerging written language skills of young children. It measures the areas of transcription, conventions of print, communication, creative expression, and record keeping. The test can be used with other measures to help identify students with mild disabilities. Its use with preschool-age children (ages 3 and 4) needs to be explored further. In fact, Shanklin (1989) questioned its overall validity.

Test of Written English

- *Age level*—Grades 1 to 6
- *Type of administration*—Group or individual
- *Technical adequacy*—The Test of Written English is a criterion-referenced instrument.
- *Scores yielded*—Approximate grade-level placement.
- *Suggested use*—The Test of Written English (TWE) (Andersen & Thompson, 1991) is a criterion-referenced test designed to measure four areas: Capitalization, Punctuation, Written Expression, and Paragraph Writing. The test was designed for use by teachers and diagnostic specialists. The Capitalization, Punctuation, and Usage items require the student to correct various errors made in sentences on the test form. The child or the student also is required to write a brief paragraph.

Writing Process Test

- *Age level*—Grades 2 to 12
- *Type of administration*—Individual
- *Technical adequacy*—Adequate reliability and validity
- *Scores yielded*—Standard scores, percentile ranks
- *Suggested use*—The Writing Process Test (WPT) (Warden & Hutchison, 1992) is a direct measure of writing that requires the student to plan and compose an article for a specific audience. There is an optional component that requires the student to edit and revise the original article. One unique feature is the comparison of ratings from the teacher and the student with guidelines for identifying significant discrepancies. Scores are provided for two composite areas—Development and Fluency—based on ten criteria.

Written Language Assessment

- *Age level*—8 to 18 and older
- *Type of administration*—Individual or group
- *Technical adequacy*—Adequate standardization, limited reliability (subtests), adequate reliability (total score), adequate validity
- *Scores yielded*—Standard scores

- *Suggested use*—The Written Language Assessment (WLA) (Grill & Kerwin, 1995) offers a direct measurement of written language through the use of writing samples. These writing samples are classified according to expressive, instructive, and creative writing. Scores are available in the areas of General Writing Ability, Productivity, Word Complexity, and Readability. An overall Written Language Quotient is also available that is a composite of the four subscores. One advantage of the Written Language Assessment is that it uses real writing tasks in a natural setting.

DIAGNOSTIC SPELLING TESTS

WHY USE DIAGNOSTIC SPELLING TESTS?

Identification of areas for further evaluation or remediation; informal determination of objectives and teaching strategies; development and evaluation of IEPs

WHO SHOULD USE THEM?

Teachers

Test of Written Spelling–3

The Test of Written Spelling–3 (TWS-3) (Larsen & Hammill, 1994) is an individually-administered and group-administered test designed to pinpoint a child's written spelling level and to specify the types of words with which a child is having problems. Its use as a group-administered instrument is somewhat limited, however. It is designed for use with children ages 6 to 18.

Description
The TWS-3 is comprised of one hundred spelling words divided into two categories: predictable and unpredictable. The "predictable" subtest includes fifty words; these conform to usual spelling rules and generalizations (for example, *bed, tardy, signal*). The "unpredictable" subtest also includes fifty words; these words do not follow the usual rules and, therefore, primarily have to be memorized (for example, *myself, eight, knife, enough*). Each word is said in isolation, used in a sentence, and repeated in isolation. The student spells the word on the form provided. Suggested starting points are provided and the testing is terminated after five consecutive errors in each section so that the student will not become frustrated.

Interpretation of Results
The raw scores for the predictable subtest, the unpredictable subtest, and the total (predictable and unpredictable) test can all be converted to percentile ranks and

standard scores or quotients (mean = 100; standard deviation = 15). Spelling ages and grade equivalents are also available, although the authors suggest that caution be used in their interpretation.

Technical Characteristics

Normative Sample.   The sample included 4,760 subjects from twenty-three states. Geographic location, grade, gender, residence, and social status of the sample are described in the manual. Most of the subjects were included in the standardization of previous editions of the TWS-3.

Reliability.   Internal consistency was good; coefficients ranged from .86 to .97 (predictable); from .86 to .97 (unpredictable); and from .94 to .99 (total test). Test-retest coefficients (for two studies) were also good, almost all were above .90. These studies were based on an earlier version of the TWS-3.

Validity.   Concurrent validity coefficients with the spelling subtest of the Durrell Analysis of Reading Difficulty, the WRAT-R, the California Achievement Tests, and the SRA Achievement Series are reported. Coefficients ranged from .72 to .93 (predictable), from .81 to .97 (unpredictable), and from .78 to .97 (total test). These data come from the original 1976 TWS, although the authors provide evidence that the two versions are comparable. Information related to content and construct validity of the TWS-3 is also provided.

Review of Relevant Research

No empirical studies on the TWS-3 were located. In reviews of the TWS-2, Erickson (1989) reported that it was an excellent screening instrument and Noyce (1989) noted that it was well constructed and easily administered. Based on the authors' data and statements regarding the equivalence of the two tests, research on the TWS might be considered relevant for the TWS-3.

- Subjects' scores from the TWS were more accurate in predicting their California Achievement Test language scores than their spelling, mathematics, or reading scores. The correlation coefficients between these two tests were small, however (from .20 to .38) (Carpenter & Carpenter, 1978).
- A computerized version of the TWS has been developed to decrease the examiner's time spent and the number of scoring errors (Hasselbring & Crossland, 1982).

OVERVIEW: TEST OF WRITTEN SPELLING–3

- *Age level*—6 through 18 years
- *Type of administration*—Individual (small group possible)

- *Technical adequacy*—Good standardization and reliability; adequate validity, although more data needed.
- *Scores yielded*—Standard scores (quotients), percentiles, age and grade equivalents
- *Suggested use*—Although the TWS-3 yields normative data, its real value lies in the informal use of the word lists. The idea of having predictable and unpredictable word lists is a good one. The reliability of the newest version has improved over the earlier version, however, which makes the normative use more appropriate. No matter how the results are used, an error analysis should also be conducted to provide additional information.

The Spellmaster Assessment and Teaching System

The Spellmaster (Greenbaum, 1987) is a criterion-referenced assessment instrument consisting of three sets of tests: Diagnostic, Irregular Word, and Homonym. The Spellmaster was field-tested on more than twenty-five hundred students and is designed for use with pupils in kindergarten through grade 8, although it can be used through adult age. The Spellmaster was developed to assist in the identification of strengths and weaknesses in spelling. It is also useful in grouping students according to their spelling needs. There are three sets of tests at eight levels that include specific types of spelling words. There are also entry-level tests that can be used to determine the most appropriate level of test to use for a particular student.

Description

Diagnostic (8 tests)—These tests include regular words, that is, words that use rules that generalize to the spelling of the majority of the words in the English language.

Irregular Words (8 tests)—These tests include words whose spelling violates basic phonics rules, thus requiring a person to master or memorize each rule and not rely on generalization.

Homonym (8 tests)—The spelling of the words on these tests can be either regular or irregular, but the correct spelling has to do with its meaning.

Interpretation of Results

Results of the Spellmaster can be used to identify strengths and weaknesses in spelling and can be used to group students according to their spelling needs (see Figure 16.3). The Spellmaster's value is in its ability to pinpoint specific types of errors. Techniques and activities are described that can be used to remediate the spelling problems identified. The name of the instrument reflects its pragmatic approach to testing and teaching spelling.

SPELLMASTER — CLASS DATA CHART — LEVEL 5

Teacher: **J. Ross**
Grade: **6**
School: **Franks**
City: **Newton**

REGULAR WORD TEST — List students in order of number of words spelled correctly.

Elements tested at this level and number of times each element is tested.

#	Student	Total Words	en	a	in	ĕa	_oy	u_e	y	al	le	tion	mis	pre	ex	ew	ōo	et	ic	ive	Additions	Omissions	Lower Level Errors
	(number tested)	40	3	3	3	3	3	3	3	3	3	3	3	3	3	3	3	3	3	3			
1	Irving G.	40																					
2	Philip C.	39																				1	
3	Sara N.	39				1																	
4	Helen B.	37													2								
5	Bruce M.	36					1	1	1						1								
6	Aaron N.	36		1	1	1																1	
7	Mary F.	35	1	1					1	1				1									
8	Joshua C.	34				1	2							1	1								1
9	Michael G.	33	1	1		1			1	1				1									1
10	Ruth J.	33	1			1	1		1				2			1							
11	Natalie F.	32		1			1					1	1	2	2							1	1
12	Rebecca C.	32	1			1				1				1		2							2
13	Benjamin C.	31				1	1							2	2	1	1		1				1
14	Paul R.	30				1	1						1	1	3	2	1						2
15	Charlene B.	30	1			1							1	3							2	2	1
16	Lisa T.	29		1	2				1	1			1	1							2	2	1
17	Emmanuel R.	28					1						1	2	2						3	1	3
18	Anne S.	28		1		1			3				1		2						2	1	2
19	Jamie L.	28	1				1				2		1	2	1						2	1	2
20	Annette F.	28				2	1						1	1	1	1					2		4
21	Abraham G.	26				2	1		1	1	2		1		3	1	1	1					3
22	Becky L.	24				2	1	2			1		2		2	2						2	3
23	Rhoda A.	24	1			1	2	1	2	1	1	1	2	1		2							2
24	David A.	24				1			1	1			1	2	1	2					2	3	3
25	Stanley S.	23		1	1	2	1		1	1			1	2	2	1	1	1	1	1			1
26	Marion W.	19		2		2			1	2	1	2		1	2	3		1	1		2	2	3
27	Joyce B.	17	2	1	1	1	1	1		1	2	2		1	3	1	1				2	2	3
28	Toni G.	15	1		2	2	1	2	2	1	1		1		2	3	2	2	1		2	3	5
29	Samuel B.	10	1		2	2	1	1		1	2	2	1	3	3	3	2	2			3	2	7
30	Susan W.	8	2	1	1	2	1	1	2	2	2	3	1	1	3	1		1	1	3	1	3	11

FIGURE 16.3   Sample Class Data Chart

From C. Greenbaum, *Spellmaster Assessment and Teaching System*. (Austin, TX: Pro-Ed, Inc., 1987).
Copyright © 1987 by C. Greenbaum.

OVERVIEW: SPELLMASTER ASSESSMENT AND TEACHING SYSTEM

■ *Age level*—Kindergarten to grade 8
■ *Suggested use*—The Spellmaster offers a series of word lists to assist a teacher in determining the type of words a student is having difficulty spelling. Care should be taken to analyze the types of errors made and not simply to group students according to spelling ability. The information related to teaching the identified spelling problems is valuable. Harrison (1990a) noted that although the Spellmaster may be useful in some classrooms, there is no evidence that the tests adequately sample spelling skills needed in schools. Wiese (1990) noted that the tests lacked technical adequacy.

INFORMAL ASSESSMENT

WHY USE INFORMAL ASSESSMENT?

Screening and identification of language problems; informal determination of objectives and teaching strategies; analysis of spontaneous use of language

WHO SHOULD USE IT?

Teachers, speech and language clinicians

Just as important as the evaluation of oral language in the natural setting is the evaluation of written language using the student's actual work products. According to Rousseau (1990), the analysis of written products should focus on the following types of errors: careless, excessive usage, verbs, nouns, pronouns, punctuation, capitalization, and paragraphs. Much of the analysis should focus on the *T-unit*, which is defined as "an independent clause including any dependent clauses attached to or embedded in it" (Rousseau, 1990, p. 94). For example, "The batter hit the baseball and the third baseman tried to catch it" is considered two T-units. Figure 16.4 provides an example of scoring procedures based on the eight previously mentioned error types.

Other areas of written language have also been recommended for error analysis. Isaacson (1988) suggested that fluency (number of words written), content (e.g., coherence and organization), convention (including spelling and handwriting), syntax, and vocabulary should be evaluated. Salvia and Hughes (1990) suggested that the two major areas of *content* and *style* be evaluated. They noted that the most common errors related to content are incomplete learning or poor proofreading skills. In the area of style, errors might be located in grammar, mechanics

Enter the name of the *Student, Age* (years and months), *Grade,* and the *Date* the student wrote the sample.

Writing Time: Record the total number of minutes allowed for writing, and the actual number of minutes the student wrote.

Picture # of Topic #: List the picture or topic number used for the writing stimulus.

1. *Total Words:* Draw a line through the title, sound effects, and end markers such as "The End." Count the total words written. Exclude words marked out.
2. *Garbled Words:* Circle garbled words. Enter the total in the space provided.
3. *Readable Words:* Subtract the number of garbled words from the total words and enter in the space provided.
4. *T-Unit:* Mark the end of each T-unit with a slash mark (/) and number the T-unit. Enter the number of T-units.
5. *Average Number of Words per T-Unit:* Divide the total readable words by the number of T-units. Round off to the nearest hundredth.
6. *Scorer:* Sign your name.

Note: FOR ALL ERROR TYPES BEGINNING WITH *OMITTED* WORDS THROUGH *INAPPROPRIATE CAPITALS* COUNT THE TOTAL ERRORS AND DIVIDE BY THE TOTAL T-UNITS TO FIND THE NUMBER PER T-UNIT.

1. *Careless Errors:*
   Omitted Words: Write omitted words in pencil above the appropriate space. Write only words that are obvious (such as *and, he, the*) and that do not change the meaning of the T-unit.
   Substituted Words: Write *sub* above substituted words.

2. *Excessive Usage:*
   Beginning of T-Unit: Count the number of T-units that begin with conjunctions.
   Within T-Unit: Underline each use of conjunctions if they appear more than once for coordination within the T-unit. Do not count conjunctions at the beginning of the T-unit in this count.

3. *Verbs:*
   Inflections: Write in the correct verb ending.
   Subject-Verb Agreement: Write *s-v* above the verb for every subject-verb errors.
   Verb Tense Changes: Place a check mark (✓) at the end of each T-unit in which the verb tense is different from the verb tense in the previous T-unit. If there are tense changes within a T-unit, place a check mark in the margin for each change. An exception is if the verb tense change occurs with a change from narrative to direct quotation.

4. *Nouns:*
   Number: Underline nouns that show incorrect form for number.
   Possession: Write *NP* above the error.

5. *Pronouns:* Write the correct pronoun above each incorrect use.

6. *Punctuation:*
   End: Write in the correct form for the omitted or incorrect punctuation and circle it.
   Within T-Units: Using a red pencil, write in the correct form for the omitted or incorrect punctuation.

7. *Capitalization:*
   Beginning: Write correct uppercase letters over lowercase letters used at the beginning of T-units.
   Proper Nouns: Write correct uppercase letters over lowercase letters used for proper nouns.
   Inappropriate: Draw an X through the incorrectly capitalized letter.

8. *Paragraphs:*
   Extraneous T-Units: Underline extraneous T-units.
   New Line for Each T-Unit: Circle *Yes* or *No.*

Summary: Count the number of each type of error and enter in the appropriate row under "# per T-unit" on the Error Analysis Form. Divide the number of each error type by the number of T-units, and enter the result in the space provided.

FIGURE 16.4   Error Analysis Scoring Instructions

From: Robert A. Gable and Jo M. Hendrickson, *Assessing Students with Special Needs: A Sourcebook for Analyzing and Correcting Errors in Academics.* Copyright © 1990 by Longman Publishing Group. Reprinted with permission.

(e.g., punctuation and capitalization), diction (word usage), and diversity (e.g., use of grammatical transformations). Identification of errors in these areas can be used to provide feedback about the incorrect aspects of the student's writing (student product) as well as the appropriate aspects (teacher model).

It is possible that the informal assessment of written expression could also directly address the five components of handwriting, spelling, mechanics, usage, and ideation. Figure 16.5 provides a checklist for evaluating the areas of ideation that were noted in Table 16.2. Spelling is a frequently analyzed component. Luts (1991) attempted to determine the most common errors in written expression made by a group of second-grade students. She found that spelling was the most common error, followed by capitalization, punctuation, grammar, and context errors. It is important, therefore, to remember the five-step process discussed in Chapter 6 regarding error analysis for spelling. Those steps are (1) obtain a sample, (2) interview the student, (3) analyze and classify the errors, (4) select a corrective strategy, and (5) implement the strategy and evaluate its impact. (See Chapter 6 for a more detailed description of these steps). Spelling can also be subjected to more sophisticated types of error analysis. For example, Hasselbring (1984) developed the *Computerized Test of Spelling Errors*. Using this approach, a teacher types in the student's spelling of forty preselected words, and the computer program analyzes the errors and generates a report.

Student's Name _____

Check the type of writing that is being evaluated:

____Friendly letter   ____Narrative   ____Expository   ____Descriptive   ____Story

____Report   ____Review   ____Essay   ____Business letter   ____Poem   ____Other

A.   **FLUENCY**—Are enough words and sentences written to:

    1.   *adequately* convey the writer's ideas and purpose?   ____YES____SOMEWHAT____NO

    2.   *appropriately* represent fluency for:

      (a)   an average, nondisabled student of the writer's same age in the regular curriculum?

                                            ____YES____SOMEWHAT____NO

      (b)   the writer?   ____YES____SOMEWHAT____NO

        (Number of words written   ____)

        (Number of sentences written   ____)

B.   **LEVEL OF MATURITY**—(Check only if writing is a narrative)

    ____Level I—Naming   ____Level II—Description

    ____Level III—Plot   ____Level IV—Issue

    Is the level appropriate for age/grade placement?   ____YES____SOMEWHAT____NO

C.   **WORD CHOICE**—Are specific words expressly chosen to achieve the writer's *purpose* for a specific *audience*, on a specific *occasion*?   ____YES____SOMEWHAT____NO

D.   **STYLE**—

    1.   *Organization:* Is the writing well organized with a clear beginning, middle, and end?

                                         ____YES____SOMEWHAT____NO

    2.   *Development:* Are the *main idea* and *purpose* clear, accurate, and complete?

                                         ____YES____SOMEWHAT____NO

      Is the *sequence* logical and orderly?   ____YES____SOMEWHAT____NO

      Is the composition *cohesive* (no superfluous ideas and no errors in logic)?

                                         ____YES____SOMEWHAT____NO

      Are sufficient *details* (examples, proofs, reasons) and *supplementary ideas* used to support or develop the main idea or purpose?   ____YES____SOMEWHAT____NO

    3.   *Comprehensibility:*

      Is the composition easily understood (no shift in tense, person, number, or point of view; no split infinitives; clear pronoun reference; proper location of modifiers, prepositional phrases, adjective clauses)?   ____YES____SOMEWHAT____NO

E.   **OVERALL IMPRESSION**

    Is the overall impression favorable (effective, interesting, creative)?   ____YES____SOMEWHAT____NO

Check any area below that requires remedial attention:

____Spelling   ____Handwriting   ____Capitalization   ____Punctuation

____Abbreviations   ____Numbers   ____Other (specify)

NOTES:

FIGURE 16.5   IDEATION Evaluation Questions

From J. Poteet, Written Expression. In J. S. Choate, B. E. Enright, L. J. Miller, J. A. Poteet, and T. A. Rakes, *Curriculum-Based Assessment and Programming* (3rd ed.). Copyright © 1995 by Allyn and Bacon. Reprinted by permission.

Instrument or Technique	Prereferral — Screening and Initial Identification	Prereferral — Informal Determination and Evaluation of Teaching Programs and Strategies	Prereferral — Determination of Current Performance Level and Educational Need	Postreferral — Decisions about Classification and Program Placement	Postreferral — IEP Goals	Postreferral — IEP Objectives	Postreferral — IEP Evaluation	Mild/Moderate	Severe/Profound	Preschool	Elementary Age	Secondary Age	Adult	Special Considerations	Educational Relevance for Exceptional Students
Test of Written Expression	X	X	X		X			X				X		Measures six areas of written expression, includes an essay section	useful
Test of Written Language–2	X	X	X		X			X				X		Measures an important and often overlooked area; technical aspects are somewhat limited	useful
Test of Early Written Language	X	X	X		X			X		X	X			Measures emerging writing skills; limited usefulness with very young children	adequate
Test of Written English		X	X		X			X			X			A criterion-referenced test that measures four areas	adequate
Writing Process Test		X	X		X			X			X	X		Student writes and then edits and revises an article	useful
Written Language Assessment		X	X		X			X			X	X		Uses writing samples to measure skill areas	adequate/useful
Test of Written Spelling–3	X	X	X		X			X			X			One of the few tests that yields normative information in spelling	useful
Spellmaster	X	X	X		X			X			X			Information from error analysis is most valuable	useful
Written Language Sampling	X	X	X		X			X			X	X	X	Helpful and easy to do because of availability of written products	very useful

Part V

SPECIAL ASSESSMENT
CONSIDERATIONS

This section will address assessment concerns related to two populations. These are *early childhood assessment* and *transitional/vocational assessment*. These areas have become increasingly important because of legislation that has mandated educational services for infants and toddlers (Public Law 99-457) and transitional services for secondary students (P.L. 101-456). The Carl D. Perkins Act also brought increased attention to vocational services for students with disabilities.

In addition to a description of a variety of instruments (formal and informal) used with these populations, discussions will also center on the type of assessment process (e.g., team assessment) and alternative procedures (e.g., play assessment, analysis of work samples) that should be considered. The format for describing instruments will be similar to the chapters in Parts III and IV. That includes the following:

1. A summary matrix presents information about specific instruments and techniques in a format that allows easy comparison of the instruments for suggested use and target population. The matrix also includes a statement of any special considerations of which a user should be aware. In addition, for each instrument, the matrix gives the educational relevance for exceptional students. The matrices are directly related to the assessment model proposed in Chapter 2.
2. A thorough review of relevant research for each norm-referenced instrument emphasizes use of the test with exceptional students.
3. An overview box for each test summarizes the age range, technical adequacy (for norm-referenced tests), and suggested use for each instrument.

AFTER READING PART V YOU SHOULD BE ABLE TO:

- Identify the reasons for needing team assessment for young children.
- Identify the importance of using play assessment for young children.
- Identify the strengths and weaknesses of a variety of screening and developmental tests.
- Identify the importance of developing transitional programs for secondary students.
- Identify the need for analyzing work samples and "on the job" assessment.
- Identify the strengths and weaknesses of a variety of vocational interest and aptitude measures.

17

EARLY CHILDHOOD ASSESSMENT

Instruments and Procedures Included

Team Assessment: A Collaborative Effort
    Natural Assessment Model
    System to Plan Early Childhood Services
Play Assessment
Screening Instruments
    AGS Early Screening Profiles
    Denver II
    Developmental Indicators for the Assessment of Learning–Revised
    Miller Assessment for Preschoolers
Developmental Tests (Norm-Referenced)
    Battelle Developmental Inventory
    Developmental Profile–II
Readiness and Preacademic Instruments
    Boehm Test of Basic Concepts–Revised
    Bracken Basic Concept Scale
Developmental Tests (Criterion-Referenced)
    Assessment Log and Developmental Progress Chart
    Behavioral Characteristics Progression
    Brigance Inventory of Early Development–Revised
    Callier–Azusa Scale
    Vulpé Assessment Battery

Additional Tests

First Grade Screening Test

Gesell School Readiness Test

Metropolitan Readiness Tests

Test of Early Reading Ability–2

Test of Early Mathematics Ability–2

Interest in the area of early childhood assessment has been increasing. This popularity is partly due to legislation that has provided increased awareness of, and has mandated increased responsibility for, the educational needs of children from birth to five years old. For example, Public Law 98-199 (the Education of the Handicapped Amendment Act of 1983) targets the expansion and improvement of services to preschool handicapped children as one of its primary initiatives. P.L. 99-457 (discussed in Chapter 1) outlines specific responsibilities for the identification and appropriate educational programming for children from birth.

It is important that young children be evaluated by a team approach. Frequently, for example, infants who have disabilities or suspected of having a disability will have medical problems that require evaluation from appropriate medical personnel. Others who might be involved are parents, psychologists, speech-language pathologists, audiologists, and physical and occupational therapists. It is important that these professionals, in conjunction with the teacher, work together to coordinate assessment results into the most viable overall educational plan. Older preschool children might be evaluated for many purposes, including screening and eligibility decisions when a less severe problem is suspected. Consequently, optimal communication is paramount among the various team members so that appropriate decisions can be made. Again, the teacher should be an active member of that team. Given the multidisciplinary nature of the assessment procedures used with young children, the instruments and techniques discussed in this chapter will focus on those used by teachers and other educational personnel.

The instruments used (norm-referenced and criterion-referenced) for infants and toddlers can be primarily considered *developmental*. Those for preschool children can be considered *developmental* (both norm-referenced and criterion-referenced), *screening*, or *preacademic*. It should be noted that many tests used in early childhood extend the entire preschool age range (usually birth to age 6 or 7).

Specific guidelines should be followed when preschool children are evaluated (Florida Department of Education, 1989). First, the rapid developmental changes that occur during the preschool years make reevaluations and continuous monitoring extremely important. Second, it is necessary to address environmental variables that have a significant influence on young children and to evaluate the home environment.

Other guidelines relate to the testing session itself. First, it should be structured in a way that allows for optimal response from the child. Subsequently, issues such as length of testing, establishing rapport, nature of instructions, and type of directions must be given extra consideration. Also, if possible, the child should not be subjected to multiple testing sessions with a number of different examiners. This may require that more than one person see the child at the same time. Finally, it might be advantageous to make the testing sessions more playlike to sustain the child's attention. In fact, it is important to observe play behavior as part of the evaluation process.

In response to the important issue of evaluating preschool children, the National Association for the Education of Young Children presented a position paper in 1988. Those points are summarized below.

1. Standardized tests used in early childhood programs must be reliable and valid.
2. Decisions that have a major impact on young children should be based on multiple scores and should never be based on any single test score. (This includes other sources of information, such as systematic observation, samples of child's work, and family information.)
3. Standardized tests should only be used for the purposes for which they are intended.
4. Test results should be interpreted cautiously and accurately to parents.
5. Tests should be chosen that match the theory, philosophy, and objectives of the available educational program.
6. Testing should be conducted by someone who is sensitive to the developmental needs of young children.
7. Testing must be sensitive to individual diversity.

Although these suggestions should be considered best practice for *all* individuals, it emphasizes the importance of carefully planning and conducting an evaluation with young children.

In this chapter, the first area to be discussed will be general assessment procedures, including those areas such as team assessment models, the assessment of play behavior, and the assessment of social behavior and interactions of young children. As noted previously, these areas are extremely important to evaluate at some point during the assessment process when working with young preschool children.

Next, the specific area of developmental screening will be discussed. Developmental screening tests provide a brief assessment of a child's abilities that are highly associated with future school success. These tests are usually administered to identify children that may need early intervention or special education services. Because of the nature of the decision being made, the issue of predictive validity is important because those decisions related to a child's future performance are made on the basis of the test results. Most developmental screening tests are quick and easy to administer and include typical developmental skills such as gross motor, fine motor, language, and conceptual skills. It should be noted that two possible erroneous outcomes can result from using developmental screening tests. These are (1) identifying as high risk a child who does not have a problem; and (2) identifying as low risk a child who does have a problem. The first type of error can lead to a waste of time and money and might result in undue anxiety for the parents and the child. The second type of error results in the lack or postponement of a necessary prevention or remediation program.

The third area that will be discussed is that of norm-referenced developmental testing. Specifically, the Battelle Developmental Inventory and the Developmental Profile II will be presented. The next area to be described is that of preacademic and readiness testing. These tests include items specifically designed to measure skills that students need to perform adequately in the early school years. Obviously, the content of many of these instruments will overlap with developmental screening tests, particularly regarding perceptual and fine motor skills that are normally developing in the preschool years. Preacademic and readiness tests, however, are more concerned with curriculum-related skills that a child has already acquired and are prerequisite for specific instructional programs (Meisels, 1987).

The last area to be discussed will be testing for educational programming. The available tools are primarily criterion-referenced inventories that have been developed specifically for the preschool age range. These instruments provide detailed skill sequences in a variety of developmental areas. It is important that those using these instruments focus only on those areas in which educational programming is necessary. In other words, the entire instrument is not administered; rather, based on data gathered from the home environment, observation, and formal test results, the appropriate curriculum areas are identified and subsequently evaluated.

It should also be noted that many of the instruments and techniques discussed in other chapters in this book are also applicable to young children. Such areas as observation, criterion-referenced testing, and curriculum-based assessment have direct relevance. Similarly, young children are represented in the standardization sample in many norm-referenced tests, making it possible to obtain scores that can be applied to that age group. Examples of this are the Kaufman-Assessment Battery for Children, the Scales of Independent Behavior, and the Differential Ability Scales. Still other instruments include a separate preschool version (usually a downward extension). Examples are the Test of Language Development–Primary and the Detroit Tests of Language Aptitude–Primary. Several assessment devices, however, are designed specifically for use with infants, toddlers, and preschool children.

TEAM ASSESSMENT: A COLLABORATIVE EFFORT

As noted previously, the evaluation of preschool children involves a number of professionals. It is extremely important that these individuals work as a team, communicating with each other to streamline the evaluation and to coordinate decision making. In some situations the child might be evaluated by an entire team, whereas in other situations the child might be evaluated by individual members although team decisions will be made. An example of each of these approaches, the Natural Assessment Model and the System to Plan Early Childhood Services, is discussed next.

Natural Assessment Model

The Natural Assessment Model was developed and implemented in the Schaumburg, Illinois, school district. In this model, the evaluation team is composed of members from different disciplines who observe the child's performance in a variety of developmental domains. Each team member receives training in the areas of intellectual, language, social-emotional, and motor development. The assessment is carried out in a play setting and involves interaction with peers, thus focusing on the child's natural interaction with the environment. Four or five children are observed simultaneously by the evaluation team for one hour. At the same time, the parent is interviewed and histories are obtained. The observation room is supplied with a variety of toys and large motor equipment.

Each team member completes a developmental checklist called the "Mini-wheel of Developmental Milestones." The areas on the Mini-wheel are primarily based on Piaget's work and measure the four major areas of intellectual, language, motor, and social-emotional development. Each area is further broken down into twelve specific skills that have accompanying definitions. The team is trained in each of the areas. Other notes are also taken by the team members related to the child's quality of performance. Ongoing communication between team members ensures that each area on the wheel is being evaluated for each child. The usual team members and their respective roles are noted below.

Speech-language pathologist—Interacts with the child and records a spontaneous language sample, observes phonological processing, and is primarily responsible for language scores on the Mini-wheel.

Preschool teacher—Observes the child's interactions, problem-solving abilities, and drawing/fine-motor ability and is primarily responsible for the social, emotional, and motor scores on the Mini-wheel.

Psychologist—Assists in determining the intellectual score on the Mini-wheel and meets with the parents, acting as the school district liaison.

Teacher assistant—Collects information from the parent and engages in motor activities with the child.

Social worker—Meets with the parents to explain the Mini-wheel and the evaluation procedures, interviews them, and obtains developmental histories.

Nurse—Conducts initial screening for vision and hearing prior to the evaluation.

After the evaluation there is a twenty- to thirty-minute meeting for the team and parents to gather and share information. Each team member relates his or her observations and ratings on the Mini-wheel, and a consensus on the child's performance is reached.

System to Plan Early Childhood Services

Another approach to team assessment uses the System to Plan Early Childhood Services (SPECS; Bagnato & Neisworth, 1990). SPECS was developed to provide a mechanism for multiple professionals to communicate results from assessment and other sources of information. There are three sections or components of SPECS: Developmental, Team, and Program. *Developmental SPECS* provides the opportunity for parents, teachers, psychologists, therapists, and other professionals to convert a variety of assessment information into mutually understood ratings regarding the child's development and educational status in nineteen areas. *Team SPECS* allows the team to compare ratings and arrive at a consensus regarding the child's level of functioning across the nineteen important areas. The nineteen areas can be clustered into developmental dimensions. Those are communication, sensorimotor, physical, self-regulation, cognition, and self/social. *Program SPECS* includes more than forty items to consider when planning a child's educational program. Each of these items is accompanied by a set of service options so that a program plan is generated. The amount of intensity required for specific services is also indicated when Program SPECS is completed. In other words, by completing all other components of SPECS, a team will have consensus on child assessment, a blueprint for the child's service plan, and an idea of the extent or intensity of needed services.

The advantage of using a system such as SPECS is that it allows each individual on the team to gather data using their preferred instruments and techniques and provides a common ground for discussing and agreeing upon the meaningfulness of those data. Figure 17.1 shows the steps that are followed in using SPECS.

PLAY ASSESSMENT

The area of play assessment is extremely important when considering the overall developmental status of young children. Although many states require the use of

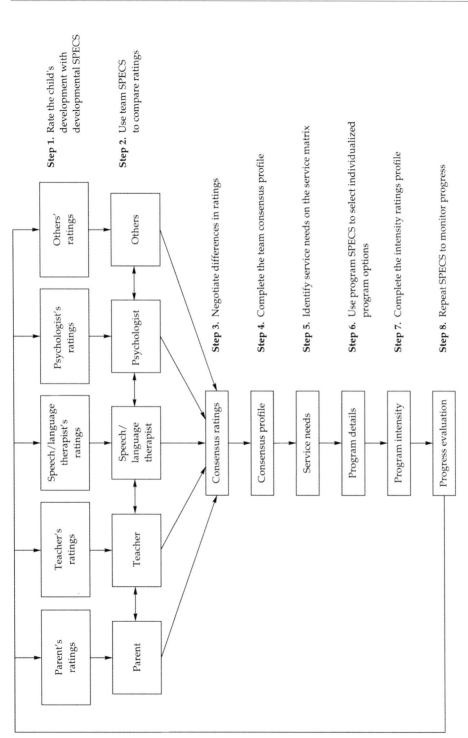

Step 1. Rate the child's development with developmental SPECS

Step 2. Use team SPECS to compare ratings

Step 3. Negotiate differences in ratings

Step 4. Complete the team consensus profile

Step 5. Identify service needs on the service matrix

Step 6. Use program SPECS to select individualized program options

Step 7. Complete the intensity ratings profile

Step 8. Repeat SPECS to monitor progress

FIGURE 17.1   Steps to Follow in Using the SPECS System

From S. Bagnato and J. Neisworth, *System to Plan Early Childhood Services.* Copyright © 1991 American Guidance Service. Reprinted with permission.

standardized tests (particularly for eligibility decisions), play assessment should be incorporated into any evaluation. Linder (1989) in her book, *Transdisciplinary Play Assessment,* provides a comprehensive and meaningful discussion of the informal and formal guidelines to follow when conducting a play assessment. For example, Linder suggests the following sequence of activities (although she notes that flexibility is a key to a successful assessment):

> *Phase I—Unstructured Facilitation:* This twenty- to twenty-five-minute period allows the child to take the lead and to choose his or her own activities.
>
> *Phase II—Structured Facilitation:* This ten- to fifteen-minute period allows the evaluator to observe such skills as puzzle making, drawing, or other areas not exhibited during the unstructured situation.
>
> *Phase III—Child–Child Interaction:* In this five- to ten-minute period two children are allowed to play in an unstructured situation. If no interaction occurs, more structure (e.g., toys, prompts) are added.
>
> *Phase IV—Parent–Child Interaction:* In this phase the parent interacts with the child for five minutes in an unstructured situation. At that point, the parent is asked to leave, and the child's reaction to the separation is observed. Finally, the parent is brought back for another five minutes in a more structured situation.
>
> *Phase V—Motor Play:* This involves a ten- to twenty-minute session of both structured and unstructured play.
>
> *Phase VI—Snack:* This final phase allows for additional observation of social interaction, self-help skills, adaptive behavior, as well as motor skills.

Linder also provides observational guidelines as well as checklists for the areas of cognitive development, social-emotional development, communication and language development, and sensorimotor development. Interested readers are encouraged to consult her book for more detailed information regarding this area.

Some specific play assessment instruments might also be used by the practitioner. These include the *Play Observation Scale* (Rogers, 1986), which allows for the assessment of sensorimotor and symbolic stages of play and includes items related to social communication, and the *Symbolic Play Checklist* (Westby, 1980), which describes a ten-step hierarchy that focuses on language, cognitive, and social aspects of play. Other examples are the *Play Assessment Checklist for Infants* (Bromwich, Fust, Khokha, and Walden, 1981), which also uses observation during free play, and *A Manual for Analyzing Free Play* (McCune-Nicholich, 1980), which provides an organized format for analyzing play using Piaget's theories. In many of these observational instruments, a specified toy set is used to structure the free play.

Other instruments are designed to evaluate the more specific area of social behaviors and interactions of young children. Table 17.1 provides a brief description of several of these instruments that are based on direct observation.

TABLE 17.1   Assessment of Social Behavior and Interaction of Young Children with Disabilities through Direct Observation

Instruments	Age Range	Behaviors Assessed	Description
Systematic Anecdotal Assessment of Social Interaction (Odom, McConnell, Kohler & Strain, 1987)	Open	Behaviors generated by the teacher	A structured anecdotal recording system for collecting social interaction information
Social Interaction Scan (Odom et al., 1988)	Preschool	Isolate/unoccupied Proximity Interactive Negative Teacher Interaction	A system for scanning classrooms of children. Designed to measure both interactive play and social integration
Observation Assessment of Reciprocal Social Interaction (McConnell, Sisson, & Sandler, 1984)	Preschool	Initiations (five behaviors listed) Response (four behaviors listed) Summative (four behaviors listed) Teacher behavior (two behaviors listed)	An interval sampling system designed to measure components and durations of social interaction of peers
Scale of Social Participation (Parten, 1932)	Preschool	Unoccupied Onlooker Solitary Parallel Associative Cooperative	An interval sampling system designed to measure young children's participation in social interaction
Parten/Smilansky Combined Scale (Rubin, 1983)	Preschool	Unoccupied Onlooker Solitary Parallel Associative Cooperative Functional Constructive Dramatic Games with rules	An interval sampling system designed to measure cognitive play within a social context
Guralnick & Groom (1987)	Preschool	Gains peer attention Uses peer as resource Leads peer in activity-positive Leads peer in activity-negative Imitates peer Expresses affection to peer Expresses hostility to peer Competes for adult attention Competes for equipment Shows pride in product Follows peer's activity without specific direction	Event recording system for measuring peer interactions
Odom, Silver, Sandler, & Strain (1983); Strain (1983); Tremblay, Strain, Hendrickson, & Shores 1980)	Preschool	Play organizer Share request Share Assistance Assistance request Affection Complimentary Negative Motor Gestural Negative Vocal Verbal	Event recording system for measuring peer social interactions

From D. Bailey and M. Wolery, *Assessing Infants and Preschoolers with Handicaps.* Copyright © 1989 Merrill Publishing Co. Reprinted with permission.

SCREENING INSTRUMENTS

WHY USE SCREENING INSTRUMENTS?

Screening

WHO SHOULD USE THEM?

Teachers, social workers, school psychologists, parent participation (often a team approach)

AGS Early Screening Profiles

The AGS Early Screening Profiles (ESP) (Harrison, 1991) is designed for use with children ages 2 through 6. Its primary purpose is to aid in the identification of those children with possible disabilities or, conversely, those who might be potentially gifted. The ESP uses an ecological approach to screening whereby numerous areas are measured and several individuals are involved in the assessment process. The child and the parent and teacher are evaluated in the ESP. The evaluation time for children ranges from fifteen to thirty minutes, while the parent and teacher questionnaires can be completed in approximately fifteen minutes. The seven sections included (Figure 17.2) are the Cognitive/Language, Motor, and Self-help/Social Profiles, and the Articulation, Home, Health History, and Behavior Surveys. Each of these will be discussed.

Description

> *Cognitive/Language Profile (78 items)*—This profile includes four subtests that are administered directly to the child. Those are verbal concepts, visual discrimination, logical relations, and basic school skills.
>
> *Motor Profile (8 items)*—This section includes both gross motor and fine motor areas. A limited number of items, however, are used in this profile (five in gross motor, three in fine motor).
>
> *Self-Help/Social Profile (120 items)*—This information is gathered through both parent and teacher reports and measures four domains. Those are communication, daily living skills, socialization, and motor skills.
>
> *Articulation Survey (20 items)*—In this survey the child is required to identify twenty common objects. The examiner notes the initial, medial, and final sounds of those words.
>
> *Home Survey (12 items)*—This questionnaire is completed by the parent and addresses such issues as types of play materials available, numbers of books in the home, and the amount of responsibility that is given to the child.

Components

ESP's three basic components, called Profiles, are supplemented by four Surveys. For most children, the total time needed for the three Profiles is under *30 minutes*. The Surveys, completed by a parent, teacher, or screening examiner, require an additional *15–20 minutes.*

Profiles	Surveys
• The **Cognitive/Language Profile** is administered individually to the child. Tasks assess reasoning skills, visual organization and discrimination, receptive and expressive vocabulary, and basic preacademic and school skills. The Profile can be separated into Cognitive (nonverbal) and Language (verbal) subscales, a useful feature for screening children with language difficulties, hearing problems, or limited English proficiency.	• The **Articulation Survey** measures the child's ability to pronounce 20 words selected to test common articulation problems in the initial, medial, and final positions of words.
	• The **Home Survey** is completed by the parent and asks noninstrusive questions about the child's home environment.
• The **Motor Profile,** also individually administered, assesses both gross and fine motor skills.	• The **Health History Survey**, also completed by the child's parent, is a brief checklist summarizing any health problems the child has had.
• The **Self-Help/Social Profile** is a questionnaire that is completed by the child's parent, teacher, or daycare provider. It assesses the child's typical performance in the areas of communication, daily living skills, socialization, and motor skills.	• The **Behavior Survey** is used by the examiner to rate the child's behavior during administration of the Cognitive/Language and Motor Profiles. The child is rated in categories such as attention span, frustration tolerance, and response style.

FIGURE 17.2   Components of the AGS Early Screening Profile

From P. Harrison, *AGS Early Screening Profile.* Circle Pines, MN: American Guidance Service, 1991. Copyright © 1991 American Guidance Service. Reprinted with permission.

> *Health History Survey (12 items)*—This also is completed by the parent and simply provides a general indication of the child's medical history, including information related to the birth of the child.
>
> *Behavior Survey (13 items)*—This survey is completed by the test administrator after the cognitive/language and motor profiles have been administered. This section can be completed in approximately two minutes and provides information related to such areas as attention span, activity level, and cooperativeness.

Interpretation of Results

The ESP has two levels of scoring. In Level I, the individual profiles and total screening are reported in screening indexes that range from one to six. Each index represents a range of performance expressed in various standard deviation units from the mean. For example, a screening index of 1 represents performance that is two standard deviations or more below the mean, whereas a screening index of 5 represents a performance one to two standard deviations above the mean. For Level II, a variety of derived scores are available, including standard scores (mean

= 100; standard deviation = 15); percentile ranks; normal curve equivalents; stanines; and age equivalents. Scores for the individual subtests and domains and the profiles are also available (both Level I and Level II scoring). Scoring of the surveys result in descriptive categories of "above average," "average," and "below average." The Health History Survey is not scored. The manual provides suggestions on ways of combining profiles and the effect this has on the referral rate. Overall, the manual discusses the issue of interpretation to a significant extent.

Technical Characteristics

Normative Sample.   More than eleven hundred children, ages 2 through 6, were included in the standardization. The sample was stratified based on gender, geographic region, socioeconomic status, and race or ethnic group. The percentage of children in the sample was similar to the 1990 U.S. census data.

Reliability.   Internal consistencies using coefficient alpha were reported in the .80s and .90s range for all Profiles and Surveys with the exception of the Motor Profile (.60s and .70s), the Home Survey (.30s to .50s), and the Behavior Survey (primarily .70s). Test-retest reliability was determined for the profiles and total screening excluding the teacher-completed Self-Help/Social Profile. Again, the coefficients were in the .80s to .90s range except for Motor, which was reported at .70. Delayed test-retest reliability coefficients were somewhat lower than expected and were primarily in the .70s and .80s range except for Motor, which was .55. Interrater reliability was determined for the Motor Profile. Those correlations were acceptable, ranging from .80 to .99 for the various items.

Validity.   A thorough discussion of validity can be found in the manual. Results of concurrent validity studies indicated moderate to good correlations with a variety of criterion measures. Results of predictive validity studies generally indicated good correlations (usually .60s and .70s). Statistical evidence of construct validity is also provided.

Review of Relevant Research

No research was located at the time this book was completed. Interested readers are referred to the ESP examiner's manual for a summary of a number of unpublished technical reports.

OVERVIEW: AGS EARLY SCREENING PROFILES

- *Age level*—2 through 6 years
- *Type of administration*—Individual (child is tested, parent and teacher interviewed)
- *Technical adequacy*—Good reliability (except for Motor); good validity
- *Scores yielded*—Screening indexes, standard scores, percentile ranks, normal curve equivalents, stanines, age equivalents

- *Suggested use*—The AGS ESP provides an ecological screening that involves direct testing of the child and participation from the parent and teacher. A close inspection of the technical data indicates that the correlations between the teacher-completed and the parent-completed Self-Help/Social Profiles were relatively low. Subsequently, the choice of informant might affect screening decisions. Another technical issue is the low correlations between the motor domain of the Self-Help/Social Profile and the Motor Profile. The relatively poor reliability of the Motor Profile adds to its questionable use.

  Several features make the ESP a valuable instrument. These include the use of multiple domains and sources of information; ease of administration and scoring; overall sound psychometric qualities; and compatibility with more inclusive instruments such as the K-ABC, the Vineland Adaptive Behavior Scales, and the Bruininks-Oseretsky Test of Motor Proficiency. (The individual authors of many of the Profiles and Surveys are the same as those of these more comprehensive instruments.) The idea of receiving multiple sources of information on which to base screening decisions is a good one. One limitation of the ESP is the use of the Motor Profile, based on the limited number of items and its relatively low reliability. Also, when interpreting the results of the ESP, the use of subtest scores (using Level II scoring) should probably be discouraged because of the lack of supportive reliability data.

Denver II

The Denver II (Frankenburg, Dodds, Archers, Bresnick, Maschka, Edelman, & Shapiro, 1990) is an individually administered instrument designed to detect developmental deviations in young children. The authors state that the Denver II should be used only for screening, not as a definitive predictor of current or future adaptive behavior or intelligence. They further state that the test should not be used to generate a diagnostic label. The test is used with children from birth to 6 years old. The items are arranged in four sections: Personal-Social, Fine Motor-Adaptive, Language, and Gross Motor. The test items are designed to measure skills that correlate with normal child development. Some test materials are meant to elicit responses in the child, although many other items can be administered through an interview with the parents.

Description

Personal-Social (25 items)—Essentially, these tasks measure a child's ability to take care of himself or herself and to relate to other people. The section includes such tasks as playing pat-a-cake, imitating activities, and dressing and undressing.

Fine Motor-Adaptive (29 items)—This section measures fine motor dexterity, drawing ability and recognition, and manipulation of objects. It includes tasks such as building a tower with blocks, reaching for objects, and scribbling.

Language (39 items)—This section measures a child's ability to perceive, understand, and express language. It includes tasks such as turning to a spoken voice, imitating speech sounds, and naming pictures.

Gross Motor (32 items)—This section measures the child's ability to sit, stand, walk, and jump.

Interpretation of Results

Each item on the Denver II is presented on the test form in a developmental sequence (Figure 17.3). A developmental age is reported at which 25 percent, 50 percent, 75 percent, and 90 percent of "normal" children passed each item. For instance, the item "Bangs 2 cubes held in hands" is passed by 25 percent of "normal" children at 6.7 months, by 50 percent at 7.5 months, by 75 percent at 10 months, and by 90 percent at 10.9 months. Each item is scored as "advanced," "normal," "caution," "delayed," or "no opportunity" and provides a developmental profile. The Denver II profile is then interpreted on the basis of advanced, caution, and delayed items. The greater the number of cautions and delayed items, the greater the probability that the child should be further evaluated. Referrals should be based on the child's past rate of development, Denver II profile, clinical picture, and the availability of further evaluation resources. A child who refuses to perform a majority of the items is considered "untestable."

Technical Characteristics

Normative Sample.   The sample included 2,096 children between the ages of 2 weeks and 6 1/2 years; only children without disabilities from Colorado were included.

Reliability.   The test-retest coefficient with thirty-eight children was .90. Interrater reliability was .99.

Validity.   The validity of the test is the accuracy with which it measures what it purports to measure—the precision in item placement. Thus it should be used like a growth curve as a basis of comparison of a given child with other children.

Review of Relevant Research

No research on the Denver II was located although research on its predecessor (the DDST) is widespread. The authors argue, however, that the two instruments are sufficiently different to warrant caution in applying these findings to the Denver II.

- The DDST failed to identify the majority of children who had failed expressive language screening even when more rigorous cutoffs were used (Glascoe & Borowitz, 1988).

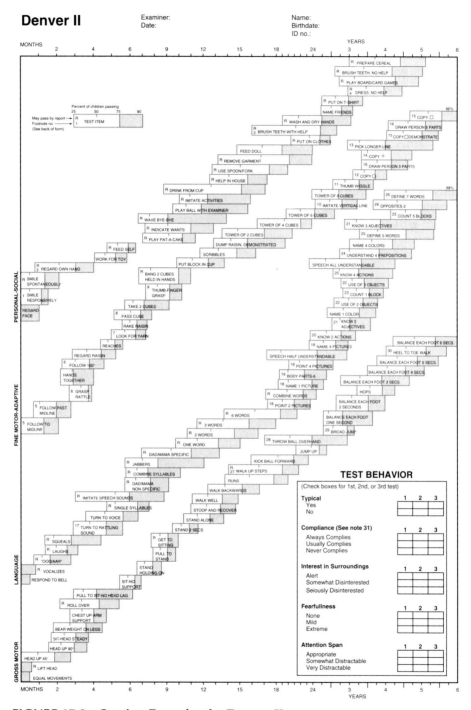

FIGURE 17.3   Scoring Form for the Denver II

- The DDST was relatively inefficient in identifying children with IQs between 50 and 70 (Nugent, 1976). In fact, Diamond (1987) found that the DDST failed to identify the majority of children who had subsequent school problems.
- The DDST was not effective in screening for children with neurological problems. It identified only 17 percent of the children found by physical examination to have organic neurologic problems. Furthermore, 56 percent of the children with neurological problems successfully passed all four DDST sections (Sterling & Sterling, 1977).
- The DDST underidentifies children needing further evaluation (McLean, McCormick, Baird, & Mayfield, 1987).
- A second level of screening should be used for children who fail the DDST (Teska & Stoneburner, 1980).
- The DDST has questionable applicability with disadvantaged children (Harper & Walker, 1983) particularly in the language areas.
- Preschool children with behavior problems scored lower on the DDST than did children without such problems (Garrity & Servos, 1978).
- Several shorter versions of the DDST have been developed. Frankenburg, Van Doorninck, Liddel, and Dick (1976) report the Preschool Developmental Questionnaire in which the parents answer ten questions about their child. An abbreviated DDST has also been developed that can be administered in less than half the time of the entire test (Frankenburg, Fandal, Sciarillo, & Burgess, 1981).
- The DDST correlates highly (.84 to .95) with various intelligence measures (Frankenburg, Camp, & Van Natta, 1971), although there are no data to support its predictive validity (Miller & Sprong, 1986).

Summary of Research Findings

Most literature on the DDST has questioned its applicability to a number of populations. It does not seem to be appropriate in the early age limits or with children with mild disabilities. Its concurrent validity seems to be adequate, although it was established by using intelligence measures as criteria. Shorter versions of the DDST are also available, although there is little evidence supporting their validity. It should be noted, however, that many of the criticisms of the DDST were based on inappropriate uses of the instrument (e.g., predicting achievement). In addition, the Denver II has attempted to address many of these criticisms (e.g., increased language items). Research on the Denver II is necessary to determine the relevance of the information available on the DDST.

OVERVIEW: DENVER II

- *Age level*—Birth through 6 years
- *Type of administration*—Individual
- *Technical adequacy*—Adequate standardization, questionable validity, acceptable reliability

- *Scores yielded*—Profile that is interpreted as "normal," "questionable," "abnormal," or "untestable"
- *Suggested use*—The Denver II is an updated version of the DDST. The DDST was criticized for several reasons including its lack of predictive validity, particularly for children with milder problems. Specifically, the DDST appeared to underidentify children in need of further evaluation. These limitations suggested that the DDST should be used cautiously. The Denver II does provide updated norms and slightly different scoring procedures. Research on this instrument is necessary.

The Developmental Indicators for the Assessment of Learning–Revised

The AGS version of the Developmental Indicators for the Assessment of Learning Revised (DIAL-R) (American Guidance Service, 1990) is a revision of the 1983 DIAL-R (Mardell-Czudnowski & Goldenberg, 1983). It represents an attempt to improve on the scoring and technical characteristics of the DIAL-R. These areas were the source of criticism in a number of reviews (e.g., Linder, 1985). Harrison (1990b) noted six major changes from the 1983 addition to the 1990 AGS addition. Those were (1) a more comprehensive manual; (2) a greater variety of methods to use in making the overall screening decisions; (3) a reanalysis of the original DIAL-R normative data using statistical weights; (4) norms for census, white, and minority groups; (5) standard errors of measurement; and (6) a wide variety of validity data. The DIAL-R is quick (twenty to thirty minutes) and easy to administer and can be used to identify a wide variety of children, from those with severe problems to those who are potentially advanced.

Description

The DIAL-R consists of twenty-four items that measure the areas of Language, Concepts, and Motor skills. The eight items in the Language area require the child to do things such as classify food and name nouns. Examples of the eight items on the Concepts section are counting and naming letters. The Motor section includes items such as catching and writing. Each of the three areas also includes a checklist of social and emotional behavior.

Interpretation of Results

A five-point scale (0–4) is used to obtain item scores. These can be combined to determine area scores and a total score. Percentile ranks and standard scores are available for both the total test and for the three areas of motor, concepts, and language. One advantage of the AGS Edition is the use of cutoff scores for plus and minus 1, 1-1/2, and 2 standard deviations as well as the fifth and ninety-fifth and tenth and ninetieth percentiles for the total and the area scores. These provide flexible alternatives for making screening decisions.

Technical Characteristics

Normative Sample.   A stratified sample of 2,447 children was used. The AGS Edition carefully reanalyzed the normative data to match the 1990 census data related to gender, geographic region, community size, ethnic background, and parents' education.

Reliability.   Internal consistency coefficients were in the .70s for the areas and .86 for the total test. Test-retest coefficients were .76 (Motor), .77 (Language), .90 (Concepts), and .87 (Total Test).

Validity.   Results of several studies determining the criterion-related validity of the DIAL-R are reported in the manual. These studies generally show a moderate correlation with a variety of criterion measures, including achievement tests and readiness tests. In addition, higher coefficients are reported with other developmental instruments such as the Learning Accomplishment Profile. The manual also includes discussions regarding the content validity and construct validity of the instrument as well. Some statistical analyses are also reported that did not support the uniqueness of the three areas suggesting that the total score is the most valid to report.

Review of Relevant Research

No research of the AGS Edition was located, although a few empirical studies and reviews on the 1983 edition of the DIAL-R were found.

Linder (1985) noted that the DIAL-R was one of the few tests that purportedly identifies young gifted students. She also noted that local school districts can choose the normative sample that is the most similar to theirs for comparison purposes. Barnett (1989) contended that the DIAL-R relied too much on the child's actual test performance and did not take advantage of parent input. Mardell-Czudnowski and Goldenberg (1988), in a longitudinal study of approximately three hundred children, found that the DIAL-R had good sensitivity and specificity but did not correspond well with subsequent special education placement. In another study, Barnett, Fowst, and Sarmir (1988) found that the profiles could not be interpreted separately with confidence, emphasizing that the total score was the best to report. Sven, Mardell-Czudnowski, and Goldenberg (1989) also reported that the total score could be used reliably but suggested that the separate profiles should not be interpreted.

OVERVIEW: DEVELOPMENTAL INDICATORS FOR THE ASSESSMENT OF LEARNING–REVISED (AGS EDITION)

- *Age level*—2 to 6 years
- *Type of administration*—Individual

- *Technical adequacy*—Good standardization; acceptable reliability and validity (particularly for total score)
- *Scores yielded*—Cutoff scores, standard scores, percentile ranks
- *Suggested use*—The AGS DIAL-R is a quick screening device for the identification of gifted children and those with disabilities. The items on the DIAL-R are a typical sample of those found on most developmental tests. Overall, this edition appears to be an improvement over the original DIAL-R, particularly in relation to technical characteristics and scoring options. The availability of separate norms for white and minority children is a nice feature. There is some evidence that the individual areas lack the technical adequacy to be interpreted separately and that the total score is the best to report. There is much discussion in the manual concerning guidelines that school districts can use to determine both screening procedures and cutoffs. In fact, there is considerable discussion regarding how to set up the screening station to administer the test. As with most screening tests, local districts should make the important determination of what cutoffs to use to indicate further evaluation. It should be noted that the DIAL-3 is currently being developed.

Miller Assessment for Preschoolers

The Miller Assessment for Preschoolers (MAP) (Miller, 1988) is designed to evaluate children ages 2 years, 9 months to 5 years, 8 months. According to the author, the MAP can be used to assess developmental status across a broad range of domains including behavioral, motor, and cognitive. The instrument can be administered in approximately thirty minutes and is used to identify children who have mild, moderate, or severe developmental delays. The MAP includes twenty-seven norm-referenced test items and a supplemental observations sheet that can be used to make appropriate use of subjective observations made during the testing session.

Description
The twenty-seven test items are categorized into five performance indices, although some test items are included in more than one index.

> *Foundations Index (10 items)*—These items measure basic sensory and motor abilities such as sense of position and movement and sense of touch.
> *Coordination Index (7 items)*—These items also measure sensory and motor abilities including gross motor and fine motor tasks.
> *Verbal Index (4 items)*—These items measure memory, sequencing, comprehension, association, and expression.
> *Nonverbal Index (5 items)*—These items measure memory, sequencing, visualization, and mental manipulations without a language component.

Complex Tasks Index (4 items)—This index includes items that require both sensorimotor and cognitive abilities involving the interpretation of visual spatial information.

Supplemental Observations (5 areas)—The supplemental observation sheet is found in the record booklet and is divided into five sections: Vision, Touch, Speech and Language, Draw a Person, and Movement. Each section is designed to help the examiner assess behaviors that might influence test performance.

Interpretation of Results

Percentile ranks are available for the MAP total score and performance index scores. In addition, cutoff scores are used on a color-coded basis. *Red* indicates that the child is functioning at or below the fifth percentile rank and needs further evaluation, *Yellow* means the child is functioning between the sixth and twenty-fifth percentile rank and should be monitored closely for developmental delays, whereas *Green* indicates that the child is above the twenty-fifth percentile and appears to be functioning at an average or above-average level. There is also a "Behavior During Testing" checklist that is not scored but simply notes whether the child's behavior was within normal limits during the testing.

Technical Characteristics

Normative Sample.   Approximately twelve hundred children were included in the standardization sample. The sample was stratified by age, gender, race, community size, and socioeconomic status. Prior to the standardization the test was administered to a tryout sample of approximately five hundred children.

Reliability.   Interrater reliability was determined using a sample of forty children. Coefficients ranged from .84 (Coordination) to .99 (Nonverbal). The total MAP yielded a coefficient of .98. Test-retest reliability was determined using a sample of eighty-one children. Those coefficients ranged from .72 to .94. The total score had a test-retest coefficient of .81. Internal reliability coefficients using the split-half method were approximately .80.

Validity.   The author discusses the content validity of the instrument by providing a thorough review of the theoretical literature on child development. Concurrent validity was determined by administering the MAP and one of four standardized instruments, including intelligence tests and other screening tests, to a group of thirty children. These correlations were variable and low. For example, the correlations between total score on the MAP with an IQ measure and language measure were .27 and .31, respectively. The correlations with a sensory integration test ranged from .02 to .17. When compared to the Denver Developmental Screening Test, the MAP identified 24 percent more children as being at risk. Predictive validity was determined by following approximately one-fourth of the children in the standardization sample and correlating their scores with later standardized instruments and school performance criteria. The coefficients were low to moderate, ranging from .17 (report card mathematics) to .50 Wechsler Intelligence Scale for Children–Revised (WISC-R full-scale IQ). Other data regarding construct validity and classification accuracy are discussed in the manual.

Review of Relevant Research

- In a review of the MAP, Padget (1985) concluded that the test's overreliance on visual-motor tasks limits its usefulness in screening for possible learning problems. Linder (1985) also noted its heavy emphasis on sensory and motor functioning. Schouten (1992) pointed out the lack of validity data.
- The MAP can consistently and correctly identify the majority of children who have later school problems (Miller, 1986) and can differentiate children with subsequent school problems from those without (Miller, 1988).
- The Foundations Index was found to be a psychometrically valuable contributor to the total MAP score (Miller & Lemerand, 1986).
- The MAP Verbal Index is less culturally biased against older preschool children than certain language tests such as the Peabody Picture Vocabulary Test–Revised (Wilderstrom, Miller, & Marzano, 1986).

Summary of Research Findings

Research on the MAP has generally supported the predictive validity of the instrument (although it should be noted that the majority of the research was conducted by the test author). Reviews of the MAP have noted its neurological base and its heavy emphasis on sensorimotor tasks.

OVERVIEW: MILLER ASSESSMENT FOR PRESCHOOLERS

- *Age level*—2 years, 9 months to 5 years, 8 months
- *Type of administration*—Individual
- *Technical adequacy*—Adequate reliability, questionable validity
- *Scores yielded*—Percentile ranks, cutoff scores
- *Suggested use*—The MAP offers an alternative to traditional developmental screening tests. It was developed by an occupational therapist and the content is heavily weighted toward sensorimotor and sensory integration tasks. It attempts to measure specific motor, language, and cognitive skills, as well as underlying neurological processing. More research is needed to determine the instrument's validity. The test should not be used for diagnostic purposes.

DEVELOPMENTAL TESTS (NORM-REFERENCED)

WHY USE NORM-REFERENCED DEVELOPMENTAL TESTS?

Screening; establishment of educational need (developmental lag); establishment of IEP goals

WHO SHOULD USE THEM?

Teachers, school psychologists, social workers

Battelle Developmental Inventory

The Battelle Developmental Inventory (BDI) (Newborg, Stock, Wnek, Guidu-baldi, & Svinicki, 1984) is an individually administered battery of tests that measures developmental skills of children from birth to age 8 years. According to the authors, the BDI can be used for four purposes. These are (1) the assessment and identification of children with disabilities, (2) the assessment of nondisabled children, (3) the planning and provision of instruction (that is, the development of IEPs), and (4) the evaluation of groups of children with disabilities. This latter purpose refers to the monitoring of progress of students who are placed in special education programs. The BDI uses three procedures for obtaining the information: traditional administration, observation, and interview. The manual indicates what type(s) of procedures are relevant for the given items.

Description
The BDI consists of 341 items that are grouped within five domains: Personal-Social, Adaptive, Motor, Communication, and Cognitive. These domains are further broken down into areas or subdomains. A screening version of the BDI consists of ninety-six items that can be used as a quick assessment of the skills covered in the five domains.

> *Personal-Social (85 items)*—Includes the areas of adult interaction, expression of feeling/affect, self-concept, peer interaction, coping, and social role.
> *Adaptive (59 items)*—Includes the areas of attention, eating, dressing, personal responsibility, and toileting.
> *Motor (82 items)*—Includes the areas of muscle control, body coordination, locomotion, fine muscle, and perceptual-motor.
> *Communication (59 items)*—The areas of receptive and expressive communication are included.
> *Cognitive (56 items)*—Includes the areas of perceptual discrimination, memory, reasoning and academic skills, and conceptual development.

Interpretation of Results

Scores from the BDI can be translated into a variety of standard scores (including developmental quotients), percentile ranks, and age equivalents. Overall, there are ten major areas for which scores are available. These are the five domains, plus fine motor, gross motor, expressive communication, receptive communication, and total. In addition, a score summary sheet provides a visual representation of the child's developmental strengths and weaknesses (Figure 17.4). Information is also available regarding suggested cutoff points to aid in educational decision making. A computerized scoring program is available.

Technical Characteristics

Normative Sample.   A total of eight hundred children from twenty-four states were included. Breakdown by age, race, and gender is available in the manual.

Score Summary

FIGURE 17.4   Summary Sheet from the Battelle Developmental Inventory

From J. Newborg, J. Stock, L. Wnek, J. Guidubaldi, and J. Svinicki, *Battelle Developmental Inventory.* Allen, TX: DLM Teaching Resources. Copyright © 1984 by LINC Associations. Reprinted with permission.

Reliability.   Test-retest coefficients were generally high (.81–.97). Interrater reliability coefficients were .95 or higher.

Validity.   Concurrent validity coefficients with a variety of criterion measures are reported in the manual. These ranged from .41 with a verbal intelligence quotient to .94 with an adaptive behavior measure. In general, these coefficients were determined from small samples. The authors also report data and provide arguments for the tests' construct and content validity.

Review of Relevant Research

- Very low correlations were reported for the BDI and the Bayley Scales of Infant Development with "at-risk" infants and toddlers (Gerken, Eliason, & Arthur, 1994).
- The pattern and strength of the correlations between the BDI and the Bayley Scales support the use of the BDI to measure development in infants with known or suspected handicaps (Boyd, Welge, Sexton, & Miller, 1989).
- Guidubaldi and Perry (1984) reported that the BDI had both high concurrent validity and predictive validity coefficients with a variety of criterion measures. They particularly noted that it was a favorable predictor of first-grade achievement when administered during kindergarten.
- Mott (1987) investigated the validity of the communications domain with speech and language-disordered children using a variety of language measures as criteria. She found that the total and expressive communication scores correlated highly with the language measures but that the receptive communication scores did not.
- Because of the way the tables are presented, a child could receive radically different scores from one day to the next despite identical performance (Boyd, 1989).
- The screening version of the BDI tends to overidentify. In one study, twenty-two of thirty-five children were identified as needing further assessment on the basis of the BDI screen. In reality only three needed extensive assessment based on results from the full BDI (McLean, McCormick, Baird, & Mayfield, 1987).
- Sheehan and Snyder (1990) noted that the BDI should not be used with young handicapped children because of the lack of appropriate items for children under two years of age. They also noted that the cutoff scores suggested in the manual should be used cautiously.
- The BDI had good test-retest reliability, ranging from .81 to .97 (McLinden, 1989). Boyd et al. (1989) reported slightly lower coefficients.
- Teachers were moderately positive about the usefulness of the BDI. They noted, however, that many of the suggested test adaptations were not appropriate (Bailey, Vandiviere, Dellinger, & Munn, 1987).
- The BDI was not a good predictive measure of social-behavior development (Merrell & Mauk, 1993).

Summary of Research Findings

In general, research on the BDI has supported its use as a valid and reliable measure of developmental skills. The screening version of the BDI, however, has been shown to significantly overidentify children as needing further evaluation. Questions related to the tables, its usefulness with very young children, and the suggested adaptations have also been brought up by researchers.

OVERVIEW: BATTELLE DEVELOPMENTAL INVENTORY

- *Age level*—Birth to 8 years
- *Type of administration*—Individual
- *Technical adequacy*—Good reliability, adequate validity
- *Scores yielded*—Standard scores, percentile ranks, age equivalents
- *Suggested use*—The BDI is a well-constructed developmental inventory. It provides a helpful profile of a child's developmental strengths and weaknesses. The manual is easy to follow and there are guidelines for adapting the test items for the evaluation of children with disabilities. There is some question, however, of whether those adaptations are useful. Overall, in fact, the test is more useful for toddlers than infants, and with children with mild, rather than severe, disabilities. Although the authors describe procedures for calculating lower standard scores from the raw scores obtained, the tables themselves do not provide low enough standard scores to differentiate performance of children with severe disabilities.

  The reliability and validity of the instruments is good. Harrington (1985), in reviewing the BDI, noted that it is rare that a developmental test meets all of the standards for test construction that are outlined in the *Standards for Educational and Psychological Tests* but that the BDI, in fact, does. Overall, it appears that the BDI can be used confidently to identify developmental strengths and weaknesses of children with and without disabilities. The use of the screening edition of the BDI is more questionable.

Developmental Profile–II

The Developmental Profile–II (DP-II) (Alpern, Boll, & Shearer, 1986) is designed to evaluate children from birth through age 9. It is meant to be used as a parent interview, which can be given in approximately twenty to forty minutes. The DP-II, however, can also be used as a self-interview that is usually completed by the teacher. The DP-II uses an age scale in which there are approximately three items per age level. An age level can encompass a five to six-month interval (e.g., twenty-five to thirty months) to a one-year interval (e.g., seventy-nine to ninety months). There are five subscales on the DP-II. An example of items (and associated age level) from each subscale follows.

Description

Physical Developmental Age Scale (39 items)—Examples of items and levels are "can the child roll from his/her stomach to his/her back and from back to stomach without help?" (0–6 months) and "can the child run fast enough to compete with a normal 8-year-old child in a race or game of tag?" (79–90 months).

Self-Help Developmental Age Scale (39 items)—Examples are "does the child try to get objects that are near but beyond reach?" (0–6 months) and "does the child take off his/her coat without help when buttons or zippers are undone?" (19–24 months).

Social Developmental Age Scale (36 items)—Examples are "does the child come when called at least 25 percent of the time?" (7–12 months) and "is the child interested in exploring new places such as a friend's house or a neighbor's yard?" (19–24 months).

Academic Developmental Age Scale (34 items)—Examples are "does the child use pencils or crayons in definite attempts to make marks on any surface?" (13–18 months) and "in the child's play, are things ever grouped together by color or form or size?" (25–30 months).

Communication Developmental Age Scale (38 items)—Examples include "does the child use at least fifteen different words in the right way?" (19–24 months) and "does the child name, not just repeat, at least twenty things seen in pictures?" (25–30 months).

Interpretation of Results

As noted previously, the DP-II uses age scores that compare a person's performance on the test to a "typical performance" by a person of the same age. These types of scores are generally discouraged for use with standardized tests. On the DP-II, items are scored as passed, failed, or no opportunity, with items from each subscale grouped together to provide an age score. The age scores are thus interpreted as either advanced or delayed, based on the actual chronological age of the child. Tables included in the manual provide methods of interpreting the significance of delays based on the point at which various percentages of the children in the standardization sample passed the various items. Overall, the interpretive procedures for the DP-II are less than adequate.

Technical Characteristics

Normative Sample. A total of more than twenty-three hundred nondisabled children, ages birth through 9 1/2, were included. Overall, the sample is not representative of the U.S. population, having significant restrictions both geographically and in terms of socioeconomic status. The normative sample for the DP-II was the same for that of the original Developmental Profile normed in 1972.

Reliability. Overall, few reliability data are offered in the test manual. More information is necessary before evaluating the reliability of the test.

Validity. The authors provide an argument for content validity of the instrument although it is somewhat unclear how the items were chosen. There is also limited evidence of concurrent validity, primarily with the Stanford-Binet Intelligence Scale (Form LM).

Review of Relevant Research

There is limited research focusing on the DP-II, although there are some studies on the original DP published in 1972. As mentioned, few changes were made in the DP-II. Some evidence indicates that the original DP was a better predictor of language delays than the Denver Developmental Screening Test (German, Williams, Herzfield, & Marshall, 1982) and that the DP, when used in conjunction with a battery of instruments, resulted in consistent clinical judgment among evaluation team members (Bagnato, 1984). In one study of the DP-II, Harris and Fagley (1987) reported significant positive correlations with later measures of self-help, physical development, and communication with a group of twenty-nine children with autism evaluated four to seven years later.

The DP-II has also been reviewed negatively in the professional literature. Huebner (1989c) noted its technical inadequacy, whereas Hightower (1989) suggested that the norm-referenced uses of the test be downplayed.

OVERVIEW: DEVELOPMENTAL PROFILE–II

- *Age level*—Birth to 9 1/2 years
- *Type of administration*—Individual (interview)
- *Technical adequacy*—Limited normative sample, reliability, and validity
- *Scores yielded*—Age score, descriptive categories
- *Suggested use*—The DP-II should be used for screening purposes only. Because of the interview format, the DP-II can be given to parents to provide some basic information and can often act as an "ice breaker." The technical inadequacy of the instrument limits its use. Further, the use of age scales is questionable and results in less than adequate interpretive value. Clearly, the DP-II should be used only in conjunction with other instruments to provide supplemental data from parental input.

READINESS AND PREACADEMIC INSTRUMENTS

WHY USE READINESS AND PREACADEMIC INSTRUMENTS?

Screening; establishment of IEP goals; grouping for instruction

WHO SHOULD USE THEM?

Teachers

Boehm Test of Basic Concepts–Revised

The Boehm Test of Basic Concepts–Revised (Boehm-R) (Boehm, 1986) is a group-administered instrument designed to measure a child's mastery of concepts that are necessary for successful performance early in school. It is used with children in kindergarten and first and second grades. The author states that the tests can be used both to identify children who have problems in the tested area and to identify specific concepts that need to be emphasized or taught. A separate preschool version called the Boehm Test of Basic Concepts–Preschool Version (BTBC-PV) includes twenty-six items designed for children ages 3 to 5.

Description

The Boehm-R has two equivalent forms, C and D, each containing fifty items, presented in separate booklets. The items are arranged in order of difficulty, and each booklet has three sample questions. The administration is straightforward: The examiner reads a passage such as, "Look at the beads and strings. Mark the bead that has a string *through* it." The child is then required to look at three pictures. One has the string around the bead, one has the string under the bead, and one has the string through the bead.

In general, the concept categories of space (twenty-four items), quantity (eighteen items), and time (six items) are measured, as well as a miscellaneous category (two items). One interesting addition to the Boehm-R is an *application booklet* that allows for the assessment of concepts used in combination, in sequences, or in making comparisons. Except for this addition, the Boehm-R is similar to the original test (seven new items were added and two old items were deleted).

The BTBC-PV is a downward extension of the Boehm-R that should be administered individually. The results of the BTBC-PV are best used informally because of the limited standardization sample on which the normative scores are based.

Interpretation of Results

Two types of scores can be derived from the Boehm-R. First, an examiner can compare to others of the same grade and socioeconomic status the percentage of students that pass each item. For instance, an average of 86 percent of the lower socioeconomic status kindergarten children passed item 1, form C. This information allows the examiner to make gross comparisons of the class's concept knowledge with the normative sample. The Boehm-R also yields percentiles for comparing individual raw scores. The author states, however, that the test should be used for teaching and screening rather than for prediction or administration; these norms, therefore, need not always be used. A class record form allows data for the entire class to be recorded on a single sheet. This record form can be used to assign students to groups or to look for concepts that the majority of the class missed.

Technical Characteristics

Normative Sample. Field testing was conducted using approximately fifteen hundred students. Standardization sample was broken down by geographic region, size of school, and socioeconomic status. Size of sample is unclear.

Reliability. Alternate-form reliability coefficients ranged from .65 (grade two) to .82 (kindergarten). Split-half coefficients ranged from .64 to .85 for form C and .73 to .83 for form D. Test-retest coefficients ranged from .75 to .88 and .55 to .85 for forms C and D, respectively.

Validity. A detailed discussion of steps taken to ensure content validity can be found in the manual. Predictive validity coefficients ranged from .38 to .64 in a series of studies.

Review of Relevant Research
Because of the similarity in format and structure, research related to the Boehm Test of Basic Concepts (BTBC) might have relevance for the Boehm-R.

- The BTBC is potentially beneficial as an indicator of receptive language in developmentally delayed children (Hutcherson, 1978).
- The BTBC has been used successfully in a battery of tests to identify gifted students (Hardman & Croyle, 1979).
- The BTBC should be used cautiously with hard-of-hearing individuals. In one study, eighteen of twenty-four hard-of-hearing students scored below the tenth percentile (Davis, 1974).
- Poor performance on the BTBC could be due to any number of factors, including the inability to focus on key words in the directions, the complexity of the directions, deficits in spatial perception, vocabulary deficits, problems with abstraction, difficulty with negative concepts, and inadequate auditory memory (Spector, 1979).
- Learning-disabled students scored lower and with greater variability on the BTBC than did students without learning disabilities. The learning-disabled

group scored lowest in the quantity, space, and miscellaneous categories, in that order (Kavale, 1982).

- The BTBC measures an overlap of cognitive and linguistic factors best described as a language-comprehension factor (Beech, 1981).
- The BTBC has low reliability with rural children and should be used cautiously with that population (Houck, Biskin, & Regetz, 1973).
- There is some evidence that the BTBC has moderate predictive validity for subsequent achievement (Estes, Harris, Moers, & Wodrich, 1976).

Summary of Research Findings

As noted previously, the similarity between the Boehm-R and the original test suggests that research on the original can be cautiously generalized to the revised version. Schwarting (1987) reviewed the Boehm-R and noted the similarities between it and the BTBC. Earlier research suggests that the BTBC has a positive relationship with academic achievement and that it can be used with a variety of special education populations. Two studies located on the Boehm-R are supportive of the previous research. In one study with black urban children the Boehm-R had appreciable test-retest reliability and moderate to substantial predictive validity (Glutting, Kelly, Boehm, & Burnett, 1989). In the other, Zucker and Riordan (1988) found significant correlations between the Boehm-R and the Bracken Basic Concept Scale. Clearly, more research is needed to replicate and extend those findings. No research was located on the BTBC-PV.

OVERVIEW: BOEHM TEST OF BASIC CONCEPTS–REVISED

- *Age level*—Kindergarten through grade 2 (preschool version available)
- *Type of administration*—Group
- *Technical adequacy*—Limited
- *Scores yielded*—Percentiles
- *Suggested use*—As a norm-referenced test, the Boehm-R would have to be judged technically inadequate. The reliability for some age groups is extremely low, and only minimal data support its validity. Furthermore, the items are too easy for children in the upper age limit of the test. After first grade, it definitely loses its sensitivity for normative decisions. The value of this test lies in its use as an informal measure. On the assumption that development of basic concepts is essential or at least important in establishing a foundation for later learning, the Boehm-R can be helpful. If used as a norm-referenced device, its purpose should primarily be as a screening instrument (Fitzmaurice & Witt, 1989). In general, these statements about the Boehm-R are relevant for the BTBC-PV as well.

Bracken Basic Concept Scale

The Bracken Basic Concept Scale (BBCS) (Bracken, 1984) is a comprehensive measure of basic concepts designed for preschool and early elementary-age children (ages 2 years 6 months through 7 years 11 months). There are two scales—a diagnostic scale that can be administered in approximately twenty to thirty minutes and a screening test. The screening test has two alternate forms (A and B) and is designed for children ages 5 to 7. The screening test can be given to small groups in approximately ten to fifteen minutes. The BBCS has also been translated into Spanish. Information on this translation and subsequent validation is available (Bracken & Fouad, 1987).

Description of Diagnostic Scale

The diagnostic scale includes 258 items that measure 11 conceptual areas. Those areas are color, letter identification, numbers/counting, comparisons, shape, direction/position, social/emotional, size, texture/material, quantity, and time/sequence. The format of the test involves the presentation of a page that has four pictures on it. The examiner states the concept, and the child must indicate which of the four pictures represents the concept. The BBCS uses basal and ceiling rules to avoid administering unnecessary items.

Interpretation of Scores

Raw scores from the BBCS can be transformed into a variety of derived scores including standard scores, percentile ranks, stanines, and age equivalents. The first five subtests (color, letter identification, numbers/counting, comparisons, and shape) are combined to form a School Readiness Composite. Each of the other six individual subtests are scored separately. A Profile Summary is also available to provide a visual representation of the child's strengths and weaknesses in the various conceptual areas.

Technical Characteristics

Normative Sample.   A sample of 1,109 children was included. The makeup of the sample was relatively close to the 1980 census regarding demographic variables.

Reliability.   Test-retest on a small sample ranged from .67 (size) to .98 (School Readiness Composite). Median split-half reliability coefficients were .96 for the total test and .85 for the subtests.

Validity.   Concurrent validity coefficients were determined using a variety of criterion measures and ranged from .68 to .88. The author does an excellent job in describing the steps that were taken to ensure content validity.

Review of Relevant Research

- Estabrook (1984) reviewed the test and considered it the most comprehensive basic concept measure available.
- Turco (1989) reviewed the test and noted that it could provide a link between assessment and remedial interventions.
- The BBCS is a better predictor of achievement than the Gesell Developmental Exam (Sterner & McCallum, 1988).
- Low to moderate correlations were reported between the BBCS and the Preschool Language Scale and Slosson Intelligence Test, suggesting that they do not measure the same abilities (Pecyna-Rhyner & Bracken, 1988).
- Children with hearing impairments score significantly lower than children without hearing impairment on the BBCS (Bracken & Cato, 1986).
- The BBCS has been translated into Spanish (Bracken & Fouad, 1987).
- Bracken, Sabers, and Insko (1987) found that black children scored approximately one-half standard deviation below white children on the test, although the pattern of their performance was similar. They discussed the possibility that the BBCS is also an intelligence measure, because most intelligence tests include the assessment of basic concepts.
- Naglieri and Bardos (1990) noted that the BBCS is a well-designed instrument that has good psychometric properties and can be used confidently as a measure of basic concepts.
- The Quantity and Time subtests should be interpreted cautiously (Frisby, 1992).

Summary of Research Findings

Although the research on the BBCS is limited, some evidence suggests that the test can be used to predict achievement. Limited data indicate that individuals with different characteristics (e.g., different disabilities, ethnic status) perform differently on the test. There is conflicting information regarding its relationship with general intelligence.

OVERVIEW: BRACKEN BASIC CONCEPT SCALE (DIAGNOSTIC)

- *Age level*—2 1/2 to 8 years
- *Type of administration*—Individual
- *Technical adequacy*—Adequate standardization, validity, and reliability
- *Scores yielded*—Standard scores, percentile ranks, age equivalents
- *Suggested use*—The BBCS is a well-constructed, comprehensive instrument designed to measure a variety of concepts. Because of the general paucity of reliability and validity data, it is probably best used to identify strong and weak areas to aid in teaching the appropriate concepts. Fur-

ther research might indicate that it could also be used for comparison purposes. The Spanish translation is also a nice feature.

DEVELOPMENTAL TESTS (CRITERION-REFERENCED)

WHY USE CRITERION-REFERENCED DEVELOPMENTAL TESTS?

Development of IEP goals and objectives; IEP evaluation

WHO SHOULD USE THEM?

Teachers

Assessment Log and Developmental Progress Chart–Infants

The Assessment Log and Developmental Progress Chart–Infants (Johnson-Martin, Jens, & Attermeier, 1986) is part of the Carolina Curriculum for Handicapped Infants and Infants at Risk. It includes items that are correlated with twenty-four curriculum sequences and is presented in a checklist format. In general, the areas included are cognition (using primarily a Piagetian approach), language/communication, self-help/social skills, fine motor, and gross motor. Within each of the twenty-four areas, sequential items are included. There is also the separate Assessment Log and Developmental Progress Chart–Preschoolers (Johnson-Martin, Attermeier, & Hacker, 1990) that consists of twenty-five skill sequences.

Description
The twenty-four areas and examples of the first and last item in each area follow.

Tactile Integration and Manipulation (11 items)—"Responds differently to warm/cold, rough/smooth" to "pokes or plays with clay."
Auditory Localization and Object Permanence (10 items)—"Quiets when noise is presented" to "turns head and looks back for two sounds." In this area, there are also alternative items for visually impaired children.
Visual Pursuit and Object Permanence (7 items)—"Visually fixates for at least three seconds" to "looks at cover under which object has disappeared."
Object Permanence-Visual Motor (12 items)—"Pulls cloth from face" to "finds object after systematic search under 3 covers."
Spatial Concepts (14 items)—"Shifts attention from one object to another" to "uses tools to deal with spatial problems (e.g., extends reach with a stick)."

Functional Use of Objects and Symbolic Play (12 items)—"Moves hand to mouth" to "talks to dolls or animals or makes them interact with one another."

Control over Physical Environment (9 items)—"Repeats activity that produces an interesting result" to "uses tools to solve problems."

Readiness Concepts (7 items)—"Matches simple geometric shapes" to "understands concept of *big*."

Responses to Communication from Others (23 items)—"Quiets to voice" to "follows 3 different 3-part commands."

Gestural Imitation (10 items)—"Looks at person talking and gesturing" to "imitates sequence of 2 signs that stand for words."

Gestural Communication (15 items)—"Shows anticipation of regularly occurring events in everyday care" to "combines signs to communicate."

Vocal Imitation (12 items)—"Vocalizing in response to person talking" to "imitates 3-syllable words."

Vocal Communication (22 items)—"Differentiates cries" to "combines 2 or more words in sentences."

Social Skills (19 items)—"Can be comforted by talking to, holding, or rocking" to "shares spontaneously with peers."

Self-Direction (6 items)—"Moves away from Mom in same room" to "explores unfamiliar places with mother present."

Feeding (19 items)—"Sucks from nipple smoothly" to "distinguishes between edible and nonedible substances."

Grooming (4 items)—"Cooperates in handwashing" to "wipes nose if given a handkerchief."

Dressing (6 items)—"Cooperates in dressing and undressing" to "puts on loose shoes or slippers."

Reaching and Grasping (11 items)—"Moves arms actively when sees or hears object" to "uses neat pincer grasp."

Object Manipulation (9 items)—"Looks at hand (or toy) to one side" to "looks toward object and visually directs reach or adjusts reach to get noisy object." This section has modifications for visually impaired children.

Object Manipulation (continued) (30 items)—This section includes items related to form manipulation, block patterns, drawing, placing pegs, and putting in and taking out objects.

Bilateral Hand Activity (14 items)—"Bats at objects at chest level" to "strings 3 large beads."

Gross Motor Activities: Prone (16 items)—"Lifts head, freeing nose; arms and legs flexed" to "crawls down stairs backward."

Gross Motor Activities: Supine (7 items)—"Turns head from side to side in response to visual and/or auditory stimuli while in supine position" to "rolls from back to stomach."

Gross Motor Activity: Upright (10 items)—"Head steady when held" to "moves from hands and knees, to hands and feet, to standing."

Gross Motor Activities: Upright (continued) (15 items)—Measures areas of stair climbing, balance, jumping, posture, and locomotion.

Name: _____
Dates: _____

☑ No norms available.   ■ Items beyond this point are necessary only for certain populations (see Assessment Log).

Sequence	0 – 3 mo.	3 – 6 mo.	6 – 9 mo.	9 – 12 mo.	12 – 15 mo.	15 – 18 mo.	18 – 21 mo.	21 – 24 mo.
Cognition								
1. Tactile Integration and Manipulation	a	b c	d e f	g h	i	j	k	
2. Auditory Localization and Object Permanence	a b c	d e	f g	h				
3. Visual Pursuit and Object Permanence	a b c d e	f	g	h	i	j	k	l
4. Object Permanence (Visual-Motor)		a b c	d e f g	h	i j	k		
5. Spatial Concepts	a b	c d	e f	g	h i	j k	l m	n
6. Functional Use of Objects and Symbolic Play	a b	c d e	f g	h	i	j	k	l
7. Control over Physical Environment	a	b c	d	e	f	g	h	i
8. "Readiness" Concepts						a b	c d	e f g
Communication/Language								
9. Responses to Communication from Others	a b	c d e f g	h i	j k	l m	n o p	q r s t	u v w
10. Gestural Imitation	a	b c	d e	f	g h	i	j	
11. Gestural Communication	a b	c d e f	g h i	j	k	l	m n	o
12. Vocal Imitation	a b c d	e	f	g	h i	j	k	l
13. Vocal Communication	a b c d e f g h	i	j	k	l m n	o	p	q r s t u v
S.S./A.*								
14. Social Skills	a b c	d e f	g h	i j k	l m	n o	p q	r s
15. Self-Direction				a	b c	d	e	f
Self-Help								
16. Feeding	a b	c d e f g h i j k l	m	n o	p q	r	s	
17. Grooming				a	b	c	d e	f
18. Dressing				a	b	c	d e	f
Fine Motor								
19. Reaching and Grasping	a b	c d e f g h i j k	II a	b c	d	e		
20. Object Manipulation	a b c d	e f	g h i	IV a b c	d e	f	g	
21. Bilateral Hand Activity	a b	c d e	f	g	h i	j k	l m	n
Gross Motor								
22. Gross Motor Activities: Stomach	a b	c d e f g h	i j k l	m n	o p	I a b	c	d
23. Gross Motor Activities: Back	a b c d	e f g				II a	b	c d
24. Gross Motor Activities Upright	a	b	c	d e f g h i	j	IV a b	c d	e

FIGURE 17.5   The Developmental Progress Chart

From N. Johnson-Martin, K. Jens, and S. Attermeier, *Assessment Log and Developmental Progress Chart for the Carolina Curriculum for Handicapped Infants and Infants at Risk.* Baltimore: Paul H. Brookes. Copyright © 1986 by Nancy Johnson-Martin, Kenneth Jens, and Susan Attermeier.

Interpretation of Results

The authors suggest that an individual be evaluated in each of the twenty-four areas, usually beginning with the first item and continuing until he or she fails three consecutive items. The obvious exceptions are those areas that cannot be measured because of the nature of an individual's disability (for example, auditory localization for a person with a significant hearing impairment). The results are then placed on the Developmental Progress Chart (see Figure 17.5). Items are scored as passed, failed, or emerging. Determination or prioritizing of instructional goals can then be accomplished. In addition, general age ranges for the various items can be determined from the results placed on the Developmental Progress Chart. These are grouped in three-month clusters from birth to 24 months. These age ranges, particularly when interpreted with students with severe or profound disabilities, must be viewed with caution.

OVERVIEW: ASSESSMENT LOG AND DEVELOPMENTAL PROGRESS CHART

- *Age level*—Birth to 24 months
- *Suggested use*—The Assessment Log and Developmental Progress Chart is used in conjunction with the Carolina Curriculum. It is a well-researched model that shows promise in determining instructional goals as well as providing instructional procedures. It should be noted that the entire model was designed for *infants*, although there is another Log and Chart designed for *preschoolers*. In general, that information suggests that many of the items might need to be adapted and that care should be taken to choose areas that are adaptive (functional) for the individual. There is a general lack of data available about the use of the curriculum and, subsequently, the assessment component with older students with severe or profound disabilities. There is mention in the manual of field-test data that did not find the use of the curriculum effective with this population on a short-term (three to six months) basis. Clearly, more research on the model is necessary.

Behavioral Characteristics Progression

The Behavioral Characteristics Progression (BCP) (VORT Corporation, 1973) is a continuum of behaviors in chart form. It contains twenty-four hundred observable traits referred to as behavioral characteristics. These *behavioral characteristics* are grouped into fifty-six criterion-referenced categories called *strands.*

This tool was intended to assist teachers of exceptional children to structure into a more coherent and manageable sequence the teaching of the various areas they are asked to cover. Particular care was take to address the self-help, emotional, and practically oriented academic skills commonly needed by the special education student. Although the BCP does include some "higher-functioning" areas, many of the strands are appropriate for individuals with severe or profound disabilities as well.

As an *assessment* tool, the BCP provides the teacher with a comprehensive chart of pupil behaviors to aid in identifying which behavioral characteristics a pupil displays or does not display. As an *instructional* tool, the BCP assists the teacher in developing individualized, appropriate learner objectives for each student. As a *communication* tool, the BCP offers a historical recording device that, throughout the education of the student, can be used to indicate progress.

Description

Strands 1–22 deal with self-help skills. Strands 23–45 include items related to social, academic, and recreational skills. Strands 46–56 involve skills specifically needed by individuals who are blind, deaf, and orthopedically impaired.

The evaluator should choose the strand or strands most appropriate for the person being evaluated. This choice is facilitated by observing the *identifying behaviors* listed in the test materials; the evaluator can use these identifying behaviors as a checklist to determine and assign priorities to the most appropriate strands.

Interpretation of Results

For each student, the strands selected are noted in an individual record booklet. A baseline for each strand is determined by measuring the behavior characteristics. The behavior characteristics are scored according to the following system: (–), behavior not displayed; (1/2), behavior exhibited, but less frequently than the recommended 75 percent required incidence level; (✔), behavior displayed at the 75 percent level with no assistance; (H), physical disability prevents demonstrations of behavior. From this information, objectives can be delineated, and progress toward them can be monitored.

OVERVIEW: BEHAVIORAL CHARACTERISTICS PROGRESSION

- *Age level*—No age provided
- *Suggested use*—The BCP is a comprehensive criterion-referenced instrument. Although it is designed for individuals with a wide range of abilities, a number of its items deal with lower-level skills. Booklets of instructional suggestions that are correlated with the strands are also available. One potential disadvantage of the test is that it can be cumbersome if the number of strands is not limited.

Brigance Inventory of Early Development–Revised

The Brigance Inventory of Early Development–Revised (Brigance, 1991) was designed for use with individuals below developmental age 7. It can be used to identify strengths and weaknesses, to determine instructional objectives, and to indicate the individual's approximate developmental level in various areas. It can also be used as an ongoing evaluation system to monitor progress. The test items were cross-referenced with texts and other tests to determine developmental-age equivalents that should be used cautiously.

Description

The Brigance Inventory of Early Development–Revised measures abilities in eleven content areas. These eleven areas include eighty-four skill sequences, which, essentially, are task analyses of the skill areas. A number of supplemental sequences are also available. One feature of the revised inventory is the inclusion of *comprehensive skill sequences*. These are more detailed sequences that can be used with children with more severe disabilities or others for whom the need for smaller steps is apparent. For example, the skill sequence of feeding/eating consists of thirty-seven items, whereas the comprehensive sequence includes sixty-seven. The author notes that the regular sequences are adequate for most children.

Preambulatory Motor Skills and Behaviors (46 items)—This content area includes four skill sequences: supine position, prone position, sitting position, and standing position.

Gross Motor Skills and Behaviors (94 items)—This content area includes ten skill sequences, beginning with standing, walking, and climbing stairs, and ending with rolling and throwing. There are three supplemental skill sequences: ball bouncing, rhythm, and wheel toys.

Fine Motor Skills and Behaviors (96 items)—This content area includes nine skill sequences, such as general manipulative skills, prehandwriting skills, and cutting with scissors. Three supplemental sequences are available.

Self-Help Skills (137 items)—This content area includes eight skill sequences, such as feeding and eating skills, undressing, dressing, toileting, and grooming.

Speech and Language Skills (179 items)—This content area includes ten skill sequences, such as prespeech, receptive language, picture vocabulary, and sentence memory, and one supplemental sequence (singing).

General Knowledge and Comprehension (218 items)—This content area includes eleven skill sequences, such as knowledge of body parts, colors, classifying, and knowing where to go for service.

Social and Emotional Development (122 items)—This section includes three skill sequences including play skills and work-related skills.

Readiness (168 items)—This content area measures four aspects of reading readiness: visual discrimination; reciting alphabet; and matching, identifying, and naming uppercase and lowercase letters.

Basic Reading Skills (78 items)—This content area includes ten skill sequences, such as auditory discrimination, initial consonants with pictures, short vowel sounds, long vowel sounds, and reading level.

Manuscript Writing (125 items)—This content area measures seven areas, including the printing of uppercase and lowercase letters sequentially and from dictation, and the printing of simple sentences.

Basic Math (open-ended number of items)—This content area includes twelve skill sequences, such as number concepts, rote counting, numerical comprehension, addition combinations, subtraction combinations, recognition of money, and time concepts.

Interpretation of Results

Figure 17.6 shows the recordkeeping system for the Brigance Inventory of Early Development–Revised. Most notable in the interpretation of results are the objectives that are spelled out according to the student's performance. These are designed for use with IEPs. Developmental-age equivalents are also assigned to certain items to give a rough estimate of the student's ability level.

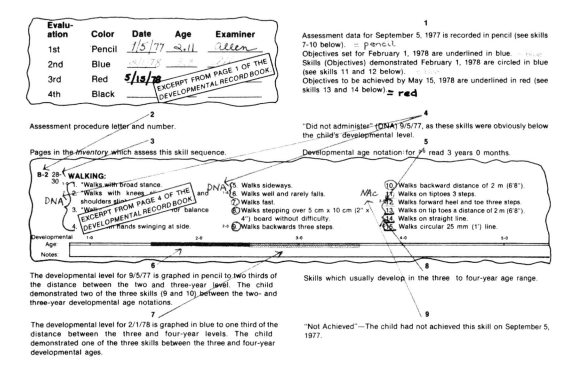

FIGURE 17.6   Illustration of the Recordkeeping System of the Brigance® Inventory of Early Development

From A. Brigance, *BRIGANCE® Inventory of Early Development.* Copyright © 1978 by Curriculum Associates, Inc. Reprinted with permission. BRIGANCE® is a registered trademark of Curriculum Associates, Inc.

OVERVIEW: BRIGANCE INVENTORY OF EARLY DEVELOPMENT– REVISED

■ *Age level*—Birth to 6 years
■ *Suggested use*—The Brigance Inventory of Early Development–Revised is a comprehensive test measuring eleven major skill areas. The test should not be given in its entirety; rather, the evaluator should choose the most appropriate areas to measure. The developmental age equivalents yielded should be considered only as estimates. The addition of the comprehensive sequences is a nice feature.

The test is not norm-referenced in the traditional sense. No reliability data are mentioned in the manual. Like the other Brigance inventories (described in Chapter 13), this one is somewhat cumbersome to administer.

Callier-Azusa Scale

The Callier-Azusa Scale (Stillman, 1978) is an individually administered instrument designed to assess the developmental level of children who are deaf-blind or have severe disabilities. It is designed to be administered by teachers or other individuals who are thoroughly familiar with the child. The author states that the child should be observed for at least two weeks, preferably in a classroom setting. The age range for the scale is from birth through approximately age 9.

Description

The Callier-Azusa Scale is comprised of eighteen subscales in five major areas. Each major area is organized into several subscales that contain sequential steps measuring the particular developmental milestones included in that subscale. In some cases the step is further broken down into as many as five separate items.

> *Motor Development*—This area includes the subscales of postural control (eighteen steps), locomotion (seventeen steps), fine motor skills (twenty steps), and visual-motor skills (twenty-one steps).
>
> *Perceptual Development*—This area includes the subscales of visual development (fifteen steps), auditory development (six steps), and tactile development (thirteen steps).
>
> *Daily Living Skills*—This area includes the subscales of undressing and dressing (sixteen steps), personal hygiene (thirteen steps), feeding skills (sixteen steps), and toileting (thirteen steps).
>
> *Cognition, Communication, and Language*—This area includes the subscales of cognitive development (twenty-one steps), receptive communication (eighteen steps), expressive communication (twenty steps), and speech development (ten steps).
>
> *Social Development*—This area includes the subscales of interaction with adults (sixteen steps), interactions with peers (seventeen steps), and interactions with environment (ten steps).

Interpretation of Results

To obtain credit for a particular step, a child must attain all the behaviors described in all items within that step. If a behavior is emerging, occurs only infrequently, or occurs only after prompting or in specific situations, credit is not given. Some items in the subscales are starred (*). According to Stillman, these items can be omitted if a "child cannot be expected to exhibit behavior because of a specific sensory or motor deficit." To score the scale, the examiner notes each subscale step that the child exhibits (a certain format for scoring is discussed in the manual). Each subscale score can be converted to a "rough" age equivalency. The author notes, however, that the behavior sequences for a child, not the age norms, provide the most important information.

OVERVIEW: CALLIER-AZUSA SCALE

■ *Age level*—Birth to 9 years
■ *Suggested use*—The Callier-Azusa Scale is one of a few scales specifically designed to use with individuals with sensory or motor deficits. Also, some of its items are designed for individuals with significant intellectual impairments. The test should be used to determine strengths and weaknesses and to identify general educational goals, rather than to assess an individual's developmental level.

Vulpé Assessment Battery

The Vulpé Assessment Battery (Vulpé, 1979) is a developmentally based system for measuring behaviors of children from birth to age 6. Information from the Vulpé can be used to determine an appropriate specific teaching approach, to indicate program goals and objectives, and to provide an accountability system for individual programs. The author states that the assessment battery is applicable to all children, including those who have multiple disabilities, are at-risk, and are "normal." She further states that the battery is extremely comprehensive, individualized, and competency-oriented. The Vulpé is divided into eight developmental skill areas or sections, and further divided into subskill areas or subsections. Each developmental skill area is sequentially based. An appendix includes a developmental reflex test and functional tests of muscle strength, motor planning, and balance.

Description

Many items on the Vulpé Assessment Battery appear in more than one of the instrument's eight skill areas or sections. In order to eliminate the need to administer an item more than once, those that are included in more than one section are cross-referenced on the assessment form. In addition, all the equipment necessary and the instructions for administering each item are included on the record form. The skill areas are as follows:

Basic Senses and Functions (16 items)—This section deals with the central nervous system functions that are considered important in performing basic activities. Included are the areas of vision, hearing, smell, balance, muscle strength, range of motion, and reflex status.

Gross Motor Behaviors (206 items)—Included in this section are items that measure such behaviors as standing, jumping, lying down, sitting, kneeling, skipping, and running.

Fine Motor Behaviors (177 items)—The items in this section deal with behaviors requiring small-muscle movements, such as eye coordination, eye-hand coordination, reaching, manipulation, and use of toys and utensils.

Language Behaviors (241 items)—This section is divided into two subsections.

Auditory Expressive Language (160 items)—This subsection includes items ranging from vocalizing noises to saying one-word sentences to using free expression.

Auditory Receptive Language (81 items)—Items in this subsection range from hearing sounds in the environment to comprehending full sentences.

Cognitive Processes and Specific Concepts (245 items)—This section is divided into thirteen subsections.

Object Concepts (17 items)—This subsection measures a child's understanding of objects. Measurement is within a developmental (for example, Piagetian) framework.

Body Concepts (32 items)—This subsection supplies information about self-image and knowledge of body parts.

Color Concepts (9 items)—This subsection includes items ranging from matching and sorting to naming and discriminating colors.

Shape Concepts (22 items)—This subsection includes items that require a child to identify shapes and to discriminate three-dimensional objects and parts of objects.

Size Concepts (6 items)—This subsection measures the child's understanding of concepts such as "bigger," "longer," and "shorter."

Space Concepts (36 items)—This subsection includes items related to the child's understanding of the relationship of his or her own body to objects in space as well as the abstract understanding of space not directly related to self.

Time Concepts (16 items)—This subsection includes items measuring a child's understanding of events that occur in the immediate present as well as the understanding of more abstract concepts of past and future.

Amount and Number Concepts (22 items)—This subsection includes counting and items that measure understanding of quantitative concepts.

Visual Memory (12 items)—This subsection includes items requiring a child to use rote memory and more complex sequential memory.

Auditory Discrimination (12 items)—This subsection requires a child to discriminate consonants, words, sounds, and tones.

Auditory Attention, Comprehension, and Memory (25 items)—This subsection includes items such as "follows one-step command," "repeats four words," "follows three-step commands," and "repeats four digits."

Cause/Effect or Means/End Behavior (12 items)—This subsection includes items such as "understands relationship of adult's presence to being lifted" and "uses parts of objects for specific purposes."

Categorizing/Combining Scheme (24 items)—This subsection includes items requiring a child to integrate information and to organize it into meaningful thoughts and actions.

Organization of Behavior (79 items)—This section is divided into four subsections.

    Attention and Goal Orientation (18 items)—This subsection deals with the ability of the child to orient and react to sensory stimuli, to selectively pay attention, to focus attention, and to maintain attention.

    Internal Control to Environmental Limits (20 items)—This subsection deals with recognition of boundaries of behavioral limits within the environment and the desire and ability to control behaviors in order to function effectively within the environment.

    Problem Solving and Learning Patterns (17 items)—This subsection includes items measuring a child's ability to react appropriately to the environment, to imitate others, and to solve problems of different complexity.

    Dependence/Independence (24 items)—This subsection measures a child's behavior along a dependence-independence continuum.

Activities of Daily Living—The items in this section are similar to those in most adaptive behavior scales measuring daily living skills. The section has seven subsections.

Feeding (47 items)
Dressing (32 items)
Social-Interaction (48 items)
Playing (50 items)
Sleeping (16 items)
Toileting (17 items)
Grooming (12 items)

Assessment of Environment (44 items)—This section is somewhat unusual for a developmental-skill instrument such as the Vulpé. It measures the interaction of the child with the environment to discover whether the child's physical and emotional needs are met by the physical and social environment.

Interpretation of Results

Each item on the Vulpé is given one of seven possible scores. A *no* score is given if the child has no apparent interest or motivation to participate in the task or cannot attend to the task. An *attention* score is given when a child shows any interest in any part of the activity but does not actively participate, whether because of physical incapacity or insufficient attention. A *physical assistance* score is used if a child actively participates in the activity when the task or environment is modified. A *social-emotional assistance* score is given when the child participates in the task when given more feedback, reinforcement, or reassurance. A *verbal assistance* score is given when the child's performance changes if verbal cues are given or the instructions repeated. An *independent* score is assigned when the student succeeds with no assistance within familiar surroundings. Finally, a *transfer* score is given when the student can perform tasks of similar complexity in different environments.

These scores can be marked directly on the Performance Analysis/Developmental Assessment scoring pad (Figure 17.7). In addition, comments about a child's performance (such as "did not perform due to sensory impairment") can be included. Age levels are provided for the items, but they represent gross indicators and should be used only to evaluate relative strengths and weaknesses.

OVERVIEW: VULPÉ ASSESSMENT BATTERY

- *Age level*—Birth to 6 years
- *Suggested use*—The Vulpé offers a highly comprehensive assessment of developmental skills of children between birth and age 6. Its comprehensiveness, in fact, might be considered one of its faults. It takes a good deal of time to administer and score all the appropriate items using the Vulpé system. The results, however, are more meaningful than those yielded from most developmental tests, particularly for use in educational programming. On the other hand, the relatively few items in certain subsections is a limitation. Venn (1987) in a review of the Vulpé, noted that it is useful for interdisciplinary assessment because of both its traditional developmental and learning content and its areas covering neurological development.

ADDITIONAL TESTS

Other tests have been used to identify children who are lagging behind in developmental areas or to identify children who might have potential problems. These tests, the First Grade Screening Test and Gesell School Readiness Test, although outdated and lacking in acceptable technical characteristics, are nonetheless used in many schools. Other tests (e.g., Metropolitan Readiness Tests) are frequently administered to large groups of students to identify readiness for the early grades.

First Grade Screening Test

Age level—End of kindergarten through beginning of first grade
Type of administration—Group
Technical adequacy—Adequate reliability, moderate predictive validity
Scores yielded—Percentiles, cutting scores
Description—The FGST (Pate & Webb, 1969) is heavily weighted toward vocabulary and language. It seems to have adequate reliability, and the limited data on its validity support its use as a screening and readiness test. The scoring format, however, seems overly rigid. For instance, the children are shown a page with six pictures on it. They are instructed to circle "all the things that you use a needle with." Some pictures must be circled,

Performance analysis/developmental assessment

Name _____ Birthdate _____

Developmental area _____

Date _____ Manual page _____

	Scale score						**Comments** Information processing and activity analysis	

No	Attention	Phys. assis.	Soc./emot. assis.	Verbal assis.	Independent	Transfer	1. Analyze activities considering component parts of each and relationship to: Basic Senses and Functions, Organizational Behaviors, Cognitive Processes and Specific Concepts, Auditory Language, Gross and Fine Motor	2. Information processing Consider:
								  Input
								  Integration
								  Feedback
								  Assimilation
								  Output

1	2	3	4	5	6	7		

Activity (item number)

1   2   3   4   5   6   7

Activity (item number)

1   2   3   4   5   6   7

Activity (item number)

1   2   3   4   5   6   7

Activity (item number)

1   2   3   4   5   6   7

Activity (item number)

1   2   3   4   5   6   7

FIGURE 17.7   Scoring Sheet from the Vulpé Assessment Battery

From S. Vulpé, *Vulpé Assessment Battery*. Copyright © 1979 by the National Institute on Mental Retardation, Ontario, Canada. Reprinted with permission.

some pictures cannot be circled, and some pictures can either be circled or not. A child must have the right responses for all six pictures in order for the item to be considered correct. This system could lead to a large number of children being considered "at risk" if they make several slight errors.

Gesell School Readiness Test

Age level—4 1/2 to 9 years old
Type of administration—Individual
Technical adequacy—Questionable reliability and validity
Scores yielded—Developmental age
Description—The GSRT (Ilg, Ames, Haines, & Gillespie, 1978) is based largely on the work of Arnold Gesell and is tied into a theory of development "which openly addresses and recommends retention" (Carstens, 1985). In other words, if a child scores low on the GSRT, it indicates that the child is developmentally young and should not be promoted. The GSRT includes items requiring the child to copy and write, manipulate cubes, name animals, identify left and right, answer basic interview questions, and demonstrate visual-memory skills. There is considerable controversy surrounding the GSRT and what it actually measures. The construction of the test leaves a lot to be desired. The value of the test depends on one's philosophical orientation towards Gesell's theories. It has both strong advocates and vocal critics.

Metropolitan Readiness Tests

Age level—Preschool to beginning first grade
Type of administration—Group
Technical adequacy—Excellent standardization, adequate reliability, questionable validity
Scores yielded—Percentile ranks, stanines, performance ratings, scaled scores, normal curve equivalents
Description—The MRT (Nurss & McGauvran, 1986) is the oldest and most widely used readiness test. The 1986 edition has maintained many of the features of earlier editions. It is heavily weighted toward preacademic skills (e.g., beginning consonants) as opposed to perceptual or developmental skills. The standardization sample was large and representative, although the predictive validity of the instrument has yet to be established. The predictive usefulness of the test, of course, depends on the specific first-grade curriculum.

Many other tests purport to measure the early academic abilities of young children, although they have questionable validity for the preschool child.

Test of Early Reading Ability–2

Age level—3 to 9 years
Type of administration—Individual
Technical adequacy—Adequate reliability, questionable validity (for preschool children)
Scores yielded—Standard score, percentile ranks, normal curve equivalent
Description—The TERA-2 (Reid, Hresko, and Hammill, 1989) was designed to measure the actual reading ability of young children. Areas such as Knowledge of Contextual Meaning, Alphabet, and Reading Conventions are measured. There are two equivalent forms of the TERA-2, A and B, which would allow examiners to test with one form and retest with another after the initiation of an intervention program. There is some question of the validity of the instrument before the age of 4 or after the age of 7. The authors, in fact, note this limitation and suggest that anyone using the instrument with those age groups establish its suitability before administration.

Test of Early Mathematics Ability–2

Age level—3 through 8 years
Type of administration—Individual
Technical adequacy—Adequate reliability, questionable validity
Scores yielded—Standard scores, percentiles, age equivalents
Description—The TEMA-2 (Ginsberg & Baroody, 1990) is a norm-referenced instrument that can also be used informally to determine specific strengths and weaknesses. According to the authors, the test can be used to monitor progress, evaluate programs, screen for readiness, identify gifted students, and guide instruction and remediation. It measures four formal areas, Knowledge of Convention (reading and writing numerals), Number Facts, Calculation (algorithms), and Base Ten Concepts, and three informal areas of Mathematics, Concepts of Relative Magnitude, Counting, and Calculation. The TEMA-2 was standardized on a somewhat limited sample, and the validity of the instrument is generally lacking. One potential advantage of the TEMA-2 is the availability of a book of remedial techniques for improving the skills that are measured.

Instrument or Technique	Suggested Use							Target Population						Special Considerations	Educational Relevance for Exceptional Students
	Preferral		Postreferral												
	Screening and Initial Identification	Informal Determination and Evaluation of Teaching Programs and Strategies	Determination of Current Performance Level and Educational Need	Decisions about Classification and Program Placement	IEP Goals	IEP Objectives	IEP Evaluation	Mild/Moderate	Severe/Profound	Preschool	Elementary Age	Secondary Age	Adult		
AGS Early Screening Profiles	X							X		X				Uses a team approach including information from the parent; motor section limited	useful
Denver II	X							X	X	X				Limited technical aspects, revision of the popular DDST	limited
Developmental Indicators for the Assessment of Learning–Revised (AGS)	X							X		X				Has been used for early identification of disabled and gifted; quick to administer	adequate
Miller Assessment for Preschoolers	X							X		X				More time consuming to administer; heavily weighted to sensorimotor and sensory integration tasks	adequate
Battelle Developmental Inventory	X	X			X			X	X	X	X			Well constructed; includes adaptations for disabled; limited with very young children	useful
Developmental Profile–II	X	X						X	X	X	X			Uses interview format; technical characteristics are limited	limited
Boehm Test of Basic Concepts–R	X	X			X			X		X	X			Best used informally; normative information of questionable relevance	useful
Bracken Basic Concept Scale	X	X			X			X		X	X			Well constructed; potentially useful basic concept scale	useful
Assessment Log and Developmental Progress Chart–Infant			X		X	X	X	X	X	X				Used in conjunction with the Carolina curriculum	useful
Behavioral Characteristics Progression			X		X	X	X	X	X	X				Books of instructional suggestions that are correlated with each item are available	useful

										Comments	
Brigance Inventory of Early Development–Revised		X	X	X	X	X	X	X		Includes objectives for each item; developmental age equivalents should be used informally only	adequate
Callier–Azusa Scale		X	X			X	X	X		Designed for use with children who are deaf-blind	adequate
Vulpé Assessment Battery		X	X	X	X	X	X	X		Has a tedious scoring system that yields important programmatic information	useful
First Grade Screening Test	X					X	X	X		Overly rigid scoring system; heavily weighted toward vocabulary skills	limited
Gesell School Readiness Test	X				X	X	X	X		Limited technical aspects; used to make retention decisions	very limited
Metropolitan Readiness Tests	X				X	X	X	X	X	Good technical aspects; comprehensive	useful
Test of Early Reading Ability–2	X				X	X	X	X	X	Limited for preschool children	limited
Test of Early Mathematics Ability–2	X				X	X	X	X	X	Limited for preschool children	limited

18

VOCATIONAL/TRANSITIONAL ASSESSMENT

Instruments and Procedures Included

Informal Procedures
> Checklists and Rating Scales
> Work Samples
> Curriculum-Based Vocational Assessment
> Direct Observation and Ecological Assessment
> Portfolio Assessment
> Outcomes Assessment

Interest and Aptitude Instruments
> Differential Aptitude Tests
> Gordon Occupational Checklists–II
> Kuder Occupational Interest Survey–Revised
> Occupational Aptitude Survey and Interest Schedule–2
> Reading-Free Vocational Interest Inventory–Revised
> Strong-Campbell Interest Inventory
> Vocational Preference Inventory–Revised
> Wide Range Interest-Opinion Test
> Work Adjustment Inventory

In recent years, the emphasis on vocational/transitional programs, particularly for secondary-level students, has increased dramatically. Along with increased emphasis on vocational programming comes an increased emphasis on vocational assessment. Although in the past the focus of vocational assessment was on the use of formal instruments, current trends in the field are toward more informal techniques that help develop a more encompassing database that can and should stretch across a student's school career. Although traditional assessment procedures have not been abandoned, this recent shift has led to a more transdisciplinary approach to vocational assessment. In turn, this has led to shared responsibilities and cooperative planning and programming that are necessary to achieve successful postschool adjustments for students with disabilities. Although the specific role that vocational assessment and education specialists might play is dictated by funding and various state and local program needs, the special education teacher can and should be familiar with the techniques included in this chapter. Aside from some of the specific tests and inventories, virtually all other procedures can be implemented by classroom teachers. If vocational assessment is conducted and the information is used appropriately, it is logical to assume that vocational programming goals and objectives on IEPs, vocational programs, and curricula and the quality of transition services will improve. With these improvements, we should also see much more positive postschool results for students with disabilities.

Vocational assessment has evolved from and employs the talents of several professional discipline areas (Stodden, 1986). Not surprisingly then, vocational assessment has traditionally involved a wide variety of procedures. These have included describing overt skills, drawing inferences about student abilities, predicting student job performance, assessing interests and aptitudes, and providing suggestions for instruction (Gaylord-Ross, 1986). More specifically, vocational assessment may rely on the use of interviews and rating scales, psychometric testing, the use of work samples, and situational assessment (Meehan & Hodell, 1986). In fact, it has been suggested that vocational assessment that relies on a single summative evaluation is probably not sufficient for accurate appraisal of the interests and attitudes of students with disabilities (Buschner, Watts, Siders, & Leonard, 1989). Others have noted that there should be increased reliance on the use of work samples (Peterson, 1986), curriculum-based vocational assessment (Conaway, 1987), and ecological assessment strategies (Falvey, 1989). Rivera (1993) suggested that performance-based (or "authentic") and portfolio assessments are emerging alternatives to traditional academic assessments. These alternative approaches have applications to vocational assessment as well.

In this chapter, the current trends in transition planning and programming will be discussed with particular reference to federal mandates that influence vocational assessment and education for students with disabilities. The steps in developing transition plans and the role of vocational assessment in that process will also be addressed. The development and use of work samples are included, as well as the basis and strategies for the use of curriculum-based vocational assessment and direct observation of students on the job. Finally, information concerning a number of relevant and commonly used psychometric instruments used in assessing students' vocational interests and aptitude will be provided.

It is worth noting that some experts differentiate between vocational assessment (i.e., gathering data) and vocational evaluation (i.e., reviewing and interpreting assessment information) (Stodden, 1986). In this chapter, the terms will be used interchangeably and are intended to include both of the above processes.

SUPPORT FOR TRANSITION SERVICES

Interest has increased in and requirements developed for providing transition services for students with disabilities that will better prepare them for the world of work. In 1984, Madeleine Will, then director of the Office of Special Education and Rehabilitative Services, wrote a position statement concerning the delivery of transition services to individuals with disabilities. She noted that the transition period includes high school, graduation, postsecondary placement, and initial years of employment. Transition planning and programming is a process that requires sound preparation and adequate support. Will stated that successful transitions require an effort that emphasizes shared responsibilities among service agencies.

Several legislative acts have supported the need for cooperative planning and service delivery to ensure successful transition programs. Such legislation has been necessary because the assimilation of people with disabilities into the mainstream workforce has yet to reach an optimal level (Johnson & Rusch, 1993; Rusch & Phelps, 1987). It should be noted, however, that many educators believe that in addition to legislative mandates, actual transition planning and programming will be required to provide better opportunities for individual students with disabilities who are leaving school and entering the "real world."

In 1983, Public Law 98-199, Section 626, "Secondary Education and Transitional Services for Handicapped Youth," was enacted specifically to increase the likelihood of successful school-to-work transitions for students with disabilities. Other legislative acts such as the Americans with Disabilities Act (P.L. 101-336) provide protection against discrimination and require reasonable accommodations in the workplace for people with handicaps (Linthicum, Cole, & D'Alonzo, 1991). In 1984, the Carl D. Perkins Vocational Education Act expanded the services provided to students with disabilities through vocational education and assessment to include transition planning and programming. More recent mandates and amendments to the Carl D. Perkins Act (e.g., Carl D. Perkins Vocational and Applied Technology Education Act of 1990, P.L. 101-392), have, however, made unclear the magnitude of the role vocational assessment personnel eventually may play within specific state and local transition programs for students with disabilities (Kochhar, 1991). Nevertheless, this law is important in understanding the relationship between vocational assessment and transition planning and programming. A more in-depth analysis of this law follows.

Carl D. Perkins Vocational and Applied Technology Education Act

Specifically, the Carl D. Perkins Act provides for an increase in the accessibility to vocational education services for special education students. Wehman, Moon, Everson, Wood, and Barcus (1988) outlined the following provisions of the Act that affect services to youths with disabilities: (1) 10 percent of a state's grant allotment be used to provide services to students with disabilities; (2) each student and his/her parents be informed of vocational opportunities available at least one year prior to the provision of vocational education services (or by the time the student reaches ninth grade); and (3) equal access be provided to vocational educational services as deemed appropriate through the IEP process. These services may include (1) vocational assessment; (2) guidance and career counseling and development; (3) adaptation of curriculum and provision of special services to meet individual needs; and/or (4) staff and counseling services to facilitate successful transitions.

It is clear from the above summary that Congress intended that special education students be afforded access to those same vocational services available to nondisabled peers. Amendments to the Carl D. Perkins Act enacted in 1990 (P.L. 101-392) may, however, have some negative impact on provision of vocational services to students with disabilities (Kochhar, 1991). Kochhar asserted that the language of the law appears to ensure that services such as those just mentioned remain intact but that program or personnel cuts due to funding changes for vocational education programs may result in changes in the provision of these services, in particular state or local programs. This act should be reauthorized by 1996, which may change current rules and regulations (Special Education Report, 1994). Interestingly, however, the importance of transitional planning was reiterated in recent legislation such as P.L. 101-476.

Public Law 101-476

Among the many provisions of P.L. 101-476 (discussed in Chapter 1), is one for a new state grant program that authorizes state education and vocational rehabilitation agencies to apply jointly for funds to develop, implement, and improve transition services for students with disabilities from age 14 through their exiting school (National Association of State Directors of Special Education [NASDSE], 1990). NASDSE reported that these funds must be used to (1) increase availability, access, and quality of transition services through development or improvement in policies, procedures, systems, and other mechanisms; (2) improve ability of professionals, parents, and advocates to work with such youth to improve transition outcomes; and (3) improve relationships among education agencies, adult service providers, families, and the private sector to identify and reach consensus on what transition services are needed and how they are to be applied. Additionally, the law mandates that transition plans be developed for all students with disabilities by age 16.

For the purposes of this chapter, it will be assumed that vocational assessment and education services will continue to be widely available. Even if this should prove not to be the case, the reader should be familiar with many of the techniques discussed for assessing vocational performance. Special education teachers should be capable of implementing, modifying, or adapting many of these practices in order to obtain vocational assessment data.

GUIDELINES FOR ESTABLISHING TRANSITION SERVICES: IMPORTANCE OF VOCATIONAL ASSESSMENT

Schriner and Bellini (1994) noted the emphasis that P.L. 101-476 placed on transition services being based on individual need and being referenced to student preferences and interests. Services may include community-based experiences, training in adult living and daily living skills, and vocational evaluation. Repetto, White, and Snauwaert (1990) reported on results of a state survey concerning the provision of transition services. These authors discovered considerable variance among states concerning the use of an Individualized Transition Plan (ITP) form, the relationship between the IEP and ITP, the age at which transition planning should begin, those to be involved in the planning, the issues to be addressed, and the expected outcomes to be emphasized. Repetto, Tulbert, and Schwartz (1993) found similar problems in a more recent statewide study but suggested that programming and planning for transition was rapidly expanding. Nevertheless, general guidelines and procedures will be offered that should serve as a model for effective vocationally related transition programming.

Transition planning and programming should begin no later than a student's first year in high school.   The more barriers a student faces (e.g., behavioral difficulties, limited employment skills), the earlier this process should begin. Planning for students with severe disabilities may begin as early as middle school. Parents might be encouraged to "brainstorm" about desired adult outcomes from a student's earliest years. Stodden and Leake (1994) argued that "transition values" should be infused across the entire curriculum and into all IEPs regardless of a child's age. These authors have suggested that such a focus would guide teachers toward not only why, what, where, and when to teach, but also how to assess within IEPs.

The assessment aspect of transition planning and programming may begin prior to the first year of high school.   Interest inventories, aptitude tests, work samples, curriculum-based vocational assessment, and even on-the-job assessment may be administered prior to the high school years. For example, Elrod, Isbell, and Braziel (1989) noted that vocational assessment may be conducted throughout the student's school career through inexpensive and easily administered procedures. Specifically, teachers and other personnel should assess prevocational competencies and relate those competencies to the basic skills curriculum (Elrod et al., 1989). For example, Elrod et al. suggested the use of short student self-evaluation scales with clear, easily understood, and brief item statements with open-ended or yes/no response requirements. Sample items requiring a yes/no response might include "I like to keep my desk neat," "I like to think about what I will be when I grow up," "I like people to count on me," and "I like to earn money" (Elrod et al., 1989). Teachers might also evaluate their efforts to improve transition/vocational outcomes through similar rating scales (Elrod et al., 1989). These authors suggested possible items using a 1–5 scale that included "I integrate transition-related skills within basic skills objectives," "I select classroom activities that are applicable to real-life settings," and "I assign classroom duties to promote proper work attitudes." Elrod et al. suggested that targeted competencies might be derived from the Life-Centered Career Education curriculum (Brolin, 1983). Because there should be emphasis on career awareness for elementary-aged students, assessment at this stage of schooling should not be ignored.

Vocational assessment becomes critical to the transition process as the student prepares for postsecondary adjustment.   During IEP and ITP discussions, a written vocational assessment report may be reviewed if available; otherwise relevant vocational assessment data should be discussed. That information should be used in deciding on vocationally related goals and objectives, daily classroom activities implemented, vocational education, and vocational training placements (Meehan & Hodell, 1986; Wisniewski, Alper, & Schloss, 1991). Wisniewski et al. also stressed that systematic assessment by a transition specialist may assist in guiding community-based instruction, as well as ensure that the vocational curriculum is functional and relevant. One manner in which this may be accomplished is through curriculum-based vocational assessment (CBVA) (Bisconer, Stodden, & Porter, 1993). Bisconer et al. noted that CBVA is "a process for determining the career/vocational needs of students based on their ongoing classroom and work experience activities and performances." CBVA is discussed in greater detail in a later section. Vocational assessment data are combined with that of other assessment specialists and educators to provide a total picture of the student's abilities, interests, and skills that might affect his or her postschool performance. According to Elrod and Sorgenfrei (1988), information collected from various personnel might include (1) psychoeducational information involving areas such as intelligence, perception, psycholinguistics, and psychomotor skills; (2) sociobehavioral information including direct observation of social conduct, personality, and psychiatric evaluation; (3) academic information including the areas of reading, mathematics, and language arts; and (4) career vocational/assessment information involving interests, needs, aptitudes, and abilities that relate to all areas of life adjustment. This latter area might include a consideration of the roles of the student in home and family, community, and workplace (Kokaska & Brolin, 1985), as well as specific vocational interests and skills. Furthermore, the specific emphasis on career/vocational assessment should increase substantially as the student enters junior and senior high school, whereas academic assessment is emphasized less (Elrod & Sorgenfrei, 1988). In one statewide survey, only 37 percent of 2,213 students with disabilities who had exited school had received in-school formal or informal vocational assessment services (Lombard, Hazelkorn, & Neubert, 1992). If the transition process is to be successful, the availability and accessibility of vocational assessment services must increase.

Halpern (1994) emphasized that the assessment process itself should involve the student with disabilities. The student should be taught whenever possible to examine and evaluate his or her own performance in academic, vocational, independent living, and personal/social skills. Halpern noted that traditional assessment data should not be discarded, but rather the "locus of interpretation" should shift from the assessment specialist to the student. That is, the assessment procedure should involve teaching self-evaluation and when a student's disabilities do not permit this, the locus should shift to the parent if possible.

Developing and Implementing the Transition Plan

Vocational assessment information is brought to the transition team meeting for sharing, discussion, and use in planning for desired outcomes and specific goals and objectives. During these meetings, the transition team will formulate an ITP that is included as part of the IEP and in some cases may be part of an Individualized Written Rehabilitation Plan (IWRP) (Repetto et al., 1990). The following are the suggested steps of Wehman et al. (1988) for implementing the transition plan and program. First, *organize the ITP teams for all transition-age students.* This step includes identifying the students according to some criteria (e.g., age and severity of barriers to postschool adjustment), identifying appropriate school personnel (i.e., individuals from different disciplines who have had recent meaningful contact with the individual), and identifying adult service agencies that may be involved in the transition process (e.g., vocational rehabilitation or Association for Retarded Citizens). Wehman et al. further noted that many adult service agencies will not have sufficient staff to participate in transition team meetings until perhaps the final two years of school. The vocational assessment specialist (or special or vocational education teacher involved in gathering relevant career/vocational assessment data) may well be the individual most qualified to suggest possible employment options, postsecondary training options, and potential employers or adult service providers. Step two involves *conducting the actual ITP meeting.* Typically, these meetings are scheduled simultaneously with the IEP for convenience and to increase the likelihood of parental and staff participation. During the actual meeting, the following procedures should be followed to formulate the ITP:

1. Open the transition meeting by introducing all present and establishing an informal, comfortable atmosphere.

2. Generate a discussion of desired outcomes and what support services are available.
3. Identify transition goals.
4. Determine steps and objectives to accomplish those goals.
5. Devise a checklist to ensure that responsible persons and time lines are identified for providing various services (e.g., referral to vocational rehabilitation, investigating application for food stamp assistance).
6. End the meeting by having all participants sign the plan.

Students with disabilities should be included as part of the IEP/ITP team whenever possible. Halpern (1994) stressed that professionals and parents alike may be too "protective" and diminish opportunities to assume responsibility and develop self-determination. Halpern noted that if "the transition process is to be successful, it must begin with helping students to gain a sense of empowerment with respect to their own transition planning" (p. 118). If students have learned self-evaluation skills, been empowered, and have been actively involved in the transition plan development, then students might also be the primary determinants of postschool goals (Halpern, 1994).

The third step is to actually *implement the plan.* This will likely involve interagency cooperation and the terms of state or local interagency agreements. The fourth step involves *ensuring that the ITP is updated at least annually* (and conceivably more frequently in the actual transition year). Follow-up procedures are also necessary to ensure goals and objectives are being addressed. The fifth and final step is to *schedule an exit meeting* just prior to the student's leaving school to discuss the continued provision of services and follow up as necessary. Those individuals involved in vocational assessment should be prepared to be responsible for assisting in referrals to appropriate agencies and programs (e.g., vocational rehabilitation), providing ongoing assessment, and providing follow-up assessment services after graduation. Follow-up assessment is a growing area of concern in vocational/transitional assessment. For example, Johnson and Rusch (1993) reviewed twenty-four follow-up studies for students who had exited special education programs. Only one of those studies addressed issues of type, quality, and degree of transition planning services. The importance of outcomes assessment is discussed in greater detail in the Informal Procedures section of this chapter.

The IEP and ITP are closely related documents. The transition plan may, however, span a multiyear period, emphasize the involvement of both educators and adult service providers, demonstrate broader scope in addressing vocational, residential, leisure, social and personal, and community living strengths and needs (Stowitschek & Kelso, 1989).The ITP is developed to facilitate entry into and maintenance of adult working and community life situations and to coordinate educational and postsecondary efforts toward this goal (Stowitschek & Kelso, 1989). A sample ITP is shown in Figure 18.1. The possible forms and formats for an ITP are many and varied (Repetto et al., 1990). IEP forms may now include a transition services and planning section for students of the appropriate age.

Student _____   Current Classroom Placement _____
Date of Plan _____   Projected Graduation Date _____

Concerns	Objective	Activities	Personnel Responsible	Completion Date
Income: Ability of person to support himself/herself				
Job & Job Training: Ability of person to hold a job on his/her own				
Living Arrangements: Ability to live independently				
Recreation & Leisure: Ability to participate in community recreation and leisure activities				
Transportation: Ability to travel from home to work, postsecondary programs, community activities, etc.				
Medical Needs: Person's medical needs are met				
Friends/Advocates: Ability to develop and maintain friendships with peers and advocates				
Long-Term Planning: Adequate provision made for long-term care/supervision needs				
Family Relationships: Person can maintain contact with his/her family				
Insurance: Adequate provision made for health and other types of insurance				

FIGURE 18.1   Transition Plan

From B. Cobb and S. Hasazi, School-aged transition services: Options for adolescents with mild handicaps. *Career Development for Exceptional Individuals, 10,* 17. Copyright © 1987 by Council for Exceptional Children. Reprinted with permission.

Assessment information used to develop IEPs and ITPs and to make other vocational programming decisions is gathered through a variety of procedures. Informal procedures include the use of checklists or rating scales and may assist the teacher in gathering preliminary information. Direct approaches such as work samples, curriculum-based vocational assessment, and observation of students on the job provide meaningful information about students' vocational interests. Finally, instruments such as career interest inventories and vocational aptitude tests might provide important information for determining career options.

INFORMAL PROCEDURES

Checklists and Rating Scales

WHY USE CHECKLISTS AND RATING SCALES?

Screening for vocational/career preferences, interests, and aptitudes; developing educational and vocational programs

WHO SHOULD USE THEM?

Teachers

A variety of informal procedures might be used to evaluate vocational skills. Elrod et al. (1989) suggested that observational data and anecdotal records might be compiled and informal interviews conducted. Sample questions might include "What job would you like to have when you finish your education?" "Do you like to work alone or with others?" and "Would you prefer a desk job or a job where you can use your physical skills?" Elrod et al. pointed out that the *Brigance Diagnostic Inventory of Essential Skills* (discussed in Chapter 13) includes components in the vocational subtest that might serve as bases for either individual or group paper and pencil tasks or for interviewing. They also suggested that informal assessment of prevocational aptitudes (for grades 7 to 12) might involve the use of rating scales completed by the teacher that include items related to placement in vocational education or in private employment. An example of such a rating scale is included in Figure 18.2. Similar rating scales might be employed at actual job placements. For example, Burnham and Housley (1992) used a different survey, but one similar to that depicted in Figure 18.2, to compare perceptions of employers, adult service providers, and students with mental or learning disabilities. They found similarities and differences in the emphasis placed by each group on various dimensions of work behavior. Later in this chapter, other examples of checklists for use in employment environments are provided. Although checklists and rating scales may be easily employed by teachers, the information gleaned from such assessments might not provide a complete portrait of a student's aptitudes and abilities. Work samples, both commercially produced and locally validated, are an example of a more formal technique that might also provide useful information.

Work Samples

WHY USE WORK SAMPLES?

Evaluate performance of specific and general work skills and worker traits and characteristics

WHO SHOULD USE THEM?

Vocational assessment personnel

Work samples are a situational assessment tool used to simulate tasks associated with jobs in the labor market. Work samples are defined in the Vocational Evaluation and Work Adjustment Association–Commission on the Accreditation of Rehabilitation Facilities (VEWAA-CARF) Vocational Evaluation and Work Adjustment Standards (1978) as

> *a well-defined work activity involving tasks, materials, and tools which are identical or similar to those in an actual job or cluster of jobs. It is used to assess an individual's vocational aptitude, worker characteristics, and vocational interests.* (p. 20)

Work samples incorporate the tools and the standards associated with the actual job. Ideally, the activities associated with work samples should be as realistic as possible (i.e., as similar as possible to the community-based work). Work samples are a component in the vocational assessment process because they emphasize performance skills and approximate work more closely than traditional psy-

Work Behavior		Rating			
1. Dresses appropriately	1	2	3	4	5
2. Is well groomed	1	2	3	4	5
3. Attends class regularly	1	2	3	4	5
4. Is punctual	1	2	3	4	5
5. Demonstrates initiative	1	2	3	4	5
6. Works well independently	1	2	3	4	5
7. Works well with peers	1	2	3	4	5
8. Works well with authority figures	1	2	3	4	5
9. Is receptive to constructive criticism	1	2	3	4	5
10. Shows pride in work	1	2	3	4	5
11. Keeps neat work area	1	2	3	4	5
12. Completes tasks on time	1	2	3	4	5
13. Asks questions, if needed	1	2	3	4	5
14. Accepts new responsibilities	1	2	3	4	5
15. Solicits additional duties when finished with a task	1	2	3	4	5

Rating Scale: 1 = Never observed; 2 = Observed sometimes; 3 = Observed about half of the time; 4 = Observed often; 5 = Always observed.

FIGURE 18.2   Prevocational Aptitude Rating Scale

From G. Elrod, C. Isbell, and P. Braziel, Assessing transition-related variables from kindergarten through grade 12. *Diagnostique, 14*, 259. Copyright © 1989 by Council for Exceptional Children. Reprinted with permission.

chometric instruments. Activities performed on a work-sample task give the evaluator an opportunity to observe work behavior in a controlled environment.

Data gathered during the work-sample activities assist the vocational evaluator in identifying strengths and weaknesses, determining a practical and realistic career goal, and assessing interest areas. They also provide the evaluator with information concerning work habits, dexterity and manipulative skills, physical abilities, interpersonal skills, and work capacity. This information may be helpful to the evaluator in analyzing vocational potential, selecting appropriate training programs, and identifying program modifications. Results obtained from using the work-sample approach assist personnel in providing vocational counseling, program development, and job placement (Sarkees & Scott, 1985).

Work-sample activities may be provided through the use of a wide variety of commercial and locally developed batteries (Peterson, 1986). Many commercial work samples provide normative data as well as information on validity and reliability. Work samples may attempt to simulate the complete range of activities associated with a single job or they may provide selected activities designed to represent a number of related tasks. Five different types of work samples are defined by the VEWAA-CARF (1978):

> *Cluster Trait Work Sample*—A single work sample developed to assess a cluster of worker traits. This type of sample is based on an analysis of an occupational area and the traits necessary for successful performance. The student's potential to perform various tasks is assessed.
>
> *Indigenous Work Samples*—This type provides activities that are used to assess the essential factors affecting performance in an occupation as it currently exists in the community.
>
> *Job Sample*—This type precisely replicates actual industrial jobs and includes the equipment, tools, raw materials, procedures, and standards used on the job.
>
> *Simulated Work Sample*—This type is similar to the job sample, but only a segment of the essential work is replicated as well as work-related factors and the use of the tools required on the job.
>
> *Single Trait Work Samples*—This type focuses assessment on a single worker trait. This trait or characteristic may be relevant to either a specific job or to a variety of jobs, but only this single isolated factor is assessed.

Sitlington and Wimmer (1978) cited eight advantages of using commercial work sample systems versus other assessment approaches.

1. Work samples provide the student with the opportunity for job exploration. Given actual simulations of work activities, individuals often begin to think seriously about the type of work they might enjoy.

2. They allow actual job simulations in the evaluation setting, where they can be conducted without the pressure that might be experienced in an actual job setting.

3. Work samples are motivating. Not only do they provide an alternative to traditional testing procedures, but they also often provide the types of tasks at which a person with a disability can be successful.

4. They may provide motivation for classroom learning by establishing relevance for certain academic skills that are related to the task.

5. Work samples allow habilitation personnel to compare an individual's abilities to those of workers employed in particular occupations.

6. They may be used as behavioral change instruments, allowing assessment and training of work habits and personal social skills.

7. Work samples allow determination of an individual's strengths and weaknesses on work-related tasks.

8. Work samples can build confidence by providing successful experiences.

Regardless of the advantages of work samples, their exclusive use in vocational assessment has significant limitations (Sax, 1973). Some of the disadvantages of the exclusive use of work samples include (1) a tendency to emphasize quality and quantity of production rather than personality factors, (2) difficulty in developing work samples for the many different jobs in the labor market, (3) problems in comparing the working environment in industry and the more controlled environment in which the work sample is collected, (4) lack of assurance that the sample is measuring the actual job skills, (5) the risk of developing a good appraisal instrument for jobs that no longer exist because work technology change is so rapid, and (6) lack of reliability and validity information for many work-sampling approaches. Sarkees and Scott (1985) specifically noted the disadvantages of using commercial work samples, among which were that the systems are often expensive and time consuming to administer and that some work samples are too simple and do not present a realistic view of the job. In addition, the norms provided for work-sample performance may not relate to the population being evaluated. Sitlington and Wimmer (1978) identified a series of questions to ask when a commercial system is considered:

1. Does the system take into account expectancy to fail?
2. Does the system take into account academic limitations?
3. Does the system take into account verbal limitations?
4. Does the system take into account experience limitations?
5. Does the system allow for more than one trial on tasks?
6. Does the system allow for repeated instructions and check for comprehension?
7. Does the system have face validity (i.e., is it an accurate assessment of the content presented)?
8. Does the system allow for appropriate conditions for testing (i.e., does it offer pleasant surroundings, orderly administration, and considerations for fatigue of individuals)?
9. Is the system adequately normed on handicapped individuals and the workers who are doing the various types of tasks?

Selection of appropriate commercial systems should also take into consideration the following factors: (1) range of jobs available in the community and scope of jobs represented in the work sample, (2) validity and reliability for the client population to be served, and (3) purpose of the evaluation including occupational information through hands-on experience, assessment of current skills and aptitudes without relating information to career functions, a thorough evaluation of student aptitude and work behaviors, occupational information and dissemination, and occupational exploration (Revell, Kriloff, & Sarkees, 1980).

Locally developed work samples can provide a more appropriate means of assessment because they are more closely associated with the limitations and demands of the local labor market than commercially developed work samples (Peterson, 1986). Work-sample activities can be developed by vocational personnel to evaluate the abilities of an individual to perform a specific task—activities that usually reflect proficiencies necessary for entry-level vocational courses associated with the program. These work samples may not always sample the total classroom curriculum, but they include tasks that suggest a potential for successful performance in the classroom and may help to point out areas for remediation (Sarkees & Scott, 1985). Pruitt (1977) noted that informal work samples can be used to provide career exploration; assess work habits, coordination, physical capacity, and interpersonal skills; assess abilities and limitations; and evaluate skills of the individual prior to placement in a job situation. An example of how a work sample might be evaluated is presented in Table 18.1. This example was taken from the Albuquerque, New Mexico, public schools.

Work samples continue to play an important role in vocational assessment programs in school and rehabilitation settings. As Peterson (1986) pointed out, the use of work (real or simulated) as a focal point in vocational assessment is both a valid and valuable process. Vocational assessment personnel and teachers have developed other procedures for evaluating work behavior and skills. Evaluators focus on performance in actual work settings, on vocational skills specifically taught, or on vocational skills embedded within the overall curriculum. Curriculum-based vocational assessment is one such procedure.

Curriculum-Based Vocational Assessment

WHY USE CURRICULUM-BASED VOCATIONAL ASSESSMENT?

Evaluate acquisition of vocational and related skills embedded within content and applied courses

WHO SHOULD USE IT?

Teachers, vocational assessment personnel

TABLE 18.1   Example of an Evaluation of a Work Sample (Written Direction Test)

Purpose	Practical assessment of functional reading ability. May also measure organizational skills of students with adequate reading comprehension.
Pertinent referral questions	1. How does this student learn best?
	2. This student has poor reading comprehension skills. Can he/she work from written directions at all?
	3. McDonald's Restaurant requires their manager trainees to read manuals. Is this an appropriate placement?
Reading level	5th or 6th grade level
Time to administer	Takes about 10 or 15 minutes to complete.
Strengths	1. Practical and quick measure of ability to follow written directions.
	2. Students seem to dislike this instrument less than other reading tests.
	3. Provides a comparison to other short tests of learning style.
Weaknesses	1. Limited norm base.
	2. Does not include a speed measure.
Possible interpretations	*High*
	1. Student may be able to work from written directions on a job.
	Low
	1. Student may lack experience in working from written directions.
	2. Student should avoid jobs requiring the use of written directions.
	3. Other methods of instruction may be appropriate.

Historically, vocational assessments have been conducted without appropriate collaboration between vocational and special education personnel and without a single, unifying funding source (Ianacone & Leconte, 1986). As a result, many programs have experienced the following problems:

1. Lack of expertise to assist in setting up vocational services
2. The use of a rehabilitation model rather than a career exploration, planning and programming, and vocational training model
3. Overreliance on the use of commercial assessment systems insensitive to local job market needs

4. Assessment in isolated settings that failed to obtain critical information concerning social and work-related behaviors
5. Emphasis on career exploration activities as opposed to more relevant assessment services
6. Lack of planning and release time for developing relevant, locally valid work samples
7. Lack of use of assessment information in making programmatic decisions
8. Lack of a uniform system for referrals, with some students being referred too early to have developed adequate motivation or concern over career goals and some too late for the assessment to have programmatic impact
9. Prohibitive transportation costs when assessments were conducted in a center
10. Lack of trained personnel with knowledge concerning vocational assessment as well as both vocational and special education (Ianacone & Leconte, 1986)

As a result of these problems, curriculum-based vocational assessment (CBVA) was offered as an alternative. This process is similar to the curriculum-based assessment procedures discussed in Chapter 7. CBVA focuses on the career/vocational needs and strengths of students based on their ongoing performance and course content, and also in work experience activities (Bisconer, Stodden, & Porter, 1993). Kohler (1994) reported on a program in Florida that incorporated the use of CBVA to determine the effectiveness of a classroom- and community-based vocational instruction program. The community-based component focused on vocational skill development and concurrent work experience. The classroom-based component focused on employment-related skills taught in school. Kohler reported that CBVA was useful as an analytical tool for measuring curricular impact on student outcomes and providing information concerning students' strengths and weaknesses. Subsequent programmatic changes could adjust for individual differences in progress. CBVA may be conducted by teachers or vocational evaluators; it may be used in the classroom or "real world" environment. It may be used to measure acquisition of course content or specific vocational skills (Conaway, 1987).

One model for CBVA, described by Porter and Stodden (1986), includes three levels of data collection. The first encompasses junior high school prevocational courses and activities. At this level, readiness and awareness skills are assessed during exploratory classes and activities. The second level begins in high school and addresses performance in vocational coursework. The third level includes assessment of work-related behaviors and both generalized vocational outcomes and specific skills in actual job placements obtained through cooperative work-experience programs (Porter & Stodden, 1986). Included in Figure 18.3 are the key steps to developing a CBVA model listed by Ianacone and Leconte (1986). Included in Figure 18.4 on page 489 is a vocational assessment rating form used in the CBVA model proposed by Porter and Stodden (1986). It is important to note that CBVA, as is curriculum-based assessment in general, is only as valid as the curriculum itself (Taylor, Willits, & Richards, 1988). That is, if the career/vocational course content is not meeting the needs of students, the assessment infor-

1. Identify key development personnel.

   • Who are the key personnel needed to conceptualize, develop, and validate a curriculum-based vocational assessment model?

   • Who are the key personnel needed to operate and develop the vocational assessment model?

   • What disciplines and administrative personnel are critical to implementation and need to be represented?

2. Conduct a comprehensive search of program models, research literature, vocational evaluation/assessment instrumentation, and pertinent legislation.

   • What research is available concerning the efficacy of vocational assessment services in school-based settings?

   • What program models currently exist and what factors have influenced their effectiveness within the local education community and employment settings?

   • What factors influence validity and reliability in the collection of assessment data?

3. Establish basic considerations for the model based on previous research; analyze and synthesize the programmative needs. These considerations include tenants, i.e., vocational assessment:

   • Should be an integrated part of the total delivery of career/vocational services.

   • Should reflect preassessment readiness needs of the student and provide developmental growth information.

   • Should be a student-centered process with a career development orientation consisting of experiences to increase one's awareness, exploration, and understanding rather than a strict predictive procedure providing isolated ability data.

   • Should be based on the assessed employment needs of the local community and the applicable skills of the student to ensure key validity and efficacy factors contributing to the structure of the model.

   • Should measure key situational factors specific to work roles that can be critical determinants of interest and performance.

   • Should produce a wide variety of demonstratively useful information that can be assessed and used by several disciplines, the student, and the parents.

   • Who should coordinate and use the assessment information to make placement and programming decisions?

   • How will this information be applied to the development of individualized educational and vocational planning and program development?

4. Establish an operational plan to implement the process.

   • Where will vocational assessment activities occur?

FIGURE 18.3   Key Steps to Curriculum-Based Vocational Assessment

Continued

FIGURE 18.3 *Continued*

- Who will be assessed?
- What information will be collected?
- How will vocational assessment information be collected (instruments, activities, techniques)?
- Who will conduct vocational assessment activities?
- How will the vocational assessment information be gathered and organized?
- Who will be responsible for coordinating information gathering, which includes facilitating, providing support, and monitoring?
- Who will analyze, synthesize, and interpret vocational assessment findings to appropriate decision-making groups?
- What time frame will be used for vocational assessment activities?
- How will data collection be integrated and formalized as part of the instructional process?
- How will the vocational assessment instrumentation be developed?
- What specific competencies and specific related behaviors will be assessed?
- How should the collected data be formatted and displayed for optimal application and use?
- What evaluation criteria will be used to measure competency attainment and behaviors?

5. Pilot and evaluate the CBVA implementation activities.

- What school(s) and personnel should be involved in field testing?
- What steps need to be taken (additional inservice training, technical assistance, and ongoing support) to ensure the appropriate climate and expertise for full integration and application of the vocational assessment process in the pilot sites?
- What criteria will be used to evaluate the process, instrumentation, and overall impact at the pilot site?
- What modifications need to be made to the process, instrumentation, or support mechanisms as a result of the pilot test?
- Who will make the modifications?

6. Implement, evaluate, and expand options.

- What additional steps need to be taken on a systemwide basis for full integration and application of the curriculum-based vocational assessment model and process?
- What specific evaluation data will be collected?
- What implementation and evaluation checkpoints need to be established?
- What additional course and activity settings would yield relevant career and vocational assessment information?
- What additional steps are needed to assist teachers to view their instructional processes and outcomes in a career or vocational context?

From R. Ianacone and P. Leconte, Curriculum-based vocational assessment. *Career Development for Exceptional Individuals, 9,* 117. Copyright © 1986 by Council for Exceptional Children. Reprinted with permission.

Entry _____ Exit _____

Student: Last name   First   M.I.   Grade   Length of term

9 weeks _____ 18 weeks _____

School

I Work related behaviors	P	M	II Generalized outcomes	P	M	III Specific skill outcomes	P	M
1 Display initiative			1 Understands oral directions			1 Compare/select products		
2 Exhibit a desire to improve			2 Can give oral directions			2 Identify product assembly procedures		
3 Display integrity			3 Understand written directions			3 Follow systematic production planning		
4 Exhibit self-confidence			4 Apply related terminology			4 Use mining processes in production		
5 Display frustration tolerance			5 Apply related measurement functions			5 Apply coating processes		
6 Exhibit flexibility			6 Apply related math computations			6 Use bonding processes		
7 Make judgements and decisions			7 Apply related science concepts			7 Prepare template		
8 Relate with peers/co-workers			8 Practice related hygienic requirements			8 Prepare a jig		
9 Relate with teachers/supervisors			9 Demonstrate safety procedures			9 Prepare a fixture		
10 Cooperate as a team member			10 Demonstrate problem solving technique			10 Identify object by shape/size		
11 Accept constructive criticism			11 Shows interest in occupational area			11 Bore hole with hand brace		
12 Work unsupervised			12 Perform equipment maintenance			12 Bore hole with portable hand drill		
13 Complete tasks accurately			13 Understand employer-employee roles			13 Cut hole with keyhole saw		
14 Complete tasks in a timely manner			14 Understand function of supervisor			14 Select proper hammer and drive nails		
15 Seek assistance appropriately			15 Understand role of employee evaluation			15 Level and plumb installations		
16 Display appropriate habits/manners			16 Understand business enterprise function			16 Apply stains/shellac/varnish		
17 Display approprite appearance						17 Operate portable drill		
18 Comply with attendance regulations						18 Operate portable sander		
19 Practice punctuality						19 Operate drill press		
20 Display appropriate conduct						20 Operate grinder		
21 Use and care of materials/equipment						21 Operate vertical band and table saw		
						22 Perform precision cutting		
						23 Operate horizontal saw		
						24 Set up and operate lathe		
						25 Demonstrate hand sawing		
						26 Demonstrate planning procedures		
						27 Demonstrate abrading procedures		

Directions

As related to your course, CIRCLE the student's overall:

Interest.........High   Medium   Low
Aptitude.........High   Medium   Low

- Please check the appropriate category.
  P = Proficient — can perform with 80% accuracy
  M = Proficient with modification — can perform with *instructor assistance* at 90% accuracy

- *Circle the number* when information *was taught* in class but student *did not achieve proficiency.*

- *Do not check or circle when information was not evaluated/covered.*

- List additional behavior'competencies. Use the blank spaces in each column for additional behaviors/ competencies relevant to your curricular area.
  - This standard of proficiency may vary in relation to course content, instructional level and degree to which competitive employment standards are used in your classroom.

Additional information

Comments

Instructor's signature – Date

FIGURE 18.4   Vocational Assessment Rating Form

From M. Porter and R. Stodden, A Curriculum-based vocational assessment procedure: Addressing the school-to-work transition needs of secondary schools. *Career Development for Exceptional Individual, 9,* 125. Copyright © 1989 by Paul Brookes. Reprinted with permission.

mation may prove of little use. Additionally, students with more severe disabilities may not be participants in vocational education as experienced by students with milder disabilities. For these students (and for students with mild disabilities as noted earlier), direct observation of student performance at community-based work-experience sites yields data that may require fewer inferences about actual vocational interests, strengths, and weaknesses. Direct observation also provides information concerning behaviors (e.g., social interaction) that affect employability as well as the specific performance of the job itself.

Direct Observation and Ecological Assessment

WHY USE DIRECT OBSERVATION AND ECOLOGICAL ASSESSMENT?

Evaluate performance of specific and general work skills and work-related behaviors; determine modifications for instruction

WHO SHOULD USE THEM?

Teachers, vocational assessment personnel, transition personnel

In general, ecological assessment may involve quantitative measures (e.g., baseline and treatment measures of how often or how long a behavior occurs) or quantitative measures (e.g., adult demands, peer expectations, conditions in the environment) (Evans, Gable, & Evans, 1993). Evans et al. emphasized that ecological assessment allows the teacher or evaluator to socially validate that a problem exists (e.g., an increase in undesirable interactions at a workplace), analyze setting events (e.g., occurrence of teasing by a coworker), and analyze consequent events (e.g., student is reprimanded by the supervisor but coworker goes unpunished).

Subsequent analyses of assessment information facilitates the identification of appropriate target behaviors that are likely to be naturally reinforced and maintained (Evans et al., 1993). Ecological assessment is a multidirectional procedure. Following are more specific strategies for the use of direct observation and ecological assessment, particularly in vocational environments. The first step involved in direct observation involves activities in the actual worksite and matching the requirements of the job to the individual student. This process is referred to as the "job match" (Falvey, 1989). As Falvey noted, it is critical that the student's abilities be adequate to the demands of the employment situation. This includes not only the specific skill requirements, but a host of other variables that may affect successful employment. A work-site analysis is then conducted to gather more in-depth information (Falvey, 1989). Figure 18.5 includes a sample job-site analysis form. Once this information is gathered, the job coach (the individual providing direct training at a job) or teacher may then proceed with breaking

Job Site Analysis

Job Site _____

Address _____

Telephone Number _____

Supervisor(s) _____

Significant Coworkers _____

_____

Teacher/Vocational Specialists _____

_____

Job Placement Staff _____

Student(s) _____

_____

Work Days/Hours _____

Relevant Information (obtain prior to student training)

  1. Location of time clock, lounge, lockers, restrooms, pay telephones, etc.: _____
      _____
      _____

  2. Location of work area and specific set up instructions: _____
      _____
      _____
      _____

  3. Location of materials and supplies: _____
      _____
      _____

  4. Required paperwork, production forms, documents, etc.: _____
      _____
      _____

  5. Procedure for obtaining required job task assignments, materials, and task priorities/
      sequence: _____
      _____
      _____

  6. Variations within the task sequence or within the job task: _____
      _____
      _____

  7. Procedure for handling finished goods and completing tasks: _____
      _____
      _____

  8. Expected work/break behavior (e.g., you can sit, eat, leave workplace): _____
      _____
      _____

FIGURE 18.5   A Sample Job Site Analysis Form

Continued

FIGURE 18.5   *Continued*

9. Person(s) to ask for answers to work questions: _____

_____

_____

10. Clean up, maintenance, or repair responsibilities: _____

_____

_____

11. The names of all things involved with the job: _____

_____

_____

12. Procedure for what to do when you run out of work or the equipment breaks down: __

_____

_____

13. Proper clothing and safety equipment: _____

_____

_____

14. Production and quality expectations: _____

_____

_____

15. Schedule for pay days: _____

16. Initial pay rate: _____

17. Details of benefits, work schedule, and procedures for notification of vacation/sick
    days: _____

_____

_____

18. Channels of communication: _____

_____

19. Job description: _____

_____

_____

20. Procedure to ensure employer communication of problems: _____

_____

Job Tasks (in order of priority): _____

_____

_____

_____

down activities and skills into teachable components as required by the student's rate of learning.

Although originally developed for students with severe disabilities, the use of ecological and student repertoire inventories (Brown et al., 1979; Brown et al., 1980; Falvey, Brown, Lyon, Baumgart, & Schroeder, 1980) are applicable to this type of training situation and with students with disabilities in general. During this process, the teacher or assessment specialist analyzes the environment in terms of what skills are required to be successful in the activities occurring in that environment and then assesses the student's performance of those skills. For example, when performing an ecological inventory, Brown et al. (1979) outlined the following general steps. First, delineate the environment itself (e.g., a fast-food restaurant). Second, delineate subenvironments where the student will be required to function successfully (e.g., up front where orders are to be taken, in the cooking area, in the storeroom, outside on the restaurant grounds and parking area). Third, the specialist delineates the activities that occur in each of those environments (e.g., taking orders, filling orders, cooking french fries and sandwiches, assembling and wrapping sandwiches, stocking shelves, picking up trash). Fourth, the specialist delineates the particular skills required to participate in each activity (e.g., greeting the customer, listening to the order, inspecting to see if the items are available or must be ordered from the cooks, telling the customer the cost, ringing up items on the cash register, giving change). The similarity between the process and task analysis discussed in Chapter 6 should not be overlooked. In fact, a completed ecological inventory may resemble an assortment of task analyses related to each of the activities and skills involved in the job. Also noted in Chapter 6, the degree to which activities and skills would be broken down would depend on the severity of the student's disability. For example, a student with mild disabilities may require fewer and "larger" steps than would an individual with a moderate or severe disability.

Falvey et al. (1980) stressed that when the ecological inventory is completed, a student repertoire inventory must be implemented. The student repertoire inventory is used to assess the student's performance compared to that of nondisabled peers on the ecologically inventoried skills. Falvey (1989) listed the following steps in conducting the student repertoire inventory. First, complete the ecological inventory delineating the skills performed by nondisabled individuals. Second, observe and record whether the student is able to perform the skills exhibited by the nondisabled individuals for a given activity. These observations should be systematic and the recording procedures suggested in Chapter 5 may be used (e.g., event recording, duration recording). Third, conduct a discrepancy analysis. This step involves analyzing whether the student is or is not able to perform the inventoried skills. If not, the assessment specialist should observe and analyze all aspects of that skill (e.g., antecedents, consequences, criteria). The student's performance is further analyzed to determine which aspects of the skill are presenting difficulty. Finally, the teacher provides intervention for these same skills using one of the following three options: teaching the skill directly, making adaptations in the skill or in how the student performs the skill, or teaching the student to perform a related skill. Suppose a student working at a fast-food restaurant is having difficulty with the skills necessary for cooking french fries. The student might be taught how to cook the potatoes through direct instruction and task analysis. The student might be provided with some adaptive device (e.g., to assist in emptying the fry basket) or taught to perform another skill that would free another worker to fry potatoes.

The advantages to using ecological and student repertoire inventories are that they assess functional skills in the actual environment where those skills will be used and that the performance is assessed in the presence of naturally occurring conditions. It should be added that this type of assessment may be used to evaluate student performance in other areas related to successful functioning such as home-living and community-living skills. This type of assessment is not, however, the only type of assessment that might be used in a vocational setting. Clearly, in an actual paid work or community-based training situation, input from the employer would also be desirable and might be obtained from a simple, 1–5 scale that is completed by the supervisor and the employee together. Figure 18.6 includes such a scale. Obviously, the teacher or trainer could adapt this scale or develop a new one to suit the particular needs of the student, employer, and teacher. It may be necessary for the teacher or trainer to spend some time with the employer or supervisor to ensure the scale is filled out as objectively as possible. It is certainly not unheard of for an employer or supervisor to either underrate or overrate a student's performance due to unduly low or high expectations. Additional types of information that might be gathered could include production rates, accuracy rate, or rate at which new skills are learned. This information could be obtained using the same observational techniques discussed in Chapter 5.

Two final procedures for informal assessment, portfolio (or authentic) assessment and outcomes assessment, may utilize many of the informal techniques already discussed. Each is closely related to CBVA in particular; both do, however, also include noteworthy characteristics aside from those discussed elsewhere.

Name: _____

Job Title: _____

Externship Site: _____

Beginning Date: _____

Completion Date: _____

Please circle the number that best represents your opinion:

1. I arrive and leave work on time.

1	2	3	4	5
Much Too Seldom	Not Often Enough	Undecided	Usually	Always

2. I maintain good attendance.

1	2	3	4	5
Much Too Seldom	Not Often Enough	Undecided	Usually	Always

3. I take my breaks and/or meals appropriately.

1	2	3	4	5
Much Too Seldom	Not Often Enough	Undecided	Usually	Always

4. I maintain a good appearance.

1	2	3	4	5
Much Too Seldom	Not Often Enough	Undecided	Usually	Always

5. My performance compares favorably with other workers' performance.

1	2	3	4	5
Much Too Seldom	Not Often Enough	Undecided	Usually	Always

6. Communication with my coworkers is not a problem.

1	2	3	4	5
Much Too Seldom	Not Often Enough	Undecided	Usually	Always

7. Communication with my supervisor is not a problem.

1	2	3	4	5
Much Too Seldom	Not Often Enough	Undecided	Usually	Always

8. I attend to my job tasks consistently.

1	2	3	4	5
Much Too Seldom	Not Often Enough	Undecided	Usually	Always

9. I take responsibility for obtaining work.

1	2	3	4	5
Much Too Seldom	Not Often Enough	Undecided	Usually	Always

10. I am performing my job as accurately as my coworkers.

1	2	3	4	5
Much Too Seldom	Not Often Enough	Undecided	Usually	Always

11. I am performing my job at the same speed as my coworkers.

1	2	3	4	5
Much Too Seldom	Not Often Enough	Undecided	Usually	Always

12. I am treated the same as my coworkers.

1	2	3	4	5
Much Too Seldom	Not Often Enough	Undecided	Usually	Always

13. My coworkers and I get along well together.

1	2	3	4	5
Much Too Seldom	Not Often Enough	Undecided	Usually	Always

14. I would like to use adaptive equipment to improve my performance.

1	2	3	4	5
Much Too Seldom	Not Often Enough	Undecided	Usually	Always

15. I enjoy my job and would like to continue working at my current job.

1	2	3	4	5
Much Too Seldom	Not Often Enough	Undecided	Usually	Always

16. I would rate my overall performance at this time as:

Please make additional comments below.

FIGURE 18.6   Joint Evaluation by Employee and Supervisor

From P. Wehman, J. Everson, R. Walker, et al., Transition services for adolescent-age individuals with severe mental retardation. *In* R. Ianacone and R. Stodden (Eds.), *Transition Issues and Directions*. Copyright © 1987 by the Council for Exceptional Children. Reprinted with permission.

Portfolio Assessment

WHY USE PORTFOLIO ASSESSMENT?

To construct a record over time of content and skills acquired, job experiences; evaluation of progress

WHO SHOULD USE IT?

Teachers, vocational assessment personnel

As noted in Chapter 8, portfolio assessment is one component of the overall current movement in assessment toward classroom- and community-based assessments (Nolet, 1992). Although experts do not agree on the specifics of what a portfolio is or what should be included in a portfolio assessment, Nolet (1992) outlined five consistently cited characteristics.

1. The portfolio includes samples of student behavior over time.
2. The samples are collected using multiple procedures (e.g., written products, videotapes of performance) and under a variety of both stimulus and response conditions.
3. Sample tasks are regularly performed in authentic or natural environments.
4. The portfolio includes raw data (i.e., actual student work samples) and summarizing data (i.e., teacher compiled data).
5. The student participates to the degree possible in selecting materials for inclusion in the portfolio.

Nolet has noted that the reliability and validity of portfolio assessment has yet to be clearly established on a broad scale; others believe there is growing consensus that portfolios may be an appropriate record of achievement for students with disabilities (Sarkees-Wircenski & Wircenski, 1994). Sarkees-Wircenski and Wircenski (1994) reported on a project in Texas in which students with disabilities were involved in constructing a "Career Portfolio" that could be used by educators and adult service providers to prepare the students for postschool opportunities. First, appropriate competencies for successful transitions were identified (e.g., employability skills, work-related social skills, independent-living skills, generalized skills such as reading or writing, and job-specific skills). Next, these competencies were validated by a variety of educators, administrators, and adult service representatives. Ultimately, the number of competencies across the above mentioned areas was reduced to 108. On each competency students were rated on a five-point continuum from having had no exposure to the competency to requiring differing degrees of supervision to achieving independence. Students and teachers would include samples of work from a variety of sources to demonstrate status on any particular competency. Sarkees-Wircenski and Wircenski suggested a number of potential uses for a career portfolio. First, a portfolio could be used for informal individual assessment prior to placement in a program. Competencies could form the basis for short- or long-term instructional objectives. Competencies could be used to formulate a "job match" between student strengths and job requirements. The portfolio could be used for vocational counseling. Students could select samples of their work. The portfolio could serve as documentation of accomplishments to a prospective employer. Finally, the portfolio could be used as a cooperative planning tool that would allow educators, service providers, and employers to identify those competencies most important for vocational success and target those same competencies for intervention (Sarkees-Wircenski & Wircenski, 1994). Although the use of portfolio assessments is not universal, its use is certain to increase. A related form of assessment is outcomes assessment.

Outcomes Assessment

WHY USE OUTCOMES ASSESSMENT?

To evaluate both individual vocational/educational outcomes and overall program effectiveness

WHO SHOULD USE IT?

Teachers, program evaluators, administrators, vocational assessment personnel

Similar to portfolio assessment, there does not appear to be a clear consensus on exactly what constitutes outcomes assessment. Destefano and Wagner (1993) stated that despite individual differences in design, measures, and data collection approaches, outcomes assessment models focus on individual achievements, statuses, or behaviors. Again, the relationship to CBVA for the case of the individual student is a close one. For the purpose of this chapter, the focus regarding outcomes assessment will be on adult outcomes and their importance in vocational/transitional assessment and programming. That is, the follow-up assessment of students who have exited from school will be highlighted.

As noted during the discussion of transition planning and assessment, the importance of determining postschool outcomes (e.g., employment status, behaviors leading to maintenance of or loss of employment, residential arrangements, accessibility of recreational opportunities, and degree of on-going supervision required to live in the community) are essential to determining program effectiveness and instructional modification. Such information also indicates areas of need for individuals as well as within communities at large.

Destefano and Wagner (1993) outlined a number of potential uses for outcomes assessment. Vocational rehabilitation agencies may use the assessment of outcomes achieved at exiting school and afterwards to (1) facilitate a smooth "hand off" of the student with disabilities from supervision by educators to the adult service provider, (2) to determine if the linkage between vocational rehabilitation and school programs is strong and well coordinated, (3) to anticipate personnel and service needs and to document systems change, and (4) to provide information for long-term planning and program improvement. These same authors also posed questions of concern. First, who will be responsible for collecting and compiling outcome data? As planning and programming issues and concerns arise, what is the process for altering the focus of the outcomes assessment? Who will provide the resources necessary to conduct outcomes assessment? How much information is needed to effectively plan, implement, and modify programs (Destefano & Wagner, 1993)? Clearly, the answers to these questions must be determined within the cohort of educators and adult service providers in each community. But, overall guidance in what and how to assess does exist in the literature. For example, Rusch, Enchelmaier, and Kohler (1994) compiled results from questionnaires completed by 106 transition project directors. These researchers (along with a panel of experts they employed) identified both outcomes and activities within those outcomes for transition to work programs. The outcomes to be assessed included those at the family and student level (e.g., placement in competitive and integrated employment), program level (e.g., upgrade skills of professionals), organization level (e.g., develop materials to encourage replication of successful practices), and at the community level (e.g., document the formal interface between school and community services). Johnson et al. (1993) listed four essential questions that may serve as the basis for formulating an individually localized outcomes assessment:

1. What are the desired outcomes for students to achieve after being out of school for one year?
2. What aspects or characteristics of current programs and transition planning support or limit students in achieving those outcomes?
3. What fundamental changes need to be made to improve outcomes?
4. What types of information should be collected and compiled to aid decision making in improving the educational and transition process?

Many models for follow-up studies that employ outcomes assessments exist in the literature (e.g., see Johnson & Rusch, 1993, for a review of twenty-four follow-up studies). The key to outcomes assessment is that data collection must not cease at the end of school careers if vocational and special education programs are to remain resilient and responsive to changes in education, technology, the economy, and the local community.

Although the focus has been on informal assessment processes to this point, the use of formal assessment procedures remains common. Data from such procedures are often incorporated into the vocational/transition counseling, planning, and programming of students with disabilities. These data are typically used to complement those obtained through informal assessments.

INTEREST AND APTITUDE INSTRUMENTS

WHY USE INTEREST AND APTITUDE INSTRUMENTS?

Screening for vocational/career interests and vocational aptitudes, developing educational/vocational programs

WHO SHOULD USE THEM?

Vocational assessment personnel

Many formal instruments have been designed to evaluate an individual's vocational interests and aptitude. These instruments are usually administered by a guidance counselor, school psychologist, or other professional involved in helping students determine their best career options. Whereas most of these instruments were designed for use with general education students (e.g., Kuder Occupational Interest Survey), some were developed specifically for students receiving special education (e.g., the Reading-Free Vocational Interest Inventory). The tests designed for students with disabilities usually do not require reading, and the format is easy to follow. Below is a brief description of several instruments that are used for career guidance purposes. Please note that this is only a brief sampling of the many instruments available.

Differential Aptitude Tests (DAT)

Age level—Grades 7 to 12 (can be used with young adults not in school)
Technical adequacy—Validity and reliability have been supported in the technical manual and in the professional literature
Areas measured—Verbal Reasoning, Numerical Ability, Abstract Reasoning, Clerical Speed and Accuracy, Mechanical Reasoning, Space Relations, Spelling, and Language Use
Types of scores—Percentile ranks, stanines, and standard scores for males, females, and combined

Suggested use—The DAT (Bennett, Seashore, & Wesman, 1990) is currently among the most widely used measures of multiple abilities. The battery is intended primarily for use in educational and vocational counseling with students in grades 7 to 12, although it is also appropriate for young adults not in school. There are two levels of the test—Level I for students in grades 7 to 9, and Level II for students in grades 10 to 12. A special large-print edition is available for the visually impaired, and several versions have been developed in other languages for use outside the United States.

The battery is designed for group administration, and it is recommended the testing be carried out in two or more sessions because the total procedure takes approximately two to three hours. A supplemental test, the Career Interest Inventory, is designed to be used with the DAT to allow the students to explore their interest in various fields of employment. The battery yields nine scores, one for each test, with an additional combined score of Verbal Reasoning and Numerical Reasoning. This combined score is used as a measure of scholastic ability and correlates highly with measures of intelligence. There is also a computerized adaptive version of the DAT that has been shown to yield scores similar to the conventional battery (Henly, Klebe, McBride, & Cudeck, 1989).

Gordon Occupational Checklists–II

Age level—Persons seeking job training below the college level
Technical adequacy—Limited reliability and validity data; this checklist is not normed in the traditional sense.
Areas measured—Business, Outdoor, Arts, Services, Technical (subdivided into Mechanical and Industrial)
Types of scores—Each item is keyed to a job title and its corresponding work group listed in the U.S. Department of Labor's *Guide for Occupational Exploration*.
Suggested use—These checklists (Gordon, 1981) provide informal information related to occupational interests. Individuals must simply underline those occupational activities that they would "like to do" and circle those that they would "like to do the very most." As noted previously, each item is correlated with a specific job title and occupational group. The checklists can be read to those examinees who do not read at the sixth-grade level.

Kuder Occupational Interest Survey–Revised (KOIS)

Age level—Grade 10 to adult
Technical adequacy—Support is generally lacking; predictive validity studies have indicated that approximately 50 percent of the students followed

found work in high-interest occupations identified by the KOIS. Relatively small studies have indicated satisfactory reliability.

Area measured—Scores are available in four areas: Dependability, Vocational Interest Estimates, Occupational, and College Majors.

Types of scores—Percentile ranks, lambda scores (similarity of response between examinee and those in various reference groups).

Suggested use—The 1985 revision of the KOIS (Kuder & Diamond, 1985) is similar to previous editions. The examinee is presented with a variety of occupational activities that he or she must mark as most preferred or least preferred. Those responses are subsequently compared to a normative group who are in 119 occupational groups. The KOIS also allows the comparison of examinee's responses to a normative group with various college majors. The Dependability scale is used to determine if the test should be considered a valid estimate of the examinee's interests (considering such things as random or omitted responses). The Vocational Interest Estimates provide a ranking of the examinee's occupational preferences. The Occupational and College Major Scales provide a comparison of the examinee's responses to various normative groups. Tenopyr (1989) noted that the revised version has a much improved report form, although the reliability and validity of the instrument need to be investigated further.

Occupational Aptitude Survey and Interest Schedule–2

Age level—Grades 8 to 12

Technical adequacy—Validity coefficients of the Aptitude Survey range from .60s to .80s. Reliability coefficients were mostly in the .80s. Reliability coefficients for the Interest Schedule ranged from middle .80s to middle .90s. The validity was determined using factor analysis to support the interest factors.

Areas measured—Aptitude Survey (General Ability, Verbal, Numerical, Spatial, Perceptual, Manual Dexterity); Interest Schedule (Artistic, Scientific, Protective, Mechanical, Industrial, Nature, Business Detail, Selling, Accommodating, Humanitarian, Leading-Influencing, Physical Performing).

Types of scores—Standard scores, percentiles

Suggested use—The OASIS-2 (Parker, 1991) measures both aptitude and interest. The six aptitude scales are related to more than twenty thousand jobs listed in the *Dictionary of Occupational Titles* and the interest factors are related to jobs listed in the *Guide of Occupational Exploration*. Profile forms are available to provide a visual summary of the student's aptitude and interests. The instrument is easy to administer; the student booklets have been reformatted in the revised edition to improve their readability. Machine scoring options are available.

Reading-Free Vocational Interest Inventory–Revised

Age level—Ages 13 to adult (The 1987 update includes additional norms for children and adults.)

Technical adequacy—Normed on both individuals with mental retardation and with learning disabilities; good test-retest reliability (adequate for those with mental retardation); adequate validity

Areas measured—Automotive, Building Trade, Clerical, Animal Care, Food Service, Patient Care, Horticulture, Housekeeping, Personal Services, Laundry Service, Materials Handling

Types of scores—T-scores, percentile ranks, profile chart is available.

Suggested use—An individual completing the Reading-Free Vocational Interest Inventory–Revised (Becker, 1987) is not required to read or give a verbal response. Rather, pictorial illustrations of individuals engaged in a variety of activities such as pumping gas or folding laundry are presented in a forced-choice format. This instrument was designed for and normed on a special education population. It is easy to administer and can be adapted for group use. The use of the profile chart provides a visual representation of the individual's interests in the eleven measured areas. Although the test was partially normed on a population with mental retardation, some evidence suggests that it was not particularly helpful for students with moderate to severe retardation (Wilgosh & Barry, 1983).

Strong-Campbell Interest Inventory

Age level—Ages 16 and older

Technical adequacy—Test-retest coefficients were moderate to strong; validity data supportive of its use.

Areas measured—Occupational Themes; Basic Interests; Occupational Scales; Special Scales (academic comfort, introversion, extroversion); Administrative Indexes

Types of scores—A variety of scores including T-scores are generated (through computer scoring only) for a variety of scales such as Basic Interest and Occupation.

Suggested use—The Strong-Campbell (Strong, Campbell, & Hansen, 1984) is intended to measure an individual's interest (not aptitude or intelligence) in various occupations. The theoretical foundation for developing the test is based on the assumption that individuals with the same occupations will have similar interests and personality characteristics. The instrument is easy to administer and can be given individually, in groups, or by mail. It takes an average of twenty-five to thirty-five minutes to complete. A computerized version is also available.

The Strong-Campbell is considered by many to be one of the best interest inventories available and is also one of the most widely used instruments for adult assessment (Harrison, Kaufman, Hickman, & Kaufman, 1988). There have been some weaknesses described, however. Tzeng (1985), for example, noted some inconsistencies between the Basic Interest and Occupational Scales and that more data supporting its construct validity are needed. Also, care should be taken when different editions of the Strong-Campbell are used, because they yield considerably different profiles (Creaser & Jacobs, 1987).

Vocational Preference Inventory–Revised (VPI-R)

Age level—Ages 14 to adult

Technical adequacy—Limited; available data support validity and reliability of earlier versions; more current research is needed to establish its technical characteristics.

Areas measured—Personality and Vocational Interests, Realistic, Investigative, Artistic, Social, Enterprising, Conventional, Self-Control, Masculinity-Femininity, Status, Infrequency, Acquiescence

Types of scores—Standard scores (T-scores)

Suggested use—The VPI-R (Holland, 1985) was designed to measure an individual's personality and vocational interests. It is based on Holland's six work typologies (first six scales listed above). The instrument is easy to administer and score. Shepard (1989) noted that it was one of the more time- and cost-efficient inventories, although it lacked current technical data. In general, support for its claim as a vocational interest inventory is greater than its claim as a personality measure.

Wide Range Interest-Opinion Test (WRIOT)

Age level—Kindergarten to adult

Technical adequacy—Large normative sample (approximately nine thousand); limited reliability and validity data available

Areas measured—Uses 450 pictures to determine examinee's preferences in 18 interest and 8 attitude areas.

Types of scores—T-scores, profile analysis

Suggested use—The WRIOT (Jastak & Jastak, 1979) is a reading-free instrument of occupational and leisure activities in which examinees must indicate among a series of three pictures that which they like least and like most. It covers a wide range of activities primarily because of the wide age range that it covers. The instrument can be individually or group administered. (A film strip is available.) Organist (1985) noted that although it is appealing for use with a variety of populations, including those with intellectual limitations or learning disabilities, its technical characteristics limit its value.

Work Adjustment Inventory

Age level—12 to 22 years

Technical adequacy—Good standardization; adequate reliability and validity

Areas measured—Activity, empathy, sociability, assertiveness, adaptability, and emotionality

Types of scores—Standard scores and an overall quotient

Suggested use—The Work Adjustment Inventory (WAI) (Gilliam, 1994) is a multidimensional instrument that measures work-related temperament. It uses a self-report format to determine an individual's temperament and adjustment to work. It requires a third-grade reading level, although the items may be read to the students. The WAI provides interesting supplemental information to many other vocational and transitional assessment instruments. The area of job-related temperament is an important one and should not be overlooked.

Instrument or Technique	Suggested Use							Target Population						Special Considerations	Educational Relevance for Exceptional Students
	Prereferral		Postreferral												
	Screening and Initial Identification	Informal Determination and Evaluation of Teaching Programs and Strategies	Determination of Current Performance Level and Educational Need	Decisions about Classification and Program Placement	ITP Goals	ITP Objectives	ITP Evaluation	Mild/Moderate	Severe/Profound	Preschool	Elementary Age	Secondary Age	Adult		
Checklists and Rating Scales		X						X			X	X	X	Informal techniques that provide preliminary data but require additional techniques for complete data	adequate
Work Samples			X		X	X						X	X	Combination of commercial and locally developed instruments is suggested although cost is a concern	useful
Curriculum-Based Vocational Assessment		X	X		X	X	X	X				X	X	Validity of vocational curriculum must be considered	very useful
Direct Observation and Ecological Assessment		X	X		X	X	X	X	X		X	X	X	Probably most adaptable and widely applicable technique	very useful
Portfolio Assessment		X	X		X	X	X	X	X		X	X	X	See Chapter 8; use of a career portfolio is helpful	useful
Outcomes Assessment		X	X				X	X	X				X	Emphasizes importance of determining postschool outcomes	useful
Differential Aptitude Tests						X		X				X	X	Widely used instrument; time consuming; computerized version available	adequate
Gordon Occupational Checklists–II						X		X				X	X	Not normed in the traditional sense; easy to administer	limited
Kuder Occupational Interest Survey						X		X				X	X	Limited technical characteristics	limited
Occupational Aptitude Survey and Interest Schedule–2						X		X				X	X	Measures aptitude and interests	adequate
Reading-Free Vocational Interest Inventory						X		X				X	X	Normed on mentally retarded and learning disabled students	adequate

Instrument or Technique	Suggested Use							Target Population						Special Considerations	Educational Relevance for Exceptional Students
	Prereferral				Postreferral										
	Screening and Initial Identification	Informal Determination and Evaluation of Teaching Programs and Strategies	Determination of Current Performance Level and Educational Need	Decisions about Classification and Program Placement	ITP Goals	ITP Objectives	ITP Evaluation	Mild/Moderate	Severe/Profound	Preschool	Elementary Age	Secondary Age	Adult		
Strong-Campbell Interest Inventory						X		X				X	X	A popular instrument that is widely researched	adequate
Vocational Preference Inventory												X	X	Based on Holland's six work typologies	limited
Wide Range Interest-Opinion Test						X		X			X	X	X	Includes occupational and leisure activities; limited technical data	limited
Work Adjustment Inventory												X	X	Measures an individual's work-related temperament	adequate

Part **VI**

EXAMPLES

In Chapter 2, a pragmatic approach to the assessment process was discussed and an assessment model provided. Throughout this book, a variety of assessment procedures have been described that can be used to implement that model. This has included both informal and formal procedures that are used for a variety of purposes. Also included has been a description of assessment instruments that are used to evaluate a variety of areas.

In this section (Chapter 19), two examples of the assessment process (from initial identification through the development and evaluation of the IEP) are presented. Both examples use a case study approach; one follows a student with mild disabilities and includes prereferral assessment data and test scores and their interpretation for documentation of educational need. The use of those test scores for labeling and classification is also discussed (noting the caveats mentioned in Chapter 4). Finally, the use of assessment data to develop the IEP is presented. The second case study involves a student with severe disabilities to permit a comparison of the similarities and differences of the assessment process with that of the student with mild disabilities.

19

EXAMPLES: PUTTING IT ALL TOGETHER

This chapter includes two case studies that follow a student with mild disabilities and a student with severe disabilities from the beginning of the assessment process (initial identification) through development of the IEP. The procedures and instruments are typical of those used in many states (although some variation, of course, will exist). These examples are meant to show the uses, as well as the limitations, of various types of assessment instruments and data.

CASE STUDY: FRANK, A STUDENT WITH MILD DISABILITIES

Frank, a 10-year-old fourth-grader, could not concentrate on most tasks for more than two or three minutes at a time. Every ten minutes or so he would turn around and talk to and bother the student behind him. His teacher had to stand over him and tap his desk every time he became disruptive. Writing was painstakingly difficult for Frank. It took him five minutes to write a five-word sentence. Most of the time he began sentences in the middle of the page. The letters were usually written very small, and some were written backwards. His script e looked like an l, and he did not dot his i's or cross his t's. When doing tasks of this type, he often got frustrated and tore his paper up. His teacher noted that Frank was a "different boy" when he was working on his science lessons. He would sit quietly, read his assignment, and wait for his turn to present the information to the rest of the class. His teacher wanted an evaluation to determine why Frank performed so well in some areas and so poorly in others. She believed that Frank had the ability to do well in all subjects and wanted information that might help her to motivate him or accommodate his learning style. In addition, she thought that he might benefit from special education.

Step One: Initial Identification

Routine curriculum-based assessment indicated that Frank was having considerable difficulty in language arts. He was significantly behind the rest of the class regarding the appropriate placement within the school's language arts curriculum. Through the use of the CBA results, observation, and evaluation of Frank's work products (including portfolio assessment), his teacher decided that further assessment was needed. One thing she noted was that Frank appeared to be off task quite often, and he frequently failed to complete assignments.

Step Two: Informal Assessment to Develop and Evaluate Teaching Programs and Strategies

Frank's teacher decided to use informal techniques to collect information prior to a formal referral. Specifically, she used observational data to document his off-task behavior and to evaluate various intervention strategies. She decided to use momentary time sampling, twice a day (during language arts and during science) for a ten-minute period. She took the following steps: (1) Define off-task behavior

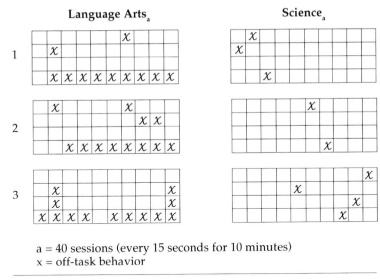

a = 40 sessions (every 15 seconds for 10 minutes)
x = off-task behavior

FIGURE 19.1   Baseline Data for Frank's Off-Task Behavior

(no eye contact during verbal tasks, not working at written task); (2) determine schedule for time samples (every fifteen seconds); (3) develop charts; (4) collect baseline data; (5) implement intervention programs; (6) observe behavior to evaluate program.

After three days, a specific pattern emerged for Frank; the baseline data are shown in Figure 19.1. This information indicated that Frank was off task approximately 30 percent of the time during the language arts sessions and only about 7 percent of the time during the science sessions. Further, it appeared that he was off task primarily near the end of the sessions.

On the basis of these observations, Frank's teacher decided to initiate a prereferral intervention program during the language-arts period. This consisted of changing the task (from spelling exercises to dictionary work). Figure 19.2 on page 512 shows the results of that intervention. This had some effect, but he was still off task approximately 15 percent of the time. His teacher then initiated a reinforcement system, whereby Frank received extra privileges for increasing his on-task behavior each day. Although this decreased his off-task behavior, Frank's teacher noted that he still was not completing the tasks. Further, his written assignments in other subjects were not being completed. She decided, therefore, to refer Frank for further evaluation.

Step Three: Referral

Frank's teacher completed the required referral form and attached the observational data that she had collected, as well as results from the CBA and examples of his work in language arts.

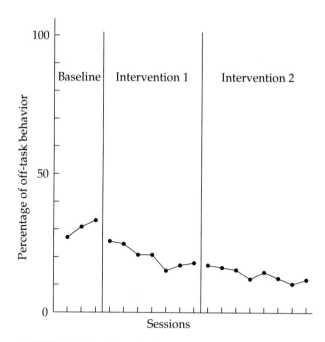

FIGURE 19.2   Graph of Prereferral Data for Frank

Step Four: Obtain Parental Permission

Before formal assessment was initiated, it was necessary to obtain parent permission.

Step Five: Formal Assessment Procedures— The IEP Process

Formal evaluation was initiated to document Frank's educational needs and to provide information for classification and placement decisions. The following tests were administered initially: Wechsler Intelligence Scale for Children–III, Kaufman Test of Educational Achievement, Vineland Adaptive Behavior Scales, Test of Visual Motor Integration–3, Test of Written Spelling–3, and the Test of Written Language–2. The following data were collected.

Wechsler Intelligence Scale for Children–Third Edition (WISC-III)
(Discussed in Chapter 9)

Full Scale IQ—105
Verbal IQ—111
Performance IQ—96

Subtest	Scaled Scores	Subtest	Scaled Scores
Information	9	Picture Completion	12
Comprehension	13	Picture Arrangement	8
Similarities	13	Block Design	11
Vocabulary	9	Object Assembly	10
Arithmetic	13	Coding	6
Digit Span	7	Mazes	7

Kaufman Test of Educational Achievement (K-TEA)
(Discussed in Chapter 13)

Subtest/Area	Standard Score
Mathematics Concepts	101
Reading Decoding	97
Spelling	73
Reading Comprehension	96
Mathematics Application	90
Reading Composite	96
Mathematics Composite	95
Battery Composite	90

Vineland Adaptive Behavior Scales (Survey Form)
(Discussed in Chapter 10)

Domain	Standard Score
Communication	104
Daily Living Skills	110
Socialization	91
Motor Skills	99
Composite	102

Test of Visual Motor Integration–Third Edition (VMI-3)
(Discussed in Appendix A)

Percentile rank–18th

Test of Written Language–2 (TOWL-2)
(Discussed in Chapter 12)

Subtests/Composite	Scaled Scores
Vocabulary	7
Spelling	6

Subtests/Composite	Scaled Scores	*(continued)*
Style	9	
Logical Sentences	9	
Sentence Combining	9	
Thematic Maturity	8	
Contextual Vocabulary	8	
Syntactic Maturity	7	
Contextual Spelling	5	
Contextual Style	7	
Overall Written Language	77	

Test of Written Spelling–3 (TWS-3)
(Discussed in Chapter 16)

Section	Spelling Quotient	Spelling Age	Grade Equivalent
Predictable	72	7–5	2.1
Unpredictable	79	8–1	2.7
Total	74	7–8	2.3

Interpretation of Results

The WISC-III and the K-TEA were administered by the school psychologist. She stated, "On the basis of the WISC-III data, the following comments are warranted. Frank is performing within the average range of intelligence. On the tests, he generally had more difficulty with visual-motor and visual-perceptual tasks than with verbal tasks. Specifically, Frank demonstrated relative strengths in areas requiring abstract thinking and social judgment. His relative weaknesses are in areas requiring sequencing and fine motor ability. There is also some evidence of a memory problem. His K-TEA scores indicate that he is slightly above average in math concepts and slightly below average in reading recognition and comprehension and in arithmetic computation, but almost two standard deviations below in spelling. These results indicate a discrepancy between his overall intellectual performance and his academic achievement, most notably in spelling."

The Vineland was administered by the school counselor to Frank's mother. The counselor reported, "Frank's overall adaptive behavior is consistent with the average student of his age in general education. Frank shows strengths in the areas of daily living skills. His lowest scores are in areas of socialization."

The learning-disabilities specialist administered the VMI-3, TOWL-2, and TWS-3. She noted that Frank "scored at a level that is approximately two years below his chronological age on visual-perceptual tasks involving a motor component. The results from the TOWL-2 indicate that the overall quality and quantity of his written language production was below average. He scored particularly low in the area of spelling. The TWS-3 confirms his deficit in this area. He was well below average in all areas of spelling."

Use of Evaluation Data in Making Decisions

A case study conference was held that included the school psychologist, the counselor, the learning-disabilities specialist, Frank's parents, and the general classroom teacher. On the basis of the test data and information from Frank's teacher, it was concluded that evidence was sufficient to warrant special-education placement for Frank.* The following profile was noted:

INTELLIGENCE—Average performance
ACHIEVEMENT—Variable performance; low in some areas
ADAPTIVE BEHAVIOR—Average performance
CLASSROOM BEHAVIOR—Variable performance
OTHER DATA (perceptual motor)—Low performance

On the basis of this available information, it was decided that Frank qualified to be in a resource room part of the day as a student with learning disabilities (see Chapter 4 for a critical discussion of the issues and problems in making classification decisions). The next step in developing an IEP for Frank was to determine goals and objectives, time lines, types of services, and IEP evaluation procedures (see Chapter 2 for a discussion of IEPs). First, however, it was necessary to give Frank a criterion-referenced test to gather more specific educational information. Portions of the Brigance Inventory of Basic Skills were therefore administered to him.

Brigance Inventory of Basic Skills
(Discussed in Chapter 13)

Area Measured	Results
Writing cursive letters—lowercase	Wrote every letter except *i, t,* and *e* correctly.
Writing cursive letters—uppercase	Wrote eight letters correctly (A, B, C, D, E, I, O, and P), but missed all the others.

---

*In actuality, Frank would need to meet the eligibility criteria established by his state.

Spelling dictation— grade-placement test	Second grade. His spelling for the sentence for second grade was "we found a blue coat and red dress." His spelling for the sentence for third grade was "the klown cood not cach th horse."
Spelling—initial consonants	Correctly wrote the beginning consonant for nineteen of twenty-one words presented. He wrote *k* for *car* and *c* for *quit*.
Spelling—initial clusters	Missed three of twenty-six two-letter initial blends. He wrote *su* for *swell*, *sc* for *sky*, and *kr* for *crack*. He missed seven out of seven three-letter initial blends. Examples include *trl* for *thrill* and *stg* for *string*.
Spelling—suffixes	Missed twenty-five out of thirty-six different suffix additions. Basically, he correctly answered only those suffixes that could be added without applying rules.
Alphabetical order	He was able to alphabetize the letters and words with 100 percent accuracy. He did, however, take a long time to complete the task.

Decisions about the IEP

During the IEP conference, the following observations and decisions were made:

From teacher's input and observational data—Frank is a distractible student, particularly during certain activities. These activities seem to be related to language arts, particularly when some type of written response is required. It is possible to increase his on-task behavior using reinforcement procedures, but he still does not complete the tasks.

From formal evaluation data for eligibility—Frank's profile is most consistent with that of a student with learning disabilities. He has average overall intelligence but has some significant academic weaknesses, most notably in spelling and other aspects of written language. Further, his problems seem to be related to the production of written language (for example, handwriting) rather than to a visual-perceptual problem. *(Note: These data alone were insufficient in establishing relevant educational objectives necessary for an IEP.)*

From criterion-referenced testing—Frank was able to write all but two lowercase letters cursively. He had more difficulty with uppercase letters (he missed eighteen of twenty-six). In terms of spelling, two patterns emerged. First, he made phonetic substitutions (for example, *k* for *c* and vice versa). Second, he had difficulty with spelling rules (for example, he wrote *hoping* for *hopping*). On a specific language arts task of alphabetizing letters and words, Frank performed at 100 percent accuracy, although it took him a long time to complete the task. This could explain why, during the pre-referral observation, he was able to decrease off-task behavior yet still not complete the task.

In Frank's IEP, therefore, the following goals and objectives were included:

Annual Goals	Evaluation Schedule
1. The student will increase his spelling grade level score from a grade level of approximately 2.5 to approximately 4.0.	Annual/use a norm-referenced test
2. When presented with pencil and paper and requested to write the lower case and uppercase cursive letters, the student will correctly and legibly write all twenty-six letters (uppercase and lowercase) in cursive script.	Annual/use a criterion-referenced test

General Objectives

1. *Objective:* When the examiner pronounces words that begin with consonants, the student will demonstrate his ability to recognize initial consonant sounds auditorily by writing the correct initial consonant for twenty-one out of twenty-one different consonants.	Every three months/use a criterion-referenced test
2. *Objective:* When the examiner pronounces words with initial blends and digraphs (clusters), the student will demonstrate his ability to recognize the initial blend and digraph sounds auditorily by	Every three months/use a criterion-referenced test

writing the letters that make up the cluster for thirty-three out of thirty-three different blends and digraphs.

3. *Objective:* When the examiner presents the student with a printed stimulus root word and requests the student to write the same root word plus a designated suffix, the student will correctly write the altered word. This task will be performed correctly for twenty-seven out of thirty-six different suffix additions (75 percent accuracy).

Every 3 months/use a criterion-referenced test

Immediate Short-Term Objectives

(Note: This section includes examples of teaching objectives. Objectives of this type are changed and updated frequently, and they are typically found in lesson plans.)

When the examiner pronounces fifteen words with the initial consonants *k, g,* and *c,* the student will demonstrate his ability to recognize initial consonant sounds by writing the correct initial consonant with 100 percent accuracy.

Weekly/use a criterion-referenced test

When the examiner pronounces fifteen words with initial blends *sw, sk,* and *cr,* the student will demonstrate his ability to recognize the initial blend by writing the correct two letters with 100 percent accuracy.

Weekly/use a criterion-referenced test

When the examiner pronounces ten words with initial three-letter blends (for example, *thr, str*), the student will demonstrate his ability to recognize each blend by writing the correct three letters with 50 percent accuracy.

Weekly/use a criterion-referenced test

When presented with three printed stimulus root words and requested to add a designated suffix (*ing* with doubled consonants; *ed* with doubled consonants; *ed* to words ending in silent *e)* to that root word, the student will correctly write the

Weekly/use a criterion-referenced test

requested word with 100 percent
accuracy.

When presented with pencil and paper, the student will correctly write all the lowercase letters in cursive script.	Weekly/use a criterion-referenced test
When presented with pencil and paper, the student will correctly write the uppercase letters A, B, C, D, E, F, G, H, I, J, K, L, M in cursive script.	Weekly/use a criterion-referenced test

In addition to adopting these goals and objectives, the decision was made to place Frank in the resource room for one hour each school day. During this time, he would receive structured one-to-one tutoring in handwriting (using stencils that would be faded gradually) and in spelling rules. In addition, his special education teacher would work with his general education teacher to incorporate the recommendations in his inclusive setting. Initially, he would be requested to complete the tasks with no time limit. After he met the criteria for mastering the skill, however, he would be required to gradually decrease the time he needed to complete the task. After one year, his progress toward the goals would be evaluated, and decisions about further steps would be made on the basis of the evaluation.

CASE STUDY: JAMES, A STUDENT WITH SEVERE DISABILITIES

James is a 6-year-old boy who has a medical diagnosis of "severe brain damage from anoxia at birth." James is nonambulatory and blind, and he has an extremely limited range of motion. He is also heavily medicated for control of seizures. James has been enrolled in a preschool program for children with disabilities for the past four years. He is no longer eligible for this program because of his age.

Step One: Initial Identification

James was identified as having severe disabilities shortly after birth. Extensive documentation from physicians, physical therapists, and other medical personnel accompanied him when he was accepted into his special preschool program. That information, as well as assessment data gathered during his four years in preschool, indicated the need for James to continue in some type of special program.

Step Two: Referral

James was referred for evaluation so that the appropriate placement and educational program could be determined and carried out.

Step Three: Obtain Parental Permission

Step Four: Formal Assessment Procedures—
The IEP Process

A formal evaluation was conducted to determine James's ability level in a number of cognitive, social, self-help, motor, and communication areas. The following instruments were administered.

Perkins-Binet Scale of Intelligence
(Discussed in Appendix B)

The psychologist reported that James was "untestable." He would not respond to the test items.

Vineland Adaptive Behavior Scales (Survey Form)
(Discussed in Chapter 10)

Domain	Percentile
Communication	2
Daily Living Skills	3
Socialization	4
Motor Skills	1
Maladaptive Behavior	2
Total Adaptive Behavior	2

TARC Assessment System
(Discussed in Chapter 10)

Area	Standard Score (Mean, 50; SD, 20)
Self-Help	12
Motor	10
Communication	32
Social	24
Total	15

Callier-Azusa Scale
(Discussed in Chapter 17)

On the basis of the data from the preceding tests, the IEP team determined that a full-day program in a class for students with severe and profound disabilities would be appropriate. Additional information was needed, however, to determine the goals and objectives for James. The psychologist decided to administer the Callier-Azusa. James was able to do the following:

Motor Development

1. Postural Control—Holds head up for indefinite periods; turns head from side to side
2. Locomotion—Rolls from stomach to back and from side to back
3. Fine Motor—Has a reflex grasp of small objects
4. Visual-Motor—Does not respond to any visual stimulus

Perceptual Development

1. Visual Development—Does not respond to any visual stimulus
2. Auditory Development—Turns head and eyes in the direction of an auditory stimulus
3. Tactile Development—Reacts to tactile stimulation but does not localize the source

Daily Living Skills

1. Undressing and Dressing—Resists being undressed or dressed
2. Personal Hygiene—Plays with toys, soap, and washcloth while being bathed
3. Feeding Skills—Allows being fed from spoon
4. Toileting—Reacts negatively to wet pants

Cognition, Communication, and Language

1. Cognitive Development—Recognizes and reacts to familiar objects (tactilely)
2. Receptive Communication—Understands simple signals that are tactilely presented
3. Expressive Communication—Nonverbally signals to indicate needs (for example, holds out arms to be picked up)

Social Development

1. Interaction with Adults—Differentiates familiar and unfamiliar adults (auditorily)
2. Interaction with Peers—Responds to peers' presence
3. Interaction with Environment—Differentiates familiar and unfamiliar environments

Setting Goals, Objectives, and Time Tables

At this point, James's current performance level has been documented, and the IEP goals and objectives, time lines, types of services, and evaluation schedule could be determined. It was decided that James would benefit from physical therapy and speech and communication therapy as part of his overall educational program. The following goals were adopted:

Annual Goals	Evaluation Schedule
1. The student will sit when supported. His head will be in midline and erect with upper trunk rounded and shoulders forward.	Annual observation by physical therapist or teacher
2. The student will crawl forward or backward on his stomach by pulling with his forearm and pushing with his foot from the opposite side.	Annual observation by physical therapist or teacher
3. The student will eat from spoon (independently, with considerable spilling) after food has been placed on it.	Annual observation by teacher
4. The student will respond appropriately to simple one-word commands.	Annual observation by teacher
5. The student will use simple gestures, signs, or vocalizations to indicate his needs (situation-specific and probably will not generalize).	Annual observation by speech therapist or teacher

Brigance Inventory of Early Development–Revised
(Discussed in Chapter 17)

Once the goals had been adopted, portions of the Brigance Inventory of Early Development–Revised were administered to obtain more information. On the basis of results of this and the previously mentioned tests, the following objectives were determined in relation to James's annual goals:

Objectives	Evaluation Schedule
1a. When placed in a sitting position, the student remains momentarily but head sags forward.	Weekly observation by the physical therapist or teacher
1b. When placed in a sitting position, the student remains momentarily; head bobs forward, but student demonstrates some evidence of support or control.	Every three months/observation by the physical therapist or teacher

1c. Same as above; head steady but not erect.

Same as above

1d. Same as above; head erect and steady.

Same as above

2a. When placed in a prone position, the student will raise chest with arm support.

Weekly/observation by the physical therapist or teacher

2b. When placed in a prone position, the student will support most body weight with hands rather than arms.

Every three months/observation by the physical therapist or teacher

2c. When placed in a prone position, the student will turn on his stomach to face in a different direction.

Same as above

3a. The student will feed himself a cracker or cookie.

Weekly/observation by the teacher

3b. The student will feed himself small pieces of food such as raisins.

Every three months/observation by the teacher

3c. The student will hold a spoon independently.

Same as above

3d. The student will put spoon to mouth (with physical guidance)

Same as above

4a. The student will respond to a few simple commands that are tactilely presented.

Weekly/observation by the teacher

4b. The student will imitate a gesture with objects present (for example, rolling a ball if the teacher makes a pushing motion).

Every three months/observation by the teacher

4c. The student will understand a gesture without objects present (for example, will find a ball to roll if teachers makes a pushing motion).

Same as above

5a. The student will imitate a gesture *while* the teacher is gesturing.

Weekly/observation by the teacher

5b. The student will imitate a gesture after the teacher stops (prompting necessary).	Every three months/observation by the teacher
5c. The student will initiate a gesture without a prompt.	Same as above

Summary

The case studies of Frank and James were intended to provide examples of the overall assessment process. As noted earlier, the choice of instruments and techniques will vary. In addition, eligibility criteria will differ from state to state. Note that with Frank, who has a mild disability, the prereferral component and the postreferral component of the assessment model were included. On the other hand, only the postreferral component was used with James because of the severity of his disabilities.

Appendix A

PROCESS INSTRUMENTS (INSTRUMENTS USED FOR MEASURING PROCESSING SKILLS)*

VISUAL-MOTOR/VISUAL-PERCEPTUAL TESTS

Bender Visual-Motor Gestalt Test (BVMGT)

(Bender, 1938)

Age level—Ages 5 to 11 years (Koppitz system)
Type of administration—Individual (group is possible)
Technical adequacy—Limited reliability, questionable validity
Scores yielded—Standard scores, percentiles, age equivalents
Description—The BVMGT requires the child to reproduce (copy) a series of nine geometric figures. Each figure is presented on a separate three-by-five-inch index card. The Koppitz scoring system is used to determine the number of developmental errors. The BVMGT has the dubious distinction of being one of the oldest tests used by special educators. This means that the test is well researched and has both strong supporters and harsh critics. The test has been used as a measure of nonverbal intelligence, brain damage, emotional status, and academic readiness as well as visual-motor ability. In general, the BVMGT might be considered a *screening device* for identifying groups of children with various problems (particularly those that have been previously identified). Its use as a clinical screening instrument should be limited to experienced trained examin-

---

*NOTE: These tests encompass a wide variety of areas but have also been used as a measure of "processing." The suggested use section addresses each test's strengths and limitations. In general, their use as a process measure is discouraged.

ers. It should not be used as a diagnostic device for any of these purposes by anyone. Special educators should note that, in general, scores on the test do not correlate significantly with reading achievement, particularly with children more than 8 years old. We have almost forgotten that the BVMGT is a test of visual-motor ability. It is probably best to remember this and use it as such.

Developmental Test of Visual-Motor Integration– Third Revision (VMI-3)

(Beery, 1989)

Age level—Ages 2 to 15 years
Type of administration—Individual (group possible)
Technical adequacy—Adequate standardization, adequate validity and reliability
Scores yielded—Standard scores, percentiles
Description—The VMI-3 also requires the individual to copy geometric figures. The VMI-3 is an extremely easy test to administer, although some degree of subjectivity is required to score the responses. A short form (ages 3 to 8) requires the child to copy fifteen geometric figures. The long form uses twenty-four figures. Its primary function should be as a screening test for visual-motor integration problems. As with other perceptual-motor instruments, the VMI-3 should not be used as an instrument for identifying students with learning disabilities or low achievement. The results from the VMI-3 should not be used as a basis for a remedial program to improve academic skills.

Developmental Test of Visual Perception–2 (DTVP-2)

(Hammill, Pearson, and Voress, 1993)

Age level—4 through 10 years
Type of administration—Individual
Technical adequacy—Adequate standardization, reliability, and validity
Scores yielded—Standard scores, percentile ranks, and age equivalents
Description—The DTVP-2 measures eight areas: eye-hand coordination, copying, visual closure, visual motor speed, figure ground, form constancy, position in space, and special relations. The original DTVP was a popular instrument when it first appeared on the market. Its popularity in later years decreased significantly. This decline was partially related to research suggesting that it failed to measure five areas of visual perception as it was supposed to, and that its relationship to academic skills (particularly reading) was practically nonexistent. According to the authors, the DTVP-2 has addressed these shortcomings by basing the test on current

theories of visual-perceptual development. In addition, the DTVP-2 includes motor-free subtests that require visual-motor integration to provide diagnostic information. This is definitely a positive addition to the revision. Research on the relationship of DTVP-2 test results to academic achievement is necessary. Until such research is available, the instrument should be used primarily to determine visual-perceptual and visual-motor abilities.

Motor-Free Visual Perception Test (MVPT)

(Colarusso & Hammill, 1972)

> *Age level*—Ages 4 to 8 years
> *Type of administration*—Individual
> *Technical adequacy*—Adequate reliability, questionable validity
> *Scores yielded*—Perceptual age, perceptual quotient
> *Description*—The MVPT measures five areas: spatial relationships, visual discrimination, figure-ground skills, visual closure, and visual memory. The MVPT is the only visual-perceptual instrument without a motor component. It can, therefore, be used in conjunction with a visual-motor test to obtain needed information. If, for instance, a child performed poorly on a test such as the VMI-3 but scored average or above on the MVPT, a fine motor or coordination problem could be the reason. Information should be used in this way only carefully, because the two tests have questionable validity and were standardized on different populations. Another concern is that although the MVPT measures five areas of visual perception, these areas are unevenly represented; for instance, fourteen items measure discrimination skills, but only five items measure perception of spatial relations. With the publication of the DTVP-2, a more recent measure of motor-free visual perception is available.

Purdue Perceptual Motor Survey (PPMS)

(Roach & Kephart, 1966)

> *Age level*—Grades 1 to 4
> *Type of administration*—Individual
> *Technical adequacy*—Limited data to support reliability and validity
> *Scores yielded*—Raw scores for comparative purposes
> *Suggested use*—There are eleven subtests on the PPMS that measure the three major areas of directionality, laterality, and perceptual-motor matching. The PPMS really should only be used for informal purposes. The scoring system is highly subjective, and the standardization sample was notably restricted. The value of the test largely depends on the user's attitudes toward and knowledge about Kephart's theory of perceptual-motor

match. Like the DTVP, the PPMS has a training program aimed at improving scores on the test. *If* this is the examiner's purpose (for example, improve balance and posture or ocular tracking ability), the test has some use. It should not be used, however, to identify children with academic problems or to develop remedial programs for academically deficient students.

AUDITORY-PERCEPTUAL/LANGUAGE TESTS

Auditory Discrimination Test (ADT)

(Wepman & Reynolds, 1986)

Age level—4 to 8 years
Type of administration—Individual
Technical adequacy—Adequate standardization, limited reliability and validity
Scores yielded—Raw score transformed into one of five levels of auditory discrimination ability
Description—This test is a revision of a popular instrument; it requires the child to listen to forty pairs of words presented by the examiner and say if the words are the same or different. The ADT is extremely easy to administer and score, although it should be used for screening purposes only. Several limitations (such as effect of dialect; child's knowledge of same-or-different concept) make its use as a diagnostic device inadvisable. Its use for children who speak non-standard English should be discouraged.

Goldman-Fristoe-Woodcock Auditory Discrimination Test (GFW)

(Goldman, Fristoe, & Woodcock, 1970)

Age level—Ages 3 1/2 to 80 years
Type of administration—Individual
Technical adequacy—Limited standardization, questionable reliability and validity
Scores yielded—Percentile ranks, T-scores
Description—The GFW uses a multiple-choice format. For example, a plate with four pictures (depicting "sack," "pack," "tack," and "shack") is shown. A tape is played in which the subject is instructed "point to tack." There is both a quiet subtest and a noisy subtest, in which the word is presented with background noise. The technical adequacy of the GFW is questionable. The evidence for its validity and reliability is limited. The idea of including a noise subtest is a good one, although the background noise supplied by the tape is so noisy that the subtest yields extremely

variable scores (probably because the individual is guessing). Like the ADT, the GFW is affected by language and dialect differences of the examiners and students. The two tests should not be used interchangeably. If the GFW is used, it should be for screening purposes only.

Illinois Test of Psycholinguistic Abilities (ITPA)

(Kirk, McCarthy, & Kirk, 1968)

Age level—Ages 2 1/2 to 10 years

Type of administration—Individual

Technical adequacy—Extremely limited

Scores yielded—Scaled scores, psycholinguistic ages, psycholinguistic quotients, and percentage scores

Description—The ITPA includes twelve subtests that measure three hypothetical components of communication. These are channels of communication (input-output modalities), psycholinguistic processes (reception, association, expression) and levels of organization (representational and automatic). The ITPA was once one of the more widely used (and abused) instruments in special education. It is based on a legitimate theoretical model, although the test does not validly measure the components of that model. The ITPA really should not be considered a measure of psycholinguistic constructs. Some research suggests that it closely resembles a measure of verbal intelligence.

Results from this test have been used in the past in a number of ways. Some have used the results to identify modality strengths and weaknesses for teaching purposes; this procedure in general has been questioned. Others have used the ITPA as a screening and diagnostic device for academic ability; this purpose is also inappropriate.

In defense of the authors, it should be noted that they, too, are critical of the way many examiners are using ITPA results. It was designed to help identify areas in need of remediation. Although its use for this purpose must also be questioned, examiners should keep the authors' purpose in mind and not "overinterpret" the results. In summary, the technical inadequacy of the ITPA seriously limits its use as a norm-referenced test.

Appendix **B**

COGNITIVE MEASURES FOR SPECIAL POPULATIONS

VISUAL IMPAIRMENT

Blind Learning Aptitude Test (BLAT)

(Newland, 1969)

> *Age range*—Ages 6 to 20 (6 to 12 is recommended)
> *Standardization*—Sample included 961 blind students
> *Technical adequacy*—Acceptable
> *Description*—The BLAT yields a learning-aptitude test age as well as a learning-aptitude test quotient. The test measures abilities such as discrimination, generalization, and sequencing using tactile stimulus items.

Haptic Intelligence Scale

(Shurrager & Shurrager, 1964)

> *Age range*—Adult
> *Standardization*—Approximately seven hundred blind adults
> *Technical adequacy*—Acceptable reliability, limited validity
> *Description*—Six subtests are included that require the subject to solve problems using tactile stimuli. These subtests (Digit Symbol, Object Assembly, Block Design, Object Completion, Pattern Board, and Bead Arithmetic) are somewhat similar to those found on the Wechsler Scales.

Perkins-Binet Intelligence Scale

(Davis, 1980)

Age range—Ages 2 to 22

Standardization—Sample included 2,153 blind and partially sighted students from day and residential programs

Technical adequacy—Good

Description—This adaptation of the Stanford-Binet has two forms: N (for those with nonusable vision) and U (for those with usable vision). Approximately 25–30 percent of the items are performance related. The test yields both mental age and intelligence quotients.

HEARING IMPAIRMENT

Arthur Adaptation of the Leiter International Performance Scale

(Arthur, 1950)

Age range—Ages 2 to 12

Standardization—The sample included 289 children without disabilities

Technical adequacy—Limited norms and validity, no reliability data

Description—The Arthur Adaptation of the Leiter is a nonverbal, untimed instrument that uses tactile stimulus items and requires motor responses. Tasks involving sequencing, analogies, and matching to sample are included. Mental ages and intelligence quotients can be determined.

Hiskey-Nebraska Test of Learning Aptitude (NTLA)

(Hiskey, 1966)

Age range—Ages 3 to 16

Standardization—The sample included 2,153 individuals (1,079 deaf and 1,074 hearing)

Technical adequacy—Limited reliability and validity

Description—The NTLA can be administered either through pantomime to deaf children or verbally to hearing children. Twelve subtests are included (for example, Memory for Color; Picture Identification; Spatial Reasoning). A learning age and a learning quotient can be determined.

NONVERBAL AND/OR PHYSICAL DISABILITY

Columbia Mental Maturity Scale (CMMS)

(Burgemeister, Blum, & Lorge, 1972)

Age range—Ages 3 1/2 to 10
Standardization—The sample included 2,600 children (stratified sample)
Technical adequacy—Acceptable reliability, limited criterion-related validity
Description—The CMMS measures the child's ability to classify visually presented items. The test yields percentile ranks, standard scores, and a maturity index (similar to a mental age).

Comprehensive Test of Nonverbal Intelligence

(Hammill, Wiederholt, & Pearson, 1995)

Age range—8 through 17 years
Standardization—Sample included more than two thousand from twenty-two states
Technical adequacy—Good reliability and validity
Description—The CTONI consists of six subtests that measure interrelated nonverbal intellectual abilities. The subtests are Pictorial Analogies, Geometric Analogies, Pictoral Categories, Geometric Categories, Pictorial Sequences, and Geometric Sequences. Also available are three composite scores, Nonverbal Intelligence, Pictorial Nonverbal Intelligence, and Geometric Nonverbal Intelligence. This CTONI is currently the most up-to-date test of nonverbal intelligence available; it is based on a well-constructed model and promises to provide valuable information in this area.

Pictorial Test of Intelligence (PTI)

(French, 1964)

Age range—Ages 3 to 8 (3 to 6 is recommended)
Standardization—Sample included 1,830 children (stratified sample)
Technical adequacy—Adequate reliability and validity
Description—The PTI has a multiple-choice format that requires only a pointing or looking response. Six areas are measured: Picture Vocabulary; Form Discrimination; Information and Comprehension; Similarities; Size and Number; and Immediate Recall.

Progressive Matrices

(Raven, 1956)

>*Age range*—Age 5 and older
>*Standardization*—Sample included 567 Veterans' Administration Hospital patients
>*Technical adequacy*—Limited norms, acceptable reliability and validity
>*Description*—Three separate tests are included: the Standard Progressive Matrices; the Colored Progressive Matrices (for young children); and the Advanced Progressive Matrices (for adults of average to above-average ability). The tests require a person to complete visual-analogy problems that vary in complexity. Percentiles can be derived from the raw scores.

Test of Nonverbal Intelligence–2

(Brown, Sherbenou, & Johnsen, 1990)

>*Age range*—Age 5 to adult
>*Standardization*—More than twenty-five hundred subjects from thirty states
>*Technical adequacy*—Adequate reliability and validity
>*Description*—There are two equivalent forms. The items essentially measure abstract problem solving, and responses do not require writing or verbalization. The areas of shape, position, direction, rotation, contiguity, shading, size, movement, and pattern are used as the basis for the problem-solving task.

REFERENCES

Achenbach, T. (1981). A junior MMPI? *Journal of Personality Assessment, 45*, 332.

Achenbach, T. M. (1986). *The Direct Observation Form.* Burlington, VT: University of Vermont Department of Psychiatry.

Achenbach, T. M. (1991a). *Manual for the Child Behavior Checklist/4–18.* Burlington, VT: University of Vermont Department of Psychiatry.

Achenbach, T. M. (1991b). *Teacher's Report Form.* Burlington, VT: University of Vermont Department of Psychiatry.

Achenbach, T. M. (1991c). *Youth Self-Report.* Burlington, VT: University of Vermont Department of Psychiatry.

Achenbach, T. M. (1992). *Child Behavior Checklist/2–3 Years.* Burlington, VT: University of Vermont Department of Psychiatry.

Achenbach, T. M., & Brown, J. S. (1991). *Bibliography of published studies using the Child Behavior Checklist and related materials: 1991 edition.* Burlington, VT: University of Vermont Department of Psychiatry.

Adams, C., & Drabman, R. (1994). BASC: A critical review. *Child Assessment News, 4*, 1–5.

Adams, G. (1986). *Normative Adaptive Behavior Checklist.* San Antonio, TX: The Psychological Corporation.

Alberto, P., & Troutman, A. (1995). *Applied behavior analysis for teachers* (4th ed.). Columbus, OH: Charles E. Merrill.

Alessi, G. (1980). Behavioral observation for the school psychologist: Responsive discrepancy model. *School Psychology Review, 9*, 31–45.

Alford, D., Moore, M., & Simon, J. (1980). A preliminary assessment of the validity and usefulness of the WRAT with visually handicapped residential school students. *Education of the Visually Handicapped, 11*, 102–108.

Algozzine, B., Eaves, R., Vance, H. B., & Mann, L. (1993). *Slosson Full Range Intelligence Test.* East Aurora, NY: Slosson Educational Publications.

Algozzine, B., & McGraw, K. (1980). Diagnostic testing in mathematics: An extension of the PIAT? *Teaching Exceptional Children, 12*, 71–77.

Algozzine, B., & Sutherland, J. (1977). The "learning disabilities" label: An experimental analysis. *Contemporary Educational Psychology, 2*, 292–297.

Alpern, G., Boll, T., & Shearer, M. (1986). *The Developmental Profile–II.* Los Angeles: Western Psychological Services.

American Guidance Service. (1990). *Developmental Indicators for the Assessment of Learning–Revised* (AGS Edition). Circle Pines, MN: American Guidance Service.

American Psychological Association. (1985). *Standards for educational and psychological testing.* Washington, D.C.: American Psychological Association.

Anastasi, A. (1988). *Psychological testing* (5th ed.). New York: Macmillan.

Anderegg, M. L., & Vergason, G. (1988). An analysis of one of the cornerstones of the Regular Education Initiative. *Focus on Exceptional Children, 20*, 1–7.

Andersen, V., & Thompson, S. (1991). *Test of Written English.* Novato, CA: Academic Therapy.

Archbald, D. A., & Newmann, F. M. (1988). *Beyond standardized testing.* Reston, VA: National Association of Secondary School Principals.

Arnold, L., Barneby, N., & Smeltzer, D. (1981). First grade norms, factor analysis and cross correlation for Conners, Daniels, and Quay-Peterson Behavior Rating Scales. *Journal of Learning Disabilities, 14*, 269–275.

Arter, J., & Jenkins, J. (1977). Examining the benefits and prevalences of modality considerations in special education. *Journal of Special Education, 11*, 281–298.

Arthur, G. (1950). *The Arthur Adaptation of the Leiter International Performance Scale.* Chicago: C. H. Stoelting.

Ashlock, R. (1990). *Error patterns in computation* (5th ed.). Columbus, OH: Charles E. Merrill.

Atkinson, L. (1990a). Intellectual and adaptive functioning: Some tables for interpreting the Vineland in combination with intelligence tests. *American Journal on Mental Retardation, 95*, 198–203.

Atkinson, L. (1990b). Standard errors of prediction for the Vineland Adaptive Behavior Scales. *The Journal of School Psychology, 28*, 355–359.

Atkinson, L. (1991). Short forms of the Stanford-Binet Intelligence Scale–Fourth Edition, for children with low intelligence. *Journal of School Psychology, 29*(2), 177–181.

Atkinson, L., Bevc, I., Dickens, S., & Blackwell, J. (1992). Concurrent validities of the Stanford-Binet (Fourth Edition), Leiter, and Vineland with developmentally delayed children. *Journal of School Psychology, 30*(2), 165–173.

Bachor, D. (1990). Review of Key-Math–Revised. *Diagnostique, 15*, 87–98.

Bacon, E. (1989). Review of Behavior Rating Profile. In J. Conoley & J. Kramer (Eds.). *Tenth Mental Measurements Yearbook.* (pp. 84–86). Lincoln, NE: University of Nebraska Press.

Bagnato, S. (1984). Team congruence in developmental diagnosis and intervention: Comparing clinical judgment and child performance measures. *School Psychology Review, 13*, 7–16.

Bagnato, S., & Neisworth, J. (1990). *System to Plan Early Childhood Services.* Circle Pines, MN: American Guidance Service.

Bahr, M. (1994). The status and impact of prereferral intervention: "We need a better way to determine success." *Psychology in the Schools, 31*, 309–318.

Bailey, D. B., Vandivere, P., Dellinger, J., & Munn, D. (1987). The Battelle Developmental Inventory: Teacher perceptions. *Journal of Psychoeducational Assessment, 3*, 271–226.

Baker, E. L. (1993). Questioning the technical quality of performance assessment. *The School Administrator, 50*(11), 12–16.

Balow, I., Farr, R., & Hogan, T. (1992). *Metropolitan Achievement Test 7.* San Antonio, TX: Psychological Corporation.

Balthazar, E. (1976). *Balthazar Scales of Adaptive Behavior.* Palo Alto, CA: Consulting Psychologists Press.

Barnett, D. (1989). Review of Developmental Indicators for the Assessment of Learning–Revised. In J. Conoley & J. Kramer (Eds.). *Tenth Mental Measurements Yearbook.* (pp. 244–246). Lincoln, NE: University of Nebraska Press.

Barnett, D. W., Faust, J., & Sarmir, M. A. (1988). A validity study of two preschool screening instruments: The LAP-D and DIAL-R. *Contemporary Educational Psychology, 13*, 26–32.

Baum, D. (1975). A comparison of the WRAT and the PIAT with learning disabled children. *Educational and Psychological Measurement, 35*, 487–493.

Bearden, D. (1994). Measurement of intelligence: The WJ-R oral language cluster as a tool for determining construct and predictive validity. *Psycho-Ed Network, 2*, 7–8, 16.

Beattie, J., & Enright, B. (1993). Problem solving: Verify the plan with action. *Teaching Exceptional Children, 26*, 60–62.

Beatty, L., Madden, R., Gardner, E., & Karlsen, B. (1985). *Stanford Diagnostic Mathematics Test.* New York: Harcourt Brace Jovanovich.

Beck, B., & Spruill, J. (1987). External validation of the cognitive triad of the Personality Inventory for Children: Cautions on interpretation. *Journal of Consulting and Clinical Psychology, 55*, 441–443.

Beck, S., Beck, A., Levitt, E., & Molish, H. (1961). *Rorschach's Test.* New York: Grune & Stratton.

Becker, R. (1987). *Reading-Free Vocational Interest Inventory.* Columbus, OH: Elbern Publications.

Beech, M. (1981). Concurrent validity of the Boehm Test of Basic Concepts. *Learning Disability Quarterly, 4*, 53–60.

Beery, K. (1989). *Developmental Test of Visual-Motor Integration–Third Edition.* Austin, TX: Pro-Ed.

Bellak, L., Bellak, S., & Haworth, M. (1974). *Children's Apperception Test.* Larchmont, NY: C.P.S., Inc.

Bender, L. (1938). A Visual Motor Gestalt Test and its clinical use. *American Orthopsychiatric Association Research Monograph*, No. 3.

Bennett, G., Seashore, H., & Wessman, A. (1990). *Differential Aptitude Tests* (5th ed.). San Antonio: Psychological Corporation.

Bensberg, G., & Irons, T. (1986). A comparison of the AAMD Adaptive Behavior Scale and the Vineland Adaptive Behavior Scales within a sample of persons classified as moderately and severely retarded. *Education and Training of the Mentally Retarded, 21*, 220–228.

Berk, R. (1981). What's wrong with using grade equivalent scores to identify LD children? *Academic Therapy, 17*, 133–140.

Berk, R. (1984). *A guide to criterion-referenced test construction.* Baltimore: Johns Hopkins Press.

Bernhardt, B. (1990). A review of the Test of Problem Solving (TOPS). *Language, Speech, and Hearing Services in Schools, 21*(2), 98–101.

Betts, E. (1946). *Foundations of reading instruction.* New York: American Book Co.

Bisconer, S. W., Stodden, R. A., & Porter, M. E. (1993). A psychometric evaluation of curriculum-based vocational assessment rating instruments used with students in mainstream vocational courses. *Career Development for Exceptional Individuals, 16*, 19–26.

Blankenship, C. (1985). Using curriculum–based assessment data to make instructional decisions. *Exceptional Children, 52*, 233–238.

Bloom A. S., Allard, A. M., Zelko, F., Brill, W., Topinka, C. W., & Pfohl, W. (1988). Differential validity of the K-ABC for lower functioning preschool children versus those of higher ability. *American Journal on Mental Retardation, 93*, 273–277.

Bloom, L., & Lahey, M. (1978). *Language development and language disorders.* New York: John Wiley & Sons.

Boehm, A. (1986). *Boehm Test of Basic Concepts–Revised.* San Antonio: Psychological Corporation.

Boehm, A., & Weinberg, R. (1987). *The classroom observer: Developing observation skills in early childhood settings* (2nd ed.) New York: Teachers College Press.

Bouchard, T. (1972). Review of the Sixteen Personality Factor Questionnaire in O. Buros (Ed.). *The seventh mental measurement yearbook* (pp. 329–332). Highland Park, NJ: Gryphon Press.

Bower, E. (1969). *Early identification of emotionally handicapped children in school* (2nd ed.). Springfield, IL: Charles Thomas.

Boyd, R. (1989). What a difference a day makes: Age-related discontinuities and the Battelle Developmental Inventory. *Journal of Early Intervention, 13,* 114–119.

Boyd, R., Welge, R., Sexton, D., & Miller, L. (1989). Concurrent validity of the Battelle Developmental Inventory: Relationship with the Bayley Scales in young children with known or suspected disabilities. *Journal of Early Intervention, 13,* 14–23.

Bracken, B. (1984). *The Bracken Basic Concept Scale.* San Antonio: The Psychological Corporation.

Bracken, B., & Cato, L. (1986). Rate of conceptual development among deaf preschool and primary children as compared to a matched group of non-hearing-impaired children. *Psychology in the Schools, 23,* 95–99.

Bracken, B., & Fouad, N. (1987). Spanish translation and validation of the Bracken Basic Concept Scale. *School Psychology Review, 16,* 94–102.

Bracken, B. A., & Howell, K. K. (1989). K-ABC subtest specificity recalculated. *Journal of School Psychology, 27,* 335–345.

Bracken, B. A., McCallum, R. S., & Crain, R. M. (1993). WISC-III subtest composite reliabilities and specificities: Interpretive aids. *Journal of Psychoeducational Assessment Monograph Series: Wechsler Intelligence Scale for Children (Third Edition),* 22–34.

Bracken, B., & Prasse, D. (1981). Comparison of the PPVT, PPVT-R and intelligence tests used for the placement of black, white and Hispanic EMR students. *Journal of School Psychology, 19,* 304–311.

Bracken, B., & Prasse, D. (1983). Concurrent validity of the PPVT-R for "at risk" preschool children. *Psychology in the Schools, 20,* 25–26.

Bracken, B., Sabers, R., & Insko, R. (1987). Performance of black and white children on the Bracken Basic Concept Scale. *Psychology in the Schools, 24,* 22–27.

Bradley-Johnson, S., Graham, D., & Johnson, C. (1986). Token reinforcement on WISC-R performance for white, low socioeconomic, upper and lower elementary school aged students. *Journal of School Psychology, 24,* 73–79.

Bramlett, R. K., & Barnett, D. W. (1993). The development of a direct observation code for use in preschool settings. *School Psychology Review, 22*(1), 49–62.

Bramlett, R., Smith, B., & Edmonds, J. (1994). A comparison of nonreferred, learning disabled, and mildly mentally retarded students utilizing the Social Skills Rating System. *Psychology in the Schools, 31,* 13–19.

Bransford, J. D., Delclos, V. R., Vye, N. J., Burns, M. S., & Hasselbring, T.S. (1987). State of the art and future directions. In C. S. Lidz (Ed.), *Dynamic assessment: An interactional approach to evaluating learning potential* (pp. 479–496). New York: Guilford Press.

Breen, M. (1983). A correlational analysis between the PPVT-R and Woodcock-Johnson achievement cluster scores for nonreferred regular education and learning disabled students. *Psychology in the Schools, 20,* 295–298.

Breen, M., & Prasse, D. (1982). A comparison of the 1976 and 1978 Wide Range Achievement Test: Implica-

tion for the learning disabled. *Journal of Learning Disabilities, 15,* 15–16.

Breuning, S., & Zella, W. (1978). Effects of individualized incentives on norm-referenced IQ test performance of high school students in special education classes. *Journal of School Psychology, 16,* 220–226.

Brigance, A. (1977). *Brigance Inventory of Basic Skills.* North Billerica, MA: Curriculum Associates.

Brigance, A. (1981). *Brigance Diagnostic Inventory of Essential Skills.* North Billerica, MA: Curriculum Associates.

Brigance, A. (1982). *Brigance Comprehensive Inventory of Basic Skills.* North Billerica, MA: Curriculum Associates.

Brigance, A. (1991). *Inventory of Early Development–Revised.* North Billerica, MA: Curriculum Associates.

Brolin, D. (1983). *Life-centered career education: A competency-based approach.* Reston, VA: Council for Exceptional Children.

Bromwich, R. M., Fust, S., Khokha, E., & Walden, M. H. (1981). *Play Assessment Checklist for Infants.* Unpublished document. Northridge, CA: State University, Northridge.

Brown, L., & Alexander, J. (1991). *Self-Esteem Index.* Austin, TX: Pro-Ed.

Brown, L., Branston, M. B., Hamre-Nietupski, S., Pumpian, I., Certo, N., & Gruenwald, L. (1979). A strategy for developing chronological age appropriate and functional curricular content for severely handicapped adolescents and young adults. *Journal of Special Education, 13,* 81–90.

Brown, L., Falvey, M., Vincent, L., Kaye, N., Johnson, F., Ferrara-Parrish, P., & Gruenwald, L. (1980). Strategies for generating comprehensive, longitudinal, and chronological-age-appropriate individualized education programs for adolescent and young-adult severely handicapped students. *Journal of Special Education, 14,* 199–215.

Brown, L., & Hammill, D. (1990). *Behavior Rating Profile–2.* Austin, TX: Pro-Ed.

Brown, L., & Leigh, J. (1986). *Adaptive Behavior Inventory.* Austin, TX: Pro-Ed.

Brown, L., & Sherbenou, R. (1981). A comparison of teacher perceptions of student reading ability, reading performance and classroom behavior. *The Reading Teacher, 34,* 557–560.

Brown, L., Sherbenou, R., & Johnsen, S. (1990). *Test of Nonverbal Intelligence–2.* Austin, TX: Pro-Ed.

Brown, V., Hammill, D., & Wiederholt, J. L. (1995). *Test of Reading Comprehension–3.* Austin, TX: Pro-Ed.

Brown, V., & McEntire, E. (1994). *Test of Mathematical Abilities–2.* Austin, TX: Pro-Ed.

Bruininks, R., McGrew, R., & Maruyama, G. (1988). Structure of adaptive behavior in samples with and without mental retardation. *American Journal on Mental Retardation, 92,* 381–384.

Bruininks, R., Woodcock, R., Weatherman, R., & Hill, B. (1984). *The Scales of Independent Behavior.* Allen, TX: DLM Teaching Resources.

Bryan, J., & Bryan, T. (1988). Where's the beef? A review of published research on the Adaptive Learning

Environment Model. *Learning Disability Quarterly,* 4, 9–14.

Bryant, B., Taylor, R., & Rivera, D. (1996). *Assessment of Adaptive Areas.* Austin, TX: Pro-Ed.

Bryant, B., & Wiederholt, L. (1991). *Gray Oral Reading Test–Diagnostic.* Austin, TX: Pro-Ed.

Bryen, D. (1982). *Inquiries into child language.* Boston: Allyn & Bacon.

Bryk, A. S., Deabster, P. E., Easton, J. Q., Luppescu, S., & Thom, Y. M. (1994). Measuring achievement gains in the Chicago Public Schools. *Education and Urban Society, 26*(3), 306–319.

Budoff, M. (1973). *Learning potential and educability among the educable mentally retarded* (Progress report, Grant No. OEG-0-8-080506-4597 from the National Institute of Education, HEW). Cambridge, MA: Research Institute for Educational Problems.

Bullock, L., Wilson, M., & Campbell, R. (1990). Inquiry into the commonality of items from seven behavior rating scales: A preliminary examination. *Behavioral Disorders, 15,* 87–99.

Burgemeister, B., Blum, L., & Lorge, I. (1972). *Columbia Mental Maturity Scale,* (3rd ed.). New York: Harcourt Brace Jovanovich.

Burger, S. E., & Burger, D. L. (1994). Determining the validity of performance-based assessment. *Educational Measurement, 13,* 9–15.

Burks, H. (1977). *Burks Behavior Rating Scales.* Los Angeles: Western Psychological Services.

Burnham, S. C., & Housley, W. F. (1992). Pride in work: Perceptions of employers, service providers and students who are mentally retarded and learning disabled. *Career Development for Exceptional Individuals, 15,* 101–108.

Burns, E. (1975). An evaluation of the Peabody Individual Achievement Test with primary age retarded children. *Psychology in the Schools, 12,* 11–14.

Burns, E. (1982). The use and interpretation of standardized grade equivalents. *Journal of Learning Disabilities, 15,* 17–18.

Burns, E., Peterson, D., & Bauer, L. (1974). The concurrent validity of the Peabody Individual Achievement Test. *Training School Bulletin, 70,* 221–223.

Burns, P., & Roe, B. (1989). *Informal Reading Inventory.* Boston: Houghton Mifflin.

Bursuk, L. (1971). Sensory mode of lesson presentation as a factor in the reading comprehension improvement of adolescent retarded readers. (ERIC Document Reproduction Service No. ED 047 435).

Buschner, P. C., Watts, M. B., Siders, J. A., & Leonard, R. L. (1989). Career interest inventories: A need for analysis. *Career Development for Exceptional Individuals, 12,* 129–137.

Butcher, J., Dahlstrom, W., Graham, A., & Kaemmer, B. (1989). *MMPI-2: Manual for administration and scoring.* Minneapolis, MN: University of Minnesota Press.

Cain, L., Levine, S., & Elzey, F. (1977). *Cain-Levine Social Competency Scale.* Palo Alto, CA: Consulting Psychologists Press.

Calnon, M. K. (1984). *Contributions of race and grade level to domain scores on the Vineland Adaptive Behavior Scales.* Unpublished manuscript. University of North Carolina, Chapel Hill.

Camp, B. (1989). Review of Scales of Independent Behavior. In J. Conoley & J. Kramer (Eds.), *Tenth mental measurement yearbook* (pp. 712–713). Lincoln, NE: University of Nebraska Press.

Campione, J. (1989). Assisted assessment: A taxonomy of approaches and an outline of strengths and weaknesses. *Journal of Learning Disabilities, 22,* 151–65.

Cancelli, A. (1985). Review of the Revised Behavior Problem Checklist. In J. Mitchell (Ed.), *Ninth mental measurements yearbook* (pp. 1274–1276). Lincoln, NE: University of Nebraska Press,

Carpenter, D., & Carpenter, S. (1978). The concurrent validity of the Larsen-Hammill Test of Written Spelling in relation to the California Achievement Test. *Educational and Psychological Measurement, 38,* 1201–1205.

Carrow, S. (1994). *Carrow Elicited Language Inventory.* McAllen, TX: DLM Resources.

Carrow-Woolfolk, E. (1985). *Test of Auditory Comprehension of Language.* McAllen, TX: DLM Resources.

Carstens, A. (1985). Retention and social promotion for the exceptional child. *School Psychology Review, 14,* 48–63.

Carter, J., & Sugai, G. (1989). Survey on prereferral practices: Responses from state departments of education. *Exceptional Children, 55,* 298–302.

Cartwright, C., & Cartwright, G. (1984). *Developing observational skills* (2nd ed.). New York: McGraw-Hill.

Carvajal, H. (1988). Relationship between scores of gifted children on the Stanford-Binet IV and the Peabody Picture Vocabulary Test–Revised. *Diagnostique, 14,* 22–25.

Carvajal, H., Parks, J., Logan, R., & Page, G. (1992). Comparisons of the I.Q. and vocabulary scores on WPPSI-R and PPVT-R. *Psychology in the Schools, 29,* 22–24.

Carvajal, H., & Weaver, K. (1989). Relationships between scores of gifted students on the Stanford-Binet IV and the Wechsler Intelligence Scale for Children–Revised. *Diagnostique, 14,* 89–93.

Cattell, R., Eber, H., & Tatsuoka, M. (1970). *Sixteen Personality Factor Questionnaire.* Champaign, IL: Institute for Personality and Ability Testing.

Cawley, J., Fitzmaurice, A., Goodstein, H., Lepore, A., Sedlak, R., & Althaus, V. (1977). *Mathematics Concept Inventory.* Tulsa, OK: Educational Development Corp.

Cebulski, L., & Bucher, B. (1986). Identification and remediation of children's subtraction errors: A comparison of practical approaches. *Journal of School Psychology, 24,* 163–180.

Chatman, S., Reynolds, C., & Willson, V. (1984). Multiple indexes of test scatter on the Kaufman Assessment Battery for Children. *Journal of Learning Disabilities, 17,* 523–531.

Cheramie, G., & Edwards, R. (1990). The AAMD Adaptive Behavior Scale, Part Two: Criterion-related validity in a behavior disorder sample. *Psychology in the Schools, 27,* 186–195.

Childs, R. (1981). A comparison of the adaptive behavior of normal and gifted five and six year old children. *Roeper Review, 4,* 41–43.

Choi, H., & Proctor, T. (1994). Error-prone subtests and error types in the administering of the SBIS–Fourth Edition. *Journal of Psychoeducational Assessment, 12,* 165–171.

Christenson, S. (1990). Review of Child Behavior Checklist. In J. Conoley & J. Kramer (Eds.), *Tenth mental measurements yearbook* (pp. 40–41). Lincoln, NE: University of Nebraska Press.

Ciardi, E. (1990). Reading comprehension and the SAT. *Journal of Reading, 33,* 558–559.

Cicchetti, D., & Sparrow, S. (1981). *Some recent research on adaptive behavior scales: Toward resolving some methodologic issues.* Paper presented at the 105th meeting of the American Association on Mental Deficiency, Detroit.

Cicchetti, D., & Sparrow, S. (1986). False conclusions about Vineland standard scores: Silverstein's Type I errors and other artifacts. *American Journal of Mental Deficiency, 91,* 5–9.

Clarizio, H. (1982). Intellectual assessment of Hispanic children. *Psychology in the Schools, 19,* 61–71.

Clark, E., Kehle, T. J., & Bullock, D. S. (1988). Personality Inventory for Children: Profiles for learning disabled, emotionally disturbed, and intellectually handicapped children. *School Psychology International, 9,* 43–48.

Clements, P., Bost, L., Dubois, Y., & Turpin, W. (1980). Adaptive Behavior Scale, Part Two: Relative severity of maladaptive behavior. *American Journal of Mental Deficiency, 84,* 465–469.

Cobb, N., & Ray, R. (1975). *Manual for coding discrete behaviors in the school setting.* Oregon Research Bulletin.

Cohen, H., & Weil, G. (1971). *Tasks of Emotional Development.* Lexington, MA: Heath.

Cohen, L. (1993). Test Review: Wechsler Individual Achievement Test. *Diagnostique, 18,* 255–268.

Cohen, L., & Spence, S. (1990). Fundamental considerations of curriculum-based assessment. In L. Cohen & J. Spruill (Eds.), *A practical guide to curriculum-based assessment for special educators* (pps. 3–14). Springfield, IL: Charles Thomas.

Colarusso, R., & Hammill, D. (1972). *The Motor-Free Test of Visual Perception.* San Rafael, CA: Academic Therapy Publications.

Cole, J., D'Alonzo, B., Gallegos, A., Giordano, G., & Stile, S. (1992). Test biases that hamper learners with disabilities. *Diagnostique, 17,* 209–225.

Coleman, L. J. (1994). Portfolio assessment: A key to identifying hidden talents and empowering teachers of young children. *Gifted Child Quarterly, 38,* 65–69.

Coleman, M., & Harmer, W. (1982). A comparison of standardized reading tests and informal placement procedures. *Journal of Learning Disabilities, 15,* 396–398.

Conaway, C. (1987). Transition: A vocational education perspective. In R. N. Ianacone & R. H. Stodden (Eds.), *Transition issues and directions* (pp. 120–124). Reston, VA: Council for Exceptional Children.

Congressional Record, October 10, 1978, H-12179.

Connolly, A. (1988). *Key Math–Revised.* Circle Pines, MN: American Guidance Service.

Cooter, R. (1988). Woodcock Reading Mastery Test–Revised. *Reading Teacher, 42,* 154–155.

Costenbader, V., & Adams, J. (1991). A review of the psychometric and administrative properties of the PIAT-R: Implications for the practitioner. *Journal of School Psychology, 29,* 219–228.

Coutinho, M., & Malouf, D. (1993). Performance assessment and children with disabilities: Issues and possibilities. *Teaching Exceptional Children, 25*(4), 62–67.

Creaser, J., & Jacobs, M. (1987). Score discrepancies between the 1981 and 1985 editions of the Strong-Campbell Interest Inventory. *Journal of Counseling Psychology, 34,* 288–292.

CTB/McGraw-Hill. (1985). *The California Achievement Tests.* Monterey, CA: CTB/McGraw-Hill.

Cullinan, D., Epstein, M., & Dembinski, R. (1979). Behavior problems of educationally handicapped and normal pupils. *Journal of Abnormal Child Psychology, 7,* 495–503.

Cullinan, D., Epstein, M., & Lloyd, J. (1981). School behavior problems of learning disabled and normal girls and boys. *Learning Disability Quarterly, 4,* 163–169.

Das, J. (1984). Simultaneous and successive processes and the K-ABC. *Journal of Special Education, 18,* 229–238.

Davis, C. (1980). *Perkins-Binet Intelligence Scale.* Watertown, MA: Perkins School for the Blind.

Davis, J. (1974). Performance of young hearing impaired children on a test of basic concepts. *Journal of Speech and Hearing Disorders, 17,* 342–351.

Dean, R. (1979). Use of the PIAT with emotionally disturbed children. *Journal of Learning Disabilities, 12,* 629–631.

Demoor-Peal, R., & Handal, P. (1983). Validity of the Personality Inventory for Children with four-year-old males and females: A caution. *Journal of Pediatric Psychology, 8,* 261–271.

Deni, J. (1985). Review of the Diagnostic Achievement Battery. In D. Keyser and R. Sweetland (Eds.), *Test critiques* (v.2). (pp. 235–240). Kansas City, MO: Test Corporation of America.

Deno, S. (1980). Direct observation approach to measuring classroom behavior. *Exceptional Children, 46,* 396–399.

Deno, S. (1985). Curriculum-based measurement: The emerging alternative. *Exceptional Children, 52,* 219–232.

Deno, S., & Fuchs, L. (1987). Developing curriculum-based measurement systems for data based special education problem solving. *Focus on Exceptional Children, 19*, 1–16.

Destefano, L., & Wagner, M. (1993). Outcome assessment in special education: Implications for decision-making and long-term planning in vocational rehabilitation. *Career Development for Exceptional Individuals, 16*, 147–158.

Diamond, K. (1987). Predicting school problems from preschool developmental screening: A four year follow-up of the Revised Denver Developmental Screening Test and the role of parent report. *Journal of the Division for Early Childhood, 11*, 247–253.

Dieffenbach, E. (1977). *Koppitz Human Figure Drawing (HFD): The reliability and clinical validity of its emotional indicators.* Ann Arbor, MI: University Microfilms International, No. 7804261.

Doll, E. (1965). *Vineland Social Maturity Scale.* Circle Pines, MN: American Guidance Service.

Dreger, R. (1981). First-, second-, and third-order factors for the children's classification project instrument and an attempt at reproachment. *Journal of Abnormal Psychology, 90*, 242–260.

Dreisbach, M., & Keogh, B. (1982). Test wiseness as a factor in readiness test performance of young Mexican-American children. *Journal of Educational Psychology, 74*, 224–229.

Drum, P. (1989). Review of Test of Word Finding. In J. Conoley & J. Kramer (Eds.), *Tenth Mental Measurements Yearbook* (pp. 857–858). Lincoln, NE: University of Nebraska Press.

Duckworth, J. C. (1991). The Minnesota Multiphasic Personality Inventory–2: A review. *Journal of Counseling and Development, 69*, 564–567.

Dudley-Marling, C., Kaufman, N., & Tarver, S. (1981). WISC and WISC-R profiles of learning disabled children: A review. *Learning Disability Quarterly, 4*, 307–319.

Duffey, L., Salvia, J., Tucker, J., & Ysseldyke, J. (1981). Nonbiased assessment: A need for operationalism. *Exceptional Children, 47*, 427–434.

Dufflemeyer, F., & Dufflemeyer, B. (1989). Are informal reading inventories passages suitable for assessing main idea comprehension? *The Reading Teacher, 42*, 358–363.

Dufflemeyer, F., Robinson, S., & Squier, S. (1989). Vocabulary questions on informal reading inventories. *The Reading Teacher, 43*, 142–148.

Dumont, R., & Faro, C. (1993). A WISC-III short form for learning-disabled students. *Psychology in the Schools, 30*(3), 12–19.

Dunbar, S., & Keith, R. (1984). Hierarchical factor analysis of the K-ABC: Testing alternate models. *Journal of Special Education, 18*, 367–375.

Dunn, L., & Dunn, L. (1981). *Peabody Picture Vocabulary Test–Revised.* Circle Pines, MN: American Guidance Service.

Dunn, L., Markwardt, F. (1988). *Peabody Individual Achievement Test–Revised.* Circle Pines, MN: American Guidance Service.

Durost, W., Gardner, E., Madden, R., & Prescott, G. (1971). *Analysis of Learning Potential.* New York: Harcourt Brace Jovanovich.

Durrant, J. F., & Porter, J. F. (1989). Screening ability of the broad-band versus narrow-band intellectual scales of the Personality Inventory for Children (PIC). *Educational and Psychological Measurement, 49*(3), 681–688.

Durrell, D., & Catterson, J. (1980). *Durrell Analysis of Reading Difficulty* (3rd ed.). New York: The Psychological Corporation.

Dusek, J., & O'Connell, E. (1973). Teacher expectancy effects on the achievement test performance of elementary school children. *Journal of Educational Psychology, 65*, 371–377.

Eaves, R. (1990). Review of Woodcock Reading Mastery Tests–Revised. *Diagnostique, 15*, 277–298.

Eaves, R., Campbell-Whatley, G., Dunn, C., Reilly, A., & Tate-Braxton, C. (1995). Statistically significant differences between standard scores on the Woodcock Reading Mastery Tests. *Diagnostique, 21*, 1–5.

Eaves, R. C., Darch, C., & Haynes, M. (1989). The concurrent validity of the Peabody Individual Achievement Test and Woodcock Reading Mastery Test among students with mild learning problems. *Psychology in the Schools, 26*, 261–266.

Eaves, R., & Simpson, R. (1986). Statistically significant differences between subtest scores on the Test of Reading Comprehension. *Psychology in the Schools, 23*, 255–258.

Edelbrock, C., & Achenbach, T. (1984). The teacher version of the Child Behavior Profile: Boys aged 6–11. *Journal of Counseling and Clinical Psychology, 52*, 207–217.

Edwards, R., & Edwards, J. L. (1993). The WISC-III: A practitioner perspective. *Journal of Psychoeducational Assessment Monograph Series: Wechsler Intelligence Scale for Children (Third Edition)*, 144–150.

Edyburn, D. L. (1994). An equation to consider: The portfolio assessment knowledge base and technology = The Grady profile. *LD Forum, 19*(4), 35–38.

Ehly, S. (1989). Review of Adaptive Behavior Inventory. In J. Conoley & J. Kramer (Eds.), *Tenth mental measurements yearbook* (pp. 20–21). Lincoln, NE: University of Nebraska Press.

Ekwall, E. (1981). *Locating and correcting reading difficulties* (3rd ed.). Columbus, OH: Charles E. Merrill.

Ekwall, E. (1986). *Ekwall Reading Inventory.* Boston: Allyn & Bacon.

Ekwall, E., & Shanker, J. (1988). *Diagnosis and remediation of the disabled reader* (3rd ed.). Boston: Allyn & Bacon.

Ellers, R., Ellers, S., & Bradley-Johnson, S. (1989). Stability reliability of the Behavior Rating Profile. *Journal of School Psychology, 27*(3), 257–263.

Elliot, C. (1990). *Differential Ability Scales.* San Antonio: The Psychological Corporation.

Elliott, S. (1994). *Creating meaningful performance assessments: Fundamental concepts.* Reston, VA: Council for Exceptional Children. (Abstracted in *Diagnostique, 20*).

Elliott, S., & Busse, R. (1990). Review of Child Behavior Checklist. In J. Conoley & J. Kramer (Eds.), *Tenth mental measurement yearbook* (Supplement). (pp. 41–45). Lincoln, NE: University of Nebraska Press.

Elliott, S., & Piersel, W. (1982). Direct assessment of reading skills: An approach which links assessment to intervention. *School Psychology Review, 11,* 267–280.

Elrod, G., Isbell, C., & Braziel, P. (1989). Assessing transition-related variables from kindergarten through grade 12: Practical applications. *Diagnostique, 14,* 247–261.

Elrod, G., & Sorgenfrei, T. (1988). Toward an appropriate assessment model for adolescents who are mildly handicapped: Let's not forget transition! *Career Development for Exceptional Individuals, 11,* 92–98.

Enright, B. (1983). *The Enright Diagnostic Inventory of Basic Arithmetic Skills.* North Billerica, MA: Curriculum Associates.

Enright, B. (1992). Basic mathematics. In J. Choate, B. Enright, L. Miller, J. Poteet, & T. Rakes (Eds), *Curriculum-based assessment and programming.* (pp. 197–230). Boston, Allyn & Bacon.

Enright, B., Beattie, J., & Algozzine, B. (1992). Helping mainstreamed students develop successful test-taking skills. *Diagnostique, 17,* 128–136.

Enright, B., Gable, R., & Hendrickson, J. (1988). How do students get answers like these? Nine steps in diagnosing computation errors. *Diagnostique, 13,* 55–63.

Erickson, D. (1989). Review of Test of Written Spelling–2. In J. Conoley & J. Kramer (Eds.), *Tenth mental measurements yearbook* (pp. 858–859). Lincoln, NE: University of Nebraska Press.

Estabrook, G. (1984). Review of Bracken Basic Concept Scale. In D. Keyser & R. Sweetland (Eds.), *Test critiques* (v. 1) (pp. 125–129). Kansas City, MO: Test Corporation of America.

Estes, G., Harris, J., Moers, F., & Wodrich, D. (1976). Predictive validity of the Boehm Test of Basic Concepts for achievement in first grade. *Educational and Psychological Measurement, 36,* 1031–1035.

Evans, L. (1990). A conceptual overview of the regression discrepancy model for evaluating severe discrepancies between IQ and achievement scores. *Journal of Learning Disabilities, 23,* 406–412.

Evans, L. (1992). Implementation of a computer-based regression discrepancy model: A survey of Montana school psychologists. *Journal of School Psychology, 30*(4), 383–393.

Evans, L., & Bradley-Johnson, S. (1988). A review of recently developed measures of adaptive behavior. *Psychology in the Schools, 25,* 276–287.

Evans, S., Evans, W., & Mercer, C. (1986). *Assessment for instruction.* Boston: Allyn & Bacon.

Evans, W. H., Gable, R. A., & Evans, S. S. (1993). Making something out of everything: The promise of ecological assessment. *Diagnostique, 18,* 175–185.

Falvey, M. (1989). *Community-based curriculum* (2nd ed.). Baltimore: Brookes.

Falvey, M., Brown, L., Lyon, S., Baumgart, D., & Schroeder, J. (1980). Strategies for using cues and correction procedures. In W. Sailor, B. Wilcox, & L. Brown (Eds.), *Methods of instruction for severely handicapped students* (pp. 109–133). Baltimore: Brookes.

Farr, R., & Tone, B. (1994). *Portfolio and performance assessment: Helping students evaluate their progress as readers and writers.* Fort Worth, TX: Harcourt Brace College Publishers.

Federal Register. (1977). Washington, D.C.: U.S. Government Printing Office, August 23, 1977.

Feuer, M., & Fulton, K. (1993). The many faces of performance assessment. *Phi Delta Kappan, 74,* 478.

Feuerstein, R., Haywood, H., Rand, Y., Hoffman, M., & Jensen, B. (1984). *Examiner manuals for the Learning Potential Assessment Device.* Jerusalem: Hadassah-WIZO-Canada Research Institute.

Fields, J., & Kumar, V. (1982). How teachers use group IQ test scores. *Journal of School Psychology, 20,* 32–38.

Finkelman, D., Ferrarese, M. H., & Garmezy, N. (1989). A factorial reliability and validity study of the Devereux Elementary School Behavior Rating Scale. *Psychological Reports, 64*(2), 535–547.

Fischer, C., & King, R. (1995). *Authentic assessment: A guide to implementation.* Thousand Oaks, CA: Corwin Press.

Fitts W. (1984). *Tennessee Self-Concept Scale.* Nashville: Counselor Recordings and Tests.

Flanagan, D. P., & Alfonso, V. C. (1993a). Differences required for a significance between Wechsler Verbal and Performance I.Q.'s and WIAT subtests and composites: The Predicted-Achievement Method. *Psychology in the Schools, 30,* 125–132.

Flanagan, D. P., & Alfonso, V. C. (1993b). WIAT subtest and composite predicted-achievement values based on WISC-III Verbal and Performance I.Q.'s. *Psychology in the Schools, 30,* 310–320.

Fleege, P. O., Charlesworth, R., Burts, D. C., & Hart, C. H. (1992). Stress begins in kindergarten: A look at behavior during standardized testing. *Journal of Research in Childhood Education, 7*(1), 20–26.

Florida Department of Education. (1989). *Prekindergarten assessment and training of the handicapped.* Tallahassee, FL: Florida Department of Education.

Fodness, R., McNeilly, J., & Bradley-Johnson, S. (1991). Relationship of the Test of Language Development–2 Primary and the Test of Language Development–2 Intermediate. *Journal of School Psychology, 29,* 167–176.

Forbes, G. R. (1987). Personality Inventory for Children: Characteristics of learning disabled children with emotional problems and of emotionally disturbed children with learning problems. *Journal of Clinical Child Psychology, 17*(9), 541–544.

Forness, S., & Knitzer, J. (1992). *A new proposed definition and terminology to replace "Serious Emotional Disturbance" in the Education of the Handicapped Act* (Report of the Work-Group on Definition, National Mental Health and Special Education Coalition). Alexandria, VA: National Mental Health Association.

Foster, R. (1974). *Camelot Behavioral Checklist.* Lawrence, KS: Camelot Behavioral Systems.

Frank, A. (1973). Breaking down learning tasks: A sequence approach. *Teaching Exceptional Children, 6,* 16–21.

Frank, A., & Gerken, K. (1990). Case studies in curriculum-based measurement. *Education and Training in Mental Retardation, 25,* 113–119.

Frank, A., Logan, H., & Martin, D. (1982). LD students' subtraction errors. *Learning Disability Quarterly, 5,* 194–196.

Frank, L. (1939). Projective methods for the study of personality. *Journal of Psychology, 8,* 389–413.

Frankenberger, W., & Fronzaglio, K. (1991). A review of states' criteria and procedures for identifying children with learning disabilities. *Journal of Learning Disabilities, 24,* 495–500.

Frankenburg, W., Camp, B., & Van Natta, P. (1971). Validity of the Denver Developmental Screening Test. *Child Development, 42,* 475–485.

Frankenburg, W., Dodds, J., Archers, P., Bresnick, B., Maschka, P., Edelman, N., & Shapiro, H. (1990). *Denver-II.* Denver, CO: Denver Developmental Materials, Inc.

Frankenburg, W., Fandel, A., Sciarillo, W., & Burgess, D. (1981). The newly abbreviated Denver Developmental Screening Test: Its accuracy as a screening instrument. *The Journal of Pediatrics, 79,* 988–995.

Frankenburg, W., Van Doorninck, W., Liddell, T., & Dick, N. (1976). The Denver Prescreening Developmental Questionnaire (PDQ). *Pediatrics, 57,* 744–753.

French, J. (1964). *Pictorial Test of Intelligence.* Boston: Houghton Mifflin.

Frisby, C. (1992). The relationship between lexicon rankings and item difficulty on the Bracken Basic Concept Scale. *Diagnostique, 17,* 115–127.

Frisby, C. L., & Braden, J. P. (1992). Feuerstein's dynamic assessment approach: A semantic, logical, and empirical critique. *Journal of Special Education, 26*(3), 281–301.

Frostig, M., Lefever, W., & Whittlesey, J. (1966). *Administration and scoring manual: Marianne Frostig Developmental Test of Visual Perception.* Palo Alto, CA: Consulting Psychologists Press.

Fuchs, D., & Fuchs, L. (1989). Effects of examiner familiarity on black, Caucasian, and Hispanic children: A metanalysis. *Exceptional Children, 55,* 303–308.

Fuchs, L. (1994). *Connecting performance assessment to instruction.* Reston, VA: Council for Exceptional Children. (Abstracted in *Diagnostique, 20*).

Fuchs, L., & Fuchs, D. (1988). Curriculum-based measurement: A methodology for evaluating and improving student programs. *Diagnostique, 14,* 3–13.

Fuchs, L., & Fuchs, D. (1990). Traditional academic assessment: An overview. In R. Gable & J. Hendrickson (Eds.), *Assessing students with special needs* (pp. 1–13). New York: Longman.

Fuchs, L., Fuchs, D., Bishop, N., & Hamlett, C. (1992). Classwide decision making strategies with curriculum-based measurement. *Diagnostique, 18,* 39–52.

Fuchs, L., Fuchs, D., & Hamlett, C. (1989). Computers and curriculum based measurement: Effects of teacher feedback systems. *School Psychology Review, 18,* 112–125.

Fuchs, L., Fuchs, D., & Hamlett, C. L. (1990). Curriculum-based measurement: A standardized, long-term goal approach to monitoring student progress. *Academic Therapy, 25,* 615–632.

Fuchs, L. S., Fuchs, D., & Hamlett, C. L. (1993). Technological advances linking the assessment of students' academic proficiency to instructional planning. *Journal of Special Education Technology, 12,* 49–62.

Fuchs, L., Fuchs, D., Hamlett, C., & Allinder, R. (1989). The reliability and validity of skills analysis within curriculum-based measurement. *Diagnostique, 14,* 203–221.

Fuchs, L., Fuchs, D., Hamlett, C., & Allinder, R. (1991). The contribution of skills analysis to curriculum-based measurement in spelling. *Exceptional Children, 57,* 443–452.

Fuchs, L., Fuchs, D., Hamlett, C., & Ferguson, C. (1992). Effects of expert system consultation within curriculum-based management using a reading maze task. *Exceptional Children, 58,* 436–450.

Fuchs, L. S., Fuchs, D., Hamlett, C. L., & Phillips, N., and Bentz, J. (1994). Classroom curriculum-based measurement: Helping general educators meet the challenge of student diversity. *Exceptional Children, 60,* 518–537.

Fuchs, L., Hamlett, C., & Fuchs, D. (1990). *Monitoring Basic Skills Progress.* Austin, TX: Pro-Ed.

Fudala, J. (1978). *Tree/Bee Test of Auditory Discrimination.* Novato, CA: Academic Therapy Publications.

Fugata, D., Clarizio, H., and Phillips, S. (1993). Referral-to-Placement ratio: A finding in need of reassessment? *Journal of Learning Disabilities, 26,* 413–416.

Fujiki, M. (1989). Review of Test of Pragmatic Skills. In J. Conoley & J. Kramer (Eds.) *Tenth mental measurement yearbook* (pp. 847–848). Lincoln, NE: University of Nebraska Press.

Gable, R. (1990). Curriculum-based measurement of oral reading: Linking assessment and instruction. *Preventing School Failure, 35,* 37–42.

Gable, R., & Coben, S. (1990). Errors in arithmetic. In R. Gable & J. Hendrickson (Eds.), *Assessing students with special needs* (pp. 30–45). New York: Longman.

Gable, R., & Hendrickson, J. (1990). *Assessing students with special needs.* New York: Longman.

Gajar, A. (1979). Educable mentally retarded, learning disabled and emotionally disturbed: Similarities and differences. *Exceptional Children, 45,* 470–472.

Galagan, J. (1985). Psychoeducational testing: Turn out the light the party's over. *Exceptional Children, 52,* 288–299.

Gall, M. (1990). *Tools for learning: A guide to teaching study skills* (ED 320126). Alexandria, VA: Association for Supervision and Curriculum Development.

Gardner, E., Rudman, H., Karlsen, B., & Merwin, J. (1982). *Stanford Achievement Test.* New York: Harcourt Brace Jovanovich.

Gardner, M. (1990a). *Receptive One-Word Picture Vocabulary Test.* Novato, CA: Academic Therapy Publications.

Gardner, M. (1990b). *Expressive One-Word Picture Vocabulary Test.* Novato, CA: Academic Therapy Publications.

Garrison, W., & Earls, F. (1985). The Child Behavior Checklist as a screening instrument for young children. *Journal of the American Academy of Child Psychiatry, 24,* 76–80.

Garrity, L., & Servos, A. (1978). Comparison of measures of adaptive behaviors in preschool children. *Journal of Consulting and Clinical Psychology, 46,* 288–293.

Gaylord-Ross, R. (1986). The role of assessment in transitional, supported employment. *Career Development for Exceptional Individuals, 9,* 129–134.

Gayton, W., Thornton, K., & Bassett, J. (1982) Utility of the Behavior Problem Checklist with preschool children. *Journal of Clinical Psychology, 38,* 325–327.

Gerken, K., Eliason, M., & Arthur, C. (1994). The assessment of at-risk infants and toddlers with the Bayley Mental Scales and the Battelle Developmental Inventory: Beyond the data. *Psychology in the Schools, 31,* 181–87.

German, D. (1986). *Test of Word Finding.* Allen, TX: DLM Teaching Resources.

German, M. L., Williams, E., Herzfield, J., & Marshall, R. M. (1982). Utility of the Revised Denver Developmental Screening Test and the Developmental Profile II in identifying preschool children with cognitive, language, and motor problems. *Education and Training of the Mentally Retarded, 17,* 319–324.

Giacobbe, G., & Traynelis-Yurek, E. (1989). Undergraduate students' errors in the administration of standardized tests. *Diagnostique, 14,* 174–182.

Gilliam, J. (1994). *Work Adjustment Inventory.* Austin, TX: Pro-Ed.

Gilliam, J. (1995a). *Attention Deficit/Hyperactivity Disorder Test.* Austin, TX: Pro-Ed.

Gilliam, J. (1995b), *Gilliam Autism Rating Scale.* Austin, TX: Pro-Ed.

Gilmore, J., & Gilmore, E. (1968). *Gilmore Oral Reading Test.* New York: Harcourt Brace Jovanovich.

Ginsburg, H., & Baroody, A. (1990). *Test of Early Mathematics Ability–2.* Austin, TX: Pro-Ed.

Ginsburg, H., & Mathews, S. (1984). *Diagnostic Test of Arithmetic Strategies.* Austin, TX: Pro-Ed.

Glascoe, F. P., & Borowitz, K. C. (1988). Improving the sensitivity of the language section of the Denver Developmental Screening Test. *Diagnostique, 13,* 76–85.

Glaub, V., & Kamphaus, R. (1991). Construction of a nonverbal adaptation of the Stanford-Binet Fourth Edition. *Educational and Psychological Measurement, 51,* 231–241.

Glutting, J. (1989). Introduction to the structure and approach of the Stanford-Binet Intelligence Scale–Fourth Edition. *Journal of School Psychology, 27,* 69–80.

Glutting, J., Kelly, M., Boehm, A., & Burnett, T. (1989). Stability and predictive validity of the Boehm Test of Basic Concepts–Revised among black kindergarteners. *Journal of School Psychology, 27,* 365–371.

Glutting, J. J., McGrath, E. A., Kamphaus, R. W. & McDermott, P. A. (1992). Taxonomy and validity of subtest profiles on the Kaufman Assessment Battery for Children. *Journal of Special Education, 26*(1), 85–115.

Goh, D. (1984). PIC profiles for learning disabled and behavior disordered children. *Journal of Clinical Psychology, 40,* 837–841.

Goldman, R., & Fristoe, M. (1986). *Goldman-Fristoe Test of Articulation.* Circle Pines, MN: American Guidance Service.

Goldman, R., Fristoe, M., & Woodcock, R. (1970). *Goldman-Fristoe-Woodcock Test of Auditory Discrimination.* Circle Pines, MN: American Guidance Service.

Good, T., & Brophy, J. (1972). Behavioral expression of teacher attitudes. *Journal of Educational Psychology, 63,* 617–624.

Goodman, K. (1977). *Miscue analysis.* Urbana, IL: ERIC, Clearinghouse on Reading and Communication Skills, National Council of Teachers of English.

Goodman, Y., & Burke, C. (1972). *Reading Miscue Inventory.* New York: Macmillan.

Goodman, Y., Watson, D., & Burke, C. (1987). *Reading miscue inventory: Alternative procedures.* New York: Richard C. Owen, Publisher.

Goodstein, H., Kahn, H., & Cawley, J. (1976). The achievement of educable mentally retarded children on the Key Math Diagnostic Arithmetic Test. *Journal of Special Education, 10,* 61–70.

Gordon, L. (1981). *Gordon Occupational Check List II.* San Antonio: Psychological Corporation.

Gough, H. (1969). *California Psychological Inventory.* Palo Alto, CA: Consulting Psychologists Press.

Graf, M., & Hinton, R. (1994). A three-year comparison study of WISC-R and WISC-III IQ scores for a sample of special education students. *Educational and Psychological Measurement, 54,* 128–133.

Graziano, W. (1982). Race of the examiner effects and the validity of intelligence tests. *Review of Education Research, 52,* 469–497.

Green, D. (1987). Interpreting grade scores from standardized tests. *National Association of Secondary Schools Bulletin, 71,* 23–35.

Greenbaum, C. (1987). *The Spellmaster Assessment and Teaching System.* Austin, TX: Pro-Ed.

Greene, A. C., Sapp, G., & Chissom, B. (1990). Validation of the Stanford-Binet Intelligence Scale: Fourth Edition with exceptional black male students. *Psychology in the Schools, 27*(1), 35–41.

Greenstein, J., & Strain, P. (1977). The utility of the Key Math Diagnostic Arithmetic Test for adolescent learning disabled students. *Psychology in the Schools, 14,* 275–282.

Gresham, F., & Elliot, S. (1990). *Social Skills Rating System.* Circle Pines, MN: American Guidance Service.

Gresham, F., Elliott, S., & Evans-Fernandez, B. (1993). *Student Self-Concept Scale.* Circle Pines, MN: American Guidance Service.

Gridley, B., & McIntosh, D. (1991). Confirmatory factor analysis of the Stanford-Binet Intelligence Scale–Fourth Edition. *Journal of School Psychology, 29,* 237–248.

Gridley, B., Miller, G., Barke, C., Fischer, W., & Smith, D. (1990). Construct validity of the K-ABC with an at-risk preschool population. *Journal of School Psychology, 28,* 39–49.

Grill, J., & Kirwin, M. (1995). *Written Language Assessment.* Novato, CA: Academic Therapy.

Gronlund, N. (1973). *Preparing criterion-referenced tests for classroom instruction.* New York: Macmillan.

Gronlund, N. (1988). *How to construct achievement tests* (4th ed.). Englewood Cliffs, NJ: Prentice-Hall.

Gronlund, N., & Linn, R. (1990). *Measurement and evaluation in teaching* (6th ed.). New York: Macmillan.

Grossman, F. (1981). Cautions in interpreting WRAT standard scores as criterion measures of achievement in young children. *Psychology in the Schools, 18,* 144–146.

Grossman, H. (Ed.). (1983). *Classification in mental retardation.* Washington, D.C.: American Association on Mental Deficiency.

Guidubaldi, J., & Perry, J. (1984). Concurrent and predictive validity of the Battelle Developmental Inventory at the first grade level. *Educational and Psychological Measurement, 44,* 977–985.

Guskey, T. R. (1994). What you assess may not be what you get. *Educational Leadership, 51*(6), 51–54.

Gutkin, T. (1979). WISC–R scatter indices: Useful information for differential diagnosis? *Journal of School Psychology, 17,* 368–371.

Guyette, T. (1989). Review of Test of Language Competence. In J. Conoley & J. Kramer (Eds.), *Tenth mental measurements yearbook* (pp. 432–434). Lincoln, NE: University of Nebraska Press.

Guzaitis, J., Carlin, J., & Juda, S. (1972). *Diagnosis: An Instructional Aid in Mathematics.* Chicago: Science Research Associates.

Hadaway, N. L., & Marek-Schroer, M. (1994). Student portfolios: Toward equitable assessments for gifted students. *Equity and Excellence in Education, 27,* 70–74.

Haddad, F. (1986). Performance of learning disabled children on the K-ABC and Bender-Gestalt. *Psychology in the Schools, 23,* 342–345.

Haines, H. (1977). *A study of the construct validity of the Woodcock Reading Mastery Tests with underachieving and slow learning fourth, fifth and sixth grade pupils.* Ann Arbor, MI: University Microfilms International, No. 7810802.

Haley, J. (1963). *Strategies of psychotherapy.* New York: Grune & Stratton.

Hall, R., & Goetz, E. (1984). Evaluation of the Kaufman Assessment Battery for Children from an information processing perspective. *Journal of Special Education, 18,* 280–296.

Hallahan, D., & Cruickshank, W. (1973). *Psychoeducational foundations of learning disabilities.* Englewood Cliffs, NJ: Prentice-Hall.

Hallahan, D., & Kauffman, J. (1976). *Introduction to learning disabilities.* Englewood Cliffs, NJ: Prentice-Hall.

Hallahan, D., & Kauffman, J. (1994). *Exceptional children* (6th ed.). Englewood Cliffs, NJ: Prentice-Hall.

Hallahan, D., Keller, C., & Ball, D. (1986). A comparison of prevalence rate variability from state to state for each of the categories of special education. *Remedial and Special Education, 7,* 8–14.

Halpern, A. S. (1994). The transition of youth with disabilities to adult life: A position statement of the Division on Career Development and Transition. *Career Development for Exceptional Individuals, 17,* 115–124.

Hammill, D. (1985). *Detroit Tests of Learning Aptitude–2,* Austin, TX: Pro-Ed.

Hammill, D. (1990). On defining learning disabilities: An emerging consensus. *Journal of Learning Disabilities, 23,* 74–84.

Hammill, D. (1991). *Detroit Tests of Learning Aptitude–3.* Austin, TX: Pro-Ed.

Hammill, D., & Larsen, S. (1988). *Test of Written Language–2,* Austin, TX: Pro-Ed.

Hammill, D., Ammer, J., Cronin, M., Mandlebaum, L., & Quinby, S. (1987). *Quick-Score Achievement Test.* Austin, TX: Pro-Ed.

Hammill, D., Brown, V., Larsen, S., & Weiderholt, L. (1994). *Test of Adolescent and Adult Language–3.* Austin, TX: Pro-Ed.

Hammill, D., & Larsen, S. (1974). The relationship of selected auditory perceptual skills and reading ability. *Journal of Learning Disabilities, 7,* 429–435.

Hammill, D., & Larsen, S. (1988). *Test of Written Language–2,* Austin, TX: Pro-Ed.

Hammill, D., Leigh, J., McNutt, G., & Larsen, S. (1981). A new definition of learning disabilities. *Learning Disability Quarterly, 4,* 336–342.

Hammill, D., Pearson, N., & Voress, J. (1993). *Developmental Test of Visual Perception–2.* Austin, TX: Pro-Ed.

Hammill, D., Wiederholt, L., & Pearson, N. (1995). *Comprehensive Test of Nonverbal Intelligence.* Austin, TX: Pro-Ed.

Hanley, T. (1995). The need for technology advances in assessments related to national education reform. *Exceptional Children, 61,* 222–229.

Hardman, J., & Croyle, G. (1979). *A kindergarten screening procedure for the identification of potentially exceptional children.* Paper presented at the 26th annual convention of the National Association for Gifted Children. Baltimore.

Hardman, M., Drew, C., Egan, M., & Wolf, B. (1993). *Human exceptionality* (3rd ed.). Boston: Allyn & Bacon.

Haring, N. (1994). Overview of special education. In N. G. Haring, L. McCormick, & T. G. Haring (Eds.), *Exceptional children and youth* (6th ed.) (pp. 1–63). New York: Merrill.

Harmer, W., & Williams, F. (1978). The Wide Range Achievement Test and the Peabody Individual Achievement Test: A comparative study. *Journal of Learning Disabilities, 11,* 65–68.

Harper, D. C., & Walker, D. P. (1983). The efficiency of the Denver Developmental Screening Test with rural disadvantaged preschool children. *Journal of Pediatric Psychology, 8,* 273–283.

Harrington, R. (1985). Review of Battelle Developmental Inventory. In D. Keyser & R. Sweetland (Eds.), *Test critiques, 2,* (pp. 72–82). Kansas City: Test Corp. of America.

Harris, D. (1963). *Children's drawings as measures of intellectual maturity.* New York: Harcourt Brace Jovanovich.

Harris, S., & Fagley, N. (1987). The Developmental Profile as a predictor of status for autistic children: Four to seven year follow up. *School Psychology Review, 16,* 89–93.

Harrison, P. (1990a). Review of Spellmaster. In J. Conoley & J. Kramer (Eds.), *Tenth mental measurements yearbook.* (Supplement) (pp. 237–239). Lincoln, NE: University of Nebraska Press.

Harrison, P. (1990b). *New prekindergarten assessment instruments.* Unpublished manuscript.

Harrison, P. (1991). *Early Screening Profiles.* Circle Pines, MN: American Guidance Service.

Harrison, P., Kaufman, A., Hickman, J., & Kaufman, N. (1988). A survey of tests used for adult assessment. *Journal of Psychoeducational Assessment, 6,* 188–198.

Harrison, P. L. (1987). Research with adaptive behavior scales. *The Journal of Special Education, 21,* 37–68.

Harrison, P. L. (1988). *K-ABC mental processing profiles for gifted referrals.* Paper presented at the Mid-South Educational Research Association Meeting, Louisville, KY.

Hart, D. (1994). *Authentic assessment.* New York: Addison-Wesley.

Hasbrouck, J. E., & Tindal, G. (1992). Curriculum-based oral reading fluency norms for students in Grades 2 through 5. *Teaching Exceptional Children, 24*(3), 41–44.

Hasselbring, T. (1984). *Computerized test of spelling errors.* Nashville, TN: Expert Systems Software, Inc.

Hasselbring, T., & Crossland, C. (1982). Application of microcomputer technology to spelling assessment of learning disabled students. *Learning Disabilities Quarterly, 5,* 80–82.

Hasselbring, T., & Goin, L. (1985). *Chronometric analysis of math strategies.* Nashville, TN: Expert Systems Software, Inc.

Hasselbring, T., & Moore, P. (1990). Computer-based assessment and error analysis. In R. Gable & J. Hendrickson (Eds.), *Assessing students with special needs* (pp. 102–116). New York: Longman.

Hayden, D. C., Furlong, M., & Linnemeyer, S. (1988). A comparison of the Kaufman Assessment Battery for Children and the Stanford-Binet IV for the assessment of gifted children. *Psychology in the Schools, 25,* 239–243.

Haynes, S. (1978). *Principles of behavioral assessment.* New York: Gardner.

Haywood, H. C., Brown, A., & Wingenfeld, S. (1990). Dynamic approaches to psychoeducational assessment. *School Psychology Review, 19*(4), 411–422.

Heath, C., & Obrzut, J. (1984). Comparison of three measures of adaptive behavior. *American Journal of Mental Deficiency, 89,* 205–208.

Heath, C., & Obrzut, J. (1986). *Trends in adaptive behavior research over the past decade.* ERIC Reproduction No. ED 270 922.

Heifetz, L. (1989). Review of Scales of Independent Behavior. In J. Conoley & J. Kramer (Eds.), *Tenth mental measurements yearbook* (pp. 713–718). Lincoln, NE: University of Nebraska Press.

Heinze, A. (1987). Assessing general psychopathology in children and youth with visual handicaps. *Australia and New Zealand Journal of Developmental Disabilities, 13*(4), 219–226.

Hendrickson, J., & Gable, R. (1990). Errors in spelling. In R. Gable & J. Hendrickson (Eds.), *Assessing students with special needs* (pp. 78–88). New York: Longman.

Henley, S., Klebe, K., McBride, J., & Cudeck, R. (1989). Adaptive and conventional versions of the DAT: The first complete test battery comparison. *Applied Psychological Measurement, 13,* 363–371.

Henson, F., & Bennett, L. (1986). The Kaufman Test of Educational Achievement. In D. Keyser & R. Sweetland (Eds.) *Test critiques* (v. 4) (pp. 368–375). Kansas City, MO: Test Corporation of America.

Herman, J., Gearhart, M., & Baker, E. (1993). Assessing writing portfolios: Issues in the validity and meaning of scores. *Educational Assessment, 1,* 201–224.

Heshusius, L. (1991). Curriculum based assessment and direct instruction: Critical reflections on fundamental assumptions. *Exceptional Children, 57,* 315–328.

Hessler, G. (1985). Review of the Kaufman Assessment Battery for Children: Implications for assessment of the gifted. *Journal for the Education of the Gifted, 8,* 133–147.

Hessler, G. (1994). *Use and interpretation of the Woodcock-Johnson–Revised.* Brandon, VT: Clinical Psychology Publishing Company.

Heward, W., & Orlansky, M. (1992). *Exceptional children* (4th ed.). Columbus, OH: Charles Merrill.

Hewitt, G. (1995). *A portfolio primer.* Portsmouth, NH: Heinemann.

Hickman, J. (1989). Review of the Gray Oral Reading Test–Revised. In J. Conoley & J. Kramer (Eds.), *Tenth mental measurements yearbook* (pp. 335–337). Lincoln, NE: University of Nebraska Press.

Hickman, J., & Bevins, S. (1990). *Learning disability discrepancy analysis.* Austin, TX: Pro-Ed.

Hightower, A. (1989). Review of Developmental Profile–II. In J. Conoley & J. Kramer (Eds.), *Tenth mental measurements yearbook.* (pp. 249–250). Lincoln, NE: University of Nebraska Press.

Hilton, L. M. (1991). Cultural bias and ecological validity in testing rural children. *Rural Educator, 12*(3), 16–20.

Hing-McGowan, J. (1994). The multicultural vocational classroom: Strategies for improving student achievement. *Journal for Vocational Special Needs Education, 16*(2), 10–15.

Hirshoren, A., & Schnittjer, C. (1979). Dimensions of problem behavior in deaf children. *Journal of Abnormal Child Psychology, 7,* 221–228.

Hishinuma, E. S., & Yamakawa, R. (1993). Construct and criterion-related validity of the WISC-III for exceptional students and those who are "At-Risk." *Journal of Psychoeducational Assessment Monograph Series: Wechsler Intelligence Scale for Children (Third Edition)*, 94–104.

Hiskey, M. (1966). *Hiskey-Nebraska Test of Learning Aptitude*. Lincoln, NE: Union College Press.

Hobbs, N. (1975). *Issues in the classification of children* (2 vols.). San Francisco: Jossey-Bass.

Hodapp, R. M., Leckman, J. F., Dykens, E. M., Sparrow, S. S., Zelinsky, D. G., & Ort, S. I. (1992). K-ABC profiles in children with Fragile X syndrome, Down syndrome and nonspecific mental retardation. *American Journal on Mental Retardation*, 97(1), 39–46.

Holland, J. (1985). *Vocational Preference Inventory–Revised*. Odessa, FL: Psychological Assessment Resources.

Hooper, S., & Hynd, G. (1986). Performance of normal and dyslexic readers on the Kaufman Assessment Battery for Children: A discriminant analysis. *Journal of Learning Disabilities*, 9, 206–209.

Hoover, H. D., Hieronymus, A. N., Frisbie, D. A., & Dunbar, S. B. (1993). *Iowa Tests of Basic Skills*. Chicago: The Riverside Publishing Company.

Hopkins, K., & Hodge, S. (1984). Review of the Kaufman Assessment Battery for Children. *Journal of Counseling and Development*, 63, 105–107.

Houck, C., Biskin, D., & Regetz, J. (1973). A comparison of urban and rural reliability estimates for the Boehm Basic Concept Test. *Psychology in the Schools*, 10, 430–432.

Howell, K. (1990). Review of Test of Mathematical Abilities. *Diagnostique*, 15, 210–217.

Howell, K. W., Bigelow, S. S., Moore, E. L., & Evoy, A. M. (1993). Bias in authentic assessment. *Diagnostique*, 19(1), 387–400.

Howell, K., & Morehead, M. (1987). *Curriculum-based evaluation for special and remedial education*. Columbus, OH: Charles E. Merrill.

Howell, K., Zucker, S., & Morehead, M. (1985). *Multilevel Academic Skills Test*. San Antonio: The Psychological Corporation.

Hoza, B. (1994). Review of the Behavior Assessment System for Children. *Child Assessment News*, 4, 5, 8–10.

Hresko, W. (1988). *Test of Early Written Language*. Austin, TX: Pro-Ed.

Hritcko, T., & Salvia, J. (1984). The K-ABC and ability training. *Journal of Special Education*, 18, 345–356.

Huberty, T. (1986). Relationship of the WISC-R factors to the Adaptive Behavior Scales School Edition in a referral sample. *Journal of School Psychology*, 24, 155–162.

Huebner, S. (1989a). Factors influencing the decision to administer psychoeducational tests. *Psychology in the Schools*, 26, 365–370.

Huebner, S. (1989b). A comparison of school psychologists' interpretations of grade equivalents, percentiles, and deviation IQs. *School Psychology Review*, 18, 51–55.

Huebner, S. (1989c). Review of Developmental Profile-II. In J. Conoley & J. Kramer (Eds.), *Tenth mental measurements yearbook* (pp. 250–251). Lincoln, NE: Unversity of Nebraska Press.

Hughes, S. (1988). Adaptive Behavior Inventory. In D. Keyser & R. Sweetland (Eds.) *Test critiques* (v. 7) (pp. 3–9). Kansas City, MO: Test Corporation of America.

Hunnicutt, L., Slate, J., Gamble, C., & Wheeler, M. (1990). Examiner errors on the Kaufman Assessment Battery for Children: A preliminary investigation. *Journal of School Psychology*, 28, 271–278.

Hunter, M., Ballash, J., & Chen A. (1992). Comparison of the Peabody Picture Vocabulary Test–Revised and the Stanford-Binet Intelligence Scale–Fourth Edition with elementary students referred for learning problems. *Diagnostique*, 17, 108–114.

Hurt, D. (1994). *Authentic assessment: A handbook for educators*. NY: Addison-Wesley.

Hutcherson, R. (1978). Correlating the Boehm and PPVT. *Academic Therapy*, 13, 285–288.

Hutt, M. (1977). *The Hutt Adaptation of the Bender-Gestalt Test* (3rd ed.). New York: Grune & Stratton.

Ianacone, R. N., & Leconte, P. J. (1986). Curriculum-based vocational assessment: A viable response to a school-based service delivery issue. *Career Development for Exceptional Individuals*, 9, 113–120.

Idol, L., Nevin, A., & Paolucci-Whitcomb, P. (1986). *Models of curriculum-based assessment*. Rockville, MD: Aspen Publishers, Inc.

Ilg, F., Ames, L., Haines, J., & Gillespie, C. (1978). *Gesell School Readiness Test*. New York: Harper and Row.

Ilmer, S., Bruininks, R. J., & Hill, B. K. (1988). Discriminant analysis of intellectual ability groups with measures of adaptive behavior. *Journal of School Psychology*, 26, 293–296.

Isaacson, S. (1988). Assessing the writing product: Qualitative and quantitative measures. *Exceptional Children*, 54(b), 528–534.

Isett, R., & Spreat, S. (1979). Test-retest and interrater reliabilities of the AAMD Adaptive Behavior Scale. *American Journal of Mental Deficiency*, 84, 93–95.

Jacobs, W. (1978). The effect of learning disability label on classroom teachers' ability objectively to observe and interpret child behaviors. *Learning Disability Quarterly*, 1, 50–55.

Jaeger, R. (1989). Review of Woodcock Reading Mastery Tests-Revised. In J. Conoley & J. Kramer (Eds.), *Tenth mental measurements yearbook* (pp. 913–916). Lincoln, NE: University of Nebraska Press.

Jastak, J., & Jastak, S. (1979). *Wide Range Interest-Opinion Test*. Wilmington, DE: Jastak Associates.

Jastak, S., & Wilkinson, G. (1984). *Wide Range Achievement Test–Revised*. Wilmington, DE: Jastak Associates.

Javorsky, J. (1993). The relationship between the Kaufman Brief Intelligence Test and the Wechsler Intelligence Scale for Children III. *Diagnostique*, 19, 377–385.

Jenkins, J. R., & Jewell, M. (1993). Examining the validity of two measures for formative teaching: Reading aloud and maze. *Exceptional Children, 59,* 421–432.

Jensen, A. (1986). The black-white difference on the K-ABC: Implications for future tests. *Journal of Special Education, 18,* 377–408.

Jensen, A. R. (1993). Spearman's hypothesis tested with chronometric information-processing tasks. *Intelligence, 17*(1), 47–77.

Jitendra, A. K., & Kameenui, E. J. (1993). Dynamic assessment as a compensatory assessment approach: A description and analysis. *Remedial and Special Education, 14*(5), 6–18.

Johns, J. (1988). *Basic Reading Inventory.* Dubuque, IA: Kendall/Hunt.

Johns, J. & VanLeirsburg, P. (1992). Teaching test-wiseness: Can test scores of special populations be improved? *Reading Psychology, 13*(1), 99–103.

Johnson, D., & Harlow, S. (1989). Using the computer in educational assessment: Can it be of any help? *Diagnostique, 14,* 274–282.

Johnson, D., & Myklebust, H. (1967). *Learning disabilities: Educational principles and practices.* New York: Grune & Stratton.

Johnson, D. R., Thompson, S. J., Sinclair, M., Krantz, G. C., Evelo, S., Stolte, K., & Thompson, J. R. (1993). Considerations in the design of follow-up and follow-along systems for improving transition programs and services. *Career Development for Exceptional Individuals, 16,* 225–238.

Johnson, J. R., & Rusch, F. R. (1993). Secondary special education and transition services: Identification and recommendations for future research and demonstration. *Career Development for Exceptional Individuals, 16,* 1–18.

Johnson-Martin, N., Attermeier, S., & Hacker, B. (1990). *Assessment Log and Developmental Progress Chart–Preschool.* Baltimore: Paul Brooks.

Johnson-Martin, N., Jens, K., & Attermeier, S. (1986). *Assessment Log and Developmental Progress Chart–Infant.* Baltimore: Paul Brooks.

Jonz, J. (1990). Another turn in the conversation: What does Cloze measure? *TESOL Quarterly, 24,* 61–83.

Karlsen, B. (1993). *Language Arts Assessment Portfolio.* Circle Pines, MN: American Guidance Service.

Kamphaus, R. (1987). Conceptual and psychometric issues in the assessment of adaptive behavior. *Journal of Special Education, 21,* 27–35.

Kamphaus, R. (1989). Review of the Diagnostic Achievement Test for Adolescents. In J. Conoley & J. Kramer (Eds.), *Tenth mental measurements yearbook* (pp. 253–254). Lincoln, NE: University of Nebraska Press.

Kamphaus, R. W., Benson, J., Hutchinson, S., & Platt, L. O. (1994). Identification of factor models for the WISC-III. *Educational and Psychological Measurement, 54*(1), 174–186.

Kamphaus, R., & Reynolds, C. (1984). Development and structure of the Kaufman Assessment Battery

for Children. *Journal of Special Education, 18,* 213–228.

Karlsen, B. (1993). *Language Arts Assessment Portfolio.* Circle Pines, MN: American Guidance Service.

Karlsen, B., & Gardner, E. (1985). *Stanford Diagnostic Reading Test.* New York: Harcourt Brace Jovanovich.

Kass, R., & Fish, J. (1991). Positive reframing and the test performance of test anxious children. *Psychology in the Schools, 28,* 43–52.

Kauffman, J. (1993). *Characteristics of children's behavior disorders* (5th ed.). Columbus, OH: Charles E. Merrill.

Kaufman, A. (1979). *Intelligent testing with the WISC-R.* New York: John Wiley.

Kaufman, A. (1981). The WISC-R and learning disabilities assessment: State of the art. *Journal of Learning Disabilities, 14,* 520–526.

Kaufman, A. (1984). K-ABC and controversy. *Journal of Special Education, 18,* 409–444.

Kaufman, A. (1994). *Intelligent testing with the WISC-III.* New York: Wiley.

Kaufman, A., & Doppelt, J. (1976). Analysis of WISC-R standardization data in terms of stratification variables. *Child Development, 47,* 165–171.

Kaufman, A., Kamphaus, R., & Kaufman, N. (1985). The Kaufman Assessment Battery for Children. In C. Newmark (Ed.), *Major psychological assessment instruments.* Boston: Allyn & Bacon.

Kaufman, A., & Kaufman, N. (1983). *The Kaufman Assessment Battery for Children.* Circle Pines, MN: American Guidance Service.

Kaufman, A., & Kaufman, N. (1985). *The Kaufman Test of Educational Achievement.* Circle Pines, MN: American Guidance Service.

Kaufman, A., & Kaufman, N. (1990). *Kaufman Brief Intelligence Test.* Circle Pines, MN: American Guidance Service.

Kaufman, A., Kaufman, N., & Dougherty, E. (1995). *Kaufman WISC-III integrated interpretive system.* Odessa, FL: PAR, Inc.

Kaufman, A., & McLean, J. (1986). K-ABC/WISC-R factor analysis for a learning disabled population. *Journal of Learning Disabilities, 19,* 145–153.

Kavale, K. (1982). A comparison of learning disabled and normal children on the Boehm Test of Basic Concepts. *Journal of Learning Disabilities, 15,* 160–161.

Kavale, K., & Mattson, D. (1983). One jumped off the balance beam: Metaanalysis of perceptual-motor training. *Journal of Learning Disabilities, 16,* 165–173.

Keenan, P., & Lachar, D. (1985). *Screening preschoolers with special problems: Use of the Personality Inventory for Children.* Eric Reproduction # ED 2802.

Keenan, P. A., & Lachar, D. (1988). Screening preschoolers with special problems: Use of the Personality Inventory for Children (PIC). *Journal of School Psychology, 26,* 1–11.

Keller, H. (1980). Issues in the use of observational assessment. *School Psychology Review, 9,* 21–30.

Kelly, E. J. (1988). Personality Inventory for Children: Selected scales in differentiating conduct-disordered and emotionally-disturbed students. *Psychological Reports, 63,* 395–401.

Kercher, A., & Sandoval, J. (1991). Reading disability and the Differential Ability Scales. *Journal of School Psychology, 29,* 293–307.

Kerlinger, F. (1986). *Foundations of behavioral research* (4th ed.). New York: Holt, Rinehart and Winston.

King-Sears, P. (1994). *Curriculum-based assessment in special education.* San Diego: Singular Publishing Group.

Kirby, E., & Porter, L. (1986). Effects of two instructional sets on the validity of the Kaufman Assessment Battery for Children–nonverbal scale with a group of severely hearing impaired children. *Psychology in the Schools, 23,* 37–43.

Kirk, S., & Gallagher, J. (1993). *Educating exceptional children* (7th ed.). Boston: Houghton Mifflin.

Kirk, S., McCarthy, J. & Kirk, W. (1968). *Illinois Test of Psycholinguistic Abilities.* Urbana, IL: University of Illinois Press.

Klanderman, J., Perney, J., & Kroeschell, Z. (1985). Comparisons of the K-ABC and WISC-R for LD children. *Journal of Learning Disabilities, 18,* 524–527.

Kline, R. (1994). New objective rating scales for child assessment, I. Parent and teachers informant inventories of the Behavior Assessment System for Children, The Child Behavior Checklist, and the Teacher Rating Form. *Journal of Psychoeducational Assessment, 12,* 289–306.

Kline, R., & Lachar, D. (1992). Evaluation of age, sex, and race bias in the Personality Inventory for Children. *Psychological Assessment, 4,* 333–339.

Klopfer, B., & Kelly, D. (1942). *The Rorschach technique.* New York: World Book Co.

Knight, B., Baker, E., & Minder, C. (1990). Concurrent validity of the Stanford-Binet: Fourth Edition and the Kaufman Assessment Battery for Children with learning disabled students. *Psychology in the Schools, 27,* 116–125.

Knight, P. (1992). How I use portfolios in mathematics. *Educational Leadership, 49*(8), 71–72.

Knoff, H. (1989). Review of Personality Inventory for Children. In J. Conoley & J. Kramer (Eds.), *Tenth mental measurements yearbook* (pp. 625–630). Lincoln, NE: University of Nebraska Press.

Knoff, H., & Prout, H. (1985). *Kinetic Drawing System for Family and School: A Handbook.* Los Angeles: Western Psychological Services.

Kochhar, C. A. (1991). Capitol connection. *Division on Career Development Network, 15.*

Kohler, P. D. (1994). On-the-job training: A curricular approach to employment. *Career Development for Exceptional Individuals, 17,* 29–40.

Kokaska, C. J., & Brolin, D. E. (1985). *Career education for handicapped individuals* (2nd ed.). Columbus, OH: Charles E. Merrill.

Koppitz, E. (1968). *Human Figure Drawing Test.* New York: Grune & Stratton.

Kratochwill, T. (1977). The movement of psychological extras into ability assessment. *Journal of Special Education, 11,* 299–308.

Kratochwill, T., & Demuth, D. (1976). An examination of the predictive validity of the Key Math Diagnostic Arithmetic Test and the Wide Range Achievement Test in exceptional children. *Psychology in the Schools, 13,* 404–406.

Krohn, E. J., & Lamp, R. E. (1989). Concurrent validity of the Stanford-Binet Fourth Edition and K-ABC for Head Start children. *Journal of School Psychology, 27,* 59–67.

Krug, D., Arick, J., & Almond, P. (1993). *Autism Screening Instrument for Educational Planning–2.* Austin, TX: Pro-Ed.

Kuder, F., & Diamond, E. (1985). *Kuder Occupational Interest Survey.* Chicago: Science Research Associates.

Kuhlmann, F., & Anderson, R. (1982). *Kuhlmann-Anderson Test.* Columbus, OH: Personnel Press.

Lachar, D., & LaCombe, J. (1983). Objective personality assessment: The Personality Inventory for Children and its application in the school setting. *School Psychology Review, 12,* 399–406.

Laffey, J., & Kelly, D. (1979). Test review: Woodcock Reading Mastery Tests. *Reading Teacher, 33,* 335–339.

Lahey, B., & Piacentini, R. (1985). An evaluation of the Quay-Peterson Revised Behavior Problem Checklist. *Journal of the American Academy of Child Psychiatry, 23,* 285–289.

Lahey, B., Schaughency, E., Strauss, C., & Frame, C. (1984). Are attention deficit disorders with and without hyperactivity similar or dissimilar disorders? *Journal of the American Academy of Child Psychiatry, 23,* 302–309.

Lambert, N. (1986). Evidence on age and ethnic status bias in factor scores and the comparison score for the AAMD Adaptive Behavior Scale–School Edition. *Journal of School Psychology, 24,* 143–153.

Lambert, N., Hartsough, C., & Sandoval, J. (1990). *Children's Attention and Adjustment Survey.* Circle Pines, MN: American Guidance Service.

Lambert, N., Leland, H., & Nihira, K. (1993). *AAMR Adaptive Behavior Scale–School Edition (Second Edition).* Austin, TX: Pro-Ed.

Lankford, F. (1972). *Some computational strategies of seventh grade pupils.* (Grant number OE6-3-72-0035.) University of Virginia: Center for Advanced Study.

Lanyon, R., and Goodstein, L. (1971). *Personality assessment.* New York: John Wiley.

Lappan, G. (1978). Review of Stanford Diagnostic Mathematics Test. In O. Buros (Ed.), *The eighth mental measurement yearbook* (pp. 436–437). Highland Park, NJ: Gryphon Press.

Larry P. et al. v. *Wilson Riles* et al. (1979). United States District Court, Northern District of California, Case No. C-71-2270-RFP.

Larsen, S., & Hammill, D. (1975). The relationship of selected visual perceptual abilities to school learning. *Journal of Special Education, 9,* 281–291.

Larsen, S., & Hammill, D. (1994). *Test of Written Spelling–3*. Austin, TX: Pro-Ed.

Larsen, S., & Poplin, M. (1980). *Methods for educating the handicapped: An individualized approach*. Boston: Allyn & Bacon.

Laughon, P. (1990). The dynamic assessment of intelligence: A review of three approaches. *School Psychology Review, 14*, 459–470.

Lazarus, B., McKenna, N., & Lynch, D. (1990). Peabody Individual Achievement Test-Revised. *Diagnostique, 15*, 135–148.

Lazarus, P., & Novoa, L. (1987). Test review: Quick Score Achievement Test. *Journal of Reading, 31*, 78–83.

Leblanc, R., & Reynolds, C. (1989). Concordance of mothers' and fathers' ratings of children's behavior. *Psychology in the Schools, 26*, 225–229.

Lee, L. (1974). *Developmental Sentence Analysis*. Evanston, IL: Northwestern University Press.

Lett, N., & Kamphaus, R. W. (1992). *Validation of the BASC Teacher Rating Scale by the BASC Student Observation Scale*. (ERIC Document Reproduction Service No. ED 357 051)

Lewandowski, L. (1985). Test review: Diagnostic Achievement Battery. *The Reading Teacher, 39*, 306–309.

Lewandowski, L., & Martens, B. (1990). Selecting and evaluating standardized reading tests (test review). *Journal of Reading, 33*, 384–388.

Lewis, T. (1991). Review of the Walker–McConnell Scales of Social Competence. *Behavioral Disorders, 16*, 159–160.

Lidz, C. (1979). Criterion-referenced assessment: The new bandwagon? *Exceptional Children, 46*, 131–132.

Linder, T. (1985). Review of the Developmental Indicators for the Assessment of Learning–Revised. In D. Keyser and R. Sweetland (Eds.). *Test critiques* (v. 4) (pp. 220–228). Kansas City, MO: Test Corporation of America.

Linder, T. (1989). *Transdisciplinary play assessment*. Baltimore: Paul Brookes.

Lindsey, J., & Armstrong, S. (1984). Performance of educably mentally retarded and learning disabled on the Brigance, Peabody and Wide Range Achievement Tests. *American Journal of Mental Deficiency, 89*, 197–201.

Lindsley, O. (1964). Direct measurement and prosthesis of retarded behavior. *Journal of Education, 14*, 62–81.

Linthicum, E., Cole, J. T., & D'Alonzo, B. (1991). Employment and the Americans with Disabilities Act of 1991. *Career Development for Exceptional Individuals, 14*, 1–13.

Lombard, R. C., Hazelkorn, M. N., & Neubert, D. A. (1992). A survey of accessibility to secondary vocational education programs and transition services for students with disabilities in Wisconsin. *Career Development for Exceptional Individuals, 15*, 179–188.

Lorge, I., Thorndike, R., & Hagen, E. (1966). *Lorge-Thorndike Intelligence Tests*. Boston: Houghton Mifflin.

Luckasson, R. (1992). *Mental retardation: Definition, classification, and systems of supports*. Washington, D.C.: American Association on Mental Retardation.

Lund, N., & Duchan, J. (1988). *Assessing children's language in naturalistic contexts* (2nd ed.). Englewood Cliffs, NJ: Prentice-Hall.

Luts, N. C. (1991). *The most common errors of second-grade story-writers*. (ERIC Document Reproduction Service No. ED 329 995)

Lyon, M., & Smith, D. (1987). Stability of the K-ABC for a sample of at risk preschool children. *Psychology in the Schools, 24*, 111–115.

MacDonald, L. (1988). Improving the reliability of a maladaptive behavior scale. *American Journal on Mental Retardation, 92*, 381–384.

MacMann, G., Plasket, C., Barnett, D., & Siler, R. (1991). Factor structure of the WISC-R for children of superior intelligence. *Journal of School Psychology, 29*, 19–36.

MacMillan, D. (1982). *Mental retardation in school and society*. Boston: Little, Brown.

MacMillan, D., Jones, R., & Aloia, G. (1974). The mentally retarded label: A theoretical analysis and review of research. *American Journal of Mental Deficiency, 79*, 241–261.

Madle, R. (1989). An Apple II series program for evaluating Stanford-Binet IV subtest scores. *Journal of School Psychology, 27*, 233–236.

Majorski, L. (1984). The K-ABC: Theory and applications for child neuropsychological assessment and research. *Journal of Special Education, 18*, 257–268.

Maller, S. J., & Braden, J. P. (1993). The construct and criterion-related validity of the WISC-III with deaf adolescents. *Journal of Psychoeducational Assessment Monograph Series: Wechsler Intelligence Scale for Children (Third Edition)*, 105–113.

Malone, D., & Christian, W. (1975). Adaptive Behavior Scale as a screening measure for special education placement. *American Journal of Mental Deficiency 79*, 367–371.

Mardell-Czudnowski, C., & Goldenberg, D. (1983). *Developmental Indicators for the Assessment of Learning–Revised*. Edison, NJ: Childcraft Education Corporation.

Mardell-Czudnowski, C., & Goldenberg, D. (1988). Predictive validity of the DIAL-R. *Diagnostique, 14*, 55–62.

Marlaire, C., & Maynard, D. (1990). Standardized testing as an interactional phenomenon. *Sociology of Education, 63*, 83–101.

Marston, D., & Magnusson, D. (1985). Implementing curriculum based measurement in special and regular education settings. *Exceptional Children, 52*, 266–276.

Martinek, T., & Zaichkowsky, L. (1977). *The Martinek-Zaichkowsky Self-Concept Scale for Children*. Jacksonville, IL: Psychologists and Educators, Inc.

Matazow, G., Kamphaus, R., Stanton, H., & Reynolds, C. (1991). Relationship of the Kaufman Assessment Battery for Children for black and white students. *Journal of School Psychology, 29,* 37–41.

Mather, N. (1989). Comparison of the new and existing Woodcock-Johnson writing tests to other measures. *Learning Disabilities Focus, 4,* 89–94.

Mather, N. (1990). *An instructional guide to the Woodcock-Johnson Psychoeducational Battery–Revised.* Brandon, VT: Clinical Psychology Publishing Co.

Mathews, J. (1990). From computer management to portfolio assessment. *The Reading Teacher, 43,* 420–421.

Mattison, R. F., Bagnato, S. J., & Strickler, E. (1987). Diagnostic importance of combined parent and teacher ratings on the Revised Behavior Problem Checklist. *Journal of Abnormal Child Psychology, 15,* 617–628.

McCaffery, L. K., & Prewett, P. N. (1993). A comparison of the Kaufman Brief Intelligence Test (K-BIT) with the Stanford-Binet, a two-subtest short form, and the Kaufman Test of Educational Achievement (K-TEA) Brief Form. *Psychology in the Schools, 30,* 299–304.

McCallum, R., & Bracken, B. (1981). Alternate form reliability of the PPVT-R for white and black preschool children. *Psychology in the Schools, 18,* 422–425.

McCarney, S. (1989). *Attention Deficit Disorders Evaluation Scale.* Columbia, MO: Hawthorne.

McCarney, S. (1993). *The prereferral intervention manual:* Columbia, MO: Hawthorne Educational Systems.

McCarney, S. (1994). *The Emotional or Behavioral Disorder Scale.* Columbia, MO: Hawthorne.

McCarney, S., Jackson, M. & Leigh, J. (1990). *Behavior Evaluation Scale–2.* Columbia, MO: Hawthorne.

McCarthy, D. (1972). *Manual for the McCarthy Scales of Children's Abilities.* New York: Psychological Corporation.

McCollough, B., & Zaremba, B. (1979). Standardized achievement tests used with learning disabled and non-learning disabled adolescent boys. *Learning Disability Quarterly, 2,* 65–70.

McCray, P. (1982). *Vocational evaluation and assessment in school settings.* Menomonie, WI: University of Wisconsin-Stout, Stout Vocational Rehabilitation Institute, Materials Development Center.

McCrowell, K., & Nagle, R. (1994). Comparability of the WPPSI-R and the SB-IV among preschool children. *Journal of Psychoeducational Assessment, 12,* 126–134.

McCune-Nicholich, B. (1980). *A manual for analyzing free play.* New Brunswick, NJ: Douglas College, Rutgers University.

McCurdy, B. L., & Shapiro, E. S. (1992). A comparison of teacher-, peer-, and self-monitoring with curriculum-based measurement in reading among students with learning disabilities. *Journal of Special Education, 26*(2), 162–180.

McDaniel, E. (1973). *Inferred Self-Concept Scale.* Los Angeles: Western Psychological Services.

McDermott, P. (1981). Sources of error in the psycho-educational diagnosis of children. *Journal of School Psychology, 19,* 31–44.

McDevitt, S., McDevitt, S., & Rosen, M. (1977). Adaptive Behavior Scale, Part II: A cautionary note and suggestions for revisions. *American Journal of Mental Deficiency, 82,* 210–212.

McGhee, R., Bryant, B., Larsen, S., & Rivera, D. (1995). *Test of Written Expression.* Austin, TX: Pro-Ed.

McGhee, T. (1986). *Structural analysis of the BASIS and K-TEA.* Proceedings of the Mid-South Educational Research Association, Memphis, TN (ED 289895).

McGrew, K., Murphy, S., & Knutson, D. (1994). The development and investigation of a graphic scoring system for obtaining derived scores for the WJ-R and other tests. *Journal of Psychoeducational Assessment, 12,* 33–41.

McIntosh, D. E., & Gridley, B. E. (1993). Differential Ability Scales: Profiles of learning-disabled subtypes. *Psychology in the Schools, 30*(1), 11–24.

McIntosh, D. E., Mulkins, R., Pardue-Vaughn, L., Barnes, L. B., & Gridley, B. E. (1992). The canonical relationship between the Differential Ability Scales upper preschool verbal and nonverbal clusters. *Journal of School Psychology, 30*(4), 355–361.

McLean, M., McCormick, K., Baird, S., & Mayfield, P. (1987). Concurrent validity of the Battelle Developmental Inventory Screening Test. *Diagnostique, 13,* 10–20.

McLinden, S. (1989). An evaluation of the Battelle Developmental Inventory for determining special education eligibility. *Journal of Psychoeducational Assessment, 7,* 66–73.

McVaugh, W., & Grow, R. (1984). Detection of faking on the Personality Inventory for Children. *Journal of Clinical Psychology, 39,* 567–573.

Mealey, D. L., & Host, T. R. (1992). Coping with test anxiety. *College Teaching, 40*(4), 147–150.

Mealor, D., & Richmond, B. (1980). Adaptive behavior: Teachers and parents disagree. *Exceptional Children, 46,* 386–389.

Meehan, K. A., & Hodell, S. (1986). Measuring the impact of vocational assessment activities upon program decision. *Career Development for Exceptional Individuals, 9,* 106–112.

Mehrens, W. (1984). A critical analysis of the psychometric properties of the K-ABC. *Journal of Special Education, 18,* 297–310.

Mehrens, W. A. (1992). Using performance assessment for accountability purposes. *Educational Measurement: Issues and Practice, 11,* 3–9, 20.

Mehrens, W. A., & Clarizio, H. F. (1993). Curriculum-based measurement: Conceptual and psychometric considerations. *Psychology in the Schools, 30,* 241–54.

Meisels, S. (1987). Uses and abuses of developmental screening and school readiness testing. *Young Children, 19,* 4–8.

Meltzer, L., & Reid, D. K. (1994). New directions in the assessment of students with special needs: The shift toward a constructivist perspective. *Journal of Special Education, 28,* 338–355.

Memory, D., Powell, G., & Calloway, B. (1980). A study of the assessment characteristics of the Woodcock Reading Mastery Tests. *Reading Improvement, 17,* 48–52.

Mercer, C., King-Sears, P., & Mercer, A. (1990). Learning disability definitions and criteria used by state education departments. *Journal of Learning Disabilities, 23,* 141–152.

Mercer, J. (1972). IQ: The lethal label. *Psychology Today, 6,* 44–47, 95–97.

Mercer, J. (1973). *Labeling the Mentally Retarded: Clinical and Social System Perspectives on Mental Retardation.* Berkeley: University of California Press.

Mercer, J., & Lewis, J. (1977). *System of Multicultural Pluralistic Assessment.* New York: Psychological Corporation.

Merrell, K. (1989). Concurrent relationships between two behavioral rating scales for teachers: An examination of self-control, social competence, and school behavioral adjustment. *Psychology in the Schools, 26,* 267–271.

Merrell, K. (1994). *School Social Behavior Scales.* Brandon, VT: Clinical Psychology Publishing Company.

Merrell, K., & Mauk, G. (1993). Predictive validity of the Battelle Developmental Inventory as a measure of social-behavioral development for young children with disabilities. *Diagnostique, 18,* 187–198.

Merz, W. (1984). Review of Kaufman Assessment Battery for Children. In D. Keyser and R. Sweetland (Eds.), *Test critiques* (v. 1) (pp. 393–405). Kansas City, MO: Test Corporation of America.

Meyers, J., & Lytle, S. (1986). Assessment of the learning process. *Exceptional Children, 53,* 138–144.

Middleton, H. A., Keene, R., & Brown, G. (1990). Convergent and discriminant validities of the Scales of Independent Behavior and the Revised Vineland Adaptive Behavior Scales. *American Journal on Mental Retardation, 94,* 669–673.

Miller, J., & Milam, C. (1987). Multiplication and division errors committed by learning disabled students. *Learning Disabilities Research, 2,* 119–122.

Miller, L. (1990). Review of the Kaufman Test of Educational Achievement. *Diagnostique, 15,* 75–86.

Miller, L., & Sprong, T. (1986). Psychometric and qualitative comparison of four preschool screening instruments. *Journal of Learning Disabilities, 19,* 480–484.

Miller, L. J. (1988). Differentiating children with school-related problems after four years using the Miller Assessment for Preschoolers. *Psychology in the Schools, 25,* 10–15.

Miller, L. J., & Lemerand, P. A. (1986). Neuromaturational variables within the Miller Assessment for Preschoolers. *Occupational Therapy Journal of Research, 6,* 123–125.

Miller, M., & Seraphine, A. (1993). Can test scores remain authentic when teaching to the test? *Educational Assessment, 1,* 119–130.

Miller, W. (1986). *Reading diagnosis kit.* West Nyack, NY: The Center for Applied Research in Education, Inc.

Millham, J., Chilcutt, J., & Atkinson, B. (1978). Comparability of naturalistic and controlled observation assessment of adaptive behavior. *American Journal of Mental Deficiency 83,* 52–59.

Mishra, S. (1981). Reliability and validity of the WRAT with Mexican-American children. *Psychology in the Schools, 18,* 154–158.

Misulis, K. E. (1989). Test of Reading Comprehension (TORC)–Revised Edition (test review). *The Journal of Reading, 33,* 228–229.

Montague, M., Bos, C., & Doucette, M. (1991). Affective, cognitive, and metacognitive attributes of eighth-grade mathematical problem solvers. *Learning Disabilities Research and Practice, 6,* 219–224.

Mooney, K., Thompson, R., & Nelson, J. (1987). Risk factors and the Child Behavior Checklist in a child mental health center setting. *Journal of Abnormal Child Psychology, 15,* 67–73.

Morsink, C., & Gable, R. (1990). Errors in reading. In R. Gable & J. Hendrickson (Eds.), *Assessing students with special needs* (pp. 46–62). New York: Longman.

Mott, S. (1987). Concurrent validity of the Battelle Developmental Inventory for speech and language disordered children. *Psychology in the Schools, 24,* 215–220.

Motta, R. W., Little, A., & Tobin, J. (1993). The use and abuse of human figure drawings. *School Psychology Quarterly, 8,* 162–69.

Motto, J., & Wilkins, G. (1968). Educational achievement of institutionalized emotionally disturbed children. *Journal of Educational Research, 61,* 218–221.

Murray, H. (1943). *Thematic Apperception Test.* Cambridge, MA: Harvard University.

Nagle, R. J., & Bell, N. L. (1993). Validation of Stanford-Binet Intelligence Scale: Fourth Edition abbreviated batteries with college students. *Psychology in the Schools, 30*(3), 227–231.

Naglieri, J. (1981). Concurrent validity of the revised Peabody Picture Vocabulary Test. *Psychology in the Schools, 18,* 286–289.

Naglieri, J. (1985). Use of the WISC-R and K-ABC with learning disabled, borderline mentally retarded, and normal children. *Psychology in the Schools, 22,* 133–141.

Naglieri, J. (1986). WISC-R and K-ABC comparison for matched samples of black and white children. *Journal of School Psychology, 24,* 81–88.

Naglieri, J. (1988). *Draw-a-Person: A Quantitative Scoring System.* San Antonio: The Psychological Corporation.

Naglieri, J., & Bardos, A. (1990). Review of Bracken Basic Concept Scale. *Diagnostique, 15,* 41–50.

Naglieri, J., Bardos, A., & LeBuffe, P. (1995). Discriminate validity of the Devereux Behavior Rating Scales–School Form for students with serious emotional disturbance. *School Psychology Review, 24,* 104–111.

Naglieri, J., Das, J., & Jarman, R. (1990). Planning, attention, simultaneous, and successive processes as a model for assessment. *School Psychology Review, 19,* 423–442.

Naglieri, J., & Kamphaus, R. (1981). Interpretation of academic strengths and weaknesses on the Peabody Individual Achievement Test. *Psychology in the Schools, 18,* 417–419.

Naglieri, J., LeBuffe, P., & Pfeiffer, S. (1993). *Devereux Behavior Rating Scales–School Form.* San Antonio, TX: Psychological Corporation.

Naglieri, J., McNeish, T., & Bardos, A. (1994). *Draw-a-Person: Screening Procedure for Emotional Disturbance.* Brandon, VT: Clinical Psychology Publishing Company.

Naglieri, J., & Naglieri, D. (1981). Comparison of the PPVT and PPVT-R for preschool children: Implications for the practitioner. *Psychology in the Schools, 18,* 434–436.

Naslund, R., Thorpe, L., & Lefever, D. (1981). *SRA Achievement Series.* Chicago: Science Research Associates.

National Association for the Education of Young Children. (1988). NAEYC position statement on standardized testing of young children 3 through 8 years of age. *Young Children, 43,* 42–47.

National Association of State Directors of Special Education. (1990). *Education of the Handicapped Act Amendments of 1990 (P.L. 101-476): Summary of major changes in parts A through H of the act.* Washington, DC: National Association of State Directors of Special Education.

Newborg, J., Stock, J., Wnek, L., Guidubaldi, J., & Svinicki, J. (1984). *Battelle Developmental Inventory.* Allen, TX: DLM Teaching Resources.

Newby, R. F., Recht, D. R., Caldwell, J. A., & Schaefer, J. (1993). Comparison of WISC-III and WISC-R IQ changes over a 2-year time span in a sample of children with dyslexia. *Journal of Psychoeducational Assessment Monograph Series: Wechsler Intelligence Scale for Children (Third Edition),* 87–93.

Newcomer, P. (1985). A comparison of two published reading inventories. *Remedial and Special Education, 6,* 31–36.

Newcomer, P. (1990). *Diagnostic Achievement Battery–2.* Austin, TX: Pro-Ed.

Newcomer, P., & Bryant, B. (1993). *Diagnostic Achievement Test for Adolescents–2* Austin, TX: Pro-Ed.

Newcomer, P., & Hammill, D. (1978). Using the Test of Language Development with language-impaired children. *Journal of Learning Disabilities, 11,* 521–524.

Newcomer, P., & Hammill, D. (1988). *Test of Language Development–2.* Austin, TX: Pro-Ed.

Newcomer, P., & Magee, P. (1977). Predictive indices of reading failure in learning disabled children. *Educational Research Quarterly, 2,* 17–23.

Newcomer, P., Noding, B., & Barenbaum, E. (1988). Teaching writing to exceptional children: Reaction and recommendations. *Exceptional Children, 54,* 559–564.

Newland, T. E. (1969). *Manual for the Blind Learning Aptitude Test: Experimental Edition.* Urbana, IL: T. Ernest Newland.

Nihira, K., Leland, H., & Lambert, N. (1993). *AAMR Adaptive Behavior Scale–Residential and Community Edition (Second Edition).* Austin, TX: Pro-Ed.

Nolet, V. (1992). Classroom-based measurement and portfolio assessment. *Diagnostique, 18*(1), 5–26.

Noyce, R. (1989). Review of Test of Written Spelling–2. In J. Conoley & J. Kramer (Eds.), *Tenth mental measurements yearbook* (pp. 860–861). Lincoln, NE: University of Nebraska Press.

Nugent, J. (1976). A comment on the efficiency of the revised Denver Developmental Screening Test. *American Journal of Mental Deficiency, 80,* 570–572.

Nurss, J., & McGauvran, M. (1986). *Metropolitan Readiness Tests, Teacher's Manual, Part II: Interpretation and Use of Test Results.* New York: Harcourt Brace Jovanovich.

Oakland, T. (1977). *Pluralistic norms and estimated learning potential.* Paper presented at the annual meeting of the American Psychological Association, San Francisco.

Obringer, J. (1988). A survey of perceptions by school psychologists of the Stanford-Binet IV. *Diagnostique, 13,* 120–122.

O'Leary, K., & Johnson, S. (1979). Psychological assessment. In H. Quay and J. Werry (Eds.), *Psychopathological disorders of childhood* (210–246). New York: John Wiley.

Olmi, J. (1994). Review of the Behavior Evaluation Scale–2. In J. Mitchell and J. Impara (Eds.), *The eleventh mental measurement yearbook* (Supplement) (pp. 74–76). Lincoln, NE: University of Nebraska Press.

O'Reilly, C. (1989). The confirmation bias in special education eligibility decisions. *School Psychology Review, 18,* 126–135.

Organist, J. (1985). Review of Wide Range Interest–Opinion Test. In D. Keyser and R. Sweetland (Eds.), *Test critiques (v.4)* (pp. 673–676). Kansas City, MO: Test Corporation of America.

Otis, A., & Lennon, R. (1989). *Otis-Lennon School Ability Test.* New York: Harcourt Brace Jovanovich.

Overton, T., & Apperson, J. (1989). Comparison of scores on the Cognitive Levels Test and the Peabody Picture Vocabulary Test–Revised. *Diagnostique, 14,* 159–162.

Padget, S. Y. (1985). Test Review: Miller Assessment for Preschoolers (MAP). *The Reading Teacher, 39,* 184–188.

Padilla, A., & Garza, B. (1975). IQ tests: A case of cultural myopia. *National Elementary Principal, 54,* 53–58.

Parker, R. (1991). *Occupational Aptitude Survey and Interest Schedule–2.* Austin, TX: Pro-Ed.

Parker, R. (1992). Greater validity for oral reading fluency: Can miscues help? *Journal of Special Education, 25,* 492–503.

Parker, R., Hasbrouck, J., & Tindal, G. (1992). The maze

as a classroom-based reading measure: Construction methods, reliability, and validity. *Journal of Special Education, 26*, 195–218.

Parrish, B. (1982). A test to test test-wiseness. *Journal of Reading, 25*, 672–675.

Partenio, I., & Taylor, R. (1985). The relationship of teacher ratings and IQ: A question of bias? *School Psychology Review, 14*, 79–83.

Pase v. *Hannon,* 506 F. Supp. 831 (N.D. Ill. 1980).

Pate, J., & Webb, W. (1969). *First Grade Screening Test.* Circle Pines, MN: American Guidance Service.

Patterson, G., Reid, J., Jones, R., & Conger, R. (1975). *A social learning approach to family intervention, V. 1: Families with aggressive children.* Eugene, OR: Castalia Publishing Co.

Paulson, F. L., Paulson, P. R., & Meyer, C. A. (1991). What makes a portfolio a portfolio? *Educational Leadership, 48*(5), 60–63.

Payette, K., & Clarizio, H. (1994). Discrepant team decisions: The effects of race, gender, school and IQ on LD eligibility. *Psychology in the Schools, 31*, 40–48.

Pearson, D. A., & Lachar, D. (1994). Using behavioral questionnaires to identify adaptive deficits in elementary school children. *Journal of School Psychology, 32*, 33–52.

Pecyna-Rhyner, P. M., & Bracken, B. A. (1988). Concurrent validity of the Bracken Basic Concept Scale with language and intelligence measures. *Journal of Communication Disorders, 21*, 479-489.

Pedriana, A., & Bracken, B. (1982). Performance of gifted children on the PPVT and PPVT-R. *Psychology in the Schools, 19*, 183–185.

Pena, E., Quinn, R., & Iglesias, A. (1992). The application of dynamic methods to language assessment: A nonbiased procedure. *Journal of Special Education, 26*, 269–80.

Perry, A., & Factor, D. C. (1989). Psychometric validity and clinical usefulness of the Vineland Adaptive Behavior Scales and the AAMD Adaptive Behavior Scale for an autistic sample. *Journal of Autism and Developmental Disorders, 19*, 41–55.

Peterson, D., & Batsche, G. (1983). School psychology and projective assessment: A growing incompatibility. *School Psychology Review, 12*, 440–445.

Peterson, D., Steger, A., Slate, J., Jones, C., & Coulter, C. (1991). Examiner errors on the WRAT-R. *Psychology in the Schools, 20*, 205–208.

Peterson, M. (1986). Work and performance sample for vocational assessment of special students: A critical review. *Career Development for Exceptional Individuals, 9*, 69–76.

Peterson, N. (1988). *Early intervention for handicapped and at-risk children.* Denver: Love Publishing.

Phelps, L. (1989). Comparison of scores for intellectualy gifted students on the WISC-R and the fourth edition of the Stanford-Binet. *Psychology in the Schools, 26*, 126–129.

Phelps, L., Leguori, S., Nisewaner, K., & Parker, M. (1993). Practical interpretations of the WISC-III with language-disordered children. *Journal of Psychoeducational Assessment Monograph Series: Wechsler Intelligence Scale for Children (Third Edition),* 71–76.

Phelps, L., Rosso, M., & Falasco, S. (1984). Correlations between the Woodcock-Johnson and the WISC-R for a behavior-disordered population. *Psychology in the Schools, 21*, 442–446.

Piers, E., & Harris, D. (1984). *The Piers-Harris Children's Self-Concept Scale.* Nashville: Counselor Recordings and Tests.

Pikulski, J. (1990). Informal reading inventories. *The Reading Teacher, 43*, 514–516.

Pikulski, J., & Pikulski, E. (1977). Cloze, maze, and teacher judgment. *The Reading Teacher, 30*, 766–770.

Plass, J., & Hill, K. (1986). Children's achievement strategies and test performance: The role of time pressure, evaluation anxiety, and sex. *Developmental Psychology, 22*, 31–36.

Platt, L., Kamphaus, R., Keltgen, J., & Gilliland, F. (1991). Overview and review of the Differential Ability Scales: Initial and current research findings. *Journal of School Psychology, 29*, 271–278.

Poplin, M., Gray, R., Larsen, S., Banikowski, A., & Mehring, T. (1980). A comparison of written expression abilities in learning disabled and non-learning disabled students at three grade levels. *Learning Disability Quarterly, 3*, 46–53.

Porter, M. E., & Stodden, R. A. (1986). A curriculum-based vocational assessment procedure: Addressing the school-to-work transition needs of secondary schools. *Career Development for Exceptional Individuals, 9*, 121–128.

Posey, C. (1989). Review of Behavior Rating Profile. In J. Conoley & J. Kramer (Eds.), *Tenth mental measurements yearbook* (pp. 86–88). Lincoln, NE: University of Nebraska Press.

Poteet, J. (1989). Review of the Test of Reading Comprehension. In J. Conoley & J. Kramer (Eds.), *Tenth mental measurements yearbook* (pp. 850–854). Lincoln, NE: University of Nebraska Press.

Poteet, J. (1990). Review of Test of Written Language–2. *Diagnostique, 15*, 228–242.

Poteet, J. (1992). Written expression. In J. Choate, B. Enright, L. Miller, J. Poteet, & T. Rakes (Eds.), *Curriculum-based assessment and programming.* Boston: Allyn & Bacon.

Poteet, J. A., Choate, J. S., & Stewart, S. C. (1993). Performance assessment and special education: Practices and prospects. *Focus on Exceptional Children, 26*(1), 1–20.

Powell, W. (1972). The validity of the instructional reading level. In R. Wilson & J. Geyer, (Eds.), *Readings for Diagnostic and Remedial Reading.* Columbus, OH: Charles E. Merrill.

Powers, D., & Pace, T. (1976). A concurrent validity study of the Key Math Diagnostic Arithmetic Test. *Mental Retardation, 4*, 48.

Prasad, S. (1994). Assessing social interaction skills of

children with disabilities. *Teaching Exceptional Children, 26,* 23–25.

Prasse, D., & Bracken, B. (1981). Comparison of the PPVT-R and WISC-R with urban educable mentally retarded students. *Psychology in the Schools, 18,* 174–177.

Prewett, P. (1992). The relationship between the Kaufman Brief Intelligence Test and the WISC-R with referred students. *Psychology in the Schools, 29,* 25–27.

Prewett, P. N., & Farhney, M. R. (1994). The concurrent validity of the Matrix Analogies Test–Short Form with the Stanford-Binet: Fourth Edition and KTEA-BF. *Psychology in the Schools, 31*(1), 20–25.

Prewett, P. N. & Matavich, M. A. (1992). Mean-score differences between the WISC-R and the Stanford-Binet Intelligence Scale: Fourth Edition. *Diagnostique, 17*(3), 195–201.

Prewett, P. N., & Matavich, M. A. (1994). A comparison of referred students' performance on the WISC-III and the SBIS–Fourth Edition. *Journal of Psychoeducational Assessment, 12,* 42–48.

Prewett, P. & McCaffery, L. (1993). A comparison of the Kaufman Brief Intelligence Test, a two subtest short form, and the Kaufman Test of Educational Achievement. *Psychology in the Schools, 30,* 299–304.

Prifitera, A., & Dersh, J. (1993). Base rates of WISC-III diagnostic subtest patterns among normal, learning-disabled, and ADHD samples. *Journal of Psychoeducational Assessment Monograph Series: Wechsler Intelligence Scale for Children (Third Edition),* 43–55.

Proger, B., Mann, L., Green, P., Bayuk, R., & Burger, R. (1975). Discriminators of clinically defined emotional maladjustment: Predictive validity of the Behavior Problem Checklist and Devereux Scales. *Journal of Abnormal Psychology, 3,* 71–82.

Pruitt, W. A. (1977). *Vocational (work) evaluation.* Menomonie, WI: Walt Pruitt Associates.

Pryor, C., Wilkinson, S., Harris, J., & Trovato, J. (1989). Grade repetition and psychological referrals in relation to Child Behavior Checklist scores for students in elementary schools. *Psychology in the Schools, 26,* 230–242.

Psychological Corporation. (1983). *Basic Achievement Skills Individual Screener.* San Antonio: Psychological Corporation.

Psychological Corporation (1992a). *Stanford Achievement Test.* San Antonio: Psychological Corporation.

Psychological Corporation (1992b). *Wechsler Individual Achievement Test.* San Antonio: Psychological Corporation.

Public Law 99-457. (Washington, D.C.: H.R. 5520, Sept. 16, 1986).

Purves, A. (1993). Setting standards in the language arts and literature classroom and the implications for portfolio assessment. *Educational Assessment, 1,* 175–199.

Putnam, M. L. (1992). The testing practices of mainstream secondary classroom teachers. *Remedial and Special Education, 13*(5), 11–21.

Quay, H., & Peterson, D. (1987). *Revised Behavior Problem Checklist.* Miami: Author.

Rainwater-Bryant, B. J. (1985). *Comparisons of parent-obtained and teacher-obtained adaptive behavior scores for handicapped children.* Unpublished doctoral dissertation, Memphis State University, Memphis.

Rankin, E., & Culhane, J. (1969). Comparable cloze and multiple choice comprehension test scores. *Journal of Reading, 13,* 193–198.

Raven, J. (1956). *Progressive Matrices.* London: H. K. Lewis & Co., Ltd.

Reed, M., & Edelbrock, C. (1983). Reliability and validity of the Direct Observation Form of the Child Behavior Checklist. *Journal of Abnormal Child Psychology, 11,* 521–530.

Reeve R., Hall, R., & Zakreski, R. (1979). The Woodcock-Johnson Tests of Cognitive Ability: Concurrent validity with the WISC-R. *Learning Disability Quarterly, 2,* 63–69.

Reid, N. (1986). Wide Range Achievement Test, 1984 Revised Edition. *Journal of Counseling and Development, 64,* 538–539.

Reid, K., Hresko, W., & Hammill, D. (1989) *Test of Early Reading Ability–2.* Austin, TX: Pro-Ed.

Reinehr, R. (1984). Review of the Wide Range Achievement Test–Revised. In D. Keyser and R. Sweetland (Eds.), *Test critiques* (v. 1) (pp. 758–761). Kansas City, MO: Test Corporation of America.

Repetto, J. B., Tulbert, B. L., & Schwartz, S. E. (1993). A statewide transition base: What's happening in Florida. *Career Development for Exceptional Individuals, 16,* 27–38.

Repetto, J. B., White, W. J., & Snauwaert, D. T. (1990). Individualized transition plans (ITP): A national perspective. *Career Development for Exceptional Individuals, 13,* 109–119.

Repp, A., Nieminen, G., Olinger, E., & Brusca, R. (1988). Direct observation: Factors affecting the accuracy of observers. *Exceptional Children, 55,* 29–36.

Reschly, D. (1978). WISC-R factor structure among Anglos, Blacks, Chicanos and Native American Papagos. *Journal of Consulting and Clinical Psychology, 46,* 417–422.

Reschly, D. (1979). Nonbiased assessment. In G. Phye & D. Reschly (Eds.), *School psychology: Perspectives and issues.* New York: Academic Press.

Reschly, D. (1980). *Nonbiased assessment.* Ames, IA: Iowa State University, ERIC Document Reproduction Service No. ED 209810 and ERIC EC 140324.

Reschly, D. (1991). The effects of placement litigation on psychological and educational classification. *Diagnostique, 17,* 6–20.

Reschly, D., Kicklighter, R., & McKee, P. (1988). Recent placement litigation part III: Analysis of differences in *Larry P.* v. *Marshall and S-1* and implications for future practices. *School Psychology Review, 17,* 39–50.

Reschly, D., & Lamprecht, M. (1979). Expectancy effects of labels: Fact or artifact? *Exceptional Children, 46,* 55–58.

Reschly, D., & Reschly, J. (1979). Validity of WISC-R factor scores in predicting teacher ratings of achievement and attention among four groups. *Journal of School Psychology, 17,* 355–361.

Reschly, D., & Ross-Reynolds, J. (1980). *Report: Iowa assessment project.* Unpublished manuscript, Department of Psychology, Iowa State University.

Revell, W., Kriloff, L., & Sarkees, M. (1980). Vocational evaluation. In P. Wehman and P. McLaughlin (Eds.), *Vocational curriculum for developmentally disabled persons.* Baltimore, MD: University Park Press.

Revell, W. G., Wehman, P., Kregel, J., West, M., & Rayfield, R. (1994). Supported employment for persons with severe disabilities: Positive trends in wages, models, and funding. *Education and Training in Mental Retardation and Developmental Disabilities, 29,* 256–264.

Reynolds, C. (1979). Factor structure of the Peabody Individual Achievement Test at five grade levels between grades one and 12. *Journal of School Psychology, 17,* 270–274.

Reynolds, C. (1983). Statistics for the enhancement of profile analysis on the Test of Language Development–Primary. *Psychology in the Schools, 20,* 5–9.

Reynolds, C. (1985). Critical measurement issues in learning disabilities. *Journal of Special Education, 18,* 451–476.

Reynolds, C. (1986). Review of the Wide Range Achievement Test–Revised. *Journal of Counseling and Development, 64,* 540–541.

Reynolds, C., & Gutkin, T. (1980). Statistics related to profile interpretation of the Peabody Individual Achievement Test. *Psychology in the Schools, 17,* 316–319.

Reynolds, C., & Kamphaus, R. (1992). *Behavior Assessment System for Children.* Circle Pines, MN: American Guidance Service.

Reynolds, C. R., Kamphaus, R. W., & Rosenthal, B. L. (1988). Factor analysis of the Stanford-Binet Fourth Edition for ages 2 years through 23 years. *Measurement and Evaluation in Counseling and Development, 21,* 52–59.

Richard, G., & Hanner, M. (1985). *Language Processing Test.* Moline, IL: Linguisystems, Inc.

Rivera, D. (1993). Performance, authentic and portfolio assessment: Emerging alternative assessment options in search of an empirical basis. *Diagnostique, 18,* 325–348.

Rivera, D., Taylor, R., & Bryant, B. (1995). Review of current trends in mathematics assessment for students with mild disabilities. *Diagnostique, 20,* 143–174.

Rivers, D., & Smith T. (1988). Traditional eligibility criteria for identifying students as specific learning disabled. *Journal of Learning Disabilities, 21,* 642–644.

Roach, E., & Kephart, N. (1996). *The Purdue Perceptual-Motor Survey.* Columbus, OH: Charles E. Merrill.

Robinson, J., & Kovacevich, D. (1984). Review of the Brigance Inventories. In D. Keyser and R. Sweetland (Eds.), *Test critiques* (v. 3) (pp. 79–98). Kansas City, MO: Test Corporation of America.

Rodriguez, R. F. (1989). *The effect of sociocultural factors on the achievement of minority children.* Proceedings of the ACRES/NRSSC Symposium, Albuquerque, NM (ED 315251).

Rogers, S. J. (1986). *Play Observation Scale.* Denver, CO: University of Colorado Health Sciences Center.

Rohde, A. (1957). *Rohde Sentence Completion Test.* Los Angeles: Western Psychological Services.

Roid, G. H., Prifitera, A., & Weiss, L. G. (1993). Replication of the WISC-III factor structure in an independent sample. *Journal of Psychoeducational Assessment Monograph Series: Wechsler Intelligence Scale for Children (Third Edition),* 6–21.

Ronka, C. S., & Barnett, D. (1986). A comparison of adaptive behavior ratings: Revised Vineland and AAMD ABS-SE. *Special Services in the School, 2,* 87–96.

Rorschach, H. (1932). *Psychodiagnostik: Methodik und Ergebnisse eines Wahrnehmungsdiagnostischen Experiments* (ed. 2). Bern, Switzerland: Huber.

Ross, L., & Gallagher, P. (1976). Devereux Scales as behavioral measures of visually impaired residential students. *New Outlook for the Blind, 70,* 251–256.

Roszkowski, M., & Bean, A. (1981). Abbreviated procedure for obtaining sum scores on the Adaptive Behavior Scale. *Exceptional Children, 48,* 265–267.

Rothlisberg, B., & McIntosh, D. (1991). Performance of a referred sample on the Stanford Binet IV and the K-ABC. *Journal of School Psychology, 29,* 367–370.

Rotholz, D. A., Kamps, D., & Greenwood, C. (1989). Ecobehavioral assessment and analysis in special education settings for students with autism. *Journal of Special Education, 23*(1), 59–81.

Rotter, J., & Rafferty, J. (1950). *The Rotter Incomplete Sentences Test.* New York: Psychological Corporation.

Rousseau, M. (1990). Errors in written language. In R. Gable & J. Hendrickson (Eds.), *Assessing students with special needs* (pp. 89–101). New York: Longman.

Rupley, W., & Blair, T. (1979). *Reading diagnosis and remediation.* Boston: Houghton Mifflin.

Rusch, F. R., Enchelmaier, J. F., & Kohler, P. D. (1994). Employment outcomes and activities for youths in transition. *Career Development for Exceptional Individuals, 17,* 1–16.

Rusch, F. R., & Phelps, L. A. (1987). Secondary special education and transition from school to work: A national priority. *Exceptional Children, 53,* 487–492.

Sailor, W., & Mix, B. (1975). *TARC Assessment System.* Lawrence, KS: H and H Enterprises.

Salvia, J., & Hughes, C. (1990). *Curriculum-based assessment: Testing what is taught.* New York: Macmillan.

Salvia, J., & Ysseldyke, J. (1995). *Assessment in special*

and remedial education (6th ed.). Boston: Houghton Mifflin.

Samuda, R. (1975). *Psychological testing of American minorities: Issues and consequences.* New York: Dodd, Mead.

Sandoval, J. (1979). The WISC-R and internal evidence of test bias with minority groups. *Journal of Consulting and Clinical Psychology, 47,* 919–927.

Sandoval, J. & Miille, M. (1980). Accuracy of judgments of WISC-R item difficulty for minority groups. *Journal of Consulting and Clinical Psychology, 48,* 249–253.

Sarbaugh, M. (1983). *Kinetic Family Drawing–School (KFD-S) Technique.* Illinois School Psychologists Association Monograph Series, 1.

Sarkees, M. D., & Scott, J. L. (1985). *Vocational special needs* (2nd ed.). Oxford, IN: American Publishers.

Sarkees-Wircenski, M., & Wircenski, J. (1994). Transition planning: Developing a career portfolio for students with disabilities. *Career Development for Exceptional Individuals, 17,* 203–214.

Sattler, J. (1989a). Review of Vineland Adaptive Behavior Scales. In J. Conoley & J. Kramer (Eds.), *Tenth mental measurements yearbook* (pp. 879–881). Lincoln, NE: University of Nebraska Press.

Sattler, J. (1989b). Review of the Kaufman Test of Educational Achievement. In J. Conoley and J. Kramer (Eds.), *Tenth mental measurements yearbook.* (pp. 412–413). Lincoln, NE: University of Nebraska Press.

Sattler, J. (1992). *Assessment of children: WISC-III and WPPSI-R Supplement.* San Diego, CA: Sattler.

Sattler, J., & Altes, L. (1984). Performance of bilingual and monolingual Hispanic children on the Peabody Picture Vocabulary Test–Revised and the McCarthy Perceptual Performance Scale. *Psychology in the Schools, 21,* 313–316.

Sattler, J., Andres, J., Squire, L., Wisely, R., & Maloy, C. (1978). Examiner scoring of ambiguous WISC-R responses. *Psychology in the Schools, 15,* 486–488.

Sattler, J., & Feldman, G. (1981). Comparison of 1965, 1976, and 1978 Wide Range Achievement Test norms. *Psychological Reports, 49,* 115–118.

Sattler, J., & Gwynne, J. (1982). White examiners generally do not impede the intelligence test performance of black children: To debunk a myth. *Journal of Consulting and Clinical Psychology, 50,* 196–208.

Sax, A. (1973). Work samples. In W. Crow (Ed.), *Positions on the practice of vocational evaluation.* Washington D.C.: Vocational Evaluation and Work Adjustment Situation.

Scannell, D. (1986). *Tests of Achievement and Proficiency.* Lombard, IL: Riverside Publishing Company.

Scannell, D., Hough, O. Lloyd, B., & Risinger, C. (1993). *Tests of Achievement and Proficiency.* Chicago: Riverside Publishing Co.

Schaefer, C., Baker, E., & Zawel, D. (1975). A factor analytic and reliability study of the Devereux Elementary School Behavior Rating Scale. *Psychology in the Schools, 12,* 295–300.

Schmidt, K. (1994). Test Review—DTLA (Third Edition). *Journal of Psychoeducational Assessment, 12,* 87–91.

Schooler, D., Beebe, M., & Koepke, T. (1978). Factor analysis of WISC-R scores for children identified as learning disabled, educable mentally impaired, and emotionally impaired. *Psychology in the Schools, 15,* 478–485.

Schopler, E., Reichler, R., & Renner, B. (1988). *The Childhood Autism Rating Scale.* Los Angeles: Western Psychological Services.

Schouten, P. (1992). Test Review: Miller Assessment for Preschoolers. *Diagnostique, 17,* 145–157.

Schriner, K. F., & Bellini, J. L. (1994). Analyzing transition policy implementation: A conceptual approach. *Career Development for Exceptional Individuals, 17,* 17–27.

Schuman, J. (1987). Test review: Diagnostic Achievement Test for Adolescents. *Journal of Reading, 31,* 186–189.

Schwarting, G. (1987). Boehm Test of Basic Concepts–Revised. In D. Keyser & R. Sweetland (Eds.), *Test critiques* (v.6) (pp. 56–59). Kansas City, MO: Test Corporation of America.

Schwean, V. L., Saklofski, D. H., Yackulic, R. A., & Quinn, D. (1993). WISC-III Performance of ADHD Children. *Journal of Psychoeducational Assessment Monograph Series: Wechsler Intelligence Scale for Children (Third Edition),* 56–70.

Science Research Associates (1980). *Mastery: An Evaluation Tool.* Chicago: Author.

Scruggs, T., & Lifson, S. (1986). Are learning disabled students "test-wise"? An inquiry into reading comprehension tests. *Educational and Psychological Measurement, 46,* 1075–1082.

Scruggs, T. E., & Marsing, L. (1988). Teaching test-taking skills to behaviorally disordered students. *Behavioral Disorders, 13*(4), 240–244.

Scruggs, T., & Mastropieri, M. (1986). Improving the test-taking skills of behavior-disordered and learning disabled children. *Exceptional Children, 53,* 63–68.

Scruggs, T., Mastropieri, M., & Argulewicz, E. (1983). Stability of performance on the PPVT-R for three ethnic groups attending a bilingual kindergarten. *Psychology in the Schools, 20,* 433–435.

Scruggs, T., Mastropieri, M., & Tolfa-Veit, D. (1986). The effects of coaching on the standardized test performance of learning disabled and behavior disordered students. *Remedial and Special Education, 7,* 37–41.

Scull, J., & Brand, L. (1980). The WRAT and the PIAT with learning disabled children. *Journal of Learning Disabilities, 13,* 64–66.

Semel, E., & Wiig, E. (1987). *Clinical Evaluation of Language Fundamentals–Revised.* San Antonio: The Psychological Corporation.

Shanahan, R., & Bradley-Johnson, S. (1992). Concurrent validity of the Cognitive Abilities Scale and the Binet-IV for nonvocal 2 and 3 year olds. *Journal of School Psychology, 30,* 395–399.

Shanklin, N. L. (1989). Test of Early Written Language. *The Reading Teacher, 42*, 630–631.

Shapiro, E. (1990). An integrated model for curriculum-based assessment. *School Psychology Review, 19*, 331–349.

Shapiro, E. S., & Eckert, T. L. (1994). Acceptability of curriculum-based assessment by school psychologists. *Journal of School Psychology, 32*(2), 167–183.

Sheehan, R., & Snyder, S. (1990). Review of Battelle Developmental Inventory. *Diagnostique, 15*, 16–30.

Shepard J. (1989). Review of the Vocational Preference Inventory. In J. Conoley & J. Kramer (Eds.), *Tenth mental measurements yearbook* (pp. 882–883). Lincoln, NE: University of Nebraska Press.

Sherrets, S., Gard, G., & Langner, H. (1979). Frequency of clerical errors on WISC protocols. *Psychology in the Schools, 16*, 495–496.

Shinn, M. (1988). Development of curriculum-based local norms for use in special education. *Journal of Special Education, 17*, 61–80.

Shinn, M. R., & Habedank, L. (1992). Curriculum-based measurement in special education problem identification and certification decisions. *Preventing School Failure, 36*(2), 11–15.

Shinn, M. R., Habedank, L., Rodden-Nord, R., & Knutson, P. (1993). Using curriculum-based measurement to identify potential candidates for reintegration into general education. *Journal of Special Education, 27*(2), 202–221.

Shinn, M., Rosenfeld, S., & Knutson, N. (1989). Curriculum based assessment: A comparison of models. *School Psychology Review, 18*, 299–316.

Shipley, K., Stone, T., & Sue, M. (1983). *Test for Examining Expressive Morphology.* Tucson, AZ: Communication Skill Builders.

Shorr, D., Jackson, N., & Robinson, H. (1980). Achievement test performance of intellectually advanced preschool children. *Exceptional Children, 46*, 646–648.

Shub, A., Carlin, J., Friedman, R., Kaplan, J., & Katien, J. (1973). *Diagnosis: An Instructional Aid in Reading.* Chicago: Science Research Associates.

Shull-Senn, S., Weatherly, M., Morgan, S. K., & Bradley-Johnson, S. (1995). Stability reliability for elementary-age students on the Woodcock-Johnson Psychoeducational Battery–Revised (Achievement Section) and the Kaufman Test of Educational Achievement. *Psychology in the Schools, 32*, 86–92.

Shulman, B. (1986). *Test of Pragmatic Skills.* Tucson, AZ: Communication Skill Builders, Inc.

Shurrager, H., & Shurrager, P. (1964). *Haptic Intelligence Scale.* Chicago, IL: Institute of Technology.

Siegel, L. (1989). IQ is irrelevant to the definition of learning disabilities. *Journal of Learning Disabilities, 22*, 506–546.

Silva, C., & Yarbrough, R. (1990). Help for young writers with spelling difficulties. *The Reading Teacher, 34*, 48–53.

Silvaroli, N. (1989). *Classroom Reading Inventory.* Dubuque, IA: Wm. C. Brown.

Silver, S., & Clampit, M. (1991). Corrected confidence intervals for quotients on the WISC-R, by level of quotient. *Psychology in the Schools, 28*, 8–14.

Silverstein, A. (1978). Note on the norms for the WRAT. *Psychology in the Schools, 14*, 152–153.

Silverstein, A. (1980). A comparison of the 1976 and 1978 norms for the WRAT. *Psychology in the Schools, 17*, 313–315.

Silverstein, A. (1981). Pattern analysis on the PIAT. *Psychology in the Schools, 18*, 13–14.

Silverstein, A. (1986a). Non-standard standard scores on the Vineland Adaptive Behavior Scales: A cautionary note. *American Journal of Mental Deficiency, 91*, 1–4.

Silverstein, A. (1986b). Organization and structure of the Detroit Tests of Learning Aptitude (DTLA-2). *Educational and Psychological Measurement, 46*, 1061–1066.

Silverthorne, P. (1994). Assessment of ADHD using ADDES. *Child Assessment News, 4*, 1–3.

Simpson, R. (1990). Review of the Revised Behavior Problem Checklist. *Diagnostique, 15*, 161–173.

Simpson, R. G. (1989). Agreement among teachers in using the Revised Behavior Problem Checklist to identify deviant behavior in children. *Behavioral Disorders, 14*, 151–156.

Simpson, R., & Arnett, K. (1987). Relationship between teacher ratings using the Revised Behavior Problem Checklist. *Diagnostique, 13*, 36–41.

Simpson, R. G., & Halpin, G. (1986). Agreement between parents and teachers in using the Revised Behavior Problem Checklist to identify deviant behavior in children. *Behavioral Disorders, 12*, 54–59.

Siskind, T. G. (1993). Teachers' knowledge about test modifications for students with disabilities. *Diagnostique, 18*(2), 145–157.

Sitlington, R., & Wimmer, D. (1978). Vocational assessment techniques for the handicapped adolescent. *Career Development for Exceptional Individuals, 1*, 78–87.

Slate, J. (1994). WISC-III correlation with the Wechsler Individual Achievement Test. *Psychology in the Schools, 31*, 278–285.

Slate, J., & Jones, C. (1990). Identifying students' errors in administering the WAIS-R. *Psychology in the Schools, 27*, 83–87.

Slate, J. R., Jones, C. H., Graham, L. S., & Bower, J. (1994). Correlations of WISC-III, WRAT-R, KM-R, and PPVT-R scores in students with specific learning disabilities. *Learning Disabilities Research and Practice, 9*(2), 104–107.

Slate, J. R., Jones, C. H., Murray, R. A., & Coulter, C. (1993). Evidence that practitioners err in administering and scoring the WAIS-R. *Measurement and Evaluation in Counseling and Development, 25*.

Slosson, R. (1991). *Slosson Intelligence Test–Revised.* Austin, TX: Pro-Ed.

Smiley, L. (1991a). Language assessment: Part one. *Learning Disability Forum, 16*, 23–26.

Smiley, L. (1991b). Language assessment: Part two. *Learning Disability Forum, 17*, 17–21.

Smith, C. (1989). Review of Adaptive Behavior Inventory. In J. Conoley & J. Kramer (Eds.), *Tenth mental measurements yearbook* (pp. 21–24). Lincoln, NE: University of Nebraska Press.

Smith, D. (1989). Review of the Enright Diagnostic Inventory of Basic Arithmetic Skills. In J. Conoley and J. Kramer (Eds.), *Tenth mental measurements yearbook* (pp. 292–293). Lincoln, NE: University of Nebraska Press.

Smith, D. K., & Bauer, J. J. (1989). *Intelligence measures in a preschool sample: SB: FE and K-ABC relationships.* Paper presented at the 97th meeting of the American Psychological Association, New Orleans, LA.

Smith, D. K., Lyon, M., Hunter, E., & Boyd, R. (1988). Relationship between the K-ABC and WISC-R for students referred for severe learning disabilities. *Journal of Learning Disabilities, 21,* 509–513.

Smith, D. K., Martin, M., & Lyon, M. (1989). A validity study of the Stanford-Binet: Fourth Edition with students with learning disabilities. *Journal of Learning Disabilities, 22,* 260–261.

Smith, T., & Smith, B. (1986). The relationship between the WISC-R and WRAT-R for a sample of rural referred children. *Journal of School Psychology, 23,* 252–254.

Smith, T., Smith, B., & Dobbs, K. (1991). Relationship between the Peabody Picture Vocabulary Test–Revised, Wide Range Achievement Test–Revised, and Wechsler Intelligence Scale for Children–Revised. *Journal of School Psychology, 29,* 53–56.

Smith, T. C., Edmonds, J., & Smith, B. (1989). The role of sex differences in the referral process as measured by the Peabody Picture Vocabulary Test–Revised and the Wechsler Intelligence Scale for Children–Revised. *Psychology in the Schools, 26,* 354–358.

Snider, M., Lima, S., & DeVito, P. (1994). Rhode Island's Literacy Portfolio Assessment Project. In S. Valencia, E. Hiebert, & P. Afflerbach (Eds.), *Authentic reading assessment: Practices and possibilities.* Newark, DE: International Reading Association.

Sowder, L. (1978). Review of Stanford Diagnostic Mathematics Test. In O. Buros (Ed.), *The eighth mental measurement yearbook* (pp. 437–439). Highland Park, NJ: Gryphon Press.

Spache, G. (1964). *Reading in the elementary school.* Boston: Allyn & Bacon.

Spache, G. (1981). *Diagnostic Reading Scales.* Monterey, CA: CTB/McGraw-Hill, Inc.

Sparrow, S., Balla, D., & Cicchetti, D. (1984). *Vineland Adaptive Behavior Scales.* Circle Pines, MN: American Guidance Service.

Sparrow, S. S., Rescorla, L. A., Provence, S., Condon, S. D., Goudreau, D., & Cicchetti, D. V. (1986). A follow-up of "atypical" children. *Journal of the American Academy of Child Psychiatry, 25,* 181–185.

Special Education Report (1994). House appropriators wary of new vocational education service rules. *Special Education Report, 20,* 3–4.

Spector, C. (1979). The Boehm Test of Basic Concepts: Exploring the test results for cognitive deficits. *Journal of Learning Disabilities, 12,* 564–567.

Spivack, G., & Swift, M. (1973). The classroom behavior of children: A critical review of teacher-adminis-

tered rating scales. *Journal of Special Education, 7,* 55–89.

Spreat, S. (1980). The Adaptive Behavior Scale: A study of criterion validity. *American Journal of Mental Deficiency, 85,* 61–68.

Spreat, S. (1982a). An empirical analysis of item weighting on the Adaptive Behavior Scale. *American Journal of Mental Deficiency, 87,* 159–163.

Spreat, S. (1982b). The AAMD Adaptive Behavior Scale: A psychometric review. *Journal of School Psychology, 20,* 45–56.

Spruill, J. (1990). Applications of CBA to P.L. 94-142. In L. Cohen & J. Spruill (Eds.), *A Practical guide to curriculum-based assessment for special educators* (pp. 25–52). Springfield, IL: Charles Thomas.

Spruill, J., & Beck, B. (1986). Relationship between the WRAT and WRAT-R. *Psychology in the Schools, 23,* 357–360.

Stack, J. (1984). Interrater reliability of the Adaptive Behavior Scale with environmental effects controlled. *American Journal of Mental Deficiency, 88,* 396–400.

Stainback, S. & Stainback, W. (1992). Schools as inclusive communities. In W. Stainback & S. Stainback (Eds.), *Controversial issues confronting special education.* Boston: Allyn & Bacon.

Stallings, J. (1977). *Learning to look: A handbook on classroom observation and teaching models.* Belmont, CA: Wadsworth.

Stavrou, E. (1990). The long-term stability of WISC-R scores in mildly retarded and learning disabled children. *Psychology in the Schools, 27,* 101–110.

Stavrou, E., & French, J. L. (1992). The K-ABC and cognitive processing styles in autistic children. *Journal of School Psychology, 30*(3), 259–267.

Stehouwer, R. (1985). Review of the Detroit Tests of Learning Aptitude–2. In D. Keyser and R. Sweetland (Eds.), *Test critiques* (v. 2) (pp. 223–230). Kansas City, MO: Test Corporation of America.

Sterling, H., & Sterling, P. (1977). Experiences with the DDST. *Academic Therapy, 12,* 339–342.

Sternberg, R. (1984). The Kaufman Assessment Battery for Children: An information-processing analysis and critique. *Journal of Special Education, 18,* 269–279.

Sterner, A. G., & McCallum, R. S. (1988). Relationship of the Gesell Developmental Exam and the Bracken Basic Concept Scale to academic achievement. *Journal of School Psychology, 26,* 297–300.

Stillman, R. (1978). *Callier-Azusa Scale.* Dallas: University of Texas at Dallas Center of Communication Disorders.

Stodden, R. A. (1986). Vocational assessment: An introduction. *Career Development for Exceptional Individuals, 9,* 67–68.

Stodden, R. A., & Leake, D. W. (1994). Getting to the core of transition: A reassessment of old wine in new bottles. *Career Development for Exceptional Individuals, 17,* 65–76.

Stone, B. (1992a). Factor analysis supports the Differential Ability Sclaes structure. *Diagnostique, 17,* 176–184.

Stone, B. (1992b). Joint confirmatory factor analysis of the Differential Ability Scales and WISC-R. *Journal of School Psychology, 30,*(2), 185–195.

Stone, B. (1994). Assessment problems in proportionate gifted identification. *Child Assessment News, 4,* 1.

Stoneburner, R., & Brown, B. (1979). A comparison of the PIAT and WRAT performances of learning disabled adolescents. *Journal of Learning Disabilities, 12,* 631–634.

Stowitschek, J. J., & Kelso, C. A. (1989). Are we in danger of making the same mistakes with ITPs as were made with IEPs? *Career Development for Exceptional Individuals, 12,* 139–151.

Strickland, B., & Turnbull, A. (1990). *Developing and implementing IEPs* (3rd ed.). Columbus, OH: Charles E. Merrill.

Strommen, E. (1988). Confirmatory factor analysis of the Kaufman Assessment Battery for Children: A reevaluation. *Journal of Special Education, 23,* 342–352.

Strong, E., Campbell, D., & Hansen, J. (1984). *Strong-Campbell Interest Inventory.* Palo Alto, CA: Consulting Psychologists Press.

Stuempfig, D. (1987). Review of Diagnostic Achievement Test for Adolescents. In D. Keyser & R. Sweetland (Eds.), *Test critiques* (v. 7) (pp. 177–184). Kansas City, MO: Test Corporation of America.

Sullivan, E., Clark, W., & Tiegs, E. (1970a). *California Test of Mental Maturity.* New York: CTB/McGraw-Hill.

Sullivan, E., Clark, W., & Tiegs, E. (1970b). *Short Form Test of Academic Aptitude.* Monterey, CA: CTB/McGraw-Hill.

Sven, H., Mardell-Czudnowski, C., & Goldenberg, D. (1989). Classification reliability of the DIAL-R preschool screening test. *Educational and Psychological Measurement, 49,* 673–680.

Swanson, H., Bradenburg-Ayres, S., & Wallace, S. (1989). Construct validity of the K-ABC with gifted children. *Journal of Special Education, 23,* 342–352.

Swezey, R. (1981). *Individual performance assessment.* Reston, VA: Reston Publishing Company.

Swicegood, P. (1994). Portfolio-based assessment practices. *Intervention, 30*(1), 6–15.

Switzer, J., & Gruber, C. (1991). *Manual for the Norris Educational Achievement Test.* Los Angeles: Western Psychological Corporation.

Tabachnick, B. (1979). Test scatter on the WISC-R. *Journal of Learning Disabilities, 12,* 626–628.

Talley, M. (1985). *Talley goals and objectives writer.* North Billerica, MA: Curriculum Associates.

Tamkin, A. (1960). A survey of educational disability in emotionally disturbed children. *Journal of Educational Research, 53,* 313–315.

Tawney, J., & Gast, D. (1984). *Single subject research in special education.* Columbus, OH: Charles E. Merrill.

Taylor, R. (1980). Use of the AAMD classification system: A review of recent research. *American Journal of Mental Deficiency, 85,* 116–119.

Taylor, R. (1984). *Assessment of exceptional students: Edu-*

cational and psychological procedures. Englewood Cliffs, NJ: Prentice-Hall.

Taylor, R. (1985). The measurement of adaptive behavior: Issues and instruments. *Focus on Exceptional Children, 18,* 1–12.

Taylor, R. (1988). Assessment instruments. In L. Sternberg (Ed.), *Educating students with severe or profound handicaps* (pp. 103–153). Austin, TX: Pro-Ed.

Taylor, R. (1990a). *Larry P.* a decade later: Problems and future directions. *Mental Retardation, 28,* iii–vi.

Taylor, R. (1990b). Review of the Woodcock-Johnson–Revised. *Diagnostique, 15,* 264–276.

Taylor, R., & Ivimey, J. (1980). Diagnostic use of the WISC-R and McCarthy Scales: A regression analysis approach to learning disabilities. *Psychology in the Schools, 17,* 327–330.

Taylor, R., & Ivimey, J. (1982). Considering alternate methods of measurement on the Adaptive Behavior Scale. *Psychology in the Schools, 85,* 116–119.

Taylor, R. L., & Kaufman, S. (1991). Trends in classification usage in the mental retardation literature. *Mental Retardation, 29*(6), 367–371.

Taylor, R., & Marholin, D. (1980). A functional approach to the assessment of learning disabilities. *Education and Treatment of Children, 3,* 271–278.

Taylor, R., & Partenio, I. (1983). *Florida norms for the SOMPA.* Tallahassee, FL: Department of Education.

Taylor, R., Smiley, L., & Ziegler, E. (1983). The effects of labels and assigned attributes on teacher perceptions of academic and social behavior. *Education and Training of the Mentally Retarded, 18,* 45–51.

Taylor, R., Sternberg, L., & Richards, S. (1995). *Exceptional children: Integrating research and teaching* (2nd ed.). San Diego: Singular Publishing Group.

Taylor, R., Warren, S., & Slocumb, P. (1979). Categorizing behavior in terms of severity: Considerations for Part Two of the Adaptive Behavior Scale. *American Journal of Mental Deficiency, 83,* 411–414.

Taylor, R. L., Willets, P., & Richards, S. B. (1988). Curriculum-based assessment: Considerations and concerns. *Diagnostique, 14,* 14–21.

Taylor, R., & Ziegler, E. (1987). A comparison of the first principal factor of the WISC-R across ethnic groups. *Educational and Psychological Measurement, 47,* 691–694.

Taylor, R., Ziegler, E., & Partenio, I. (1984). Investigation of WISC-R verbal-performance discrepancies as a function of ethnic status. *Psychology in the Schools, 21,* 436–444.

Taylor, R., Ziegler, E., & Partenio, I. (1985). Factor structure of the WISC-R across ethnic groups: An investigation of construct validity. *Diagnostique, 11,* 9–13.

Telzrow, C. (1984). Practical applications of the K-ABC in the identification of handicapped preschoolers. *Journal of Special Education, 18,* 311–324.

Tenopyr, M. (1989). Review of the Kuder Occupational Interest Survey. In J. Conoley & J. Kramer (Eds.), *Tenth mental measurements yearbook* (pp. 427–429). Lincoln, NE: University of Nebraska Press.

Terman, L. (1925). *Genetic studies of genius, vol. 1: Mental and physical traits of a thousand gifted children*. Stanford, CA: Stanford University Press.

Terman, L., & Oden, M. (1959). *Genetic studies of genius, vol. 5: The gifted group at midlife*. Stanford, CA: Stanford University Press.

Teska, J. A., & Stoneburner, R. L. (1980). The concept and practice of second level screening. *Psychology in the Schools, 17*, 192–195.

Thomas, P. (1990). Review of Scales of Independent Behavior. *Diagnostique, 15*, 174–182.

Thomas, V. (1979). *Teaching spelling* (2nd ed.). Calgary, Canada: Gage Publishing Ltd.

Thompson, J., & Sones, R. (1973). *Education Apperception Test*. Los Angeles: Western Psychological Services.

Thorndike, R., & Hagen, E. (1994). *Cognitive Abilities Test*. Boston: Houghton Mifflin.

Thorndike, R., Hagen, E., & Sattler, J. (1986). *Stanford-Binet Intelligence Scale: Fourth Edition*. Chicago: Riverside Publishing Company.

Tierney, R. (1989). Review of Test of Reading Comprehension. In J. Conoley & J. Kramer (Eds.), *Tenth mental measurements yearbook* (pp. 854–855). Lincoln, NE: University of Nebraska Press.

Tinney, F. (1975). A comparison of the Key Math Diagnostic Arithmetic Test and the California Arithmetic Test with learning disabled students. *Journal of Learning Disabilities, 8*, 57–59.

Trahan, D., & Strickland, A. (1979). Bender-Gestalt emotional indicators and acting out behavior in young children. *Journal of Personality Assessment, 43*, 365–375.

Tucker, J. (1985). Curriculum-based assessment: An introduction. *Exceptional Children, 52*, 199–204.

Tukey, J. (1977). *Exploratory data analysis*. Reading, MA: Addison-Wesley.

Turco, T. (1989). Review of Bracken Basic Concept Scale. In J. Conoley & J. Kramer (Eds.), *Tenth mental measurements yearbook* (pp. 102–104). Lincoln, NE: University of Nebraska Press.

Tur-Kaspa, H., & Bryan, T. (1995). Teachers' ratings of the social competence and school adjustment of students with learning disabilities in elementary and junior high school. *Journal of Learning Disabilities, 287*, 44–52.

Turner, B., Beidel, D., Hughes., S., and Turner, M. (1993). Test anxiety in African American school children. *School Psychology Quarterly, 8*, 140–152.

Tymitz-Wolf, B. (1982). Guidelines for assessing goals and objectives. *Teaching Exceptional Children, 14*, 198–201.

Tzeng, O. (1985). Review of the Strong-Campbell Interest Inventory. In D. Keyser & R. Sweetland (Eds.), *Test critiques*, v. 2 (pp. 737–749). Kansas City, MO: Test Corporation of America.

Ulissi, S. M. (1989). Use of the Kaufman Assessment Battery for Children with the hearing impaired. *American Annals of the Deaf, 134*(4), 283–287.

Ullman, R., Sleator, E., & Sprague, R. (1991). *ADD-H Comprehensive Teacher's Rating Scale–Second Editon*. Los Angeles: Western Psychological Services.

Underhill, R., Uprichard, A., & Heddens, J. (1982). Di-

agnosing mathematical difficulties. Columbus, OH: Charles E. Merrill.

Valencia, R. (1984). Concurrent validity of the Kaufman Assessment Battery for children in a sample of Mexican-American children. *Educational and Psychological Measurement, 44*, 365–372.

Valencia, R. R., & Rankin, R. J. (1988). Evidence of bias in predictive validity on the Kaufman Assessment Battery for Children in samples of Anglo and Mexican American children. *Psychology in the Schools, 25*, 257–263.

Valencia, S. (1990). A portfolio approach to classroom reading assessment: The why's, what's, and how's. *The Reading Teacher, 43*, 142–148.

Vallecorsa, A., & Tittle, C. (1985). Adaptive Behavior Scale–School Edition. *Journal of Counseling and Development, 63*, 532–534.

Vance, B., Mayes, L., Fuller, G., & Abdullah, A. (1994). A preliminary study of the relationship of the WISC-III and WRAT-3 with a sample of exceptional students. *Diagnostique, 19*, 15–22.

Vance, B., & Stone, J. (1990). Review of Peabody Picture Vocabulary Test–Revised. *Diagnostique, 15*, 149–160.

Vandergriff, D. V., Hester, J., & Mandra, D. (1987). Composite ratings on the AAMD Adaptive Behavior Scale. *American Journal of Mental Deficiency, 92*, 203–206.

Van Etten, C., & Watson, B. (1978). Arithmetic skills: Assessment and instruction. *Journal of Learning Disabilities, 11*, 155–162.

VanRoekel, B. (1978). Review of Stanford Diagnostic Reading Test. In O. Buros (Ed.), *The eighth mental measurements yearbook* (pp. 1298–1300). Highland Park, NJ: The Gryphon Press.

Vavrus, L. (1990). Put portfolios to the test. *Instructor, 100*(1), 48–53.

Venn, J. (1987). Vulpé Assessment Battery. In D. Keyser & R. Sweetland (Eds.), *Test critiques* (v. 6) (pp. 622–628). Kansas City, MO: Test Corporation of America.

Vernon, P. (1990). An overview of chronometric measures of intelligence. *School Psychology Review, 19*, 399–410.

Vitali, G. J. (1993). *Factors influencing teachers' assessment and instructional practices in an assessment-driven educational reform*. (Doctoral dissertation, University of Kentucky).

Von Isser, A., Quay, H., & Love, C. (1980). Interrelationships among three measures of deviant behavior. *Exceptional Children, 46*, 272–276.

VORT Corporation. (1973). *Behavioral Characteristics Progression*. Palo Alto, CA: VORT Corporation.

Vulpé, S. (1979). *Vulpé Assessment Battery*. Toronto, Canada: National Institute on Mental Retardation.

Wade, H. L., Kutsick, K., & Vance, B. (1988). A comparison of preschool children's performance on the Kaufman Assessment Battery for Children–Nonverbal Scale and the Wechsler Preschool and Primary Scale of Intelligence Performance Scale. *Diagnostique, 13*, 98–104.

Walker, H. (1978). Observing and recording child behavior in the classroom. In Smith (Ed.), *Iowa perspective*. Des Moines: Iowa Department of Public Instruction.

Walker, H. (1983). *Walker Problem Behavior Identification Checklist*. Los Angeles: Western Psychological Services.

Walker, H., & Hops, H. (1976). Use of normative peer data as a standard for evaluating classroom treatment effects. *Journal of Applied Behavior Analysis, 9,* 159–168.

Walker, H., & McConnell, S. (1995). *Walker-McConnell Scale of Social Competence and School Adjustment*. San Diego: Singular Publishing Group.

Wall, S., & Paradise, L. (1981). A comparison of parent and teacher reports of selected adaptive behaviors of children. *Journal of School Psychology, 19,* 73–77.

Wallace, G., & Hammill, D. (1994). *Comprehensive Receptive and Expressive Vocabulary Test*. Austin, TX: Pro-Ed.

Wang, M., & Birch, J. (1984). Comparison of a full-time mainstreaming program and a resource room approach. *Exceptional Children, 51,* 33–40.

Wang, M., & Zollers, N. (1990). Adaptive instruction: An alternative service delivery model. *Remedial and Special Education, 11,* 7–21.

Watanabe, A., & Algozzine, B. (1989). Who discovered America? How many seeds in a watermelon? Tips for modifying teacher made tests. *Diagnostique, 14,* 191–197.

Watkins, M., & Kush, J. (1988). *Manual for rational WISC-R analysis*. Phoenix, AZ: Southwest Educational Psychology Services, Inc.

Webber, J., Scheuermann, B., & Wheeler, L. (1992). Relationship among students scores on four social skills measures. *Diagnostique, 17,* 244–254.

Webster, R. E., Hewett, H., & Crumbacker, H. (1989). Criterion related validity of the WRAT-R and K-TEA with teacher estimates of actual classroom academic performance. *Psychology in the Schools, 26,* 243–248.

Wechsler, D. (1991). *Manual for the Wechsler Intelligence Scale for Children–Third Edition*. San Antonio: Psychological Corporation.

Wehman, P., Moon, M. S., Everson, J. M., Wood, W., & Barcus, J. M. (1988). *Transition from school to work*. Baltimore, MD: Brookes.

Weibe, M. (1986). Test review: The Kaufman Assessment Battery for Children. *Education and Training of the Mentally Retarded, 3,* 76–79.

Wepman, J. (1967). The perceptual basis for learning. In E. C. Frierson & W. B. Barbe (Eds.), *Educating children with learning disabilities: Selected readings*. New York: Appleton-Century-Crofts.

Wepman, J., & Reynolds, J. (1986). *Auditory Discrimination Test*. Chicago: Language Research Associates.

Wesson, C. L., & King, R. P. (1992). The role of curriculum-based measurement in portfolio assessment. *Diagnostique, 18*(1), 27–38.

Wesson, C., Vierthaler, J., & Haubrich, P. (1989). The discriminant validity of curriculum-based measures for establishing reading groups. *Reading Research and Instruction, 29,* 23–32.

Westby, C. E. (1980). Assessment of cognitive and language abilities through play. *Language, Speech, and Hearing Services in the School, 11,* 154–168.

White, O., & Haring, N. (1980). *Exceptional teaching* (2nd ed.). Columbus, OH: Charles E. Merrill.

White, O., & Liberty, K. (1976). Behavioral assessment and precise educational measurement. In N. Haring & R. Schiefelbusch (Eds.), *Teaching special children*. New York: McGraw-Hill.

Wiederholt, L., & Bryant, B. (1986). *Gray Oral Reading Test–Revised*. Austin, TX: Pro-Ed.

Wiederholt, L., & Bryant, B. (1992). *Gray Oral Reading Test-3*. Austin, TX: Pro-Ed.

Wiese, M. (1990). Review of Spellmaster. In J. Conoley & J. Impara (Eds.), *Tenth mental measurements yearbook* (Supplement) (pp. 239–240). Lincoln, NE: University of Nebraska Press.

Wiggins, G. (1989). A true test: Toward more authentic and equitable assessment. *Phi Delta Kappan, 70,* 703–13.

Wiig, E., & Secord, W. (1985). *Test of Language Competence*. San Antonio: The Psychological Corporation.

Wilderstrom, A. H., Miller, L. J., and Marzano, R. J. (1986). Sex and race differences in the identification of communicative disorders in preschool children as measured by the Miller Assessment for Preschoolers. *Journal of Communication Disorders, 19,* 219–226.

Wilgosh, L., & Barry, M. (1983). Assessment of vocational interests of TMH students. *Mental Retardation and Learning Disability Bulletin, 11,* 79–84.

Wilkinson, G. (1993). *Wide Range Achievement Test–3*. Wilmington, DE: Wide Range, Inc.

Wilkinson, S. C. (1993). WISC-R profiles of children with superior intellectual ability. *Gifted Child Quarterly, 37*(2), 84–91.

Will, M. (1986). Educating children with learning problems: A shared responsibility. *Exceptional Children, 52,* 411–416.

Will, M. C. (1984). *OSERS Program for the transition of youth with disabilities: Bridges from school to working life*. Washington, DC: Office of Special Education and Rehabilitative Services, U.S. Department of Education.

Williams, R. (1972). *Black Intelligence Test of Cultural Homogeneity*. St. Louis, MO: Williams and Associates.

Williamson, A. (1976). *An analysis of error patterns of disabled readers at secondary level*. Ann Arbor, MI: University Microfilms International, catalogue no. 77-764.

Willis, J., Smithy, D., & Holliday, S. (1979). Item level difficulty of the Devereux Elementary School Behavior Rating Scale. *Journal of Abnormal Child Psychology, 7,* 327–336.

Willson, V. L., Nolan, R., Reynolds, C., & Kamphaus, R. (1989). Race and gender effects on item functioning on the Kaufman Assessment Battery for Children. *Journal of School Psychology, 27,* 289–296.

Wilson, M. J., & Bullock, L. M. (1988). Agreement among teachers in using the Revised Behavior Problem Checklist to identify deviant behavior in children. *Behavioral Disorders, 14,* 186–200.

Wilson, W. M. (1992). The Stanford-Binet: Fourth Edition and Form L-M in assessment of young children with mental retardation. *Mental Retardation, 30*(2), 81–84.

Wirt, R., Lachar, D., Klinedinst, J., & Seat, P. (1984). *Manual for the Personality Inventory for Children.* Los Angeles: Western Psychological Services.

Wisniewski, L. A., Alper, S., & Schloss, P. (1991). Work-experience and work-study programs for students with special needs. *Career Development for Exceptional Individuals, 14,* 43–58.

Witt, J., & Martens, B. (1984). Adaptive behavior: Tests and assessment issues. *School Psychology Review, 13,* 478–484.

Wodrich, D., & Barry, C. (1991). A survey of school psychologists' practices for identifying mentally retarded students. *Psychology in the Schools, 28,* 165–170.

Wolf, D. P., LeMahieu, P. G., & Eresh, J. (1992). Good measure: Assessment as a tool for educational reform. *Educational Leadership, 49*(8), 8–13.

Wolfram, W. (1990). *Dialect differences and testing.* Washington: Office of Educational Research and Improvement (ED 323813).

Wolman, C., Thurlow, M., & Bruininks, R. (1989). Stability of categorical designations for special education students: A longitudinal study. *Journal of Special Education, 23,* 13–22.

Wong, B., & Roadhouse, A. (1978). The Test of Language Development: A validation study. *Learning Disability Quarterly, 1,* 48–61.

Wood, D. (1991). Discrepancy formulas and classification and identification issues that affect diagnoses of learning disabilities. *Psychology in the Schools, 28,* 219–225.

Woodcock, R. (1987). *Woodcock Reading Mastery Tests–Revised.* Circle Pines, MN: American Guidance Service.

Woodcock, R., & Johnson, W. B. (1989). *Woodcock-Johnson–Revised.* Allen, TX: DLM Teaching Resources.

Woods, M., & Moe, A. (1989). *Analytical Reading Inventory.* Columbus, OH: Charles E. Merrill.

Woodward, C., Santa-Barbara, J., & Roberts, R. (1975). Test-retest reliability of the Wide Range Achievement Test. *Journal of Clinical Psychology, 31,* 81–84.

Warden, M. R., & Hutchison, T. (1992). *Writing Process Test.* Chicago: Riverside Publishing Company.

Worthern, B. R. (1993). Critical issues that will determine the future of alternative assessment. *Phi Delta Kappan, 74*(6), 444–454.

Worthing, R., Phye, G., & Nunn, G. (1984). Equivalence and concurrent validity of the PPVT-R Forms L and M for school age children with special needs. *Psychology in the Schools, 21,* 296–299.

Worthington, C. (1987). Kaufman Test of Educational Achievement, Comprehensive and Brief Form. *Journal of Counseling and Development, 65,* 325–327.

Worthington, L., & Harrison, P. (1990). Review of the Walker-McConnell Scale of Social Competence and School Adjustment. *Diagnostique, 15,* 243–253.

Wright, D. (1983). The effectiveness of the PPVT-R for screening gifted students. *Psychology in the Schools, 20,* 25–26.

Yell, M., Deno, S., & Marston, D. (1992). Barriers to implementation of curriculum-based measurements. *Diagnostique, 18,* 99–112.

Ysseldyke, J. (1989). Review of the Diagnostic Achievement Test for Adolescents. In J. Conoley & J. Kramer (Eds.), *Tenth mental measurements yearbook* (pp. 254–256). Lincoln, NE: University of Nebraska Press.

Ysseldyke, J., Algozzine, B., Regan, R., & McGue, M. (1981). The influence of test scores and naturally occurring pupil characteristics on psychoeducational decision making with children. *Journal of School Psychology, 19,* 167–177.

Ysseldyke, J., & Christenson, S. (1987). Evaluating students' instructional environments. *Remedial and Special Education, 8,* 17–24.

Ysseldyke, J., & Christenson, S. (1992). *The Instructional Environment Scale.* Longmont, CO: Sopris West.

Ysseldyke, J., Sabatino, D., & Lamanna, J. (1973). Convergent and discriminant validity of the Peabody Individual Achievement Test with educable mentally retarded children. *Psychology in the Schools, 10,* 200–204.

Zachman, L., Jorgensen, C., Huisingh, R., & Barrett, M. (1984). *Test of Problem Solving.* Moline, IL: Linguisystems, Inc.

Ziffer, R., & Shapiro, L. (1995). *The Self-Report and Projective Inventory.* Circle Pines, MN: American Guidance Service.

Zucker, S., & Riordan, J. (1988). Concurrent validity of new and revised conceptual language measures. *Psychology in the Schools, 25,* 252–256.

AUTHOR INDEX

SUBJECT INDEX

The abbreviations *t* and *f* stand for table and figure, respectively.

TEST INDEX

The abbreviations *t* and *f* stand for table and figure, respectively.